INTERNATIONAL MARITIME CONVENTIONS
VOLUME III:
Protection of the Marine Environment

MARITIME AND TRANSPORT LAW LIBRARY

MARITIME AND TRANSPORT LAW LIBRARY

International Maritime Conventions
Volume Three
Protection of the Marine Environment
by Francesco Berlingieri
(2015)

International Maritime Conventions
Volume Two
Navigation, Securities, Limitation of Liability
and Jurisdiction
by Francesco Berlingieri
(2014)

Maritime Law
3rd edition
edited by Yvonne Baatz
(2014)

Offshore Contracts and Liabilities
by Bariş Soyer and Andrew Tettenborn
(2014)

Marine Insurance Fraud
by Bariş Soyer
(2014)

International Maritime Conventions
Volume One
The Carriage of Goods and Passengers by Sea
by Francesco Berlingieri
(2014)

International Carriage of Goods by Road: CMR
6th Edition
by Malcolm A. Clarke
(2014)

The Maritime Labour Convention:
International Labour Law Redefined
edited by Jennifer Lavelle
(2013)

Modern Maritime Law:
Volume 2: Managing Risks and Liabilities
3rd Edition
by Aleka Mandaraka-Sheppard
(2013)

Modern Maritime Law:
Volume 1: Jurisdiction and Risks
3rd Edition
by Aleka Mandaraka-Sheppard
(2013)

Uni-Modal and Multi-Modal Transport in
The 21st Century
edited by Bariş Soyer and Andrew Tettenborn
(2013)

The Law of Yachts and Yachting
by Filippo Lorenzon and Richard Coles
(2012)

Freight Forwarding and Multimodal Transport
Contracts
2nd edition
by David A. Glass
(2012)

Marine Insurance Clauses
5th Edition
by N. Geoffrey Hudson, Tim Madge and
Keith Sturges
(2012)

Pollution at Sea: Law and Liability
edited by Bariş Soyer and Andrew Tettenborn
(2012)

Contracts of Carriage by Air
2nd Edition
by Malcolm A. Clarke
(2012)

Places of Refuge: International Law and the
CMI Draft Convention
by Eric Van Hooydonk
(2010)

Maritime Fraud and Piracy
by Paul Todd
(2010)

The Carriage of Goods by Sea under the
Rotterdam Rules
edited by D. Rhidian Thomas
(2010)

The International Law of the Shipmaster
by John A. C. Cartner, Richard P. Fisk
and Tara L. Leiter
(2009)

The Modern Law of Marine Insurance:
Volume 3
edited by D. Rhidian Thomas
(2009)

The Rotterdam Rules: A Practical Annotation
by Yvonne Baatz, Charles Debattista, Filippo
Lorenzon, Andrew Serdy, Hilton Staniland
and Michael Tsimplis
(2009)

The Evolving Law and Practice of Voyage Charters
Edited by D. Rhidian Thomas
(2009)

Risk and Liability in Air Law
by George Leloudas
(2009)

Legal Issues Relating to Time Charterparties
edited by D. Rhidian Thomas
(2008)

Contracts of Carriage by Land and Air
2nd Edition
by Malcolm A. Clarke and David Yates
(2008)

Bills of Lading and Bankers' Documentary Credits
4th Edition
by Paul Todd
(2007)

Liability Regimes in Contemporary Maritime Law
edited by D. Rhidian Thomas
(2007)

Marine Insurance: The Law in Transition
edited by D. Rhidian Thomas
(2006)

Commencement of Laytime
4th Edition
edited by D. Rhidian Thomas
(2006)

General Average: Law and Practice
2nd Edition
by F. D. Rose
(2005)

War, Terror and Carriage by Sea
by Keith Michel
(2004)

Port State Control
2nd Edition
by Oya Ozcayir
(2004)

Modern Law of Marine Insurance:
Volume Two
edited by Francis Rose
(2002)

Commercial and Maritime Statutes
edited by Peter Macdonald Eggers and
Simon Picken
(2002)

Bills of Lading: Law and Contracts
by Nicholas Gaskell, Regina Asariotis and
Yvonne Baatz
(2000)

Shipbrokers and the Law
by Andrew Jamieson
(1997)

INTERNATIONAL MARITIME CONVENTIONS

VOLUME III

Protection of the Marine Environment

FRANCESCO BERLINGIERI

informa law
from Routledge

Published 2015
by Informa Law from Routledge
2 Park Square, Milton Park, Abingdon, Oxon OX14 4RN

and by Informa Law from Routledge
711 Third Avenue, New York, NY 10017

Informa Law from Routledge is an imprint of the Taylor & Francis Group, an Informa business

© 2015 Francesco Berlingieri

The right of Francesco Berlingieri to be identified as author of this work has been asserted by him in accordance with sections 77 and 78 of the Copyright, Designs and Patents Act 1988.

All rights reserved. No part of this book may be reprinted or reproduced or utilised in any form or by any electronic, mechanical, or other means, now known or hereafter invented, including photocopying and recording, or in any information storage or retrieval system, without permission in writing from the publishers.

Whilst every effort has been made to ensure that the information contained in this book is correct, neither the author nor Informa Law can accept any responsibility for any errors or omissions or for any consequences arising therefrom.

Trademark notice: Product or corporate names may be trademarks or registered trademarks, and are used only for identification and explanation without intent to infringe.

British Library Cataloguing in Publication Data
A catalogue record for this book is available from the British Library

Library of Congress Cataloging in Publication Data
Berlingieri, Francesco, author.
International maritime conventions / by Francesco Berlingieri
p. cm. -- (Maritime and transport law library
ISBN 978-0-415-71984-1 (hardback) -- ISBN 978-1-315-79645-1 (ebook) 1. Maritime law. I. Title
K1150.B47 2013
341.4'5--dc23
2013038767

ISBN: 978-0-415-71987-2
eISBN 978-1-315-77829-7

Typeset in Plantin by
Servis Filmsetting Ltd, Stockport, Cheshire

Printed and bound in Great Britain by
TJ International Ltd, Padstow, Cornwall

CONTENTS

Glossary	xix
Introduction	xxi
Table of Conventions	xxv
Table of Legislation	xxxv
Table of Cases	xxxvii

Volume III

Part I   The Preventive Conventions

Chapter 1	International Convention relating to Intervention on the High Seas in Cases of Oil Pollution Casualties, 1969 and Protocol of 1973	3

Section I – The Convention of 1969	3
1 The history of the Convention	3
2 The scope of application of the Convention	4
2.1 The notion of 'maritime casualty'	4
2.2 The area in which the measures may be taken	6
2.3 The notion of 'ship'	6
3 The conditions under which the measures may be taken	7
3.1 Grave and imminent danger of pollution or threat of pollution	7
3.2 The pollution must be by oil	8
3.3 The danger must affect the coastline and related interests	8
3.4 The pollution must reasonably be expected to entail major harmful consequences	9
4 The obligations of the State that takes the measures allowed by art. 1	10
4.1 Obligations prior to taking the measures	10
4.2 Optional advice	12
4.3 When compliance with the obligations under (a) and (b) is not required	12
4.4 The manner in which the measures ought to be taken	13
4.5 Guidelines for the selection of the measures	13
4.5.1 Measures proportionate to the damage	14
4.5.2 Measures necessary to achieve their purpose	15

CONTENTS

5   Compensation due for the damage caused by the measures taken
pursuant to art. I   15
6   Compulsory conciliation and arbitration of disputes   16

Section II – The Protocol of 1973   17
7   The history of the Protocol   17
8   The scope of application of the Protocol   20
9   The relationship between the Protocol and the Convention   20
10   The procedure for updating the list of the substances   21

Chapter 2   International Convention on Oil Pollution Preparedness,
Response and Cooperation, 1990 (OPRC Convention) with its
Protocol of 2000 (OPRC-HNS Protocol)   23

Section I – The Convention of 1990   23
1   Introduction   23
2   The scope of application of the Convention   23
3   An analysis of the possible conflict between the OPRC Convention
and the Intervention Convention   24

Section II – The Protocol of 2000   26
4   The Protocol of 2000 to the OPRC Convention   26
5   A comparison of the provisions of the Protocol with those of the
Convention   27

Chapter 3   International Convention for the Prevention of Pollution
from Ships (MARPOL) and Protocol of 1978   29
1   Introduction   29
2   General scope of application   30
    2.1   Ships to which the Convention applies   30
3   The main purpose of MARPOL   31
4   General obligations of the States Parties to the Convention   32
5   Provisions on the inspection of the ships to which the Convention
applies   33
6   Overview of the relevant provisions of the Annexes   35
    6.1   Introduction to the overview   35
    6.2   A summary of the Annexes   35
        6.2.1   Annex I: Regulations for the Prevention of Pollution
by Oil   35
        6.2.2   Annex II: Regulations for the Control of Pollution by
Noxious Liquid Substances in Bulk   36
        6.2.3   Annex III: Regulations for the Prevention of Pollution by
Harmful Substances Carried by Sea in Packaged Form   36
        6.2.4   Annex IV: Regulations for the Prevention of Pollution by
Sewage from Ships   37
        6.2.5   Annex V: Regulations for the Prevention of Pollution by
Garbage from Ships   37

viii

CONTENTS

6.2.6	Annex VI: Regulations for prevention of air pollution from ships	37

Chapter 4 International Convention for the Safety of Life at Sea, 1974 (SOLAS) — 38

Chapter 5 Convention on the Prevention of Marine Pollution by Dumping of Wastes and Other Matter, 1972 as Amended by the Protocol of 1996 — 41

1 Introduction — 41
2 The scope of application of the Convention and of the Protocol — 43
  2.1 Vessels and aircraft to which national implementing legislation must apply — 43
  2.2 Vessels and aircraft to which national legislation does not apply — 44
3 The activities regulated by the Convention and the Protocol — 44
4 The obligations of the Contracting Parties — 46
  4.1 General obligations — 46
  4.2 The obligation of States Parties to prohibit or regulate dumping of wastes or other matters — 47
  4.3 The exceptions to such obligations — 48
5 The directives to States Parties for the implementation of the rules on dumping — 50
6 Instructions to States Parties on the issuance of permits and reporting — 51
  6.1 The designation and the tasks of the appropriate authority — 51
  6.2 The duties of the appropriate authority — 52
  6.3 The duty of Contracting States to report to IMO — 53

Chapter 6 International Convention for the Control and Management of Ships' Ballast Water and Sediments, 2004 — 55

1 Introduction — 55
2 Scope of application — 55
  2.1 Ships to which the Convention applies — 55
  2.2 Ships to which the Convention does not apply — 56
  2.3 The matter to which the Convention applies — 58
3 The manner in which such purpose is achieved — 58
4 The technique adopted for the implementation of the provisions of the Convention — 59

Chapter 7 International Convention on Standards of Training, Certification and Watchkeeping for Seafarers, 1978 — 62

1 The object of the control of ships, while in the ports of a State Party, by officers of that State — 62
2 The provisions in the Code in which reference is made to the protection of the environment — 63

CONTENTS

Chapter 8   Nairobi International Convention on Removal of Wrecks
            18 May 2007   79
1   Introduction   79
2   Scope of application   79
    2.1   The subject matter of the Convention   79
    2.2   The notion of 'wreck'   80
    2.3   The notion of 'hazard'   81
          2.3.1   A general analysis of the relevant rules in this and
                  in other Conventions   81
    2.4   The notion of 'Convention area'   83
          2.4.1   The party who may determine whether a wreck
                  poses a hazard   83
          2.4.2   The criteria to be taken into account   84
    2.5   The voluntary extension of the geographical scope and the
          provisions excluded from the extension   86
3   General obligations of States to be complied with when they become
    Parties to the Convention   88
4   Obligations of States Parties in case of a casualty resulting in a wreck   89
    4.1   Obligation of the State in respect of a ship flying its flag to
          report involvement in a wreck   89
5   Obligations of the State in whose Convention area the wreck is
    located   90
    5.1   Locating wrecks   90
    5.2   Marking wrecks   90
    5.3   Removal of wrecks   91
6   Obligations and liabilities of the owner of the wreck   92
    6.1   Obligations   92
    6.2   Liabilities   93
    6.3   Exceptions to liabilities   94
7   Compulsory insurance or other financial security   95
    7.1   Minimum tonnage of ships for which compulsory insurance is
          obligatory   95
    7.2   Nationality of ships by which insurance must be provided   95
    7.3   Conditions of issue and validity of the certificate   96
    7.4   Claims brought against the insurer and defences available   96
8   Time limits   96
9   Settlement of disputes between States Parties   97

Chapter 9   Port State Control: The Paris Memorandum of Understanding
            and the European Directive 2009/16/EC   99
1   Introduction   99
    I   The Paris Memorandum of Understanding on Port State Control   100
1   The criteria for adherence to the Memorandum   100
2   The organisational structure of the Paris MoU   101
3   The ships to which the Paris MoU applies   102
4   The inspection commitments of the Maritime Authorities   102

CONTENTS

5	The duties and powers of the Port Authorities when deficiencies are detected	103
	5.1 The detention of the ship subject to inspection	104
	5.2 The suspension of an inspection	104
	5.3 The refusal of access	105
6	Information system on inspections	105
	II The European Directive on Port State Control	106
1	The origin and purpose of the Directive	106
2	Ships to which the Directive applies	107
	2.1 Ships included within the scope of application of the Directive	107
	2.2 Ships excluded from the scope of application of the Directive	107
3	The inspection commitments of the Member States	107
	3.1 The general rule	107
	3.2 Frequency of inspections	108
	3.3 The detention of the ship subject to inspection	109
4	The refusal of access	109
	4.1 Refusal based on the records of a ship	109
	4.2 Refusal based on prior failure to comply with conditions determined by authorities	110

Chapter 10 European Traffic Monitoring and Information System: Directive
2002/59/EC of 27 June 2002 — 111

Part II The Liability Conventions

	Chapter 11 International Convention on Civil Liability for Oil Pollution Damage, 1992 (CLC 1992)	117
1	Introduction	117
2	The scope of application of the CLC 1992	119
	2.1 Ships subject to the Convention	119
	2.2 Ships excluded from the scope of application of the Convention	121
	2.3 The definition of 'oil'	122
	2.4 The notion of pollution damage	122
3	The geographical scope of the Convention	125
4	The person liable for the pollution damage	127
	4.1 Whether the owner of the ship or the owner of the cargo should be liable	127
	4.2 The definition of owner of the ship	127
	4.3 The rule on the channelling of liability	128
5	The basis of liability	133
6	The limitation of liability of the owner	135
	6.1 The limit of liability	135
	6.2 The amendment of the limits	137
	6.3 The limitation fund	138
	6.3.1 When and where it must be constituted	138

xi

CONTENTS

	6.3.2	How it must be constituted	139
	6.3.3	Bar to other actions	139
7	The distribution of the fund		140
	7.1	The general rule	140
	7.2	The right of subrogation	141
	7.3	The protection of the owner or other person that may be compelled to effect payment of compensation	141
	7.4	Preventive measures taken by the owner	142
8	The loss of the right to limit		142
9	The liability insurance		143
	9.1	The party who is bound to insure	145
	9.2	The nature and amount of the security required	146
	9.3	The sum insured or secured	146
	9.4	Evidence of the insurance or other financial security	146
		9.4.1 Principal place of business	147
		9.4.2 Period of validity	148
	9.5	Conditions of issue and validity of the certificate	149
	9.6	Language of the certificate	149
	9.7	Period of validity of the certificate	149
	9.8	International validity of the certificate	150
	9.9	Direct action against the insurer or guarantor	150
	9.10	Ships owned by a Contracting State	151
10	Time for suit		152
11	Jurisdiction		153
12	Recognition and enforcement of judgments		154
13	Conflict with other conventions		155
	13.1	Convention on Limitation of Liability 1957	155
	13.2	LLMC Convention as amended	155

Chapter 12	International Convention on the Establishment of an International Fund for Compensation for Oil Pollution Damage, 1992, as amended by its Protocol of 2000 and its Supplementary Protocol of 2003 (the Fund Convention)	156
1	Introduction	156

Section A – The International Fund			161
2	The establishment of the International Fund		161
3	Scope of application of the Fund		161
4	Structure of the Fund Convention		161
5	Rules governing payment of compensation for pollution damage		162
	5.1	When payment of compensation is due	162
	5.2	When payment of compensation by the Fund is not due	165
	5.3	The amount of compensation available under the Fund Convention	167

xii

CONTENTS

5.4	Distribution of the amount available under the 1992 Fund Convention when claims are in excess of the compensation payable	170
5.5	Payment of compensation when the owner has not constituted a fund	170
5.6	Extinction of the right to compensation	170
5.7	Jurisdiction	171
	5.7.1 The courts of competent jurisdiction	171
	5.7.2 Exclusive jurisdiction of the competent court	172
	5.7.3 The right of the Fund to intervene in proceedings brought against the owner	173
	5.7.4 When a judgment or a settlement is not binding on the Fund	173
	5.7.5 Right of the Fund to intervene in the proceedings against the owner	173
6	The contributions to the Fund	174
6.1	Introduction	174
6.2	Who is bound to make contribution	175
6.3	The currency in which contributions must be paid	176
6.4	The basis of the assessment of the amount of annual contributions	177
6.5	The breach by persons liable of their obligations and the action to be taken by the Fund	178
6.6	The cooperation of Contracting States	179
6.7	Voluntary assumption by Contracting States of the obligations of the persons liable	180
7	Organisation and administration of the Fund	180
7.1	The organs of the Fund	180
Section B – The Supplementary Fund		182
8	The establishment of the Supplementary Fund	182
9	The entry into force of the Supplementary Fund and the claims in respect of which it is available	183
10	The rules governing payment by the Supplementary Fund	184
10.1	When payment is due	184
10.2	The conditions precedent to the payment by the Supplementary Fund	185
10.3	The amount of compensation available under the Supplementary Fund	185
10.4	Distribution of the amount available under the Supplementary Fund when claims are in excess of the compensation payable	185
11	Extinction of the right to compensation	186
12	Contributions to the Supplementary Fund	187
12.1	Who is bound to make contributions	187
12.2	The assessment of annual contributions	188

xiii

CONTENTS

12.3	The breach by persons liable of their payment obligations, the cooperation of Contracting States and the voluntary assumption by them of the payment obligations	188

Chapter 13 International Convention on Civil Liability for Bunker Oil Pollution Damage, 2001 — 189

1 Introduction — 189
2 Scope of application — 190
    2.1 Geographical scope — 190
    2.2 The notion of pollution damage — 190
    2.3 Ships subject to the Convention — 191
    2.4 Ships excluded from the scope of application of the Convention — 191
3 The person(s) liable for the pollution damage — 192
4 The basis of liability and the exclusions from liability — 196
5 Limitation of liability — 196
6 Compulsory insurance or financial security — 199
    6.1 Who is bound to insure — 199
    6.2 The nature and amount of the security provided — 200
    6.3 Evidence of the insurance or other financial security — 201
    6.4 Authorities that may issue the certificate and notices required — 201
    6.5 Language of the certificate — 202
    6.6 International validity of the certificate — 203
    6.7 The obligation for the ships to carry on board the certificate — 203
    6.8 Direct action against the insurer or guarantor — 204
    6.9 Ships owned by a Contracting State — 205
    6.10 Facultative exclusion of ships operating exclusively within the area of a State — 205
7 Time for suit — 205
8 Jurisdiction — 206
9 Recognition and enforcement of judgments — 206
10 Supersession Clause — 207

Chapter 14 International Convention on Liability and Compensation for Damage in Connection with the Carriage of Hazardous and Noxious Substances by Sea, 1996 — 208

1 The history of the Convention — 208
2 The structure of the Convention — 210
    I General Provisions — 210
3 Scope of application — 210
    3.1 Nature of the damage — 211
    3.2 Substances causing the damage — 212
    3.3 Area in which the damage is caused — 215
    3.4 Exclusions from the scope of application — 216
        3.4.1 Exclusions related to the basis of the claims — 216
        3.4.2 Exclusions based on the character or the cause of the damage — 216

xiv

CONTENTS

	3.4.3 Exclusion of warships and ships owned or operated by States	217
	3.4.4 Exclusions allowed to States Parties	217
II	Liability of the owner	218
4	The definition of 'owner'	218
5	The basis of liability and the allocation of the burden of proof	218
6	The rule on the channelling of liability	220
7	The limitation of liability of the owner	220
7.1	The limits of liability	220
7.2	The limitation fund	222
	7.2.1 Where the fund may be constituted	222
	7.2.2 How the fund may be constituted	222
	7.2.3 The distribution of the fund	223
7.3	The loss of the right to limit	224
8	The compulsory insurance of the owner	224
8.1	Who is bound to insure	224
8.2	The nature and amount of the security required	225
8.3	Evidence of the insurance or other financial security	225
	8.3.1 The name given to the document	226
	8.3.2 The identification of the ship	226
	8.3.3 The effect of the cessation of validity of the certificate	227
8.4	Conditions of issue and validity of the certificate	228
8.5	Language of the certificate	228
8.6	International validity of the certificate	228
8.7	Direct action against the insurer or guarantor	229
8.8	Ships owned by a State Party	230
8.9	When the obligation for ships to carry on board a certificate is compulsory	230
III	Compensation by the International HNS Fund	231
9	Establishment of the Fund	231
10	When compensation must be paid by the Fund	231
10.1	Conditions required for the payment by the Fund	232
10.2	When payment of compensation is not due	232
10.3	The amount of compensation payable by the Fund	233
	10.3.1 The general structure of the relevant rules	233
	10.3.2 The general aggregate amount	233
	10.3.3 Distribution among the claimants of the amount available	235
10.4	Related tasks of the HNS Fund	235
10.5	Contributions	235
IV	Claims and actions	236
11	Limitation of actions	236
12	Jurisdiction	238
12.1	Jurisdiction in respect of actions against the owner	238
12.2	Jurisdiction in respect of actions against the HNS Fund or actions taken by the Fund	239

xv

CONTENTS

12.3	Whether and to what extent a judgment rendered against the owner is binding on the Fund	240
13	Recognition and enforcement of judgments	240
13.1	Judgements against the owner	241
14	Judgments against the HNS Fund	241
15	Subrogation and recourse	241
15.1	Subrogation of the Fund in the rights against the owner or guarantor	241
15.2	Right of recourse or subrogation of the Fund against other persons	242
15.3	Right of subrogation or recourse against the Fund	242
16	Supersession clause	243
V	Transitional provisions	243
VI	Final clauses	244
17	Signature, ratification, acceptance, approval and accession	244
17.1	General provisions	244
17.2	Submission of data on total quantities of contributing cargo	244
17.2.1	Initial submission of data on total quantities of contributing cargo	245
17.2.2	Subsequent submission of data on total quantities of contributing cargo	245
17.3	Withdrawal of the consent to be bound	246
18	Entry into force of the Convention	246
19	Amendment of limits	247
20	Termination	248

Appendices

Part I   The Preventive Conventions

1	International Convention relating to Intervention on the High Seas in Cases of Oil Pollution Casualties, 1969 and Protocol of 1973	251
2	International Convention on Oil Pollution Preparedness, Response and Co-operation, 1990 (OPRC Convention) with its Protocol of 2000 (OPRC-HNS Protocol)	264
3	International Convention for the Prevention of Pollution from Ships (MARPOL), 1973 and Protocol of 1978	282
4	International Convention for the Safety of Life at Sea, 1974 and Protocol of 1988 (SOLAS)	294
5	Convention on the Prevention of Marine Pollution by Dumping of Wastes and Other Matter, 1972 and Protocol of 1996	304
6	International Convention for the Control and Management of Ships' Ballast Water and Sediments, 2004	331
7	International Convention on Standards of Training, Certification and Watchkeeping for Seafarers, 1978	353
8	Nairobi International Convention on the Removal of Wrecks, 2007	361

CONTENTS

Part II The Liability Conventions

9   International Convention on Civil Liability for Oil Pollution Damage,
    1992 (CLC 1992)   375
10 Consolidated text of the International Convention on the Establishment
    of an International Fund for Compensation for Oil Pollution Damage,
    1992, as amended by its Protocol of 2000 and its Supplementary
    Protocol of 2003 (the Fund Convention)   386
11 International Convention on Civil Liability for Bunker Oil Pollution
    Damage, 2001   417
12 International Convention on Liability and Compensation for Damage
    in Connection with the Carriage of Hazardous and Noxious Substances
    by Sea, 1996   425

Index   465

GLOSSARY

Arrest Convention 1952: International Convention Relating to the Arrest of Sea-Going
Ships, 1952

Arrest Convention 1999: International Convention on Arrest of Ships, 12 March 1999

Ballast Water and Sediments: International Convention for the Control and Management of
Ships' Ballast Water and Sediments, 2004

Bunker Oil Convention: International Convention on Civil Liability for Bunker Oil
Pollution Damage, 2001

CLC 1969: International Convention on Civil Liability for Oil Pollution Damage, 1969

CLC 1992: International Convention on Civil Liability for Pollution Damage, 1992 as
amended on 18 October 2000

Convention on Dumping of Wastes: Convention on the Prevention of Marine Pollution by
Dumping of Wastes and Other Matters, 1972. As amended by the Protocol of 1996

Convention on Registration of Ships: United Nations Convention on Conditions for
Registration of Ships, 1986

Fund Convention 1971: International Convention on the Establishment of an International
Fund for Compensation for Oil Pollution Damage, 1971

Fund Convention 1992: International Convention on the Establishment of an International
Fund for Compensation for Oil Pollution Damage, 1992 and the Amendments of the
Limits of Liability, 2000

HNS 1996: International Convention on Liability and Compensation for Damage in
Connection with the Carriage of Hazardous and Noxious Substances by Sea, 1996 as
amended by the Protocol of 2010

IBC Code: IMO International Code for the Construction and Equipment of Ships Carrying
Dangerous Chemical in Bulk

IGC Code: IMO International Code for the Construction and Equipment of Ships
Carrying Liquefied Gases in Bulk

IMDG Code: International Dangerous Goods Code

IMSBC Code: International Maritime Solid Bulk Cargoes Code

Immunity Convention 1926: International Convention for the Unification of Certain Rules
Relating to the Immunity of State-Owned Ships, 1926

Intervention Convention 1969: International Convention Relating to Intervention oh the
High Seas and Protocol of 1973 Relating to Intervention on the High Seas in Cases of
Pollution by Substances Other than Oil

ISM Code: International Safety Management Code

LLMC Convention: Convention on Limitation of Liability for Maritime Claims, 1976 as
amended by the Protocol of 2 May 1996

MARPOL: International Convention for the Prevention of Pollution from Ships, 1973 and
Protocol of 1978

Nairobi Convention: Nairobi International Convention on the Removal of Wrecks, 2007

OPRC Convention 1990 with OPRC-HNS Protocol 1990: International Convention on Oil Pollution Preparedness, Response and Co-operation, 1990, with Protocol of 2000 Relating to Pollution Incidents by Hazardous and Noxious Substances in Cases of Oil Pollution Casualties

Paris MoU: Paris Memorandum of Understanding on Port State Control 1982

Port State Control: European Directive 2009/16/EC of 23 April 2009

Rotterdam Rules: United Nations Convention on Contracts for the International Carriage of Goods Wholly or Partly by Sea, 2008

SOLAS: International Convention for the Safety of Life at Sea, 1974

Supplementary Fund: Protocol of 2002 to the Fund Convention 1992

Traffic Monitoring and Information System: European Directive 2002/59/EC

STCW Code: International Convention on the Standards of Training, Certification and Watch-keeping for Seafarers, 1978

UNCLOS: United Nations Convention on the Law of the Sea, 1980

Vienna Convention: Vienna Convention on the Law of Treaties, 1969

INTRODUCTION

The need for preventative measures governing liability for loss or damage caused by pollution of the sea by oil was brought to the world's attention by the grounding of the *Torrey Canyon* on 18 March 1967.

The *Torrey Canyon* was a single screw tanker built in 1959 of 61,263 gross tons and 48,437 net tons with a deadweight capacity of 120,890 tons on her winter marks. Loaded with 119,328 tons of crude oil shipped by BP Trading Limited, her ultimate destination being Milford Haven, Wales, she went aground on the Seven Stones reef between the Scilly Isles and Lands End. In the opinion of the Board of Investigation set up by the Liberian Government, the stranding was due solely to the negligence of the master.

The stranding damaged many of the cargo tanks and by 20 March it was estimated that 30,000 tons of oil had spilled into the sea. On 25 March, oil began to arrive on Cornish beaches, 100 miles of coastline being affected. On 26 March, high seas and strong winds caused the ship to break her back, releasing, it was estimated, a further 30,000 tons of crude oil. Between 28 and 30 March, the ship was bombed by British Naval and Air Forces to open the remaining tanks and release the rest of the oil into the sea. The oil was then set on fire by dropping aviation fuel, napalm and sodium chlorate devices; it is believed that all the oil in the vicinity of the wreck was destroyed by 30 March. Some oil also reached the coast of Brittany where it did considerable damage.

The reaction of the international shipping community was twofold: to create an international instrument with the view to governing the liability for loss or damage caused by oil pollution and to create an international instrument to govern the right of States to intervene outside their territory (including their territorial waters) to prevent, mitigate or eliminate danger to their coasts from sea pollution. In respect of the liability aspect of the problem, two instruments were adopted by the IMCO in 1969 and 1971: the Convention on Civil Liability for Oil Pollution Damage 1969 (CLC 1969) and the Convention on the Establishment of an International Fund for Compensation for Oil Pollution Damage 1971 (Fund 1971). The Convention Relating to Intervention on the High Seas in cases of casualties of oil pollution was adopted concurrently with the CLC 1969 in respect of the right of intervention. Concern soon widened, and it was felt necessary to protect the environment where other hazardous and noxious substances were involved. The Protocol relating to the Intervention on the Highs Seas in cases of Pollution by Substances other than Oil was introduced in 1973. More than twenty years later, in 1996, a general convention

INTRODUCTION

governing liability and compensation for damage caused by hazardous and noxious substances was adopted.

Meanwhile, attention was drawn to the importance of uniform rules on precautionary measures aiming at preventing oil pollution. This problem was, in various degrees, the object, or one of the objects, of several conventions aiming at generally ensuring safety at sea, reference to which is made hereafter.[1] The action aimed at preventing pollution of the sea and the coastline by oil and generally by hazardous and noxious substances may relate to the construction, maintenance and operation of ships, therefore relevant provisions may be found in a great many of such conventions and other instruments that will be considered in the first part of this volume. The second part, will consider the conventions that regulate the liability of persons responsible for loss or damage caused by oil pollution or by hazardous and noxious substances and the limitations on such liability.

The conventions and other instruments of the first group (the Preventive Conventions) are:

(a) the International Convention relating to Intervention on the High Seas in Cases of Oil Pollution Casualties, 1969 with its Protocol of 1973;

(b) the International Convention on Oil Pollution Preparedness, Response and Cooperation, 1990 (OPRC) with its Protocol of 2000 (OPRC-HNS Protocol);

(c) the International Convention for the Prevention of Pollution from Ships, 1973 as amended by the Protocol of 1978 (MARPOL);

(d) the International Convention for the Safety of Life at Sea, 1974 (SOLAS), albeit marginally;

(e) the Convention on the Prevention of Marine Pollution by Dumping of Wastes and Other Matter, 1972, as amended by the Protocol of 1996;

(f) the International Convention for the Control and Management of Ship's Ballast Water and Sediments, 2004;

(g) the International Convention on Standards of Training, Certification and Watchkeeping for Seafarers;

(h) the Nairobi International Convention on the Removal of Wrecks, 2007;

(i) the Paris Memorandum of Understanding on Port State Control and the European Directive on Port State Control 2009/16/EC of 23 April 2009; and

(j) the European Directive 2002/59/EC on Vessel Traffic Monitoring and Information System, as amended.

The conventions of the second group (the Liability Conventions) are:

(a) the International Convention on Civil Liability for Oil Pollution Damage, 1992 (the CLC Convention);

(b) the International Convention on the Establishment of an International Fund for Compensation for Oil Pollution Damage, 1992, as amended by its Protocol of 2000 and its Supplementary Protocol of 2003 (the Fund Convention);

---

1 On pollution of the sea generally see Gregory J. Timagenis, *International Control of Marine Pollution*, Oceana Publications, 1980, Vol. I, p. 21.

(c) the International Convention on Civil Liability for Bunker Oil Pollution Damage, 2001 (the Bunker Oil Convention); and

(d) the International Convention on Liability and Compensation for Damage in Connection with the Carriage of Hazardous and Noxious Substances by Sea, 1996, with its 2010 Protocol (the HNS Convention).

TABLE OF CONVENTIONS

Arrest Convention, 1952 *see*
  International Convention
  Relating to the Arrest of Sea-
  Going Ships
Arrest Convention, 1999 *see*
  International Convention on
  Arrest of Ships
Athens Convention Relating to the
  Carriage of Passengers and
  their Luggage by Sea, 1974
  as amended by its Protocols
  of 1990 and 2002 (Athens
  Convention)................... 145, 171, 247
  art. 4*bis*.............................. 95, 202, 228
  art. 4*bis*(1), (2), (5), (9), (13)............. 145
  art. 13 143
  art. 16(2)... 97
  art. 16(3)... 153
  2002 Protocol...................... 26, 225, 228
  art. 23 21
  art. 23(5), (10).................................. 22
Bunker Oil Convention *see*
  International Convention on
  Civil Liability for Bunker Oil
  Pollution Damage, 2001
CLC 1969, CLC PROT 1992
  (Civil Liability Convention)
  see International Convention
  on Civil Liability for Pollution
  Damage, 1969 as amended by its
  Protocols of 1984 and 1992 158
Collision Convention, 1910 *see*
  International Convention for
  the Unification of Certain Rules
  of Law Relating to Collision
  between Vessels
Convention for the Unification
  of Certain Rules Relating to

International Carriage by Air
  1929 amended by the Hague
  Protocol 1955 142
  art. 26 224
Convention on Civil Liability for
  Damage Caused during Carriage
  of Dangerous Goods by Road,
  Rail and Inland Navigation
  Vessels 1989 (CRDT)
  art. 5(4)(c) 219
  art. 5(7).. 131
Convention on Civil Liability for
  Nuclear Damage 1963 and
  Protocol of 1997
  art. IV 94
  art. IV(1)... 94
Convention on Limitation of
  Liability for Maritime Claims,
  1976 and Protocol of 1996
  (LLMC Convention)...............88, 121,
  133, 135, 138, 140, 143, 155, 195, 199,
  200, 201, 222, 223, 235, 241, 243, 247
  art. 1(2)... 193
  art. 2(1)(c) 198
  art. 3(a) 93
  art. 3(b)... 155
  art. 6 223
  art. 6(1), (2) 223
  art. 12(1)..................................170, 223
  art. 12(2).. 141
  art. 12(4).......................... 141, 142, 223
  art. 13(2).. 140
  art. 15(2)(b) 191
  art. 18(1).. 243
  1996 Protocol...............26, 135, 200, 201
  art. 7 243
  art. 8 21
  art. 8(4), (9) 22

xxv

TABLE OF CONVENTIONS

Convention on the Liability of
Operators of Nuclear Ships, 1962..... 96
art. V(1)... 97
Convention on the Prevention of
Marine Pollution by Dumping of
Wastes and Other Matter, 1972
and Protocol of 1996 ...... 32, 37, 41, 80
art. III(1)(a) 45
art. III(1)(b) 45
art. III(2)... 43
art. III(4)... 45
art. IV 47, 49
art. V 48
art. V(1), (2) 49
art. VI.. 50
art. VI(1) 50, 51
art. VI(1)(a) 48
art. VI(1)(b)..................................... 50
art. VI(1)(c) 50, 52
art. VI(2), (3) 51, 52
art. VI(4) 51, 53
art. VII.. 144
art. VII(1) 42, 43, 56
art. VII(1)(d) 43, 52
art. VII(4) 43, 44
arts VIII–XXII 42
Annex II.. 48
Annex III...................................... 50, 53
1996 Protocol.................................... 80
art. 1 42
art. 1.1.4 48
art. 1.1.7 48
art. 1.4 45
art. 1.4.2 45
art. 1.5 45
art. 1.6 43
art. 1.8 45
art. 2 .... 42, 46, 48
art. 3 46
art. 3.1 .... 46, 48
art. 3.2 47
art. 3.3 47
art. 3.4 .... 37, 47
art. 4 .... 47, 50, 53
art. 8.1 49
art. 8.2 49
art. 9 .... 50, 51
art. 9.1 .... 50, 51
art. 9.1.2 .... 51, 52, 54
art. 9.1.3 .... 51, 54

art. 9.2 .... 50, 52
art. 9.3 50
art. 9.4 .... 51, 53, 54
art. 9.4.2 .... 51, 54
art. 9.4.3 .... 51, 54
art. 9.5 53
art. 10 42
art. 10.1 43
art. 10.4 44
arts 11–18 42
art. 23 41
Annex 1... 47, 51
Annex 2.................................... 48, 51, 53
Fund Convention, 1971 *see*
International Convention on the
Establishment of an International
Fund for Compensation for Oil
Pollution Damage
Fund Convention 1992 *see*
International Convention on the
Establishment of an International
Fund for Compensation for
Oil Pollution Damage, 1992 as
amended by the Protocol of 2000
and Supplementary Protocol of 2003
Hamburg Rules *see* United Nations
Convention on the International
Carriage of Goods by Sea
HNS Convention *see* International
Convention on Liability and
Compensation for Damage in
Connection with the Carriage
of Hazardous and Noxious
Substances, 1996
Immunity Convention *see* 1926
International Convention for
the Unification of Certain Rules
Concerning the Immunity of
State-owned Vessels
International Convention for the
Control and Management of
Ships' Ballast Water and
Sediments, 2004 (BWM) 32, 55, 101
art. 1(1).. 60
art. 1(2).. 58
art. 1(8).. 58
art. 1(11)..................................... 56, 58
art. 2(1).. 59
art. 2(3).. 60
art. 3(1).. 55

xxvi

TABLE OF CONVENTIONS

art. 3(2)..56
art. 3(2)(a), (b) 56
art. 3(2)(c), (d), (e) 57
art. 3(2)(f) 58
art. 3(3)......................................56, 57
art. 4 ....55, 58, 59
art. 4(2)..60
art. 5 ....58, 59, 60
art. 8 ....59, 60
art. 9 ....55, 59
art. 10 55
art. 10(2)..60
Annex, section B, regs B-1, B-2 59
Annex, section D 59
International Convention for the
  Prevention of Pollution from
  Ships, 1973, as modified by
  Protocol of 1978 (MARPOL
  73/78)... 29,
            37, 39, 101, 107, 111, 149
art. 1(1).......................................31, 32
art. 2(2), (3) 32
art. 2(3)(b)(i)....................................32
art. 2(4)..31, 32
art. 2(5)..33
art. 3 30
art. 3(1)..56
art. 3(1)(b) 60
art. 3(3)..31
art. 4 32
art. 4(4)..33
art. 5 ....33, 102
art. 6 34
art. 11 106
art. 11(1)(b) 29
Annex I 29, 30, 35
Annex I, App. 1 213
Annex I, regs 7, 9, 11, 12, 12A, 13,
    14, 15, 16, 18, 28, 31, 35, 37,
    38, 40..30
Annex I, chap. 1, reg. 1.....................35
Annex I, chap. 2, reg. 11.............. 35, 103
Annex I, chap. 3, reg. 12(2) 35
Annex I, chap. 3, reg 18(1) 36
Annex II..29
Annex II, regs 1–5............................36
Annex II, reg. 1.10 213
Annex II, regs 6.1, 6.2, 6.3 213
Annex III...29
Annex III, reg. 1.1............................36

Annex IV.....................................29, 30
Annex IV, chaps 1–5 37
Annex V 29, 30
Annex V, reg. 1.................................37
Annex VI 29, 30
Annex VI, chap. 1, reg. 1.1................37
1978 Protocol...................................29
art. I...29
International Convention for the
  Safety of Life at Sea, 1974
  (SOLAS 74).................................38,
            39, 100, 107, 111, 149
Annex
chap. I, part A-1 39
chap. I, part B...................................39
chap. I, reg. 3(h) 39
chap. 1, reg. 11 39
chap. II-1, part A, reg. 2 39
chap. II-1, part A, reg. 3 39
chap. II-1, part A, reg. 3–1................39
chap. II-1, part A, reg. 29 39
chap. II-2...39
chap. II-2, parts A, D 39
chap. VII...40
chap. VII, parts A, B, C.....................40
International Convention for the
  Safety of Life at Sea, 1974
  (SOLAS PROT 78).....................100
International Convention for the
  Safety of Life at Sea, 1974
  (SOLAS PROT 88).....................101
International Convention for the
  Unification of Certain Rules
  Concerning the Immunity
  of State-owned Vessels, 1926
  (Immunity Convention)............. 44, 57
arts 1, 2 121
art. 3(1)..............................44, 121, 192
International Convention for the
  Unification of Certain
  Rules of Law Relating to
  Assistance and Salvage
  at Sea, 1910 246
International Convention for the
  Unification of Certain Rules of
  Law Relating to Bills of Lading,
  1924 (Brussels Convention
  1924) as amended by the Visby
  Protocol of 1968 (The Hague-
  Visby Rules)............... 26, 27, 142, 246

xxvii

TABLE OF CONVENTIONS

art. 4(5)(e) 224
Protocol 42
International Convention for the
   Unification of Certain Rules
   of Law Relating to Collision
   between Vessels, 1910 .... 5, 171, 246
art. 10 153
art. 13 (draft) 6
International Convention for the
   Unification of Certain Rules
   Relating to Penal Jurisdiction in
   Matters of Collision or Other
   Incidents of Navigation, 1952 5
International Convention on Arrest of
   Ships, 1999 (Arrest Convention,
   1999) 56, 147, 246
art. 1(1)(d) 82
art. 8(1) 56
art. 8(4), (5), (6) 147
International Convention on Civil
   Liability for Bunker Oil Pollution
   Damage, 2001 (Bunker Oil
   2001) 101, 189, 247
art. 1(1) 191
art. 1(3) 193, 194, 199
art. 1(5), (9) 190
art. 2 190
art. 2(a)(i) 200
art. 2(a)(ii) 83
art. 3(1) 191, 194, 196
art. 3(2) 192, 194
art. 3(3) 95, 196
art. 3(4), (5) 196
art. 3(6) 195
art. 4 191
art. 4(1) 190, 191
art. 4(2), (3), (4) 191, 192
art. 6 .... 93, 196, 198, 205, 206
art. 7 .... 195, 199
art. 7(1) 194, 195, 199, 204
art. 7(2) 201, 203
art. 7(3) 201
art. 7(3)(a) 201
art. 7(3)(b) 202
art. 7(4) 202
art. 7(5) 204
art. 7(9) 203, 204
art. 7(10) 204
art. 7(11) 203
art. 7(12), (13) 203, 204

art. 7(14) 205
art. 7(15) 200, 205
art. 8 205
art. 10 206
art. 11 .... 155, 207, 243
International Convention on Civil
   Liability for Oil Pollution
   Damage, 1969 (CLC 1969)
   as amended by its Protocols of
   1984 and 1992 (CLC PROT
   1992) 5, 8,
   15, 16, 27, 28, 94, 101, 107, 117, 129,
   156, 157, 162, 165, 182, 198, 211
art. I(6) 122
art. II 125
art. V(10) 136
1992 CLC PROT 26, 27, 101, 117,
   119, 141, 159, 248
International Convention on Civil
   Liability for Pollution Damage,
   1992 (CLC 1992) 161, 172,
   182, 186, 187, 189, 191, 195, 196,
   199, 200, 202, 204, 208, 210, 215, 220,
   221, 222, 224, 225, 231, 236, 237, 243,
   247
art. I 133
art. I(1) 119, 191
art. I(2) 193
art. I(3) 127, 145
art. I(5) 119, 123, 213, 216
art. I(6) 123, 142, 143, 211
art. I(6)(b) 211
art. I(7) 46, 124, 133, 142, 143
art. II 123, 125, 161, 172, 190
art. II(a)(ii) 83, 138
art. II(3) draft 128, 129
art. II(4) 190
art. III draft 143
art. III(1) 127
art. III(1)(a) 166
art. III(2) 93, 94,
   134, 135, 163, 169, 172, 219
art. III(2)(a) 134, 169
art. III(2)(b), (c) 135
art. III(3) 134, 135, 167, 218, 219
art. III(4) 129, 130, 131, 132, 141, 220
art. III(4)(a) 131
art. III(4)(b) 132
art. III(4)(c) 130, 132, 133
art. III(4)(d), (e), (f) 133

xxviii

TABLE OF CONVENTIONS

art. IV 166
art. V 146
art. V(1).......143, 146, 151, 152, 229, 248
art. V(1)(a), (b) 137
art. V(2).............................. 132, 143, 151
art. V(3).............. 138, 139, 151, 167, 222
art. V(4)–(8) 140
art. V(4).............................. 140, 170, 223
art. V(5).............................. 141, 142, 223
art. V(6), (7) 141
art. V(8)... 142
art. V(9)... 136
art. V(10)... 136
art. VI... 139
art. VI(1) 137
art. VI(2) 139, 144, 145
art. VII.. 95,
  143, 146, 148, 151, 152, 199, 224
art. VII(1) 143, 145, 152
art. VII(2) 145, 146, 148, 149, 201
art. VII(2)(a)..................................... 226
art. VII(2)(d), (e) 147
art. VII(3) 149, 228
art. VII(4) 43, 44, 145, 203
art. VII(5) 148, 149
art. VII(6)..............................149, 228
art. VII(7) 144, 145, 150
art. VII(8) 14, 150, 229
art. VII(10) 145
art. VII(11) 144, 145, 147, 150
art. VII(12) 151, 152, 205, 230
art. VIII 152, 153, 170, 206
art. IX 138, 140, 153, 171, 172
art. IX(1)....................138, 154, 172, 222
art. IX(3)... 154
art. X 154, 207, 241
art. XI 121, 166, 217
art. XI(1)... 192
art. XI(2)....................................121, 152
art. XII.............................. 155, 207, 243
art. 15 .... 21, 119, 137
art. 15(5)... 248
International Convention on
 Liability and Compensation for
 Damage in Connection with
 the Carriage of Hazardous and
 Noxious Substances, 1996 with
 its Protocol of 2010 (HNS
 Convention) 125, 126, 189,
  191, 200, 202, 204, 208, 221, 247

chap. II 231
chap. IV....................................... ..238
art. 1(1)... 215
art. 1(3)... 218
art. 1(5)........................... 209, 212, 219
art. 1(5)(a) 40, 215
art. 1(5)(a)(i) 212
art. 1(5)(a)(iii), (v) 40
art. 1(5)(b) 215
art. 1(6).....................................211, 215
art. 1(6)(a), (b), (c) 224, 237
art. 3 215
art. 3(b)......................83, 238, 239, 240
art. 3(c) 240
art. 4(1).....................................212, 216
art. 4(2)... 212
art. 4(3).....................................211, 216
art. 4(3)(b) 216
art. 4(4).....................................192, 217
art. 4(5), (6) 217
art. 5(1).....................................217, 218
art. 5(1)(a), (b), (c) 217
art. 5(2).....................................217, 218
art. 5(5)... 218
art. 7(1)... 218
art. 7(2).........................94, 219, 233
art. 7(2)(a), (b), (c), (d)..............219, 233
art. 7(2)(a) 234
art. 7(2)(b), (c), (d)......................... 242
art. 7(3).....................................219, 233
art. 7(4)... 219
art. 7(5).....................................220, 223
art. 7(6)... 220
art. 9 .... 209, 225, 229
art. 9(1)............. 220, 225, 226, 229, 248
art. 9(2)... 224
art. 9(3)... 222
art. 9(4).....................................223, 235
art. 9(7)... 223
art. 11 .... 221, 230, 235
art. 11(1)... 226
art. 11(2)... 226
art. 11(4)... 226
art. 12 .... 95, 199, 224, 225, 230
art. 12(1)............. 224, 225, 227, 229, 230
art. 12(2)........................... 201, 225, 230
art. 12(2)(a)..................................... 227
art. 12(3)..............................149, 228
art. 12(4)..................202, 203, 225, 227
art. 12(5)... 227

TABLE OF CONVENTIONS

art. 12(6).. 227
art. 12(7).. 228
art. 12(8)......................................224, 229
art. 12(10).. 230
art. 12(11)......................................225, 230
art. 12(12).. 205
art. 13 .... 199, 231, 235
art. 13(1)... 231
art. 14 ....231, 241
art. 14(1)...................231, 232, 233, 242
art. 14(1)(a), (b), (c) 242
art. 14(2).. 232
art. 14(3).......................................231, 232
art. 14(3)(a)... 234
art. 14(4).......................................231, 232
art. 14(5)–(7)..................................231, 233
art. 14(5).......................................241, 248
art. 14(5)(a)... 233
art. 14(5)(b) 234
art. 14(5)(d) 234
art. 14(6)........................... 235, 241, 242
art. 14(7)... 234
art. 15 235
arts 16–23 235
art. 16(1)–(4) 235
art. 18 236
art. 18(1)... 236
art. 18(1)(a), (c) 247
art. 18(2)... 236
art. 19 244
art. 19(2), (3) 236
arts 20–29 243
art. 21 244
art. 37 236
art. 37(1).......................................236, 237
art. 37(2)... 237
art. 37(3)... 238
art. 38 222
art. 38(1), (2) 238, 239
art. 39(1).......................................239, 240
art. 39(2)... 240
art. 39(4), (5) 239
art. 39(7).......................................237, 240
art. 40 240
art. 40(1), (2), (3) 241
art. 41(1)... 241
art. 41(2), (3) 242
art. 42 .... 155, 207, 243
art. 44 243
art. 45 ....243, 244

art. 45(1)–(3).............................244, 245
art. 45(4)....................................244, 246
art. 45(5).. 245
art. 45(6) 244, 245, 246
art. 45(7).. 245
art. 45(8).. 246
art. 46 .... 208, 244, 245
art. 46(1).. 247
art. 48 247
art. 48(7)(a).. 248
art. 51 248
Annex I 226, 230
2010 Protocol........................209, 210,
221, 222, 225, 245
art. 9(1)... 221
art. 45 ....210, 243
art. 45(4), (5) 210
International Convention on Load
Lines, 1966 (LL PROT 88) 100
International Convention on Load
Lines, 1966 (LOAD LINES
66)...100, 107
art. 21 106
International Convention on
Maritime Liens and Mortgages,
1926 (MLM Convention, 1926)..... 247
International Convention on
Maritime Liens and Mortgages,
1993 (MLM Convention, 1993)..... 247
art. 16 .... 43, 56
International Convention on Oil
Pollution Preparedness, Response
and Cooperation, 1990 (OPRC
Convention) with its Protocol of
2000 (OPRC-HNS Protocol)........... 23
art. 1(1).. 27
art. 2(2).. 82
art. 2(3).. 24
art. 3 23
art. 4 .... 23, 28
art. 5 .... 25, 28
art. 5(1)(a), (b) 25
art. 5(1)(c) 26
art. 5(2), (3) 26
art. 6 .... 23, 28
art. 7 .... 23, 25, 26, 28
art. 8 .... 23, 28
art. 9 .... 23, 28
art. 10 .... 23, 28
art. 11 ....25, 26, 28

TABLE OF CONVENTIONS

art. 12 23
art. 13 27
art. 13(1) 27, 28
2000 Protocol 26, 27
art. 1(1) 27
art. 1(4) 28
art. 2 28
art. 3 28
art. 3(3) 28
arts 4–10 28

International Convention on Salvage,
    1989 .... 44, 92, 119, 133
art. 1(a) 80
art. 1(d) 82
arts 9, 11 113

International Convention on
    Standards of Training,
    Certification and Watchkeeping
    for Seafarers, 1978 (STCW
    Convention) 62, 101, 107
art. X 62, 106
art. X(3) 62
Annex
Reg. I/4, para 3 62
Reg. I/5(1) 62
Reg. I/14 62

International Convention on the
    Control of Harmful Anti-Fouling
    Systems on Ships, 2001 (AFS
    2001) 101

International Convention on the
    Establishment of an International
    Fund for Compensation for Oil
    Pollution Damage, 1971 (Fund
    Convention, 1971) as amended
    by the International Maritime
    Organization Protocol of 1992
    (Fund 92) 28,
         119, 129, 157, 160, 161, 182
art. 2(2) 183
art. 4(5) 140
art. 10 160
1992 Protocol 168, 180
art. 17 180
art. 30(1)(b) 160

International Convention on the
    Establishment of an International
    Fund for Compensation for
    Oil Pollution Damage, 1992 as
    amended by the Protocol

of 2000 and Supplementary
    Protocol of 2003 (Fund
    Convention, 1992) 156,
       189, 208, 210, 216, 231, 247
art. 2 .... 161, 183
art. 2(1) 157
art. 2(1)(a) 162
art. 2(2) 183
art. 3(a)(ii) 83
art. 4(1) 142, 160,
     162, 163, 167, 170, 183, 232
art. 4(1)(b) 163, 164
art. 4(2) 166, 167, 232
art. 4(2)(a) 166, 167
art. 4(2)(b) 166
art. 4(3) 166, 167, 232
art. 4(4) 167, 168, 233, 248
art. 4(4)(a) 159, 168, 169
art. 4(4)(b) 159, 169
art. 4(4)(c) 167, 169
art. 4(4)(d), (e) 169
art. 4(5) 186, 233
art. 4(6) 166, 170, 233
art. 7(1), (2) 171
art. 7(3) 172
art. 7(4) 173
art. 7(5) 170, 173
art. 7(6) 171, 173, 238, 240
art. 10 .... 175, 178, 179
art. 10(1) 169
art. 12 .... 177, 178, 188
art. 12(1)(i)(a), (b) 188
art. 12(1)(ii)(a), (b), (c) 179
art. 12(2) 179
art. 12(4) 180
art. 13 .... 178, 179
art. 13(2) 179
art. 13(3) 181
art. 14 .... 179, 180
art. 15 174
art. 16 180
art. 18 181
art. 18(7) 169, 181
art. 18(9) 181
art. 21 181
arts 22–27 181
art. 22(2)(a) 181
art. 28(2) 181
art. 29(1), (2) 181
art. 29(2)(a), (b), (c) 181

TABLE OF CONVENTIONS

art. 29(2)(d), (e), (f), (g), (h) 182
art. 33(6) 160
art. 37 156
art. 38 248
2003 Protocol 183, 247
art. 1(8)
art. 2 182
art. 4 187
art. 4(1) 184
art. 4(2)(a) 185
art. 5 .... 185, 186
art. 6 186
art. 10 187
art. 10(1), (2) 187
art. 11 188
art. 14 187
art. 15(2), (3) 185
recitals 3, 4, 5 183
International Convention on Tonnage
   Measurement of Ships, 1969
   (TONNAGE 69) 101, 107
International Convention Relating to
   Intervention on the High Seas in
   Cases of Oil Pollution Casualties,
   1969 (Intervention Convention)
   and Protocol of 1973 3,
                            23, 24, 27, 111
art. I 15, 16, 25
art. I(1) 4, 5, 9, 10, 14, 20
art. II(1) 4, 6
art. II(2) 6
art. II(3) 8
art. II(4) 9
art. II (4)(a), (b), (c) 9
art. III 10, 13, 25, 26, 49
art. III(a), (b) 10, 12, 13, 26
art. III(c), (d) 12, 13
art. III(e) 13
art. IV 12
art. V 13, 14, 16
art. V(1) 14, 15
art. V(2) 15
art. V(3) 15
art. V(a), (b), (c) 14
art. VI 15
art. VIII 16
art. VIII(1) 17
Annex
arts 10, 13(2) 17
1973 Protocol 17, 19, 27

art. I(1) 20
art. I(2) 20
art. I(2)(b) 20
art. I(3) 20
art. II 21
art. III 21
art. III(1)–(7) 21
International Convention Relating
   to the Arrest of Sea-Going
   Ships, 1952 (Arrest Convention,
   1952) 147, 246
art. 8(1) 56
International Convention Relating
   to the Limitation of Liability of
   Owners of Sea-Going Ships
   1957 .... 136, 140,
                    155, 195, 200, 243, 247
art. 3(3) 141
art. 3(4) 223
Intervention Convention, 1969
   see International Convention
   Relating to Intervention on
   the High Seas in Cases of Oil
   Pollution Casualties
International Regulations for
   Preventing Collisions at Sea,
   1972 (COLREG 72) 101, 107
Limitation Convention, 1957 see
   International Convention
   Relating to the Limitation of
   Liability of Owners of Sea-Going Ships
LLMC (Limitation) Convention,
   1976 see Convention on
   Limitation of Liability for
   Maritime Claims, 1976, and
   Protocol of 1996
Maritime Labour Convention, 2006
   (MLC 2006) 101
MARPOL 73/78 see International
   Convention for the Prevention
   of Pollution from Ships, 1973, as
   modified by Protocol of 1978
Merchant Shipping (Minimum
   Standards) Convention, 1976
   (ILO Convention No. 147) (ILO
   147) 101, 108
Merchant Shipping (Minimum
   Standards) Convention, 1976
   (ILO Convention No. 147) (ILO
   147 PROT 96) 101

xxxii

TABLE OF CONVENTIONS

MLM (Maritime Liens and
Mortgages) Convention, 1926
see International Convention on
Maritime Liens and Mortgages, 1926

MLM (Maritime Liens and
Mortgages) Convention, 1993
see International Convention on
Maritime Liens and Mortgages, 1993

Nairobi International Convention
on the Removal of Wrecks,
2007 ....32, 79, 145
art. 1(1).................................... 83, 84
art. 1(3), (4) 80
art. 1(5)...................................82, 91
art. 1(6)..82
art. 1(10).......................................89
art. 2(1)................................... 79, 81
art. 2(2), (3) 81
art. 2(4)...86
art. 3(1)..79
art. 3(2)...............................83, 87, 93
art. 3(3)...83
art. 4(4)...86
art. 4(4)(a) 86
art. 4.4(b).......................................87
art. 5(1)...............................81, 89, 91
art. 5(2) 89, 91
art. 5(2)(a)–(e) 89
art. 6 83
art. 6(a)–(d)....................................84
art. 6(e)–(l)....................................85
art. 6(m)–(o) 85
art. 6(o)...84
art. 7 ....87, 90, 91
art. 7(1), (2) 90
art. 8 ....87, 90, 91
art. 8(1)..83
art. 9 .... 87, 93
art. 9(1).......................81, 83, 86, 90, 91
art. 9(2)–(4) 92
art. 9(2), (3) 87, 91
art. 9(4)...87
art. 9(5)....................................86, 91
art. 9(6)....................................81, 91
art. 9(6)(a), (b), (c) 92
art. 9(7)....................................81, 91
art. 9(8)....................................81, 92
art. 9(9)...81
art. 9(10).......................................87
art. 10 ....81, 88, 93

art. 10(1)................................90, 94, 95
art. 10(2).......................................94
art. 10(9).......................................88
art. 10(9)(2), (3) 88
art. 11 .... 81, 94
art. 11(2).......................................93
art. 12 ....88, 93, 95
art. 12(1)........................ 88, 95, 96, 145
art. 12(2), (5) 145
art. 12(7).......................................96
art. 12(9)..................................... 145
art. 12(10).....................................96
art. 12(11)................................... 145
art. 12(12).....................................95
art. 13 96
art. 15 .... 87, 97
art. 15(1), (2) 97
art. 15(3)................................... 97, 98
art. 15(4).......................................98

OPRC Convention *see* International
Convention on Oil Pollution
Preparedness, Response and
Cooperation, 1990

Penal Jurisdiction Convention, 1952
see International Convention for
the Unification of Certain Rules
Relating to Penal Jurisdiction in
Matters of Collision or Other
Incidents of Navigation

Rotterdam Rules, 2008 *see* United
Nations Convention on the
International Carriage of Goods
Wholly or Partly by Sea

Salvage Convention, 1910 *see*
International Convention for the
Unification of Certain Rules of
Law Relating to Assistance and
Salvage at Sea

Salvage Convention, 1989 *see*
International Convention on Salvage

SOLAS 1974 *see* International
Convention for the Safety of Life at Sea

STCW Convention *see* International
Convention on Standards of
Training, Certification and
Watchkeeping for Seafarers, 1978

UNCLOS *see* United Nations
Convention on the Law of the Sea

United Nations Convention on
Conditions for Registration of

TABLE OF CONVENTIONS

Ships, 1986 43
art. 4(2) 56
United Nations Convention on the
High Seas, 1958
art. 6(1) 4, 6
United Nations Convention on
the International Carriage of
Goods by Sea, 1978 (Hamburg
Rules) 153, 171, 246
United Nations Convention on
the International Carriage of
Goods Wholly or Partly by Sea
2008 (Rotterdam Rules) 153,
171, 225, 246
art. 63 153
United Nations Convention on
the Law of the Sea, 1982
(UNCLOS) 41, 126
Part XV... 97
arts 29–32 .... 44, 192

art. 32 57
art. 57 126
art. 211(6)(a)..................................... 84
art. 287 .... 97, 98
art. 287(1)... 97
Annex VII.. 98
Vienna Convention on the Law of
Treaties, 1969, as amended by
Protocol of 1997............................. 16
art. 28 183
art. 30(4)... 155
art. 30(4)(b) 207, 243
Warsaw Convention, 1929 *see*
Convention for the Unification
of Certain Rules Relating to
International Carriage by Air

TABLE OF LEGISLATION

Europe
Commission Directive
No. 2011/15/EC of
23 February 2011 111
Council Directive No. 2002/59/EC
of 27 June 2002 on European
Traffic Monitoring and
Information System................... 111
   art. 1.. 111
   art. 2(2) 111
   art. 3(g) 111
   art. 12... 112
   art. 13... 112
   art. 16..............................112, 113
   art. 17... 113
   art. 17(1) 113
   art. 19... 113
   art. 20a 113, 114
   art. 20a(1)................................... 114
   art. 20b....................................... 114
   recitals 17, 18, 19 114
   Annex IV 113
Council Directive No. 2009/16/EC
of 23 April 2009 on Port State
Control....................................... 99
   art. 1.. 106
   art. 2(1) 107
   art. 2(5) 107
   art. 3(4) 107
   art. 5(2) 107

   art. 5(2)(b)................................... 107
   art. 11... 108
   art. 11(b) 108
   art. 12(a), (b) 107
   art. 16(1) 109, 110
   art. 19(2) 109, 110
   art. 19(4) 110
   art. 19(8) 109
   art. 21(4) 110
   recitals 13, 14.............................. 106
   Annex I................................108, 109
   Annex I, section 1......................... 108
Council Directive No. 2009/17/EC
of 23 April 2009.......... 111, 112, 113
Council Directive No. 2009/18/EC
of 23 April 2009...................... 111

France
Arrêtê 14 March 1969
   art. 97...81

Italy
Navigation Code
   art. 97...81

United Kingdom
Merchant Shipping Act 1995
   s. 9(3) 81

TABLE OF CASES

France
Erika, The (2012) DMF 985, Cour de Cassation, 25 September 2012 132
Prestige, The (2014) DMF 599, Court of Appeal of Rennes, 11 March 2014 .... 183, 184

Italy
International Oil Pollution Compensation Fund, Venha Maritime Ltd and The United
    Kingdom Mutual Steam Ship Assurance Association (Bermuda) Ltd v. Commune
    of Varazze and Others (*The Haven* case) (1996) Dir. Mar. 407, Court of Appeal
    of Genoa, 30 March 1996 139

Sweden
Sweden v. Latvian Shipping (*Tsesis* case) (1984) Dir. Mar. 381, Swedish Supreme
    Court (Högsta Domstolen), 13 January 1983 135

United Kingdom
Landcatch Ltd v International Oil Pollution Compensation Fund and Landcatch Ltd
    v. Braer Corporation and Others (The '*Braer*') [1998] 2 Lloyd's Rep 552 164

USA
United Nations Relief and Rehabilitation Administration v. Steamship Mormacail
    and Others (1951) AMC 1152, U.S.D.C. Southern District of New York,
    7 May 1951 153

PART I

THE PREVENTIVE CONVENTIONS

CHAPTER 1

International Convention relating to Intervention on the High Seas in Cases of Oil Pollution Casualties, 1969 and Protocol of 1973

SECTION I – THE CONVENTION OF 1969

1 THE HISTORY OF THE CONVENTION

On 18 March 1967, the *Torrey Canyon*, a single screw tanker built in 1959 of 61,263 gross tons and 48,437 net tons, with a deadweight capacity of 120,890 tons on her winter marks, loaded with 119,328 tons of crude oil shipped by BP Trading Limited of the United Kingdom, her ultimate destination being Milford Haven, Wales, ran aground on the Seven Stones reef between the Scilly Isles and Lands End. In the opinion of the Board of Investigation set up by the Liberian Government, the stranding was due solely to the negligence of the master.

The stranding damaged many of the cargo tanks and by 20 March it was estimated that 30,000 tons of oil had spilled into the sea. On 25 March, oil began to arrive on Cornish beaches, 100 miles of coastline being affected. On 26 March high seas and strong winds caused the ship to break her back, releasing an estimated further 30,000 tons of crude oil. Between 28 and 30 March, the ship was bombed by British Naval and Air Forces in order to open the remaining tanks and release the rest of the oil into the sea. The oil was then set on fire by dropping aviation fuel, napalm and sodium chlorate devices; it is believed that all the oil in the vicinity of the wreck was destroyed by 30 March. Some oil also reached the coast of Brittany, where it caused considerable damage.

Not long after the commencement of the work aiming at adopting uniform rules on the liability for oil pollution damage the attention was called within IMCO to the need to carry out studies aimed at adopting measures that could strengthen the safety of navigation and obviate the danger of pollution.[1] Two alternative approaches were considered: either to recommend national action or to adopt international rules. These were the object of a guidance paper of the United States, in which the advantages and disadvantages of both alternatives were considered.[2] Another guidance paper was submitted by the United Kingdom[3] and comments thereon were

---

1 Conclusions of the Council on the action to be taken on the problems brought to light by the loss of the '*Torrey Canyon*', document C/ED.III/5 of 8 May 1967.

2 Document LEG/WG(I).WP.3 of 15 August 1967.

3 Document LEG/WG(I).I/WP.1 of 15 August 1967. This document consisted of a questionnaire covering the circumstances in which action could be taken, the scope of action permitted, the need for consultation or notice and the right of compensation.

3

submitted to the Working Group constituted by the IMCO's Legal Committee by several governments.[4] Such documents were considered by the Working Group at its first session and, at its second session, the Working Group, after discussing the agenda items,[5] prepared a Report to the Council enclosing draft articles on the right of a coastal State to intervene in case of a casualty occurring outside its territorial sea which causes, or might cause, pollution by oil.[6] The need for an international convention arose from the fact that pursuant to art. 6(1) of the International Convention on the High Seas 1958, no State could take police action beyond its territorial waters against ships flying a foreign flag: the jurisdiction over vessels when sailing on the high seas pertained exclusively to the flag State.[7]

The draft articles (except art. VIII) were adopted by the International Conference held in November 1969 with very few changes.

2 THE SCOPE OF APPLICATION OF THE CONVENTION

Article I(1) states:

Parties to the present Convention may take such measures on the high seas as may be necessary to prevent, mitigate or eliminate grave and imminent danger to their coastline or related interests from pollution or threat of pollution of the sea by oil, following upon a maritime casualty or acts related to such casualty, which may reasonably be expected to result in major harmful consequences.

It is not easy to draw a distinction between the rules on the scope of application of the Convention and the rules that set out the conditions under which the measures necessary to prevent, mitigate or eliminate grave and imminent danger to the coastline or related interests from pollution or threat of pollution of the sea by oil may be adopted. It is suggested, however, that the rules that pertain to the scope of application of the Convention are those that relate to the notion of 'maritime casualty', to the area in which the measures may be taken and to the notion of ship.

2.1 The notion of 'maritime casualty'

Maritime casualty is defined in art. II(1) as follows:

'Maritime casualty' means a collision of ships, stranding or other incident of navigation, or other occurrence on board a ship or external to it resulting in material damage or imminent threat of material damage to a ship or cargo.

During the Conference, the Canadian delegate objected to this definition, which had already appeared in the draft articles prepared by the Legal Committee, on

---

4 *Inter alia*, there were comments by the Federal Republic of Germany (LEG/WG (I).I/WP.4) and France (LEG/WG(I).I/WP.7).

5 For a summary of such discussion see LEG/WG(I).II/2 of 6 April 1968.

6 Document LEG III/WP.22 of 14 June 1968, Annex I.

7 Article 6(1) of the Convention so provides:

 1. Ships shall sail under the flag of one State only and, save in exceptional cases expressly provided for in international treaties or in these articles, shall be subject to its exclusive jurisdiction on the high seas.

the ground that the purpose of the Convention was not to protect the ship and cargo, but to protect the coastline and related interests; the coastal State should not be compelled to prove that the incident which had occurred had caused material damage to the ship.[8] The Syrian delegate then suggested that the words 'a ship or cargo' at the end of the sentence should be replaced by 'a coastal State or States'.[9] There followed a long and not very constructive debate, during which perhaps the most significant comment against the Canadian proposal was made by the Irish delegate, who stated that the words the deletion of which was suggested were essential, 'otherwise a slight incident of navigation, such as a mere change of course, might be interpreted as justifying an intervention'.[10] Both the concern about the wording of this provision, and that about the effect of its suggested amendment had some justification. The definition of maritime casualty must be read into art. I(1) from which it appears that the danger must arise from either a casualty or acts related to such a casualty. The 'material damage' is definitely a constituent element of the notion of 'maritime casualty', even if it is not required that such material damage has occurred. It is sufficient that there is an 'imminent threat' of its occurrence, as would be the case for a tanker grounded on rocks in calm sea that has not suffered any damage, but would suffer significant damage if the weather had turned from calm to stormy. The danger may follow, rather than from a maritime casualty, from an act related to it, as would be the case if unskilful attempts to refloat a grounded ship were made. But, in any event, there must be either material damage or an imminent threat of material damage to a ship or her cargo. Since the cargo is oil, the damage to the cargo may occur in case of fire or of discharge of the oil into the sea. It appears that the type of occurrence to which the Convention does not apply is that of voluntary discharge of oil (or oil residues) from a ship except where it is made for the purpose of salving the ship.

The 'maritime casualty' must therefore involve a ship or her cargo. Its nature is described in rather loose terms, since reference is made, in addition to collision and stranding, to other incidents of navigation or other occurrence either on board a ship or external to it. 'Incident in navigation' is an expression previously used also in the 1952 Convention on Penal Jurisdiction: while in the contemporary Civil Jurisdiction Convention reference is made to collision only, in the Penal Jurisdiction Convention there is added, after collision, the reference to 'other incidents of navigation'. Although no explanation may be found in the *travaux préparatoires* for the reason of such addition, a precedent may be found in those of the 1910 Collision Convention, from which it appears that, following a proposal by the Belgian

---

8 This objection was raised by the Canadian delegate who so stated (Official Records of the International Legal Conference, p. 314):

> . . . a coastal State, when exercising its right to intervene under the Convention, should not be compelled to prove for that purpose that the incident which had occurred had caused material damage to ship and cargo. A coastal State had a legitimate interest in protecting its coastline. If the text proposed by the Canadian delegation (that text consisted in the addition at the end of the sentence of the words 'resulting in danger to the coastline or related interest'), a different wording would be acceptable, provided that it respected the fundamental principle that the criterion for intervention should be the danger to the coastline and not the danger to the ship or cargo.

9 Official Records, *supra*, note 8, p. 313.
10 *Ibid.*, p. 318.

delegate to extend the scope of application of the Convention to other incident of navigation,[11] there was in the draft convention an article – art. 13 – that provided that the Convention applied also to the making good of damages which a vessel has caused to another vessel, or to goods on board either of them by the execution of a manoeuvre or by the non-observance of regulations. It appears, therefore, that a similar meaning must be given to the phrase 'other incident of navigation' in the definition of 'maritime casualty'.

However the cause of danger of pollution is further extended by the subsequent words 'or other occurrence' and the statement that such occurrence may take place either on board the ship or be 'external' to the ship. An occurrence on board may consist of a fire or of an explosion. An occurrence on the high seas external to the ship, that could justify the taking of measures against that ship, is more difficult to conceive.

2.2 The area in which the measures may be taken

The geographic scope of application of the Convention is the high seas. The reason for this is twofold. Pursuant to the International Convention for the Prevention of Pollution of the Sea by Oil, as amended, the coastal State has full competence to act within its territorial waters and, as previously stated, a State has, pursuant to art. 6(1) of the Convention on the High Seas 1958, exclusive jurisdiction over ships flying its flag.[12]

2.3 The notion of 'ship'

Article II(2) provides the following definition of ship:

'ship' means:
  (a) any sea-going vessel of any type whatsoever, and
  (b) any floating craft, with the exception of an installation or device engaged in the exploration and exploitation of the resources of the sea-bed and the ocean floor and the subsoil thereof.

The first question that arises relates to the notion of 'sea-going vessel'. The reason why this reference has been made is unclear. Since, in fact, the Convention applies to measures taken on the high seas, there was no reason to qualify the relevant vessel as 'sea-going' since it is obvious that such vessel was 'going' at sea, failing which

---

11 Volume I, Chapter 1, para. 2.1.

12 At the fifth meeting of the Committee of the Whole during the IMCO Conference of 1969 the Spanish delegate so stated (Official Records, *supra*, note 8, p. 301):

> Mr Munoz (Spain) said that his delegation had proposed its amendment partly to answer the problem raised on the previous day by the Cameroon representative. It stated where measures might be taken – on the high seas – but left to be understood that those measures could be taken whether the casualty occurred on the high seas or in the territorial sea. The purpose of the Convention was to legitimate the taking of measures on the high seas: it was already understood that they could be taken in the territorial sea.

The Spanish proposal, that was adopted, consisted of moving the reference to the high seas from the original place, after the words 'maritime casualty' to the initial part of the provision, where it appears the text of art.1 (1) as adopted by the Conference.

the Convention would not apply. Since it would not make sense to exclude from the scope of application of the Convention ships registered in an inland navigation register if at the relevant time they were navigating on the high seas, the conclusion can only be that that expression is redundant, and that the Convention applies to all ships, wherever registered, whether mainly intended for navigation on the sea or in inland waters, that at the relevant time are sailing on the high seas.

The term 'floating craft', as well as the French term '*engin flottant*' embraces almost anything that floats, such as boats, barges, pontoons, etc. And the intention to use the term in its widest meaning is confirmed by the initial word 'any (floating craft)' and in the French text '*tout (engin flottant)*' as well as by the express exclusion of 'an installation or device engaged in the exploration and exploitation of the resources of the sea-bed', therefore with the implied inclusion of such installations and devices while they are not engaged in the exploration and exploitation.

3 THE CONDITIONS UNDER WHICH THE MEASURES MAY BE TAKEN

There are four such conditions:

(a) there must be a grave and imminent danger of pollution or threat of pollution;
(b) the pollution must be by oil;
(c) the danger must affect the coastline and related interests; and
(d) the pollution must reasonably be expected to entail major harmful consequences.[13]

3.1 Grave and imminent danger of pollution or threat of pollution

It is not clear what is the difference between danger of pollution and threat of pollution, since one of the various meanings of 'threat' is danger or peril.[14] The only explanation could be that the words 'grave and imminent' qualify the danger, but not the threat of pollution; but that does not appear to be possible, because the threat must also be qualified. The conjunction 'or' should introduce an alternative, but in this case 'danger' and 'threat' are not alternatives. They are qualified both in respect of the level, that must be grave, *viz.* important, and the time when it may

---

13 The reason why the United Kingdom in its general comments on the draft convention (Official Records, *supra*, note 8, p. 192) quoted below, mentioned only three conditions without referring to pollution by oil was that at that time, in draft art. 1 the words 'by oil' were in square brackets:

> It is clear from the second recital of the preamble that the purpose of the Convention is to describe the measures of an exceptional character which a coastal State may take under extreme circumstances. The situation in which the coastal State may act is further described in article 1. That article indicates that at least three tests must be fulfilled:
>
> (a) grave and imminent danger to the coastline or related interests;
> (b) pollution or threat of pollution of the sea; and
> (c) reasonable expectation of major or catastrophic consequences.

14 *Shorter Oxford Dictionary.*

materialise. This should be very short – 'imminent' qualifies something that is about to happen.

3.2 The pollution must be by oil

In the draft article the words 'by oil' were placed in brackets, since there had been conflicting opinions as to whether the Convention ought to apply only to pollution by oil or ought to apply generally to all noxious and hazardous substances. That conflict was settled during the conference when it was agreed to limit the immediate scope of application of the Convention to pollution by oil, but to consider its extension to pollution by any other agent. A resolution to that effect was adopted by the Conference[15] and a Protocol, giving effect to that Resolution, was adopted on 2 November 1973.[16] Oil is defined in art. II(3) as:

3 'Oil' means crude oil, fuel oil, diesel oil and lubricating oil.

This definition had been suggested by Sweden.[17] It differs from that adopted in the contemporary CLC in that it does not qualify the oil as 'persistent'. The Swedish delegation explained that that word had been omitted since it believed that non-persistent oil might cause considerable damage during the time needed to remove it.[18] The definition, initially included in brackets,[19] was subsequently adopted.

3.3 The danger must affect the coastline and related interests

'Coastline' is not defined in the Convention, probably because it is a term that has various meanings.[20] In the *Shorter Oxford Dictionary* it is defined as the 'contour of a coast'. It may also be considered a synonym of 'sea shore' that is 'the land lying adjacent to the sea' or 'the ground actually washed by the sea at high tides'. The former definition is very likely the more appropriate for the purposes of this Convention,

---

15 The Resolution was the following (Official Records, *supra*, note 8, p. 184):

The States represented at the Conference,
IN ADOPTING the International Convention Relating to Intervention on the High Seas in Cases of Oil Pollution Casualties (hereinafter referred to as 'the Convention');
NOTING that pollution may be caused by agents other than oil;
RECOGNIZING that the limitation of the Convention to oil is not intended to abridge any right of a coastal State to protect itself against pollution by any other agent;
PENDING the entry into force of an international Instrument concerning pollution by such other agents or that there should be an extension of the Convention to such pollution;
RECOMMEND that the Inter-Governmental Maritime Consultative Organization should intensify its work, in collaboration with all interested international organizations, on all aspects of pollution by agents other than oil;
FURTHER RECOMMEND that Contracting States which become involved in a case of pollution danger by agents other than oil cooperate as appropriate in applying wholly or partially the provisions of the Convention.

16 For a commentary on such Protocol see *infra*, paras. 7–10.
17 Official Records, *supra*, note 8, p. 250.
18 *Ibid.*, p. 324.
19 *Ibid.*, p. 325.
20 It suffices to download the pages of Wikipedia on 'coast' to realise that that is the case. In the French text, the word used is *côte*: a word that has definitely a much wider meaning than 'coastline'.

OIL POLLUTION CASUALTIES CONVENTION, 1969

in consideration of the fact that the relevant danger is not referred to the coastline only, but also that the object of the danger may be, in addition to the coastline, also the 'related interests' that widen considerably the area in respect of which the danger from pollution or threat of pollution is relevant for the purposes of the Convention.

'Related interests' are so defined in art. II(4):

4 'related interests' means the interests of a coastal State directly affected or threatened by the maritime casualty, such as:
    (a) maritime, coastal, port or estuarine activities, including fisheries activities, constituting an essential means of livelihood of the persons concerned;

In the draft articles, reference was made to 'maritime coastal or port activities constituting essential means of livelihood of the persons concerned'. During the conference, a reference to activities in estuaries was added following a proposal from the Australian delegate who stated that such activities could be taken to constitute an essential means of livelihood.[21] Reference to fisheries was added following a proposal from the Japanese delegate, who stated that fisheries constituted the essential means of livelihood of large populations in many countries, including his own.[22]

(b) tourist attractions of the area concerned;

This expression has not been the object of any comment and that suggests that its meaning was clear to the delegates. It appears that it includes seaside resorts of any kind, hotels, swimming facilities etc. The 'area concerned' had been the object of a comment by Canada, to the effect that it was 'considered in Canada to include at least the territorial sea and exclusive fishing zone'.[23] In the Summary Records there appears only the following statement: 'Subject to the comment of the Canadian Government (LEG/CONF/3) sub-paragraph (b) was approved.'[24]

(c) the health of the coastal population and the well-being of the area concerned, including conservation of living marine resources and of wildlife.

In the draft articles the second part of this sub-paragraph was so worded: 'including conservation of fish and wildlife'.[25] Japan had stated that since the 'related interests' should include the interests of fishing industries, in this sub-paragraph, reference should be made to 'conservation of living marine resources'.[26] This proposal was carried.[27]

3.4 The pollution must reasonably be expected to entail major harmful consequences

Pursuant to art. I(1), the danger 'may reasonably be expected to result in major harmful consequences'. In the draft articles, the level of the consequences was

---

21 Official Records, *supra*, note 8, p. 320.
22 *Ibid.*
23 Official Records, *supra*, note 8, p. 205.
24 *Ibid.*, p. 322.
25 *Ibid.*, p. 205.
26 *Ibid.*, p. 206.
27 *Ibid.*, p. 323.

even higher, since it was provided that the casualty 'may reasonably be expected to result in major or catastrophic consequences'.[28] Objections against that wording were raised by Canada which suggested its deletion, but the prevailing view was that the danger ought to be qualified[29] even though it was agreed to replace the word 'catastrophic' by 'harmful'. The original wording did not make much sense, as it contained a rather inappropriate alternative between 'major' and 'catastrophic' consequences. The wording ultimately adopted qualifies instead the harmful consequences by requiring that they must be 'major': that the harm that would have been caused should have been major: it would not suffice that a harm would have been caused (e.g. pollution of a small beach) but it would have been necessary for the area polluted to be extensive.

4 THE OBLIGATIONS OF THE STATE THAT TAKES THE MEASURES ALLOWED BY ART. I

Article III sets out rules on the obligations a State must comply with before taking the measures allowed by art. I(1), on the advice it may seek on the situations where prior compliance with that obligation is not required, on the manner in which the action should be taken and on the duty to give notice of the measures that it has taken.

4.1 Obligations prior to taking the measures

Art. III states in sub-paragraphs (a) and (b):

(a) before taking any measures, a coastal State shall proceed to consultations with other States affected by the maritime casualty, particularly with the flag State or States;
(b) the coastal State shall notify without delay the proposed measures to any persons physical or corporate known to the coastal State, or made known to it during the consultations, to have interests which can reasonably be expected to be affected by those measures. The coastal State shall take into account any views they may submit;

This appears to be a two-phase procedure: first a consultation with other States, secondly a notification of proposed measures seeking the views of interested persons. The persons involved in the first phase are (i) other States that have an interest similar to that of the coastal State who intends to take measures in order to prevent or mitigate danger to the coastline, as they are States that are or may be affected by the casualty; and (ii) the flag State or States of the ship or ships against which the measure would be taken: two groups with possible conflicting interests. In any

---

28 *Ibid.*, p. 195.
29 The Swedish delegate so stated (Official Records, *supra*, note 8, p. 305):

Mr Voss said that at first it might appear logical to delete the final phrase of the paragraph, on the grounds that it was unnecessary further to qualify the danger already described. But on further reflection it appeared that some reference to the consequences of that danger was essential if the coastal State was to be sufficiently justified in taking action to protect itself. He was sure it had been the intention of the Legal Committee to make reference to the consequences of the danger in addition to the danger itself.

event there does not appear to be any obligation of the coastal State to adopt the suggestions that may be given.

The second phase assumes that the coastal State has reached a conclusion on the kind of measures that ought to be taken and requires the coastal State to notify such measures to the persons that it is aware 'can reasonably be expected to be affected by such measures'. The meaning of the term used – affected (*compromis* in the French text) – is twofold: a person may be affected positively (and have an advantage) or negatively (to suffer a loss): any person who may suffer a loss on account of pollution may avoid or minimise such loss if the measure is successful or see its loss materialise or increase if it is unsuccessful, while the owner of the ship or of its cargo would almost always suffer a greater loss (e.g. because his ship has been sunk or his cargo destroyed).

The coastal State has two obligations: first to notify without delay the proposed measures to any persons known to have an interest and secondly to take into account their views. The burden of proof in case of the breach of the first of such obligations, in respect of which a distinction is made between persons known and persons made known during the consultations (a distinction difficult to understand, since the notification takes place after the period of consultations) should rest on the claimant. The claimant should prove that the person to whom the coastal State failed to notify the proposed measures was known to have an interest which could reasonably be expected to be affected by those measures, as well as the damages caused by such non-compliance.

The second obligation has been the object of a debate during the Conference and various proposals were made, including the deletion of the sentence,[30] the replacement of 'shall take into account' by 'may take into account'[31] and the replacement of 'take into account' by 'take into consideration'.[32] The Chairman ignored the second and third proposals and only put the first to the vote.[33] That was rejected, whereupon he stated that the sentence was adopted unchanged and no objection was made. It appears, therefore, that the coastal State has an obligation to take into account any view that may be submitted by the persons to whom it had notified the proposed measures. However, apart from the fact that the views submitted, that include those submitted by other States during the consultations, may be conflicting with one another, to 'take into account' (the words used in the French text are *'prendre en consideration'*) does not entail an obligation to accept, but merely to take the views into consideration in deciding the measures, if any, that should be adopted. The coastal State must make a sound assessment of such views, taking into consideration the threat of damage to its coastline. There is also a time element that plays an important role: since all this happens when there is an imminent danger to its coast and to the related interest, the coastal State must take a quick decision; therefore, it cannot wait long for such views to come.

---

30 By Guatemala (Official Records, *supra*, note 8, p. 333).
31 By Indonesia and Cameroon (Official Records, *supra*, note 8, pp. 333 and 334).
32 By the United Kingdom (Official Records, *supra*, note 8, p. 333).
33 Official Records, *supra*, note 8, p. 335.

4.2 Optional advice

Art. III(c) so provides:

(c)   before any measure is taken, the coastal State may proceed to a consultation with independent experts, whose names shall be chosen from a list maintained by the Organization;

Canada had suggested redrafting this paragraph to recognise that coastal States maintained the right of consulting experts other than those listed by the Organization.[34]
However, during the conference, the Canadian delegate stated that he withdrew the
amendment since 'on reflection . . . he had realized that the original draft text did
in fact allow for the possibility of a coastal State consulting experts other than those
listed by the Organization'.[35] This statement, that did not give rise to any comment,
appears to be correct, the difference between consulting an expert chosen from an
official list and a private expert being that, in this latter case, the decision on the
action to be taken would remain a decision of the coastal State, whereas a decision
based on the advice of an expert chosen from the official list would provide a strong
argument against the different actions resulting from the consultations, reference to
which is made under (a) and (b).

The setting up of the official list of experts is the object of an express rule in art.
IV of the Convention which provides:

1   Under the supervision of the Organization, there shall be set up and maintained the list
of experts contemplated by article III of the present Convention, and the Organization
shall make necessary and appropriate regulations in connection therewith, including the
determination of the required qualifications.
2   Nominations to the list may be made by Member States of the Organization and by
Parties to this Convention. The experts shall be paid on the basis of services rendered
by the States utilizing those services.

A proposal for the amendment of this provision, the wording of which is the same
as that in the draft article submitted to the Conference, was made by the United
States,[36] such amendment consisting of the list of experts prepared by Member
States of the Organization and by States Parties to the Convention, that however
would become the official list, being only a list from which the Organization would
choose the experts that would appear in the official list. Although there was some
support of the US proposal, the majority was in favour of the wording suggested by
the Legal Committee.[37]

4.3 When compliance with the obligations under (a) and (b) is not required

Art. III(d) so provides:

(d)   in cases of extreme urgency requiring measures to be taken immediately, the coastal State
may take measures rendered necessary by the urgency of the situation, without prior
notification or consultation or without continuing consultations already begun;

---

34 *Ibid.*, p. 207.
35 *Ibid.*, p. 335.
36 LEG/CONF/3; Official Records, *supra*, note 8, pp. 209–210.
37 Official Records, *supra*, note 8, pp. 341–344.

The only question that was discussed during the Conference concerned the placement of this provision within art. III, Canada having suggested, with the support of some other delegations, that it should come first, since the case of extreme urgency would be the most usual. The view prevailed that its placement was appropriate, since it was an exception to the general rule.[38] The fact remains that the whole of the Convention aims to regulate an exceptional situation: the situation in which there is a grave and imminent danger from pollution or threat of pollution. This fact justifies some doubts in respect of the feasibility of the complicated and apparently rather lengthy procedure described in paragraphs (a) and (b), complemented by the optional procedure in paragraph (c). It would not be a nonsense to state that any case in which there is a grave and imminent danger of pollution is one which requires urgent action. That would entail that art. III(d) is the general rule and art. III(a) and (b) is the exception applicable when the danger is not really 'imminent'.

4.4 The manner in which the measures ought to be taken

Art. III(e) so provides:

(e)   a coastal State shall, before taking such measures and during their course, use its best endeavours to avoid any risk to human life, and to afford persons in distress any assistance of which they may stand in need, and in appropriate cases to facilitate repatriation of ships' crews, and to raise no obstacle thereto.

This paragraph originates from a provision, proposed by the USSR delegation, that was aimed at protecting the crew of a ship involved in a maritime casualty and of other persons on board that ship.[39] This proposal was supported by several delegations and it was decided to set up a small working group with the task of drafting a revised text of that provision.[40] Its scope was extended by the Working Group to cover the duty to avoid any risk to human life and to afford assistance to any persons in distress, with a specific mention of the crew.

4.5 Guidelines for the selection of the measures

Such guidelines are set out in art. V and are basically twofold: the measures must be proportionate to the damage and must not go beyond what is reasonably necessary to achieve their purpose.

---

38 *Ibid.*, pp. 334 and 335.

39 The wording of the provision submitted by the USSR delegation, as subsequently amended by that delegation, was the following (LEG/CONF/C.1/WP.7/Rev. 1, Official Records, *supra*, note 8, p. 252):

E. If the measures to be taken could affect the safety of the crew and other persons on board a ship involved in a maritime casualty, a coastal State shall, before taking any such measures, move the crew and other persons from the ship to a safe place and shall not prevent their return to the ship as soon as it is safe or to the port of the ship's registry or to their home country.

40 Official Records, *supra*, note 8, p. 340.

4.5.1 *Measures proportionate to the damage*

Art. V states, in paragraphs 1 and 3, the wording of which is the same as in the draft articles:

1 Measures taken by the coastal State in accordance with article I shall be proportionate to the damage actual or threatened to it.

  . . .

3 In considering whether the measures are proportionate to the damage, account shall be taken of:
   (a) the extent and probability of imminent damage if those measures are not taken; and
   (b) the likelihood of those measures being effective; and
   (c) the extent of the damage which may be caused by such measures.

The principle of proportionality has not given rise to any comment, nor do any comments appear to have been made in respect of sub-paragraph (a). There is, however, a difference between art. V(3)(a) and art. I(1): whilst pursuant to art. I(1) States Parties to the Convention may take the measures to prevent, mitigate or eliminate grave and imminent danger from pollution which may reasonably be expected to result in major harmful consequences, pursuant to art. V(3)(a) what is required to be 'imminent' is not the danger, but the damage. Therefore, in the chain of events the danger is bypassed. Although the time gap may not be considerable, the requirements under art. V(3) are still stricter than those under art. I(1).

In so far as the guidelines under sub-paragraphs (b) and (c) are concerned, critical comments have been made by Canada. In respect of sub-paragraph (b), Canada[41] observed that the likelihood of the measures being effective must be assessed taking into account the actual situation pertaining at the time of emergency, and that options taken in the heat of the moment might well be seriously questioned afterwards.[42] This was correct, but that is what sub-paragraph (b) says: the 'likelihood' of the measures being effective cannot but be assessed at the time when the measures are decided and are taken, on the basis of the information available at that time.[43]

In so far as sub-paragraph (c) is concerned, the Canadian delegate said that it referred to the actions of a coastal State as viewed in retrospect when all the facts were available and suggested that sub-paragraph (c) could be deleted. It is suggested that the position is similar to that relating to sub-paragraph (b). The extent of the damage which may be caused by the measures must be assessed at the time they are taken: the provision in fact refers to the damage that 'may be caused' and not to the

---

41 The alternative wording suggested for para. (b) had been the following (Official Records, *supra*, note 8, p. 211):

  The likelihood of those measures being effective having regard the exigencies of the situation.

42 Official Records, *supra*, note 8, p. 345.

43 This was what the UK delegate meant when, obviously having in mind the bombing of the '*Torrey Canyon*' by the RAF, he stated (Official Records, *supra*, note 8, p. 346):

  . . . sub-paragraph (ii) meant that if drastic action were contemplated – such as bombing for example – and it appeared that as a result of that action there would still be as much pollution as before, that factor must be taken into account. In such a case the likelihood of those measures being effective was not very great.

OIL POLLUTION CASUALTIES CONVENTION, 1969

damage that 'has been caused'. In this respect, the comments made by the German delegate appear appropriate.[44]

4.5.2 Measures necessary to achieve their purpose

Article V(2) provides:

2　Such measures shall not go beyond what is reasonably necessary to achieve the end mentioned in article I and shall cease as soon as that end has been achieved; they shall not unnecessarily interfere with the rights and interests of the flag State, third States and of any persons, physical or corporate, concerned.

The purpose of this provision, adopted without any discussion, as that of the provisions in paragraphs 1 and 3, is to ensure a reasonable balance between the interests of those persons who may suffer damages as a consequence of the casualty and those of the owners of and other persons having an interest in the ship or ships involved in the casualty, including the flag State or States.

5 COMPENSATION DUE FOR THE DAMAGE CAUSED BY THE MEASURES TAKEN PURSUANT TO ART. I

Art. VI so provides:

Any party which has taken measures in contravention of the provisions of the present Convention causing damage to others, shall be obliged to pay compensation to the extent of the damage caused by measures which exceed those reasonably necessary to achieve the end mentioned in article I.

The original text of this provision, as it appeared in the draft articles, was the following:[45]

Any State which, within the scope of the present Convention, has taken measures in contravention of its provisions, causing damage to others, shall be obliged to pay compensation.

That provision met with strong opposition from Canada and some other delegations on the ground that it would have been unfair to make the State who has taken measures liable if the State claiming damages were not bound by the private law convention in preparation (the CLC) and the proposal was made by Canada to link the two conventions by providing that a State party to the public law convention

---

44　He so stated (Official Records, *supra*, note 8, p. 347):

> Mr Hinz (Federal Republic of Germany) said that, while sympathizing with the Canadian point of view, his delegation was in favour of retaining sub-paragraph (iii), which represented the hard core of the principle of proportionality. The cost of the prevention of pollution had to be weighed against the damage to the ship and cargo. No government and no judge could evade trying to strike a balance. Furthermore, a balance must be struck between the importance of the cleanliness of the coastal State's seashore and all other interests on the high seas which might be affected. In that connexion, he recalled that after the 'Torrey Canyon' incident a group of scientists had produced a report in which they came to the conclusion that the harmful effects of the chemicals used to combat the pollution were worse than the noxious effects of the oil itself.

45　Official Records, *supra*, note 8, p. 212.

INTERNATIONAL MARITIME CONVENTIONS

might declare not to consider itself bound by this article to States which do not become parties to the private law convention.[46] That proposal was rejected,[47] but a second joint Canadian and United States proposal was adopted, pursuant to which liability of the party (and not the State) which has taken the measures would exist to the extent that the measures went beyond what was reasonably necessary to achieve the end mentioned in art. I.[48] This provision is thereby linked to that in the previous art. V and liability exists only where the relevant party is in breach of obligations under that article, but it applies irrespective of the person liable for the pollution damage being subject to the CLC or not.

6 COMPULSORY CONCILIATION AND ARBITRATION OF DISPUTES

Art. VIII so provides:

1 Any controversy between the Parties as to whether measures taken under article I were in contravention of the provisions of the present Convention, to whether compensation is obliged to be paid under article VI, and to the amount of such compensation shall, if settlement by negotiation between the Parties involved or between the Party which took the measures and the physical or corporate claimants has not been possible, and if the Parties do not otherwise agree, be submitted upon request of any of the Parties concerned to conciliation or, if conciliation does not succeed, to arbitration, as set out in the Annex to the present Convention.
2 The Party which took the measures shall not be entitled to refuse a request for conciliation or arbitration under provisions of the preceding paragraph solely on the grounds that any remedies under municipal law in its own courts have not been exhausted.

The principle of compulsory conciliation and arbitration, adopted in paragraph 1 of this article, had been the object of a rather lengthy debate. It had been stated by some delegations that it was out of place in a public law convention, since a multi-lateral agreement could not subject sovereign States to compulsory arbitration[49] and was in conflict with the Vienna Convention.[50] However, a large majority was instead of the view that art. VIII was not an 'important' derogation from the principle of State sovereignty[51] and was compatible with the Vienna Convention.[52]

Some doubts could arise in respect of the meaning in paragraph 2 of the words 'shall not be entitled to refuse a request for conciliation or arbitration *solely on the grounds* that any remedies under its own municipal law have not been exhausted'. The adverb 'solely' might be deemed to imply that a request of conciliation or arbitration might be refused on other grounds. However, if it is considered that this paragraph is a redraft of the first sentence of the text contained in the draft articles

---

46 *Ibid.*
47 *Ibid.*, at p. 351.
48 *Ibid.*, at pp. 351 and 380.
49 See the statement of the USSR delegate, Official Records, *supra*, note 8, p. 365 and the statement of the Romanian delegate at p. 366.
50 Official Records, *supra*, note 8, p. 360.
51 See the statement of the US delegate, Official Records, *supra*, note 8, p. 367.
52 See the statement of the delegates of the Netherlands and New Zealand, Official Records, *supra*, note 8, p. 368.

submitted to the Conference, it appears that such interpretation has no basis. In fact the result of the debate on the more lengthy provision contained in square brackets in the draft articles,[53] that had taken place during the Conference, had been that the first sentence of that paragraph should be retained, but not in the present form and the second sentence should instead be deleted.[54] Since the first sentence provided that States parties might undertake the procedures provided for in the preceding paragraph before local remedies have been exhausted, while the second sentence, the deletion of which had been decided, provided that the procedures mentioned in paragraph 1 would be held in abeyance pending final disposition in the forum of the coastal State, it appears that the adverb 'solely' is a surplus.

The rules on conciliation and arbitration annexed to the Convention will not be the object of a specific commentary since the likelihood of such procedures taking place is rather remote. Suffice it to mention that pursuant to art. 13(2), where conciliation is unsuccessful a request for arbitration may only be made within a period of 180 days following the failure of conciliation, and that pursuant to art. 10, a conciliation shall be deemed unsuccessful if, 90 days after the Parties have been notified of the recommendation, either Party shall not have notified the other Party of its acceptance of the recommendation or if the Conciliation Commission shall not have issued its recommendation within one year from the date on which the Chairman of the Commission was nominated. It would appear, therefore, that since conciliation and arbitration are compulsory, a claim becomes barred if a request for arbitration is not made within the aforesaid period of 180 days. However, no time limit is set in the Convention in respect of the request of conciliation, and, therefore, that time limit depends on the relevant rules of the applicable law.

SECTION II – THE PROTOCOL OF 1973

7 THE HISTORY OF THE PROTOCOL

The history of this Protocol appears very clearly from a Note of the IMCO Secretariat prepared for the Twelfth Session of the Legal Committee held in March 1972.[55] An extract is quoted below:

1 The International Legal Conference on Marine Pollution Damage, 1969, in adopting the International Convention Relating to Intervention on the High Seas in Cases of Oil Pollution Casualties, noted that pollution may be caused by agents other than oil and recognized that the Convention was not intended to abridge the right of a coastal State to protect itself against pollution by any other agent.

---

53 Its wording was the following (Official Records, *supra*, note 8, p. 217):

[The Contracting Parties may undertake the procedures provided for in the preceding paragraph before local remedies have been exhausted. However, where claims for compensation can be pursued against the coastal State in its own courts or in some other way provided by agreement under its national law, and the coastal State waives any defences under its own law based on the fact that the action it took was the act of a sovereign State, the procedures provided for in the preceding paragraph shall be held in abeyance pending final disposition in the forum of the coastal State].

54 Official Records, *supra*, note 8, pp. 378–379.

55 Document LEG XII/2 of 13 March 1972.

INTERNATIONAL MARITIME CONVENTIONS

2   The Conference accordingly established a Working Group to explore the means by which the Convention could be extended to cover pollution by agents other than oil. The discussions of the problem of extension revealed, however, that more study of the problem would be needed, in particular with a view to identifying these agents of pollution.

3   The consensus at the Conference was that, until all aspects of pollution by substances other than oil could be investigated, a blanket extension of the Convention to all noxious and hazardous cargoes without specification would be unwise. Similarly, it was felt that the mere attachment, to the Convention, of a list of polluting agents other than oil to which the Convention might be made applicable would not be a useful addition to that instrument, in the absence of some clear indication of some of the essential characteristics of these substances which would help in determining the possibility and extent of the applicability of the Convention to the various substances. It was also felt that it would be useful and necessary to have criteria by reference to which such a list of substances might be enlarged or decreased in response to developments.

4   In view of these and other considerations, the Conference did not adopt the suggestion for a protocol or additional act by which the 'Public Law' Convention would or could be extended to cover agents of pollution other than oil (see LEG/CONF/C.1/WP.8 and LEG/CONF/C.1/SR.18 and 19). It decided instead to recommend that, pending the entry into force of an instrument concerning pollution by such other agents – or an extension of the Convention at some future time to such pollution –the Organization (i.e. IMCO) should intensify its work, in collaboration with all interested international organizations, on all aspects of pollution by agents other than oil. Finally the Conference recommended that the Convention should be applied in whole or in part to cases of pollution danger by such agents of pollution through appropriate cooperation by the States involved (see Resolution of the Conference: Attachment 3 to the Final Act).

5   It is safe to assume, therefore, that the Conference was in large measure convinced of the applicability of the 'Public Law' Convention to situations in which grave pollution danger might reasonably be expected to result from a maritime casualty not involving oil. It was felt that, since the Convention was intended primarily to provide a framework of law to govern self-protective measures of exceptional character, the limitation of its provisions to grave and imminent danger from oil pollution or its threat might ultimately lead to the undesirable and unintended inference that unregulated and disproportionate measures could be taken with impunity in respect of maritime casualties involving danger from other polluting substance, while casualties involving oil alone were subject to uniform international law. It was the view of the Conference that action should be taken to discourage this result.

Following the discussion that took place in the Legal Committee during its twelfth session, a working party was created with the task of presenting draft texts of a Protocol taking into account the approaches suggested by the Committee.[56] The first of such approaches was to extend the Convention to cover substances other than oil and the second was to restrict the extension to substances enumerated in a list. The Working Party submitted a concise summary of such two approaches, called Formula A and Formula B[57] and added a third alternative, which consisted in

---

56 Legal Committee – 16th session, Consideration of the Extension of the Convention Relating to Intervention on the High Seas in Cases of Oil Pollution Casualties to Noxious and Hazardous Substances Other than Oil – Note by the Secretariat, document LEG XVI/2 of 23 November 1972.

57 They were worded as follows:

(LEG XVI/2, Annex I):
Formula A
Article I

Parties to the present Protocol may take such measures on the high seas as may be necessary to prevent, mitigate or eliminate grave and imminent danger to their territory including the territorial sea or related

OIL POLLUTION CASUALTIES CONVENTION, 1969

a combination of such approaches by having both a general clause and a list, called Formula C.[58]

At its sixteenth session, the Legal Committee considered the three alternatives submitted by the working group and the majority felt that the Formula C approach, suggested by the working group, was more likely to find general acceptance and decided to use it as a basis of further work. It also decided that the new instrument should take the form of a protocol to the Convention of 1969.[59] With the assistance of the Working Group the Committee prepared a Draft Protocol as well as an Annex to it with a list of substances that had been established by the Marine Environmental Protection Committee of IMCO (MEPC), circulated to governments. The Draft Protocol and such list were considered by the Diplomatic Conference convened in October 1973 and adopted on 2 November 1973. As of 31 May 2014, 54 of the 87 States parties to the Convention were also parties to the Protocol.[60]

---

interests from pollution or threat of pollution of the environment by substances other than oil following upon a maritime casualty or acts related to such a casualty, which may reasonably be expected to result in major harmful consequences.

Article II

The provisions of paragraph 2 of article I and article II *et seq.* of the Convention and the Annexes thereto as they relate to oil shall be applicable with regard to the substances referred to in article I of this Protocol.

Formula B
Article I

1 Parties to the present Protocol may take such measures on the high seas as may be necessary to prevent, mitigate or eliminate grave and imminent danger to their territory including the territorial sea or related interests from pollution or threat of pollution of the environment by substances other than oil following upon a maritime casualty or acts related to such a casualty, which may reasonably be expected to result in major harmful consequences.

2 'Substances other than oil' as referred to in paragraph 1 shall be those substances enumerated in a list maintained for the purposes by the Maritime Safety Committee of the Organization.

Article II

The provisions of paragraph 2 of article I and article II *et seq.* of the Convention and the Annexes thereto as they relate to oil shall be applicable with regard to the substances referred to in article I of this Protocol.

58 Its wording was the following:

(LEG XVI/2, Annex I, p. 3 and 4):
Formula C
Article I

1 Parties to the present Protocol may take such measures on the high seas as may be necessary to prevent, mitigate or eliminate grave and imminent danger to their territory including the territorial sea or related interests from pollution or threat of pollution of the environment by substances other than oil following upon a maritime casualty or acts related to such a casualty, which may reasonably be expected to result in major harmful consequences.

2 'Substances other than oil' as referred to in paragraph 1 shall be:

(a) those substances enumerated in a list maintained for the purpose by the Maritime Safety Committee of the Organization; and

(b) those substances which, by their nature or characteristics, bioaccumulation, damage to living resources, hazard to human health, reduction of amenities or interference with other uses of the sea, substantially degrade the environment.

3 With regard to the provisions of articles V, VI, VII and VIII of the Convention, the intervening Party where it intervenes with regard to a substance not set forth under (a) shall have the burden of establishing that the substance was, at the time and location, capable of substantially degrading the environment.

59 Document LEG XVI/4, p. 3, para. 11.

60 The States parties to the Convention are the following (those parties also to the Protocol are printed in italics): *Algeria*, Angola, Argentina, *Australia*, *Bahamas*, Bangladesh, *Barbados*, *Belgium*, Benin, *Brazil*, *Bulgaria*, Cameroon, *Chile*, *China*, Côte d'Ivoire, *Croatia*, Cuba, *Denmark*, Djibouti, Dominican Republic, Ecuador, *Egypt*, Equatorial Guinea, *Estonia*, Fiji, *Finland*, *France*, Gabon, *Georgia*, *Germany*,

INTERNATIONAL MARITIME CONVENTIONS

8 THE SCOPE OF APPLICATION OF THE PROTOCOL

Article I states in paragraphs 1 and 2:

1 Parties to the present Protocol may take such measures on the high seas as may be necessary to prevent, mitigate or eliminate grave and imminent danger to their coastline or related interests from pollution or threat of pollution by substances other than oil following upon a maritime casualty or acts related to such a casualty, which may reasonably be expected to result in major harmful consequences.
2 'Substances other than oil' as referred to in paragraph 1 shall be:
   (a) those substances enumerated in a list which shall be established by an appropriate body designated by the Organization and which shall be annexed to the present Protocol, and
   (b) those other substances which are liable to create hazards to human health, to harm living resources and marine life, to damage amenities or to interfere with other legitimate uses of the sea.

The Protocol does not apply only to substances enumerated in the list annexed to the Protocol, that may be amended from time to time, but also to other substances that have the characteristics mentioned in paragraph 2(b), which are liable to create hazards. However, in order that the Protocol apply in such case, the burden of proving the above character is on the person invoking the application of the Protocol. Paragraph 3 of art. 1 so in fact provides:

Whenever an intervening Party takes action with regard to a substance referred to in paragraph 2(b) above that Party shall have the burden of establishing that the substance, under the circumstances present at the time of the intervention, could reasonably pose a grave and imminent danger analogous to that posed by any of the substances enumerated in the list referred to in paragraph 2(a) above.

The terms used are those used in art. I(1) of the Convention, but since it is likely that the substances enumerated in the list will not pose precisely the same level of grave imminent danger, the problem arises whether it would suffice that the relevant substance would pose a danger similar to that posed by a substance at the bottom of the list in respect of its dangerous character. It is suggested that that should be the case.

9 THE RELATIONSHIP BETWEEN THE PROTOCOL AND THE CONVENTION

The purpose of this Protocol differs from that of most of the other protocols to maritime conventions. Its purpose is not to amend provisions of the Convention, but to extend the scope of its application and, therefore, the Protocol is autonomous. In

---

Ghana, Guyana, Iceland, India, *Ireland, Iran (Islamic Republic of)*, *Italy, Jamaica*, Japan, Kuwait, *Latvia*, Lebanon, *Liberia, Marshall Islands, Mauritania, Mauritius, Mexico, Monaco, Montenegro, Morocco, Namibia, Netherlands*, New Zealand, *Nicaragua*, Nigeria, *Norway, Oman, Pakistan*, Panama, Papua New Guinea, *Poland, Portugal*, Qatar, *Russian Federation*, St Kitts and Nevis, *St Lucia, St Vincent & The Grenadines*, Senegal, *Serbia, Slovenia, South Africa*, Spain, Sri Lanka, Suriname, *Sweden, Switzerland*, Syrian Arab Republic, *Tanzania, Tonga*, Trinidad and Tobago, *Tunisia*, Ukraine, United Arab Emirates, *United Kingdom, United States, Vanuatu, Yemen*.

fact, it incorporates all the relevant provisions of the Convention, as appears from art. II which provides:

1 The provisions of paragraph 2 of article I and of articles II to VIII of the Convention Relating to Intervention on the High Seas in Cases of Oil Pollution Casualties, 1969, and the Annex thereto as they relate to oil, shall be applicable with regard to the substances referred to in article I of the present Protocol.
2 For the purpose of the present Protocol the list of experts referred to in articles III(c) and IV of the Convention shall be extended to include experts qualified to give advice in relation to substances other than oil. Nominations to the list may be made by Member States of the Organization and by Parties to the present Protocol.

10 THE PROCEDURE FOR UPDATING THE LIST OF THE SUBSTANCES

Art. III so provides:

1 The list referred to in paragraph 2(a) of article I shall be maintained by the appropriate body designated by the Organization.
2 Any amendment to the list proposed by a Party to the present Protocol shall be submitted to the Organization and circulated by it to all Members of the Organization and all Parties to the present Protocol at least three months prior to its consideration by the appropriate body.
3 Parties to the present Protocol whether or not Members of the Organization shall be entitled to participate in the proceedings of the appropriate body.
4 Amendments shall be adopted by a two-thirds majority of only the Parties to the present Protocol present and voting.
5 If adopted in accordance with paragraph 4 above, the amendment shall be communicated by the Organization to all Parties to the present Protocol for acceptance.
6 The amendment shall be deemed to have been accepted at the end of a period of six months after it has been communicated, unless within that period an objection to the amendment has been communicated to the Organization by not less than one-third of the Parties to the present Protocol.
7 An amendment deemed to have been accepted in accordance with paragraph 6 above shall enter into force three months after its acceptance for all Parties to the present Protocol, with the exception of those which before that date have made a declaration of non-acceptance of the said amendment.

The provision in paragraph 1 cannot be read in isolation, but rather in conjunction with the provisions in paragraph 2, that set out the procedure to be followed for the amendments of the list. The 'appropriate body' designated by IMO does not have the power to update the list, but paragraph 3 indicates that its task is to conduct the procedure for the amendments accepted by the States Parties in accordance with the procedure set out in paragraphs 2–7. Such procedure, that is the predecessor of those adopted for the amendments of the limits in art. 15 of CLC 1992, art. 8 of the Protocol of 1996 to LLMC Convention 1976 and art. 23 of the Protocol of 2002 to the Athens Convention of 1974, leaves to the Parties to the Protocol the initiative to propose the amendments to the 'appropriate body', and provides that the proposed amendments must be circulated to all States Members of IMO as well as to all States Members of the Protocol. The proposed amendments are then adopted by a two-thirds majority of all such latter States present and voting, irrespective of how many they were, and shall be deemed to have been accepted unless, prior to the lapse of six months from the date of communication, objections are made by not less than one-third of all States Parties to the Protocol. Although, therefore, it is conceivable that their adoption occurs even if the States Parties present are relatively few, double protection is granted to the other States Parties both because the amendments are deemed to have been accepted only if objections by at least one-third of all States Parties are not communicated to IMO before the lapse of six months and because, in any event, they are not binding for the States Parties which before the lapse of three months from the date of their deemed acceptance have made a declaration of non-acceptance. A rather cumbersome procedure, that would create two categories of States Parties, the first in respect of which the amended list applies, and the second in respect of which the un-amended list applies. This problem has been overcome in the provisions subsequently adopted in other conventions, in which the States Parties present and voting must comprise at least one-half of the States Parties, but all States Parties are bound by the amendments unless they denounce the Protocol.[61]

The first revision of the list was adopted by the Marine Environment Protection Committee with resolution MEPC 49(31) of 4 July 1996 followed by resolution MEPC 72(38) of 10 July 1996. After the restructuring of the Annex to the Protocol approved by MEPC, the list of substances was amended by resolution MEPC 100/48 of 11 October 2002. All the amendments were approved by sessions of the MEPC with the required two-thirds majority of States Parties to the Intervention Protocol.

---

61 Articles 8(4) and (9) of the 1996 Protocol of the LLMC 1976; art. 23(5) and (10) of the 2002 Protocol to the Athens Convention 1974; art. 8(4) and (9) of the 1996 Protocol to the LLMC Convention 1976.

CHAPTER 2

International Convention on Oil Pollution Preparedness, Response and Cooperation, 1990 (OPRC Convention) with its Protocol of 2000 (OPRC-HNS Protocol)

SECTION I – THE CONVENTION OF 1990

1 INTRODUCTION

This Convention is relevant because some of its provisions apply either to a phase that precedes that to which the provisions of the Intervention Convention apply or to the same phase, and therefore may overlap them[1] and in both cases the question arises whether such provisions need to be coordinated.

2 THE SCOPE OF APPLICATION OF THE CONVENTION

Before considering whether the provisions of the first category are relevant in connection with the situations covered by the Intervention Convention and whether those of the second category may be in conflict with the provisions of the Intervention Convention, it should be noted that the scope of application of the OPRC Convention is wider than that of the Intervention Convention. This is because it includes rights and obligations not related to incidents, namely those regulated by:

- art. 3 on Oil pollution emergency plans;
- art. 6 on National and regional systems for preparedness and response;
- art. 7 on International cooperation in pollution response;
- art. 8 on Research and development;
- art. 9 on Technical cooperation;
- art. 10 on Promotion of bilateral and multilateral cooperation in preparedness and response; and
- art. 12 on Institutional arrangements.

---

1 Out of the 87 States parties to the Intervention Convention, 70 are also parties to the OPRC Convention. They are: Algeria, Angola, Argentina, Australia, Bahamas, Bangladesh, Benin, Brazil, Bulgaria, Cameroon, Chile, China, Côte d'Ivoire, Croatia, Cuba, Denmark, Djibouti, Ecuador, Egypt, Estonia, Finland, France, Gabon, Georgia, Germany, Ghana, Guyana, Iceland, India, Ireland, Iran (Islamic Republic of), Italy, Jamaica, Japan, Latvia, Lebanon, Liberia, Marshall Islands, Mauritania, Mauritius, Mexico, Monaco, Morocco, Namibia, Netherlands, New Zealand, Nigeria, Norway, Oman, Pakistan, Poland, Portugal, Qatar, Russian Federation, St Kitts and Nevis, St Lucia, Senegal, Slovenia, Spain, Suriname, Sweden, Switzerland, Syrian Arab Republic, Tanzania, Tonga, Trinidad and Tobago, Tunisia, United Kingdom, United States, Vanuatu.

23

Its scope is wider geographically, because it also covers incidents occurring in territorial waters. Finally, it is wider because in the definition of 'ships' in art. 2(3), reference is made to hydrofoil boats, hydrofoils, air-cushion vehicles and submersibles and the Convention applies also to offshore units.

3 AN ANALYSIS OF THE POSSIBLE CONFLICT BETWEEN THE OPRC CONVENTION AND THE INTERVENTION CONVENTION

In Conference Resolution No. 1 it is recognised that the measures introduced by the OPRC Convention take into account the provisions of other important conventions developed by the International Maritime Organization and it is stated that the OPRC Convention needs to supplement and not to duplicate the important provisions adopted by or under the auspices of IMO. Although reference is made only to MARPOL, there are other Conventions in respect of which the principle that the OPRC Convention intends to supplement and not to duplicate the provisions of other conventions applies and, it should be emphasised, that it is important to avoid any conflict with other such conventions. Reference will be made hereafter to the Intervention Convention of 1969.

The provisions of the OPRC Convention that apply to a phase that precedes that to which the Intervention Convention applies are those of art. 4, which provides:

Oil pollution reporting procedures

(1) Each Party shall:
- (a) require masters or other persons having charge of ships flying its flag and persons having charge of offshore units under its jurisdiction to report without delay any event on their ship or offshore unit involving a discharge or probable discharge of oil:
    - (i) in the case of a ship, to the nearest coastal State;
    - (ii) in the case of an offshore unit, to the coastal State to whose jurisdiction the unit is subject;
- (b) require masters or other persons having charge of ships flying its flag and persons having charge of offshore units under its jurisdiction to report without delay any observed event at sea involving a discharge of oil or the presence of oil:
    - (i) in the case of a ship, to the nearest coastal State;
    - (ii) in the case of an offshore unit, to the coastal State to whose jurisdiction the unit is subject;
- (c) require persons having charge of sea ports and oil handling facilities under its jurisdiction to report without delay any event involving a discharge or probable discharge of oil or the presence of oil to the competent national authority;
- (d) instruct its maritime inspection vessels or aircraft and other appropriate services or officials to report without delay any observed event at sea or at a sea port or oil handling facility involving a discharge of oil or the presence of oil to the competent national authority or, as the case may be, to the nearest coastal State;
- (e) request the pilots of civil aircraft to report without delay any observed event at sea involving a discharge of oil or the presence of oil to the nearest coastal State.

(2) Reports under paragraph (1)(a)(i) shall be made in accordance with the requirements developed by the Organization and based on the guidelines and general principles adopted by the Organization. Reports under paragraph (1)(a)(ii), (b), (c) and (d) shall be made in accordance with the guidelines and general principles adopted by the Organization to the extent applicable.

The duty to report any event involving a discharge or probable discharge of oil may trigger the decision of the coastal State to take measures in accordance with art. I of the Intervention Convention, but may also accelerate the consultation proceedings reference to which is made in art. III of that Convention and entail the possible reduction of the impact of the measures that should be taken.

The provisions of the OPRC Convention that overlap, or may overlap, those of the Intervention Convention are arts. 5 and 7. The question of a possible conflict is settled by art. 11 of the OPRC Convention which so provides:

Nothing in this Convention shall be construed as altering the rights or obligations of any Party under any other convention or international agreement.

It appears, however, that no such conflict is conceivable, and that from a comparison of the provisions of the OPRC with those of the Intervention Convention, the provisions of the former overlap those of the latter, and therefore are complied with through the compliance of those of the latter, or cover areas not covered by the latter and, therefore, must be complied with, if mandatory.

Art. 5 of the OPRC Convention so provides:

Action on receiving an oil pollution report
(1) Whenever a Party receives a report referred to in article 4 or pollution information provided by other sources, it shall:
    (a) assess the event to determine whether it is an oil pollution incident;
    (b) assess the nature, extent and possible consequences of the oil pollution incident; and
    (c) then, without delay, inform all States whose interests are affected or likely to be affected by such oil pollution incident, together with
        (i) details of its assessments and any action it has taken, or intends to take, to deal with the incident, and
        (ii) further information as appropriate, until the action taken to respond to the incident has been concluded or until joint action has been decided by such States.
(2) When the severity of such oil pollution incident so justifies, the Party should provide the Organization directly or, as appropriate, through the relevant regional organization or arrangements with the information referred to in paragraph (1)(b) and (c).
(3) When the severity of such oil pollution incident so justifies, other States affected by it are urged to inform the Organization directly or, as appropriate, through the relevant regional organizations or arrangements of their assessment of the extent of the threat to their interests and any action taken or intended.
(4) Parties should use, in so far as practicable, the oil pollution reporting system developed by the Organization when exchanging information and communicating with other States and with the Organization.

In order to consider taking the measures mentioned in art. 1 of the Intervention Convention, a State must make an assessment of the gravity and imminence of the danger to its coastline or related interests from pollution and threat of pollution and in so doing it will also comply with art. 5(1)(a) and (b) of the OPRC Convention.

By proceeding to consultation with other States affected by the maritime casualty and with the flag State or States, as required by art. III(a) on the Intervention Convention and by notifying the proposed measures as required by art. III(b) a State will comply with art. 5(1)(c) of the OPRC Convention.

Although the provisions in art. 5(2) and (3), which however are not mandatory, have no counterpart in the Intervention Convention, they are not in conflict with the rules of such Convention and, therefore, compliance with them would not trigger the application of art. 11 of the OPRC Convention.

Art. 7 of the OPRC Convention in turn provides:

International cooperation in pollution response

(1) Parties agree that, subject to their capabilities and the availability of relevant resources, they will cooperate and provide advisory services, technical support and equipment for the purpose of responding to an oil pollution incident, when the severity of such incident so justifies, upon the request of any Party affected or likely to be affected. The financing of the costs for such assistance shall be based on the provisions set out in the Annex to this Convention.

(2) A Party which has requested assistance may ask the Organization to assist in identifying sources of provisional financing of the costs referred to in paragraph (1).

(3) In accordance with applicable international agreements, each Party shall take necessary legal or administrative measures to facilitate:

   (a) the arrival and utilization in and departure from its territory of ships, aircraft and other modes of transport engaged in responding to an oil pollution incident or transporting personnel, cargoes, materials and equipment required to deal with such an incident; and

   (b) the expeditious movement into, through, and out of its territory of personnel, cargoes, materials and equipment referred to in subparagraph (a).

It is conceivable that during the consultations reference to which is made in art. III of the Intervention Convention one or more States Parties to the OPRC Convention may offer their cooperation in taking the measures deemed advisable in order to prevent, mitigate or eliminate the danger of pollution, in which event, as provided in art. III(b), the coastal State must take into account the views that will accompany that offer. Nor would that be in conflict with art. 11 of the OPRC Convention.

It appears, therefore, that where a State Party to the Intervention Convention that intends to avail itself of its provisions is party also to the OPRC Convention, it must comply also with the additional provisions of such latter Convention previously considered, none of which appears to be in conflict with the Intervention Convention.

SECTION II – THE PROTOCOL OF 2000

4 THE PROTOCOL OF 2000 TO THE OPRC CONVENTION

Among maritime conventions there are various kinds of protocols. Some, that could be qualified as the typical protocols, aims at amending the convention to which they refer as is the case for the Visby Protocol to the 1924 Brussels Convention on Bills of Lading, the Protocol of 2002 to the Athens Convention of 1974, the Protocol of 1996 to the LLMC Convention 1976 and the Protocol of

1992 to the CLC. The effect they achieve may differ, according to whether they are States Parties to the original convention only and States Parties to the original convention as amended by the protocol, as is the case for the Hague-Visby Rules, or all States Parties to the original convention have become parties to the Protocol, as is the case for the CLC 1969 as amended by the Protocol of 1992. Other protocols cover an area close to that of the original convention, of which they incorporate by reference most of the provisions, as is the case for the Intervention Convention of 1969 and its Protocol of 1973. Still others regulate an area close to that of the convention to which they refer and reproduce most of its provisions, but have a distinct scope of application. This is the case for the Protocol of 2000 to the OPRC Convention.

The purpose of this Protocol, that entered into force on 14 June 2007,[2] is similar to that of the 1973 Protocol to the Intervention Convention, as well as to that of the HNS Convention 1996 but the technique adopted differs from that adopted in both of these cases. Whilst, in fact, the 1973 Protocol incorporates the provisions of the Intervention Convention and the HNS Convention is autonomous from the CLC, the OPRC Protocol is formally linked to the OPRC Convention since from the Preamble[3] and from art. 13[4] it appears that only States Parties to the OPRC Convention may become Parties to the Protocol; but at the same time it is independent of the Convention, since it contains a wholly distinct regime for hazardous and noxious substances, albeit with almost identical wording, as will be shown in the following discussion.

5 A COMPARISON OF THE PROVISIONS OF THE PROTOCOL WITH THOSE OF THE CONVENTION

Art. 1 – *General provisions*
The wording is almost the same, save that in paragraph 1 of the Convention reference is made to 'oil pollution incident' and in paragraph 1 of the Protocol to 'pollution incident by hazardous and noxious substances'. Also, the wording of

---

2 As of 31 August 2014, States Parties are the following: Algeria, Australia, Chile, China, Colombia, Denmark, Ecuador, Egypt, Estonia, France, Germany, Greece, Iran (Islamic Republic of), Japan, Liberia, Malaysia, Malta, Netherlands, Norway, Palau, Poland, Portugal, Korea Republic of, Singapore, Slovenia, Spain, Sweden, Syria, Turkey, Uruguay, Vanuatu, Yemen.

3 The Preamble opens with the following statements:

THE PARTIES TO THE PRESENT PROTOCOL
BEING PARTIES to the International Convention on Oil Pollution Preparedness, Response and Cooperation, done in London on 30 November 1990.

4 Art 13(1) so provides:

(1) This Protocol shall remain open for signature at the Headquarters of the Organization from 15 March 2000 until 14 March 2001 and shall thereafter remain open for accession. Any State Party to the OPRC Convention may become Party to this Protocol by:
(a) signature without reservation as to ratification, acceptance or approval; or
(b) signature subject to ratification, acceptance or approval, followed by ratification, acceptance or approval; or
(c) accession.

the Annex is identical to that of the Convention, except that the last sentence of paragraph 4, which requires that special attention be paid to the CLC 1969 and the Fund Convention 1971, has been omitted.

Art. 2 – *Definitions*

The definition in no. 1 of 'oil' is replaced in no. 2 by that of 'hazardous and noxious substances' and that in no. 2 of 'oil pollution incident' is replaced in no. 1 by that of 'pollution incident by hazardous and noxious substances' subsequently referred to as 'pollution incident'.

The definition in no. 5 of 'sea ports and oil handling facilities' is replaced in no. 3 by that of 'sea ports and hazardous and noxious substances handling facilities'.

The definition of 'off-shore unit' is obviously omitted and that of 'OPRC Convention' is added. It is worthwhile to observe that reference to the OPRC Convention is only made once, in art. 13(1), in which it is specified how a State Party to the OPRC Convention may become Party to the Protocol.

Art. 3 – *Emergency plans and reporting*

This title has replaced the Convention title 'Oil Pollution Emergency Plan' and in the text, which differs in some respects, reference is made to 'pollution incident emergency plan' in lieu of 'oil pollution emergency plan'. While no reference is made to offshore units, a provision is added in paragraph 3 whereby when authorities of a Party learn of a pollution incident (that stands for pollution incident by hazardous and noxious substances), they shall notify other States whose interests are likely to be affected by such incident. Some provisions that in the Convention are included in the subsequent art. 4, such as that whereby Parties must require Masters or other persons having charge of ships to report, are included in this article and arts 4 and 5 of the Convention are omitted.

Art. 4 – *National and regional systems for preparedness and response*

This article reproduces with minimal variations art. 6 of the Convention, the only change being the replacement of the words 'oil pollution incident' with the words 'pollution incident'.

Art. 5 – *International cooperation in pollution response*

This article reproduces art. 7 of the Convention, the only change being the replacement of the words 'oil pollution incident' with the words 'pollution incident'.

Art. 6 – *Research and development*

Art. 7 – *Technical cooperation*

Art. 8 – *Promotion of bilateral and multilateral cooperation in preparedness and response*

Art. 9 – *Relation to other conventions and other agreements*

These articles reproduce arts. 8 through to 11 of the Convention, the only change being also for them the replacement of 'oil pollution' with 'pollution'.

Art. 10 – *Institutional arrangements*

In this case the change consists in the omission of the reference in parenthesis to specific articles preceded by the words 'see for example'.

CHAPTER 3

International Convention for the Prevention of Pollution from Ships (MARPOL) and Protocol of 1978

1 INTRODUCTION

The International Convention for the Prevention of Pollution from Ships, adopted in 1973, was followed by a Protocol, adopted in 1978. Since at the time of its adoption the 1973 Convention had not yet entered into force, it was given effect by the Protocol, subject to a postponement of the entry into force of Annex II to the Convention and the amendment of art. 11(1)(b).[1]

Art. I of the Protocol so provides:

Article I – General obligations
(1) The Parties to the present Protocol undertake to give effect to the provisions of:
    (a) the present Protocol and the Annex hereto which shall constitute an integral part of the present Protocol; and
    (b) the International Convention for the Prevention of Pollution from Ships, 1973 (hereinafter referred to as 'the Convention'), subject to the modifications and additions set out in the present Protocol.
(2) The provisions of the Convention and the present Protocol shall be read and interpreted together as one single instrument.
(3) Every reference to the present Protocol constitutes at the same time a reference to the Annex hereto.

The Protocol, and with it the Convention, globally referred to as 'MARPOL', entered into force on 2 October 1983. As with most of the preventive conventions considered in this Part of Volume III, MARPOL sets out rules on the prevention of pollution by oil and harmful and noxious substances as well as on the discharge from ships of harmful substances. The operational and technical rules are set out in its six Annexes, being:

- Annex I with Regulations for the Prevention of Pollution by Oil;
- Annex II with Regulations for the Control of pollution by Noxious Liquid Substances in Bulk;
- Annex III with Regulations for Prevention of Pollution by Harmful Substances carried by Sea in Packaged Form;

---

1 The Convention was further amended by a Protocol adopted on 26 September 1997 the purpose of which had been only the addition of Annex VI entitled Regulations for the Prevention of Air Pollution from Ships. Subsequently, amendments to Annex III were adopted by resolution MEPC. 193/61 and entered into force on 1 January 2014, and amendments to Annexes IV, V and VI were adopted by resolutions MEPC. 202(62) and MEPC. 203(62) and entered into force on 1 January 2013. For a meticulous analysis of this Convention and its history see Gregory J. Timagenis, *International Control of Marine Pollution*, Dobbs Ferry, New York, pp. 319–574.

29

- Annex IV with Regulations for the Prevention of Pollution by Sewage from Ships;
- Annex V with Regulations for the Prevention of Pollution by Garbage from Ships;
- Annex VI with Regulations for the Prevention of Air Pollution from Ships.

The most relevant of these is Annex I in which the following matters are the object of specific regulations:

- international oil pollution prevention certificates (regulations 7, 9 and 11);[2]
- tanks for oil residues (regulation 12);[3]
- oil fuel tanks protection (regulation 12A);[4]
- oil filtering equipment (regulation 14);[5]
- control of discharge of oil (regulation 15);[6]
- segregation of oil and water ballast and carriage of oil in forepeak tanks (regulation 16);[7]
- requirements for the cargo area of oil tankers (regulation 18);[8]
- prevention of oil pollution from oil tankers carrying heavy grade oil as cargo (regulation 13);[9]
- subdivision and damage stability (regulation 28);[10]
- oil discharge monitoring and control system (regulation 31);[11]
- crude oil washing operations (regulation 35);[12]
- oil pollution emergency plan (regulation 37);[13]
- reception facilities (regulation 38);[14]
- prevention of pollution during transfer of oil cargo between oil tankers at sea (regulation 40).[15]

2 GENERAL SCOPE OF APPLICATION

2.1 Ships to which the Convention applies

Art. 3 of MARPOL so provides:

Article 3 – Application
(1) The present Convention shall apply to:

---

2 MARPOL, Consolidated Edition 2011, pp. 53, 55.
3 MARPOL, Consolidated Edition 2011, p. 56.
4 MARPOL, Consolidated Edition 2011, p. 56.
5 MARPOL, Consolidated Edition 2011, p. 64.
6 MARPOL, Consolidated Edition 2011, p. 66.
7 MARPOL, Consolidated Edition 2011, p. 67.
8 MARPOL, Consolidated Edition 2011, p. 69.
9 MARPOL, Consolidated Edition 2011, p. 78.
10 MARPOL, Consolidated Edition 2011, p. 92.
11 MARPOL, Consolidated Edition 2011, p. 98.
12 MARPOL, Consolidated Edition 2011, p. 100.
13 MARPOL, Consolidated Edition 2011, p. 102.
14 MARPOL, Consolidated Edition 2011, p. 103.
15 MARPOL, Consolidated Edition 2011, p. 107.

(a) ships entitled to fly the flag of a Party to the Convention; and
(b) ships not entitled to fly the flag of a Party but which operate under the authority of a Party.
(2) Nothing in the present article shall be construed as derogating from or extending the sovereign rights of the Parties under international law over the sea-bed and subsoil thereof adjacent to their coasts for the purposes of exploration and exploitation of their natural resources.
(3) The present Convention shall not apply to any warship, naval auxiliary or other ship owned or operated by a State and used, for the time being, only on government non-commercial service. However, each Party shall ensure by the adoption of appropriate measures not impairing the operations or operational capabilities of such ships owned or operated by it, that such ships act in a manner consistent, so far as is reasonable and practicable, with the present Convention.

The ships to which the Convention applies are identified, as in some other conventions of this group, on the basis of their nationality by means of a reference to their entitlement to fly the flag of a State Party to the Convention. The subsequent reference to 'ships not entitled to fly the flag of a Party but which operate under the authority of a Party' is due to the following very wide definition of ship in art. 2(4):

(4) Ship means a vessel of any type whatsoever operating in the marine environment and includes hydrofoil boats, air-cushion vehicles, submersibles, floating craft and fixed or floating platforms.

Therefore, a craft or platform that is not entitled to fly the flag of the State under the authority of which it operates is covered by the above provision.

The exclusion from the application of the Convention of warships and the other ships mentioned in paragraph 3 is not, as in various private law conventions, absolute, for the State to which they belong is required, pursuant to paragraph 3, to ensure that such ships act in a manner consistent with the Convention, such rule being, however, subject to a double condition. First, the 'appropriate measures' adopted by the State should not impair the operations or operational capabilities of such ships. It must be assumed that, although the burden of proof is on the State, the statement that that would be the case suffices to justify the failure to comply with this rule, as certainly would be the case for warships. Secondly, that action in a manner consistent with the Convention is 'reasonable and practicable'. The burden of proof is also in this case on the State, but again, at least in so far as warships are concerned, in all likelihood a mere declaration of the State should suffice.

3 THE MAIN PURPOSE OF MARPOL

Art. 1(1) of the Convention so provides:

The Parties to the Convention undertake to give effect to the provisions of the present Convention and those Annexes thereto by which they are bound, in order to prevent the pollution of the marine environment by the discharge of harmful substances or effluents containing such substances in contravention of the Convention.

The pollution of the marine environment, that MARPOL aims to prevent is the discharge of harmful substances and since this is also the purpose – or one of the purposes – of other conventions, such as that on the Control and Management of Ships' Ballast Water and Sediments 2004, that on Removal of Wrecks 2007 and that on Dumping of Wastes 1972, it is important to establish whether there may be a conflict between the Convention now under consideration and one or more of the above-mentioned conventions – and, if so, what may be the consequences of such a conflict.

There are two definitions in MARPOL that are helpful in this respect – those relating to 'discharge' and 'harmful substances'. These are set out in art. 2(2) and 2(3) in the following terms:

(2)   Harmful substance means any substance which, if introduced into the sea, is liable to create hazards to human health, to harm living resources and marine life, to damage amenities or to interfere with other legitimate uses of the sea, and includes any substance subject to control by the present Convention.

(3)(a) Discharge, in relation to harmful substances or effluents containing such substances, means any release howsoever caused from a ship and includes any escape, disposal, spilling, leaking, pumping, emitting or emptying;

(b)   Discharge does not include:

  (i)   dumping within the meaning of the Convention on the Prevention of Marine Pollution by Dumping of Wastes and Other Matter, done at London on 13 November 1972; or

 (ii)   release of harmful substances directly arising from the exploration, exploitation and associated offshore processing of sea-bed mineral resources; or

(iii)   release of harmful substances for purposes of legitimate scientific research into pollution abatement or control.

A conflict with the Convention on Dumping of Wastes, otherwise almost certain, is expressly excluded by the above provision under paragraph 3(b)(i) by which priority is given to such Convention.

A conflict with the Convention on Control and Management of Ships' Ballast Water and Sediments 2004 does not seem to be conceivable, given the definition of 'sediments' as 'matters settled out of Ballast Water'.

Nor is a conflict conceivable with the Convention on Removal of Wrecks, since MARPOL applies to ships as defined in its art. 2(4).

4 GENERAL OBLIGATIONS OF THE STATES PARTIES TO THE CONVENTION

Article 1(1), previously quoted, expressly states what in private law conventions is implied, namely that the Parties undertake to implement the provisions of the Convention. However, the Convention goes further, for, after having stated that the 'requirements' of the Convention are mandatory, it provides that the State of which the ship flies the flag must establish sanctions for any violation of such requirements.

Art. 4 so provides:

(1)   Any violation of the requirements of the present Convention shall be prohibited and sanctions shall be established therefor under the law of the Administration of the ship concerned wherever the violation occurs. If the Administration is informed of such a violation and is satisfied that sufficient evidence is available to enable proceedings to be

brought in respect of the alleged violation, it shall cause such proceedings to be taken as soon as possible, in accordance with its law.

(2) Any violation of the requirements of the present Convention within the jurisdiction of any Party to the Convention shall be prohibited and sanctions shall be established therefor under the law of that Party. Whenever such a violation occurs, that Party shall either:

   (a) cause proceedings to be taken in accordance with its law; or
   (b) furnish to the Administration of the ship such information and evidence as may be in its possession that a violation has occurred.

(3) Where information or evidence with respect to any violation of the present Convention by a ship is furnished to the Administration of that ship, the Administration shall promptly inform the Party which has furnished the information or evidence, and the Organization, of the action taken.

(4) The penalties specified under the law of a Party pursuant to the present article shall be adequate in severity to discourage violations of the present Convention and shall be equally severe irrespective of where the violations occur.

The 'Administration' to which reference is made in this article is defined in art. 2(5):

(5) Administration means the Government of the State under whose authority the ship is operating. With respect to a ship entitled to fly a flag of any State, the Administration is the Government of that State. With respect to fixed or floating platforms engaged in exploration and exploitation of the sea-bed and subsoil thereof adjacent to the coast over which the coastal State exercises sovereign rights for the purposes of exploration and exploitation of their natural resources, the Administration is the Government of the coastal State concerned.

The nature of the sanctions the Parties are required to establish is subsequently indicated, because art. 4(4) makes reference to the 'penalties' specified under the law of the relevant State and this suggests that the sanctions should be of a criminal nature. The nature of the penalties is indicated in general terms in paragraph 4, which requires that they are 'adequate in severity to discourage violations'. The owners of ships to which the Convention applies are therefore subject, in case of violations of the requirements of the Convention as implemented in the national law, to the sanctions established by national law.

5 PROVISIONS ON THE INSPECTION OF THE SHIPS TO WHICH THE CONVENTION APPLIES

Such ships are also subject, in any State Party, to inspections by duly authorised officers of that State. There are two situations in which such inspection may be carried out. The first is a routine inspection, which is normally limited to verifying whether there is on board the ship a valid certificate issued by the competent authority of a Party to the Convention. Art. 5 stipulates in this respect:

(1) Subject to the provisions of paragraph (2) of the present article a certificate issued under the authority of a Party to the Convention in accordance with the provisions of the regulations shall be accepted by the other Parties and regarded for all purposes covered by the present Convention as having the same validity as a certificate issued by them.

(2) A ship required to hold a certificate in accordance with the provisions of the regulations is subject, while in the ports or offshore terminals under the jurisdiction of a Party, to

inspection by officers duly authorized by that Party. Any such inspection shall be limited to verifying that there is on board a valid certificate, unless there are clear grounds for believing that the condition of the ship or its equipment does not correspond substantially with the particulars of that certificate. In that case, or if the ship does not carry a valid certificate, the Party carrying out the inspection shall take such steps as will ensure that the ship shall not sail until it can proceed to sea without presenting an unreasonable threat of harm to the marine environment. That Party may, however, grant such a ship permission to leave the port or offshore terminal for the purpose of proceeding to the nearest appropriate repair yard available.

(3) If a Party denies a foreign ship entry to the ports or offshore terminals under its jurisdiction or takes any action against such a ship for the reason that the ship does not comply with the provisions of the present Convention, the Party shall immediately inform the consul or diplomatic representative of the Party whose flag the ship is entitled to fly, or if this is not possible, the Administration of the ship concerned. Before denying entry or taking such action the Party may request consultation with the Administration of the ship concerned. Information shall also be given to the Administration when a ship does not carry a valid certificate in accordance with the provisions of the regulations.

(4) With respect to the ships of non-Parties to the Convention, Parties shall apply the requirements of the present Convention as may be necessary to ensure that no more favourable treatment is given to such ships.

It appears, therefore, that if the ship does not carry a valid certificate, it may be detained if there is a danger that she may harm the environment.

The second situation is that in which there appears to be an emergency, since a ship is suspected to have discharged harmful substances. That situation is covered by art. 6 of the Convention which states:

(1) Parties to the Convention shall cooperate in the detection of violations and the enforcement of the provisions of the present Convention, using all appropriate and practicable measures of detection and environmental monitoring, adequate procedures for reporting and accumulation of evidence.

(2) A ship to which the present Convention applies may, in any port or offshore terminal of a Party, be subject to inspection by officers appointed or authorized by that Party for the purpose of verifying whether the ship has discharged any harmful substances in violation of the provisions of the regulations. If an inspection indicates a violation of the Convention, a report shall be forwarded to the Administration for any appropriate action.

(3) Any Party shall furnish to the Administration evidence, if any, that the ship has discharged harmful substances or effluents containing such substances in violation of the provisions of the regulations. If it is practicable to do so, the competent authority of the former Party shall notify the master of the ship of the alleged violation.

(4) Upon receiving such evidence, the Administration so informed shall investigate the matter, and may request the other Party to furnish further or better evidence of the alleged contravention. If the Administration is satisfied that sufficient evidence is available to enable proceedings to be brought in respect of the alleged violation, it shall cause such proceedings to be taken in accordance with its law as soon as possible. The Administration shall promptly inform the Party which has reported the alleged violation, as well as the Organization, of the action taken.

(5) A Party may also inspect a ship to which the present Convention applies when it enters the ports or offshore terminals under its jurisdiction, if a request for an investigation is received from any Party together with sufficient evidence that the ship has discharged harmful substances or effluents containing such substances in any place. The report of such investigation shall be sent to the Party requesting it and to the Administration so that the appropriate action may be taken under the present Convention.

MARPOL

6 OVERVIEW OF THE RELEVANT PROVISIONS OF THE ANNEXES

6.1 Introduction to the overview

It is not the purpose of this chapter to carry out an analysis of the regulations contained in the Annexes to MARPOL; nor would the author be competent to carry it out. Its purpose is only to mark the great importance that MARPOL, and the regulations contained in most, if not all, its Annexes have within the general scope of Part I of this volume, in which all conventions aiming at preventing damage to the marine environment caused by ships are considered. For this reason, the present paragraph merely seeks to provide an overview of the Regulations; and as such it will be limited to a description of the Regulations of a legal and administrative nature, without trespassing into the area of Regulations of a more technical nature.

6.2 A summary of the Annexes

6.2.1 Annex I: Regulations for the Prevention of Pollution by Oil[16]

This is a fundamental Annex that consists of 39 regulations divided into seven chapters and followed by several appendices.

Chapter 1 regulation 1 contains various definitions, including those of various types of oil, that of 'special area' (i.e. 'a sea area where for recognized technical reasons in relation to its oceanographical and ecological condition and to the particular character of its traffic the adoption of special mandatory methods for the prevention of sea pollution by oil is required', such special areas including *inter alia* the Mediterranean Sea area, the Baltic Sea area, the Black Sea area), and the definitions of tankers of various characteristics and size.

Chapter 2 sets out rules on surveys and certification, and regulation 11 provides that a ship when in a port or an offshore terminal of another Party is subject to inspection by officers duly authorised by such Party concerning operational requirements under Annex I.

Chapter 3 sets out special rules on discharge into the sea of oil and oil mixtures. Such rules relate first to the requirements for the machinery spaces of all ships of 400 GT and above[17] and requirements for the cargo area of oil

---

16 MARPOL, Consolidated Edition 2011, p. 41.
17 Regulation 12(2) so provides:

> 2 Oil residue (sludge) may be disposed of directly from the oil residue (sludge) tank(s) through the standard discharge connection referred to in regulation 13, or any other approved means of disposal. The oil residue (sludge) tank(s):
>
> 1 shall be provided with a designated pump for disposal that is capable of taking suction from the oil residue (sludge) tank(s); and
>
> 2 shall have no discharge connections to the bilge system, oily bilge water holding tank(s), tank top or oily water separators except that the tank(s) may be fitted with drains, with manually operated self-closing valves and arrangements for subsequent visual monitoring of the settled water, that lead to an oily bilge water holding tank or bilge well, or an alternative arrangement, provided such arrangement does not connect directly to the bilge piping system.

tankers.[18] They relate subsequently to the limits and the conditions under which such discharge is permitted and vary in respect of the discharge outside special areas and discharge in special areas.

Those relating to discharge outside special areas are as follows:

2 Any discharge into the sea of oil or oily mixtures from ships of 400 gross tonnage and above shall be prohibited except when all the following conditions are satisfied:
1 the ship is proceeding *en route*;
2 the oily mixture is processed through an oil filtering equipment meeting the requirements of regulation 14 of this Annex;
3 the oil content of the effluent without dilution does not exceed 15 ppm;
4 the oily mixture does not originate from cargo pump-room bilges on oil tankers; and
5 the oily mixture, in case of oil tankers, is not mixed with oil cargo residues.

Those relating to discharge in special areas are as follows:

3 Any discharge into the sea of oil or oily mixtures from ships of 400 gross tonnage and above shall be prohibited except when all of the following conditions are satisfied:
1 the ship is proceeding *en route*;
2 the oily mixture is processed through an oil filtering equipment meeting the requirements of regulation 14.7 of this Annex;
3 the oil content of the effluent without dilution does not exceed 15 ppm;
4 the oily mixture does not originate from cargo pump-room bilges on oil tankers; and
5 the oily mixture, in case of oil tankers, is not mixed with oil cargo residues.

The first appendix contains a list of oils, the second contains the form of the International Oil Pollution Prevention Certificate and the third the Form of Oil Record Book.

6.2.2 Annex II: Regulations for the Control of Pollution by Noxious Liquid Substances in Bulk[19]

After the definitions in regulation 1, regulations 2, 3, 4 and 5 deal with the scope of application, the exceptions, the exemptions and equivalent materials. There follow rules on surveys and certification.

6.2.3 Annex III: Regulations for the Prevention of Pollution by Harmful Substances Carried by Sea in Packaged Form[20]

Pursuant to regulation 1.1 'harmful substances are those substances which are identified as marine pollutants in the IMDG Code or which meet the criteria in the Appendix to Annex III'. The subsequent regulations set out rules on the packing, marking and labelling, documentation stowage and quantity limitations.

---

18 Pursuant to Regulation 18 para. 1, every crude oil tanker of 20,000 tons deadweight and above and every product carrier of 30,000 tons deadweight and above must be provided with segregated ballast tanks and comply with the specific rules set out in the subsequent paras. 2 through 5 as appropriate.

19 MARPOL, Consolidated Edition 2011, p. 165. Paragraph 12 requires that segregated ballast tanks located within the cargo ranks length must be arranged in accordance with the requirements of the subsequent paras. 13, 14 and 16 to provide a measure of protection against oil outflow in the event of grounding or collision.

20 MARPOL, Consolidated Edition 2011, p. 215.

6.2.4 Annex IV: Regulations for the Prevention of Pollution by Sewage from Ships[21]

Chapter 1 – General sets out definitions and rules on the scope of application. There follows in chapter 2 rules on surveys and certification, in chapter 3 rules on equipment and control of discharge, in chapter 4 rules on reception facilities, in chapter 5 rules on port State control and as an appendix the form of International Sewage Pollution Prevention Certificate.

6.2.5 Annex V: Regulations for the Prevention of Pollution by Garbage from Ships[22]

Regulation 1 includes the following definition of garbage:

'Garbage' means all kinds of victual, domestic and operational waste excluding fresh fish and parts thereof, generated during the normal operation of the ship and liable to be disposed of continuously or periodically except those substances which are defined or listed in other Annexes to the present Convention.

Since under this definition 'garbage' must be deemed to be included in the definition of 'wastes or other matters' in the Dumping of Wastes Convention 1972, as amended by the Protocol of 1996, both Conventions apply in this case. However, there does not appear to be any conflict between that Convention, as amended and MARPOL, as it provides in art. 3(4) of its Protocol:

No provision of this Protocol shall be interpreted as preventing Contracting Parties from taking, individually or jointly, more stringent measures in accordance with international law with respect to prevention, reduction and where practicable elimination of pollution

and the provisions of MARPOL are more stringent than those of the Dumping of Wastes Convention.

As an Appendix there follows the form of the Garbage Record Book.

6.2.6 Annex VI: Regulations for prevention of air pollution from ships

After several definitions, chapter 1 sets out rules on exceptions and exemptions, and the exceptions are worthy of mention. Regulation 1.1 provides:

1 Regulations of this Annex shall not apply to:
  1 any emission necessary for the purpose of securing the safety of a ship or saving life at sea; or
  2 any emission resulting from damage to a ship or its equipment:
    2.1 provided that all reasonable precautions have been taken after the occurrence of the damage or discovery of the emission for the purpose of preventing or minimizing the emission; and
    2.2 except if the owner or the master acted either with the intent to cause damage, or recklessly with knowledge that damage would probably result.

---

21 MARPOL, Consolidated Edition 2011, p. 223.
22 MARPOL, Consolidated Edition 2011, p. 241.

CHAPTER 4

International Convention for the Safety of Life at Sea, 1974 (SOLAS)

The International Convention for the Safety of Life at Sea, adopted by the International Conference on Safety of Life at Sea on 1 November 1974, replaced the International Convention for the Safety of Life at Sea 1960 and entered into force on 25 May 1980. It has since been amended by means of Protocols,[1] by resolutions adopted either by the IMO's Maritime Safety Committee,[2] or by conferences of Contracting Governments.[3]

The Convention contains only general rules on the manner of implementation of its provisions and of the annexes thereto; on the manner in which it may be amended; and on the obligation of Contracting Governments to communicate and to deposit with the Secretary General of IMCO (now IMO) a list of non-governmental agencies authorised to act on their behalf in the administration of measures for safety of life at sea and of the text of laws, decrees orders and regulations which would be promulgated on the matters within the scope of the Convention.

The rules aiming at ensuring safety of life are almost all based on safety of ships and are contained in the annex to the Convention, which at present consists of the following twelve chapters:

- I   General provisions
- II   Construction
- III   Life-saving appliances and arrangements
- IV   Radio communications
- V   Safety of navigation
- VI   Carriage of cargoes
- VII   Carriage of dangerous goods
- VIII Nuclear ships
- IX   Management for the safe operation of ships
- X   Safe measures for high-speed craft
- XI   Special measures to enhance maritime safety
- XII   Additional safety measures for bulk carriers.

---

1 Protocol of 17 February 1978, entered into force on 1 May 1981; Protocol of 11 November 1988, entered into force on 3 February 2000 replaced and abrogated the 1978 Protocol as between the Parties to the 1988 Protocol; Protocol of 11 November 1988, entered into force on 1 February 1992.

2 A summary of all such amendments is available on IMO Website in the document 'SOLAS 1974: Brief History – List of amendments to date and where to find them'.

3 Diplomatic Conference on Maritime Security 13 December 2002. The amendments entered into force on 1 July 2004 and included new chapter XI-2 on Special Measures to Enhance Maritime Security.

Of course, the rules contained in many of these chapters have an impact on compliance with the specific rules adopted by the preventive conventions, such as the regulations on surveys and certificates[4] and on maintenance of conditions after survey,[5] the regulations on the structure of ships,[6] those on corrosion prevention of seawater ballast tank,[7] and on suppression of fire.[8]

As for MARPOL,[9] a commentary on all such regulations is beyond the scope of this book, but it is also appropriate to mention that SOLAS is of primary importance in respect of the prevention of environmental damage. Some examples:

- in chapter I, regulation 3 there is under (h) the following definition of 'tanker':

  (h) A *tanker is a cargo ship constructed or adapted for the carriage on bulk of liquid cargoes of an inflammable nature.*

- in chapter II-1, part A, regulation 2 there is the following definition of 'oil tanker':

  12. An *oil tanker* is the oil tanker defined in regulation 1 of Annex I of the Protocol of 1978 relating to the International Convention for the Prevention of Pollution from Ships, 1973.

- in chapter II-1, part A, regulation 3 there is the following definition of 'chemical tanker':

  19 *Chemical tanker* is a cargo ship constructed or adapted and used for the carriage in bulk of any liquid product listed in either:
  1 chapter 17 of the International Code for Construction and Equipment of Ships Carrying Dangerous Chemicals in Bulk adopted by the Maritime Safety Committee by resolution MSC.4(48), hereunder referred to as 'the International Bulk Chemical Code', as may be amended by the Organization; or
  2 chapter VI of the Code for the Construction and Equipment of Ships carrying Dangerous Chemicals in Bulk adopted by the Assembly of the Organization by resolution A.212(VII), hereafter referred to as 'the Bulk Chemical Code', as has been or may be amended by the Organization;

- in chapter II-1 part A, regulation 3-6 applies to access to and within spaces in cargo area of oil tankers and bulk carriers;
- in chapter II-1 part C, regulation 29 sets out in paragraphs 16–20 rules on steering gears of tankers;
- in chapter II-2 on Construction-Fire protection, fire detection and fire extinction there are set out in Part A – General rules on fire protection, fire detection and extinction in ships and there are set out in Part D fire safety measures for tankers.

---

4 Chapter I, Part B.
5 Chapter I, Regulation 11.
6 Chapter I, Part A-1.
7 Chapter II-1, Regulation 3-1.
8 Chapter II-2.
9 *Supra*, Chapter 1.

- in chapter VII there are set out rules on carriage of dangerous goods and specifically:

  - in Part A rules on carriage of dangerous goods in packaged form or in solid form in bulk reference is made to the IMDG Code to which reference is also made in art. 1(5)(a) of the HNS Convention;
  - in Part B rules on construction and equipment of ships carrying dangerous liquid chemicals in bulk that make mandatory the requirements of the International Code for the Construction and Equipment of Ships Carrying Dangerous Chemicals in Bulk, reference to which is made in art. 1(5)(a)(iii) of the HNS Convention;[10]
  - in Part C rules on construction and equipment of ships carrying liquefied gases in bulk that make mandatory the provisions of the International Code for the Construction and Equipment of Ships Carrying Liquefied Gases in Bulk, reference to which is made in art. 1(5)(a)(v) of the HNS Convention.[11]

---

10 *Infra*, Chapter 14, para. 3.2.
11 *Infra*, Chapter 14, para. 3.2.

CHAPTER 5

Convention on the Prevention of Marine Pollution by Dumping of Wastes and Other Matter, 1972 as Amended by the Protocol of 1996

1 INTRODUCTION

This Convention, adopted on 29 December 1972, entered into force on 30 August 1975.[1] On 7 November 1996 a Protocol was adopted, the purpose of which was entirely to replace the text of 1972. Art. 23 of the Protocol so in fact provides:

This Protocol will supersede the Convention as between Contracting Parties to this Protocol which are Parties to the Convention.

Since, however, of the 87 States Parties to the Convention of 1972 only 34 are Parties to the Protocol,[2] which entered into force on 24 March 2006, the commentary that follows indicates the changes and additions brought to the original text by the Protocol. The provisions replaced or deleted by the Protocol are crossed out and the *changes and additions are in italics*.

The purpose of the Convention is stated in the two last paragraphs of the Preamble to the 1972 Convention, worded as follows:

BEING CONVINCED that international action to control the pollution of the sea by dumping can and must be taken without delay but that this action should not preclude

---

1 Provisions on pollution by dumping have subsequently been adopted in art. 210 of UNCLOS.

2 Since, pursuant to its art. 23, the Protocol supersedes the Convention as between Contracting Parties to the Protocol which are also Parties to the Convention and the Protocol entered into force on 26 March 2006, as of that date the States Parties to the Convention have been reduced to those that are not parties to the Protocol. The States Parties to the Convention that have become Parties to the Protocol still appear in the list that follow but are crossed out:

Afghanistan, Antigua and Barbuda, Argentina, ~~Australia~~, Azerbaijan, Barbados, Belarus, ~~Belgium~~, Benin, Bolivia, Brazil, ~~Bulgaria~~, ~~Canada~~, Cape Verde, ~~Chile~~, ~~China~~, Costa Rica, Côte d'Ivoire, Croatia, Cuba, Cyprus, Congo Democratic Republic of the, ~~Denmark~~, Dominican Republic, ~~Egypt~~, Equatorial Guinea, Finland, ~~France~~, Gabon, ~~Germany~~, Greece, Guatemala, Haiti, Honduras, Hungary, ~~Iceland~~, Iran (Islamic Republic of), ~~Ireland~~, ~~Italy~~, Jamaica, ~~Japan~~, Jordan, ~~Kenya~~, Kiribati, Libya, ~~Luxembourg~~, Malta, ~~Mexico~~, Monaco, Montenegro, Morocco, Nauru, ~~Netherlands~~, ~~New Zealand~~, ~~Nigeria~~, ~~Norway~~, Oman, Pakistan, Panama, Papua New Guinea, Peru, ~~Philippines~~, Poland, Portugal, ~~Republic of Korea~~, Russian Federation, Saint Lucia, Saint Vincent and the Grenadines, Serbia, Seychelles, ~~Sierra Leone~~, ~~Slovenia~~, Solomon Islands, ~~South Africa~~, ~~Spain~~, ~~Suriname~~, ~~Sweden~~, ~~Switzerland~~, Syrian Arab Republic, ~~Tonga~~, Tunisia, Ukraine, United Arab Emirates, ~~United Kingdom~~, United Republic of Tanzania, United States, ~~Vanuatu~~.

As of 30 June 2014, the States Parties to the Protocol were the following

Angola, Australia, Barbados, Belgium, Bulgaria, Canada, Chile, China, Congo, Denmark, Egypt, Estonia, France, Georgia, Germany, Ghana, Iceland, Ireland, Italy, Japan, Kenya, Luxembourg, Marshall Islands, Mexico, New Zealand, Netherlands, Nigeria, Norway, Philippines, Republic of Korea, Saint Kitts and Nevis, Saudi Arabia, Sierra Leone, Slovenia, South Africa, Spain, Suriname, Sweden, Switzerland, Tonga, Trinidad and Tobago, United Kingdom, Uruguay, Vanuatu, Yemen.

discussion of measures to control other sources of marine pollution as soon as possible; and

WISHING to improve protection of the marine environment by encouraging States with a common interest in particular geographical areas to enter into appropriate agreements supplementary to this Convention

replaced in the Protocol by the following paragraph:

BEING CONVINCED that further international action to prevent, reduce and where practicable eliminate pollution of the sea caused by dumping can and must be taken without delay to protect and preserve the marine environment and to manage human activities in such a manner that the marine ecosystem will continue to sustain the legitimate uses of the sea and will continue to meet the needs of present and future generations

it is then further stated in art. 1 that:

Contracting Parties shall individually and collectively promote the effective control of all sources of pollution of the marine environment, and pledge themselves especially to take all practicable steps to prevent the pollution of the sea by the dumping of waste and other matter that is liable to create hazards to human health, to harm living resources and marine life, to damage amenities or to interfere with other legitimate uses of the sea

replaced in the Protocol by the following art. 2:

Contracting Parties shall individually and collectively protect and preserve the marine environment from all sources of pollution and take effective measures, according to their scientific, technical and economic capabilities, to prevent, reduce and where practicable eliminate pollution caused by dumping or incineration at sea of wastes or other matter. Where appropriate, they shall harmonize their policies in this regard.

The Convention, therefore, does not set out obligations addressed to individuals, that must be implemented by Contracting States, but creates obligations on States to adopt the measures required in order prevent pollution caused by dumping of wastes. A clear example of the difference is given by the chapeau of art. VII(1), that became art. 10 in the Protocol, quoted below in paragraph 2.1.

The distinction between this technique, employed to ensure international uniformity, and that used in most maritime conventions is very subtle, for also in respect of such other conventions one of the methods of implementation is the translation of their rules into terms of national law,[3] in which event the result is similar to that achieved under the convention now under consideration.

The provisions of the Convention and of the Protocol[4] that will be considered are only those that affect the rights and obligations of the persons who may be involved in the dumping or incineration of wastes or other matter. Consideration of those relating exclusively to the relations between Contracting Parties (arts. VIII–XXII of the Convention and 11–18 of the Protocol) will be omitted.

---

3 F. Berlingieri, *Arrest of Ships*, 5th ed., p. 17. This method is expressly referred to in the Protocol of signature of the Bills of Lading Convention 1924 which provides in its English translation:

> The High Contracting Parties may give effect to this Convention either by giving it the force of law or by including in their national legislation in a form appropriate to that legislation the rules adopted under this Convention.

4 Additions to the text of the Convention made by the Protocol appear in *italics* and phrases and words which have been deleted are crossed out.

MARINE POLLUTION CONVENTION, 1972

2 THE SCOPE OF APPLICATION OF THE CONVENTION AND OF THE PROTOCOL

2.1 Vessels and aircraft to which national implementing legislation must apply

Art. VII(1) of the Convention (now art. 10.1 of the Protocol) so provides:

1 Each Contracting Party shall apply the measures required to implement the present ~~Convention~~ _Protocol_ to all:
~~(a)~~ 1   vessels and aircraft registered in its territory or flying its flag;
~~(b)~~ 2   vessels and aircraft loading in its territory ~~or territorial seas~~ *wastes or other* matter which ~~is~~ *are* to be dumped *or incinerated at sea*;
~~(c)~~ 3   vessels, ~~and~~ aircraft and ~~fixed or floating~~ platforms *or other man-made structures* ~~under its jurisdiction~~ believed to be engaged in dumping *or incinerating at sea in areas within which it is entitled to exercise jurisdiction in accordance with international law.*

These rules do not define the scope of application of the Convention, but that of the national laws that will implement the obligations of Contracting States arising out of their ratification of or accession to the Convention. Therefore, the phrase 'This ~~Convention~~ *Protocol* shall not apply . . .' in paragraph 4 appears to be inappropriate.

The vessels and aircraft to which the national implementing legislation must apply are divided into three groups.

The first group covers all vessels and aircraft registered in the territory of each Contracting State or flying its flag. It appears that the alternative between registration and flag applies to both ships and aircraft. As regards ships, although the general rule is that ships fly the flag of the State in whose registers they are registered, there are States that allow ships registered in another State to fly their flag; and that situation is now recognised in all the States in which temporary change of flag is permitted.[5] It is significant that in the UN Convention on Conditions for Registration of Ships 1986 there are separate definitions of Flag and State of registration. In the Convention now under consideration the following definition of 'vessels and aircraft' is given in art. III(2), which has become in the Protocol art. 1(6):

'Vessels and aircraft' means waterborne or airborne craft of any type whatsoever. This expression includes air cushioned craft and floating craft, whether self-propelled or not.

The term 'floating craft' must be given a wide meaning, since in the definition of 'dumping', that will be considered subsequently, reference is made to the disposal of wastes from 'platforms or other man-made structures'.

The second group covers vessels and aircraft of any nationality or registration that are loading in the territory (or territorial seas under the Convention) of the relevant Contracting State (wastes or other) matter which is to be dumped.[6] Therefore, Contracting States must take appropriate actions in order to prevent such ships sailing out of their territorial sea with on-board wastes that would be dumped (or incinerated under the Protocol) at sea.

The third group in (c), in addition to vessels and aircraft, also covers fixed or

---

5 Reference is made to art. 16 of the MLM Convention 1993. See vol. II, chapter 7, para. 7.
6 For the definition of 'dumping' see para. 3.

43

floating platforms, of whatever nationality, that are believed to be engaged in dumping (or incineration). The relevant area in which dumping (or incineration) would take place is referred to in the Convention as the 'jurisdiction' of the relevant State, whilst in the Protocol it is more appropriately identified as that within which the relevant State is '*entitled to exercise its jurisdiction in accordance with international law*'.

2.2 Vessels and aircraft to which national legislation does not apply

Art. VII(4) of the Convention (art. 10.4 of the Protocol), so provides:

4 This ~~Convention~~ *Protocol* shall not apply to those vessels and aircraft entitled to sovereign immunity under international law. However, each Party shall ensure by the adoption of appropriate measures that such vessels and aircraft owned or operated by it act in a manner consistent with the object and purpose of this ~~Convention~~ *Protocol* and shall inform the Organization accordingly.

The wording used in order to identify vessels entitled to sovereign immunity is similar to that used in art. 4(1) of the Salvage Convention 1989, except that in that Convention it follows a specific reference to warships. In order to identify generally the vessels entitled to sovereign immunity reference must be made to the Convention of 1926 on Immunity of State-Owned Ships and to arts. 29–32 of UNCLOS. In art. 3(1) of the 1926 Immunity Convention the exception to the general rule that ships owned or operated by States are subject to the same rules of liability and to the same obligations as are applicable to privately owned ships, applies to 'warships, State-owned yachts, Coastguard vessels, hospital ships, fleet auxiliaries, supply vessels and other vessels owned or operated by a State and employed exclusively on governmental and non-commercial service'. Art. 32 of UNCLOS provides generally that with the exceptions contained in subsection A and in arts. 30 and 31[7] nothing in the Convention affects the immunities of warships and other government ships operated for non-commercial purposes. The provision now under consideration requires Contracting States to ensure that State ships 'act in a manner consistent with the object and purpose of the Convention and inform the Organization accordingly'. It is not clear if by that it is meant that States should merely confirm having done so, or whether they should provide details on the manner in which they ensured compliance with such rule.

3 THE ACTIVITIES REGULATED BY THE CONVENTION AND THE PROTOCOL

There is a difference between the scope of the Convention and that of the Protocol, since the Convention applies only to dumping, whilst the Protocol applies to dumping and incineration.

---

7 Art. 31 provides:

The flag State shall bear international responsibility for any loss or damage to the coastal State resulting from the non-compliance by a warship or other government ship operated for non-commercial purposes with the laws and regulations of the coastal State concerning passage through the territorial sea with the provisions of this Convention or other rules of international law.

MARINE POLLUTION CONVENTION, 1972

Dumping is defined in art. III(1)(a) of the Convention and art. 1.4 of the Protocol:

(a) 'Dumping' means:
(i)1 Any deliberate disposal at *into the* sea of wastes or other matter from vessels, aircraft, platforms or other man-made structures at sea;
(ii)2 Any deliberate disposal at *into* sea of vessels, aircraft, platforms or other man-made structures at sea;
  3 *any storage of wastes or other matter in the seabed and the subsoil thereof from vessels, aircraft, platforms or other man-made structures at sea; and*
  4 *any abandonment or toppling at site of platforms or other man-made structures at sea, for the sole purpose of deliberate disposal.*

'Disposal' is the action of getting rid of something and 'disposal at sea' indicates that the manner of getting rid of wastes is to throw them in the sea. The reference to disposal from vessels, aircraft, platforms or other man-made structures indicates that the wastes must be carried on any one of such craft and therefore disposal from ashore is not covered by the Convention. The 'other matter' is not the object of a specific definition in the Convention and in the Protocol. There is only the following definition of both in art. III(4) and art. 1.8 of the Protocol:

'Wastes or other matter' means material and substance of any kind, form and description.

For the purpose of the definition of 'dumping' the Convention and the Protocol then set out as follows in art. III(b) and art. 1.4.2 of the Protocol the actions that are not included in the notion of dumping:

(b)2 'Dumping' does not include:
(i)1 the disposal at sea of wastes or other matter incidental to, or derived from the normal operations of vessels, aircraft, platforms or other man-made structures at sea and their equipment, other than wastes or other matter transported by or to vessels, aircraft, platforms or other man-made structures at sea, operating for the purpose of disposal of such matter or derived from the treatment of such wastes or other matter on such vessels, aircraft, platforms or structures;
(ii)2 placement of matter for a purpose other than the mere disposal thereof, provided that such placement is not contrary to the aims of this Convention.
  3 *notwithstanding paragraph 4.1.4. abandonment in the sea of matter (e.g., cables, pipelines and marine research devices) placed for a purpose other than the mere disposal thereof.*
(c) The disposal *or storage* of wastes or other matter directly arising from, or related to the exploration, exploitation and associated off-shore processing of sea-bed mineral resources will not be covered by the provisions of this ~~Convention~~ *Protocol*.

Incineration is so defined in art. 1(5) of the Protocol:

1 *'Incineration at sea' means the combustion on board a vessel, platform or other man-made structure at sea of wastes or other matter for the purpose of their deliberate disposal by thermal destruction.*
2 *'Incineration at sea' does not include the incineration of wastes or other matter on board a vessel, platform, or other man-made structure at sea if such wastes or other matter were generated during the normal operation of that vessel, platform or other man-made structure at sea.*

The clarification under sub-paragraph 2 was needed since there is a similar clarification under the previous paragraph 1(4)(2) of the Protocol in respect of 'dumping'.

INTERNATIONAL MARITIME CONVENTIONS

4 THE OBLIGATIONS OF THE CONTRACTING PARTIES

4.1 General obligations

Art. 3 of the Protocol (no similar provision exists in the Convention) so provides:

1 *In implementing this Protocol, Contracting Parties shall apply a precautionary approach to environmental protection from dumping of wastes or other matter whereby appropriate preventative measures are taken when there is reason to believe that wastes or other matter introduced into the marine environment are likely to cause harm even when there is no conclusive evidence to prove a causal relation between inputs and their effects.*
2 *Taking into account the approach that the polluter should, in principle, bear the cost of pollution, each Contracting Party shall endeavour to promote practices whereby those it has authorized to engage in dumping or incineration at sea bear the cost of meeting the pollution prevention and control requirements for the authorized activities, having due regard to the public interest.*
3 *In implementing the provisions of this Protocol, Contracting Parties shall act so as not to transfer, directly or indirectly, damage or likelihood of damage from one part of the environment to another or transform one type of pollution into another.*
4 *No provision of this Protocol shall be interpreted as preventing Contracting Parties from taking, individually or jointly, more stringent measures in accordance with international law with respect to the prevention, reduction and where practicable elimination of pollution.*

This article sets out directives to States on the manner in which they must implement the provisions of the Convention.

The preventative (the word used in other conventions, such as the CLC, is 'preventive') measures, reference to which is made in paragraph 1, are defined in art. I(7) of the CLC as 'reasonable measures taken by any person after an incident has occurred to prevent or minimize pollution damage'. In this Convention, much more specific directions are provided. First, the Convention specifies in which circumstances the measures ought to be adopted: they are when there is 'reason to believe' that the wastes or other matter 'are likely to cause harm'. Although there is no indication as to what would be harmed, the previous reference to a precautionary approach to environmental protection and the general reference in art. 2 to the effect that the objective of the Convention is the protection and preservation of the marine environment, indicate clearly that the purpose is to avoid harm being caused to the environment. However the level of the precautionary action[8] appears to be significantly reduced by the final words of paragraph 1, pursuant to which there must be a 'reason to believe' that there may be a risk of harm 'even when there is no conclusive evidence to prove a causal relation between inputs and their effect', a rather obscure wording for dumping and harm. Although in fact the need for conclusive evidence is excluded, this wording suggests that there ought to be a sufficiently high level of proof, and this appears to be in conflict with the general principle that dumping is generally prohibited.

In any event, the wording of paragraph 1 is such that States ought to adopt flexible rules and give their competent authorities a rather high level of discretion in their decision, that must be based on the circumstances of the specific situation.

---

8 In 'Focus on IMO' of July 1997 attention is drawn (at p. 12) to the fact that this provision 'shifts the burden of proof by making it necessary for those wishing to carry out dumping operations to prove that it is safe, not for those opposing it to prove that is unsafe'.

Paragraph 2 is complementary to paragraph 1, in that States ought to charge the persons applying for a dumping or incineration permit with all costs to be incurred in taking the appropriate precautionary measures aiming at avoiding any possible damage to the environment.

Paragraph 3 lays down an important rule that should constitute a guide in granting a permit to dump any of the wastes or other matter listed in Annex 1: such dumping should not merely transfer damage or likelihood of damage from one part of the environment to another or transform one type of pollution into another. It is a fact that, in general, the wastes or other matter are already causing damage to the environment where they lie prior to being loaded on a ship for subsequent dumping or incineration, and the purpose of dumping or incinerating is to prevent further damage. Therefore, a comparison must be made between the existing level of environmental damage and that, if any, occurring after the expensive dumping or incinerating process. The question that arises is whether the level of environmental damage should be significantly reduced, albeit not wholly excluded.

The provisions in paragraph 4 stress a (possible) difference between the classic uniform law conventions and the conventions that create obligations on States to legislate in accordance with the rules laid down therein: such latter conventions may not ensure uniformity, but rather a minimum level of protection of the environment.

4.2 The obligation of States Parties to prohibit or regulate dumping of wastes or other matters

Art. IV of the Convention and art. 4 of the Protocol so provide:

1   ~~In accordance with the provisions of this Convention Contracting Parties shall prohibit~~
    ~~the dumping of any wastes or other matter in whatever form or condition except as~~
    ~~otherwise specified below:~~
        ~~(a)   the dumping of wastes or other matter listed in Annex I is prohibited;~~
        ~~(b)   the dumping of wastes or other matter listed in Annex II requires a prior special~~
            ~~permit;~~
        ~~(c)   the dumping of all other wastes or matter requires a prior general permit.~~
2   ~~Any permit shall be issued only after careful consideration of all the factors set forth in~~
    ~~Annex III, including prior studies of the characteristics of the dumping site, as set forth~~
    ~~in sections B and C of that Annex.~~
1   *.1 Contracting Parties shall prohibit the dumping of any wastes or other matter with the exception of those listed in Annex 1.*
    .2 The dumping of wastes or other matter listed in Annex 1 shall require a permit. Contracting Parties shall adopt administrative or legislative measures to ensure that issuance of permits and permit conditions comply with provisions of Annex 2. Particular attention shall be paid to opportunities to avoid dumping in favour of environmentally preferable alternatives.
3.2 No provision of this Convention is to be interpreted as preventing a Contracting Party from prohibiting, insofar as that Party is concerned, the dumping of wastes or other matter not mentioned in Annex I. That *Contracting* Party shall notify *the Organization of* such measures ~~to the Organization.~~

The most significant change brought by the Protocol to the original text of the Convention has been the replacement of the division of wastes or other matter into three groups, the first of the wastes the dumping of which is prohibited, the second of the wastes the dumping of which requires a prior *special* permit and the third of the wastes the dumping of which requires a prior *general* permit, by a general prohibition of dumping any wastes or other matter save those listed in Annex 1, the dumping of which however requires a permit.

The distinction in the Convention between a general permit, that may be granted in advance, and a special permit appears to be based on the fact that the wastes and other matter of the latter group require special care.[9]

The chapeau of Annex 1 to the Protocol provides:

The following wastes or other matter are those that may be considered for dumping being mindful of the Objectives and General Obligations of this Protocol set out in articles 2 and 3.

This wording indicates clearly that the permission to effect dumping is not granted outright.

Article 2 in fact provides that Contracting Parties shall take effective measures 'to prevent reduce and where practicable eliminate pollution caused by dumping or incineration at sea of wastes and other matter' and art. 3(1) provides that Contracting Parties must apply a precautionary approach to environmental protection from dumping.[10] In addition, for vessels and platforms or other man-made structures at sea (under paragraph 1.4) and bulky items primarily comprising iron, steel, concrete etc (under paragraph 1.7) the following requirements are set out:

The wastes or other matter listed in paragraphs 1.4 and 1.7 may be considered for dumping, provided that material capable of creating floating debris or otherwise contributing to pollution of the marine environment has been removed to the maximum extent and provided that the material dumped poses no serious obstacle to fishing or navigation.

General directives are then contained in Annex 2, the opening paragraph of which is significant:

1 The acceptance of dumping under certain circumstances shall not remove the obligations under this Annex to make further attempts to reduce the necessity for dumping.

Rules are then set out on the Waste Prevention Audit, the Consideration of Waste Management Options, the need for a description of 'Chemical, Physical and Biological Properties', the need for States to develop an 'Action List', Dump-Site Selection and other matters.

4.3 The exceptions to such obligations

Art. V of the Convention and art. 8 of the Protocol so provide:

1 The provisions of ~~article IV~~ *articles 4.1. and 5* shall not apply when it is necessary to secure the safety of human life or of vessels, aircraft, platforms or other man-made structures at sea in cases of force majeure caused by stress of weather, or in any case which constitutes a danger to human life or a real threat to vessels, aircraft, platforms or other man-made structures at sea, if dumping *or incineration* appears to be the only way of averting the threat and if there is every probability that the damage consequent upon such dumping

---

9 Annex II to the Convention contains the following statement that precedes the list of wastes and other material: 'The following substances and materials requiring special care are listed for the purposes of article VI(1)(a).'

10 *Supra*, para. 4(1).

MARINE POLLUTION CONVENTION, 1972

will be less than would otherwise occur. Such dumping *or incineration* shall be so conducted as to minimize the likelihood of damage to human or marine life and shall be reported forthwith to the Organization.

2   A Contracting Party may issue a special permit as an exception to ~~article IV(1)(a)~~ *articles 4.1 and 5*, in emergencies, posing unacceptable risk relating to human health, *safety, or the marine environment* and admitting no other feasible solution. Before doing so the Party shall consult any other country or countries that are likely to be affected and the Organization which, after consulting other Parties, and *competent* international organizations as appropriate, shall, in accordance with article ~~XIV~~ *18.1.6*, promptly recommend to the *Contracting* Party the most appropriate procedures to adopt. The *Contracting* Party shall follow these recommendations to the maximum extent feasible consistent with the time within which action must be taken and with the general obligation to avoid damage to the marine environment and shall inform the Organization of the action it takes. The Parties pledge themselves to assist one another in such situations.

3   Any Contracting Party may waive its rights under paragraph (2) at the time of, or subsequent to ratification of, or accession to this ~~Convention~~ *Protocol*.

The difference between the situations envisaged in paragraph 1 and the situation envisaged in paragraph 2 seems to be that paragraph 1 applies where dumping or incineration is necessary to secure the safety of human life or of vessels, aircraft, platforms or other man-made structures as well as in any case that constitutes a danger to human life or a real threat to vessels, etc. and paragraph 2 instead applies in emergencies posing an unacceptable risk to human health and, according to the text as amended by the Protocol, also to safety and the marine environment. In the first case immediate State action without compliance with art. IV is allowed, while in the second case it must be preceded by a rather cumbersome and lengthy procedure. Although health is less important than life, nevertheless it is important and may even affect life. The subsequent reference to 'safety' generally, raises doubts as to what the subject matter of such safety may be, considering that in paragraph 1 reference is made only to the safety of human life.

The distinction between the two situations gives rise to serious doubts on its justification, in particular since the rapid procedure under paragraph 1 applies also in the case of danger to vessels, aircraft etc., that may also occur without a danger to human life. There is a certain analogy between the situations envisaged in these provisions and those envisaged in art. III of the Intervention Convention, where, however, what is at risk is property and not life and action without previous consultations is allowed in cases of extreme urgency.[11]

As previously stated, the procedure indicated in paragraph 2 appears to be in blatant conflict with the first of the situations envisaged, described as an emergency posing unacceptable risk relating to human health and generally to 'safety'. Such procedure consists of several successive stages: first, consultation with other countries likely to be affected and the Organization (IMO); secondly, consultation between IMO and other Parties to the Convention and international organisations (which should they be?); thirdly, prompt recommendation to the Party involved of the most appropriate procedure to adopt. It is not known whether that procedure has ever been tested, but it appears unlikely that it would be appropriate for an action required in an emergency.

---

11 Chapter 1.

49

INTERNATIONAL MARITIME CONVENTIONS

5 THE DIRECTIVES TO STATES PARTIES FOR THE IMPLEMENTATION OF THE RULES ON DUMPING

Art. VI, which has been the object of significant amendments accompanied by needed clarifications in the Protocol (in which it is numbered 9), provides in its first four paragraphs (which are followed below by a short commentary):

1 Each Contracting Party shall designate an appropriate authority or authorities to:
(a) 1 issue ~~special~~ permits ~~which shall be required prior to, and for, the dumping of matter listed in Annex II and in the circumstances provided for in article V(2)~~); *in accordance with this Protocol*;
(b) ~~issue general permits which shall be required prior to, and for, the dumping of all other matter;~~
(c) 2 keep records of the nature and quantities of all *wastes and other* matter *for which dumping permits have been issued and where practicable the quantities actually dumped* ~~permitted to be dumped~~ and the location, time and method of dumping;
(d) 3 monitor individually, or in collaboration with other Parties and competent international organizations, the condition of the seas for the purposes of this ~~Convention~~ *Protocol*.

This paragraph sets out the powers and duties of the authority to be designated by Contracting Parties. The changes made in the Protocol are mostly consequent on the changes in the situations in which dumping of wastes and other matter is permitted, except that the obligation of keeping records as to quantities now also includes records of quantities actually dumped, 'where practicable'. The conditions of the sea must be monitored in connection with the dumping, and they refer to the conditions at the time of and subsequent to the dumping, because they can affect its consequences.

2 The appropriate authority or authorities of a contracting Party shall issue ~~prior special or general~~ permits in accordance with ~~paragraph (1)~~ *this Protocol* in respect of *wastes and other* matter intended for dumping *or, as provided for in article 8.2, incineration at sea*:
(a)1 loaded in its territory; *and*
(b)2 loaded by a vessel or aircraft registered in its territory or flying its flag, when the loading occurs in the territory of a State not *a Contracting* Party to this ~~Convention~~ *Protocol*.

This paragraph, the amendments to which are consequential on the amendments to the rules on permits, requires that records be kept by the appropriate authority of a Contracting Party in respect of all wastes and other matter intended for dumping and incineration at sea loaded in its territory on ships or aircraft of whatever nationality, as well as of all wastes and other matter intended for dumping and incineration at sea loaded on ships or aircraft registered in its territory, or flying its flag in a territory of a State not a Contracting Party.

3 In issuing permits ~~under sub-paragraphs (1)(a) and (b) above~~, the appropriate authority or authorities shall comply with ~~Annex III~~ *the requirements of article 4*, together with such additional criteria, measures and requirements as they may consider relevant.

This paragraph in the Convention requires compliance with Annex III (which enumerates the provisions to be considered in establishing criteria governing the issue of permits for the dumping of matter at sea); and in the Protocol requires

50

MARINE POLLUTION CONVENTION, 1972

compliance with the requirements of art. 4 (in which reference is made to Annex 1 in respect of the wastes and other matter the dumping of which may permitted, and to Annex 2 in respect of conditions to be complied with for the issue of a permit).[12]

4 Each Contracting Party, directly or through a Secretariat established under a regional agreement, shall report to the Organization, and where appropriate to other Parties ~~the information specified in sub-paragraphs(c) and (d) of paragraph (1) above, and the criteria, measures and requirements it adopts in accordance with paragraph (3) above. The procedure to be followed and the nature of such reports shall be agreed by the Parties in consultation.~~:

   1 the information specified in paragraphs 1.2 and 1.3;

   2 the administrative and legislative measures taken to implement the provisions of this Protocol, including a summary of enforcement measures; and

   3 the effectiveness of the measures referred to in paragraph 4.2 and any problems encountered in their application.

The information referred to in paragraphs 1.2 and 1.3 shall be submitted on an annual basis. The information referred to in paragraphs 4.2 and 4.3 shall be submitted on a regular basis.

This paragraph, which in the Convention sets out concisely the object of the report to be made by Contracting Party to IMO, enumerates in more detail the matters in respect of which report must be made and most helpfully specifies the frequency with which the reports must be made in respect of the information referred to in paragraphs 1.2 and 1.3 (on an annual basis) and in respect of the information referred to in paragraphs 4.2 and 4.3 (on a regular basis).[13]

6 INSTRUCTIONS TO STATES PARTIES ON THE ISSUANCE OF PERMITS AND REPORTING

Art. VI of the Convention (art. 9 of the Protocol) is divided into three parts: the first sets out instructions to Contracting Parties as regards designating an authority to carry out the task of issuing permits, the nature of which differs in the Convention and in the Protocol; the second sets out the directions to such authority; and the third the obligations to report to IMO. They will be considered separately in respect of both the Convention and the Protocol.

6.1 The designation and the tasks of the appropriate authority

~~1 Each Contracting Party shall designate an appropriate authority or authorities to:~~

  ~~(a) issue special permits which shall be required prior to, and for, the dumping of matter listed in Annex II and in the circumstances provided for in article V(2);~~

  ~~(b) issue general permits which shall be required prior to, and for, the dumping of all other matter;~~

1 Each Contracting Party shall designate an appropriate authority or authorities to:

  1 issue permits in accordance with this Protocol;

---

12 *Supra*, para. 2.2.
13 For comments on this expression see *infra*, para. 6.3.

51

The difference between the text in the Convention and that in the Protocol is due to the fact that under the Protocol there is only one kind of permit.

(c) keep records of the nature and quantities of all matter permitted to be dumped and the location, time and method of dumping;

2   keep records of the nature and quantities of all wastes or other matter for which dumping permits have been issued and where practicable the quantities actually dumped and the location, time and method of dumping; and

The first difference relates to the permit, that is always required under the Protocol. The second relates to the requirement under the Protocol to keep records not only of the nature and quantity for which a dumping permit has been issued, but also of the quantities actually dumped and the location, time and method of dumping. That additional information is of great importance, because there may be a significant difference between the quantities the dumping of which is permitted and the quantities actually dumped; and the method of dumping is also very important. The obligation to keep records in that latter respect is not absolute, but subject to issues of practicality: that seems to imply that there are circumstances in which it is not feasible to keep records of what has actually been dumped, when and where. Although the scope of the Protocol has been widened, and covers also incineration, no records are apparently required in respect of the quantities that have been incinerated.

3   monitor individually, or in collaboration with other Parties and competent international organizations, the condition of the seas for the purposes of this Convention.

Monitoring the conditions of the seas is certainly important, because a risk of pollution to the environment may arise from the dumping of wastes and other matter.

6.2 The duties of the appropriate authority

2   The appropriate authority or authorities of a contracting Party shall issue prior special or general permits in accordance with paragraph (1) in respect of matter intended for dumping:
(a) loaded in its territory;
(b) loaded by a vessel or aircraft registered in its territory or flying its flag, when the loading occurs in the territory of a State not party to this Convention.
3   In issuing permits under sub-paragraphs (1)(a) and (b) above, the appropriate authority or authorities shall comply with Annex III, together with such additional criteria, measures and requirements as they may consider relevant.

2   The appropriate authority or authorities of a Contracting Party shall issue permits in accordance with this Protocol in respect of wastes or other matter intended for dumping or, as provided for in article 8.2, incineration at sea:
   1   loaded in its territory; and
   2   loaded onto a vessel or aircraft registered in its territory or flying its flag, when the loading occurs in the territory of a State not a Contracting Party to this Protocol.
   3   In issuing permits, the appropriate authority or authorities shall comply with the requirements of article 4, together with such additional criteria, measures and requirements as they may consider relevant.

The competence of the appropriate authority has remained unchanged. There are two connecting factors. The first is geographical: they are competent to issue permits in respect of wastes or other matters intended for dumping, irrespective of when and where, loaded in their territory and, when the Protocol is applicable, also for wastes and other matter intended for incineration at sea, on any ship, of whatever nationality. By 'territory' is meant the jurisdiction of the appointing State. The second connecting factor is based on the place of registration or the flag of the ship on which the loading takes place: the appropriate authorities are also competent when the loading occurs outside their territory when the ship is registered in their territory or flies the flag of the State by which they have been appointed, provided it occurs in the territory of a State not party to the Convention or to the Protocol. If in fact it occurs in the territory of a State party to either, it is the appropriate authority of that State that will be competent.

Annex III, compliance with which is required by the Convention, sets out (a) the characteristics and composition of the matter, requiring that in issuing a permit the Contracting Parties should consider whether an adequate scientific basis exists concerning characteristics and composition of the matter, and (b) requires that the characteristics of the dumping site and method of deposit be specified.

Art. 4, compliance with which is required by the Protocol, requires in paragraph 1(2) that the issuance of permits and permit conditions comply with the provisions of Annex 2, which in turn sets out rules on the dump-site selection, the assessment of potential effects of dumping, the conditions under which a permit may be issued and the data and information that must be specified in the permit. A comparison between the requirements under the Convention and the Protocol shows that they have been made wider and more strict in the Protocol.

6.3 The duty of Contracting States to report to IMO

Art. VI(4) of the Convention so provides:

> ~~Each Contracting Party, directly or through a Secretariat established under a regional agreement, shall report to the Organization, and where appropriate to other Parties, the information specified in sub-paragraphs (c) and (d) of paragraph (1) above, and the criteria, measures and requirements it adopts in accordance with paragraph (3) above. The procedure to be followed and the nature of such reports shall be agreed by the Parties in consultation.~~

Art. 9(4) and (5) of the Protocol instead provides:

> 4 *Each Contracting Party, directly or through a secretariat established under a regional agreement, shall report to the Organization and where appropriate to other Contracting Parties:*
> 1 *the information specified in paragraphs 1.2 and 1.3;*
> 2 *the administrative and legislative measures taken to implement the provisions of this Protocol, including a summary of enforcement measures; and*
> 3 *the effectiveness of the measures referred to in paragraph 4.2 and any problems encountered in their application.*
> *The information referred to in paragraphs 1.2 and 1.3 shall be submitted on an annual basis. The information referred to in paragraphs 4.2 and 4.3 shall be submitted on a regular basis.*
> 5 *Reports submitted under paragraphs 4.2 and 4.3 shall be evaluated by an appropriate subsidiary body as determined by the Meeting of Contracting Parties. This body will report its conclusions to an appropriate Meeting or Special Meeting of Contracting Parties.*

The matters on which report to IMO must be made by the Contracting Parties appear to be more detailed in the relevant provisions of the Protocol than those of the Convention. But very helpful is the indication at the end of paragraph 4 of the Protocol as to the frequency with which the information must be provided. This is on an annual basis as referred to in paragraphs 1.2 and 1.3; and on a regular basis as referred to in paragraphs 4.2 and 4.3. The meaning of 'regular basis' is less clear. It is suggested that, with respect to new administrative and legislative measures, it means each time new measures are adopted. This should not be the case with respect to the effectiveness of the measures and problems encountered in their application. It is suggested that the frequency must be decided by the relevant Contracting Party, but should then always be the same: therefore 'regular basis' would mean at 'fixed intervals'.

CHAPTER 6

International Convention for the Control and Management of Ships' Ballast Water and Sediments, 2004

1 INTRODUCTION

This is another public law convention that creates obligations on States Parties to enact legislation that is necessary in order to ensure compliance by ships with the requirements set forth therein. Its art. 4 provides:

Control of the Transfer of Harmful Aquatic Organisms and Pathogens through Ships' Ballast Water and Sediments

1   Each Party shall require that ships to which this Convention applies and which are entitled to fly its flag or operating under its authority comply with the requirements set forth in this Convention, including the applicable standards and requirements in the Annex, and shall take effective measures to ensure that those ships comply with those requirements.
2   Each Party shall, with due regard to its particular conditions and capabilities, develop national policies, strategies or programmes for Ballast Water Management in its ports and waters under its jurisdiction that accord with, and promote the attainment of the objectives of this Convention.

There are, however, also rules that are enforceable directly on ships, to which the Convention applies, that are in ports or offshore terminals of a State Party other than that of which they are flying the flag, including their detention.[1]

2 SCOPE OF APPLICATION

Since the purpose of the Convention is to ensure the control and management of ballast water and sediments of ships, its scope of application is linked with the ships that are subject to its rules and to the notion of ballast water and of sediments.

2.1 Ships to which the Convention applies

Art. 3.1 so provides:

1   Except as expressly provided otherwise in this Convention, this Convention shall apply to:
   (a)   ships entitled to fly the flag of a Party; and

---

1   Rules in this respect are set out in art. 9, pursuant to which ships may be subject to inspection (*infra*, para. 3) and in art. 10, pursuant to which ships may also be detained (*infra*, para. 4).

55

(b) ships not entitled to fly the flag of a Party but which operate under the authority of a
Party.

There is no consistency in the manner in which the linkage of ships to a State is described. Whilst also in art. 3(1) of the Convention for Prevention of Pollution of 1973 reference is made to ships entitled to fly the flag of a State Party and in art. 4(2) of the Convention on Registration of Ships it is provided that ships 'have the nationality of the State whose flag they are entitled to fly', in art. VII(1) of the Convention on Dumping of Wastes reference is made to vessels registered in or flying the flag of a State and in art. 8(1) of both the 1952 and 1999 Arrest Conventions reference is made to ships flying the flag of a Contracting State.[2] The reference to the entitlement to flying the flag rather than to the flag the vessel is flying is more secure, because it is connected with a document, which is normally the register in which the ship is registered, rather than – at least formally – on a fact. But in practice there is no difference, because a court in order to establish what flag the ship is flying, would require evidence of the registry in which she is registered. What is meant by operation 'under the authority' of a State Party is not clear. That description would probably fit with the situation where a ship flying the flag of a State is operated, on the basis, for example, of a demise charter, by a company having its principal place of business in another State.

Art. 3(3) so provides:

3 With respect to ships of non-Parties to this Convention, Parties shall apply the requirements of this Convention as may be necessary to ensure that no more favourable treatment is given to such ships.

The phrase 'ships of non-Parties' is an abridged formulation of the phrase 'ships entitled to fly the flag of non-Parties' and the flexible formula used in this provision seems in practice to entail a rather wide application of the Convention to such ships, since all provisions aiming at ensuring the control and management of ballast water and sediments would apply.

2.2 Ships to which the Convention does not apply

It is appropriate to consider *seriatim* the rather long list of such ships enumerated in art. 3(2).

(a) ships not designed or constructed to carry Ballast Water;

The question that might be asked is whether ships not designed or constructed to carry ballast water may nevertheless do so. Apparently the answer is no. Another question might be why no reference is made to sediments: this time the answer is based on the definition of sediments in art. 1(11) as 'matter settled out of ballast water within a ship': therefore if there is not ballast water there cannot be sediments.

(b) ships of a Party which only operate in waters under the jurisdiction of that Party, unless the Party determines that the discharge of Ballast Water from such ships would impair

---

2 This is the so-called 'bareboat charter registration', permitted in several jurisdictions, and regulated under the name of 'temporary change of flag' in art. 16 of the MLM Convention 1993 (see vol. II, chapter 7, para. 7).

CONTROL OF SHIPS' BALLAST WATER AND SEDIMENTS CONVENTION, 2004

or damage their environment, human health, property or resources, or those of adjacent or other States.

As previously observed in connection with paragraph 3, 'ships of a Party' is an abridged formulation of 'ships entitled to fly the flag of a State Party'. The basic exclusion is due to the fact that in the case considered there would normally be no element of internationality. But such element would instead materialise if the discharge of ballast water could impair or damage the environment, human health, property or resources of an adjacent State or other States. It does not seem appropriate that in such case the decision to apply the Convention be only that of the Party State the flag of which the ship is entitled to fly. However it appears that the risk of such impairment would entail a violation of the basic purpose of the Convention and might give rise to a dispute between States Parties.

(c) ships of a Party which only operate in waters under the jurisdiction of another Party, subject to the authorization of the latter Party for such exclusion. No Party shall grant such authorization if doing so would impair or damage their environment, human health, property or resources, or those of adjacent or other States. Any Party not granting such authorization shall notify the Administration of the ship concerned that this Convention applies to such ship;

The situation would be similar where the authorisation is granted by the State in the waters of which the ship would operate and damage would occur in the waters of other States.

(d) ships which only operate in waters under the jurisdiction of one Party and on the high seas, except for ships not granted an authorization pursuant to sub-paragraph (c), unless such Party determines that the discharge of Ballast Water from such ships would impair or damage their environment, human health, property or resources, or those of adjacent of other States;

It is not clear what is the distinction between this case and the previous one, but it appears that also in this case the waters in which the ship would operate are not those of the State of which the ship is entitled to fly the flag and the reference to the authorisation of the State in whose waters the ship operates seems to confirm this. The difference could be that in a case covered by sub-paragraph (d), the ship would also operate on the high seas, save that in that case the ship is not granted an authorisation by the State in the waters of which she would operate.

(e) any warship, naval auxiliary or other ship owned or operated by a State and used, for the time being, only on government non-commercial service. However, each Party shall ensure, by the adoption of appropriate measures not impairing operations or operational capabilities of such ships owned or operated by it, that such ships act in a manner consistent, so far as is reasonable and practicable, with this Convention;

The wording of this exclusion is based on art. 32 of the Law of the Sea Convention, to which there has been added the reference to 'naval auxiliary', reference to which is also made, as 'fleet auxiliaries', in the Immunity Convention 1926. However States are not released from all obligations in respect of the ships mentioned in this provision, but their compliance with them is conditional on their non-impairment of the 'operations or operational capabilities' of such ship. It is suggested that where States fail to comply with the rules of the Convention, they have the burden of proving that such compliance would have impaired such operational capabilities. It is also suggested that this is unlikely to be the case in respect of ships owned or operated by States on government non-commercial service.

(f)   permanent Ballast Water in sealed tanks on ships, that is not subject to discharge.

Compliance with the requirements of this Convention is conceivable if there is a discharge of ballast water and sediments, but it is not where ballast has a permanent character and the tanks in which ballast is loaded are sealed.

2.3 The matter to which the Convention applies

The matter to which the Convention applies is the ballast water of ships as defined in art. 1.2:

2   'Ballast Water' means water with its suspended matter taken on board a ship to control trim, list, draught, stability or stresses of the ship.

The suspended matter reference to which is made in the above definition is called 'sediments', as defined in art. 1.11:

11   'Sediments' means matter settled out of Ballast Water within a ship.

The ballast water is the object of the Convention because of the matter that is suspended therein and specifically because of the danger that such matter may include harmful aquatic organisms and pathogens as defined in art. 1.8:

8   'Harmful Aquatic Organisms and Pathogens' means aquatic organisms or pathogens which, if introduced into the sea including estuaries, or into fresh water courses, may create hazards to the environment, human health, property or resources, impair biological diversity or interfere with other legitimate uses of such areas.

The purpose of the Convention is to prevent the risk of such hazard through a controlled discharge of ships' ballast water, as appears from the following sentence in its premise:

CONSCIOUS that the uncontrolled discharge of Ballast Water and Sediments from ships has led to the transfer of Harmful Aquatic Organisms and Pathogens, causing injury or damage to the environment, human health, property and resources . . .

3 THE MANNER IN WHICH SUCH PURPOSE IS ACHIEVED

That purpose is achieved by providing that States Parties (a) require all ships entitled to fly their flag or operating under their authority to comply with the provisions of the Convention and its Annex and, (b) take all necessary actions with a view to ensuring that adequate facilities be provided in their ports for the reception of ballast water from ships and to ensuring that ships comply with the requirement of the Convention. Articles 4 and 5 of the Convention so provide:

Article 4 Control of the Transfer of Harmful Aquatic Organisms and Pathogens Through Ships' Ballast Water and Sediments

1   Each Party shall require that ships to which this Convention applies and which are entitled to fly its flag or operating under its authority comply with the requirements set forth in this Convention, including the applicable standards and requirements in the Annex, and shall take effective measures to ensure that those ships comply with those requirements.

2   Each Party shall, with due regard to its particular conditions and capabilities, develop national policies, strategies or programmes for Ballast Water Management in its ports and waters under its jurisdiction that accord with, and promote the attainment of the objectives of this Convention.

Article 5 Sediment Reception Facilities

1   Each Party undertakes to ensure that, in ports and terminals designated by that Party where cleaning or repair of ballast tanks occurs, adequate facilities are provided for the reception of Sediments, taking into account the Guidelines developed by the Organization. Such reception facilities shall operate without causing undue delay to ships and shall provide for the safe disposal of such Sediments that does not impair or damage their environment, human health, property or resources or those of other States.

2   Each Party shall notify the Organization for transmission to the other Parties concerned of all cases where the facilities provided under paragraph 1 are alleged to be inadequate.

The compliance by ships with the provisions of art. 4, or more precisely with the provisions enacted in each State Party along the lines of those of that article, is ensured by: (a) the regulations adopted in section B of the Annex to the Convention on the Management and Control Requirements for Ships, which in Regulation B-1 requires each ship to have on board and implement a Ballast Water Management plan and in Regulation B-2 to have on board a Ballast Water record book; (b) by the Standards for Ballast Water Management set out on section D.

Pursuant to art. 8 sanctions must be established under the law of the State of the flag in respect of any violation of the requirement of the Convention, and pursuant to art. 9 ships to which the Convention applies may be subject to inspection by officers duly authorised in any port or offshore terminal of another State Party.

4 THE TECHNIQUE ADOPTED FOR THE IMPLEMENTATION OF THE PROVISIONS OF THE CONVENTION

In the Convention and in its Annex, reference to which has been made above, there are set out specific rules on the control and management of ballast water and sediments and it is provided that States Parties are bound to implement them. The obligations of States Parties are set out in general terms in art. 2(1) which provides:

1   Parties undertake to give full and complete effect to the provisions of this Convention and the Annex thereto in order to prevent, minimize and ultimately eliminate the transfer of Harmful Aquatic Organisms and Pathogens through the control and management of ships' Ballast Water and Sediments.

2   The Annex forms an integral part of this Convention. Unless expressly provided otherwise, a reference to this Convention constitutes at the same time a reference to the Annex.

But States are allowed to adopt more stringent measures. Art. 2(3) in fact provides:

3 Nothing in this Convention shall be interpreted as preventing a Party from taking, individually or jointly with other Parties, more stringent measures with respect to the prevention, reduction or elimination of the transfer of Harmful Aquatic Organisms and Pathogens through the control and management of ships' Ballast Water and Sediments, consistent with international law.

The actions required of States relate both to ships flying their flag and to the port and terminal installations.

Compliance with the requirements set forth in the Convention may be ensured by transforming the rules of the Convention into domestic rules. But the taking of effective measures in order to ensure such compliance appears to be a very flexible rule of a rather vague character: would the mandatory character of the domestic rules satisfy the obligations of States Parties, or should a penalty for the breach of the obligation be provided? If so, how serious should be such penalty in order to qualify as an effective measure? As regards the ships in respect of which such measures must be taken, it is not clear what are ships 'operating under the authority' of a State,[3] other than those flying its flag. Even more generic is the obligation set out in paragraph 2 of art. 4: what is meant by due regard to the conditions and capabilities of a State? Which authority is competent to assess compliance with this obligation?

Rules are then set out in art. 8 in respect of the violation of the requirements of the Convention and of the sanctions that must be established 'under the law of the Administration of the ship concerned' – by which is meant the law of the State of which the ship is flying the flag.[4] In fact, the object of the violation will not be the requirements of the Convention, but rather the requirement of the national law enacted in compliance with the obligations of the relevant State to enact rules that comply with its obligations under the Convention.

The provisions of art. 5 exclusively create obligations on States Parties and in this case a failure to comply with them might entitle shipowners to bring claims for damages against the State in breach of its obligations.

Additional actions are permitted to, but not required by, the State of which the ship is flying the flag. Art. 10(2) states:

2 If a ship is detected to have violated this Convention, the Party whose flag the ship is entitled to fly, and/or the Party in whose port or offshore terminal the ship is operating, may, in addition to any sanctions described in article 8 or any action described in article 9, take steps to warn, detain, or exclude the ship. The Party in whose port or offshore terminal the ship is operating, however, may grant such a ship permission to leave the port or offshore terminal for the purpose of discharging Ballast Water or proceeding to the nearest

---

3 The same language is used in art. 3(1)(b) of MARPOL, *supra*, chapter 3, para. 2.1.
4 Art.1(1) provides the following definition of 'Administration':

1 'Administration' means the Government of the State under whose authority the ship is operating. With respect to a ship entitled to fly a flag of any State, the Administration is the Government of that State. With respect to floating platforms engaged in exploration and exploitation of the sea-bed and subsoil thereof adjacent to the coast over which the coastal State exercises sovereign rights for the purposes of exploration and exploitation of its natural resources, including Floating Storage Units (FSUs) and Floating Production Storage and Offloading Units (FPSOs), the Administration is the Government of the coastal State concerned.

appropriate repair yard or reception facility available, provided doing so does not present a threat of harm to the environment, human health, property or resources.

The provisions of this article apply not only to ships flying the flag of the State in which the violation of the Convention (or, more precisely, of the national rules by which the provisions of the Convention have been implemented), wherever the violation has been committed, but also to any other ship, of whatever nationality, operating within the ports or offshore terminals of a State Party.

CHAPTER 7

International Convention on Standards of Training, Certification and Watchkeeping for Seafarers, 1978

One of the purposes of the Convention and of the Seafarers' Training, Certification and Watchkeeping (STCW) Code is to require that seafarers acquire expertise in order to ensure the protection of the environment, as discussed in the following review of their provisions.

1 THE OBJECT OF THE CONTROL OF SHIPS, WHILE IN THE PORTS OF A STATE PARTY, BY OFFICERS OF THAT STATE

Art. X of the Convention provides in paragraph 1 that ships are subject, while in the ports of a Party, to control by officers duly authorised by that Party to verify that all seafarers serving on board are certificated by the Convention and then provides in paragraph 3 that if the deficiencies referred to in paragraph 3 of Regulation 1/4[1] are not corrected and it is determined that this fact poses a danger, *inter alia*, to the environment, the Party carrying out the control shall take steps to ensure that the ship will not sail unless and until such requirements are met to the extent that the danger is removed.

Regulation I/5 of the Annex to the Convention, as amended by the Manila Conference of 2010,[2] provides in paragraph 1:

1   Each Party shall establish processes and procedures for the impartial investigation of any reported incompetence, act, omission or compromise to security *that may pose a direct threat to safety of life or property at sea or to the marine environment* by the holders of certificates or endorsements issued by that Party in connection with their performance of duties related to their certificates and for the withdrawal, suspension and cancellation of such certificates for such cause and for the prevention of fraud.

Regulation I/14, as amended, provides that each Administration shall require every company to ensure, *inter alia*, that the ship's complement can effectively coordinate their activities in an emergency situation and in performing functions vital to safety or to the prevention or mitigation of pollution.

---

1 Regulation 1/4 includes in para. 3, among the objects of the control, the assessment of the ability of seafarers to maintain watchkeeping standards as required by the Convention if there are clear grounds for believing that such standards cannot be maintained for any of the reasons subsequently mentioned, including a discharge of substances from the ship when under way, at anchor or at berth which is illegal.

2 Attachment 1 to the Final Act of the Conference, doc. STCW/CONF.2/33 of 1 July 2010.

2 THE PROVISIONS IN THE CODE IN WHICH REFERENCE IS MADE TO THE PROTECTION OF THE ENVIRONMENT

The last of the recitals of Resolution 2, by which the Conference has adopted the STCW Code, is so worded:

DESIRING to achieve and maintain the highest practicable standard for the safety of life and property at sea and in port and for the protection of the environment

and reference to the need for the protection of the environment is frequently made in the chapters of the Code as it appears from the review that follows.

Chapter II – Standards regarding the master and deck department

Section A-II/1 – Mandatory minimum requirements for certification of officers in charge of a navigational watch on ships of 500 gross tonnage or more

Table A-II/1 – 'Specification of minimum standard of competence for officer in charge of a navigational watch on ships of 500 gross tonnage or more'

In respect of the function 'Controlling the operation of the ship and care for persons on board at the operational level' the following entries appear:[3]

Column 1	Column 2	Column 3	Column 4
Competence	Knowledge, understanding and proficiency	Methods for demonstrating competence	Criteria for evaluating competence
Ensure compliance with pollution prevention requirements	*Prevention of pollution of the marine environment and anti-pollution procedures* *Knowledge of the precautions to be taken to prevent pollution of the marine environment* *Anti-pollution procedures and all associated equipment* *Importance of proactive measures to protect the marine environment*	Examination and assessment of evidence obtained from one or more of the following: 1 approved in-service experience 2 approved training ship experience 3 approved training	Procedures for monitoring shipboard operations *and ensuring compliance with MARPOL requirements are fully observed* *Actions to ensure that a positive environmental reputation is maintained*

and[4]

---

3 STCW/CONF.2/34, p. 44.
4 At p. 45.

Column 1	Column 2	Column 3	Column 4
Competence	Knowledge, understanding and proficiency	Methods for demonstrating competence	Criteria for evaluating competence
Monitor compliance with legislative requirements	Basic working knowledge of the relevant IMO conventions concerning safety of life at sea, security *and protection of the marine environment*	Assessment of evidence obtained from examination or approved training	Legislative requirements relating to safety of life at sea, security *and protection of the marine environment are correctly identified*

Section A-II/2 – Mandatory minimum requirements for certification of masters and chief mates on ships of 500 gross tonnage or more
Paragraph 3 of the introduction so provides:[5]

3　Bearing in mind that the master has ultimate responsibility for the safety and security of the ship, its passengers, crew and cargo, *and for the protection of the marine environment against pollution by the ship*, and that a chief mate shall be in a position to assume that responsibility at any time, assessment in these subjects shall be designed to test their ability to assimilate all available information that affects the safety and security of the ship, its passengers, crew or cargo, *or the protection of the marine environment.*

Table A-II/2 – 'Specification of minimum standard of competence for masters and chief mates of ships of 500 gross tonnage or more'
In respect of the function 'Cargo handling and stowage at the management level', the following entries are made:[6]

Column 1	Column 2	Column 3	Column 4
Competence	Knowledge, understanding and proficiency	Methods for demonstrating competence	Criteria for evaluating competence
(. .. .. .)	(. .. .. .)	(. .. .. .)	(. .. .. .)
Carriage of dangerous goods	*International regulations, standards, codes and recommendations on the carriage of dangerous cargoes, including the International Maritime Dangerous Goods (IMDG) Code and the International Maritime Solid Bulk Cargoes (IMSBC) Code Carriage of dangerous, hazardous and harmful cargoes; precautions during loading and unloading and care during the voyage*	Examination and assessment of evidence obtained from one or more of the following: 1 approved in-service experience 2 approved simulator training, where appropriate 3 approved specialist training	Planned distribution of cargo is based on reliable information and is in accordance with established guidelines and legislative requirements *Information on dangers, hazards and special requirements is recorded in a format suitable for easy reference in the event of an incident*

---

5 At p. 48.
6 At p. 58.

and in respect of the function 'Controlling the operation of the ship and care for persons on board at the management level' the following entries are made:[7]

Column 1	Column 2	Column 3	Column 4
Competence	Knowledge, understanding and proficiency	Methods for demonstrating competence	Criteria for evaluating competence
Monitor and control compliance with legislative requirements and measures *to ensure safety of life at sea, security and the protection of the marine environment*	Knowledge of international maritime law embodied in international agreements and conventions Regard shall be paid especially to the following subjects: (. . . . .) *4 responsibilities under the International Convention for the Prevention of Pollution from Ships, as Amended* (. . . . .) *7 methods and aids to prevent pollution of the marine environment by ships*	Examination and assessment of evidence obtained from one or more of the following: 1 approved in-service experience 2 approved training ship experience 3 approved simulator training, where appropriate	Procedures for monitoring operations and maintenance comply with legislative requirements Potential non-compliance is promptly and fully identified Planned renewal and extension of certificates ensures continued validity of surveyed items and equipment

Table A-II/3 – Specification of minimum standard of competence for officers in charge of a navigational watch and for masters on ships of less than 500 gross tonnage engaged on near-coastal voyages

In respect of the function 'Cargo handling and stowage at the operational level' the following entries are made:[8]

Column 1	Column 2	Column 3	Column 4
Competence	Knowledge, understanding and proficiency	Methods for demonstrating competence	Criteria for evaluating competence
Monitor the loading, stowage, securing and unloading of cargoes and their care during the voyage	*Cargo handling, stowage and securing* Knowledge of safe handling, stowage and securing of cargoes, *including dangerous, hazardous and harmful cargoes, and their effect on the*	Examination and assessment of evidence obtained from one or more of the following: 1 approved in-service experience 2 approved training ship experience	Cargo operations are carried out in accordance with the cargo plan or other documents and established safety rules/regulations, equipment operating instructions and shipboard stowage limitations

7 At p. 60.
8 At p. 72.

INTERNATIONAL MARITIME CONVENTIONS

	safety of life and of the ship *Use of the International Maritime Dangerous Goods (IMDG) Code*	3 approved simulator training, where appropriate	*The handling of dangerous, hazardous and harmful cargoes complies with international regulations and recognized standards and codes of safe practice*

and in respect of the function 'Controlling the operation of the ship and care for persons on board at the operational level' the following entries are made:[9]

Column 1	Column 2	Column 3	Column 4
Competence	Knowledge, understanding and proficiency	Methods for demonstrating competence	Criteria for evaluating competence
Ensure compliance with pollution prevention requirements	*Prevention of pollution of the marine environment and anti-pollution procedures* *Knowledge of the precautions to be taken to prevent pollution of the marine environment* *Anti-pollution procedures and all associated equipment*	Examination and assessment of evidence obtained from one or more of the following: 1 approved in-service experience 2 approved training ship experience	*Procedures for monitoring shipboard operations and ensuring compliance with MARPOL requirements are fully observed*

Table A-II/5 – 'Specification of minimum standard of competence of ratings as able seafarer deck'

In respect of the function 'Controlling the operation of the ship and care for persons on board at the support level' the following entries are made:[10]

Column 1	Column 2	Column 3	Column 4
Competence	Knowledge, understanding and proficiency	Methods for demonstrating competence	Criteria for evaluating competence
Apply precautions and contribute to the prevention of pollution of the marine environment	*Knowledge of the precautions to be taken to prevent pollution of the marine environment* *Knowledge of the use and operation of anti-pollution equipment* *Knowledge of the approved methods for disposal of marine pollutants*	Assessment of evidence obtained from one or more of the following: 1 approved in-service experience 2 practical training 3 examination 4 approved training ship experience	*Procedures designed to safeguard the marine environment are observed at all times*

---

9 At p. 72.
10 At p. 82.

SEAFARER STANDARDS CONVENTION, 1978

Chapter III – Standards regarding engine department

Section A-III/1 – Mandatory minimum requirements for certification of officers in charge of an engineering watch in a manned engine-room or as designated duty engineers in periodically unmanned engine-room

Table A-III/1 – 'Specification of minimum standards of competence for officers in charge of an engineering watch in a manned engine-room or designated duty engineers in periodically unmanned engine-room'

In respect of the function 'Marine engineering at the operational level' the following entries are made:[11]

Column 1	Column 2	Column 3	Column 4
Competence	Knowledge, understanding and proficiency	Methods for demonstrating competence	Criteria for evaluating competence
Operate fuel, lubrication, ballast and other pumping systems and associated control systems	Operational characteristics of pumps and piping systems, including control systems Operation of pumping systems: 1 routine pumping operations 2 operation of bilge, ballast and cargo pumping systems Oily-water separators (or-similar equipment) requirements and operation	Examination and assessment of evidence obtained from one or more of the following: 1 approved in-service experience 2 approved training ship experience 3 approved simulator training, where appropriate 4 approved laboratory equipment training	*Operations are planned and carried out in accordance with operating manuals, established rules and procedures to ensure safety of operations and avoid pollution of the marine environment* Deviations from the norm are promptly identified and appropriate action is taken

In respect of the function 'Controlling the operation of the ship and care for persons on board at the operational level' the following entries are made:[12]

Column 1	Column 2	Column 3	Column 4
Competence	Knowledge, understanding and proficiency	Methods for demonstrating competence	Criteria for evaluating competence
Ensure compliance with pollution prevention requirements	*Prevention of pollution of the marine environment Knowledge of the precautions to be taken to prevent pollution of the marine environment*	Examination and assessment of evidence obtained from one or more of the following: 1 approved in-service experience	*Procedures for monitoring shipboard operations and ensuring compliance with MARPOL requirements are fully observed*

11 At p. 89.
12 At p. 93.

	Anti-pollution procedures and all associated equipment Importance of proactive measures to protect the marine environment	2 approved training ship experience 3 approved training	to ensure that a positive environmental reputation is maintained

Table A-III/2 – 'Specification of minimum standard of competence for chief engineer officers and second engineer officers on ships powered by main propulsion machinery of 3,000 kW propulsion power or more'

In respect of the function 'Marine engineering at the management level' the following entries are made:[13]

Column 1	Column 2	Column 3	Column 4
Competence	Knowledge, understanding and proficiency	Methods for demonstrating competence	Criteria for evaluating competence
Manage fuel, lubrication and ballast operations	Operation and maintenance of machinery, including pumps and piping systems	Examination and assessment of evidence obtained from one or more of the following: 1 approved in-service experience 2 approved training ship experience 3 approved simulator training, where appropriate	*Fuel and ballast operations meet operational requirements and are carried out so as to prevent pollution of the marine environment*

In respect of the function 'Controlling the operation of the ship and care for persons on board at the management level' the following entries are made:[14]

Column 1	Column 2	Column 3	Column 4
Competence	Knowledge, understanding and proficiency	Methods for demonstrating competence	Criteria for evaluating competence
Monitor and control compliance with legislative requirements and measures to ensure safety of life at sea, security and protection	*Knowledge of relevant international maritime law embodied in international agreements and conventions* Regard shall be paid especially to the following subjects:	Examination and assessment of evidence obtained from one or more of the following: 1 approved in-service experience	Procedures for monitoring operations and maintenance comply with legislative requirements Potential non-compliance is

---

13 At p. 101.
14 At p. 104.

| the marine environment | 1 certificates and other documents required to be carried on board ships by international conventions, how they may be obtained and the period of their legal validity
2 responsibilities under the relevant requirements of the International Convention on Load Lines, 1966, as amended
3 responsibilities under the relevant requirements of the International Convention for the Safety of Life at Sea, 1974, as amended | 2 approved training ship experience
3 approved simulator training, where appropriate | Procedures for monitoring operations and maintenance comply with legislative requirements
Potential non-compliance is promptly and fully identified
Requirements for renewal and extension of certificates ensure continued validity of survey items and equipment |
| Monitor and control compliance with legislative requirements and measures to ensure safety of life at sea and protection of the marine Environment (continued) | 4 responsibilities under the International Convention for the Prevention of Pollution from Ships, as amended
5 maritime declarations of health and the requirements of the International Health Regulations
6 responsibilities under international instruments affecting the safety of the ships, passengers, crew or cargo
7 methods and aids to prevent pollution of the environment by ships
8 knowledge of national legislation for implementing international agreements and conventions | | |

Table A-III/5 – 'Specification of minimum standard of competence for ratings as able seafarer engine in a manned engine-room or designated to perform duties in a periodically unmanned engine-room'

In respect of the function 'Marine engineering at the support level' the following entries are made:[15]

---

15 At p. 114.

Column 1	Column 2	Column 3	Column 4
Competence	Knowledge, understanding and proficiency	Methods for demonstrating competence	Criteria for evaluating competence
Contribute to bilge and ballast operations	*Knowledge of the safe function, operation and maintenance of the bilge and ballast systems, including: 1 reporting incidents associated with transfer operations 2 ability to correctly measure and report tank levels*	Assessment of evidence obtained from one or more of the following: 1 approved in-service experience 2 practical training 3 examination 4 approved training ship experience Assessment of evidence obtained from practical demonstration	*Operations and maintenance are carried out in accordance with established safety practices and equipment operating instructions and pollution of the marine environment is avoided* Communications within the operator's area of responsibility are consistently successful

In respect of the function 'Controlling the operation of the ship and care for persons on board at the support level' the following entries are made:[16]

Column 1	Column 2	Column 3	Column 4
Competence	Knowledge, understanding and proficiency	Methods for demonstrating competence	Criteria for evaluating competence
Contribute to the handling of stores	Knowledge of procedures for safe handling, stowage and securing of stores	Assessment of evidence obtained from one or more of the following: 1 approved in-service experience 2 practical training 3 examination 4 approved training ship experience	Stores operations are carried out in accordance with established safety practices and equipment operating instructions *The handling of dangerous, hazardous and harmful stores complies with established safety practices* Communications within the operator's area of responsibility are consistently successful
Apply precautions and contribute to the prevention of pollution of the marine environment	*Knowledge of the precautions to be taken to prevent pollution of the marine environment Knowledge of use and operation of anti-pollution equipment Knowledge of approved methods for disposal of marine pollutants*	Assessment of evidence obtained from one or more of the following: 1 approved in-service experience 2 practical training 3 examination 4 approved training ship experience	*Procedures designed to safeguard the marine environment are observed at all times*

---

16 At p. 116.

SEAFARER STANDARDS CONVENTION, 1978

Table A-III/6 – 'Specification of minimum standard of competence for electro-technical officers'

In respect of the function 'Controlling operation of the ship and care for persons on board at the operational level' the following entries are made:[17]

Column 1	Column 2	Column 3	Column 4
Competence	Knowledge, understanding and proficiency	Methods for demonstrating competence	Criteria for evaluating competence
Ensure compliance with pollution prevention requirements	*Prevention of pollution of the marine environment* *Knowledge of the precautions to be taken to prevent pollution of the marine environment* *Anti-pollution procedures and all associated equipment* *Importance of proactive measures to protect the marine environment*	Examination and assessment of evidence obtained from one or more of the following: 1 approved in-service experience 2 approved training ship experience 3 approved training	*Procedures for monitoring shipboard operations and ensuring compliance with pollution-prevention requirements are fully observed* *Actions to ensure that a positive environmental reputation is maintained*

Table A-III/7 – 'Specification of minimum standard of competence for electro-technical ratings'

In respect of the function 'Controlling the operation of the ship and care for persons on board at the support level' the following entries are made:[18]

Column 1	Column 2	Column 3	Column 4
Competence	Knowledge, understanding and proficiency	Methods for demonstrating competence	Criteria for evaluating competence
Contribute to the handling of stores	Knowledge of procedures for safe handling, stowage and securing of stores	Assessment of evidence obtained from one or more of the following: 1 approved in-service experience 2 practical training 3 examination 4 approved training ship experience	Stores stowage operations are carried out in accordance with established safety practices and equipment operating instructions *The handling of dangerous, hazardous and harmful stores complies with established safety practices* Communications within the operator's area of responsibility are consistently successful

---

17 At p. 126.
18 At p. 133.

71

| Apply precautions and contribute to the prevention of pollution of the marine environment | Knowledge of the precautions to be taken to prevent pollution of the marine environment Knowledge of use and operation of anti-pollution equipment/agents Knowledge of approved methods for disposal of marine pollutants | Assessment of evidence obtained from one or more of the following: 1 approved in-service experience 2 practical training 3 examination 4 approved training ship experience | Procedures designed to safeguard the marine environment are observed at all times |

Chapter V – Standards regarding special training requirements for personnel on certain types of ships

Section A-V/1-1 'Mandatory minimum requirements for the training and qualification of masters, officers and ratings on oil and chemical tankers'

Table A-V/1-1-1 – 'Specification of minimum standard of competence in basic training for oil and chemical tanker cargo operations'

The following entries are made:[19]

Column 1	Column 2	Column 3	Column 4
Competence	Knowledge, understanding and proficiency	Methods for demonstrating competence	Criteria for evaluating competence
Take precautions to prevent pollution of the environment from the release of oil or chemicals	Basic knowledge of the effects of oil and chemical pollution on human and marine life Basic knowledge of shipboard procedures to prevent pollution Basic knowledge of measures to be taken in the event of spillage, including the need to: 1 report relevant information to the responsible persons 2 assist in implementing shipboard spill-containment procedures	Examination and assessment of evidence obtained from one or more of the following: 1 approved in-service experience 2 approved training ship experience 3 approved simulator training 4 approved training programme	Procedures designed to safeguard the environment are observed at all times

---

19 At p. 144.

SEAFARER STANDARDS CONVENTION, 1978

Table A-V/1-1-2 – 'Specification of minimum standard of competence in advanced training for oil tanker cargo operations'

The following entries are made:[20]

Column 1	Column 2	Column 3	Column 4
Competence	Knowledge, understanding and proficiency	Methods for demonstrating competence	Criteria for evaluating competence
Familiarity with physical and chemical properties of oil cargoes	*Knowledge and understanding of the physical and chemical properties of oil cargoes* Understanding the information contained in a Material Safety Data Sheet (MSDS)	Examination and assessment of evidence obtained from one or more of the following: 1 approved in-service experience 2 approved training ship experience 3 approved simulator training 4 approved training programme	*Effective use is made of information resources for identification of properties and characteristics of oil cargoes and related gases, and their impact on safety, the environment and vessel operation*
Respond to emergencies	*Knowledge and understanding of oil tanker emergency procedures, including:* *1 ship emergency response plans* *2 cargo operations emergency shutdown* *3 actions to be taken in the event of failure of systems or services essential to cargo* *4 fire-fighting on oil Tankers* 5 enclosed space rescue 6 use of a Material Safety Data Sheet (MSDS) Actions to be taken following collision, grounding, or spillage Knowledge of medical first aid procedures on board oil tankers	Examination and assessment of evidence obtained from one or more of the following: 1 approved in-service experience 2 approved training ship experience 3 approved simulator training 4 approved training programme	*The type and impact of the emergency is promptly identified and the response actions conform with established emergency procedures and contingency plans* *The order of priority, and the levels and time-scales of making reports and informing personnel on board, are relevant to the nature of the emergency and reflect the urgency of the problem* Evacuation, emergency shutdown and isolation procedures are appropriate to the nature of the emergency and are implemented promptly The identification of and actions taken in a medical emergency conform to current recognized first aid practice and international guidelines

---

20 At p. 147.

73

Take precautions to prevent pollution of the environment	*Understanding of procedures to prevent pollution of the atmosphere and the environment*	Examination and assessment of evidence obtained from one or more of the following: 1 approved in-service experience 2 approved training ship experience 3 approved simulator training 4 approved training programme	*Operations are conducted in accordance with accepted principles and procedures to prevent pollution of the environment*
Monitor and control compliance with legislative requirements	*Knowledge and understanding of relevant provisions of the International Convention for the Prevention of Pollution from Ships (MARPOL), as amended, and other relevant IMO instruments, industry guidelines and port regulations as commonly applied*	Examination and assessment of evidence obtained from one or more of the following: 1 approved in-service experience 2 approved training ship experience 3 approved simulator training 4 approved training programme	*The handling of cargoes complies with relevant IMO instruments and established industrial standards and codes of safe working practice*

Table A-V/1-1-3 – 'Specification of minimum standard of competence in advanced training for chemical tanker cargo operations'

The following entries are made:[21]

Column 1	Column 2	Column 3	Column 4
Competence	Knowledge, understanding and proficiency	Methods for demonstrating competence	Criteria for evaluating competence
Ability to safely perform and monitor all cargo operations	*Design and characteristics of a chemical tanker* *Knowledge of chemical tanker designs, systems, and equipment, including:* *(. . . . . .)*	Examination and assessment of evidence obtained from one or more of the following: 1 approved in-service experience 2 approved training ship experience 3 approved simulator training 4 approved training programme	*Communications are clear, understood and successful* *Cargo operations are carried out in a safe manner, taking into account chemical tanker designs, systems and equipment* *Cargo operations are planned, risk is managed and carried out in accordance with accepted principles and procedures to ensure safety of operations and avoid pollution of the marine environment*

---

21 At p. 151.

and:[22]

Column 1	Column 2	Column 3	Column 4
Competence	Knowledge, understanding and proficiency	Methods for demonstrating competence	Criteria for evaluating competence
Familiarity with physical and chemical properties of chemical cargoes	*Knowledge and understanding of the chemical and the physical properties of noxious liquid substances, including:* *1 chemical cargoes categories (corrosive, toxic, flammable, explosive)* *2 chemical groups and industrial usage* *3 reactivity of cargoes* *Understanding the information contained in a Material Safety Data Sheet (MSDS)*	Examination and assessment of evidence obtained from one or more of the following: 1 approved in-service experience 2 approved training ship experience 3 approved simulator training 4 approved training programme	*Effective use is made of information resources for identification of properties and characteristics of noxious liquid substances and related gases, and their impact on safety, environmental protection and vessel operation*

and:[23]

Column 1	Column 2	Column 3	Column 4
Competence	Knowledge, understanding and proficiency	Methods for demonstrating competence	Criteria for evaluating competence
Take precautions to prevent pollution of the environment	*Understanding of procedures to prevent pollution of the atmosphere and the environment*	Examination and assessment of evidence obtained from one or more of the following: 1 approved in-service experience 2 approved training ship experience 3 approved simulator training 4 approved training programme	*Operations are conducted in accordance with accepted principles and procedures to prevent pollution of the environment*

---

22 At p. 154.
23 At p. 157.

INTERNATIONAL MARITIME CONVENTIONS

Table A-V/1-2-1 – 'Specification of minimum standard of competence in basic training for liquefied gas tanker cargo operations'
The following entries are made:[24]

Column 1	Column 2	Column 3	Column 4
Competence	Knowledge, understanding and proficiency	Methods for demonstrating competence	Criteria for evaluating competence
Take precautions to prevent pollution of the environment from the release of liquefied gases	*Basic knowledge of the effects of pollution on human and marine life* *Basic knowledge of shipboard procedures to prevent pollution* *Basic knowledge of measures to be taken in the event of spillage, including the need to:* *1 report relevant information to the responsible persons* *2 assist in implementing shipboard spill-containment procedures* *3 prevent brittle fracture*	Examination and assessment of evidence obtained from one or more of the following: 1 approved in-service experience 2 approved training ship experience 3 approved simulator training 4 approved training programme	*Procedures designed to safeguard the environment are observed at all times*

Table A-V/1-2-2 – 'Specification of minimum standard of competence in advanced training for liquefied gas tanker cargo operations'
The following entries are made:[25]

Column 1	Column 2	Column 3	Column 4
Competence	Knowledge, understanding and proficiency	Methods for demonstrating competence	Criteria for evaluating competence
Ability to safely perform and monitor all cargo operations	*Design and characteristics of a liquefied gas tanker* *Knowledge of liquefied gas tanker design, systems, and equipment, including:* *(. . . . . .)*	Examination and assessment of evidence obtained from one or more of the following: (. . . . . .)	*Communications are clear, understood and successful* *Cargo operations are carried out in a safe manner, taking into account liquefied gas tanker designs, systems and equipment* *Pumping operations are carried out in accordance with accepted principles and procedures and are relevant to the type of cargo*

---

24 At p. 163.
25 At p. 164.

SEAFARER STANDARDS CONVENTION, 1978

			Cargo operations are planned, risk is managed and carried out in accordance with accepted principles and procedures to ensure safety of operations and avoid pollution of the marine environment

and:[26]

Column 1	**Column 2**	**Column 3**	**Column 4**
Competence	Knowledge, understanding and proficiency	Methods for demonstrating competence	Criteria for evaluating competence
Take precautions to prevent pollution of the environment	*Understanding of procedures to prevent pollution of the environment*	Assessment of evidence obtained from one or more of the following: 1 approved in-service experience 2 approved training ship experience 3 approved simulator training 4 approved training programme	*Operations are conducted in accordance with accepted principles and procedures to prevent pollution of the environment*
Monitor and control compliance with legislative requirements	*Knowledge and understanding of relevant provisions of the International Convention for the Prevention of Pollution from Ships (MARPOL) and other relevant IMO instruments, industry guidelines and port regulations as commonly applied Proficiency in the use of the IBC and IGC Codes and related documents*	Assessment of evidence obtained from one or more of the following: 1 approved in-service experience 2 approved training ship experience 3 approved simulator training 4 approved training programme	*The handling of liquefied gas cargoes complies with relevant IMO instruments and established industrial standards and codes of safe working practices*

Chapter VI – Standards regarding emergency, occupational safety, security, medical care and survival functions

Section A-VI-1 'Mandatory minimum requirements for safety familiarization, basic training and instruction for all seafarers'

---

26 At p. 171.

Table A-VI/1-4 – 'Specification of minimum standard of competence in personal safety and social responsibilities'

The following entries are made:[27]

Column 1	Column 2	Column 3	Column 4
Competence	Knowledge, understanding and proficiency	Methods for demonstrating competence	Criteria for evaluating competence
Take precautions to prevent pollution of the marine environment	*Basic knowledge of the impact of shipping on the marine environment and the effects of operational or accidental pollution on it* *Basic environmental protection procedures* *Basic knowledge of complexity and diversity of the marine environment*	*Assessment of evidence obtained from approved instruction or during attendance at an approved course*	*Organizational procedures designed to safeguard the marine environment are observed at all times*

Chapter VIII – Standards regarding watchkeeping

Section A-VIII/2 – 'Watchkeeping arrangements and principles to be observed'

In Part 4 the following provision is made:[28]

Protection of marine environment

12 *The master, officers and ratings shall be aware of the serious effects of operational or accidental pollution of the marine environment and shall take all possible precautions to prevent such pollution, particularly within the framework of relevant international and port regulations.*

---

27 At p. 171.
28 At p. 186.

CHAPTER 8

Nairobi International Convention on Removal of Wrecks 18 May 2007

1 INTRODUCTION

Wrecks of sunken ships and parts thereof may not only be dangerous for navigation, but also to the marine environment. Oil and other hazardous and noxious substances may be released from a sunken ship even years after the casualty. Whilst their removal within the territorial waters of a State belongs to the jurisdiction of such State, if wrecks lie beyond territorial waters their removal is not and its law is not applicable. Nor has that State any specific obligations to care for the marking and removal of such wrecks or right of action against their owners. The Nairobi Convention was adopted with a view to filling this gap in international public maritime law. Although the majority of wrecks lie within territorial waters, there are in fact wrecks beyond them that may constitute a hazard to navigation as well as a threat to the marine environment; this would certainly be the case for sunken tankers and, generally, for the bunker oil of any ship. As of July 2014, the Convention has been ratified by 11 States and, the instrument of ratification of the tenth State having been deposited on 14 April 2014, the Convention has entered into force on 14 April 2015.

2 SCOPE OF APPLICATION

2.1 The subject matter of the Convention

The subject matter of the Convention is the removal of wrecks. Art. 2(1) so provides:

1 A State Party may take measures in accordance with this Convention in relation to the removal of a wreck which poses a hazard in the Convention area.

And art. 3(1) so provides:

1 Except as otherwise provided in this Convention, this Convention shall apply to wrecks in the Convention area.

The three basic conditions for the Convention to apply are therefore: (a) that there is a wreck; (b) that such wreck poses a hazard to navigation; and (c) that the hazard is located in the Convention area.

2.2 The notion of 'wreck'

Pursuant to art. 1(4), the definition of 'wreck' is linked to the nature of the event from which it has resulted. Art.1(4) in fact provides in its chapeau:

4 'Wreck', following upon a maritime casualty, means:

Therefore, a wreck may be so qualified only if it is the consequence of a maritime casualty, so defined in art. 1(3):

3 'Maritime casualty' means a collision of ships, stranding or other incident of navigation, or other occurrence on board a ship or external to it resulting in material damage or imminent threat of material damage to a ship or its cargo.

While incidents involving a ship are all covered, doubts may arise in respect of matters carried on board that are voluntarily thrown overboard, with the intention of getting rid of them. That action would probably be covered by the Convention on the Prevention of Marine Pollution by Dumping of Wastes and Other Matter, as amended by its Protocol of 1996.[1]

A description of the alternative nature of a wreck is provided in the four sub-paragraphs of paragraph 4 that may be convenient to consider *seriatim*:

(a) a sunken or stranded ship
Although a stranded ship is unlikely to cause a hazard to navigation, it may instead pose a hazard in respect of the marine environment if there is a danger that oil may be released from her bunker and, if a tanker, from her cargo tanks.

(b) any part of a sunken or stranded ship, including any object that is or has been on board such ship
In so far as ships are concerned, this requires that the ship before sinking or stranding has broken into two or more parts. In so far as objects are concerned, the liaison with the ship reference to which is made appears clearly from the words 'that is or has been on board'. If such object is still on board, it must obviously be on the part of that ship considered in this sub-paragraph. If it is not on board anymore, in order that it poses a hazard, its characteristics vary according to the type of hazard.

(c) any object that is lost at sea from a ship and that is stranded, sunken or adrift at sea
The conjunction 'and' (that is stranded, etc.) indicates that what is stranded, sunken or adrift at sea is the object, and not the ship. The nature of the object varies according to whether the hazard affects navigation or the environment. In the first case, its dimensions must be significant, in the second case, the quantity must be such as to entail major harmful consequences to the marine environment or damage to the coastline or related interests.

---

1 *Supra*, Chapter 3.

(d) a ship that is about, or may reasonably be expected, to sink or to strand, where effective measures to assist the ship or any property in danger are not already being taken

There could be a potential conflict in this case between this Convention and the Salvage Convention 1989 and the wording of this sub-paragraph must be compared with that of art. 1(a) of this latter Convention: what prevents the operation of the Nairobi Convention is the prior taking of effective measures to assist the ship or property in danger; what entails the coming into being of salvage operations is any act or activity undertaken to assist a vessel or other property in danger. By accepting a request of assistance, the salvor undertakes to assist the vessel or property, but can it be stated that 'effective measures' to assist such ship or property have already been taken? It is suggested that the answer should be affirmative, even if 'to undertake to assist' means only to agree to perform.

Although, therefore, the nature of the wreck may vary considerably, the general assumption in most of the provisions of this Convention is that the wreck is a sunken or stranded ship or a part thereof, since reference is frequently made to the master or operator of the ship (art. 5 para. 1), to the ship's registry and to the registered owner (art. 9 paras. 1, 6, 7, 8 and 9; art.10; art. 11). Of course, the reference to the ship's registry is inappropriate when the ship has been deregistered because of its having become a wreck[2] and the reference to registered owner is equally inappropriate. However, it must be understood that those expressions have been intended to cover all such situations.

2.3 The notion of 'hazard'

2.3.1 A general analysis of the relevant rules in this and in other Conventions

Although certain provisions of the Convention apply to wrecks generally, whether or not they pose a hazard, the core of the Convention is the protection against wrecks that pose a hazard. That is stated in art. 2, in which the objectives and general principles are set out. Paragraphs 1, 2 and 3 so provide:

1   A State Party may take measures in accordance with this Convention in relation to the removal of a wreck which poses a hazard in the Convention area.
2   Measures taken by the Affected State in accordance with paragraph 1 shall be proportionate to the hazard.
3   Such measures shall not go beyond what is reasonably necessary to remove a wreck which poses a hazard and shall cease as soon as the wreck has been removed; they shall

---

2 Article 163 of the Italian Navigation Code provides that a ship is deregistered when it has been lost or has been demolished. Article 97 of the French Arrêté 14 March 1969 provides that in case of loss or sale abroad of a French ship the owner is bound to return the *acte de francisation* (pursuant to which the ship is granted the French nationality) and to request the annulment of the *fiche matricule* (certificate of registration). Section 9(3) of the English Merchant Shipping Act 1995 provides: 'The registrar may, nevertheless, if registration regulations so provide, refuse to register or terminate registration of a ship if, having regard to any relevant requirements of this Act, he considers it would be inappropriate for the ship to be or, as the case may be, to remain registered' and in footnote 3 (at p. 9 of *Merchant Shipping Act 1995: An Annotated Guide* by Nevil Phillips, LLP 1996) it is stated: 'Registration may clearly be terminated when the vessel is no longer owned by persons qualified to own a British-registered vessel, reflecting section 61(2) of the 1988 Act.'

not unnecessarily interfere with the rights and interests of other States including the State of the ship's registry, and of any person, physical or corporate, concerned.

The following definition of hazard is given in art. 1(5):

5 'Hazard' means any condition or threat that:
  (a) poses a danger or impediment to navigation; or
  (b) may reasonably be expected to result in major harmful consequences to the marine environment, or damage to the coastline or related interests of one or more States.

The danger in the navigation is a physical danger due to the risk of ships sailing above the wreck or colliding with it. The impediment consists of the obligation of a ship sailing in the area in which there is a sunken wreck, to deviate from its course in order to avoid the risk of collision.

Major harmful consequences to the marine environment and damage to the coastline or related interests appear to be considered in this provision as alternative consequences of a hazard. In art. I(1) of the Intervention Convention 1969 they appear instead to be strictly related, the grave and imminent danger to the coastline and related interests from pollution or threat of pollution being expected to result in major harmful consequences.[3] This is also the case for the Salvage Convention 1989, in art. 1(d) of which damage to the environment is defined as:

(e) Damage to the environment means substantial physical damage to human health or to marine life or resources in coastal or inland waters or areas adjacent thereto, caused by pollution, contamination, fire, explosion or similar major incidents.

A distinction appears instead to have been made in art. 1(1)(d) of the Arrest Convention 1999:

(d) damage or threat of damage caused by a ship to the environment, coastline or related interests; measures taken to prevent, minimize, or remove such damage, compensation for such damage; costs of reasonable measures of reinstatement of the environment actually undertaken or to be undertaken; loss incurred or likely to be incurred by third parties in connection with such damage; and damage, costs, or loss of a similar nature to those identified in this subparagraph (d).

Finally a clearer distinction is made in the OPRC Convention 1990, art. 2(3) of which defines oil pollution incident as:

1 'Oil pollution incident' means an occurrence or series of occurrences having the same origin, which results or may result in a discharge of oil and which poses or may pose a threat to the marine environment, or to the coastline or related interest of one or more States, and which requires emergency action or other immediate response.

Since the coastline covers an area definitely different from and more inland than that covered by the 'marine environment', the distinction appears appropriate and this is confirmed by the reference to the 'related interests', that are thus defined in art. 1(6):

6 'Related interests' means the interests of a coastal State directly affected or threatened by a wreck, such as:
  (a) maritime, coastal, port and estuaries activities, including fisheries activities, constituting an essential means of livelihood of the persons concerned;

---

3 *Supra*, Chapter 1, para. 3.3.

(b) tourist attractions and other economic interests of the area concerned;
(c) the health of the coastal population and the well-being of the area concerned, including conservation of marine living resources and of wildlife; and
(d) offshore and underwater infrastructure.

It appears, therefore, that the coastline is an area near the coast, the depth of which depends on the connection between the life in that area and the sea: this is precisely what is meant in France when reference is made to the Côte d'Azur.

2.4 The notion of 'Convention area'

'Convention area' is defined in art. 1(1) as:

'Convention area' means the exclusive economic zone of a State Party, established in accordance with international law or, if a State Party has not established such a zone, an area beyond and adjacent to the territorial sea of that State determined by that State in accordance with international law and extending not more than 200 nautical miles from the baseline from which the breadth of its territorial sea is measured.

The area referred to in this provision is the same as that defined in art. II(a)(ii) of the CLC 1992, in art. 3(a)(ii) of the Fund Convention 1992, in art. 3(b) of the HNS Convention and in art. 2(a)(ii) of the Bunker Oil Convention.[4]

Where a State Party has extended, pursuant to art. 3(2), the application of the Convention to wrecks located within its territory, including its territorial sea,[5] pursuant to art. 3(3), the notion of 'Convention area' includes the territory, including the territorial sea, of that State.

2.4.1 The party who may determine whether a wreck poses a hazard

From several provisions of the Convention it appears that that party is the Affected State and that its determination cannot be challenged.

Art. 6, an analysis of which will be made below, so provides in its chapeau:

When determining whether a wreck poses a hazard, the following criteria should be taken into account by the Affected State:

Art. 8(1) so provides:

If the Affected State determines that a wreck constitutes a hazard, that State shall ensure that all reasonable steps are taken to mark the wreck.

Art. 9(1) so provides:

If the Affected State determines that a wreck constitutes a hazard, that State shall immediately:
(a) inform the State of the ship's registry and the registered owner; and
(b) proceed to consult the State of the ship's registry and other States affected by the wreck regarding measures to be taken in relation to the wreck.

---

4 Reference is therefore made to Chapter 13, para. 2.3.

5 Since not all the provisions of the Convention apply, in case of such voluntary extension of the scope of application of the Convention the analysis of its effect will be considered after the review of all the provisions of the Convention: *infra*, para. 2(5).

2.4.2 The criteria to be taken into account

Such criteria are enumerated in art. 6 and from the last paragraph worded:

(o)   any other circumstances that might necessitate the removal of the wreck

it appears that the list is open-ended.

The various criteria enumerated clearly apply in different circumstances. They will be briefly considered hereafter.

(a) the type, size and construction of the wreck
This criterion appears to be of general application, irrespective of the wreck being a ship, a part of a ship or an object lost from a ship, such as a container.

(b) depth of the water in the area
The 'area', reference to which is made in several criteria, is not the 'Convention area' as defined in art.1(1), but the area in which the wreck is located. The depth of the water is always important, because the greater it is, the less danger there is of a ship hitting the wreck.

(c) tidal range and currents in the area
The tidal range is similarly important, as the currents may cause a shifting of the wreck away from its original position.

(d) particularly sensitive sea areas identified and, as appropriate, designated in accordance with guidelines adopted by the Organization, or a clearly defined area of the exclusive economic zone where special mandatory measures have been adopted pursuant to article 211, paragraph 6, of the United Nations Convention on the Law of the Sea, 1982.
It is not clear why the plural is used, because the wreck is not located in various areas, but the sense of this criterion is the fact that the wreck is located in one of the particularly sensitive areas identified by the IMO or in a 'clearly defined area' where special mandatory measures have been adopted pursuant to art. 211(6) of UNCLOS. This article sets out in (a) the procedure the coastal State must follow in order to obtain from the competent organisation (in our case the IMO) confirmation that the special mandatory rules suggested are required.[6]

---

6 Art. 211(6)(a) so provides:

6(a) Where the international rules and standards referred to in paragraph 1 are inadequate to meet special circumstances and coastal States have reasonable grounds for believing that a particular, clearly defined area of their respective exclusive economic zones is an area where the adoption of special mandatory measures for the prevention of pollution from vessels is required for recognized technical reasons in relation to its oceanographical and ecological conditions, as well as its utilization or the protection of its resources and the particular character of its traffic, the coastal States, after appropriate consultations through the competent international organization with any other States concerned, may, for that area, direct a communication to that organization, submitting scientific and technical evidence in support and information on necessary reception facilities. Within 12 months after receiving such a communication, the organization shall determine whether the conditions in that area correspond to the requirements set out above. If the organization so determines, the coastal States may, for that area, adopt laws and regulations for the prevention, reduction and control of pollution from vessels implementing such international rules and standards or navigational practices as are made applicable, through the organization, for special

(e) proximity of shipping routes or established traffic lanes
The proximity of the wreck to shipping routes or lanes increases the probability of an accident.

(f) traffic density and frequency
This is also the case where the density of the traffic is considerable.

(g) type of traffic
The basic distinction of type of traffic is between liner trade and bulk trade, a distinction that has been adopted recently in the Rotterdam Rules in which reference is made to 'liner transportation'[7] and 'non-liner transportation'.

(h) nature and quantity of the wreck's cargo, the amount and types of oil (such as bunker oil and lubricating oil) on board the wreck and, in particular, the damage likely to result should the cargo or oil be released into the marine environment
This criterion is relevant for the risk of damage to the environment.

(i) vulnerability of port facilities
This criterion is relevant for the assessment of the risk of damage to the environment and, specifically, to port facilities the oil might reach.

(j) prevailing meteorological and hydrographical conditions
The meteorological and hydrographical conditions may affect the possible shifting of the wreck as well as the direction the oil may take and the speed with which it may reach the coastline.

(k) submarine topography of the area
The topography of the area may be relevant for the assessment of a risk of the wreck shifting away from its original position.

(l) height of the wreck above or below the surface of the water at lowest astronomical tide
The qualification of the tide as 'astronomical' is due to the gravitational force between the earth and the moon and, to a lesser extent, the sun, which creates a rise and fall of sea levels. There are also geological variations in sea level, but their effects are very insignificant compared to those caused by the moon and the sun.[8] The height of the wreck below the surface of the sea is the vertical distance between the highest part of the wreck and the surface of the sea: the greater the distance, the lesser the danger of a collision between the ships passing by and the wreck. If the

---

areas. These laws and regulations shall not become applicable to foreign vessels until 15 months after the submission of the communication to the organization.

7 See Volume I, p. 116. Liner transportation has been defined as follows in art. 1.3:

'Liner transportation' means a transportation service that is offered to the public through publication or similar means and includes transportation by ships operating on a regular schedule between specified ports in accordance with publicly available timetables of sailing dates.

8 It appears that in a century, between 1850 and 1950, the geological change in sea level has been 10 cm (*Encyclopaedia Britannica*, under word 'Tides', sec. VII.)

wreck emerges from the sea level, then the larger the part that emerges, the smaller the danger of not being noticed by passing ships.

(m) acoustic and magnetic profiles of the wreck
Information in this respect might facilitate detecting the wreck with sonar and similar devices.

(n) proximity of offshore installations, pipelines, telecommunications cables and similar structures
Probably such proximity would increase the danger of the wreck causing damage to such structures if the wreck were to shift due to currents, tides or a storm.

(o) any other circumstances that might necessitate the removal of the wreck
As previously stated, this last criterion makes the list open to any specific situation that might affect the prospects of an occurrence.

2.5 The voluntary extension of the geographical scope and the provisions excluded from the extension

Art. 3(2) so provides:

A State Party may extend the application of this Convention to wrecks located within its territory, including the territorial sea, subject to article 4, paragraph 4. In that case, it shall notify the Secretary General accordingly, at the time of expressing its consent to be bound by this Convention or at any time thereafter. When a State Party has made a notification to apply this Convention to wrecks located within its territory, including the territorial sea, this is without prejudice to the rights and obligations of that State to take measures in relation to wrecks located in its territory, including the territorial sea, other than locating, marking and removing in accordance with this Convention. The provisions of articles 10, 11 and 12 of this Convention shall not apply to any measures so taken other than those referred to in articles 7, 8 and 9 of this Convention.

Art. 4(4), reference to which is made in art. 3(2), indicates in sub-paragraph (a) the provisions that do not apply in the territory, including the territorial sea, of a State that has given notice of its decision to extend the application of the Convention to wrecks located in in its territory, including the territorial sea. They will be considered *seriatim*:

(i) Article 2, paragraph 4
This provides:

4. The application of this Convention within the Convention area shall not entitle a State Party to claim or exercise sovereignty or sovereign rights over any part of the high sea.

The exclusion is obvious, since a State does exercise sovereign rights over its territorial sea.

(ii) Article 9, paragraphs 1, 5, 7, 8, 9 and 10
Art. 9(1) requires the Affected State, which has determined that a wreck constitutes a hazard, to inform the State of the ship's registry and the registered owner and

to proceed to consultations: such obligation has been deemed unjustified where the wreck is located in the territorial sea of the Affected State. Art. 9(5) deals with the right of intervention of the Affected State in the removal of a wreck: since the Affected State is defined as the State in whose Convention area the wreck is located, this provision does not apply to the removal of a wreck situated within the territorial sea.

Art. 9(7) grants the Affected State the right to remove the wreck only if the registered owner does not do so within the deadline set by the Affected State: a condition that it has not been deemed appropriate if the wreck lies in the territorial waters of the Affected State.

Art. 9(8) regulates situations in which immediate action is required, with the consequent right of the Affected State to remove the wreck.

Art. 9(9) provides that States Parties must take appropriate measures under their national law to ensure compliance by the registered owners with their obligations under paragraphs 2 and 3; no such obligation is conceivable in respect of wrecks in the territorial waters, that are subject to the legislation of the State to which such waters belong.

Art. 9(10) provides that States Parties must give their consent to the Affected State to act: no consent is obviously required in respect of actions of a State Party within its territorial waters.

(iii) Article 15

This article regulates the settlement of disputes arising between two or more States Parties regarding the interpretation or application of the Convention. In case of voluntary extension of the application of the Convention to disputes relating to wrecks located within the territorial waters of a State Party, it has been deemed convenient to exclude the application of this article, in consideration of the general principle that events within the territorial waters are subject to the jurisdiction of the State to which such waters belong.

Art. 4(4) quotes in sub-paragraph (b) the amended text of art. 9(4), which sets out rules relating to the salvage contract stipulated by the registered owner of the wreck, in so far as it applies to the territory, including the territorial sea of a State Party. The amendment consists only of making the provision subject to the national law of the Affected State:

(b)　Article 9, paragraph 4, insofar as it applies to the territory, including the territorial sea of a State Party, shall read:
Subject to the national law of the Affected State, the registered owner may contract with any salvor or other person to remove the wreck determined to constitute a hazard on behalf of the owner. Before such removal commences, the Affected State may lay down conditions for such removal only to the extent necessary to ensure that the removal proceeds in a manner that is consistent with considerations of safety and protection of the marine environment.

The provisions in the second sentence of art. 3(2) are meant to make clear that in respect of wrecks situated within the territorial sea, a State Party may cover in its national law matters other than those covered by arts. 7, 8 and 9.

3 GENERAL OBLIGATIONS OF STATES TO BE COMPLIED WITH WHEN THEY BECOME PARTIES TO THE CONVENTION

Pursuant to art. 10(9), States Parties are required to take appropriate measures under their national law to ensure that registered owners comply with paragraphs 2 and 3 of that article which provide:

2 The registered owner shall remove a wreck determined to constitute a hazard.
3 When a wreck has been determined to constitute a hazard, the registered owner, or other interested party, shall provide the competent authority of the Affected State with evidence of insurance or other financial security as required by article 12.

In order to comply with such provisions States must, when they become parties to the Convention, enact rules pursuant to which owners of ships to which the Convention applies are bound to remove the wrecks of their ships that have become a hazard and are required to maintain insurance or other financial security to cover liability under the Convention as provided by art. 12. The insurance or other financial security is compulsory in respect of all ships of 300 gross tonnage and above flying the flag of a State Party.

Art. 12(1) so provides:

The registered owner of a ship of 300 gross tonnage and above and flying the flag of a State Party shall be required to maintain insurance or other financial security, such as a guarantee of a bank or similar institution, to cover liability under this Convention in an amount equal to the limits of liability under the applicable national or international limitation regime, but in all cases not exceeding an amount calculated in accordance with article 6(1)(b) of the Convention on Limitation of Liability for Maritime Claims, 1976, as amended.

Pursuant to art. 10, the registered owner is liable for the costs of locating, marking and removing the wreck but since no limits are set in the Convention to such liability, the amount of the insurance or other financial security is, similarly to the Bunker Oil Convention, based on the general limits of liability under the applicable national or international limitation regime. However, in order to ensure some degree of uniformity, it is provided that such limit shall not exceed that provided by the LLMC Convention, as amended by its Protocol of 1996, in respect of claims other than claims for loss of life or personal injury.[9] Art.12(1) does not state which is the applicable national or international regime, but it appears that in respect of a ship registered in a State Party, it should be that in force in the State Party in which the ship is – or was – registered and that should also be the case if the action is brought against the insurer or provider of other financial security.

---

9 For a comment of the limits under the LLMC Convention 1976 as amended see vol. II, chapter 11, para. 8.1.2.

4 OBLIGATIONS OF STATES PARTIES IN CASE OF A CASUALTY RESULTING IN A WRECK

4.1 Obligation of the State in respect of a ship flying its flag to report involvement in a wreck

Art. 5(1) so provides:

1 A State Party shall require the master and the operator of a ship flying its flag to report to the Affected State without delay when that ship has been involved in a maritime casualty resulting in a wreck. To the extent that the reporting obligation under this article has been fulfilled either by the master or the operator of the ship, the other shall not be obliged to report.

The question that arises is whether this provision applies when a ship flying the flag of a State party has been involved in a maritime casualty resulting in a wreck, or it applies generally in respect of all ships flying the flag of a State Party. The first alternative is supported by the obligation to require the master and the operator of a ship flying its flag to report 'when that ship has been involved in a maritime casualty'. It appears, therefore, that the State, upon being informed that a ship flying its flag has already been involved in a maritime casualty and that casualty has resulted in a wreck, must instruct the master or the operator to report to the 'affected State', so defined in art. 1.10:

'Affected State' means the State in whose Convention area the wreck is located.

The purpose of the report and the information it must provide are stated as follows in paragraph 2:

2 Such reports shall provide the name and the principal place of business of the registered owner and all the relevant information necessary for the Affected State to determine whether the wreck poses a hazard in accordance with article 6, including:
   (a) the precise location of the wreck;
   (b) the type, size and construction of the wreck;
   (c) the nature of the damage to, and the condition of, the wreck;
   (d) the nature and quantity of the cargo, in particular any hazardous and noxious substances; and
   (e) the amount and types of oil, including bunker oil and lubricating oil, on board.

Notwithstanding the wide definition of 'wreck', the information listed in this provision applies almost exclusively to ships; in many jurisdictions only ships are registered in a public register, and only ships carry a cargo and have on board bunker and lubricating oil. The information enumerated under (b), (d) and (e) is available ashore and may be provided by the office of the owner. The information under (a) may be provided from ashore if the master had informed the owner of the incident, provided that the communications system on board was still operating; but this may not always be the case. The information under (c) may be more difficult to provide if the ship had sunk and would probably require an underwater inspection of the ship, which would very likely be impossible in bad weather conditions. Therefore, the information mentioned in this provision would, in serious incidents, be provided in successive stages, when circumstances permit.

5 OBLIGATIONS OF THE STATE IN WHOSE CONVENTION AREA THE WRECK IS LOCATED

According to circumstances, the obligations of the Affected State are to locate the wreck, warn mariners and States, mark the wreck and, where necessary, take appropriate action for its removal.

5.1 Locating wrecks

Art. 7 so provides:

1 Upon becoming aware of a wreck, the Affected State shall use all practicable means, including the good offices of States and organizations, to warn mariners and the States concerned of the nature and location of the wreck as a matter of urgency.
2 If the Affected State has reason to believe that a wreck poses a hazard, it shall ensure that all practicable steps are taken to establish the precise location of the wreck.

Although the Affected State has no liability in connection with the wreck, nevertheless it has two obligations[10] that arise out of the fact that the wreck is within its economic zone or the area adjacent to its territorial sea: to warn mariners[11] and 'States concerned'. Their identification may be based on art. 9(1) pursuant to which if the Affected State determines that the wreck constitutes a hazard it must consult the State of the ship's registry and other States 'affected by the wreck': such States are obviously those whose economic zones are adjacent to that of the Affected State. Since the information must include both the location and the nature of the wreck, a preliminary submarine inspection of the wreck would probably be required. In consideration of this it is not clear what is the difference between the manner in which the location must be established in order to comply with paragraph 1 and that in which such location must be established in order to comply with paragraph 2 relating to the situation where the wreck poses a hazard,[12] since in paragraph 1 reference is made merely to the 'location' whilst in paragraph 2, reference is made to the 'precise location'. The location can only be established through its coordinates, and that is always a 'precise location'. Therefore it is not clear what more should be done in order to comply with the requirements of paragraph 2.

5.2 Marking wrecks

Art. 8 so provides:

1 If the Affected State determines that a wreck constitutes a hazard, that State shall ensure that all reasonable steps are taken to mark the wreck.

---

10 However the costs incurred in order to fulfil them must, pursuant to art. 10(1), be settled by the owner of the wreck, save in the cases mentioned thereunder. *Infra*, para. 6(2).

11 Such warning should be made through a Notice to Mariners. In B. Dutton, *Navigation and Nautical Astronomy*, the following description is given of such notice: '*Notice to Mariners*, issued weekly, gives changes in aids to navigation (lights, buoyage, harbour constructions), dangers to navigation (rocks, shoals, banks, bars), important new soundings, and, in general, all such information as affects the mariner's charts, manuals, and Sailing Directions (Pilots).'

12 For the notion of 'hazard' see *supra*, para. 2.3.

2 In marking the wreck, all practicable steps shall be taken to ensure that the markings conform to the internationally accepted system of buoyage in use in the area where the wreck is located.
3 The Affected State shall promulgate the particulars of the marking of the wreck by use of all appropriate means, including the appropriate nautical publications.

The obligation of the Affected State to mark the wreck arises only if, in the judgment of that State, the wreck constitutes a hazard. In this connection out of the two notions of 'hazard' given in art. 1(5) the relevant one is the first: 'a condition or threat that poses a danger or impediment to navigation'.

5.3 Removal of wrecks

The removal of the wreck is required if it constitutes a hazard.
Art. 9 so provides:

1 If the Affected State determines that a wreck constitutes a hazard, that State shall immediately:
   (a) inform the State of the ship's registry and the registered owner; and
   (b) proceed to consult the State of the ship's registry and other States affected by the wreck regarding measures to be taken in relation to the wreck.

The sequence of the actions appears to be the following: first, pursuant to art. 5(1), the master or the operator of the ship involved in a maritime casualty resulting in a wreck must report to the Affected State and provide the information specified in art. 5(2); secondly, the Affected State must, pursuant to art. 7, warn mariners and if it determines that the wreck constitutes a hazard, pursuant to art. 8, must ensure that all reasonable steps are taken to mark the wreck; thirdly, pursuant to art. 9(1), must inform the State of the ship's registry and the registered owner, whereupon, pursuant to art. 9(3), the registered owner (or other interested party) must provide the competent authority of the Affected State with evidence of insurance or other financial security and, pursuant to art. 9(2), must remove the wreck.

Paragraphs 5, 6, 7 and 8 set out rights and obligations of the Affected State in connection with the removal of the wreck by or for the account of the registered owner. They so provide:

5 When the removal referred to in paragraphs 2 and 4 has commenced, the Affected State may intervene in the removal only to the extent necessary to ensure that the removal proceeds effectively in a manner that is consistent with considerations of safety and protection of the marine environment.
6 The Affected State shall:
   (a) set a reasonable deadline within which the registered owner must remove the wreck taking into account the nature of the hazard determined in accordance with article 6;
   (b) inform the registered owner in writing of the deadline it has set and specify that, if the registered owner does not remove the wreck within that deadline, it may remove the wreck at the registered owner's expense; and
   (c) inform the registered owner in writing that it intends to intervene immediately in circumstances where the hazard becomes particularly severe.
7 If the registered owner does not remove the wreck within the deadline set in accordance with paragraph 6(a), or the registered owner cannot be contacted, the Affected State may remove the wreck by the most practical and expeditious means available, consistent with considerations of safety and protection of the marine environment.

8 In circumstances where immediate action is required and the Affected State has informed the State of the ship's registry and the registered owner accordingly, it may remove the wreck by the most practical and expeditious means available, consistent with considerations of safety and protection of the marine environment.

The use in some of the above provisions of the word 'shall' and in others of the word 'may' appears to indicate that in the first case the Affected State must comply with the action mentioned, while in the second case, the Affected State has the right, but not the obligation, to perform the action described.[13]

The Affected State is bound to perform the actions described in paragraph 6(a), (b) and (c). Those under (a) and (b) are merely notices that must be given by the Affected State to the registered owner, whereas that under (c), albeit it appears to be merely a notice, entails the taking over by the Affected State of the removal operations. Nor is the consequential obligation of the Affected State excluded or lessened by paragraph 8, in which it is provided that the Affected State 'may remove the wreck by the most practical and expeditious means available', for the liberty given to the Affected State is only to choose the means of removal, but not whether or not to carry it out. And the previous reference to the circumstance where 'immediate action is required' confirms this conclusion.

6 OBLIGATIONS AND LIABILITIES OF THE OWNER OF THE WRECK

6.1 Obligations

Art. 9 so provides in paragraphs 2–4:

2 The registered owner shall remove a wreck determined to constitute a hazard.
3 When a wreck has been determined to constitute a hazard, the registered owner, or other interested party, shall provide the competent authority of the Affected State with evidence of insurance or other financial security as required by article 12.
4 The registered owner may contract with any salvor or other person to remove the wreck determined to constitute a hazard on behalf of the owner. Before such removal commences, the Affected State may lay down conditions for such removal only to the extent necessary to ensure that the removal proceeds in a manner that is consistent with considerations of safety and protection of the marine environment.

Timewise, the obligation in paragraph 3 to provide evidence of insurance or financial security is the first to be fulfilled. Paragraph 2 provides generally that the registered owner must remove the wreck and paragraph 4 provides that the removal may be entrusted to a salvor. The subsequent alternative reference to 'other person' is due to the fact that probably, in many cases, the wreck has a small value, in which event no salvor would be interested in carrying out the removal on a 'no cure no pay' basis and, if so, the services rendered could not be qualified as salvage services and the Convention of 1989 would not apply.

---

13 The imperative mood is realised in the French text of the Convention with the use of the present tense (*'fixe un délais raisonnable'* in sub-para. (a) and *'informe par écrit'* in paras. (b) and (c) and in Spanish with the use of the future tense (*'fijarà'* and *'informarà'*).

Reference to salvage is also made in art. 11(2) which states:

2 To the extent that measures under this Convention are considered to be salvage under applicable national law or an international convention, such law or convention shall apply to questions of the remuneration or compensation payable to salvors to the exclusion of the rules of this Convention.

If the removal of the wreck may be qualified as salvage, the LLMC Convention, reference to which is made in art. 10, would not apply pursuant to its art. 3(a).

6.2 Liabilities

Art. 10(1) so provides:

1 Subject to article 11, the registered owner shall be liable for the costs of locating, marking and removing the wreck under articles 7, 8 and 9, respectively, unless the registered owner proves that the maritime casualty that caused the wreck:
(a) resulted from an act of war, hostilities, civil war, insurrection, or a natural phenomenon of an exceptional, inevitable and irresistible character;
(b) was wholly caused by an act or omission done with intent to cause damage by a third party; or
(c) was wholly caused by the negligence or other wrongful act of any Government or other authority responsible for the maintenance of lights or other navigational aids in the exercise of that function.

Except for the different drafting, since the term 'exceptions to liability' is used only in respect of conflict with other conventions, this provision adopts the same allocation of the burden of proof and the same exonerations from liability already adopted in art. III(2) of the CLC 1992, and therefore reference is made to the comments under that article.[14]

The benefit of limitation of liability is granted to the registered owner in the same terms in which it is granted to the shipowner in art. 6 of the Bunker Oil Convention 2001,[15] except that thereunder the benefit is expressly granted also to the person providing insurance or other financial security. However such benefit, albeit in different terms, is subsequently granted under art. 12 in which the rules on compulsory insurance are set out.[16] Art.10(2) so provides:

2 Nothing in this Convention shall affect the right of the registered owner to limit liability under any applicable national or international regime, such as the Convention on Limitation of Liability for Maritime Claims, 1976, as amended.
3 No claim for the costs referred to in paragraph 1 may be made against the registered owner otherwise than in accordance with the provisions of this Convention. This is without prejudice to the rights and obligations of a State Party that has made a notification under article 3, paragraph 2, in relation to wrecks located in its territory, including the territorial sea, other than locating, marking and removing in accordance with this Convention.

The general provisions of the Convention are those in arts. 9 and 10. The special provisions are those in art. 3(2), wherein it is provided that the notification by

---

14 *Infra*, Chapter 11, para. 4.
15 *Infra*, Chapter 13, para. 5.
16 *Infra*, para. 7.

a State Party of the extension of the Convention also to wrecks located within its territory, including the territorial sea is without prejudice to the right and obligations of that State to take measures other than locating, marking and removing them.

6.3 Exceptions to liabilities

Art. 11 so provides:

1   The registered owner shall not be liable under this Convention for the costs mentioned in article 10, paragraph 1 if, and to the extent that, liability for such costs would be in conflict with:
   (a)   the International Convention on Civil Liability for Oil Pollution Damage, 1969, as amended;
   (b)   the International Convention on Liability and Compensation for Damage in Connection with the Carriage of Hazardous and Noxious Substances by Sea, 1996, as amended;
   (c)   the Convention on Third Party Liability in the Field of Nuclear Energy, 1960, as amended, or the Vienna Convention on Civil Liability for Nuclear Damage, 1963, as amended; or national law governing or prohibiting limitation of liability for nuclear damage; or
   (d)   the International Convention on Civil Liability for Bunker Oil Pollution Damage, 2001, as amended; provided that the relevant convention is applicable and in force.
2   To the extent that measures under this Convention are considered to be salvage under applicable national law or an international convention, such law or convention shall apply to questions of the remuneration or compensation payable to salvors to the exclusion of the rules of this Convention.

An attempt will be made to identify the situations in which there could be such a conflict with any one of the conventions mentioned in paragraph 1 of this article.

(a) CLC 1992
As previously stated, the exonerations from liability adopted in art. III(2) of the CLC 1992 are the same as those adopted in art. 10(1) of the Nairobi Convention.

(b) HNS 1996 as amended
The position is the same as for the CLC 1992, the exonerations under art. 7(2) being the same as those under art. 10(2) of the Nairobi Convention.

(c) Convention on Civil Liability for Nuclear Damage of 21 May 1963, as amended by the Protocol of 12 September 1997
Although the theoretical possibility of an application of this Convention in a case to which also the Nairobi Convention applies is minimal, it appears that the exonerations of the operator under its art. IV are more restricted than those under the Nairobi Convention, considering also that the basic rule under art. IV(1) is that the liability of the operator is absolute.

(d) Bunker Oil Convention 2001

The exonerations from liability of the shipowner under art. 3(3) coincide with those under art. 10(1) of the Nairobi Convention.

7 COMPULSORY INSURANCE OR OTHER FINANCIAL SECURITY

Compulsory insurance has now become a standard provision in all uniform maritime law conventions that regulate aspects of the liability of shipowners in areas such as carriage of passengers, loss or damage in case of pollution by oil and removal of wrecks. Since an analysis has been made of the very similar provision in art. 4bis of the Athens Convention and in respect of the provisions of art. 12 of the Nairobi Convention as well as of those in art. VII of the CLC 1992 and of art. 12 of the HNS Convention attention will be drawn only to the particular provisions of each of such Conventions.

In so far as the Nairobi Convention is concerned, they are the following.

7.1 Minimum tonnage of ships for which compulsory insurance is obligatory

All ships of 300 gross tons and above are required to maintain insurance. It is difficult to understand why so low a tonnage has been adopted while in the CLC the minimum tonnage is not only a carrying capacity of more than 2,000 tons, but also the actual carriage of more than 2,000 tons, both because one of the purposes of the Nairobi Convention is to prevent harmful consequences to the marine environment and because the level of the danger or impediment to navigation of the wreck of a ship of 300 tons deadweight appears to be rather modest.

7.2 Nationality of ships by which insurance must be provided

Paragraph 1 of art. 12 requires that insurance must be maintained in respect of ships flying the flag of a State Party. However paragraph 2 provides in its relevant part:

A certificate attesting that insurance or other financial security is in force in accordance with the provisions of this Convention shall be issued to each ship of 300 gross tonnage and above by the appropriate authority of the State of the ship's registry after determining that the requirements of paragraph 1 have been complied with. With respect to a ship registered in a State Party such certificate shall be issued or certified by the appropriate authority of the State of the ship's registry; with respect to a ship not registered in a State Party it may be issued or certified by the appropriate authority of any State Party.

Paragraph 12 provides:

Subject to the provisions of this article, each State Party shall ensure, under its national law, that insurance or other security to the extent required by paragraph 1 is in force in respect of any ship of 300 gross tonnage and above, wherever registered, entering or leaving a port in its territory, or arriving at or leaving an offshore facility in its territorial sea.

The difference between ships registered in a State Party and ships registered elsewhere is that for the former insurance or other security as provided by paragraph 1 is compulsory and for the latter it is a condition for their entering or leaving ports or offshore facilities in the territorial sea of States Parties and that means it is a condition for their trading with State Parties.

7.3. Conditions of issue and validity of the certificate

Paragraph 7 states:

The State of the ship's registry shall, subject to the provisions of this article *and having regard to any guidelines adopted by the Organization on the financial responsibility of the registered owners,* determine the conditions of issue and validity of the certificate.

The part of this paragraph in italics is a novelty: it does not appear in the corresponding provisions of other conventions.

7.4 Claims brought against the insurer and defences available

Whilst in respect of other conventions in which there are specific rules on the limitation of liability of the owner reference is made to such rules, in this convention, in which there are not (nor could there be) any such rules, there is a general reference to the limitation of liability in force in the State. Paragraph 10 states in its relevant part:

In such a case the defendant may invoke the defences (other than the bankruptcy or winding up of the registered owner) that the registered owner would have been entitled to invoke, including limitation of liability under any applicable national or international regime. Furthermore, even if the registered owner is not entitled to limit liability, the defendant may limit liability to an amount equal to the amount of the insurance or other financial security required to be maintained in accordance with paragraph 1.

Since the defendant is the insurer or the guarantor, the last part of this provision seems to be redundant, for obviously his liability is limited to the amount of the guarantee. This is clearly stated in paragraph 1.

8 TIME LIMITS

Art. 13 so provides:

Rights to recover costs under this Convention shall be extinguished unless an action is brought hereunder within three years from the date when the hazard has been determined in accordance with this Convention. However, in no case shall an action be brought after six years from the date of the maritime casualty that resulted in the wreck. Where the maritime casualty consists of a series of occurrences, the six-year period shall run from the date of the first occurrence.

The double *dies a quo* has become customary where the basic date from which the period is calculated may not be known to the claimant. Probably the first convention in which it has been provided is the Convention on the Liability of Operators of

9 SETTLEMENT OF DISPUTES BETWEEN STATES PARTIES

In this Convention there are no provisions on jurisdiction and recognition and enforcement of judgments, even though they appear more likely to occur than disputes between States. Art. 15 provides, in its first three paragraphs:

1 Where a dispute arises between two or more States Parties regarding the interpretation or application of this Convention, they shall seek to resolve their dispute, in the first instance, through negotiation, enquiry, mediation, conciliation, arbitration, judicial settlement, resort to regional agencies or arrangements or other peaceful means of their choice.
2 If no settlement is possible within a reasonable period of time not exceeding twelve months after one State Party has notified another that a dispute exists between them, the provisions relating to the settlement of disputes set out in Part XV of the United Nations Convention on the Law of the Sea, 1982, shall apply *mutatis mutandis*, whether or not the States party to the dispute are also States Parties to the United Nations Convention on the Law of the Sea, 1982.
3 Any procedure chosen by a State Party to this Convention and to the United Nations Convention on the Law of the Sea, 1982, pursuant to article 287 of the latter shall apply to the settlement of disputes under this article, unless that State Party, when ratifying, accepting, approving or acceding to this Convention, or at any time thereafter, chooses another procedure pursuant to article 287 for the purpose of the settlement of disputes arising out of this Convention.

The provisions in paragraph 1 are based on those in art. 2(3) of the Charter of the United Nations:

All Members shall settle their international disputes by peaceful means in such a manner that international peace and security, and justice, are not endangered.

Pursuant to paragraph 2, the time allowed in order to settle a dispute by any of the peaceful means mentioned in paragraph 1 is one year from the notification of one party to the other that a dispute existed, failing which recourse must be made to the provisions of Part XV of UNCLOS and that entails the application of its section 2 and specifically of art. 287, reference to which is made in paragraph 3.

Since paragraph 1 of that article, which enumerates four alternative means for the settlement of disputes,[19] applies only to declarations made when ratifying or

---

17 Art. V(1) so provided:

> Rights of compensation under this Convention shall be extinguished if an action is not brought within ten years from the date of the nuclear incident. If, however, under the law of the licensing State the liability of the operator is covered by insurance or other financial security or State indemnification for a period longer than ten years, the applicable national law may provide that rights of compensation against the operator shall only be extinguished after a period which may be longer than ten years but shall not be longer than the period for which his liability is covered under the law of the licensing State. However, such extension of the extinction period shall in no case affect the right of compensation under this Convention of any person who has brought an action for loss of life or personal injury against the operator before the expiry of the aforesaid period of ten years.

18 Volume I – *The Carriage of Goods and Passengers by Sea*, p. 281.
19 Art. 287 (1) of UNCLOS so provides:

INTERNATIONAL MARITIME CONVENTIONS

acceding to the relevant Convention or, subsequently, prior to a dispute having arisen,[20] pursuant to paragraph 3, a State Party is deemed to have accepted arbitration in accordance with Annex VII to UNCLOS.

Art. 287 of UNCLOS also applies where a State Party to the Nairobi Convention is not a party to UNCLOS. It states:

4   A State Party to this Convention which is not a Party to the United Nations Convention on the Law of the Sea, 1982, when ratifying, accepting, approving or acceding to this Convention or at any time thereafter shall be free to choose, by means of a written declaration, one or more of the means set out in article 287, paragraph 1, of the United Nations Convention on the Law of the Sea, 1982, for the purpose of settlement of disputes under this article. Article 287 shall apply to such a declaration, as well as to any dispute to which such State is party, which is not covered by a declaration in force. For the purpose of conciliation and arbitration, in accordance with Annexes V and VII of the United Nations Convention on the Law of the Sea, 1982, such State shall be entitled to nominate conciliators and arbitrators to be included in the lists referred to in Annex V, article 2, and Annex VII, article 2, for the settlement of disputes arising out of this Convention.

---

1 When signing, ratifying or acceding to this Convention or at any time thereafter, a State shall be free to choose, by means of a written declaration, one or more of the following means for the settlement of disputes concerning the interpretation or application of this Convention:
(a)   the International Tribunal for the Law of the Sea established in accordance with Annex VI;
(b)   the International Court of Justice;
(c)   an arbitral tribunal constituted in accordance with Annex VII;
(d)   a special arbitral tribunal constituted in accordance with Annex VIII for one or more of the categories of disputes specified therein.

20 That is implied by para. 3 which provides:

A State Party, which is a party to a dispute not covered by a declaration in force, shall be deemed to have accepted arbitration in accordance with Annex VII.

CHAPTER 9

Port State Control: The Paris Memorandum of Understanding and the European Directive 2009/16/EC

1 INTRODUCTION

Although compliance with the compulsory provisions of the Conventions and Codes previously considered ought to be enforced by the States in the registers of which the ships are registered, it has been established that a great contribution in this respect could be provided by the competent authorities of the ports at which the ships are calling during their operation. The first initiative worldwide to organise such control on an international plane was made with the adoption in January 1982 by the Maritime Authorities of 14 European States of an administrative agreement, named the Paris Memorandum of Understanding on Port State Control (the Paris MoU), pursuant to which they undertook to carry out inspections on board the merchant ships calling at their ports with a view to establishing whether they complied with the standards laid down in compulsory provisions of the principal instruments on safety of life at sea, maritime labour and protection of the environment adopted by IMO and ILO. As of 31 December 2013, 27 Maritime Authorities were signatories of the Paris Memorandum.[1] The purpose of the inspections is stated in the first paragraph of the introduction, which stresses the need 'to increase maritime safety and the protection of the marine environment and the importance of improving living and working conditions on board ships'. Reference to the protection of the marine environment is also made in section 1(5), in which it is stated that port authorities must immediately inform the Authority of the port State or the coastal State, as appropriate, 'whenever they learn ... that there are apparent anomalies which may prejudice the safety of the ship, or which may pose a threat of harm to the marine environment'.

Similar regional Port State Control Agreements are at present in force in the Asia/Pacific Region,[2] the Latin America Region,[3] the Caribbean,[4] West and Central

---

1 Belgium, Bulgaria, Canada, Croatia, Cyprus, Denmark, Estonia, Finland, France, Germany (Federal Republic of), Greece, Iceland, Ireland, Italy, Latvia Lithuania, Malta, Netherlands, Norway, Poland, Portugal, Romania, Russian Federation, Slovenia, Spain, Sweden, United Kingdom.

2 Named the 'Tokyo MoU' between the Maritime Authorities of Australia, Canada, Chile, China, Fiji, Hong Kong, China, Indonesia, Japan, Republic of Korea, Malaysia, Marshall Islands, New Zealand, Papua New Guinea, Philippines, Russian Federation, Singapore, Solomon Islands, Thailand, Vanuatu and Vietnam.

3 Named 'Acuerdo de Viña del Mar', between Argentina, Bolivia, Brazil, Colombia, Chile, Ecuador, Mexico, Panama, Peru, Uruguay and Venezuela.

4 Named the 'Memorandum of Understanding on Port State Control', between Antigua & Barbuda, Aruba, the Bahamas, Barbados, Belize, The Cayman Islands, Curaçao, Cuba, Grenada, Guyana, Jamaica, the Netherlands, St Kitts and Nevis, Suriname and Trinidad and Tobago.

Africa,[5] the Black Sea Region,[6] the Mediterranean Region[7] and the Gulf Region.[8] A Directive on Port State Control was adopted on 23 April 2009 by the European Parliament.[9] There follows a commentary of the Paris MOU and of the European Union Directive.

I – THE PARIS MEMORANDUM OF UNDERSTANDING ON PORT STATE CONTROL[10]

1 THE CRITERIA FOR ADHERENCE TO THE MEMORANDUM

The first basic criterion indicated in section 9.2 of the Memorandum is geographic. Section 9.2 so provides:

A Maritime Authority of a European coastal State and a coastal State of the North Atlantic basin from North America to Europe, which complies with the criteria specified in Annex 5, may adhere to the Memorandum with the consent of all Authorities participating in the Memorandum.

Several other criteria are set out in Annex 5 to the Memorandum, entitled 'Qualitative Criteria for Adherence to the Memorandum', and among them it is worth mentioning paragraph 2 which provides:

Such Maritime Authority will have ratified all relevant instruments in force, before adherence shall be accomplished.

Of course, ratification is made by the State to which the relevant Maritime Authority belongs and the Memorandum binds the States to which the Authorities belong, as is made clear by Annex 11, which in its first heading refers to 'Inspection commitments of Member States' and then in the text of paragraph 1 sets out the 'inspection commitments of each Authority'.

The 'relevant instruments' are enumerated in section 2 of the Memorandum which provides in section 2.1:

For the purposes of the Memorandum 'relevant instruments' are the following:
1   the International Convention on Load Lines, 1966 (LOAD LINES 66);
2   the Protocol of 1988 relating to the International Convention on Load Lines, 1966 (LL PROT 88);
3   the International Convention for the Safety of Life at Sea, 1974 (SOLAS);
4   the Protocol of 1978 relating to the International Convention for the Safety of Life at Sea, 1974 (SOLAS PROT 78);

---

5 Named the 'West and Central Africa Memorandum of Understanding on Port State Control', between Angola, Benin, Cameroon, Cape Verde, Congo, Cote d'Ivoire, Gabon, Ghana, Guinea, Liberia, Mauritania, Namibia, Nigeria, Senegal, Sierra Leone, South Africa, São Tomé and Principe, Democratic Republic of Congo, Guinea Bissau, Gambia and Togo.

6 Named the 'Black Sea Memorandum of Understanding on Port State Control', between Bulgaria, Georgia, Romania, Russian Federation, Turkey and Ukraine.

7 Named the 'Mediterranean MOU on PSC' between Algeria, Cyprus, Egypt, Israel, Jordan, Lebanon, Malta, Morocco, Tunisia and Turkey.

8 Named the 'Riyadh MOU' between Bahrain, Kuwait, Oman, Qatar, Saudi Arabia an UAE.

9 Directive 2009/16/EC.

10 See https://www.parismou.org/about-us/memorandum.

5 the Protocol of 1988 relating to the International Convention for the Safety of Life at Sea, 1974 (SOLAS PROT 88);
6 the International Convention for the Prevention of Pollution from Ships, 1973, as modified by the Protocol of 1978 relating thereto, and as further amended by the Protocol of 1997 (MARPOL);
7 the International Convention on Standards of Training, Certification and Watchkeeping for Seafarers, 1978 (STCW 78);
8 the Convention on the International Regulations for Preventing Collisions at Sea, 1972 (COLREG 72);
9 the International Convention on Tonnage Measurement of Ships, 1969 (TONNAGE 69);
10 the Merchant Shipping (Minimum Standards) Convention, 1976 (ILO Convention No. 147) (ILO 147);
11 the Protocol of 1996 to the Merchant Shipping (Minimum Standards) Convention, 1976 (ILO Convention No. 147) (ILO P147);
12 the Maritime Labour Convention, 2006 (MLC, 2006);
13 the International Convention on Civil Liability for Oil Pollution Damage, 1969 (CLC1969);
14 Protocol of 1992 to amend the International Convention on Civil Liability for Oil Pollution Damage, 1969 (CLC PROT 1992);
15 International Convention on the Control of Harmful Anti-Fouling Systems on Ships, 2001 (AFS2001);
16 the International Convention on Civil Liability for Bunker Oil Pollution Damage, 2001;
17 the International Convention for the Control and Management of Ships' Ballast Water and Sediments (BWM).

Such instruments apply to the extent to which they are in force in the State to which each Maritime Authority belongs. This is expressly stated in section 2.3:

Each Authority will apply those relevant instruments which are in force and to which its State is a Party. In the case of amendments to a relevant instrument each Authority will apply those amendments which are in force and which its State has accepted. An instrument so amended will then be deemed to be the 'relevant instrument' for that Authority.

2 THE ORGANISATIONAL STRUCTURE OF THE PARIS MOU

In section 7 of the MoU it is provided that a Committee would be established, consisting of representatives of each of the Authorities and of the European Union and that a secretariat provided by the Netherlands' Ministry of Infrastructures and the Environment would be set up. From the Annual Report for 2013 it appears that the MoU has a President and a Secretary General, an Advisory Board whose task is to advise the Port State Control Committee consisting of delegates of the Maritime Authorities of the European Commission and of observers nominated by IMO, ILO and other MoUs and a Staff. There is also a Paris Secretariat and a Technical Evaluation Group.

3 THE SHIPS TO WHICH THE PARIS MOU APPLIES

There does not appear to be too much consistency in the terminology used throughout the Memorandum and its Annexes. In section 1, reference is made to 'foreign merchant ships'; in section 3, which deals with the reporting requirements, reference is made to 'each ship' and subsequently to 'ship'; in section 4.1, reference is made again to 'foreign merchant ship' and then to 'ship'; in section 4.2, reference is made to 'foreign ship'; in the heading of Annex 1 reference is made to 'ships of non-Parties'; in Annex 3.1 reference is made to the selection of 'foreign flag ships' and in other Annexes reference is mainly made to 'ship' or 'ships'. Perhaps definitions might have been helpful. In any event it is suggested that the only basic distinction that must be made is between 'ships' and 'foreign ships', in that when the term used is 'ship' the provisions apply to all ships, of any nationality, including that of the State to which the relevant Authority belongs; while when reference is made to 'foreign ships' the intention is to refer to ships of any nationality except that of the State to which the relevant Authority belongs. The distinction between ships of States Parties and ships on non-Parties appears to apply only to the specific provisions in connection with which that term is used.

4 THE INSPECTION COMMITMENTS OF THE MARITIME AUTHORITIES[11]

Section 1.3 states:

Each Authority will carry out an inspection on every foreign merchant ship of Priority I calling at one of its ports or anchorages, subject to the flexibility and regional commitment as described in Annex 11. Each Authority will carry out a total number of inspections of foreign merchant ships of Priority I and Priority II which corresponds at least to its annual inspection commitment determined in accordance with Annex 11. Authorities should refrain from selecting Priority II periodic inspections when these are not required in order to meet their annual commitment.[12]

Pursuant to Annex 11(1) the inspection commitments of each Maritime Authority are the following:

(a) to carry out an inspection on every ship calling at one of its ports and anchorages with a Priority I status; and
(b) to carry out a number of inspections on Priority I and Priority II ships which corresponds at least to its annual inspection commitment.

The basis of the priority is indicated in Annex 8(6) which states:

The selection scheme is divided into two priorities:
   Priority I: ships must be inspected because either the time window has closed or there is an overriding factor.
   Priority II: ships may be inspected because they are within the time window or the port State considers an unexpected factor warrants an inspection.

---

11 From the Paris MoU Annual Report 2013, it appears that 17,687 inspections were made in 2013.
12 Rules on inspection of ships are also contained in art. 5 of MARPOL: *supra*, chapter 3, para. 5.

The 'time window' indicates the frequency of the inspections to which ships must be subject by the Maritime Authorities of the States members of the Paris Memorandum, that varies according to the risk profile of the ships, established on the basis of the criteria set out in Table 1 of Annex 7. Ships are consequently classified as 'High Risk Ships (HRS)', 'Low Risks Ship (LRS)' and 'Standard Risk Ships (SRS)'. The time window is set out in Annex 8(6) as follows:

Ships become due for periodic inspection in the following time windows:
For HRS – between 5–6 months after the last inspection in the Paris MoU region.
For SRS – between 10–12 months after the last inspection in the Paris MoU region.
For LRS – between 24–36 months after the last inspection in the Paris MoU region.

5 THE DUTIES AND POWERS OF THE PORT AUTHORITIES WHEN DEFICIENCIES ARE DETECTED

Section 3.4 provides that Port Authorities will endeavour to secure the rectification of all deficiencies that have been detected. A distinction is then made between deficiencies which are or are not 'clearly hazardous to safety, health or the environment'. In the negative, on condition that 'all possible efforts have been made to rectify the deficiencies' the ship may be allowed to proceed to another port where they can be rectified; in the affirmative the Port Authority will, 'except as provided in 3.8', ensure that the hazard is removed 'before the ship is allowed to proceed to sea'.

Since even if the deficiencies are not hazardous, it is required that all possible action be made to rectify them, there will be situations in which the requirement that they be removed will be impossible to comply with. This is precisely what section 3.8 considers in the first place, since it provides that where the deficiencies cannot be remedied in the port of inspection, the Maritime Authority may allow the ship to proceed to the nearest appropriate repair yard available. Since, where all possible efforts have been unsuccessful in rectifying the deficiencies, the conclusion must be that the deficiencies cannot be remedied in the port where the ship lies, it may appear questionable whether a distinction between hazardous and non-hazardous deficiencies was really necessary. But that solution has probably been chosen since in section 3.8 there are included other specific situations, the first relating to the decision to send the ship to a repair yard due to lack of compliance with IMO Resolution A.1049(27)[13] and the

---

13 By Resolution A 27/Res.1049 of 30 November 2011 the Assembly of IMO has adopted the International Code on the Enhanced Programme of Inspections During Surveys of Bulk Carriers and Oil Tankers, 2011 (2011 ESP Code), with 15 Annexes, that regulates Renewal Surveys, Annual Surveys, Intermediate Surveys and Preparation for Survey.

Special rules on the detention of oil tankers are set out in MARPOL Annex I, chapter 2, regulation 11 which provides:

Port State control on operational requirements
1 A ship when in a port or an offshore terminal of another Party is subject to inspection by officers duly authorized by such Party concerning operational requirements under this Annex, where there are clear grounds for believing that the master or crew are not familiar with essential shipboard procedures relating to the prevention of pollution by oil.
2 In the circumstances given in paragraph 1 of this regulation, the Party shall take such steps as will ensure that the ship shall not sail until the situation has been brought to order in accordance with the requirements of this Annex.

second relating to the situation where the vessel is detained because it is not equipped with a functioning data recorder system when its use is compulsory.[14]

5.1 The detention of the ship subject to inspection[15]

Section 3.4, after stating that the Port Authority must ensure that the hazard is removed before the ship is allowed to proceed to sea, states:

For this purpose appropriate action will be taken, which may include detention or a formal prohibition of a ship to continue an operation due to established deficiencies which, individually or together, would render continued operation hazardous. In deciding on the appropriate action to be taken Port State Control Officers will be guided by a PSCC Instruction.

The instructions of the PSCC (Port State Control Committee), established pursuant to section 7 of the Memorandum, are not ad hoc instructions, but general instructions, reference to which is made in the tasks of the Committee listed in section 7.3 of the Memorandum.

In addition to the situations in which the ship is allowed to proceed to another port where a suitable repair yard is available, pursuant to section 3.5 detention is not permissible where its ground is the result of accidental damage suffered on the ship's voyage to a port or during cargo operations, subject to the conditions mentioned therein.[16]

5.2 The suspension of an inspection

A Maritime Authority may, pursuant to section 3.6, suspend an inspection where the overall condition of a ship and its equipment is found to be obviously sub-standard,

---

3 Procedures relating to the port State control prescribed in article 5 of the present Convention shall apply to this regulation.

4 Nothing in this regulation shall be construed to limit the rights and obligations of a Party carrying out control over operational requirements specifically provided for in the present Convention.

14 Section 3.8 states in its third paragraph:

If the vessel is detained because it is not equipped with a functioning voyage data recorder system, when its use is compulsory, and this deficiency cannot be readily rectified in the port of detention, the authority may allow the ship to proceed to the appropriate repair yard or port nearest to the port of the detention where it shall be readily rectified or require that the deficiency is rectified within a maximum period of 30 days.

15 From the Paris MoU Annual Report 2013, it appears that there were 668 detentions in that year.

16 Section 3.5 provides:

Where the ground for a detention is the result of accidental damage suffered on the ship's voyage to a port or during cargo operations, no detention order will be issued, provided that:

1 due account has been given to the requirements contained in Regulation I/11(c) of SOLAS regarding notification to the flag Administration, the nominated surveyor or the recognized organization responsible for issuing the relevant certificate;

2 prior to entering a port or immediately after a damage has occurred, the master or ship owner has submitted to the port State control authority details on the circumstances of the accident and the damage suffered and information about the required notification of the flag Administration;

3 appropriate remedial action, to the satisfaction of the Authority, is being taken by the ship, and

4 the Authority has ensured, having been notified of the completion of the remedial action, that deficiencies which were clearly hazardous to safety, health or the environment have been addressed to the satisfaction of the Authority.

in which event it must immediately notify the flag Administration. The suspension lasts until that Authority has been informed that the ship complies with the relevant requirements.

5.3 The refusal of access

Section 4.1 sets out rules on refusal of access in respect of foreign merchant ships flying the flag of States appearing in the grey and black lists[17] following their multiple detentions. As previously indicated,[18] foreign (merchant) ships are ships flying the flag of States other than that in which ships are detained. The detention is decided by the relevant Port Authority, but when the conditions set out in section 4.1.1 materialise, detention is 'recommended'. The condition for the refusal of access to operate is that a ship must have been detained 'more than twice'; and that means that she must have been detained at least three times. The difference between ships flying the flag of States appearing in the grey or black list relates to the period during which the detentions have occurred: 24 months for ships flying the flag of States appearing in the grey list and 36 months for ships flying the flag of States appearing in the black list. Therefore ship owners may be induced not to register their ships in States entered in the black or grey areas.

The period is reduced in both cases to 12 months in respect of ships that are subject to a second refusal of access, and where access of a ship has been refused three times, pursuant to art. 4.5 refusal of access becomes permanent.

6 INFORMATION SYSTEM ON INSPECTIONS

An information system has been established by the MoU in order to assist the Port Authorities in the selection of the foreign flag ships that ought to be inspected. This is managed by a manager on the basis of an agreement adopted by the Committee, reference to which is made in section 7 of the MoU. Its tasks are set out in Annex 3, paragraph 3 of which states:

The information system will include the following functionalities:
- Incorporate PSC inspection and port call data of Member States;
- Provide data on the ship risk profile and inspection priority;
- Calculate the inspection commitments for each Member State;
- Produce data for the calculation of the white as well as the grey and black list of flag States and the performance table of the Recognized Organizations;
- Calculate the performance of companies;

---

17 States are entered by the Committee established pursuant to section 7.1 into three different lists on the basis of the performance of the ships flying their flag, such performance being assessed with reference to the inspection and detention history of the ship. Annex 7 provides:
Black, grey and white list
The black, grey and white list for flag State performance is established annually taking account of the inspection and detention history over the preceding three calendar years and is adopted by the Paris MoU Committee.
From the Paris MoU Annual Report 2013 it appears that 46 States were included in the white list, 19 were included in the grey list and 14 were included in the black list.
18 *Supra*, para. 3.

- Identify the items in risk areas to be checked at each inspection;
- Provide batch transfer (in and out) of PSC inspection and port call data to and from a Member State.

The cooperation of the MoU with IMO and ILO is evidenced by paragraphs 11 and 12 of that Annex which state:

11 With the consent of the Authority, the information system manager will, on behalf of that Authority, submit data as agreed by the Committee to the International Maritime Organization in accordance with Regulation I/19 of SOLAS, Article 11 of MARPOL, Article 21 of LOADLINES 66 and Article X of STCW 78.
12 With the consent of the Authority, the information system manager will, on behalf of that Authority, submit data as agreed by the Committee to the International Labour Organization in accordance with Standard A5.2.1 or Article 4 of ILO 147 if applicable.

II – THE EUROPEAN DIRECTIVE ON PORT STATE CONTROL

1 THE ORIGIN AND PURPOSE OF THE DIRECTIVE

The original Directive 95/21/EC on Port State Control of 19 June 1995, having been amended several times,[19] was replaced by Directive 2009/16/EC of 23 April 2009.

Its linkage with the Paris MOU is stated clearly in the following recitals 13 and 14:

(13) The inspection system set up by this Directive takes into account the work carried under the Paris MoU. Since any developments arising from the Paris MoU should be agreed at Community level before being made applicable within the EU, close coordination should be established and maintained between the Community and the Paris MoU in order to facilitate as much convergence as possible.
(14) The Commission should manage and update the inspection database, in close collaboration with the Paris MoU. Until the Community maritime information system, SafeSeaNet, is fully operational and allows for an automatic record of the data concerning ships' calls in the inspection database, Member States should provide the Commission with the information needed to ensure a proper monitoring of the application of this Directive, in particular concerning the movements of ships. On the basis of the inspection data provided by Member States, the Commission should retrieve from the inspection database data on the risk profile of ships, on ships due for inspections and on the movement of ships and should calculate the inspection commitments for each Member State. The inspection database should also be capable of interfacing with other Community maritime safety databases.

The purpose of the Directive is stated in art. 1, which states:

The purpose of this Directive is to help to drastically reduce substandard shipping in the waters under the jurisdiction of Member States by:
    (a) increasing compliance with international and relevant Community legislation on maritime safety, maritime security, protection of the marine environment and onboard living and working conditions of ships of all flags;

---

19 The original Directive was amended by Council Directive 95/21/EC, Commission Directive 98/42/EC, Commission Directive 1999/97/EC, Directive 2001/106/EC and Directive 2001/84/EC.

(b) establishing common criteria for control of ships by the port State and harmonizing procedures on inspection and detention, building upon the expertise and experience under the Paris MoU;

(c) implementing within the Community a port State control system based on the inspections performed within the Community and the Paris MoU region, aiming at the inspection of all ships with a frequency depending on their risk profile, with ships posing a higher risk being subject to a more detailed inspection carried out at more frequent intervals.

2 SHIPS TO WHICH THE DIRECTIVE APPLIES

2.1 Ships included within the scope of application of the Directive

There is no direct definition of 'ship' in the Directive, but only one by reference to several conventions enumerated in art. 2(1).[20] Art. 2(5) states:

5. 'Ship' means any seagoing vessel to which one or more of the Conventions apply, flying a flag other than that of the port State.

2.2 Ships excluded from the scope of application of the Directive

Art. 3.4 so provides:

Fishing vessels, warships, naval auxiliaries, wooden ships of a primitive build, government ships used for non-commercial purposes and pleasure yachts not engaged in trade shall be excluded from the scope of this Directive.

Although it is certainly of a very limited application, 'wooden ships of a primitive build' is a description of doubtful meaning. Doubts may also arise in respect of the meaning of 'pleasure yachts not engaged in trade': while carriage of goods with payment of freight would come under that description, would yachts carrying passengers for a reward also be deemed to be engaged in trade? And, if so, what would be the dividing line between those yachts, and yachts chartered with a crew?

3 THE INSPECTION COMMITMENTS OF THE MEMBER STATES

3.1 The general rule

The obligations of States Parties are very similar to those set out in section 1.3 of the Paris MoU.[21] Art. 5(2) of the Directive states:

---

20 The chapeau of art. 2(1) states:

'Conventions' means the following Conventions, with Protocol and amendments thereto, and related codes of mandatory status, in their up-to-date version:

The conventions enumerated thereafter are the Load Line Convention 1966, SOLAS, MARPOL, STCV 78/95, Colreg 1972, Tonnage Measurement 1969, ILO No. 147, CLC 1992.

21 *Supra*, section I, para. I-4.

2 In order to comply with its annual inspection commitment, each Member State shall:
  (a) inspect all Priority I ships, referred to in article 12(a), calling at its ports and anchorages; and
  (b) carry out annually a total number of inspections of Priority I and Priority II ships, referred to in article 12(a) and (b), corresponding at least to its share of the total number of inspections to be carried out annually within the Community and the Paris MoU region. The inspection share of each Member State shall be based on the number of individual ships calling at ports of the Member State concerned in relation to the sum of the number of individual ships calling at ports of each State within the Community and the Paris MoU region.

The distinction between 'Priority I' ships and 'Priority II' ships, for which reference is made to art. 12(a) and (b), originates, as a great many of the terms used in the Directive, from the Paris MoU in which they are clearly defined.[22] Their definition is not so clear in art. 12(a) and (b), reference to which is made in art. 5(2)(b), but there is no doubt that it is based on whether the period by which inspection is required has elapsed or not.

3.2 Frequency of inspections

Article 11 sets out rules on the frequency of inspections, such inspections being of two kinds: periodic inspections and additional inspections.

The periodic inspections must be carried out, as provided in the Paris MoU, at predetermined intervals, depending on the risk profile of the ship that is determined, pursuant to Annex I, by a combination of the generic and historic parameters set out in its section I, the combination of which determines three levels of risk, that correspond to those indicated in Annex 7 of the Paris MoU:[23] high risk, low risk and standard risk. The parameters specified in Annex I correspond to those indicated in Table I of the Paris MoU's Annex 7, and the ensuing periods of inspection are approximately the same:

  (a) for ships with a high-risk profile: inspection is required when they have not been inspected within the Community during the last six months, such ships becoming eligible for inspection as from the fifth month;
  (b) for ships with a standard-risk profile: inspection is required when they have not been inspected within the Community during the last 12 months, such ships becoming eligible for inspection as from the tenth month;
  (c) for ships with a low-risk profile: inspection is required when they have not been inspected within the Community during the last 36 months, such ships becoming eligible for inspection as from the twenty-fourth month.

The notion of 'additional inspections' – a term that indicates that they can be carried out in addition to the periodic inspection – is based in art. 11(b) which states:

(b) Ships shall be subject to additional inspections regardless of the period since their last periodic inspection as follows:

---

22 *Supra*, section I, para. I-4.
23 *Ibid.*

- the competent authority shall ensure that ships to which overriding factors listed in Annex I, Part. II 2A, apply are inspected;
- ships to which unexpected factors listed in Annex I, Part II 2B, apply may be inspected. The decision to undertake such an additional inspection is left to the professional judgment of the competent authority.

This term also originates from the Paris MoU, Annex 8 of which refers to 'Overriding or unexpected factors' that might trigger an inspection between periods of inspections. Such factors are enumerated in Annex I of the Directive under paragraphs 2A and 2B and it appears that, in both cases, the list is a closed list. A similar enumeration is made in Annex 8 to the Paris MoU in paragraphs 11 and 12 and a comparison between them shows that they are almost the same.

3.3 The detention of the ship subject to inspection

The general cause of detention is the discovery during the inspection of deficiencies that are hazardous to safety, health or the environment. Art. 19(2) so provides:

2. In the case of deficiencies which are clearly hazardous to safety, health or the environment, the competent authority of the port State where the ship is being inspected shall ensure that the ship is detained or that the operation in the course of which the deficiencies are revealed is stopped. The detention order or stoppage of an operation shall not be lifted until the hazard is removed or until such authority establishes that the ship can, subject to any necessary conditions, proceed to sea or the operation be resumed without risk to the safety and health of passengers or crew, or risk to other ships, or without there being an unreasonable threat of harm to the marine environment.

This provision is similar to that in the Paris MoU which in section 3.4 provides that 'In the case of deficiencies which are clearly hazardous to safety, health or the environment, the Maritime Authority will, except as provided in 3.8, ensure that the hazard is removed before the ship is allowed to proceed at sea.' Section 3.8 deals with the situation where the deficiencies cannot be remedied in the port of inspection. It provides that the Authority may allow the ship to proceed to the nearest appropriate repair yard and sets out specific rules where the decision is due to a lack of compliance with IMO Resolution A.1049(27), or the ship is detained because it is not equipped with a functioning voyage data recorder system when its use is compulsory.

Detention because the ship is not equipped with a functioning voyage recorder is also mentioned in section 3.8 of the Paris MoU.

In the same way as the Paris MoU, the Directive provides in art. 19(8) that all possible efforts must be made to avoid a ship being unduly detained or delayed and also provides that where that happens, the owner or operator are entitled to compensation.

4 THE REFUSAL OF ACCESS

4.1 Refusal based on the records of a ship

Such refusal is based on the records of a particular ship concerning her prior detention. Article 16(1) of the Directive reproduces verbatim section 4.1 of the Paris

MOU,[24] save that under section 4.1 refusal of access is recommended, while under art. 16(1) of the Directive refusal of access is obligatory.

4.2 Refusal based on prior failure to comply with conditions determined by authorities

Refusal of access of ships to a port or anchorage in a Member State may also be consequential on a failure to carry out the rectification of the deficiencies in compliance with the provisions of art. 19(2) and (4). Art. 21(4) so provides:

4. Member States shall take measures to ensure that access to any port or anchorage within the Community is refused to ships referred to in paragraph 1 which proceed to sea:
   (a) without complying with the conditions determined by the competent authority of any Member State in the port of inspection; or
   (b) which refuse to comply with the applicable requirements of the Conventions by not calling into the indicated repair yard.
   Such refusal shall be maintained until the owner or operator provides evidence to the satisfaction of the competent authority of the Member State where the ship was found defective, demonstrating that the ship fully complies with all applicable requirements of the Conventions.

Also, in this case, refusal by the competent authorities of Member States is obligatory, while under the Paris MoU it is not. The difference lies in the legal nature of the Paris MoU, which is merely an administrative agreement between States.

---

24 *Supra*, section I, para. 5.3.

CHAPTER 10

European Traffic Monitoring and Information System Directive 2002/59/EC of 27 June 2002

On 27 June 2002, Directive 2002/59/EC[1] establishing a European Union vessel traffic monitoring and information system was adopted and was subsequently amended by Directives 2009/17/EC of 23 April 2009[2] and 2009/18/EC of 23 April 2009[3] and by Commission Directive 2001/15/EU of 23 February 2011.[4]

The importance of this directive in connection with the uniform measures aiming at preventing environmental damage clearly appears from its art. 1 which states:

The purpose of this Directive is to establish in the Community a vessel traffic monitoring and information system with a view to enhancing the safety and efficiency of maritime traffic, improving the response of authorities to incidents, accidents or potentially dangerous situations at sea, including search and rescue operations, and contributing to a better prevention and detection of pollution by ships. Member States shall monitor and take all necessary and appropriate measures to ensure that the masters, operators or agents of ships, as well as shippers or owners of dangerous or polluting goods carried on board such ships, comply with the requirements under this Directive.

From its scope there are excluded ships that are also excluded in several IMO Conventions. Art. 2(2) provides:

2   Unless otherwise provided, this Directive shall not apply to:
    (a)   warships, naval auxiliaries and other ships owned or operated by a Member State and used for non-commercial public service;
    (b)   fishing vessels, traditional ships and recreational craft with a length of less than 45 metres;
    (c)   bunkers on ships below 1000 gross tonnage and ships' stores and equipment for use on board all ships.

The linkage with IMO Conventions is evidenced from the reference in art. 3, among the relevant international instruments, to MARPOL, SOLAS, the Intervention Convention of 1969, the ISM Code,[5] the IMDG Code,[6] the IBC Code[7] and the IGC Code,[8] as well as by the following definition of dangerous goods in art. 3(g):

---

1   OJ L 208, 5.8.2002, p. 10.
2   OJ L 131, 28.5.2009, p. 101.
3   OJ L 131, 28.5.2009, p. 114.
4   OJ L 49, 24.2.2011, p. 33.
5   International Safety Management Code.
6   International Maritime Dangerous Goods Code.
7   IMO International Code for the Construction and Equipment of Ships carrying Dangerous Chemicals in Bulk.
8   IMO International Code for the Construction and Equipment of Ships Carrying Liquefied Gases in Bulk.

(g) 'dangerous goods' means:
- goods classified in the IMDG Code,
- dangerous liquid substances listed in Chapter 17 of the IBC Code,
- liquefied gases listed in Chapter 19 of the IGC Code,
- solids referred to in Appendix B of the BC Code.

Also included are goods for the carriage of which appropriate preconditions have been laid down in accordance with paragraph 1.1.3 of the IBC Code or paragraph 1.1.6 of the IGC Code.

Member States were required to bring into force the laws, regulations and administrative provisions necessary to comply with Directive 2009/17/EC by 30 November 2010.

Among the provisions that appear of particular importance for the protection of the environment, there are those relating:

(a) to the information that must be provided in connection with the transport of dangerous goods;

(b) to the notification of dangerous polluting goods carried on board;

(c) to the monitoring of hazardous ships;

(d) to the reporting of incidents and accidents at sea;

(e) to measures relating to incidents or accidents at sea; and

(f) to ships in need of assistance.

(a) Information concerning the transport of dangerous goods
Art. 12 provides that no dangerous or polluting goods shall be offered for carriage or taken on board any ship, irrespective of its size, in the port of a Member State unless a declaration has been delivered to the master or operator before the goods are taken on board containing information, *inter alia*, in respect of the emergency numbers of the shipper or any other person or body in possession of information on the physic-chemical characteristics of the products and on the action to be taken in an emergency.

(b) Notification of dangerous polluting goods carried on board
Art. 13 requires that the operator, agent or master of a ship carrying dangerous or polluting goods coming from a port located outside the European Union and bound for a port of a Member State or an anchorage located in a Member State's territorial waters shall, at the latest upon departure from the loading port or as soon as the port of destination or the location of the anchorage is known, notify the correct technical names of the dangerous or polluting goods, the United Nations (UN) numbers where they exist, the IMO hazard classes in accordance with the IMDG, IBC and IGC Codes and, where appropriate, the class of the ship as defined by the INF Code, the quantities of such goods, their location on board and, if they are being carried in cargo transport units other than tanks, the identification number thereof.

(c) Monitoring of hazardous ships
Art. 16 provides that Member States holding relevant information on the planned route of ships posing a potential hazard to shipping or a threat to maritime safety, the safety of individuals or the environment, must communicate such information to

the coastal States located along the planned route of such ships. Such ships include those which in the course of the voyage have been involved, *inter alia*, in incidents affecting their safety or a situation liable to lead to pollution of the waters or shore of a Member State.

(d) Reporting of incidents and accidents at sea

Art. 17 provides that Member States must monitor and take all appropriate measures to ensure that the master of a ship sailing within their search and rescue region/ exclusive economic zone or equivalent area immediately reports to the coastal station responsible for that geographical area any incident or accident, *inter alia*, affecting the safety of the ship or creating a situation, such as discharge or threat of discharge of polluting product into the sea, liable to lead to pollution of the waters or shore of a Member State.[9]

(e) Measures relating to incidents or accidents at sea

Pursuant to art. 19, in the event of incidents or accidents at sea as referred to in art. 17, Member States shall take all appropriate measures consistent with international law, where necessary to ensure the safety of shipping and of persons and to protect the marine and coastal environment. A non-exhaustive list of measures available to Member States pursuant to that article is set out in Annex IV.

(f) Ships in need of assistance

The possible conflict between salvage operations and the protection of the environment has been considered, but not settled,[10] by the Salvage Convention in its arts. 9 and 11. Art. 20a, which has been added by Directive 2009/17/EC, provides directions that attempt to reach a compromise between the performance of salvage

---

9 Art. 16 so provides:

 1 Ships meeting the criteria set out below shall be considered to be ships posing a potential hazard to shipping or a threat to maritime safety, the safety of individuals or the environment:
  (a) ships which, in the course of their voyage:
   – have been involved in incidents or accidents at sea as referred to in Article 17; or
   – have failed to comply with the notification and reporting requirements imposed by this Directive; or
   – have failed to comply with the applicable rules in ships' routing systems and VTS placed under the responsibility of a Member State;
  (b) ships in respect of which there is proof or presumptive evidence of deliberate discharges of oil or other infringements of the MARPOL Convention in waters under the jurisdiction of a Member State;
  (c) ships which have been refused access to ports of the Member States or which have been the subject of a report or notification by a Member State in accordance with Annex I-1 to Council Directive 95/21/EC of 19 June 1995 on port State control of shipping;
  (d) ships which have failed to notify, or do not have, insurance certificates or financial guarantees pursuant to any Community legislation and international rules; and
  (e) ships which have been reported by pilots or port authorities as having apparent anomalies which may prejudice their safe navigation or create a risk for the environment.

Art. 17(1) requires Member States to monitor and take all appropriate measures to ensure that the master of a ship sailing within their search and rescue region/exclusive economic zone immediately reports, *inter alia*, '(c) any situation liable to lead to pollution of the waters or shore of a Member State such as discharge or threat of discharge of polluting products into the sea':

10 See Volume II, chapter 5, para. 5.2.2.

operations and the protection of the environment as well as the general interest of the coastal State within the territorial waters of which is located the place of safety where the operations are terminated.[11] This has been done by requiring Member States to draw up plans for the accommodation of ships in need of assistance and providing directions to this effect. Such plans will be the basis, pursuant to art. 20b, on which the authorities designated by Member States 'shall decide on the acceptance of a ship in a place of refuge following a prior assessment of the situation carried out on the basis of the plans referred to in article 20a'. Art. 20a so provides in paragraph 1:

1. Member States shall draw up plans for the accommodation of ships in order to respond to threats presented by ships in need of assistance in the waters under their jurisdiction, including, where applicable, threats to human life and the environment. The authority or authorities referred to in article 20(1) shall participate in drawing up and carrying out those plans.

---

11 Recitals 17, 18 and 19 provide a clear outline of the duties of Member States:

    17 Plans for accommodating ships in need of assistance should describe precisely the decision-making chain with regard to alerting and dealing with the situation in question. The authorities concerned and their remits should be clearly described, as should the means of communication between the parties involved. The applicable procedures should ensure that an appropriate decision can be taken quickly on the basis of specific maritime expertise and adequate information available to the competent authority.

    18 Ports which accommodate a ship should be able to rely on prompt compensation in respect of costs and any damage arising from the operation. To that end, it is important that the relevant international conventions be applied. Member States should endeavour to put in place a legal framework under which they could, in exceptional circumstances and in accordance with Community law, compensate a port or other entity for costs and economic loss suffered as a result of accommodating a ship. Moreover, the Commission should examine existing mechanisms within Member States for the compensation of potential economic loss suffered by a port or a body and should, on the basis of this examination, put forward and evaluate different policy options.

    19 When drawing up the plans, Member States should gather information on potential places of refuge on the coast so as to allow the competent authority, in the event of an accident or incident at sea, to identify clearly and quickly the most suitable areas for accommodating ships in need of assistance. This relevant information should contain a description of certain characteristics of the sites under consideration and the equipment and installations available to make it easier to accommodate ships in need of assistance or deal with the consequences of an accident or pollution.

PART II

THE LIABILITY CONVENTIONS

CHAPTER 11

International Convention on Civil Liability for Oil Pollution Damage, 1992 (CLC 1992)

1 INTRODUCTION

The CLC 1969, from which the CLC 1992 originates, was a direct consequence of the pollution of the shores of the United Kingdom and France resulting from the grounding on 18 March 1967 of the *Torrey Canyon* on Pollard Rock, off the English coast between the Isles of Scilly to the west and Lands End to the east and her subsequent sinking.[1]

The British Government asked the Inter-Governmental Maritime Consultative Organisation (IMCO) to study the problems exposed by the *Torrey Canyon* disaster and to recommend solutions. The Council of IMCO met in Extraordinary Session on 4 May 1967. Recognising that some of the problems were essentially legal in character, an ad hoc Committee was established which met for its first session on 21 and 22 June 1967. By the time of its second session in November 1967 the ad hoc Legal Committee had become a permanent organ of IMCO.

Also, in May 1967, the Comité Maritime International (CMI) appointed an International sub-Committee with Lord Devlin as chairman to study the problems posed by the *Torrey Canyon* disaster. CMI applied for and was granted consultative status by IMCO, and thus began the close cooperation and consultation between these two organisations which has existed ever since. The system of maritime law which prevailed up to 1969 had been reasonably adequate to deal with the ordinary maritime casualty, but the loss of the *Torrey Canyon* demonstrated that the ordinary rules of maritime law might no longer be adequate to provide a satisfactory remedy for victims of oil pollution on a massive scale.

The Conference, which was organised by IMCO, met in Brussels on 10 to 29 November 1969. The two fundamental issues upon which the Conference had to reach a decision were: (a) the nature of the liability, and (b) the party who should bear that liability. States which had coastlines particularly vulnerable to oil pollution demanded a legal remedy which would ensure that they could recover clean-up costs and compensation for damage to resources within their territory, including their territorial seas. Nothing short of strict, if not absolute, liability could effectively guarantee such a remedy, but on whom should such liability rest? Maritime States with large tanker fleets demanded that if the ship was to be liable, such liability

---

1 On this incident see Chapter 1, para. 1. See also Colin de la Rue and Charles B. Anderson, *Shipping and the Environment*, 1998, p. 11.

117

should be based on fault. These States were prepared to consider a system of strict or absolute liability only if that liability were placed on cargo.

The possibility of obtaining a convention acceptable to two-thirds of the delegations present looked rather remote. Many delegations had become convinced that only a system of strict liability would provide an adequate remedy and doubted the feasibility of establishing an oil pollution compensation fund based on a levy on cargoes of persistent oil moving on the oceans of the world. A Working Group had been set up to consider this concept during the Conference, but it was obvious that it would not be able to complete its work in the time available. The deadlock was eventually broken on 24 November 1969 when a compromise was reached on the basis of a proposal of the United Kingdom delegation,[2] supported by many other delegations,[3] that the convention be founded on strict liability of the ship, compulsory insurance and a limit of liability of 1,900 Poincaré francs per ton with a ceiling of 210 million, insurance up to the limits being obtainable on the London market. As an agreed and essential part of the compromise the Conference adopted a resolution whereby, in consideration of the fact that in order to ensure that adequate compensation be available to the victims of large-scale oil pollution incidents a compensation scheme based upon the existence of an international fund should be elaborated, IMCO should be requested to convene an International Legal Conference not later than 1971, to consider and adopt such compensation scheme taking into account as a foundation the following principles:

1 Victims should be fully and adequately compensated under a system based on the principle of strict liability.
2 The fund should in principle relieve the shipowners of the additional financial burden imposed by the present Convention.[4]

---

2 Document LEG/CONF/C.2/WP.35, Official Records of the International Legal Conference on Marine Pollution Damage, 1969, p. 596.

3 Official Records, *supra*, note 2, pp. 727–738.

4 The full text of the resolution was as follows (Official Records, *supra*, note 2, p. 185):

The International Legal Conference on Marine Pollution Damage, 1969,

NOTING that the International Convention on Civil Liability for Oil Pollution Damage, 1969, although it lays down the principle of strict liability and provides for a system of compulsory insurance or other financial guarantee for ships carrying oil in bulk as cargo, does not afford full protection for victims in all cases,

RECOGNIZING the view having emerged during the Conference that some form of supplementary scheme in the nature of an international fund is necessary to ensure that adequate compensation will be available for victims of large-scale oil pollution incidents,

TAKING ACCOUNT of the report submitted by the working party set up by the Committee of the Whole II to study the problems relating to the constitution of an international compensation fund,

REALIZING, however, that the time available for the Conference has not made it possible to give full consideration to all aspects of such a compensation scheme,

REQUESTS the Inter-Governmental Maritime Consultative Organization to elaborate as soon as possible, through its Legal Committee and other appropriate legal bodies, a draft for a compensation scheme based upon the existence of an international fund,

CONSIDERS that such a compensation scheme should be elaborated taking into account as a foundation the following principles:

1 Victims should be fully and adequately compensated under a system based upon the principle of strict liability.

2 The fund should in principle relieve the shipowner of the additional financial burden imposed by the present Convention.

REQUESTS IMCO to convene, not later than the year 1971, an International Legal Conference for the consideration and adoption of such a compensation scheme.

The CLC 1969 entered into force on 19 June 1975 and after the replacement of the original money of account, the franc Poincaré, by the Special Drawing Right by a Protocol adopted on 19 November 1976,[5] was the object of an in-depth review by a Protocol adopted on 25 May 1984. That Protocol never entered into force, and was replaced by a new Protocol adopted on 19 November 1992,[6] that entered into force on 30 May 1996. The Convention, as amended by that Protocol, replaced for all purposes the CLC 1969, all State parties to it having ratified or acceded to the Protocol and became known as CLC 1992. On 18 October 2000 the limits of liability were increased by the IMO Legal Committee, pursuant to the procedure set out in art. 15.

2 The scope of application of the CLC 1992

The scope of application of the Convention must be considered from the standpoint of the ships subject to the Convention, of the area in which the Convention applies (geographical scope) and of the characteristics of the oil pollution damage the compensation of which is governed by the Convention.

2.1 Ships subject to the Convention

The following definition of ship[7] is given in art. I(1):

1. 'Ship' means any sea-going vessel and seaborne craft of any type whatsoever, *constructed or adapted for the carriage of oil in bulk as cargo, provided that a ship capable of carrying oil and other cargoes shall be regarded as a ship only when it is* actually carrying oil in bulk as cargo *and during any voyage following such carriage unless it is proved that it has no residues of such carriage of oil in bulk aboard.*

The part of the definition in italics was added by the Protocol of 1992. The wording adopted in 1969 relates to the type of vessel: it may be a vessel or a craft. If a vessel it must be sea-going; if a craft it must be seaborne. The words 'of any type whatsoever' that follow the terms 'vessel' and 'ship' are used in maritime conventions in a manner that does not help to understand their precise meaning, as it appears from the fact that while in this Convention the term 'ship' is given a meaning wider than 'vessel' since it includes crafts of any type, in the Salvage Convention 1989 the relationship between such terms is reversed: 'vessel' in fact is a term which is given a wider meaning,[8] since it includes 'any ship or craft or structure capable of navigation'. It is suggested that in each convention, such terms have been used merely for

---

5 Entered into force on 8 April 1981.

6 By resolution A.729(17), adopted by the IMO Assembly on 7 November 1991, the Legal Committee had been requested to consider:

(a) the draft Protocols modifying the CLC 1969 and the Fund Convention 1971;

(b) the draft Conference resolutions attached to document LEG 66/5; and

(c) whether there should be introduced in the Fund Convention a system of setting a cap on contributions payable by oil receivers in any given State for a transitional period.

7 On the definition of ship see also C. de la Rue and C.B. Anderson, *Shipping and the Environment, supra*, note 1, p. 79.

8 Reference is made to the analysis of these terms in Kennedy and Rose *Law of Salvage*, 8th edition, pp. 93–97.

the purpose of covering the craft to which each convention was intended to apply, and that a comparison between the various conventions would be inappropriate. Limiting therefore the enquiry to the original definition in the CLC, it is convenient to consider at the same time its wording in the French text of the Convention, which was the following:

'Navire' signifie tout bâtiment de mer ou engin marin, quel qu'il soit, qui transporte effectivement des hydrocarbures en vrac en tant que cargaison.

The first question which arises is whether the words 'of any type whatsoever' (*'quel qu'il soit'* in the French text) are related to both the preceding terms – 'any sea-going vessel and seaborne craft' – or only to the latter. Although the comma that appears in the French text after *'engin marin'* (seaborne craft) would support the first alternative, the fact that it does not appear in the English text and that the word 'vessel' could embrace a variety of meanings if it were not qualified by the word 'sea-going', supports the second alternative. The fact that the 'craft' is qualified by the word 'seaborne', in opposition to the word 'sea-going' which qualifies the term 'vessel', indicates that the craft is not self-propelled: it may, for example, be a barge or a tank. The term *'engin'* has an even greater variety of meanings, that actually are not sufficiently restricted by the word *'marin'*, as also a fishing gear is an *'engin marin'* and its interpretation needs the support of the English term 'seaborne craft'.

The Convention, however, according to the original definition applied only where a ship at the time of the incident was actually carrying oil as cargo and, therefore, it did not apply in respect of pollution damage caused by oil residues of previous cargoes and by bunker.

When the Legal Committee considered the revision of the Convention, it was discussed, *inter alia*, whether it should also apply to combination carriers which had carried oil as cargo and still had residues on board and the following draft of a new definition of 'ship', with some alternative wording, was adopted for submission to the diplomatic conference:[9]

1 'Ship' means any sea-going vessel and seaborne craft of any type whatsoever, constructed or adapted for the carriage of oil in bulk as cargo, provided that a ship capable of carrying oil and other cargoes shall be regarded as a ship only when it is actually carrying oil in bulk and during [the] [any] voyage following such carriage unless it is proved that it has no residues of such carriage of oil in bulk aboard.

At the diplomatic conference held in May 1984 this wording was adopted with the deletion of the definite article 'the' before 'carriage of oil' and of the square brackets around the word 'any'.[10]

A distinction is therefore now made between a ship constructed or adapted to carry only oil in bulk as cargo and a ship capable of carrying either oil or other cargoes as is the case with ships capable of carrying oil or ore. In the first case, the Convention always applies, provided pollution damage has occurred. If, therefore, at the time of the incident the ship was sailing in ballast and pollution damage was

---

9 Official Records of the International Conference on Liability and Compensation for Damage in connection with the Carriage of Certain Substances by Sea, 1984 and the International Conference on the Revision of the 1969 Civil Liability Convention and the 1971 Fund Convention, 1992, vol. 1, p. 134.

10 Official Records, *supra* note 8, vol. 3, p. 204.

OIL POLLUTION DAMAGE CONVENTION, 1992

caused by bunker oil, the Convention applies, as made clear by the reference in the definition of 'oil' to any persistent hydrocarbon 'whether carried on board the ship as cargo or in the bunkers of such ship'. In the second case, the Convention applies only if, when the pollution damage occurred, the ship or craft was actually carrying oil in bulk as cargo and during 'any voyage' following such carriage, except where it is proved that it had no residues of such carriage of oil in bulk, in which event the mere carriage of oil in the bunker does not entail the application of the Convention. The burden of proof rests on the party who invokes the application of the Convention: it may be the claimant, in order to benefit from the rules on the strict liability of the carrier, or the owner, in order to benefit from the limitation of liability, even though he may very likely also invoke the limitation under the LLMC Convention.

2.2 Ships excluded from the scope of application of the Convention

Art. XI so provides:

1 The provisions of this Convention shall not apply to warships or other ships owned or operated by a State and used, for the time being, only on government non-commercial service.
2 With respect to ships owned by a Contracting State and used for commercial purposes, each State shall be subject to suit in the jurisdictions set forth in article IX and shall waive all defences based on its status as a sovereign State.

In the draft articles submitted by the Legal Committee to the Conference there was a provision in art. XI based on that in art. 3(1) of the Convention on Immunity of State-owned Ships of 1926, pursuant to which the Convention would not apply to warships or ships owned or operated by a State and used for the time being only on government non-commercial services.[11] During the Conference the proposal was made by the United States[12] to add the following paragraph:

With respect to ships owned or operated by a State and used on commercial purposes, each Contracting State shall be subject to suit in the jurisdiction set forth in article VIII and shall waive all defences based on its status as sovereign State.

Subsequently the above wording was included in art. XI of the revised draft articles prepared by the Secretariat.[13]

Reference to the United States proposal was made during the thirteenth meeting of the Committee of the Whole, when it was adopted[14] and art. XI, as amended by the United States, was approved during the fifteenth meeting.[15] The rules laid down in paragraph 2 are the same as those laid down in arts. 1 and 2 of the Immunity Convention of 1926.

---

11 Official Records, *supra*, note 2, p. 535.
12 Document LEG/CONF/C.2/WP.14, Official Records, *supra*, note 2, pp. 569–570.
13 Document LEG/CONF/C.2/WP.22/Rev.1, Official Records, *supra*, note 2, p. 576, at p. 582.
14 Official Records, *supra*, note 2, p. 701.
15 *Ibid.*, p. 719.

2.3 The definition of 'oil'

Art. 1.5 of the CLC 1992 states:

5 'Oil' means any persistent hydrocarbon mineral oil such as crude oil, fuel oil, heavy diesel oil and lubricating oil, whether carried on board a ship as cargo or in the bunkers of such ship.

This definition differs from that adopted in the CLC 1969 in that the mere reference to 'oil' has been replaced by a reference to 'hydrocarbon mineral oil' and the inclusion of 'whale oil' has been deleted. When the draft Protocol was discussed at the Conference held in March 1986 these changes were considered. The replacement of 'oil' by 'hydrocarbon mineral oil' was suggested on the ground that non-mineral oils were not carried in sufficient quantities; if they were considered to pose a threat they should be covered by the HNS Convention not by the CLC.[16] The deletion of the reference to 'whale oil' was stated to be due to the fact that pollution caused by such oil was no longer a problem.[17] A much longer debate followed the proposal of the addition to a reference to 'non persistent oil'. In support of that addition it was also stated that non-persistent oils were capable of causing serious damage and that even if damage by such oil was due to its toxic nature, it could still be considered as contamination.[18] Against the argument, it was pointed out that their inclusion would considerably extend the CLC to types and numbers of vessels to which the CLC might apply and thus extend the scope of compulsory insurance, thereby causing significant burden upon governments;[19] it was also stated that it would be difficult to extend to such oils the scope of application of the Fund Convention. An alternative proposal[20] had been that of adopting a more general definition, in which reference would be made only to 'hydrocarbon oils'. Since the majority had supported the reference to 'persistent oil',[21] that addition was adopted.

2.4 The notion of pollution damage

'Pollution damage' was defined in art. 1(6) of the CLC 1969:

6 'Pollution damage' means loss or damage caused outside the ship carrying oil by contamination resulting from the escape or discharge of oil from the ship, wherever such escape or discharge may occur, and includes the costs of preventive measures and further loss or damage caused by preventive measures.

At the Conference held in 1984 for the revision of the CLC 1969 and the Fund Convention of 1971 that definition was considered by the Committee of the Whole II in charge of the revision of the CLC and the following text was adopted:

---

16 Summary Record of the third meeting of the Committee of the Whole (LEG/CONF.6/C.2/SR.3, p. 5).

17 Summary Record, *supra*, note 16, p. 9.

18 *Ibid.*, p. 9.

19 *Ibid.*, p. 6.

20 By Canada, Summary Record, *supra*, note 16, p. 10.

21 Summary Record, *supra*, note 16, p. 15.

OIL POLLUTION DAMAGE CONVENTION, 1992

6 'Pollution damage' means:

(a) loss or damage caused outside the ship by contamination resulting from the escape or discharge of oil from the ship, wherever such escape or discharge may occur, <u>provided that compensation for impairment of the environment other than loss of profit from such impairment shall be limited to costs of reasonable measures of reinstatement actually undertaken or to be undertaken;</u>

(b) the costs of preventive measures and further loss or damage caused by preventive measures.

The first part of the definition, that is not underlined, has remained unchanged and the following general comments may be made on it.

(i) The terms 'loss' and 'damage' are used in a great many conventions and, therefore their interpretation may be based, in addition to the context in which they are used in this provision, on their general meaning in all conventions. 'Damage' has a physical connotation, even though it may also entail a loss, as it appears from the second part of the definition, in which reference is made to the impairment of the environment, which may consist of damage but the subsequent words 'other than loss of profit from such impairment' indicate that it may have economic consequences other than those connected with the reinstatement of the environment. 'Loss' instead may consist in a physical loss or in a financial loss.

(ii) The location where the loss or damage may occur is indicated by way of exclusion: it must occur outside the ship, and consequently any loss or damage that may occur on board the ship is not relevant for the purposes of this Convention.

(iii) The cause of the loss or damage is contamination by oil as defined in art. 1(5) and contamination implies a physical alteration of something outside the ship: it may be the environment or another ship or craft, etc.

(iv) The oil which causes the contamination must have escaped or have been discharged from a ship, as defined in art. 1.1. The escape is natural, as is the case where the hull is breached by the ship stranding on rocks or colliding with another ship. The discharge requires an intentional act, such as the opening of a valve; however it would appear that the term 'discharge' is meant in the OPRC Convention to cover also the escape of oil from a ship.

(v) The place where the escape or discharge occurs is irrelevant, but the loss or damage caused by the contamination is subject to the CLC, pursuant to art. II, only if it is caused in the territory or in the exclusive economic zone of a Contracting State.

The second underlined part of the definition was worded as follows in the draft prepared by the Legal Committee:

(b) economic loss actually sustained as a direct result of contamination as set out in (a).[22]

---

22 The wording of sub-para. (a) was that of the original text in the Convention of 1969.

Although it had been stated[23] that the existing definition covered also damage to the environment, it was stressed[24] that an express reference to costs arising out from the restoration of the environment was needed. The United Kingdom had made the following comment on that draft definition:[25]

10   The UK would favour the development of a more precise definition of pollution damage, but would be concerned if this were to eliminate types of claims which are generally accepted as legitimate at present. It is for consideration whether the desired result would not be achieved even with the present definition, by the addition of a proviso to CLC Article III.1 as follows:
'Provided that compensation for reinstatement of the environment shall not exceed the costs of reasonable measures actually undertaken or to be undertaken.'

After a debate it was decided to instruct a working group to consider the possible wording of the global definition of pollution damage and two alternative definitions were prepared, in which the relevant part relating to compensation for reinstatement of the environment was identical, its terms being as follows:[26]

provided that compensation for impairment of the environment other than loss of profit from such impairment shall be limited to costs of reasonable measures of reinstatement actually undertaken or to be undertaken.

The subsequent debate obviously had as its object the initial part of the two definitions and no comment of interest was made in respect of the second part quoted above, that was adopted by the Committee of the Whole at its sixteenth meeting.[27] The only change as respects the draft submitted by the United Kingdom has been, therefore, the addition of the words 'other than loss of profit from such impairment', that is not related to the cost of reinstatement. It, is, however, related to the time required for the reinstatement of the environment and the question arises whether the failure to take a timely action for such reinstatement might affect the claim for the loss caused by the environmental damage.

Recourse to the concept of reasonability is made in international conventions in all situations in which it is impossible to provide a specific description.[28]

'Preventive measures' are defined in art. I(7) as:

7   'Preventive measures' means any reasonable measures taken by any person after an incident has occurred to prevent or minimize pollution damage.

---

23 By Canada, during the fourth meeting of the Committee of the Whole: LEG/CONF.6/C.2/SR.4, p. 2.
24 By Poland: LEG/CONF.6/C.2/SR.4, p. 2.
25 Official Records, *supra* note 16, vol. 1, p. 365.
26 CONF.6/C. 2/2, Official Records, *supra* note 16, vol. 2, p. 188.
27 Official Records, *supra* note 16, vol. 2, p. 491.
28 On the notion of reasonableness and the use of this term in international conventions see F. Berlingieri, 'Flexibility, foreseeability, reasonableness and other relevant instruments', paper delivered at the VII European Colloquium on Maritime Law Research, published in (2013) Dir. Mar. 1017 and in Marius No. 424 (2013), 69. For a specific analysis of the notion of reasonableness as used in the definitions of 'pollution damage' and 'preventive measures' in the CLC 1992, applicable also to the Fund Convention 1992 pursuant to its art. 1(2), see Jacobsson, 'The International Liability and Compensation Regime for Oil Pollution from Ships – International Solutions for a Global Problem', (2007) *Tulane Maritime Law Journal*, 1, p. 21.

This definition has been kept unvaried since it had been adopted in the draft article submitted by the Legal Committee to the 1969 Conference and does not appear to require any comment.

3 THE GEOGRAPHICAL SCOPE OF THE CONVENTION

Art. II so provides:

This Convention shall apply exclusively:
(a) to pollution damage caused:
  (i) in the territory, including the territorial sea, of a Contracting State, and
  (ii) in the exclusive economic zone of a Contracting State, established in accordance with international law, or, if a Contracting State has not established such a zone, in an area beyond and adjacent to the territorial sea of that State determined by that State in accordance with international law and extending not more than 200 nautical miles from the baselines from which the breadth of its territorial sea is measured;
(b) to preventive measures, wherever taken, to prevent or minimize such damage.

The CLC 1969 provided in art. II that the Convention applied exclusively to pollution damage caused in the territory including the territorial sea of a Contracting State and to preventive measures taken to prevent or minimise such damage. When the geographical scope was discussed in Committee II of the Conference held in March 1984, by which the draft revision of the CLC Convention was being considered, that issue had already been discussed in Committee I in respect of the draft HNS Convention. Committee I favourably considered the need for widening the scope of application of the draft beyond the territorial sea to the exclusive economic zone, on the ground that accidents involving hazardous and noxious substances were likely to occur beyond the territorial sea.[29] However, in the draft revision of the CLC 1969 prepared by the Legal Committee the following new, rather vague, text of art. II had been suggested:[30]

This Convention shall apply exclusively:

(a) to pollution damage caused on the territory, including the territorial sea, of a Contracting State [or in the area in which, under international law, a Contracting State may exercise sovereign rights over natural resources], and
(b) to preventive measures, wherever taken, to prevent or minimize such damage.

That draft had given rise to a prolonged debate between delegations that supported the maintenance of the original text of art. II and those that instead deemed it necessary to extend the scope of the Convention to the exclusive economic zone. The former stated, *inter alia*, that the concept of pollution damage under the CLC was not the same as under the HNS Convention,[31] that while in the context of the

---

29 LEG/CONF.6/C.1/SR.4, paras. 58–98; LEG/CONF.6/C.1/SR.5, paras. 1–27; LEG/CONF.6/C.1/SR.6, paras. 18–30 and LEG/CONF.6/C.1/SR.8, paras. 23 and 24.

30 Official Records of the International Conference on Liability and Compensation for Damage in Connection with the Carriage of Certain Substances by Sea, 1984 and the International Conference on the Revision of the 1969 Civil Liability Convention and the 1971 Fund Convention, 1992, vol. 1, p. 57, at p. 59.

31 Official Records, *supra*, note 16, vol. 2, p. 364, para. 13.

HNS Convention it was clear that hazardous and noxious substances might cause significant damage beyond the territorial sea, in the case of oil no such evidence was available.[32] The latter stated, *inter alia*, that it was impossible to ignore that UNCLOS provided for States to exercise their jurisdiction in the EEZ in order to preserve the marine environment,[33] that there are States, such as the United States, that have substantial natural marine resources in areas beyond the territorial sea[34] and that generally States were making increasing use of the waters outside the territorial seas: consequently there was no reason why pollution damage to such waters should not be recognised in the same way as damage to the territorial sea.[35] Some of the delegations that favoured the extension of the scope of application beyond the territorial sea suggested, however, that while supporting in principle the text in square brackets in the draft, a clearer interpretation of the extension might be developed by the working group.[36] After discussions on the geographical scope had taken place in an informal working group composed by the delegations (that appeared to be the majority) which were in favour of expanding the geographical application of the CLC, the following draft text[37] was approved by a large majority[38] of the delegations:

This Convention shall apply exclusively:

1. To pollution damage caused:
    (a)   in the territory, including the territorial sea, of a Contracting State;
    (b)   in the exclusive economic zone of a Contracting State; and
    (c)   on the continental shelf of a Contracting State, including artificial islands, installations and structures under the jurisdiction of that Contracting State in accordance with international law.
2. To preventive measures, wherever taken, to prevent or minimize such damage.

However, as a consequence of subsequent discussions on the provision under (c), it was agreed to delete it on the understanding that the Drafting Committee would consider it so as to meet the concerns of those delegations which could not accept the expression 'exclusive economic zone'.[39] That was done by adding, for the benefit of the States that had not established an exclusive economic zone, a reference to an area beyond and adjacent to the territorial sea of the relevant State determined by that State extending no more than 200 nautical miles from the baselines from which the breadth of the territorial sea is measured: an area, therefore, the breadth of which corresponds to the maximum extension of the exclusive economic zone pursuant to art. 57 of UNCLOS.

---

32 *Ibid.*, p. 366, paras. 23–25.
33 *Ibid.*, p. 367, para. 35.
34 *Ibid.*, p. 366, para. 28.
35 *Ibid.*, p. 372, para. 71.
36 *Ibid.*, p. 366, para. 29.
37 LEG/CONF.6/C.2/WP.27, Official Records, *supra*, note 16, vol. 2, p. 288.
38 Thirty-four delegations were in favour, 16 were against, with 6 abstentions. Official Records, *supra*, note 16, vol. 2, p. 523.
39 CONF.6/C.2/SR.24, paras. 5–26 (Official Records, *supra*, note 16, vol. 2, pp. 566–568).

OIL POLLUTION DAMAGE CONVENTION, 1992

4 THE PERSON LIABLE FOR THE POLLUTION DAMAGE

4.1 Whether the owner of the ship or the owner of the cargo should be liable

Art. III (1) so provides:

1 Except as provided in paragraphs 2 and 3 of this article, the owner of a ship at the time of an incident, or, where the incident consists of a series of occurrences, at the time of the first such occurrence, shall be liable for any pollution damage caused by the ship as a result of the incident.

The issue of whether the owner of the ship or the owner of the cargo should be liable for pollution damage and the question of whether liability should be based on fault or be strict had been the object of debate at the Conference. Four alternatives were put forward: (a) strict liability of the ship, (b) liability of the ship based on fault, (c) strict liability of the cargo and (d) joint strict liability on ship and cargo with first liability up to a fixed amount on ship and the remaining liability on cargo.[40] The alternative under (d) received particular attention when it was combined with the proposal, submitted by Belgium, as a supplement (or an alternative) to the liability of the cargo, of the establishment of an international fund for the compensation of pollution damage.[41] The subsequent issue to be considered was that relating to the order in which the claimants should address their claims against the ship and the fund and out of the alternatives put forward, that pursuant to which the claimants should address their claims first to the ship and, once the limit of liability had been exhausted, against the fund, was chosen.[42] There followed further discussions on the basis of liability, and on the possible adoption of a Fund Convention concurrently with the Civil Liability Convention and when it appeared that, although the Working Group set up by the Committee of the Whole had submitted a report,[43] such adoption would have not been possible within the time allowed for the completion of the work of the Conference, it was agreed to finalise the work for the Civil Liability Convention and, on the basis of a proposal of the Scandinavian delegations, to adopt a resolution whereby IMCO be requested to convene, not later than the year 1971, an International Legal Conference for the establishment of an international fund.[44]

4.2 The definition of owner of the ship

The owner of a ship is defined in art. I(3) as:

3. 'Owner' means the person or persons registered as the owner of the ship or, in the absence of registration, the person or persons owning the ship. However in the case of a ship owned by a State and operated by a company which in that State is registered as the ship's operator, 'owner' shall mean such company.

---

40 Official Records, *supra*, note 2, pp. 647–648.
41 Document LEG/CONF/C.2/WP.2, Official Records, *supra*, note 2, p. 553.
42 Official Records, *supra*, note 2, p. 674.
43 LEG/CONF/C.2/WP.45; Official Records, *supra*, note 2, p. 604.
44 LEG/CONF/C.2/WP.44, Official Records, *supra*, note 2, p. 603.

In the course of the debates on whether liability should rest on the owner of the ship or of the cargo, reference was frequently made to liability of the ship or of the cargo. But when it had been decided that liability should rest on the ship, the alternative as to whether the registered owner or the operator ought to be liable was considered and although several delegates were of the view that the person liable ought to be the operator,[45] rather than the owner, it was pointed out that claimants could easily identify the registered owner, but not the operator, for in the majority of maritime countries the name of the operator is not mentioned in the ships register and, therefore, it was agreed that it would have been preferable to place the liability on the registered owner. It was, however, pointed out by the delegate of the USSR that in the socialist countries, the owner was the State and the operator a State-owned company and that consequently, liability for the operation rested on such latter company.[46] In order to take that situation into account it was decided to provide in the definition that where a ship is owned by a State and is operated by a company which is registered as the operator, 'owner', for the purposes of the Convention, would mean such company.

4.3 The rule on the channelling of liability[47]

In the draft of art. III prepared by Working Group II of the IMCO Legal Committee convened on January 7, 1969, that rule was worded as follows:[48]

4 No claim for compensation for pollution damage shall be made against the owner otherwise than in accordance with this Convention.
5 Nothing in this Convention shall prejudice the question whether a person liable for damage in accordance with its provisions has a right of recourse against any other person.

In the Draft Articles prepared by the Legal Committee and submitted to the Diplomatic Conference held from 10 to 26 November 1969 paragraphs 4 and 5 of art. III, which had become art. II (3),were merged into one single paragraph worded as follows:[49]

3 No claim for compensation for pollution damage shall be made against the owner otherwise than in accordance with the provisions of this Convention. No claim for pollution damage, under this Convention or otherwise, may be made against the servants or agents of the owner.

During the Diplomatic Conference held in November 1969 the Delegation of the Netherlands proposed an amendment to draft art. II(3)[50] consisting in the

---

45 Official Records, *supra*, note 2, p. 692.

46 *Ibid.*, p. 693.

47 The expression 'channelling of liability' has been used during the discussions because it was considered that only the owner, with the exclusion of his servants or agents and subsequently also of other persons that participated in the operation of the ship, should be liable, *inter alia*, in order to avoid a duplication of liability insurances. That, of course, entailed a prohibition of bringing claims against such other persons, but although this regime has been also qualified as a prohibition of action (see Måns Jacobsson, 'The International Liability and Compensation regime for Oil Pollution from Ships – International Solutions for a Global Problem', *supra*, note 28, p. 5), it has been deemed more appropriate to consider the problem from the standpoint of the persons who must be held liable, rather from that of the persons who instead should not be held liable.

48 The Report is also published in the CMI Documentation 1960-III, p. 90.

49 Official Records, *supra*, note 2, p. 459.

50 In document LEG/CONF/4/Add.6 of 19 November 1969, Official Records, *supra* note 2, p. 544.

OIL POLLUTION DAMAGE CONVENTION, 1992

addition, after 'servants or agents', of the words 'independent contractors'. In turn the Japanese Delegation proposed an amendment[51] consisting in the replacement of the draft text of art. II(3) with the following text:

No claim for compensation for pollution damage shall be made against the person or persons for whose action the owner shall be liable in accordance with the provision of paragraph 1 of the present article.

After both amendments had been rejected, draft art. II(3) became, without any change, paragraph 4 of art. III of the Convention adopted by the Diplomatic Conference.

Subsequently, after the entry into force of the CLC 1969, on 19 June 1975, the channelling of liability was discussed by an Informal Working Group that met in Washington at the invitation of the Government of the United States to consider a possible revision of the CLC 1969 and of the Fund Convention 1971. From the Report of the Chairman[52] it appears that while the organisations representing the oil industry and shipping and insurance interests were of the opinion that the CLC and the Fund Convention should constitute a comprehensive, simple and all-inclusive regime for compensation for pollution damage, and that it was particularly important that a more extensive channelling be introduced,[53] some delegations were opposed to the introduction in the CLC of channelling to a larger extent than presently provided in art. III.

A second Informal Meeting was held in Stockholm from 7 to 11 December 1981. In the Report[54] it was stated that after an exchange of views on the issue of channelling of liability the meeting decided to submit the following new wording of art. III(4) for consideration by IMCO, indicating that the text was drafted on the basis of the corresponding text of art. 3.5 of the draft Convention on Liability and Compensation in Connexion with Carriage of Noxious and Hazardous Substances by Sea:[55]

---

51 In document LEG/CONF/C.2/WP.31 of 23 November 1969, Official Records, *supra*, note 2, p. 593.

52 Report of the Chairman of the Informal Working Group on the revision of the Civil Liability Convention and the Fund Convention, IMO document LEG XLVI/3/1 of 15 July 1981.

53 The following statement is made in the Report (para. 49):

> It was in their view particularly important that channelling was introduced in the Civil Liability Convention as regards bareboat charterers, but there was a need to protect also other persons, e.g. salvors and those taking preventive measures, from claims for pollution damage. It was suggested that such a system of channelling of liability had the advantage of eliminating the need for persons other than the shipowner to take out insurance for oil pollution damage.

54 Report of the Chairman of the Second Informal Meeting on the revision of the Civil Liability Convention and the Fund Convention, IMCO document LEG 48/2/2 of 22 January 1982.

55 The discussion on the channelling of liability was summarised as follows in paras. 80–82:

> 80. The meeting considered whether the Civil Liability Convention should be amended so as to provide for channelling of liability to the shipowner to a larger extent than currently provided (art. III.4 and 5).
> 81. A number of participants expressed themselves in favour of introducing more far-reaching channelling of liability in the Convention. It was suggested that a system of channelling of liability had the advantage of eliminating the need for persons other than the shipowner to take out insurance for pollution damage. The observers representing oil industry, shipping and insurance interests supported this view, as they considered that the Civil Liability and Fund Conventions should constitute a comprehensive, simple and all-inclusive regime for compensation for pollution damage and that no claim for compensation

No claim for pollution damage under this Convention or otherwise may be made against:

(a) the servants or agents of the owner or the members of the crew;
(b) the pilot or any other person who, without being a member of the crew, performs services for the ship;
(c) the charterer, manager or operator;
(d) any person performing salvage operations with the consent of the owner;
(e) any person performing salvage operations on the instructions of a competent public authority;
(f) any person taking preventive measures;
(g) all servants or agents of persons mentioned in sub-paragraphs (c), (d), (e) and (f) unless the damage resulted from their act or omission, committed with the intent to cause such damage or recklessly and with knowledge that such loss would probably result.

The channelling of liability was subsequently discussed during the 48th session of the Legal Committee in March 1982. From the Report of that session[56] it appears that opposite views existed in respect of the extension of the channelling provision of CLC 1969, but that it was ultimately agreed to retain, with brackets, the text proposed by the Informal Working Group. The position of the bareboat charterer was the object of considerable discussion, some delegates being in favour of the concept of joint and several liabilities for the owner and the bareboat charterer, while others were against and no consensus was reached on this question.

The text prepared by the Informal Working Group appears, still in brackets, in a Note by the IMCO Secretariat of 6 May 1982[57] and in the Report of the third meeting of the Informal Working Group held at IMO from 2 to 4 June 1982.[58]

Following a proposal by the CMI,[59] the issue relating to bareboat charterers was decided by adding in art. III(4)(c) an express reference to them as well as to managers and operators. The text of sub-paragraph (c) was, therefore, amended as follows:

(c) any charterer (howsoever described, including bareboat charterers), manager and operator.

Except for that change, the revised text of art. III(4)(c) as drafted by the Informal Working Group was adopted by the Legal Committee and included in the draft Protocol submitted to the Diplomatic Conference.

During the Diplomatic Conference draft art. 4(3) of the Protocol, setting out the amended text of art. III(4) of the CLC, was considered in the course of the

---

should be allowed outside these Conventions. It was in their view particularly important that channelling was introduced as regards bareboat charterers. Some participants considered that other persons also needed protection from claims for pollution damage (e.g. salvors and those taking preventive measures).
82. Some participants were of the view that the question of channelling was linked with the increase of the amounts laid down in the two Conventions. A system of channelling of liability deprived victims of the right to make claims against persons other than the shipowner, and in their view a far-reaching channelling could be accepted only if the revised limitation amounts were sufficiently high.

56 Report of the Legal Committee on the work of its forty-eighth session, document LEG/48/6 of 19 March 1982.
57 Document LEG 49/3 of 6 May 1982, Annex 1.
58 Report of the Chairman of the Third Informal Meeting on the revision of the 1969 Civil Liability Convention and the 1971 Fund Convention, document LEG 49/3/1 of 26 July 1982.
59 Position Paper submitted by the CMI, document LEG 50/4/10 of 18 February 1983, para. 28. See also Report of the Legal Committee of the work of its fiftieth session, document LEG 50/8 of 17 March 1983.

11th meeting of the Committee of the Whole. Several delegates, including those of Canada, United Kingdom and United States, stated that there was a close link between the channelling of liability and the liability limits and that they were willing to favourably consider the draft provision on channelling, provided the limits to be adopted were high. After three proposals of amendments to the draft prepared by the Legal Committee had been rejected,[60] that draft was adopted without any change, with the deletion of all square brackets.[61]

The 1984 Protocol never entered into force owing to the strict conditions required for its entry into force and was replaced by the 1992 Protocol, which contains the same substantive provisions of the 1984 Protocol.

The groups of persons listed in art. III(4) will be considered *seriatim*.

(a)   the servants or agents of the owner or the members of the crew;

The terms 'servants' and 'agents' may have a variety of meanings in civil and common law. It is suggested, however, that for the purposes of this Convention the term 'servant' (*préposé* in the French text of the Convention) connotes a person who acts in the course of his employment and the consequences of his action entail the responsibility of the principal pursuant to the rule *respondeat superior*. The term 'agent' may have different meanings in English law, but the relevant meaning in this Convention is given by the use in the French text of the term '*mandataire*', which connotes a person who acts on behalf of another. Basically the servant performs physical work, while the agent performs intellectual work and assumes obligations on behalf of his principal.[62]

The term 'crew' in common parlance indicates the ratings: clause 10(b) of Barecon 2001 provides that 'the Master, officers and crew of the vessel shall be the servants of the Charterers'. However, in civil law countries the corresponding term *equipage, equipaje, equipaggio* includes all personnel on board a ship: master, officers and crew.

---

60 Official Records, *supra* note 8, vol. 2, p. 437.

61 A similar rule on channelling was subsequently adopted in the Convention on Civil Liability for Damage Caused during Carriage of Dangerous Goods by Road, Rail and Inland Navigation Vessels (CRDT), art. 5(7) of which provides:

> 7 Subject to paragraph 9 of this article and to articles 6 and 7, no claim for compensation for damage under this Convention or otherwise may be made against:
> (a) the servants or agents of the carrier or the members of the crew;
> (b) the pilot of the ship or any other person who, without being a member of the crew, performs services for the vehicle;
> (c) the owner, hirer, charterer, user, manager or operator of the vehicle, provided that he is not the carrier;
> (d) any person performing salvage operations with the consent of the owner of the ship:
> (e) any person performing salvage operations on instruction of a competent public authority;
> (f)   any person other than the carrier taking preventive measures for damage caused by those measures;
> (g) any servants or agents of the persons mentioned under (b), (c), (d), (e) and (f),
> unless the damage resulted from their personal act or omission, committed with intent to cause such damage or recklessly and with knowledge that such damage would probably result.

62 The legal nature of the agent is defined in *Halsbury's Laws of England* (4th edn, Vol. 16, p. 313) as follows:

> The terms 'agency' and 'agent' have in popular use a number of different meanings, but in law the word 'agency' is used to connote the relation which exists where one person has an authority or capacity to create legal relations between a person occupying the position of principal and third parties.

It is obvious that in the context of this provision the term 'crew' includes all sea-farers on board a ship.

(b)   the pilot or any other person who, without being a member of the crew, performs services for the ship;

A wide interpretation of this sub-paragraph has been given in what could be described as an *obiter* by the French Cour de Cassation in *The Erika*.[63] The Court in fact stated that although the Court of Appeal had been wrong in holding that a classification society could not benefit of the provisions of art. III(4) of CLC 1992, that benefit should be excluded anyhow because the classification society had committed a *'faute de témérité'*,[64] thereby intending to refer in an abridged form to the action that pursuant to art. V(2) of CLC 1992 entails the loss of the right to limit. The action, described in the English text of the CLC 1992 as 'committed . . . recklessly and with knowledge that such damage would probably occur', is described in the French text as *'commis témèrairement et avec conscience qu'en tel dommage en résulterait probable-ment'*. The Court did not provide any explanation why a classification society could enjoy the protection of art. III(4) and which of its sub-paragraphs would have been applicable. In any event it appears that the statement quoted above has no basis.[65] In fact the category of other persons performing services for the ship, theoretically very wide, is limited twice in the context of this provision. First, it is limited because the person who performs services for the ship is a person *other* than the pilot, and that clearly indicates, pursuant to the *ejusdem generis* rule, that such other person must have a legal relationship with the owner pursuant to which he performs services for the ship similar to those of the pilot. Secondly, it is limited because such other person must be a person performing services for the ship 'without being a member of the crew'. That means that such person, although not a member of the crew, per-forms services similar to those performed by the crew: such services must, therefore, be performed on board the ship in the course of navigation, such as the services of the hotel personnel.[66] This is confirmed by the separate reference under (c) to the

---

63 Cour de Cassation 25 September 2012, (2012) DMF 985.

64 The statement made by the Court (at p. 992) was as follows:

> Attendu que, si c'est à tort que l'arrêt énonce qu'une société de classification ayant délivré des certificats de classe en exécution d'un contrat avec l'armateur ne peut bénéficier de la canalisation, cette décision n'encourt pas la censure dès lors que la faute retenue au titre de l'action publique contre cette société caractérise une faute de témérité au sens de la Convention CLC 69/92, qui la prive nécessairement de la possibilité d'invoquer un tel bénéfice et rend par là même les critiques inopérantes; d'où il suit que le moyen doit être écarté..
>
> *Whereas, although the judgment had wrongly stated that a classification society that has issued a class certificate in the performance of a contract with the operator cannot benefit from the channelling, that decision does not incur a blame since the fault established in the public action against that company has the character of a reckless fault under the CLC 69/92, that necessarily excludes the possibility of invoking that benefit and makes the criticisms inoperative; it follows therefrom that the ground of appeal must be rejected.*

65 This view has been held by P. Bonassies, 'L'arrêt Erika' (2012 Dir. Mar. 1271) and F. Berlingieri, 'Les sociétés de classification peuvent-elles bénéficier de la canalisation prévue à l'article III.2 de la CLC 1992?' (2012 DMF 1015).

66 Under the shipowner's traditional Protection & Indemnity (P&I) insurance coverage for third-party liability claims, besides the crew, operates for persons aboard the vessel or who are otherwise involved in the navigation of the vessel on a voyage and the risks covered are reflected in the premium paid by the shipowner. Such other persons, besides hotel staff, include, for example, passengers, the

manager and operator who are definitely persons performing services in connection with the operation of the ship, but ashore and not on board.

(c)   any charterer (howsoever described, including bareboat charterers), manager and operator;

From the *travaux préparatoires* it appears that all types of charterers are included, such as, in addition to the bareboat charterer, the time and voyage charterer as well as, probably, the slot charterer. Reference to manager and operator is also made in the LLMC Convention 1976 as persons who, together with the owner, can invoke the benefit of limitation of liability. Manager is the person or company who takes care of the management of the ship as agent for the owner (or operator). Operator is the person, other than the owner, who operates the ship for his own account, normally on the basis of a bareboat charter party; if that is the case, channelling is already granted by the reference to the bareboat charterer.

(d)   any person performing salvage operations with the consent of the owner or on the instructions of a competent public authority;

The salvor already enjoys the benefit of the general limitation of liability under the 1989 Salvage Convention and the protection under CLC 1992 is granted for similar reasons. There are, however, situations where, although the salvor is entitled to a reward, he may not have the protection granted by this provision. In fact, salvage operations may take place without the consent of the owner of the salved vessel and even in case of prohibition of the owner, provided such prohibition is not reasonable.

(e)   any person taking preventive measures;[67]

The scope of this provision is clear, 'preventive measures' being defined in art. I(7) of CLC 1992.

(f)   all servants or agents of persons mentioned in subparagraphs (c), (d) and (e);

The terms 'servants or agents' must obviously have the same meaning as in sub-paragraph (a) and the fact that reference in this sub-paragraph (f) is not made to sub-paragraph (b) confirms that the persons to whom reference is made in such latter sub-paragraph are individuals.

5 THE BASIS OF LIABILITY

The debate on the basis of the liability for pollution damage took place jointly with that on whom, either the owner of the ship or the owner of the cargo, should be liable, and that whether liability should be limited or not. A compromise solution was found, at the end of a long debate, when it was agreed to make first the shipowner liable, but only for a limited amount, and the damage in excess of the

---

pilot, tugs used for towing or docking and salvors who are considered borrowed servants. Including such persons is consistent with the goal of the CLC to avoid duplicate insurances.

67 Under CLC art. 1 '"preventive measures" means any reasonable measures taken by any person after an incident has occurred to prevent or minimize pollution damage'.

limit being borne by an international fund. It was also agreed that the liability of the owner should be strict.[68] Strict, but not absolute. Arts III(2) and (3) state:

2   No liability for pollution damage shall attach to the owner if he proves that the damage:

    (a) resulted from an act of war, hostilities, civil war, insurrection or a natural phenomenon of an exceptional, inevitable and irresistible character, or

    (b) was wholly caused by an act or omission done with intent to cause damage by a third party, or

    (c) was wholly caused by the negligence or other wrongful act of any Government or other authority responsible for the maintenance of lights or other navigational aids in the exercise of that function.

3   If the owner proves that the pollution damage resulted wholly or partially either from an act or omission done with intent to cause damage by the person who suffered the damage or from the negligence of that person, the owner may be exonerated wholly or partially from his liability to such person.

Paragraph 2(a), which consists of two entirely different series of events that are beyond the control of the owner, originates from the following text in alternative B of the draft articles prepared by the Secretariat:[69]

No liability shall attach to the owner with respect to pollution damage resulting directly from an act of war, hostilities, civil war, insurrection or a grave natural disaster of an exceptional character.

While the first series of events has not given rise to significant comments, in respect of the second – 'a grave natural disaster of an exceptional character' – there has been a proposal of amendment by the USSR,[70] to replace the words 'grave natural disaster of an exceptional character', by 'natural phenomenon of an unforeseeable, inevitable and irresistible character' that was supported by the United States[71] which however suggested the inclusion of the term 'exceptional', and by Italy[72] which instead suggested to delete the term 'unforeseeable' and both such amendments were approved. The changes in the USSR text, evidenced by the following, are significant for the correct interpretation of the second part of sub-paragraph (a):

natural phenomenon of an **exceptional** ~~unforeseeable~~, inevitable and irresistible character

The term 'exceptional' indicates that the inevitable and irresistible character of a natural phenomenon is not sufficient in order to exonerate the owner from liability. A ship sailing across the ocean cannot avoid a storm, but this should not by itself justify the owner's exoneration from liability, for storms are ordinary events in the seas and the term 'irresistible' may simply qualify a storm as being strong: but again this should not suffice to exonerate the owner when his liability is strict. It is instead the exceptional character of the storm that marks the difference between ordinary and extraordinary events.

---

68 Official Records, *supra*, note 2, pp. 674 and 676.
69 Official Records, *supra*, note 2, p. 578.
70 *Ibid.*, p. 601.
71 *Ibid.*, p. 742.
72 *Ibid.*

Paragraph 2(b) was not included in the draft articles prepared by the Legal Committee and was added following a proposal of the United Kingdom[73] as a complement to the exemption in respect of pollution damage resulting from act or omission by the person who suffered damage, that instead did appear in the draft articles.[74] The difference, that did not exist in the proposal but does exist in the final text, is that while the intentional act is required in respect of an act of a third party, in respect of an act of the person who suffered the damage, the negligent character of the act suffices.

Also paragraph 2(c) was not included in the draft articles prepared by the Legal Committee and was added following a proposal from the United Kingdom,[75] which does not appear to have been the object of any objection or discussion. It has instead been the object of a decision in the *Tsesis* case by the Swedish Supreme Court (Högsta Domstolen)[76] that held that nautical charts are navigational aids for the purposes of this provision, with the consequent exoneration of liability of the owner of a tanker who went aground on a rock that had not been marked on the chart issued by the Swedish Hydrographic Office.

Paragraph 3 in its original wording restricted the exemption from liability only to the case where pollution resulted from an act or omission of the person who had suffered damage done with the intent to cause damage.[77] A rather unlikely event. The alternative reference also to the negligence of that person had been suggested by the USSR,[78] and that suggestion was approved during the eighteenth meeting of the Committee of the Whole.

In all the situations covered by paragraph 2 and in that covered by paragraph 3, the burden of proof is on the owner.

6 THE LIMITATION OF LIABILITY OF THE OWNER

6.1 The limit of liability

Under art. V of the CLC 1969 the limit of liability was 2,000 units of account for each ton of the ship's tonnage, but the aggregate amount of the limit could not exceed 210 million units of account – an amount that would be the limit for a tanker of 105,000 GT. Therefore the gradual increase would occur only up to ships of such tonnage. The original unit of account, as in the LLMC Convention 1976,[79] was 'a unit consisting of 65.5 milligrams of gold of millesimal fineness 900', called 'franc Poincaré'; this was replaced in the Protocol of 1976 by the Special Drawing Right (SDR), a unit of account created by the International Monetary Fund, and the conversion was made on the basis of the ratio between the gold content of the

---

73 *Ibid.*, p. 597.

74 Alternative B(3), Official Records, *supra*, note 2, p. 520.

75 Official Records, *supra*, note 2, p. 597.

76 *Sweden* v *Latvian Shipping*, 13 January 1983, (1984) Dir. Mar. 381. For an analysis of this judgment see also C. de la Rue and C. B. Anderson, *Shipping and the Environment, supra*, note 1, p. 89.

77 Alternative B (3), Official Records, *supra*, note 2, p. 520.

78 Official Records, *supra*, note 2, p. 601.

79 Volume II, Part V, Chapter 11, para. 8.

two moneys of account, such ratio being 15. The limit per ton thus became 133 SDRs and the global maximum liability 14 million SDRs. The previous unit of account was still maintained for Contracting States which were not members of the International Monetary Fund, whose law did not permit the application of the Special Drawing Right.[80]

Pursuant to art. V(10) for the purpose of calculating the limit of liability the tonnage of the ship was, as in the Limitation Convention of 1957,[81] the net tonnage of the ship with the addition of the amount deducted from the gross tonnage on account of the engine room space for the purpose of ascertaining the net tonnage.[82]

The 1992 Protocol brought about significant changes to the above provisions: for all ships not exceeding 5,000 units of tonnage the limit became 4,510,000 SDRs; for ships with a tonnage in excess thereof, 631 SDRs would be added for each ton in excess, but the aggregate amount could not exceed 89,770,000 SDRs. That amount would be the limit for a tanker of 135,118 GT: therefore the gradual increase would occur only up to ships of such tonnage. That would not adversely affect the persons who have suffered damage from the pollution, for the global losses in excess of that sum would be settled by the International Fund, within the limits of the amount of compensation available at the relevant time.[83]

Furthermore, the method of calculating the tonnage was changed. Art. V(10) states:

10   For the purpose of this article the ship's tonnage shall be the gross tonnage calculated in accordance with the tonnage measurement regulations contained in Annex I of the International Convention on Tonnage Measurement of Ships, 1969.

The gross tonnage calculated pursuant to that Convention is almost certainly greater than the tonnage calculated with the method adopted pursuant to art. V(10) of the CLC 1969.[84]

The rules on the conversion into national currency of the limits are set out in art. V(9) which provides:

The amounts mentioned in paragraph 1 shall be converted into national currency on the basis of the value of that currency by reference to the Special Drawing Right on the date of the constitution of the fund referred to in paragraph 3. The value of the national currency, in terms of the Special Drawing Right, of a Contracting State which is a member of the International Monetary Fund shall be calculated in accordance with the method of valuation applied by the International Monetary Fund in effect on the date in question for its operations and transactions. The value of the national currency, in terms of the Special Drawing Right, of a Contracting State which is not a member of the International Monetary Fund shall be calculated in a manner determined by that State.

---

80 As of 31 March 2014 only two of the States Parties to the CLC 1992 were not members of the International Monetary Fund: the Cook Islands and Monaco.

81 Volume II, Chapter 11, para. 8.

82 For an analysis of the limitation tonnage and its calculation see also C. de la Rue and C.B. Anderson, *Shipping and the Environment, supra*, note 1, p. 101.

83 *Infra*, Chapter 12 para. 5.3.

84 A table was produced during the LLMC Conference showing sample increase in tonnage due to the measurement in accordance with the 1969 Tonnage Measurement Convention (Vol. II, Chapter 11, note 79), in which, however, mention is made only of dry cargo ships. Probably some indication of the increase for tankers may be provided by the variation in tonnage for an OBO of 73,608 GT, such increase being of 8%.

OIL POLLUTION DAMAGE CONVENTION, 1992

The last provision of this paragraph has a very limited scope of application since as of 31 March 2014, the only States Parties to CLC 1992 not members of the International Monetary Fund were Cook Islands and Monaco.

6.2 The amendment of the limits

Article 15 of the CLC 1992 sets out the procedure for the amendment of the limits, which is structured as follows:

(i) An amendment proposal may be submitted to the Secretary General of IMO by at least one quarter of the States Parties to the Protocol (para. 1).

(ii) The proposal must then be circulated by the Secretary General to all Member States and to all the Contracting States and shall be submitted to the Legal Committee for consideration at a date at least six months after the date of circulation (para. 2).

(iii) All Contracting States, whether or not Members of IMO, shall be entitled to participate in the proceeding of the Legal Committee for consideration and adoption of the amendment (para. 3).

(iv) Amendments shall be adopted by a two-thirds majority of the Contracting States present and voting in the Legal Committee, provided that at least one half of the Contracting States shall be present at the time of voting.

(v) Any amendment adopted will be notified to all Contracting States and shall be deemed to have been accepted after eighteen months after the date of notification (para.7).

(vi) Such amendment deemed to have been accepted shall enter into force eighteen months after its acceptance (para. 8).

A proposal to increase the limits of liability[85] adopted with the Protocol of 1992 was considered by the IMO Legal Committee at its eighty-second session and on 18 October 2000 a resolution[86] was adopted pursuant to which:

- the limit for ships not exceeding 5,000 units of tonnage set in art. V(1) (a) of the Convention, as amended by art. 6(1) of the Protocol of 1992, was increased from 3 million units of account to 4,510,000 units of account;
- the limit of 420 units of account set in art. V(1)(b) for each additional unit of tonnage was increased to 631 units; and
- the ceiling of 59,700,000 units of account was increased to 89,770,000 units.

The increase of the limits has been, therefore, slightly less than 50.24% and, having been deemed accepted on 1 May 2002 since no declaration of non-acceptance by

---

85 In the Report of the Legal Committee (document LEG 8/12 of 6 November 2000), the term used in the table of contents and in the heading of para. J(a) is 'limits of compensation'. This term appears to be inappropriate, as it appears to refer to the right of the victim, rather than to the obligation of the person responsible; the right to compensation is not limited under the CLC, what is limited is the liability of the owner.

86 IMO Resolution LEG.1(82).

the required number of Contracting States had been made, entered into force on 1 November 2003.

6.3 The limitation fund

6.3.1 When and where it must be constituted

Art. V(3) states:

For the purpose of availing himself of the benefit of limitation provided for in paragraph 1 of this article the owner shall constitute a fund for the total sum representing the limit of his liability with the Court or other competent authority of any one of the Contracting States in which action is brought under article IX or, if no action is brought, with any Court or other competent authority in any one of the Contracting States in which an action can be brought under article IX.

While under the LLMC Convention the constitution of the fund is optional, under the CLC it is required in order that the owner may invoke the benefit of the limitation of liability. Three rules are set out in this article in respect of the court or courts in which the fund must be constituted.

(a) If an action has already been brought in a Court having jurisdiction pursuant to art. IX the fund must be constituted with that Court or, if under the *lex fori* the limitation fund must be constituted with a different authority, with such authority.

(b) If various actions have been brought in the Courts of various Contracting States having jurisdiction pursuant to art. IX, the owner may constitute the fund in any one of such Courts.

(c) If no action has yet been brought, the owner may constitute the fund in any one of the Contracting States having jurisdiction pursuant to art. IX.

Article IX(1) provides:

1 Where an incident has caused pollution damage in the territory, including the territorial sea or an area referred to in article II, of one or more Contracting States or preventive measures have been taken to prevent or minimize pollution damage in such territory including the territorial sea or area, actions for compensation may only be brought in the Courts of any such Contracting State or States. Reasonable notice of any such action shall be given to the defendant.

More than one Contracting State may have jurisdiction if either pollution damage has occurred or preventive measures have been taken in the territory, including the territorial sea or exclusive economic zone, or in any of the areas of the relevant States mentioned in art. II(a)(ii). Where one or more actions for compensation have been brought, the owner would be aware of that, and would therefore know where he could constitute the fund. If no action has yet been brought, the owner must carry out enquiries in that respect and would have the burden of proving to the chosen court that it has jurisdiction for the constitution of the fund.

There is no time limit by which the fund must be constituted, but the owner would be interested, in order to exclude actions of the claimants against his assets, in taking such action where it appears that the damages likely to have

OIL POLLUTION DAMAGE CONVENTION, 1992

been caused or to be caused in the future by the pollution exceed the limit of his liability.

6.3.2 How it must be constituted

Art. V(3) states in its last sentence:

The fund can be constituted either by depositing the sum or by producing a bank guarantee or other guarantee, acceptable under the legislation of the Contracting State where the fund is constituted, and considered to be adequate by the Court or other competent authority.

The words 'considered to be adequate' refer to the amount. It has been held by the Court of Appeal of Genoa in *The Haven* case[87] that if the fund is provided by means of a bank guarantee, the amount must include interest. Other guarantees, that are considered to be acceptable in various jurisdictions, are those of P&I Clubs members of the International Group.

6.3.3 Bar to other actions

Art. VI states:

1 Where the owner, after an incident, has constituted a fund in accordance with article V, and is entitled to limit his liability:

(a) no person having a claim for pollution damage arising out of that incident shall be entitled to exercise any right against any other assets of the owner in respect of such claim;

(b) the Court or other competent authority of any Contracting State shall order the release of any ship or other property belonging to the owner which has been arrested in respect of a claim for pollution damage arising out of that incident, and shall similarly release any bail or other security furnished to avoid such arrest.

2 The foregoing shall, however, only apply if the claimant has access to the Court administering the fund and the fund is actually available in respect of his claim.

These are the conditions for the operation of this provision: (a) the owner must be entitled to limit his liability; (b) the fund must have been constituted; (c) the claimant who has exercised or intend to exercise his claim on other assets of the owner must have access to the Court administering the fund. The allocation of the burden of proof appears to be the following:

(a) Since the general rule is that the owner is entitled to limit his liability and the burden of proving the loss of such right is on the claimant, this condition is presumed to exist.

(b) The owner who invokes the protection of this provision has the burden of proving that he has constituted a fund with a competent court in the amount and in the manner prescribed by art. V(3).

(c) Since paragraph 2 provides that the bar to other actions applies only if the

---

87 Court of Appeal of Genoa 30 March 1996, *International Oil Pollution Compensation Fund, Venha Maritime Ltd and The United Kingdom Mutual Steam Ship Assurance Association (Bermuda) Ltd v Commune of Varazze and Others* (1996) Dir. Mar. 407.

INTERNATIONAL MARITIME CONVENTIONS

claimant has access to the court administering the fund and such fund is actually available in respect of his claim, the burden of proving that such conditions actually exist is on the owner.

(d) Contrary to what happens in respect of the corresponding provision in the LLMC Convention, pursuant to which the release of a ship or other property already arrested is conditional on the fund having been constituted at one of the places specified in art. 13(2),[88] in the case now under consideration the release must always take place, the reason being that the fund must be constituted with one of the Courts having jurisdiction in respect of actions for compensation pursuant to art. IX or with other authority within such jurisdiction.

7 THE DISTRIBUTION OF THE FUND

The provisions applicable in respect of the distribution of the limitation fund are contained in paragraphs 4 to 8 of art. V. They will be considered *seriatim*.

7.1 **The general rule**

Art. V(4) states:

4 The fund shall be distributed among the claimants in proportion to the amounts of their established claims.

The rule pursuant to which no priority should be recognised in respect of the claims subject to limitation had already been adopted in the Limitation Convention of 1957 and the wording used was the same: the fund must be distributed in proportion to the amounts of the established claims. That wording has subsequently been adopted in the LLMC Convention. The word 'established' indicates that the claim cannot be disputed and, in connection with limitation proceedings, it implies that it has been accepted by the court. The words '*créances admises*' used in the French text of the Convention confirm that: the claims are '*admises*' ('allowed'), by the court administering the fund. Similar wording is used in the Fund Convention. Art. 4(5) so in fact provides:

5 Where the amount of established claims against the Fund exceeds the aggregate amount of compensation payable under paragraph 4, the amount available shall be distributed in such a manner that the proportion between any established claim and the amount of compensation actually recovered by the claimant under this Convention shall be the same for all claimants.

In that provision the word in the French text is not '*admises*' but '*établies*' which literally corresponds to the word 'established'. Probably that is due to the fact that while in the limitation proceedings under the CLC the fund is administered by a Court, under the Fund Convention the aggregate amount of compensation is distributed by the Fund.

---

88 *Supra*, vol. II, Part 5, Chapter 11, para. 10.3.2.

140

7.2 The right of subrogation

Art. V(5) states:

5 If before the fund is distributed the owner or any of his servants or agents or any person providing him insurance or other financial security has as a result of the incident in question, paid compensation for pollution damage, such person shall, up to the amount he has paid, acquire by subrogation the rights which the person so compensated would have enjoyed under this Convention.

This provision is based on that in art. 12(2) of the LLMC Convention which, in turn, is based on that in art. 3(3) of the 1957 Limitation Convention and appears to protect persons who, under the Convention, are liable for the pollution damage. Such persons include the providers of insurance or other financial security against whom a direct action of the claimants is permitted by art. VII(8). After the entry into force of the Protocol of 1992 the reference to servants or agents no longer appears to have any basis in view of the adoption of the new art. III(4), pursuant to which no claim for compensation for pollution damage may be made against the servants or agents of the owner or the members of the crew. It is, in fact, difficult to conceive that a person who is protected by the rules on channelling of liability on the owner (and his insurer) voluntarily pays compensation for pollution damage.
Art. V(6) states:

6 The right of subrogation provided for in paragraph 5 of this article may also be exercised by a person other than those mentioned therein in respect of any amount of compensation for pollution damage which he may have paid but only to the extent that such subrogation is permitted under the applicable national law.

The distinction between this provision and that preceding it is based on the fact that while pursuant to paragraph 6 the right of subrogation is recognised by the Convention, the right of subrogation of persons other than those mentioned in paragraph 5 must be recognised by the applicable law.

7.3 The protection of the owner or other person that may be compelled to effect payment of compensation

Art. V(7) states:

7 Where the owner or any other person establishes that he may be compelled to pay at a later date in whole or in part any such amount of compensation, with regard to which such person would have enjoyed a right of subrogation under paragraphs 5 or 6 of this article, had the compensation been paid before the fund was distributed, the Court or other competent authority of the State where the fund has been constituted may order that a sufficient sum shall be provisionally set aside to enable such person at such later date to enforce his claim against the fund.

The situation covered by this provision differs from that covered by paragraphs 5 and 6 in that in such paragraphs, payment had been made prior to the distribution of the limitation fund, while in this provision, no payment has been made prior to the distribution of the fund, but a payment is likely to be subsequently required.

This provision is identical to that in art. 12(4) of the LLMC Convention, which in turn is based on that in art. 3(4) of the Limitation Convention 1957. As for that in art. 12(4) of the LLMC Convention, this provision is a complement of that in the preceding paragraph 5. However, even if the reference to 'any other person' originally covered all the persons mentioned in the preceding paragraph 5, including the owner's servants or agents, after the adoption of the rule on channelling of liability it can no longer include them.

7.4 Preventive measures taken by the owner

Art. V(8) so provides:

8   Claims in respect of expenses reasonably incurred or sacrifices reasonably made by the owner voluntarily to prevent or minimize pollution damage shall rank equally with other claims against the fund.

The purpose of these measures is the same as that of the preventive measures defined in art. I.7 of the Convention, but their nature is specifically indicated: whilst in fact the preventive measures are defined generically as 'reasonable measures taken to prevent or minimise pollution damage', those taken by the owner must consist of expenses reasonably incurred or sacrifices reasonably made. However, the extent of the cover appears similar to that of the claims for pollution damage, since in the definition of pollution damage there are included under I.6 both the preventive measures and 'further loss or damage caused by preventive measures' and in art. V(8) reference is made to 'sacrifices reasonably made'.

The following provision, almost identical to that in art. V(8), may be found in the last sentence of art. 4(1) of the Fund Convention 1992 as amended:

Expenses reasonably incurred or sacrifices reasonably made by the owner voluntarily to prevent or minimize pollution damage shall be treated as pollution damage for the purposes of this article.

This latter provision does not entail the implied abrogation of that in art. V(8) of the CLC Convention. The owner therefore remains entitled to participate in the distribution of the CLC Fund and then claim the outstanding balance, if any, from the Compensation Fund.

8 THE LOSS OF THE RIGHT TO LIMIT

The rules on the loss of the right to limit liability have become standard since their adoption in the Visby Protocol of 1968 to the 1924 Convention on Bills of Lading (Hague-Visby Rules) on the basis of those adopted in the Hague Protocol of 1955 to the Warsaw Convention of 1929. The only difference that exists in the wording relates to the reference to the damage of which the person liable had knowledge: in some conventions reference is only made to damage while in others reference is made to 'such' damage:[89] the addition of that word clearly restricts the situations in which the loss of the right may occur and renders the burden of proof on the claimant heavier.

---

89 The word 'such' does not appear in the Warsaw Convention of 1929 as amended by the Hague Protocol of 1955 and in the Hague-Visby Rules (Vol. I, Chapter 2, para. 7.1). It appears instead in art.

OIL POLLUTION DAMAGE CONVENTION, 1992

This is the case for the CLC 1992, art. V(2) of which states:

2   The owner shall not be entitled to limit his liability under this Convention if it is proved
    that the pollution damage resulted from his personal act or omission, committed with the
    intent to cause such damage, or recklessly and with knowledge that such damage would
    probably result.

How much heavier the burden of proof may be depends on whether the words 'such damage' mean the specific damage suffered by a specific claimant[90] or generally pollution as defined in art. I(6). Obviously the first alternative would render the operation of art. V(2) impossible and that cannot have been the intention. However, if the knowledge that triggers the loss of the right to limit would relate merely to the fact that the escape or discharge of oil could have caused pollution of the sea, the conditions for the loss of the right to limit would always or almost always materialise, for it is difficult to conceive of a situation where the owner would ignore the possible consequences of the escape or discharge of oil from his ship. It is suggested, therefore, that for the purposes of this Convention, what would trigger the loss of the benefit of limitation and should be proved by the claimants is that the owner acted recklessly in the knowledge that the escape or discharge of oil would probably have entailed pollution damage of the character of that in respect of which claims have been brought.

9 THE LIABILITY INSURANCE

The compulsory insurance of the liability of the shipowner had been one of the basic elements on which the consensus on the draft convention had been reached.[91] The need for the compulsory insurance of the shipowner had already been discussed by the Legal Committee and most of the provisions now contained in art. VII of the Convention were already contained in art. III of the Draft Articles adopted by the Legal Committee.[92]

Art. VII(1) states:

1   The owner of a ship registered in a Contracting State and carrying more than 2,000 tons
    of oil in bulk as cargo shall be required to maintain insurance or other financial security,
    such as the guarantee of a bank or a certificate delivered by an international compensation
    fund, in the sums fixed by applying the limits of liability prescribed in article V, paragraph
    1 to cover his liability for pollution damage under this Convention.

The reference to the 'limits of liability' is not appropriate, because there is only one limit. Art. V(1) sets out the manner of calculation of the limit, but the limit is that which results from such calculation.

---

13 of the Athens Convention of 1974 (Vol. I, Chapter 4, para. 7.10) and in the LLMC Convention 1976 (Vol. II, Part V, Chapter 11, para. 7).

90 Reference is made to the analysis in respect of the LLMC Convention in Vol. II, Chapter 11, para. 7.

91 *Supra*, para. 1.

92 Official Records, *supra*, note 2, p. 442, at pp. 465–470. Draft art. III was accompanied by the following note:

> The Legal Committee did not take a decision on the principle of compulsory insurance. There was a division of opinion on this issue. However, a majority of the Committee were in favour of submitting a draft article to the Conference.

Although the obligation to maintain an insurance or other financial security applies only to the owners of ships registered in a Contracting State, the rules adopted by the Convention also affect ships that are not registered in a Contracting State. This result is achieved by providing that Contracting States are bound to ensure under their national legislation that the liability insurance as provided in art. VII is in force in respect of all ships carrying more than 2,000 tons of oil in bulk as cargo entering or leaving a port in their territory or an off-shore terminal in their territorial sea, irrespective of whether they are registered in a Contracting State or not. Art.VII(11) states:

11 Subject to the provisions of this article, each Contracting State shall ensure, under its national legislation, that insurance or other security to the extent specified in paragraph 1 of this article is in force in respect of any ship, wherever registered, entering or leaving a port in its territory, or arriving at or leaving an off-shore terminal in its territorial sea, if the ship actually carries more than 2,000 tons of oil in bulk as cargo.

Working Group II had submitted to the Legal Committee the proposal to add two provisions to the provision pursuant to which a Contracting State should not permit a ship under its flag to trade unless a certificate of insurance or other guarantee had been issued: the first pursuant to which a Contracting State might or should refuse a ship of another Contracting State to enter its ports unless such ship had been issued a certificate of insurance or other guarantee and the second pursuant to which such refusal should or could be enforced in respect of ships of non-Contracting States.[93] Such provisions were included by the Legal Committee in the draft Convention annexed to the Progress Report on the work of its fifth session[94] and were subsequently merged in one provision only, in which the refusal appeared as an obligation of each Contracting State and applied to 'any ship', thereby indicating that it applied both to ships registered in other Contracting States and to ships registered in non-Contracting States. That provision appears to have been approved by the Conference without any opposition.

The fact that, in order to ensure protection of the persons who have suffered pollution damage (as defined in the Convention) it is necessary to require compliance with the obligation to maintain insurance or other financial security by the owners of all ships, whether registered in a Contracting State or not, is confirmed: (a) by the reference in paragraph 2 to the issue of a certificate attesting that insurance or other financial security is in force in respect of ships not registered in a Contracting State and (b) by the provision in paragraph 7 pursuant to which certificates issued or certified under the authority of a Contracting State in accordance with paragraph 2 shall be accepted by other Contracting States and shall be regarded by other Contracting

---

93 Report of Working Group II to the Legal Committee on its third session, CMI Documentation 1969, III, p. 134. Such draft provisions, appearing in square brackets, were worded as follows:

[9 A contracting States (may) (shall) refuse to permit a ship of another contracting State to enter its ports unless such ship has been issued a certificate under paragraphs 2 or 11 of this Article.]
[10 A contracting State (may) (shall) refuse to permit a ship of a non-contracting State to enter its ports unless such ship maintains insurance or other financial security approved by the contracting State and adequate to cover liability for pollution damage within the limits set forth in Article V.]

94 Progress Report of the Legal Committee on the work of its fifth session held from 4 to 7 March 1969, CMI Documentation 1969, III, p. 134.

States as having the same force as certificates issued or certified by them 'even if issued or certified in respect of a ship not registered in a Contracting State'.

The global application of the rules on compulsory insurance is a feature common in all conventions in which the rule on compulsory liability insurance has been adopted, such conventions being, in addition to the CLC, the Athens Passengers Convention of 1974 as amended by its Protocol of 2002 and the Nairobi Wreck Removal Convention of 2007, as it appears from the following summary:

(i)   The obligation to insure liability applies only to owners of ships registered in Contracting States:

CLC 1992   Athens 2002   Nairobi 2007
art. VII(1)   art. 4*bis* (1)   art. 12(1)

(ii)   The party by whom the insurance certificate in respect both of ships registered in Contracting and non-Contracting States must be issued:

CLC 1992   Athens 2002   Nairobi 2007
art. VII(2)   art. 4bis (2)   art. 12(2)

(iii) The authority with which a copy of the certificate must be deposited;

CLC 1992   Athens 2002   Nairobi 2007
art. VII(4)   art. 4bis (5)   art. 12(5)

(iv)   Acceptance of certificates by other Contracting States:

CLC 1992   Athens 2002   Nairobi 2007
art. VII(7)   art. 4bis(9)   art. 12(9)

(v)   Obligation of States to ensure that insurance is in force:

CLC 1992   Athens 2002   Nairobi 2007
art. VII(11)   art. 4bis(13)   art 12(11)

9.1 The party who is bound to insure

The person liable for pollution damage under the CLC is the owner, as defined in art. 1(3): he will normally be the registered owner of the ship except where the ship is owned by a State and is operated by a company registered as the ship's operator.[95]

The obligation exists only in respect of ships carrying more than 2,000[96] tons of oil as cargo. Therefore, it is not based on the carrying capacity of the ship, but on the actual carriage of more than 2,000 tons of oil as cargo. For the purposes of this Convention a tanker having a carrying capacity of more than 2,000 tons but actually carrying less than 2,000 tons as cargo, irrespective of the oil carried as bunker, is not bound to maintain insurance. It is however not easy to reconcile this interpretation of paragraph 1 with paragraph 10 which states:

---

95 *Supra*, para. 3.2.

96 This figure appeared, in square brackets, in the draft approved by the Legal Committee. The original figure included in the draft had been 500 tons (see the comments of Finland, in Official Records, *supra*, note 2, p. 466).

10 A Contracting State shall not permit a ship under its flag to which this article applies to trade unless a certificate has been issued under paragraph 2 or 12 of this article.

To this effect it would be necessary to exclude that a tanker that sails in ballast bound to a place where she will load 30,000 tons of oil is trading, for the purposes of art. VII.

In practice, however, the owner of a tanker with a carrying capacity of over 2,000 tons will always be insured in compliance with this provision, also during ballast voyages, for it would be difficult to effect insurance cover in respect of each loaded voyage and to timely provide the ship with the required certificate.

9.2 The nature and amount of the security required

In the draft submitted by the Legal Committee[97] reference was made only to 'insurance or other financial security'. The words 'such as the guarantee of a bank or a certificate delivered by an international compensation fund' were added, without any comment, following a proposal of the French delegation,[98] and it appears that no discussion on that proposal took place at the Conference. In any event the addition, being preceded by the words 'such as', might have only the effect of applying the *ejusdem generis* rule. But the reference to a guarantee of a bank would extend the categories of the possible guarantors to a great variety of financial institutions. It is likely that the reference to certificates of an international compensation fund was added having in mind the future convention on the international fund, reference to which was made in the resolution to be adopted by the Conference, but its scope is different. In any event pursuant to art. VII(2), the guarantor must be approved by the appropriate authority of the Contracting State of the ship's registry or, for ships not registered in a Contracting State, by the appropriate authority of any Contracting State.

9.3 The sum insured or secured

The sum insured or secured is equal to the limits of liability of the shipowner resulting from art. V. It is not clear why the plural is used, since under art. V(1) the limit is one, being the aggregate amount calculated pursuant to that provision.

9.4 Evidence of the insurance or other financial security

Art. VII(2) states:

2 A certificate attesting that insurance or other financial security is in force in accordance with the provisions of this Convention shall be issued to each ship after the appropriate authority of a Contracting State has determined that the requirements of paragraph 1 have been complied with. With respect to a ship registered in a Contracting State such certificate shall be issued or certified by the appropriate authority of the State of the ship's registry; with respect to a ship not registered in a Contracting State it may be issued or

---

97 *Supra*, note 85.
98 Document LEG/CONF./C.2/WP.37, Official Records, *supra*, note 2, p. 599.

OIL POLLUTION DAMAGE CONVENTION, 1992

certified by the appropriate authority of any Contracting State. This certificate shall be in the form of the annexed model and shall contain the following particulars:

(a) name of ship and port of registration;
(b) name and principal place of business of owner;
(c) type of security;
(d) name and principal place of business of insurer or other person giving security and, where appropriate, place of business where the insurance or security is established;
(e) period of validity of certificate which shall not be longer than the period of validity of the insurance or other security.

The particulars which deserve some comments are those under (d) and (e).

9.4.1 Principal place of business

Reference in (d) to the principal place of business only, while in other conventions, such as the Arrest Conventions 1952 and 1999,[99] reference is made both to the habitual residence and principal place of business, is almost certainly due to the fact that the insurer or provider of security must be a legal person. Questions may instead arise in respect of the subsequent words 'where appropriate, place of business where the insurance or security is established'. In this context 'established' means the issuance or creation of the insurance or security as confirmed by the use in the French text of the Convention of the words '*a été souscrite*'. As regards the circumstances in which it would be 'appropriate' to refer to that place, it is suggested that that should be the case where the insurance or security is not issued in the place where the insurer or guarantor has its principal place of business, but somewhere else, where it has a branch or an office or where the agent who has issued the insurance or guarantee has its seat.

The question whether the relevant State should be the flag State or the State of the principal place of business of the insurer or guarantor, had been considered by Group II of the Legal Committee and the majority had been in favour of the first alternative.[100] As regards the ships in respect of which certificates should be issued, no discussion took place in respect of the possible issuance of such certificates also for ships not registered in a Contracting State, but there was instead discussion as to whether it should be mandatory on Contracting States to refuse access to their ports to such ships.[101] That question was settled by generally providing in paragraph 11 that each Contracting State shall ensure that insurance or other security is maintained in respect of 'any ship, wherever registered'. The problem

---

99 Respectively in art. 8(4), (5) and (6).

100 Report of Working Group II to the Legal Committee on its third session, *supra*, note 85, p. 90.

101 Report of Working Group II to the Legal Committee on its third session, *supra*, note 85, p. 96, para. 13. The discussion was summarised as follows:

> 13 *Enforcement of the convention against ships of other States.* There was a difference of view as to whether it should be mandatory on States to refuse access to their ports to ships of non-contracting States which could not show evidence of financial security, whether this should be expressed as a discretionary power or whether any provision was necessary at all. It was pointed out that if it was expressed as a discretionary power it would be adding nothing to existing principles of international law, but that the possibility of making mandatory the obligation to refuse access might have to be considered in the light of obligations to third countries.

of the issuance of such certificate in respect of ships not registered in Contracting States was considered during the Conference and settled by including in this paragraph the reference to ships not registered in a Contracting State and providing that the certificate may be issued or certified by the appropriate authority of any Contracting State.

Paragraph 2 also provides that it shall be in the form of the annexed model. By comparing the particulars enumerated in paragraph 2 and the model there appear to be the following slight differences:

- in the model there is also a box where the distinctive number or letters of the ship must be indicated: this is an additional, albeit obvious, piece of information since the distinctive IMO number permits prompt identification of a ship, whatever its nationality may be;
- in the model the information relating to the insurer or guarantor includes a reference to their name and address, whilst in paragraph 2 the information that must be provided includes also 'where appropriate, place of business where the insurance or security is established': this additional information was not mentioned in the draft article on compulsory insurance (then numbered III) attached to the draft articles annexed to the Report on the third session of Group II to the Legal Committee held on 7 January 1969. There was already annexed to that article a draft of the certificate of insurance, the wording of which was kept unaltered when the information on the insurer or guarantor previously mentioned was added.

9.4.2 Period of validity

The term 'period' entails two dates: that on which the period starts to run and that on which it terminates and the need for such two dates is clear in respect of an insurance cover: the date on which the insurance certificate is issued is not necessarily that on which the cover begins to run. The need for an initial and final date perhaps is normally not so important for a financial security, but since the same term is used, it appears that also where a financial security is issued, there needs to be an initial and final date. In the model of certificate mention is made first to the 'duration' of the security and then to the date when validity of the certificate expires. The term 'duration' does not necessarily entail an initial and final date: what is required is a final date, even if the initial date must precede the date of issue of the certificate, for pursuant to the opening sentence the policy of insurance or other financial security must be already in force when the certificate is issued. However, in the subsequent paragraph 5 reference is made to the expiry of the 'period' of validity of the insurance or other financial security.

Then the certificate must indicate the date on which its validity expires. A date that must not be subsequent to that of the 'duration' of the security, whilst it may be precedent to that when the security expires.

There appears to be a lack of coordination between the terminology used in art. VII of the Convention and that used in the model of certificate, but that used in the model of certificate must be interpreted in the light of that used in art. VII.

9.5 Conditions of issue and validity of the certificate

Art. VII(6) states:

6   The State of registry shall, subject to the provisions of this article, determine the conditions of issue and validity of the certificate.

This provision must be read in the light of the preceding paragraph 2 from which it appears that the State of registry has an obligation to issue the certificate. Therefore, the conditions for the issue of the certificate should not be such as to entail a full discretion of the State: such conditions must be reasonable, and such as to be complied with by the owner of a ship that complies with the requirements of SOLAS and MARPOL. Although reference is made only to the State of registry, where the certificate is issued in respect of a ship that is not registered in a Contracting State a greater flexibility is granted to the State by which the certificate is issued: paragraph 2 in fact provides that in such case the certificate 'may be issued or certified' by a Contracting State.

9.6 Language of the certificate

Art. VII(3) states:

3   The certificate shall be in the official language or languages of the issuing State. If the language used is neither English nor French, the text shall include a translation into one of these languages.

The reason why reference is made (only) to English and French is probably due to the fact that these were the two official languages in which the Convention was adopted. But since this requirement has not been amended by the Protocol of 1992, which instead has been established in Arabic, Chinese, English, French, Russian and Spanish, the reason now must be deemed to be the fact that at least one of these languages is spoken in all maritime countries of the world. However, in art. 12(3) of the HNS Convention 1996, Spanish has been added to English and French.

9.7 Period of validity of the certificate

Art. VII(5) states:

5   An insurance or other financial security shall not satisfy the requirements of this article if it can cease, for reasons other than the expiry of the period of validity of the insurance or security specified in the certificate under paragraph 2 of this article, before three months have elapsed from the date on which notice of its termination is given to the authorities referred to in paragraph 4 of this article, unless the certificate has been surrendered to these authorities or a new certificate has been issued within the said period. The foregoing provisions shall similarly apply to any modification which results in the insurance or security no longer satisfying the requirements of this article.

The provisions of this paragraph are addressed to the authorities of the Contracting States by which the certificates may be issued. Such authorities must verify the terms of the insurance or other financial security in order to make sure that the requirements of this provisions are met. It appears that the simplest way to carry out such verification and avoid any responsibility of that authority or of the State by

9.8 International validity of the certificate

Art. VII(7) states:

7 Certificates issued or certified under the authority of a Contracting State in accordance with paragraph 2 shall be accepted by other Contracting States for the purposes of this Convention and shall be regarded by other Contracting States as having the same force as certificates issued by them even if issued or certified in respect of a ship not registered in a Contracting State. A Contracting State may at any time request consultation with the issuing or certifying State should it believe that the insurer or guarantor named in the certificate is not financially capable of meeting the obligations imposed by this Convention.

The provision in the first sentence is a necessary complement to the rule of paragraph 11 pursuant to which each Contacting State is required to ensure under its national legislation that insurance or other security is in force in respect of any ship, wherever registered, entering or leaving a port in its territory: compliance with this rule entails necessarily that each State accepts certificates issued by other Contracting States, both in respect of ships registered in such States and of ships registered in non-Contracting States.

9.9 Direct action against the insurer or guarantor

Art. VII(8) so provides:

8 Any claim for compensation for pollution damage may be brought directly against the insurer or other person providing financial security for the owner's liability for pollution damage. In such case the defendant may, even if the owner is not entitled to limit his liability according to article V, paragraph 2, avail himself of the limits of liability prescribed in article V, paragraph 1. He may further avail himself of the defences (other than the bankruptcy or winding up of the owner) which the owner himself would have been entitled to invoke. Furthermore, the defendant may avail himself of the defence that the pollution damage resulted from the wilful misconduct of the owner himself, but the defendant shall not avail himself of any other defence which he might have been entitled to invoke in proceedings brought by the owner against him. The defendant shall in any event have the right to require the owner to be joined in the proceedings.

The question whether the claimant should have a direct action against the insurer or guarantor was discussed by the Legal Committee and three possibilities were discussed, namely: (a) no direct action should be granted; (b) direct action should be granted only in the event of the insolvency of the owner; and (c) direct action should be granted in any event. The last one was ultimately chosen, provided the insurer or guarantor should have the same defences and rights of limitation of the owner.[102]

---

102 This problem was discussed during the third session of Working Group II of the Legal Committee

The provision pursuant to which the insurer or guarantor may avail itself of the limits of liability prescribed in art. V(1) entails that such persons may act as the owner would have acted. Therefore, they may invoke the benefit of limitation as the owner would have done, and pursuant to art. V(3) they must constitute a limitation fund. However, contrary to the owner, the benefit of limitation cannot be challenged by the claimants on the basis of art. V(2).

The fourth sentence was not included in the draft articles submitted to the Conference by the Legal Committee. It was added following the observation that it was a general rule that liability insurance does not cover loss or damage caused by the wilful misconduct of the assured.[103] There appears anyhow to be some difficulties in reconciling this provision with that of the second sentence, pursuant to which the insurer or guarantor may avail himself of the limits of liability even if the owner is not entitled to do so. When this provision was adopted in the original text of art. VII, the loss by the owner of the benefit of limitation was provided in case the incident occurred as a result of his actual fault, a behaviour that differs from wilful misconduct, the terms used in the French text being '*faute personnelle*' in the first case and '*faute intentionnelle*' in the second case; but the distinction (if it is still possible) is more subtle now, since pursuant to art. V(2) the loss by the owner of the right to limit requires an act or omission committed with the intent to cause *such* damage or recklessly and with knowledge that *such* damage would probably result.

It would appear that where the pollution damage resulted from a personal act or omission of the owner committed with the intent to cause such damage the insurer or guarantor has two options: either to reject the claim on the basis of the fourth sentence or to invoke the benefit of limitation on the basis of the second sentence.

9.10 Ships owned by a Contracting State

Art. VII(12) so provides:

12. If insurance or other financial security is not maintained in respect of a ship owned by a Contracting State, the provisions of this article relating thereto shall not be applicable to such ship, but the ship shall carry a certificate issued by the appropriate authorities

---

held on 7 January 1969 and the following report was made to the Legal Committee (Report of Working Group II to the Legal Committee on its third session, *supra*, note 85, p. 95):

> It was argued that direct recourse was necessary in the event of the insolvency of the owner, and that to allow it otherwise might embarrass the insurer or guarantor in the conduct of claims, since he would find it more difficult to control the owner concerned, which might involve an increase in premium rates. Against this, it was argued that in any event the owner was always contractually bound to act in relation to claims against himself in accordance with the directions of the insurer and that to permit direct actions would give the claimant a convenient and direct means of gaining access to the person with the actual funds from which he would be compensated. As a basis for future discussion it was decided to include a provision embodying (c) in the draft article, but it was also agreed that it should be made clear that the insurer or guarantor should have the same defences and right of limitation as an owner himself except those which would arise by reason of the owner's own bankruptcy.

103 Lords Devlin stated (Official Records. *supra* note 2, p. 727):

> The insurance underwriters had indicated, however, that they would have preferred such a provision and that the very minimum they would insist upon if they were to be able to insure the limits quoted was that an insurer could disclaim liability where 'the pollution damage resulted from the wilful misconduct of the owner himself'.

INTERNATIONAL MARITIME CONVENTIONS

of the State of the ship's registry stating that the ship is owned by that State and that the ship's liability is covered within the limits prescribed by article V, paragraph 1. Such a certificate shall follow as closely as practicable the model prescribed by paragraph 2 of this article.

Paragraph 12, the wording of which is practically the same as that appeared in art. III of the draft articles submitted to the Conference by the Legal Committee, only applies to ships owned by Contracting States and used for commercial purposes, reference to which is made in art. XI(2).[104] Therefore Contracting States are subject to all the provisions of the Convention and, in particular, to those of art. VII, in respect of ships operated by them and used for commercial purposes. Pursuant to the provisions of this paragraph, States have the choice, in respect of ships owned by them and used for commercial purposes, between maintaining an insurance or financial security as provided by art. VII, in which event all its provisions shall apply, and accept to bear directly the liability that under art. VII is covered by the insurer or guarantor. In such latter case they are required, pursuant to paragraph 12, to provide the ship with a certificate that contains the declaration mentioned in this paragraph. The wording used is not legally correct, for the liability covered is not that of the ship but rather that of the State, that would exist anyhow. It would have been more appropriate to require the State to declare that it assumes liability in respect of the operation of the ship within the same limits prescribed by art. VII(1), in which in turn reference is made to the limits of liability prescribed by art. V(1).

10 TIME FOR SUIT

Art. VIII so provides:

Rights of compensation under this Convention shall be extinguished unless an action is brought thereunder within three years from the date when the damage occurred. However, in no case shall an action be brought after six years from the date of the incident which caused the damage. Where this incident consists of a series of occurrences, the six years' period shall run from the date of the first such occurrence.

In the draft articles submitted by the Legal Committee to the Conference of 1969[105] the text of this article (then art. VII) consisted only of the first sentence and the date from which the period started to run was the date of the incident. The second and third sentences were added following a Norwegian proposal based on the possible lapse of some time between the accident and the pollution.[106] Therefore, while the replacement of the date of the incident by the date when the damage occurred protects the victims, the addition of a second longer term (initially suggested as ten years and then reduced to six) from the date of the incident was made in order to

---

104 *Supra*, para. 2.2.
105 Official Records, *supra*, note 2, p. 490.
106 The Norwegian delegate stated (Official Records, *supra*, n. 2, pp. 722–723):

> The purpose of the amendment was to protect victims in cases where damage occurred long after the incident which had caused it; for example, when a ship had sunk it could remain on the sea bed for several years before pollution occurred.

ensure certainty in respect of the time by which actions may be brought, that is the purpose of the time limit.

Nothing is said in this provision, on whether the periods provided for therein may be subject to suspension or interruption or not. Although in several conventions it is expressly stated that national rules apply in this respect,[107] it appears that that would be the cause of a significant lack of uniformity as well as of uncertainty, and it is for that reason that in the Rotterdam Rules it has been expressly provided in art. 63 that the period of the time for suit is not subject to suspension or interruption. It appears that the global interpretation of art. VIII impliedly excludes the possibility of suspension or interruption of the terms. In fact, as regards the six-year term, the statement that 'in no case' shall an action be brought after six years, since the suspension or interruption of the running of the term would exclude the application of national law in that respect. Such conclusion applies also to the three years term for two reasons: first, because the application of a different regime to the two terms would have required an express provision; secondly, because the granting of a second term would not have been required if the first term might be subject to suspension or interruption.

The further question that is not settled by this provision, nor could have been settled, and it is not settled by similar provisions in other conventions, is when an action must be deemed to be brought: a question the answer to which depends on the procedural law of the State in which the action is brought. For example, in some civil law jurisdictions an action is deemed to be brought when service of the summons is made to and the summons is actually received by the defendant,[108] while in some common law jurisdictions, proceedings begin when the claim form is issued (not when it is served),[109] or it suffices that the libel be filed with the Chancery of the Court.[110]

11 JURISDICTION

Art. IX states:

1 Where an incident has caused pollution damage in the territory, including the territorial sea or an area referred to in article II, of one or more Contracting States or preventive measures have been taken to prevent or minimize pollution damage in such territory including the territorial sea or area, actions for compensation may only be brought in the Courts of any such Contracting State or States. Reasonable notice of any such action shall be given to the defendant.
2. Each Contracting State shall ensure that its Courts possess the necessary jurisdiction to entertain such actions for compensation.
3 After the fund has been constituted in accordance with article V the Courts of the State

---

107 This is the case for art. 10 of the Collision Convention of 1910 (Vol. II, Part I, Chapter 1, para. 6.3), for art. 16 of the Hamburg Rules (Vol. I, Chapter 2, para. 13) and for art. 16(3) of the Athens Convention (Vol. I, Part II, Chapter 3, para. 12).

108 This is the case in Italy and France.

109 This is the case in England.

110 This is the case in the United States: *United Nations Relief and Rehabilitation Administration* v *Steamship Mormacail and Others*, U.S.D.C. Southern District of New York, 7 May 1951, (1951) AMC 1152.

in which the fund is constituted shall be exclusively competent to determine all matters relating to the apportionment and distribution of the fund.

It appears from paragraph 1 that where pollution damage has occurred or preventive measures have been taken in more than one State, any claimant may decide to bring an action against the owner or his insurer/guarantor in the courts of any such States, whether he is domiciled in such State or not. Although that is not expressly stated, it appears to be a logical consequence of this provision that declaratory actions must be brought in the courts of any such States. The question that remains is whether courts of different States may be seised by different claimants. That does not appear to be possible after the fund has been constituted, for pursuant to paragraph 3 of this article only the courts of the State where the fund has been constituted are competent to determine all matters relating to the apportionment and distribution of the fund and that implies also the assessment of the claim, since if by 'apportionment' would be meant the calculation of the percentage of the claims payable to each claimant, the action of the court would be limited to a mathematical operation. The further question is whether after the fund has been constituted actions brought in the courts of the other State or States competent pursuant to paragraph 1 of this article may be decided by such courts or must be removed to the court in which the fund has been constituted. It appears that pursuant to paragraph 3 of this article they should be so removed.

12 RECOGNITION AND ENFORCEMENT OF JUDGMENTS

Art. X so provides:

1 Any judgment given by a Court with jurisdiction in accordance with article IX which is enforceable in the State of origin where it is no longer subject to ordinary forms of review, shall be recognized in any Contracting State, except:
   (a) where the judgment was obtained by fraud; or
   (b) where the defendant was not given reasonable notice and a fair opportunity to present his case.
2 A judgment recognized under paragraph 1 of this article shall be enforceable in each Contracting State as soon as the formalities required in that State have been complied with. The formalities shall not permit the merits of the case to be re-opened.

Situations in which there would be the need for a judgment given by a court in a contracting State to be enforced in another Contracting State appear to be limited. That would be the case where the owner of the ship that has caused the pollution does not invoke the benefit of limitation. If he does avail himself of such benefit, he must concurrently constitute the fund, whereupon the court in which the fund is constituted acquires exclusive jurisdiction. Of course, the need for enforcement of judgments delivered by a court of another Contracting State would exist if, contrary to the view expressed in the preceding paragraph, the apportionment reference to which is made in art. IX(3) consists only in the material calculation of the percentage of the recognised claims payable out of the fund.

13 CONFLICT WITH OTHER CONVENTIONS

Art. XII so provides:

This Convention shall supersede any International Conventions in force or open for signature, ratification or accession at the date on which the Convention is opened for signature, but only to the extent that such Conventions would be in conflict with it; however, nothing in this article shall affect the obligations of Contracting States to non-Contracting States arising under such International Conventions.

The last sentence of this article is meant to comply with the provisions of art. 30(4)(b) of the Vienna Convention on the Law of Treaties.[111] Since rules on the limitation of liability of the shipowner are contained also in the Convention on Limitation of Liability 1957 and on the LLMC Convention 1976–1996, it is necessary to consider what is the effect of the above provision if an action is brought in a State party to the CLC against the owner of a ship registered in a State party to one of such conventions that is not a party to the CLC.

13.1 Convention on Limitation of Liability 1957

Since claims for pollution damage may be qualified as claims in respect of infringement of rights caused by the act, neglect or default of any person on board the ship, they would be subject to the Convention on Limitation of Liability, and its provisions would prevail over those of the CLC if the State party to the CLC in which action is brought is also party to the Convention on Limitation of Liability.[112]

13.2 LLMC Convention as amended

No conflict is conceivable, since pursuant to art. 3(b) of the CLC its rules do not apply to claims for oil pollution damage 'within the meaning' of the CLC.

---

111 An identical provision is included in the HNS Convention (art. 42) and in the Bunker Oil Convention (art. 11).

112 That would be the case for Belize, Fiji, Ghana, Grenada, Iran, Israel, Lebanon, Madagascar, Monaco, Papua New Guinea, Portugal, St Vincent and the Grenadines, Seychelles and Solomon Islands.

CHAPTER 12

International Convention on the Establishment of an International Fund for Compensation for Oil Pollution Damage, 1992, as amended by its Protocol of 2000 and its Supplementary Protocol of 2003 (the Fund Convention)

1 INTRODUCTION

As indicated in the introduction to the CLC 1969, one of the conditions for accepting the primary liability of the owner on a strict basis had been that a limit to such liability should be fixed and then the balance of the damages caused by pollution should be borne by the cargo owner through the adoption of an international compensation scheme based upon the existence of an international fund.[1]

A draft of the Convention was prepared by the Legal Committee of IMCO[2] and was submitted to the Conference convened by the Assembly of IMCO from 29 November to 18 December 1971, by which the Convention was adopted. The basic structure of such draft was as follows:[3]

(i) linkage with the CLC: the States may become parties to the Fund Convention if they are parties to the CLC: its art. 37 provides that the Convention is open for signature by the States which have signed or which accede to the CLC and by any State represented at the Conference;

(ii) the establishment of an International Fund for compensation of pollution damage to be recognised as a legal person;

(iii) its purpose to be twofold: (a) partial relief of the owner, under certain conditions; and (b) compensation of the victims when damages exceed the owner's liability;

(iv) a global limit on the aggregate amount of compensation payable by the Fund;

(v) assumption of the obligation of guarantor in respect of part of the owner's liability;

(vi) jurisdiction for actions against the Fund;

(vii) criteria for contributions to the Fund by Contracting States;

(viii) functions of the Assembly, Executive Committee and Secretary.

---

1 *Supra*, Chapter 11, para. 1 and for the full text of the resolution note 4.

2 At its seventh session held in January 1970 the Legal Committee decided to appoint a Working Group to examine the question of the establishment on an International Compensation Fund for Oil Pollution Damage. The report of its work is made by the Secretariat in document LEG IX/2 of 5 October 1970.

3 For the full text see Official Records of the Conference on the Establishment of an International Compensation Fund for Oil Pollution Damage, 1971.

The Convention, as adopted on 18 December 1971, follows the general lines of the draft. It contains rules on the compensation and indemnification of the victims, on the relief to the owner, on contributions by Contracting States and on the organisation and administration of the Fund.

Its linkage with the CLC is stated in the following subtitle of the Convention attached to the Final Act of the Conference of 1971:

(Supplementary to the International Convention on Civil Liability for Oil Pollution Damage, 1969)

and from the following considerations in its Preamble:

CONSIDERING that the International Convention of 29 November 1969, on Civil Liability for Oil Pollution Damage, by providing a regime for compensation for pollution damage in Contracting States and for the costs of measures, wherever taken to prevent or minimize such damage, represents a considerable progress towards the achievement of the aim,

CONSIDERING HOWEVER that this regime does not afford full compensation for victims of oil pollution damage in all cases while it imposes an additional financial burden to shipowners,

CONSIDERING FURTHER that the economic consequences of oil pollution damage resulting from the escape or discharge of oil carried in bulk at sea by ships should not exclusively be borne by the shipping industry but should in part be borne by the oil cargo interests.

The linkage appears also from its art. 2(1) which describes the aims of the Convention as follows:

(a) to provide compensation for pollution damage to the extent that the protection afforded by the Liability Convention is inadequate;
(b) to give relief to shipowners in respect of the additional financial burden imposed on them by the Liability Convention, such relief being subject to conditions designed to ensure compliance with safety at sea and other conventions;
(c) to give effect to the related purposes set out in this Convention.

The relief to shipowners was provided in art. 5(1) of the Convention as follows:

1   For the purpose of fulfilling its functions under article 2, paragraph 1(b), the Fund shall indemnify the owner and his guarantor for that portion of the aggregate amount of liability under the liability Convention which:

(a) is in excess of an amount equivalent to 1,500 francs[4] for each ton of the ship's tonnage or of an amount of 125 million francs, whichever is the less, and
(b) is not in excess of an amount equivalent to 2,000 francs for each ton of the said tonnage or an amount of 210 million francs, whichever is the less,

provided, however, that the Fund shall incur no obligation under this paragraph where the pollution damage resulted from the wilful misconduct of the owner himself.

The Convention entered into force on 16 October 1978. By a Protocol of 19 September 1976 (entered into force on 22 November 1994), the original unit of account (the Poincaré franc) was replaced by the Special Drawing Right, as it had been done on the same date for the CLC 1969.

Prior to the Conference held from 30 April to 25 May 1984 by which draft Protocols to revise the 1969 CLC and the 1971 Fund Convention were adopted,

---

4 In the CLC 1969, the limits were expressed in Poincaré francs and were replaced by limits in Special Drawing Rights by the Protocol of 1976, on the basis of the ratio 15:1. *Supra*, Chapter 11, para. 5.1.

the contribution of ships and cargoes to the settlement of pollution damage was the object of an in-depth discussion within the Legal Committee.[5] Different views were expressed in respect of whether and to which extent the increase should be borne by the owner of the ship or by the owners of the cargo. It was stated on behalf of the shipowners' interests that in respect of the twelve years 1970 to 1981, 74 per cent of the cost of the claims had been borne by shipowners and that out of more than 17,000 individual oil spills less than 1 per cent had exceeded the 1969 Civil Liability Convention limits.[6] It was stated on behalf of the cargo interests that a very significant amount of pollution damage had been caused by small ships and that it was desirable to introduce a specified minimum liability for ships below a certain tonnage;[7] it was also stated that the relief of the shipowner was not justified and that the tonnage criterion should be abandoned.[8] A consensus was ultimately reached on the abolishment of the relief in favour of shipowners[9] and on the adoption in the CLC of a fixed minimum tonnage for limitation purposes.[10] The levels of contribution by shipowners and cargo to the settlement of damages were also discussed and suggestions were made.[11]

---

5 See Interim Report of the Working Group to the Legal Committee of 10 June 1970, doc. LEG/WG(FUND) I/4; Report to the Legal Committee of 30 September 1970, doc. LEG/WG(FUND) II/4; Consideration of Questions relating to the Establishment of an International Compensation Fund for Oil Pollution Damage – Note by the Secretariat of 5 October 1970, doc. LEG IX/2.

6 Official Records of the International Conference on Liability and Compensation for Damage in Connexion with the Carriage of Certain Substances by Sea, 1984 and the International Conference on the Revision of the 1969 Civil Liability Convention, 1992, vol. 1, p. 171.

7 Official Records, *supra*, note 6, vol. 1, p. 162.

8 Official Records, *supra*, note 6, vol. 1, p. 164 and 175.

9 The reason for the adoption of the relief to shipowners and for its possible present abolishment were explained during the 50th session of the Legal Committee by the President of the CMI (at that time the author of this book). Official Records, *supra*, note 6, vol. 1, p. 169, para. 3), as follows:

> If the limits were not subject to too large an increase, then, in the view of the CMI, the provision for 'roll-back' provision (article 5) of the 1971 Fund Convention was made necessary because the 1969 Convention had greatly increased the shipowner's per ton liability for oil pollution beyond that of the 1957 Limitation Convention for other types of property damage. However, since it was currently foreseen that both conventions may be revised simultaneously, the same 'roll-back' provision might not be necessary, particularly if the shipowner's liability for oil pollution claims was not greatly in excess of its liability for other types of property damage claims. Only if such excess liability were decided upon, would it be necessary, in CMI's view, that the 'roll-back' provision of the Fund Convention should be retained in such a way that the limit of the shipowner's liability after the 'roll-back' would be co-ordinated with the limits of 1976 Convention on Limitation of Liability for Maritime Claims, just as the 1971 Fund Convention was co-ordinated with the 1957 Limitation Convention.

10 The comment made by the CMI in this connection was reported as follows (Official Records, *supra*, note 6, vol. 1, p. 170, para. 10):

> The CMI took the view that the argument advanced by OCIMF that small ships can, on occasion, cause sufficiently large and expensive oil pollution problems so that a mere monetary amount per ton limit would not be adequate to compensate claims, was not without merit. However, in the CMI view, the argument did not have such validity that it would warrant abandoning the time-honoured and thoroughly tested tonnage system for limitation of liability. Further, it could be argued that it was not practical to involve the Fund with respect to relatively minor claims. For these reasons, it was the position of the CMI that the solution would be to set a reasonable minimum tonnage.

11 A proposal had been made by OCIMF that the shipowner would be responsible for the first $50 million for pollution damage per incident and the cargo-related compensation fund, the IOPC Fund, would provide a supplement coverage of $75million per incident (Official Records, *supra*, note 6, vol. 1, p. 170, para. 6).

The Conference held from 30 April to 25 May 1984 adopted a Protocol to the CLC 1969 by which a minimum limit of 3 million SDRs was provided for ships not exceeding 5,000 GT, increased for ships with tonnage in excess thereof by 420 SDRs for each ton in excess, with a ceiling of 59.7 million SDRs. It also adopted a Protocol to the Fund Convention pursuant to which the owner's relief was excluded and the ceiling in art. 4(4)(a) and (b) was increased from 450 million francs (corresponding to 30 million SDRs) to 135 million SDRs, with the addition of a further global ceiling of 200 million.[12]

The Protocols adopted in 1984 for both the CLC and the Fund Convention never entered into force[13] and were replaced by almost identical Protocols adopted by a Conference held from 23 November to 2 December 1992. The Preamble to the Protocols clearly indicated that their purpose was to enact the provisions of the Protocols of 1984. The wording of the Protocol to the Fund Convention is in fact as follows:[14]

HAVING CONSIDERED the International Convention on the Establishment of an International Fund for Compensation for Oil Pollution Damage, 1971, and the 1984 Protocol thereto,

HAVING NOTED that the 1984 Protocol to that Convention which provides for improved scope and enhanced compensation, has not entered into force,

AFFIRMING the importance of maintaining the viability of the international oil pollution liability and compensation system,

AWARE OF the need to ensure the entry into force of the content of the 1984 Protocol as soon as possible,

RECOGNIZING the advantage for the States parties of arranging for the amended Convention to co-exist with and be supplementary to the original Convention for a transitional period,

CONVINCED that the economic consequences of pollution damage resulting from the carriage of oil in bulk by sea by ships should continue to be shared by the shipping industry and by the oil cargo interests,

BEARING IN MIND the adoption of the Protocol of 1992 to amend the International Convention on Civil Liability for Oil Pollution Damage, 1969 . . .

The changes as respects the Protocol of 1984 were minimal. They consisted of:

(a)   the deletion of art. 12(1)(b) of the Convention;[15]
(b)   the addition of a new article 36*ter* pursuant to paragraph 1 of which the maximum increase in the aggregate amount of contributions payable in respect of contributing oil received in a single Contracting State in respect

---

12 For an analysis of art. 4 see *infra*, para. 5. For the history of this Protocol and the influence of the United States for its adoption see Måns Jacobsson, 'The International Liability and Compensation Regime for Oil Pollution from Ships – International Solutions for a Global Problem', 32 *Tulane Maritime Law Journal* (2007), 2 at p. 11.

13 Jacobsson (*supra*, note 12, p. 12) explains that the entry into force conditions had been drafted in such a way that the Protocol for its entry into force required the ratification of Japan and the United States and indicates the five reasons for which the United States had decided to abstain.

14 Official Records, *supra*, note 6, vol. 4, pp. 97–98 and 111.

15 This provision provided:

(b) payments to be made by the Fund in the relevant year for the satisfaction of claims against the Fund due under article 4 or 5, including repayments on loans previously taken by the Fund for the satisfaction of such claims, to the extent that the aggregate amount of such claims in respect of any one incident does not exceed 15 million francs.

of a given calendar year should not exceed 27.5 per cent of the total contributions in respect of that calendar year;[16]

(c) the reduction from 600 million tons to 450 million tons of the global quantity received during the preceding calendar year by the persons who would be liable to contribute pursuant to art. 10 of the 1971 Fund Convention;[17]

(d) the dates before which amendments of the limits may not be considered pursuant to art. 33(6).

The Protocol to the Fund Convention entered into force on 30 May 1996. By a further Protocol of 27 September 2000, entered into force on 27 June 2001, it was provided that the 1971 Fund Convention would terminate on the date when the number of Contracting States falls below twenty-five, or twelve months following the date on which the Assembly would note that the total quantity of contributing oil received in the remaining Contracting States would fall below 1,000 million tons. The Fund Convention 1971 ceased to be in force on 24 May 2002[18] and only the Convention as amended by the Protocol of 1992, remained in force being referred to as Fund 1992. The limits adopted in 1992 were amended on 18 October 2000 by a resolution of the Legal Committee and the new limits entered into force on 1 November 2003.

In view, however, of the fact that the maximum compensation afforded by the Fund Convention 1992 might be insufficient to meet compensation needed in certain circumstances in some Contracting States, a further Protocol was adopted on 16 May 2003.[19] Its purpose was not to amend the Fund Convention 1992, but to create a Supplementary Fund that would ensure additional payments to the persons who have not received full settlement for oil pollution damage. Its purpose is stated in art. 4(1) as follows:

The Supplementary Fund shall pay compensation to any person suffering pollution damage if such person has been unable to obtain full and adequate compensation for an established claim for such damage under the terms of the 1992 Fund Convention, because the total damage exceeds, or there is a risk that it will exceed, the applicable limit of compensation laid down in article 4, paragraph 4, of the 1982 Fund Convention in respect of any one incident.

The 1992 Fund Convention and the Supplementary Fund Protocol will therefore be considered separately, in sections A and B of this Chapter.

---

16 That provision, however, pursuant to the subsequent para. 4, operates until the total quantity of contributing oil received in all Contracting States in a calendar year has reached 750 million tons or until a period of five years after the date of entry into force of the 1992 Protocol has elapsed, whichever occurs earlier.

17 Article 30(1)(b) of the Protocol.

18 Jacobsson, *supra*, note 12, p. 3.

19 Jacobsson, *supra*, note 12, p. 14.

THE FUND CONVENTION

SECTION A – THE INTERNATIONAL FUND

2 THE ESTABLISHMENT OF THE INTERNATIONAL FUND

Art. 2 so provides:

1 An International Fund for compensation for pollution damage, to be named 'The International Oil Pollution Compensation Fund 1992' and hereinafter referred to as 'the Fund', is hereby established with the following aims:

    (a)   to provide compensation for pollution damage to the extent that the protection afforded by the 1992 Liability Convention is inadequate;

    (b)   to give effect to the related purposes set out in this Convention.

2 The Fund shall in each Contracting State be recognized as a legal person capable under the laws of that State of assuming rights and obligations and of being a party in legal proceedings before the courts of that State. Each Contracting State shall recognize the Director of the Fund (hereinafter referred to as 'The Director') as the legal representative of the Fund.

The Fund must be deemed to have been established concurrently with the entry into force of the Convention, because it is only at that time that art. 2(2) will become effective. Therefore, the 1971 Fund Convention was established on 16 October 1978 and the 1992 Fund was established on 30 May 1996.

3 SCOPE OF APPLICATION OF THE FUND

Art. 3 so provides:

This Convention shall apply exclusively:
    (a)   to pollution damage caused:
         (i)   in the territory, including the territorial sea, of a Contracting State, and
        (ii)   in the exclusive economic zone of a Contracting State, established in accordance with international law, or, if a Contracting State has not established such a zone, in an area beyond and adjacent to the territorial sea of that State determined by that State in accordance with international law and extending not more than 200 nautical miles from the baselines from which the breadth of its territorial sea is measured;
    (b)   to preventive measures, wherever taken, to prevent or minimize such damage.

The scope of application of the Fund Convention is obviously the same as that of CLC 1992 since it is complementary to it and, therefore, reference is made to the comments on art. II of the CLC.[20]

4 STRUCTURE OF THE FUND CONVENTION

The Fund Convention consists of three parts: the first contains rules on the payment of compensation to the persons suffering pollution damage; the second contains

---

20 *Supra*, Chapter 11, para. 3.

161

5 RULES GOVERNING PAYMENT OF COMPENSATION FOR POLLUTION DAMAGE

5.1 When payment of compensation is due

Art. 4(1) so provides:

1 For the purpose of fulfilling its function under article 2, paragraph 1(a), the Fund shall pay compensation to any person suffering pollution damage if such person has been unable to obtain full and adequate compensation for the damage under the terms of the 1992 Liability Convention,

  (a) because no liability for the damage arises under the 1992 Liability Convention;
  (b) because the owner liable for the damage under the 1992 Liability Convention is financially incapable of meeting his obligations in full and any financial security that may be provided under Article VII of that Convention does not cover or is insufficient to satisfy the claims for compensation for the damage; an owner being treated as financially incapable of meeting his obligations and a financial security being treated as insufficient if the person suffering the damage has been unable to obtain full satisfaction of the amount of compensation due under the 1992 Liability Convention after having taken all reasonable steps to pursue the legal remedies available to him;
  (c) because the damage exceeds the owner's liability under the 1992 Liability Convention as limited pursuant to Article V, paragraph 1, of that Convention or under the terms of any other international Convention in force or open for signature, ratification or accession at the date of this Convention.

Expenses reasonably incurred or sacrifices reasonably made by the owner voluntarily to prevent or minimize pollution damage shall be treated as pollution damage for the purposes of this article.

  (a) While in art. 2(1)(a) it is stated that the aim of the Fund was to provide compensation to the extent that the protection afforded by the CLC is inadequate, in art. 4(1) it is stated that the obligation of the Fund arises where a person suffering pollution damage has been unable to obtain 'full and adequate' compensation.[21] The double requirement appears to be due to the fact that compensation may be paid in full, but its amount

---

21 This double qualification originates from the Resolution adopted by the Legal Conference of 1969 by which the CLC 1969 was adopted (see Chapter 11, para. 4) and was quoted in the first Interim Report of the Working Group appointed by the Legal Committee of IMCO (LEG/WG (FUND) I/4 of 10 June 1970, in which the following statement was made (at pp. 3–4):

> The Working Group unanimously agreed that one of the basic purposes of an international compensation fund was to ensure that victims of oil pollution incidents would be able in principle to have full and adequate compensation as promptly as possible. To achieve this it was agreed that the Fund should provide victims, in appropriate cases, with: (a) compensation which would be additional to what would be available to them under the 1969 Convention on Civil Liability for Oil Pollution Damage, and (b) compensation where no compensation would be due to them under the 1969 Convention.

THE FUND CONVENTION

is not adequate or it may instead be adequate but it has not been paid in full.

The three reasons that could have prevented payment of such 'full and adequate' compensation enumerated in art. 4(1) will be considered *seriatim*.

(a[1]) The cases in which no liability of the owner arises are those specified in art. III(2) of the CLC[22] and the liability of the Fund would exist if the damage resulted from a natural phenomenon of an exceptional, inevitable and irresistible character, was wholly caused by an act or omission done with intent to cause damage by a third party or by the negligence or other wrongful act of any Government or other authority responsible for the maintenance of lights or other navigational aids in the exercise of that function.

(a[2]) Two distinct cases in which either the owner or the provider of security have failed to provide full and adequate compensation are mentioned thereunder:

  (i) the case where the owner is financially incapable of meeting his obligation in full, and

  (ii) the case where the financial security does not cover or is insufficient to satisfy the claims for compensation.

  The inability of the owner to meet his obligation in full does not mean that in order that such situation materialises it is necessary that at least the owner must meet his obligation in part: this provision applies both where the obligation is not met in full, or at all.

(b) The compensation was adequate, but was not paid or was not paid in full: the owner or the provider of security have failed to provide full and adequate compensation because the owner is financially incapable of meeting his obligation in full, and the insurance or other financial security does not cover or is insufficient to satisfy the claims for compensation.

(c) The compensation was inadequate. In this case it may be that: (i) it was paid; (ii) it was not paid in full; or (iii) it was not paid at all.

In order to avail themselves of these situations, pursuant to art. 4(1)(b) the claimants have the burden of proving that they have taken 'all reasonable steps to pursue the legal remedies available to them'. This requirement did not exist in the draft submitted to the Conference and was added following a proposal of the Scandinavian delegations.[23] When it was discussed, it met only with the objection of the Polish delegate, who said that it placed too heavy an obligation on the victim of damage by pollution, but the proposal was adopted almost unanimously.[24] Indeed, the wording of this condition is so generic, that it might have created many disputes: what in fact are all the legal remedies the victims must adopt prior to being entitled to claim payment from the Fund? And what are the reasonable steps?[25] Should the

---

22 *Supra*, Chapter 11, para. 4.

23 LEG/CONF. 2/C.1/WP.55, Official Records, *supra*, note 6, p. 285.

24 Official Records, *supra*, note 6, pp. 516–517.

25 In connection with this problem see Måns Jacobsson, 'How clean is clean? The Concept of "Reasonableness" in the Response to Tanker Oil Spills', in *Scritti in Onore di Francesco Berlingieri, Il Diritto Marittimo*, 2010, p. 565.

victims proceed judicially against the shipowner and/or the guarantor and unsuccessfully enforce a judgment against any of them? In *Landcatch Ltd v International Oil Pollution Compensation Fund and Landcatch Ltd v Braer Corporation and Others – The 'Braer'*[26] the Outer House of the Court of Session (Scotland) held:[27]

On the pursuers' averment it cannot be said at this stage what the extent of the obligations of the owners or of the insurers will be, still less that those obligations cannot be met in full. Until the liability of the owner or guarantor has been determined under the 1971 Act, it cannot be known whether the Fund will have any liability at all ... For these reasons I consider that unless waiver or personal bar applies the court cannot grant decree against the Fund until the condition set out in section 4(1)(1)b) of the 1974 Act has been satisfied.

However from the information available in the IOPC Funds' Decisions database it appears that the Fund's governing bodies had adopted a rather pragmatic approach on the assessment of the conditions for the operation of art. 4(1)(b).[28]

---

26 [1998] 2 Lloyd's Rep 552.

27 At p. 563.

28 In the *Milad* incident the claimants were unable to trace the owners and the following analysis of a claim of the Marine Emergency Mutual Aid Centre (MEMAC) by the Executive Committee is reported in FUND/EXC.3/7 of 29 April 1999:

> 3.2.6 A number of delegations expressed the view that there were various additional steps which MEMAC could take to trace the shipowner. It was suggested that enquiries could be made of the Belize Registry regarding the status of the vessel and whether it was free from mortgages, any other registered encumbrances and other liens or charges. It was pointed out that a vessel of the size of the *Milad 1* should comply with SOLAS and the ISM Code and that the accompanying ISM certificate should identify a physical person representing the vessel. Those delegations considered that, notwithstanding the small amount of money involved, important principles were at stake and that every effort should be made to protect the 1992 Fund's interests in respect of MEMAC's claim.
>
> 3.2.7 Many delegations, whilst noting that other steps could be taken, considered that the question of proportionality should not be overlooked and drew attention to the fact that the amount claimed was only £33,000. They expressed the view that in this particular situation MEMAC had taken all reasonable steps to trace the shipowner. Those delegations made the point that the 1992 Fund was in a better position to pursue the shipowner by recourse action.
>
> 3.2.8 The Executive Committee decided that, taking all factors into account, MEMAC had taken all reasonable steps to pursue the legal remedies available to it and that MEMAC's claim was therefore admissible.

In the *Kinhu* incident (this vessel was registered in Estonia) the following analysis was made by the Director in respect of a claim against the Fund by the Finnish Government (71 FUND/EXC.52/5 of 3 February 1997, para. 5.4):

> 5.4 The Director makes the following analysis as to whether the Finnish Government has fulfilled the requirement laid down in article 4.1(b) of the 1971 Fund Convention to take all reasonable steps to pursue the legal remedies available to it.
>
> Estonia was not Party to the 1969 Civil Liability Convention and the 1971 Fund Convention, nor did it have any domestic law governing liability for oil pollution. It appears very unlikely, therefore, that the Finnish Government would have been able to recover its costs for preventive measures from the shipowner, the bare-boat charterer or the insurer by taking legal action in Estonia. In any event, a judgment rendered by an Estonian court would not have been rendered under the 1969 Civil Liability Convention.
>
> The Finnish Government could have taken action in Finland against the registered owner (Tallinn Port Authority) under the Finnish legislation implementing the 1969 Civil Liability Convention. However, Finland does not have any agreement with Estonia in respect of enforcement of judgments, and Estonia is not Party to any treaty relating to recognition and enforcement of judgments which would be applicable in this case. It is unlikely, therefore, that a judgment rendered by a Finnish Court against the shipowner could have been enforced in Estonia. It would have been theoretically possible to enforce such a judgment against the shipowner's assets in any State Party to the 1969 Civil Liability Convention. However, it is almost certain that the Tallinn Port Authority would not have assets outside Estonia.

It may be added that the wording of the third case, described as that where the damage exceeds the owner's liability under the CLC,[29] is far from accurate; it is in fact not the damage suffered by 'any person', reference to which is made in the chapeau of paragraph 1, that exceeds the owner's liability, but the global pollution damage caused by an incident.

5.2 When payment of compensation by the Fund is not due

A thorough analysis of the possible exceptions from the general responsibility of the Compensation Fund was made by the Working Group appointed by the Legal Committee of IMCO in the Spring of 1970 on the basis of the questions raised by the Delegations on the Netherlands and Norway.[30] Such questions, based on the exclusions of the liability of the owner under the CLC 1969, are reproduced below, followed by views of the Working Group.

Question 1: Should the Fund indemnify the victims in cases where the damage resulted from an act of war, hostilities, civil war or insurrection?
The general view of the Working Group was that the victims should not be entitled to compensation in such cases.
Question 2: Should the Fund indemnify the victims in cases where the damage resulted from a natural phenomenon of an exceptional, inevitable and irresistible character?
The general view of the Working Group was that the victims should be entitled to compensation in these cases.
Question 3: Should the Fund indemnify the victims in cases where the damage was wholly caused by an act or omission done with intent to cause damage by a third party?
The Working Group was of the unanimous view that the victims should be able to claim compensation in such cases.
Question 4: Should the Fund indemnify the victims in cases where the damage was wholly caused by the negligence or other wrongful act of any Government or other authority responsible for the maintenance of lights or other navigational aids in the exercise of that function?

The Finnish Act implementing the 1969 Civil Liability Convention provides for a channelling of liability which goes further than the channelling provided in article III.4 of the Convention. The channelling in this Act is similar to that contained in article III.4 of the 1992 Civil Liability Convention. Claims for compensation for pollution damage failing within the scope of the Act may not be brought against, *inter alia*, any person who in the place of the registered owner operates the ship. For this reason, it would not have been possible for the Government to bring legal action against the bare-boat charterer under this Act, nor under any other legal provisions.

The insurer has opposed the action against it in Finland on the ground that there was no right of direct action, since the insurance was not issued under article VII.1 of the 1969 Civil Liability Convention. As mentioned above, the insurance had been taken out by the bare-boat charterer and not by the registered owner. It is unlikely, therefore, that the Finnish Court will accept a direct action against the P & I insurer, since Finnish law does not allow direct action against insurers except in cases specifically provided by statute. It is improbable that a direct action against the insurer in the Turks & Caicos Islands (a United Kingdom dependency), where the insurer has its registered office, would be successful, again because the insurance was not issued under article VII.1 and United Kingdom law does not allow direct action against an insurer, except in cases specifically provided by statute.

5.5 For the reasons set out above, the Director takes the view that the Finnish Government has taken all reasonable steps to pursue the legal remedies available to it to recover its costs from parties other than the 1971 Fund.

The Author is indebted to the former Director of the Fund, Mr Måns Jacobsson, for having kindly drawn his attention on these incidents and on the decisions of the Fund.

29 On this paragraph see also the comments of the Rapporteur, in Official Records, *supra*, note 6, p. 331.
30 LEG/WG(FUND) I/4, Annex II.

A large majority of the Working Group considered that the victims should be able to claim compensation in these cases.

Question 5: Should the Fund indemnify the victims in cases where the pollution damage resulted wholly or partially from an act or omission done with intent to cause damage by the person who suffered the damage?

Question 6: Should the Fund indemnify the victims in cases where the pollution damage resulted wholly or partially from the negligence of the person who suffered the damage?

The Working Group was of the view that these questions should be answered in exactly the same way as they were dealt with under the 1969 Convention.

Question 7: Should the Fund indemnify the victims in cases where the guarantor may refuse to pay on the grounds that the pollution damage resulted from the wilful misconduct of the owner himself (see Article VII, paragraph 8 of the Civil Liability Convention, 1969)?

The general consensus was that the victims should be entitled to compensation from the Fund in these cases.

Question 8: Should the Fund indemnify the victims in cases where the ship or guarantor is not financially capable of fulfilling the guarantee or indemnifying the victims?

The Working Group considered that the Fund should indemnify the victims in such cases.

Question 9: Should the Fund indemnify the victims in cases where quantities of oil of less than 2,000 tons carried aboard a ship causes pollution damage, and the shipowner is not financially capable of indemnifying the victims (see Article VII, 1969 Civil Liability Convention)?

Subject to the outcome of the further consideration to be given by the Working Group to the problems contained in paragraphs 24 to 27 of the Report, the general consensus in the Working Group was that the victims should be entitled to claim compensation in such cases.

There are three provisions in art. 4 that are relevant for the purpose of establishing when payment of compensation is not due by the Fund: those set out in paragraphs 2, 3 and 6. They will be considered *seriatim*.

2 The Fund shall incur no obligation under the preceding paragraph if:

  (a) it proves that the pollution damage resulted from an act of war, hostilities, civil war or insurrection or was caused by oil which has escaped or been discharged from a warship or other ship owned or operated by a State and used, at the time of the incident, only on Government non-commercial service; or

  (b) the claimant cannot prove that the damage resulted from an incident involving one or more ships.

The phrase in sub-paragraph 2 'shall incur no obligation' is tantamount at the same time to exoneration from liability and to exclusion from the scope of application. The exclusion in sub-paragraph (a) in respect of pollution damage resulting from act of war, hostilities, civil war or insurrection corresponds to the exoneration from liability of the owner under art. III(1)(a) of the CLC, whilst in respect of pollution damage caused by oil which has escaped or been discharged from a warship or other ship owned or operated by a State and used only on Government non-commercial service it corresponds to the exclusion of those ships from the scope of application of the CLC pursuant to its art. XI.

The exclusion of any obligation in sub-paragraph (b) where the claimant cannot prove that the damage resulted from an incident involving one or more ships, apart from the unusual negative formulation of the rule, does not find any corresponding provision in the CLC, but it is clear that also under the CLC the claimant has the burden of proving that the pollution causing the damage has been due to an incident involving two or more ships, reference to which is made in art. IV of the CLC. Since the burden of proof is on the claimants, their entitlement to compensation from the Fund arises first upon proof by them that one of the conditions indicated in paragraph 1 exists and secondly upon proof that damage resulted from an incident involving one or more ships. It is only upon such evidence having been provided that the defence indicated in paragraph 2(a) may be raised.

3   If the Fund proves that the pollution damage resulted wholly or partially either from an act or omission done with the intent to cause damage by the person who suffered the damage or from the negligence of that person, the Fund may be exonerated wholly or partially from its obligation to pay compensation to such person. The Fund shall in any event be exonerated to the extent that the owner may have been exonerated under article III, paragraph 3, of the 1992 Liability Convention. However, there shall be no such exoneration of the Fund with regard to preventive measures.

This defence is also based on the identical defence available to the owner pursuant to art. III(3) of the CLC 1992. The purpose of the subsequent reference to that provision, that appears as a repetition of the same rule already enunciated in the first sentence, is probably that of relieving the Fund of the burden of proof placed on it by the first sentence and allowing it to obtain the same result by proving that the owner had been exonerated (wholly or partially) from liability pursuant to art. III(3) of the CLC.

6   The Assembly of the Fund may decide that, in exceptional cases, compensation in accordance with this Convention can be paid even if the owner of the ship has not constituted a fund in accordance with article V, paragraph 3, of the 1992 Liability Convention. In such case paragraph 4(c) of this article applies accordingly.[31]

It is difficult to understand the logic of this provision, since pursuant to the preceding paragraph 1 the Fund is required to pay adequate compensation if the owner is incapable of meeting his obligation in full and in such event it is hardly conceivable he will constitute a fund in accordance with art. V(3) of the CLC.

The provisions of art. 4(2) and (3) previously considered cover the situations dealt with in questions 1, 5 and 6. The provisions of art. 4(1) expressly or impliedly cover the situations dealt with in questions 2, 3, 4, 7 and 8, for in all the situations envisaged thereunder the Fund must pay compensation to any person suffering pollution damage. It is suggested that art. 4(1) also impliedly affirms the obligation of the Fund in respect of damage caused by oil carried in a quantity of less than 2,000 tons, irrespective of whether the carrying capacity of the ship is below or above 2,000 tons: in art. 4(1) reference is made under (b) to the situation where the insurance or financial security does not cover the claims for compensation.

5.3 The amount of compensation available under the Fund Convention

Art. 4(4) so provides:

4   (a)   Except as otherwise provided in sub-paragraphs (b) and (c) of this paragraph, the aggregate amount of compensation payable by the Fund under this article shall in respect of any one incident be limited, so that the total sum of that amount and the amount of compensation actually paid under the 1992 Liability Convention for pollution damage within the scope of application of this Convention as defined in article 3 shall not exceed 203,000,000 units of account.

---

31   Paragraph 4(c) is considered *infra*, in para 5.3.

INTERNATIONAL MARITIME CONVENTIONS

(b) Except as otherwise provided in sub-paragraph (c), the aggregate amount of compensation payable by the Fund under this article for pollution damage resulting from a natural phenomenon of an exceptional, inevitable and irresistible character shall not exceed 203,000,000 units of account.

(c) The maximum amount of compensation referred to in sub-paragraphs (a) and (b) shall be 300,740,000 units of account with respect to any incident occurring during any period when there are three Parties to this Convention in respect of which the combined relevant quantity of contributing oil received by persons in the territories of such Parties, during the preceding calendar year, equalled or exceeded 600 million tons.

(d) Interest accrued on a fund constituted in accordance with article V, paragraph 3, of the 1992 Liability Convention, if any, shall not be taken into account for the computation of the maximum compensation payable by the Fund under this article.

(e) The amounts mentioned in this article shall be converted into national currency on the basis of the value of that currency by reference to the Special Drawing Right on the date of the decision of the Assembly of the Fund as to the first date of payment of compensation.

The provisions comprised in paragraph 4 will be considered *seriatim*.

The provision in sub-paragraph (a)

The global character of the compensation to be granted for pollution damage to the victims is enhanced by the fact that the total compensation is unique and the compensation payable by the Fund is basically complementary to that payable by the owner or his guarantor under the CLC: whatever is the compensation, if any, payable under the CLC, the Fund must make available a sum such as to ensure a total compensation of 203 million SDRs. That entails that the share payable by the Fund varies according to the tonnage of the ship from which the oil has escaped or has been discharged: where the ship's tonnage is 5,000 GT and the limit is 3 million SDRs the maximum complement payable by the Fund would be 200 million SDR; where the ship's tonnage is 140,000 GT, the maximum sum payable by the owner being 59,700,000 SDRs, the maximum complement payable by the Fund would be 143,300,000 SDRs.[32]

Although the comparison between the contributions of the ship and of the cargo appears at first sight striking, it is necessary to consider what is the percentage of incidents in respect of which the claims are below the limit of the owner's liability and which are above such limit and, consequently, which are the global contributions paid by the ship and by the cargo.[33]

---

32 A summary of the contributions by the ship and the cargo had been made by the delegate of the United Kingdom at the sixth meeting of the Committee of the Whole (Official Records, *supra*, note 6, vol. 2, p. 275) and a table with a list of the cases involving the largest total payments in the years from 1979 to 2008 has been published by Måns Jacobsson, 'The International Liability Compensation Regime for Oil Pollution from Ships', *supra* note 12, p. 8.

33 At the time of the adoption of the Protocols to the CLC and the Fund Convention by the Conference on May 1984 statistics were provided by the International Group of P and I Clubs (LEG/CONF.6/14, in Official Records, *supra*, note 6, vol. 2, pp. 15–31) and by France (LEG/CONF.6/C.2/WP.4, Official Records, *supra*, note 6, vol. 2, p. 245). Reference to such statistics has been made by the observer of International Group at the sixth meeting of the Committee of the Whole (Official Records, *supra*, note 6, vol. 2, p. 377) and a summary of those provided by France has been made by the French delegate at that meeting (Official Records, *supra*, note 6, vol. 2, p. 379).

168

THE FUND CONVENTION

The provision in sub-paragraph (b)
The provision in sub-paragraph (b), pursuant to which the aggregate amount of compensation payable by the Fund for pollution damage resulting from a natural phenomenon of an exceptional, inevitable and irresistible character shall not exceed the total compensation indicated in sub-paragraph (a), aims at ensuring the same protection to the victims in a case where the owner is not liable under art. III(2)(a) of the CLC but, unlike the other cases enumerated in art. III(2),[34] does not justify the exclusion of the obligation of the Fund.

The provision in sub-paragraph (c)
The amount of compensation indicated under sub-paragraphs (a) and (b), has been determined with reference to a prudent estimate of the quantity of contributing oil likely to be received by persons in the Contracting States bound to contribute pursuant to art. 10(1). It has, however, been deemed appropriate to increase such amount if the global quantity of contributing oil would be in excess of such estimate and it has been decided to increase the maximum contribution to 300,740,000 SDRs where the global contributing oil received by persons in three Contracting States had been equal to or greater than 600 million tons.

The provision in sub-paragraph (d)
No provision on interest is made in the CLC and since the owner has the option of constituting the fund by depositing the sum or by producing a bank guarantee, it appears that also where this second alternative is chosen, the guarantee will be for an amount corresponding to the limit and, therefore, interest will not mature. This is the reason why reference is made in sub-paragraph (d) to 'interest . . . if any'.

The provision in sub-paragraph (e)
Article 18 includes among the functions of the Assembly the following:

7 To approve settlements of claims against the Fund, to take decisions in respect of the distribution among claimants of the available amount of compensation in accordance with article 4, paragraph 5, and to determine the terms and conditions according to which provisional payments in respect of claims shall be made with a view to ensuring that victims of pollutions damage are compensated as promptly as possible.

These functions are entrusted by the Internal Regulations[35] to the Director. Regulation 7 so provides:

7.2 The Director shall promptly satisfy any claims for pollution damage under article 4 of the 1992 Fund Convention which have been established by judgment against the 1992 Fund enforceable under article 39 of the 1992 Fund Convention.
7.4 Where the Director is satisfied that the 1992 Fund is liable under the 1992 Fund Convention to pay compensation for pollution damage, he or she may, without the prior approval of the Assembly, make final settlement of any claim, if he or she estimates that the total cost to the 1991 Fund of satisfying all claims arising out of the relevant incident is not likely to exceed 2,5 million SDRs. The Director may in any case make final settlement of claims from individuals and small businesses up to an aggregate amount of

---

34 On which see *supra*, Chapter 11, para. 4.3.
35 As amended by the Administrative Council at its 29th session held from 15 to 19 October 2012.

INTERNATIONAL MARITIME CONVENTIONS

1 million SDRs in respect of any one incident. The relevant date of conversion shall be the date of the incident in question.

5.4 Distribution of the amount available under the 1992 Fund Convention when claims are in excess of the compensation payable

Art. 7(5) states:

5 Where the amount of established claims against the Fund exceeds the aggregate amount of compensation payable under paragraph 4, the amount available shall be distributed in such a manner that the proportion between any established claim and the amount of compensation actually recovered by the claimant under this Convention shall be the same for all claimants.

Whilst the initial part of this provision appears to be due to the fact that, contrary to what happens in respect of the CLC as well as of the LLMC Convention, the Fund is basically intended to ensure the full satisfaction of the claims, it is not clear why the wording of the final part differs from that of art. V(4) of the CLC and of art. 12(1) of the LLMC Convention: would it in fact not have been simpler and clearer just to provide that 'the amount available shall be distributed among the claimants in proportion to their established claims'?

5.5 Payment of compensation when the owner has not constituted a fund

Art. 4(6) so provides:

6 The Assembly of the Fund may decide that, in exceptional cases, compensation in accordance with this Convention can be paid even if the owner of the ship has not constituted a fund in accordance with article V paragraph 3, of the 1992 Liability Convention. In such case paragraph 4 (e) of this article applies accordingly.

Since art. 4(1) provides that the Fund shall pay compensation, *inter alia*, because no liability for the damage arises under the CLC or the owner is incapable of meeting his obligation and the financial security does not cover the claim, payment by the Fund constitutes the fulfilment of its functions and, therefore, it is not clear why such cases should be qualified as 'exceptional' and a decision of the Assembly be required.

5.6 Extinction of the right to compensation

Art. 6 so provides:

Rights to compensation under article 4 shall be extinguished unless an action is brought thereunder or a notification has been made pursuant to article 7, paragraph 6, within three years from the date when the damage occurred. However, in no case shall an action be brought after six years from the date of the incident which caused the damage.

As mentioned in respect of art. VIII of the CLC, the time when an action may be deemed to be brought may vary between jurisdictions and in particular between civil law and common law jurisdictions.[36] The need for an action to be brought

---

36 *Supra*, Chapter 11, para. 10. See also C.de la Rue and C.B. Anderson, *Shipping and the Environment, supra*, Chapter 11, note 1.

170

against the Fund in order to avoid the extinction of the right of compensation is not required where the claimant has brought proceedings against the owner or his guarantor under the CLC and has given notice of such action to the Fund, thereby enabling the Fund to intervene in such proceedings. Art.7(6) states:

6 Without prejudice to the provisions of paragraph 4, where an action under the 1992 Liability Convention for compensation for pollution damage has been brought against an owner or his guarantor before a competent court in a Contracting State, each party to the proceedings shall be entitled under the national law of that State to notify the Fund of the proceedings. Where such notification has been made in accordance with the formalities required by the law of the court seized and in such time and in such a manner that the Fund has in fact been in a position effectively to intervene as a party to the proceedings, any judgment rendered by the court in such proceedings shall, after it has become final and enforceable in the State where the judgment was given, become binding upon the Fund in the sense that the facts and findings in that judgment may not be disputed by the Fund even if the Fund has not actually intervened in the proceedings.

Whilst in most maritime conventions the lapse of time extinguishes or 'bars' the exercise of the action,[37] in this Convention, as well as in the CLC, the lapse of time extinguishes the right.[38]

Pollution may occur quite some time after an incident that has caused the sinking of a tanker with her cargo or a part of it. It was therefore necessary to ensure certainty by adding to the period running from the time when the damage occurred, a (longer) period running from the time of the incident, for otherwise it would be impossible for the period to fulfil its function – that is, to be sure of the existence of claims or their termination. This rule applies both to the time by which the action may be brought and to the time when the notification to the Fund under art. 7(6) may be given.

5.7 Jurisdiction

5.7.1 The courts of competent jurisdiction

Art. 7 states in its paragraphs 1 and 2:

1 Subject to the subsequent provisions of this article, any action against the Fund for compensation under article 4 of this Convention shall be brought only before a court competent under article IX of the 1992 Liability Convention in respect of actions against the owner who is or who would, but for the provisions of article III, paragraph 2, of that Convention, have been liable for pollution damage caused by the relevant incident.
2 Each Contracting State shall ensure that its courts possess the necessary jurisdiction to entertain such actions against the Fund as are referred to in paragraph 1.

The need for the court in which actions against the Fund must be brought to be the same in which actions against the owner may be brought under art. IX of the CLC

---

37 This is so for the Collision Convention 1910 (Vol. II, Chapter 1, para. 6), the Hamburg Rules (Vol. I, Chapter 2, para. 13), the Rotterdam Rules (Vol. I, Chapter 3, para. 15), the Athens Convention (Vol. I, Chapter 4, para. 12).
38 For a comparative analysis of the various provisions see Vol. I, Chapter 2, para 13.

is obvious, for in the ordinary situations the Fund must integrate the indemnity payable by the owner. The reference to the court which would have been competent 'but for the provisions of art. III paragraph 2' is due to the fact that there are enumerated thereunder the situations in which the owner is not liable, but in one of which (that of pollution damage wholly caused by an act or omission of a third party done with the intent to cause damage) the Fund would be. Perhaps, given that also in the other two the Fund would not be liable, the specific reference to that in which instead it would be liable might have been preferable.

5.7.2 Exclusive jurisdiction of the competent court

Art. 7(3) so provides:

3 Where an action for compensation for pollution damage has been brought before a court competent under article IX of the 1992 Liability Convention against the owner of a ship or his guarantor, such court shall have exclusive jurisdictional competence over any action against the Fund for compensation under the provisions of article 4 of this Convention in respect of the same damage. However, where an action for compensation for pollution damage under the 1992 Liability Convention has been brought before a court in a State Party to the 1992 Liability Convention but not to this Convention, any action against the Fund under article 4 of this Convention shall at the option of the claimant be brought either before a court of the State where the Fund has its headquarters or before any court of a State Party to this Convention competent under article IX of the 1992 Liability Convention.

Pursuant to art. IX(1) of the CLC several courts may have jurisdiction over claims against the owner for pollution damage caused by the same incident where such damage has occurred or preventive measures have been taken in the territory or area of several States reference to which is made in art. II. Once an action has been brought in any one of the courts of competent jurisdiction, only that court will be competent for actions against, and actions by, the Fund. In this provision the case has already been considered of an action being brought against the owner in a court of a State party to the CLC 1992 but not party to the Fund 1992, in which event the action at the option of the claimant may be brought either in the court of the State in which the Fund has its headquarters, such State being at present England, or before any court of a State Party to the Fund Convention competent under art. IX of the CLC 1992. But it would be conceivable that none of the States Parties to the CLC competent under art. IX of such Convention be party to the Fund Convention, in which event the only court of competent jurisdiction would be that in the State in which the Fund has its headquarters.

As of 10 April 2015, 15 of the 133 States Parties to the CLC 1992 were not parties to the Fund Convention 1992,[39] and, therefore, it is rather unlikely that none of the States the court of which might be competent under art. IX of the CLC 1992, would not be party to the Fund Convention 1992.

---

39 These States are: Azerbaijan, Chile, Egypt, El Salvador, Indonesia, Kuwait, Lebanon, Moldova, Mongolia, Pakistan, Romania, Saudi Arabia, Solomon Islands, Togo, Ukraine, Vietnam and Yemen.

THE FUND CONVENTION

5.7.3 The right of the Fund to intervene in proceedings brought against the owner

Art. 7(4) so provides:

4   Each Contracting State shall ensure that the Fund shall have the right to intervene as a party to any legal proceedings instituted in accordance with article IX of the 1992 Liability Convention before a competent court of that State against the owner of a ship or his guarantor.

This is a provision that requires an express implementation by the States Parties, save that the right of intervention in proceedings pending in national courts is generally recognised to parties having an interest.

5.7.4 When a judgment or a settlement is not binding on the Fund

Art. 7(5) so provides:

5   Except as otherwise provided in paragraph 6, the Fund shall not be bound by any judgment or decision in proceedings to which it has not been a party or by any settlement to which it is not a party.

This provision, as all the others in this article, already existed in the draft articles prepared by the Legal Committee for consideration by the Conference held in December 1971[40] and does not call for any comment. It is in fact a fundamental principle that the finding of facts on the basis of which a judgment is issued as well as the judgment itself are only binding on the parties.

5.7.5 Right of the Fund to intervene in the proceedings against the owner

Art. 7 so provides in paragraph 6:

6   Without prejudice to the provisions of paragraph 4, where an action under the 1992 Liability Convention for compensation for pollution damage has been brought against an owner or his guarantor before a competent court in a Contracting State, each party to the proceedings shall be entitled under the national law of that State to notify the Fund of the proceedings. Where such notification has been made in accordance with the formalities required by the law of the court seized and in such time and in such a manner that the Fund has in fact been in a position effectively to intervene as a party to the proceedings, any judgment rendered by the court in such proceedings shall, after it has become final and enforceable in the State where the judgment was given, become binding upon the Fund in the sense that the facts and findings in that judgment may not be disputed by the Fund even if the Fund has not actually intervened in the proceedings.

The rules laid down in this paragraph are exceptions to the general rule of the previous paragraph 6 and the basis of such exception is the strict link between the CLC and the Fund Convention. It is logical that the Fund, which is bound to integrate, within a specified limit, the sum payable by the shipowner, has a direct interest following the settlement negotiations between the victims and the shipowner as well as the judicial proceedings that may be brought by the victims against the shipowner. It would therefore be unfair if the victims were bound to join the Fund in the

---

40 *Supra*, note 3, p. 149.

proceedings pending against the shipowner, and instead it makes sense leaving to the Fund, that has been informed that proceedings are pending, the liberty to join such proceedings or not.

6 THE CONTRIBUTIONS TO THE FUND

6.1 Introduction

The question whether the Fund or the individual Contracting States should take all actions necessary in order to obtain payment of the contributions by the persons who, in each Contracting State, receive in a given year an amount of oil equal or greater than the minimum required in order to trigger the obligation to pay his contribution could be answered either by leaving the entire responsibility to the Fund, leaving it to each Contracting States or placing it on both the Fund and the Contracting States. The solution adopted has been, quite reasonably, the latter. The Contracting States provide their cooperation in order to enable the Fund to collect the contribution and are only liable if they fail to do that at a time and in the manner prescribed in the Internal Regulations.

Art. 15 so provides:

1 Each Contracting State shall ensure that any person who receives contributing oil within its territory in such quantities that he is liable to contribute to the Fund appears on a list to be established and kept up to date by the Director in accordance with the subsequent provisions of this article.
2 For the purposes set out in paragraph 1, each Contracting State shall communicate, at a time and in the manner to be prescribed in the Internal Regulations, to the Director the name and address of any person who in respect of that State is liable to contribute to the Fund pursuant to article 10, as well as data on the relevant quantities of contributing oil received by any such person during the preceding calendar year.
3 For the purposes of ascertaining who are, at any given time, the persons liable to contribute to the Fund in accordance with article 10, paragraph 1, and of establishing, where applicable, the quantities of oil to be taken into account for any such person when determining the amount of his contribution, the list shall be prima facie evidence of the facts stated therein.
4 Where a Contracting State does not fulfil its obligations to submit to the Director the communication referred to in paragraph 2 and this results in a financial loss for the Fund, that Contracting State shall be liable to compensate the Fund for such loss. The Assembly shall, on the recommendation of the Director, decide whether such compensation shall be payable by that Contracting State.

In connection with the obligations of Contracting States mentioned in para 2, Regulation 4 of the Internal Regulations provides in section 4.5:

4.5 The Director shall, not later than 15 January of each year, invite Member States to submit the reports referred to in Internal Regulation 4.1. The Director shall send these States an appropriate number of the forms mentioned in that Regulation.

It then provides in sections 4.1 and 4.2:

4.1 Each Member State shall forward annually to the Director reports on contributing oil receipt, using the form annexed to these Internal Regulations. The reports shall reach the Director not later than 30 April each year. They shall specify the names and addresses of all persons who, in the preceding calendar year, received within the territory of the Member State concerned oil in respect of which contributions are liable to be paid in accordance with article 10 of the 1992 Convention, together with details of the quantities of contributing oil received by all such persons during that year.

4.2 The reports shall be completed by the contributors concerned, taking into account the explanatory notes attached to the form referred to in Internal Regulation 4.1. The reports shall be signed by a competent officer of the entity which received the oil and by a Government official.

Therefore each Contracting State must act as agent for the Fund and deliver the Contributing Oil Report Forms to all the persons who received within its territory a quantity of oil exceeding 150,000 tons, collect such forms duly filled in and deliver them to the Fund.[41] However the fact that the form must be countersigned by a government official entails an implied guarantee of the government that the information provided therein is correct.

6.2 Who is bound to make contribution

Art. 10 so provides:

1 Annual contributions to the Fund shall be made in respect of each Contracting State by any person who, in the calendar year referred to in article 12, paragraph 2(a) or (b), has received in total quantities exceeding 150,000 tons:

(a) in the ports or terminal installations in the territory of that State contributing oil carried by sea to such ports or terminal installations; and

(b) in any installations situated in the territory of that Contracting State contributing oil which has been carried by sea and discharged in a port or terminal installation of a non-Contracting State, provided that contributing oil shall only be taken into account by virtue of this sub-paragraph on first receipt in a Contracting State after its discharge in that non-Contracting State.

2(a) For the purposes of paragraph 1, where the quantity of contributing oil received in the territory of a Contracting State by any person in a calendar year when aggregated with the quantity of contributing oil received in the same Contracting State in that year by any associated person or persons exceeds 150,000 tons, such person shall pay contributions in respect of the actual quantity received by him notwithstanding that that quantity did not exceed 150,000 tons.

(b) 'Associated person' means any subsidiary or commonly controlled entity. The question whether a person comes within this definition shall be determined by the national law of the State concerned.

This article creates a direct obligation of the persons who in each Contracting State receive oil to effect payment of their contributions to the Fund.[42] The reason why annual contributions are payable only by persons who have received in the rel-

---

41 Attention was drawn in 2007 by the then Director of the Fund, Mr Måns Jacobsson, to the fact that a number of Member States did not fulfil their treaty obligations to present their reports, thereby rendering impossible for the Fund to levy contributions with respect to the receivers of oil in their countries (M. Jacobsson, 'The International Liability Compensation Regime for Oil Pollution from Ships', *supra* note 12, p. 7.

42 The levy of contributions depends on reports of the amounts of oil received by individual contributors, which the governments of Member States are obliged to submit annually to the Secretariat of the Fund.

evant year total quantities exceeding 150,000 tons has been to limit the number of contributors, thereby reducing administrative costs.[43] However for the purposes of establishing whether that minimum quantity has been received by any given person account must be taken first of the oil discharged in a non-Contracting State and carried therefrom to the relevant Contracting States by means other than a ship (e.g. by a pipeline) and secondly also of oil received in the relevant Contracting State by a person associated to the relevant person. The treatment of that oil differs, since in the first case it is relevant for the calculation of the actual amount of the contribution, while in the second case it is only relevant for the purposes of triggering the obligation of payment of the contribution, but not for the calculation of its amount, which must be made with reference only to the quantity, lower than 150,000 tons actually received by that person.

6.3 The currency in which contributions must be paid

Regulation 3 of the Internal Regulations provides:

Contributions
3.1 The fixed sum on the basis of which annual contributions shall be calculated under article 12.2 of the 1992 Fund Convention shall be determined in Pounds Sterling.
3.2 Annual contributions shall be payable in Pounds Sterling. However, the Director may require a contributor to pay his or her annual contribution or a portion thereof in the national currency of the State within whose territory the relevant quantities of contributing oil were received. In the latter case, conversion from Pounds Sterling to the currency in which payment is to be made shall be at the mid-market rate of exchange applied by the Bank of England on the first day of the month of the invoice.
3.3 For the purposes of calculating the annual contributions, the relevant date for conversion of the figure of 4 million SDRs laid down in article 12.1(i)(b) and (c) of the 1992 Fund Convention shall be the date of the incident in question.

The choice of the pound sterling as the currency of payment is due to the fact that the seat of the Headquarters of the Fund 1992 is in England pursuant to a Headquarters Agreement between the Government of the United Kingdom and the Fund 1992.

---

43 The following comments were made by the Rapporteur at the thirteenth meeting of the Committee of the Whole established by the Conference held from 29 November to 18 December 1971 (Official Records of the Conference on the Establishment of an International Compensation Fund for Oil Pollution Damage, 1971, p. 404):

Mr Nordenson, Rapporteur, explaining the general principle of the system of contributions set out in article 10, said that under paragraph 1 initial and annual contributions were to be made in respect of each contracting State only by persons who, in the course of the year as defined in articles 11 and 12 of the draft, had received total quantities of contributing oil exceeding an amount of tons to be determined. The purpose of that provision was to limit the number of contributors in order to reduce administrative costs. The contributions were payable in respect of contributing oil carried by sea and discharged in a port or terminal installation of a Contracting State or in any installation on the territory of a non-Contracting State and thereafter transported by pipe-line or otherwise into the territory of a Contracting State. Contributions had to be made every time there was a movement, for example, when a delivery of crude oil was followed by a delivery of fuel oil produced from that crude oil. In addition, contributing oil received by any branches or entities commonly controlled by any person referred to in paragraph 1, was, under the terms of paragraph 2, considered as having been received by such person for the purpose of calculating the quantity of oil referred to in paragraph 1. The tons referred to in the article were metric tons.

THE FUND CONVENTION

6.4 The basis of the assessment of the amount of annual contributions

Art. 12 so provides:

1 With a view to assessing the amount of annual contributions due, if any, and taking account of the necessity to maintain sufficient liquid funds, the Assembly shall for each calendar year make an estimate in the form of a budget of:

(i) *Expenditure*
> (a) costs and expenses of the administration of the Fund in the relevant year and any deficit from operations in preceding years;
>
> (b) payments to be made by the Fund in the relevant year for the satisfaction of claims against the Fund due under article 4, including repayment on loans previously taken by the Fund for the satisfaction of such claims, to the extent that the aggregate amount of such claims in respect of any one incident does not exceed four million units of account;
>
> (c) payments to be made by the Fund in the relevant year for the satisfaction of claims against the Fund due under article 4, including repayments on loans previously taken by the Fund for the satisfaction of such claims, to the extent that the aggregate amount of such claims in respect of any one incident is in excess of four million units of account;

(ii) *Income*
> (a) surplus funds from operations in preceding years, including any interest;
>
> (b) annual contributions, if required to balance the budget;
>
> (c) any other income.

2 The Assembly shall decide the total amount of contributions to be levied. On the basis of that decision, the Director shall, in respect of each Contracting State, calculate for each person referred to in article 10 the amount of his annual contribution:

(a) in so far as the contribution is for the satisfaction of payments referred to in paragraph 1(i)(a) and (b) on the basis of a fixed sum for each ton of contributing oil received in the relevant State by such persons during the preceding calendar year; and

(b) in so far as the contribution is for the satisfaction of payments referred to in paragraph 1(i)(c) of this article on the basis of a fixed sum for each ton of contributing oil received by such person during the calendar year preceding that in which the incident in question occurred, provided that State was a Party to this Convention at the date of the incident.

3 The sums referred to in paragraph 2 above shall be arrived at by dividing the relevant total amount of contributions required by the total amount of contributing oil received in all Contracting States in the relevant year.

4 The annual contribution shall be due on the date to be laid down in the Internal Regulations of the Fund. The Assembly may decide on a different date of payment.

5 The Assembly may decide, under conditions to be laid down in the Financial Regulations of the Fund, to make transfers between funds received in accordance with article 12.2(a) and funds received in accordance with article 12.2(b).

The following analysis of the draft of this provision, that did not differ significantly from that adopted by the Conference and quoted above, was made by the Rapporteur at the fourteenth meeting of the Committee of the Whole, held on 8 December 1971:[44]

Mr Nordenson, Rapporteur, explained that article 12 dealt with the question of annual contribution to the Fund: namely, contributions designed firstly to supplement, if so required, the working capital constituted by the initial contribution, secondly, to cover administrative

---

44 Official Records, *supra*, note 6, p. 413.

expenses for the relevant year, and thirdly, to meet obligations arising during the year in respect to indemnification of owners or insurers or compensation of victims. The basic principle underlying the provisions was that no party receiving oil in the territory of a Contracting State should be liable to contribute towards claims arising out of an incident that occurred prior to the country where the oil was received becoming a party to the Convention. Since a State might adhere to the Convention in the interim between an incident and the call on the Fund to disburse indemnification or compensation in respect thereof, the question had arisen as to the liability of an oil receiver in such a State. In that regard, it had been considered appropriate, in order to facilitate administration of the Fund, to differentiate between major and minor incidents as the source of claims. In the case of a minor incident involving amounts below a level to be agreed upon, contributions would be payable by all oil receivers liable to contribute to the Fund in the year in question, even though their countries of origin might not have been parties to the convention at the time of its occurrence. On the other hand, in the case of a major incident entailing obligations on the Fund above that level, contributions would be made only by those receivers whose countries were parties to the convention at the time of the incident. The borderline to be drawn between the two categories of incident was of course an arbitrary one, but the IMCO Legal Committee and Working Group had come to the conclusion that 15 million francs would be a fair amount to be specified for the purpose.

Since the levy of contributions depends on the amounts of oil received in each Member State by individual contributors, the global amount of contributions paid by persons in a Member State varies considerably according to the quantity of contributing oil received in each Member State.[45]

6.5 The breach by persons liable of their obligations and the action to be taken by the Fund

Art. 13 so provides:

1 The amount of any contribution due under article 12 and which is in arrears shall bear interest at a rate which shall be determined in accordance with the Internal Regulations of the Fund, provided that different rates may be fixed for different circumstances.

. . .

3 Where a person who is liable in accordance with the provisions of articles 10 and 12 to make contributions to the Fund does not fulfil his obligations in respect of any such contribution or any part thereof and is in arrears, the Director shall take all appropriate action against such person on behalf of the Fund with a view to the recovery of the amount due. However, where the defaulting contributor is manifestly insolvent or the circumstances otherwise so warrant, the Assembly may, upon recommendation of the Director, decide that no action shall be taken or continued against the contributor.

Art.12(4) provides that the annual contribution is due on the date laid down in the Internal Regulation of the Fund. Regulation 3.5 provides that the Director 'shall promptly issue to every person liable to pay contributions under articles 10, 12 and

---

45 From the information available on the website of the Fund www.iopcfunds.org, it appears that 77 per cent of contributions for 2014, based on 2013 oil receipts, were made by the following ten States, in the percentages shown for each of them:

Japan 15%	Singapore 7%
India 13%	Spain 5%
Republic of Korea 9%	France 4%
Netherlands 8%	United Kingdom 4%
Italy: 8%	Canada 4%.

THE FUND CONVENTION

14 of the 1992 Fund Convention[46] an invoice in respect of the sums for which he or she is liable' and then indicates the contents of the invoice including the date by which payment must be made. Regulation 3.6 then provides:

Payment of annual contribution shall be due on 1 March of the year following that in which the Assembly decides on the levy of annual contributions, unless the Assembly decides otherwise.

The date that must be stated should therefore be that indicated in Regulation 3.6. It is, however, implied that in order to enable the person liable to make payment by that date the invoice must be issued and received by the person liable reasonably in advance. Perhaps this should have been explicitly stated in that Regulation.

6.6 The cooperation of Contracting States

Art. 13(2) so provides:

2 Each Contracting State shall ensure that any obligation to contribute to the Fund arising under this Convention in respect of oil received within the territory of that State is fulfilled and shall take any appropriate measures under its law, including the imposing of such sanctions as it may deem necessary, with a view to the effective execution of any such obligation; provided, however, that such measures shall only be directed against those persons who are under an obligation to contribute to the Fund.

The question that arises is whether pursuant to this provision Contracting States become the guarantors of the persons liable. Although this article taken in isolation might be interpreted in that sense, the subsequent provision in art. 14 that States may assume the obligations incumbent on the persons liable appears to exclude that interpretation of art. 13(2). However, they cannot wash their hands and just leave to the Fund the initiative of prosecuting the persons liable. They must in fact enact provisions that bind the persons liable to fulfil their obligations: it does not appear that the action required of them is performed by merely giving the force of law to the Convention: they must enact domestic rules that bind the persons liable, including sanctions[47] for their breach. It would appear, therefore, that direct liability of Contracting States would arise if they fail to enact such rules and the persons liable are in breach of their obligation. Should the Fund hold a Contracting State liable for the breach of its obligations under art. 13, the question of the allocation of the burden of proof would arise: should the Fund merely prove the failure of the Contracting State to comply with the provisions of art. 13(2), or should it also prove that such failure has been the cause of the breach by the person liable of his obligations? It is suggested that the first alterative is correct.

---

46 Art. 10 of the 1992 Convention sets out the general rule pursuant to which annual contribution is due by any person who in the relevant calendar year has received in total quantities exceeding 150,000 tons. Art. 12(2) provides that the Assembly decides the total amount of contributions to be levied and that on the basis of that decision the Director shall in respect of each State calculate for each person the amount of his total contribution in respect of each of the three items of income specified in para. 1(ii)(a), (b) and (c). Reference to art. 14 becomes relevant only where a Contracting State declares that it will assume obligations that are incumbent on any person who is liable to contribute to the Fund.

47 In the Draft Articles submitted to the Conference, after the sentence 'including the imposing of such sanctions' there followed the words 'under civil or criminal law'. The discussion on this provision during the Conference appears to have been limited to the deletion of those words, that indeed were not necessary (Official Records, *supra*, note 6, p. 424).

179

6.7 Voluntary assumption by Contracting States of the obligations of the persons liable

Art. 14 so provides:

1   Each Contracting State may at the time when it deposits its instrument of ratification or accession or at any time thereafter declare that it assumes itself obligations that are incumbent under this Convention on any person who is liable to contribute to the Fund in accordance with article 10, paragraph 1, in respect of oil received within the territory of that State. Such declaration shall be made in writing and shall specify which obligations are assumed.
2   Where a declaration under paragraph 1 is made prior to the entry into force of this Convention in accordance with article 40, it shall be deposited with the Secretary-General of the Organization who shall after the entry into force of the Convention communicate the declaration to the Director.
3   A declaration under paragraph 1 which is made after the entry into force of this Convention shall be deposited with the Director.
4   A declaration made in accordance with this article may be withdrawn by the relevant State giving notice thereof in writing to the Director. Such notification shall take effect three months after the Director's receipt thereof.
5   Any State which is bound by a declaration made under this article shall, in any proceedings brought against it before a competent court in respect of any obligation specified in the declaration, waive any immunity that it would otherwise be entitled to invoke.

The wording of this article as it appeared in the Draft Articles[48] has not given rise to any comment during the Conference and has been adopted without any change. It is questionable whether the flexibility granted to Contracting States is not excessive and may lead to cumbersome administrative actions. In fact States may not only, pursuant to paragraph 1, specify which obligations of any given person they assume, but may also, pursuant to paragraph 4, withdraw their declaration, albeit with a three-month notice. The use of the plural in respect of the obligation to contribute of any person who has received quantities of oil exceeding 150,000 tons is due to the fact that pursuant to art. 12(4) the annual contribution is payable in two tranches.

7 ORGANISATION AND ADMINISTRATION OF THE FUND

7.1 The organs of the Fund

Originally there were three organs of the Fund: the Assembly, the Secretariat and the Executive Committee. However the Executive Committee, consisting of one-third of the members of the Assembly, was impliedly suppressed by the Protocol of 1992. Art. 16 of the Convention, which in its original text provided:

The Fund shall have an Assembly, a Secretariat headed by a Director and, in accordance with the provisions of article 21, an Executive Committee.

was replaced in art. 17 of the Protocol of 1992 by the following text:

The Fund shall have an Assembly and a Secretariat headed by a Director.

---

48 Official Records, *supra*, note 6, p. 101.

Nor has the Executive Committee ever been established. This is confirmed by the fact that art. 21 provided that the Executive Committee would be established at the first regular session of the Assembly after the date on which the number of Contracting States reached 15 and that article and the subsequent articles from 22 to 27 which set out rules of the functioning of the Executive Committee have been equally suppressed without any provision on the dissolution of that organ. A more flexible rule was instead adopted by the aforesaid Protocol, which in its art. 18 provided, *inter alia*, the replacement in art. 18, in which the functions of the Assembly are set out, of its paragraph 9 which provided:

9 to establish any temporary or permanent subsidiary body it may consider to be necessary

with the following text:

9 to establish any temporary or permanent subsidiary body it may consider to be necessary, to define its terms of reference and to give it the authority needed to perform the functions entrusted to it; when appointing the members of such body, the Assembly shall endeavour to secure an equitable geographical distribution of members and to ensure that the Contracting States, in respect of which the largest quantities of contributing oil are being received, are appropriately represented; the Rules of Procedure of the Assembly may be applied, *mutatis mutandis*, for the work of such subsidiary body;

The equitable geographical distribution of members was also a fundamental criterion for the choice of the members of the Executive Committee according to art. 22(2)(a).

The main function of the Assembly, in addition to those required for its operation, such as the election of the Chairman and Vice-chairmen, the appointment of the Director and of the auditors and the approval of the accounts, is that of superintending the settlement of claims against the Fund. Paragraph 9 of art. 18 provides:

7 to approve settlements of claims against the Fund, to take decisions in respect of the distribution among claimants of the available amount of compensation in accordance with article 4, paragraph 5, and to determine the terms and conditions according to which provisional payments in respect of claims shall be made with a view to ensuring that victims of pollution damage are compensated as promptly as possible;

But the pivot of the fund is the Director. He in fact, besides being, pursuant to art. 28(2), the legal representative of the Fund and pursuant to art. 29(1) the chief administrative officer of the Fund, is given by art. 29(2) the following very wide powers and high responsibilities (comments are added, where deemed appropriate):

(a) appoint the personnel required for the administration of the Fund;
(b) take all appropriate measures with a view to the proper administration of the Fund's assets;
(c) collect the contributions due under this Convention while observing in particular the provisions of article 13, paragraph 3;

The express reference to art. 13(4) draws the attention to a particularly delicate function of the Director, namely that of deciding the actions to be taken when contributions are not timely paid. It states:

3 Where a person who is liable in accordance with the provisions of articles 10 and 12 to make contributions to the Fund does not fulfil his obligations in respect of any such contribution or any part thereof and is in arrears, the Director shall take

all appropriate action against such person on behalf of the Fund with a view to the recovery of the amount due. However, where the defaulting contributor is manifestly insolvent or the circumstances otherwise so warrant, the Assembly may, upon recommendation of the Director, decide that no action shall be taken or continued against the contributor.

Although, of course, the Director would seek the opinion of legal advisors when necessary, the responsibility of choosing the actions which in each particular situation appear the most appropriate is his and so is the decision to abstain from any action when the contributor is 'manifestly insolvent': an assessment which is sometimes difficult to make.

(d) to the extent necessary to deal with claims against the Fund and carry out the other functions of the Fund, employ the services of legal, financial and other experts;
(e) take all appropriate measures for dealing with claims against the Fund within the limits and on conditions to be laid down in the Internal Regulations, including the final settlement of claims without the prior approval of the Assembly where these Regulations so provide;

This is even more delicate, for the assessment of the conditions under which a claim may be deemed to be justified and its appropriate amount requires not only great experience, but also a political assessment of the consequences that delays in the settlement of claims may entail. Also in this case legal and financial advices are normally sought, but the final responsibility is that of the Director.

(f) prepare and submit to the Assembly the financial statements and budget estimates for each calendar year;
(g) prepare, in consultation with the Chairman of the Assembly, and publish a report of the activities of the Fund during the previous calendar year;
(h) prepare, collect and circulate the papers, documents, agenda, minutes and information that may be required for the work of the Assembly and subsidiary bodies.

SECTION B – THE SUPPLEMENTARY FUND

8 THE ESTABLISHMENT OF THE SUPPLEMENTARY FUND

Art. 2 of the Protocol of 2003 to the Fund Convention 1992 provides:

1 An International Supplementary Fund for compensation for pollution damage, to be named 'The International Oil Pollution Compensation Supplementary Fund, 2003' (hereinafter the 'Supplementary Fund'), is hereby established.
2 The Supplementary Fund shall in each Contracting State be recognized as a legal person capable under the laws of that State of assuming rights and obligations and of being a party in legal proceedings before the courts of that State. Each Contracting State shall recognize the Director of the Supplementary Fund as the legal representative of the Supplementary Fund.

This article differs from those of the 1971 and of the 1992 Fund Conventions in that it does not set out its aims, that in any event are different from those of the 1971 and 1992 Fund Conventions: while the aims of such Conventions were to provide compensation for pollution damage to the extent that the protection afforded by the 1969 or 1992 Liability Conventions is inadequate, the aim of the Supplementary

Fund Protocol is to pay compensation to persons who have been unable to obtain full and adequate compensation under the terms of the 1992 Fund Convention. That aim is not set out in art. 2, but in art. 4(1).

9 THE ENTRY INTO FORCE OF THE SUPPLEMENTARY FUND AND THE CLAIMS IN RESPECT OF WHICH IT IS AVAILABLE

In consideration of the wording of art. 2(2) being the same as that of art. 2(2) of the 1971 and 1992 Fund Conventions, the Supplementary Fund must be deemed to have been established concurrently with the entry into force of the 2003 Protocol, such entry into force having taken place on 3 March 2005.

But the question that arises in respect of the Supplementary Fund is whether it applies to any pollution damage in respect of which the Liability and Fund Conventions 1992 apply, or it applies only to pollution damage that occurred after the entry into force of the Protocol of 2003 and thus after 3 March 2005. In a recent case relating to claims for pollution damage caused by the shipwreck of the *Prestige*, which occurred on 13 November 2002, the Court of Appeal of Rennes held[49] that the Protocol of 2003 by which the Supplementary Fund was created could apply only to events subsequent to its entry into force and invoked in support of its opinion art. 28 of the Vienna Convention on the Law of Treaties. This decision, however, is unpersuasive. It must in fact be considered that the general rule laid down by art. 28 of the Vienna Convention, pursuant to which the provisions of a treaty do not bind a party in relation to any act or fact that took place before the date of its entry into force, applies 'unless a different intention appears from the treaty'; and that is precisely the case for the Protocol of 2003, the declared purpose of which is to ensure that victims of oil pollution damage be 'compensated in full for their loss or damage' and to 'alleviate the difficulties faced by victims in cases where there is a risk that the amount of compensation available under the 1992 Liability and the 1992 Fund Conventions will be insufficient to pay established claims in full'. This had been considered by a number of Contracting States to the 1992 Liability and Fund Conventions as a matter of urgency.[50]

It is suggested therefore that, except when claims have been finally settled, the

---

49 Court of Appeal of Rennes 11 March 2014 (2014) DMF 599.
50 The third, fourth and fifth recital of the Protocol are worded as follows:

> NOTING that the maximum compensation afforded by the 1992 Fund Convention might be insufficient to meet compensation needs in certain circumstances in some Contracting States to that Convention,
> RECOGNIZING that a number of Contracting States to the 1992 Liability and 1992 Fund Conventions consider it necessary as a matter of urgency to make available additional funds for compensation through the creation of a supplementary scheme to which States may accede if they so wish,
> BELIEVING that the supplementary scheme should seek to ensure that victims of oil pollution damage are compensated in full for their loss or damage and should also alleviate the difficulties faced by victims in cases where there is a risk that the amount of compensation available under the 1992 Liability and 1992 Fund Conventions will be insufficient to pay established claims in full and that as a consequence the International Oil Pollution Compensation Fund, 1992, has decided provisionally that it will pay only a proportion of any established claim . . .

Supplementary Fund should be available from the date of its entry into force to all victims of oil pollution damage to which the 1992 Liability and Fund Conventions apply,[51] as would be the case also in respect of the claims for oil pollution damage caused by the breaking and sinking of the *Erika* in December 1999.

10 THE RULES GOVERNING PAYMENT BY THE SUPPLEMENTARY FUND

10.1 When payment is due

Art. 4(1) of the Protocol so provides:

1 The Supplementary Fund shall pay compensation to any person suffering pollution damage if such person has been unable to obtain full and adequate compensation for an established claim for such damage under the terms of the 1992 Fund Convention, because the total damage exceeds, or there is a risk that it will exceed, the applicable limit of compensation laid down in article 4, paragraph 4, of the 1992 Fund Convention in respect of any one incident.
2 (a) . . .
(b) . . .
3 Where the amount of established claims against the Supplementary Fund exceeds the aggregate amount of compensation payable under paragraph 2, the amount available shall be distributed in such a manner that the proportion between any established claim and the amount of compensation actually recovered by the claimant under this Protocol shall be the same for all claimants.

It is not clear in which circumstances payment should be made not only when the total damage exceeds the applicable limit under the Fund Convention, but also when there is a risk the it will exceed such limit. The inability of the claimant to obtain 'full and adequate compensation' at a time when there is only a risk that the total damage exceeds the limit would not in fact be definitive and would so become when such inability will become definitive.

These aspects are, however, clarified by the Internal Regulations of the Supplementary Fund that so provide in Regulation 7:

7.5 Where a claim has been submitted to the 1992 Fund and agreement has been reached between the 1992 Fund and the claimant as to the value of the majority of items of the claim, but further investigation is considered necessary with respect to the remaining items, the Director may make payment in respect of the agreed items to the extent that these items are not paid under the 1992 Civil Liability Convention and the 1992 Fund Convention. Internal Regulation 7.4 applies correspondingly.
7.7 If in the Director's view the Supplementary Fund should make provisional payments in order to mitigate financial hardship to victims, the Director shall refer the matter to the Assembly for decision.
7.8 As a condition of making a provisional payment in respect of a claim, the Director shall obtain from the claimant concerned a transfer to the Supplementary Fund of any right that such a claimant may enjoy under the 1992 Civil Liability Convention against the owner or his or her guarantor, up to the amount of the provisional payment to be made by the Supplementary Fund to that claimant.

---

51 This is also the opinion of Professor Pierre Bonassies. Reference is made to his analysis of the judgment of the Court of Appeal of Rennes: (2014) DMF 604.

THE FUND CONVENTION

10.2 The conditions precedent to the payment by the Supplementary Fund

Art.15(2) and (3) provide:

2 No compensation shall be paid by the Supplementary Fund for pollution damage in the territory, territorial sea or exclusive economic zone or area determined in accordance with article 3(a)(ii), of this Protocol, of a Contracting State in respect of a given incident or for preventive measures, wherever taken, to prevent or minimize such damage, until the obligations to communicate to the Director of the Supplementary Fund according to article 13, paragraph 1 and paragraph 1 of this article have been complied with in respect of that Contracting State for all years prior to the occurrence of that incident. The Assembly shall determine in the Internal Regulations the circumstances under which a Contracting State shall be considered as having failed to comply with its obligations.

3 Where compensation has been denied temporarily in accordance with paragraph 2, compensation shall be denied permanently in respect of that incident if the obligations to communicate to the Director of the Supplementary Fund under article 13, paragraph 1 and paragraph 1 of this article, have not been complied with within one year after the Director of the Supplementary Fund has notified the Contracting State of its failure to report.

10.3 The amount of compensation available under the Supplementary Fund

Art. 4(2)(a) so provides:

2(a) The aggregate amount of compensation payable by the Supplementary Fund under this article shall in respect of any one incident be limited, so that the total sum of that amount together with the amount of compensation actually paid under the 1992 Liability Convention and the 1992 Fund Convention within the scope of application of this Protocol shall not exceed 750 million units of account.

The criterion adopted in the Fund Convention is followed also in respect of the Supplementary Fund.[52] There is no fixed limit to the amount payable by the Supplementary Fund: that amount is such as to ensure the global availability of the sum of 750 million SDRs. But since:

pursuant to the Fund Convention the aggregate amount of compensation payable by the Fund is limited to the sum necessary in order to ensure a global amount available for the settlement of pollution damage in respect of any one incident, added to the amount actually paid under the 1992 CLC, of 203,000,000 SDRs, or 300,740,000 SDRs in respect of any one incident when there are three parties under the Fund Convention in respect of which the combined relevant quantity of contributing oil received by persons in their territory equalled or exceeded 600 million tons,

the amount that the Supplementary Fund may be required to make available shall not exceed 547,000,000 SDRs in the first case or 449,250,000 in the second case.

10.4 Distribution of the amount available under the Supplementary Fund when claims are in excess of the compensation payable

Art. 5 states:

The Supplementary Fund shall pay compensation when the Assembly of the 1992 Fund has considered that the total amount of the established claims exceeds, or there is a risk that the

---

52 For an analysis of the provisions on the Supplementary Fund see M. Jacobsson, 'The International Liability Compensation Regime for Oil Pollution from Ships', *supra* note 12, p. 14.

185

total amount of established claims will exceed the aggregate amount of compensation available under article 4, paragraph 4, of the 1992 Fund Convention and that as a consequence the Assembly of the 1992 Fund has decided provisionally or finally that payments will only be made for a proportion of any established claim. The Assembly of the Supplementary Fund shall then decide whether and to what extent the Supplementary Fund shall pay the proportion of any established claim not paid under the 1992 Liability Convention and the 1992 Fund Convention.

This rule is the same as that in art. 4(5) of the Fund Convention and this is obvious, for the 'established claims', reference to which is made therein, are so defined in art. 1(8):

8 'Established claim' means a claim which has been recognised by the 1992 Fund or been accepted as admissible by decision of a competent court binding upon the 1992 Fund not subject to ordinary forms of review and which would have been fully compensated if the limit set out in article 4, paragraph 4, of the 1992 Fund Convention had not been applied to that incident;

If the amount of the Supplementary Fund is sufficient for the full settlement of any established claim not paid under the CLC 1992, no apportionment will of course be required. If instead the global amount of the balance of such claims is higher than the sum available under the Supplementary Fund, only a proportion of such outstanding claims will be paid.

This provision clarifies the meaning of art. 4(1) for, besides the need for a decision of the Assembly, it states that the likelihood of the total damage exceeding the total limit laid down in art. 4(5) of the Fund Convention is such as to trigger a decision of the Assembly of the 1992 Fund to the effect that 'provisionally or finally' such payments will be made, but shall be only for a proportion of the established claims. And the Assembly of the Supplementary Fund has discretion as 'to whether and to what extent' the Supplementary Fund should contribute.

11 EXTINCTION OF THE RIGHT TO COMPENSATION

Art. 6 states:

1 Subject to article 15, paragraphs 2 and 3, rights to compensation against the Supplementary Fund shall be extinguished only if they are extinguished against the 1992 Fund under article 6 of the 1992 Fund Convention.
2 A claim made against the 1992 Fund shall be regarded as a claim made by the same claimant against the Supplementary Fund.

Quite logically, there is no independent rule on the extinction of rights of compensation against the Supplementary Fund, since the right of compensation is only one, and is the right to seek payment of a sum complementary to that paid under the CLC. While therefore there are distinct rights of compensation against the owner and the Fund, and separate rules apply to their extinction, there is a global right of compensation against the Fund and, where the conditions established in art. 5 materialise, against the Supplementary Fund.

THE FUND CONVENTION

12 CONTRIBUTIONS TO THE SUPPLEMENTARY FUND

12.1 Who is bound to make contributions

Art. 10 of the Protocol states:

1 Annual contributions to the Supplementary Fund shall be made in respect of each Contracting State by any person who, in the calendar year referred to in article 11, paragraph 2(a) or (b), has received in total quantities exceeding 150,000 tons:
   (a) in the ports or terminal installations in the territory of that State contributing oil carried by sea to such ports or terminal installations; and
   (b) in any installations situated in the territory of that Contracting State contributing oil which has been carried by sea and discharged in a port or terminal installation of a non-Contracting State, provided that contributing oil shall only be taken into account by virtue of this sub-paragraph on first receipt in a Contracting State after its discharge in that non-Contracting State.
2 The provisions of article 10, paragraph 2, of the 1992 Fund Convention shall apply in respect of the obligation to pay contributions to the Supplementary Fund.

Paragraph 1 of this article is a reproduction word for word of art. 10(1) of the Fund Convention, while its paragraph 2 is instead incorporated in paragraph 2. The criteria on the basis of which contribution is made to the Supplementary Fund are therefore the same.

The fundamental difference is that recourse to the Supplementary Fund may be made only if, and to the extent to which, claimants are unable to obtain full and adequate compensation under the terms of the 1992 Fund Convention. Therefore, in the years in which that does not occur, annual contributions may not be required except for the payment of costs and expenses of the administration of the Supplementary Fund.[53]

The operation of this provision is, however, conditional on a minimum receipt by a Contracting State of one million tons on contributing oil. Art. 14 stipulates:

1 Notwithstanding article 10, for the purposes of this Protocol there shall be deemed to be a minimum receipt of 1 million tons of contributing oil in each Contracting State.
2 When the aggregate quantity of contributing oil received in a Contracting State is less than 1 million tons, the Contracting State shall assume the obligations that would be incumbent under this Protocol on any person who would be liable to contribute to the Supplementary Fund in respect of oil received within the territory of that State in so far as no liable person exists for the aggregated quantity of oil received.

If, therefore, the quantity of oil received is less than one million tons the persons who have received a quantity of oil in excess of 150,000 have no obligation to contribute, but such obligation is assumed by the relevant State; and that entails that the Supplementary Fund is bound to pay compensation to the persons suffering pollution damage, when the conditions stated in art. 4 materialise.

---

53 From the Annual Report of the International Oil Pollution Compensation Funds for the year 2013 p. 15, it appears that no contributions were due during 2012; nor were any contributions levied for payment in 2013, the total obligations incurred in 2012 being £63,100 of which £59,500 was in respect of the management fee and the total obligations incurred in 2013 being £36,600 of which £33,000 was in respect of the management fee.

187

12.2 The assessment of annual contributions

The provisions in art. 11 on the budget of expenditure and income and the decisions on the total amount of contribution to be levied reproduced those in art. 12 of the Fund Convention except for those in paragraph (i) on expenditure, the variations to which appear in the following text (i.e. the text that is crossed out being that which is not reproduced in the Protocol):

(i) Expenditure

    (a) costs and expenses of the administration of the *Supplementary* Fund in the relevant year and any deficit from operations in preceding years;

    (b) payments to be made by the *Supplementary* Fund in the relevant year for the satisfaction of claims against the *Supplementary* Fund due under article 4, including repayment on loans previously taken by the *Supplementary* Fund for the satisfaction of such claims, ~~to the extent that the aggregate amount of such claims in respect of any one incident does not exceed four million units of account;~~

    ~~(c) payments to be made by the Fund in the relevant year for the satisfaction of claims against the Fund due under Article 4, including repayments on loans previously taken by the Fund for the satisfaction of such claims, to the extent that the aggregate amount of such claims in respect of any one incident is in excess of four million units of account;~~

The provisions in (a) and (b) of the Fund Convention 1992 in the part in which they draw a distinction between claims the aggregate amount of which in respect of any one incident does not exceed four million units of account and claims the aggregate amount of which is instead in excess of four million units of account have not been reproduced.

12.3 The breach by persons liable of their payment obligations, the cooperation of Contracting States and the voluntary assumption by them of the payment obligations

The provisions of the Fund Convention on all such aspects[54] are incorporated in the Protocol by its art. 12, which provides:

1 The provisions of article 13 of the 1992 Fund Convention shall apply to contributions to the Supplementary Fund.
2 A Contracting State itself may assume the obligation to pay contributions to the Supplementary Fund in accordance with the procedure set out in article 14 of the 1992 Fund Convention.

---

54 *Supra, para.* 6.5.

CHAPTER 13

International Convention on Civil Liability for Bunker Oil Pollution Damage, 2001

1 INTRODUCTION

Pollution damage caused by bunker oil is covered by the CLC 1992 only where it is caused by bunker oil of tankers, whether loaded or in ballast. The compensatory regime ensured by the CLC 1992 and the Fund Convention, extended generally to hazardous and noxious substances by the HNS Convention 1996 as amended by the Protocol of 2010, left a gap in respect of damage caused by bunker of dry cargo ships, that was excluded from their scope of application, even though bunker oil of dry cargo ships as well as of passenger ships, that in large ships can be of thousands of tons,[1] can cause considerable pollution damage. That gap has been filled by the International Convention on Civil Liability for Bunker Oil Pollution Damage, adopted on 23 March 2001 and entered into force on 21 November 2008. As of July 2014, there were 77 States Parties to this Convention.[2]

The structure of this Convention[3] differs from that of the CLC because there are no provisions on the limitation of liability of the owner, nor is it complemented by a Fund Convention.

---

1 It was pointed out by Australia in its Consideration of Compensation for Pollution from Ships' Bunkers (LEG 73/12, 13 July 1995) that large bulk carriers may carry as much as 10,000 tons of fuel oil. From the diagrams elaborated by Lloyd's Register and sent to IMO on 5 December 2000 (LEG/CONF.12/4), it appears that crude oil tankers may have a bunker capacity of 15,000 tons and container vessels a bunker capacity of up to 8,000 tons.

2 The States Parties are the following: Albania, Antigua and Barbuda, Australia, Austria, Azerbaijan, Bahamas, Barbados, Belgium, Belize, Bulgaria, Canada, China, Congo, Cook Islands, Côte d'Ivoire, Croatia, Cyprus, Czech Republic, Denmark, Egypt, Estonia, Ethiopia, Finland, France, Germany, Greece, Hungary, Iran (Islamic Republic of), Ireland, Italy, Jamaica, Jordan, Kiribati, Korea (Democratic People's Republic of), Korea (Republic of), Latvia, Liberia, Lithuania, Luxembourg, Malaysia, Malta, Marshall Islands, Mauritius, Mongolia, Montenegro, Morocco, Netherlands, New Zealand, Nicaragua, Nigeria, Niue, Norway, Palau, Panama, Poland, Romania, Russian Federation, Saint Kitts and Nevis, Saint Vincent and the Grenadines, Samoa, Serbia, Sierra Leone, Singapore, Slovakia, Slovenia, Spain, Sweden, Switzerland, Syrian Arab Republic, Togo, Tonga, Tunisia, Turkey, Tuvalu, United Kingdom, Vanuatu, Vietnam.

3 On which see generally Patrick Griggs, 'International Convention on Civil Liability for Bunker Oil Pollution Damage', http://www.bmla.org.uk/documents/imo-bunker-convention.htm; Michael N. Tsimplis, 'The Bunker Pollution Convention 2001: Completing and Harmonizing the Liability Regime for Oil Pollution from Ships?', (2005) LMCLQ 83.

INTERNATIONAL MARITIME CONVENTIONS

2 SCOPE OF APPLICATION

2.1 Geographical scope

Art. 2 so provides:

This Convention shall apply exclusively:

(a)   to pollution damage caused:
    (i)   in the territory, including the territorial sea, of a State Party, and
    (ii) in the exclusive economic zone of a State Party, established in accordance with
        international law, or, if a State Party has not established such a zone, in an
        area beyond and adjacent to the territorial sea of that State determined by that
        State in accordance with international law and extending not more than 200
        nautical miles from the baselines from which the breadth of its territorial sea is
        measured;
(b)   to preventive measures, wherever taken, to prevent or minimize such damage.

This provision is identical to that in art. II of the CLC and therefore reference is made to the comments made thereunder.[4]

2.2 The notion of pollution damage

Pollution damage is so defined in art. 1(9) of the Convention:

9 'Pollution damage' means:

(a)   loss or damage caused outside the ship by contamination resulting from the escape or
    discharge of bunker oil from the ship, wherever such escape or discharge may occur,
    provided that compensation for impairment of the environment other than loss of profit
    from such impairment shall be limited to costs of reasonable measures of reinstatement
    actually undertaken or to be undertaken; and
(b)   the costs of preventive measures and further loss or damage caused by preventive
    measures.

Although this definition is identical to that in art. 2(4) of the CLC, the pollution damage to which the Bunker Oil Convention applies differs. Art. 4(1) in fact provides:

1   This Convention shall not apply to pollution damage as defined in the Civil Liability
    Convention, whether or not compensation is payable in respect of it under that Convention.

This provision may be misleading, since the definition of pollution damage is the same in both conventions. What differs are the combined definitions of 'ship' and of 'oil'. Whilst under the CLC 'ship' is only a sea-going vessel or seaborne craft constructed or adapted for the carriage of oil as cargo and actually carrying oil in bulk as cargo or during any following voyage, under the Bunker Oil Convention 'ship' is generally a sea-going vessel or seaborne craft; and whilst under the CLC 'oil' is generally any persistent hydrocarbon mineral oil whether carried on board a ship as cargo or in the bunkers of such ship, under the Bunker Oil Convention 'oil' is only 'bunker oil', so defined in art. 1.5:

---

4 Chapter 11, para. 3.

190

5 'Bunker oil' means any hydrocarbon mineral oil, including lubricating oil, used or intended
to be used for the operation or propulsion of the ship, and any residues of such oil.

Oil carried in the bunkers of ships as defined in art. I.1 of the CLC 1992 is excluded by art. 4.1, which provides:

1 This Convention shall not apply to pollution damage as defined in the Civil Liability Convention, whether or not compensation is payable in respect of it under that Convention.

However the term 'bunker oil', which suggests that the oil to which the Convention applies is only the oil carried in the bunker of a ship, does not cover all the oils to which the Convention applies, since in the definition reference is made both to oil used for the propulsion and operation (as is the case for the oil used for the genera-tors) of the ship and to lubricating oil, that is not normally carried in the bunkers of the ship. Therefore, the word 'bunker' has been used in order to draw a distinction between the oil carried on board for the use of the ship and the oil carried as cargo: oil carried in barrels and intended to be used as lubricating oil is therefore covered by the Convention, whereas oil carried in barrels as cargo is not.[5]

2.3 Ships subject to the Convention

The following definition of ship is given in art. 1(1):

'Ship' means any seagoing vessel and seaborne craft, of any type whatsoever.

Except that there is no reference to the cargo, this definition is identical to that in the CLC and also that in the HNS Convention. The qualification of the ship or craft as 'seagoing' does not, also in this case, refer to the type of register in which the ship or craft is registered, but rather to the requirement that the ship or craft must be 'going' at sea at the relevant time. The (standard) qualification of the craft as 'seaborne' (and not 'seagoing') also aims at including non self-propelled craft. The words used in all conventions in their French text is *'engin marin'* which also suggests a very general description of the craft, that only requires the *'engin'* to be employed at sea.[6]

Size is not relevant; nor is there any provision in the Convention, as there is in some other conventions, such as the LLMC Convention in its art. 15(2)(b), allowing States to exclude from the scope of its application ships below a specified tonnage (e.g. 300 tons).

2.4 Ships excluded from the scope of application of the Convention

Art. 4 so provides in paragraphs 2, 3 and 4:

2 Except as provided in paragraph 3, the provisions of this Convention shall not apply to warships, naval auxiliary or other ships owned or operated by a State and used, for the time being, only on Government non-commercial service.

---

5 The distinction made by M.N. Tsimplis, *supra*, note 3, p. 86, between cargo and bunkers, does not appear to be correct and appears to be misleading.

6 Reference is made to the wider discussion on the definition of 'ship' in the chapter on the CLC (*supra*, Chapter 11, para. 2.1).

INTERNATIONAL MARITIME CONVENTIONS

3 A State Party may decide to apply this Convention to its warships or other ships described in paragraph 2, in which case it shall notify the Secretary-General thereof specifying the terms and conditions of such application.[7]

4 With respect to ships owned by a State Party and used for commercial purposes, each State shall be subject to suit in the jurisdictions set forth in article 9 and shall waive all defences based on its status as a sovereign State.

Article 4(2) differs from art. XI(1) of the CLC in that, in addition to warships, reference is made to naval auxiliaries. An addition has also been made in art. 4(4) of the HNS Convention and originates from art. 3(1) of the Immunity Convention 1926 in which the terminology slightly differed, since reference was made therein to 'fleet auxiliaries'. That addition is difficult to understand, considering also that in its provisions on immunity of Government ships UNCLOS refers to 'warships and other government ships'.[8]

3 THE PERSON(S) LIABLE FOR THE POLLUTION DAMAGE

Arts 3(1) and (2) provide:

1 Except as provided in paragraphs 3 and 4, the shipowner at the time of an incident shall be liable for pollution damage caused by any bunker oil on board or originating from the ship, provided that, if an incident consists of a series of occurrences having the same origin, the liability shall attach to the shipowner at the time of the first of such occurrences.

2 Where more than one person is liable in accordance with paragraph 1, their liability shall be joint and several.

---

7 A decision to this effect has been made by Norway and notice has been given to the Secretary-General of IMO in the following terms:

> In accordance with article 4, paragraph 3 of the Convention, Norway will apply the Convention to warships, naval auxiliary ships or other ships owned or operated by the Norwegian State and used, for the time being, only on Government non-commercial service. The rules of the Convention will apply generally to such ships. For such ships owned by the Norwegian State, it follows by Section 186, third paragraph of the Norwegian Maritime Act of June 24, 1994, no. 39, that if insurance or other financial security is not maintained in respect of such a ship, the ship may instead carry a certificate issued by the appropriate authority of the State, stating that the ship is owned by the State and that the ship's liability is covered within the limit prescribed in accordance with article 7, paragraph 1.

A similar decision has been made by Sweden and notice has been given to the Secretary-General of IMO in the following terms:

> In accordance with article 4, paragraph 3 of the Convention, Sweden will apply the Convention to warships, naval auxiliary ships and other ships owned or operated by a State and used for the time being only on Government non-commercial service. The rules of liability in the Convention will apply generally when such ships cause pollution damage in the territory, including the territorial sea of Sweden, or in the exclusive economic zone of Sweden or preventive measures have been taken to prevent or minimize pollution damage in the territory of Sweden or in the exclusive economic zone of Sweden. Such ships will not be required to maintain insurance or other financial security according to article 7 in the Convention and will not be required to hold a certificate according to article 7, paragraph 2 or 14 of the Convention. Judgments on matters covered by the Convention, when given by a court of another Member State of the European Union, with the exception of Denmark, shall be recognized and enforced in Sweden according to the relevant internal Union rules on the subject.

8 Articles 29–32.

The definition of shipowner in art. 1(3) is as follows:

'Shipowner' means the owner, including the registered owner, bareboat charterer, manager and operator of the ship.

When the need for the adoption of an international regime for liability and compensation for damage caused by oil from ships' bunkers was first considered by the IMO Legal Committee one of the issues requiring analysis had been that of the possibility of attaching liability not only to the shipowner but also to parties responsible for the day-to-day operation of the ship.[9] Although the original draft submitted to the IMO Legal Committee by Australia, Canada, Norway, South Africa and the United Kingdom reproduced that adopted in art. 1(2) of the CLC and in art. 1(2) of the HNS Convention,[10] in a subsequent draft submitted two years later to the Legal Committee by Australia, Canada, Finland, Norway, South Africa and the United Kingdom[11] there were included four alternative options for such definition, in all of which persons other than the owner of the ship were included. The first of these options was worded as follows: '"Shipowner" means the owner [, charterer, manager and operator] of the ship'.[12] A very similar definition, followed by an alternative one, was included, this time without square brackets, in a draft of the Bunker Oil Convention submitted three years later by Australia, Canada, Finland, Ireland, Malta, the Netherlands, Norway, South Africa, Sweden and the United Kingdom. It was worded:

'Shipowner' means the owner, including the registered owner, bareboat and demise charterer, manager and operator of the ship.

In the comment that followed it was stated that such definition was based on that in art. 1(2) of the LLMC Convention.[13] That indeed was correct, but, besides the addition of the words 'including the registered owner', the purpose of the extended definition was very different: in the LLMC Convention it was the extension of the benefit of limitation to other persons involved in the operation of the vessel and in the draft Bunker Oil Convention it was the extension of the liability for damage by bunker oil to persons other than the (registered) owner. Instead the reason why in the CLC and in the HNS Convention the definition is restricted to the registered owner is that of channelling the liability to the registered owner only.

---

9 Legal Committee, 74th session, June 1996, LEG 74/13, para. 13, p. 5.
10 Legal Committee, 77th session, Annex to LEG 77/6/1, p. 2.
11 Legal Committee, 78th session, LEG 78/5/2, p. 4.
12 The other three options were drafted as follows:

Option 2
'Shipowner' means the owner, charterer, manager and operator of the ship; and 'Responsible party' means the owner of the ship, or any other organisation or person who or which has assumed responsibility for compliance with the insurance requirements of this Convention. (Note: This definition is based on the definition of 'company' in the ISM Code.)
Option 3
'Shipowner' means the owner of the ship, or any other organization; or person who or which has assumed responsibility for the operation of the ship.
Option 4
'Shipowner' means the person or persons registered as the shipowner or, in the absence of registration, the person or persons owning the ship. However, in the case of a ship owned by a State and operated by a company which in that State is registered as the ship's operator, 'shipowner' shall mean such company.

13 LEG 80/4/1, Annex, p. 2.

From the standpoint of the wording, the definition in the Bunker Oil Convention is peculiar, because it is on two different levels: it provides first that 'shipowner' means 'owner' and secondly that 'owner' includes 'the registered owner, bareboat charterer, manager and operator of the ship'. The primary term appears, therefore, to be 'owner' and the secondary or subordinate term appears to be 'registered owner': exactly the opposite of the CLC.

Finally, at a subsequent session of the Legal Committee (the 81st session) a new draft convention was submitted by Australia, Canada, Finland, Ireland, Malta, the Netherlands, Norway, South Africa, Sweden and the United Kingdom in which only the definition of 'shipowner' previously quoted was included, albeit with a minor change, the words 'bareboat and demise charterer' being quite rightly linked also by the conjunction 'or'.[14]

From the standpoint of the substance of the definition, from the *travaux prépara-toires* it appears that the reason for the extension was, albeit with significant opposition, that of increasing the number of the persons that could be held liable, for better protection of the victims. This was the interpretation, apparently unchallenged, of the International Group of P&I Clubs which suggested that the other parties in the definition should be liable only when it had not been possible to obtain compensation from the registered owner or his insurer.[15] The same interpretation was given to art. 3(1) by the International Chamber of Shipping, which suggested that proper channelling provisions should be included, stating that even though the requirement in art. 7(1) for the registered owner to insure his potential liability should result, in practice, in claims being channelled to him, the joint and several liability provision would invite claimants to sue the range of parties in the 'shipowner' definition.[16]

If the term 'shipowner' in art. 3(1) is replaced by the definition in art. 1.3, art. 3(1) would read: 'Except as provided in paragraphs 3 and 4, the owner, *registered owner, bareboat charterer, manager and operator* at the time of the incident shall be liable for pollution damage.' If at the time of the incident there is no bareboat charterer, manager or operator, since the ship is directly operated by the registered owner, of course the only person liable is the registered owner. And this is impliedly recognised by art. 3(2), which provides:

2 Where more than one person is liable in accordance with paragraph 1, their liability shall be joint and several.

Although that is not entirely clear, it must be assumed that the situation covered by art. 3(2) is that in which the ship is bareboat chartered or where the owner (or the

---

14 Legal Committee, 81st session, LEG 81/4.

15 LEG/CONF.12/9.

16 LEG/CONF. 12/10. The statement made by the ICS under the heading 'Channelling' was the following:

> 3 For practical reasons and reasons of consistency with other pollution conventions, proper channelling provisions should be included in the proposed convention. Even though the requirement in article 7, paragraph 1, for the registered owner to insure his potential liability under the draft convention should result, in practice, in claims being channelled to the registered owner, the joint and several liability provisions invite claimants to sue the range of parties in the 'shipowner' definition. As pointed out in the International Group of P&I Clubs' submission (LEG/CONF.12/9), there are likely to be disputes in practice at the time of a spill about the apportionment of liability between the various parties. This could delay response.

bareboat charterer – the co-existence of a bareboat charterer and an operator is difficult to conceive) has appointed a manager, in which event the registered owner would continue to be liable. This provision, however, gives rise to some problems. First, while the identity of the registered owner is easy to establish, that is not the case for the bareboat charterer or the manager. And the burden of proof would lie on the claimant.

Secondly, if, for example, the ship is bareboat chartered and pursuant to the charter party the owner is liable for bunker oil pollution damage – which would make sense, since the owner is required to maintain insurance or other financial security to cover liability for pollution damage – claimants would nevertheless be entitled to bring a claim against the bareboat charterer, who apparently[17] is not required to maintain insurance or financial security. In any event, if he does, the claimants may not have a direct action against the insurer or provider of security, unless a direct action is provided by the applicable law. In addition, it is conceivable that under the applicable national liability regime (on the assumption that neither the 1957 limitation convention nor the LLMC Convention are in force in the relevant jurisdiction) the bareboat charterer may not enjoy the benefit of limitation. The result could be that where the ship is bareboat chartered and its management is entrusted by the charterer to a manager, there would be three persons who should maintain insurance or other financial security, thereby tripling the insurance costs: a result that under the CLC has been avoided by channelling the liability to the registered owner.

Thirdly, whether, on the assumption that the ship whose bunker oil has caused pollution damage is bareboat chartered and the persons who have suffered pollution damage claim compensation from the registered owner, the registered owner, in the event that under the applicable law or under the contract the person liable is the bareboat charterer, would have a right of recourse against him under the Convention or under that law or the contract. That situation is probably governed by art. 3(6) which provides:

6 Nothing in this Convention shall prejudice any right of recourse of the shipowner which exists independently of this Convention.

This is another reason for which the bareboat charterer, the manager and the operator (if a distinction between bareboat charterer and operator is conceivable in practice) would be compelled to insure their liability.

---

17 Although initially in art. 7(1) reference is made as the person required to maintain insurance or other financial security to the 'registered owner', subsequently the term frequently used in art. 7 is 'shipowner', as it appears in particular from para. 10, quoted hereafter, in which the various references to the owner are printed in italics:

> Any claim for compensation for pollution damage may be brought directly against the insurer or other person providing financial security for the *registered owner's* liability for pollution damage. In such a case the defendant may invoke the defences (other than bankruptcy or winding up of the *shipowner*) which the *shipowner* would have been entitled to invoke, including limitation pursuant to article 6. Furthermore, even if the *shipowner* is not entitled to limitation of liability according to article 6, the defendant may limit liability to an amount equal to the amount of the insurance or other financial security required to be maintained in accordance with paragraph 1. Moreover, the defendant may invoke the defence that the pollution damage resulted from the wilful misconduct of the *shipowner*, but the defendant shall not invoke any other defence which the defendant might have been entitled to invoke in proceedings brought by the *shipowner* against the defendant. The defendant shall in any event have the right to require the *shipowner* to be joined in the proceedings.

4 THE BASIS OF LIABILITY AND THE EXCLUSIONS FROM LIABILITY

Art. 3 so provides in paragraphs 3 and 4:

3 No liability for pollution damage shall attach to the shipowner if the shipowner proves that:

   (a) the damage resulted from an act of war, hostilities, civil war, insurrection or a natural phenomenon of an exceptional, inevitable and irresistible character; or
   (b) the damage was wholly caused by an act or omission done with the intent to cause damage by a third party; or
   (c) the damage was wholly caused by the negligence or other wrongful act of any Government or other authority responsible for the maintenance of lights or other navigational aids in the exercise of that function.
4 If the shipowner proves that the pollution damage resulted wholly or partially either from an act or omission done with intent to cause damage by the person who suffered the damage or from the negligence of that person, the shipowner may be exonerated wholly or partially from liability to such person.

The combination of the rules on the liability of the shipowner under art. 3(1) and on the exclusions from liability under art. 3(3) and (4), identical to those under the CLC, indicates that his liability is strict. But, as the liability of the owner for pollution damage under the CLC, it is governed exclusively by the provisions of this Convention. Art.3(5) provides:

5 No claim for compensation for pollution damage shall be made against the shipowner otherwise than in accordance with this Convention.

5 LIMITATION OF LIABILITY

Art. 6 so provides:

Nothing in this Convention shall affect the right of the shipowner and the person or persons providing insurance or other financial security to limit liability under any applicable national or international regime, such as the Convention on Limitation of Liability for Maritime Claims, 1976, as amended.

It is worth summarising the history of this provision in order to understand its purpose and its meaning.

In a paper submitted to the 76th session of the Legal Committee by Australia, the Netherlands, Norway, Sweden and the United Kingdom[18] the attached draft convention text included the following provision on limitation of liability:

The shipowner shall be entitled to limit liability in accordance with the applicable international convention or the national law of the State the courts of which have jurisdiction in accordance with article 9, paragraph 5.

Another paper was submitted at the 77th session of the Legal Committee by Australia, Canada, Norway, South Africa and the United Kingdom[19] in which,

---

18 LEG 76/4/1, 8 August 1997.
19 LEG 77/6/1, 13 February 1998.

in view of a number of delegations being of the opinion that the draft convention should contain its own limitation figures, two options were submitted, the first providing for the right of the shipowner to limit liability in accordance with the LLMC Convention as amended by the Protocol of 1996 and the second providing independent limitation rules.[20] However, the suggestion to include independent rules on limitation of liability was subsequently withdrawn and in the revised draft of the convention submitted by several delegations at the 80th session of the Legal Committee the provision on limitation of liability (art. 6) was worded as follows:[21]

Nothing in this Convention shall affect the right of the shipowner to limit liability under any applicable national or international regime, such as the Convention on Limitation of Liability for Maritime Claims, 1976, as amended.[22]

At the subsequent session of the Legal Committee the delegation of the United Kingdom on behalf of all six sponsoring delegations, introduced document LEG 81/4/3 containing a draft conference resolution urging States to become Party to the 1996 Protocol to the LLMC 1976 and to denounce the 1924, 1956 or 1976 liability Conventions, as appropriate, with effect from the entry into force of the 1996 Protocol to the LLMC Convention.[23] The draft resolution, introduced again at the 82nd session,[24] was approved by the Conference.[25]

Since it has been stated to be strongly arguable that the LLMC may give no

---

20 The two alternatives were formulated as follows:

Option 1
[The shipowner shall be entitled to limit liability in accordance with the Convention on Limitation of Liability for Maritime Claims 1976, as amended by the Protocol of 1996. [, or the national law of the State the courts of which have jurisdiction in accordance with article 9, paragraph 6.]]
Option 2
[(1) The owner of a ship shall be entitled to limit his liability under this Convention in respect of any one incident to an aggregate amount calculated as follows:
(a) 3 million units of account for a ship not exceeding 5,000 units of tonnage;
(b) for a ship with a tonnage in excess thereof, for each additional unit of tonnage, 420 units of account in addition to the amount mentioned in subparagraph (a);
provided, however, that this aggregate amount shall not in any event exceed 59.7 million units of account.
(2) The owner shall not be entitled to limit his liability under this Convention if it is proved that the pollution damage resulted from his personal act or omission, committed with the intent to cause damage, or recklessly and with knowledge that such damage would probably result.
(3) For the purpose of availing himself of the benefit or limitation provided for in paragraph 1 of this Article the owner shall constitute a fund . . .

(*there follow rules on the distribution of the fund*).
21 LEG 80/4/1-Annex. p. 5.
22 The text was accompanied by the following comment:

See LEG 78/WP.4. An informal working group which reported to LEG 78 agreed that the substantive aspects of limitation of liability would be dealt with by other applicable national and international liability regimes such as LLMC 76 as amended from time to time including by the 1996 Protocol. This wording reflects this point and was suggested by the working group. It has also been suggested that as the current wording would allow for limitation to the 1924 and 1957 LLMC limits, there is a need to specify the 1996 LLMC but allow for other national regimes).

23 LEG 81/11, para. 18.
24 LEG 82/3/3.
25 LEG/CONF.12/18. It was worded follows:
THE CONFERENCE,
HAVING ADOPTED the International Convention on Civil Liability for Bunker Oil Pollution Damage, 2001 (hereinafter 'the Convention'),

general right of limitation for bunker pollution claims,[26] it appears of considerable importance to verify whether the LLMC would apply or not. The statement that nothing in the Bunker Oil Convention affects the right of the shipowner and the person providing insurance or other financial guarantee to limit liability under the applicable national or international regime 'such as' the LLMC Convention suggests that in the opinion of those who drafted and subsequently approved this provision, the LLMC would apply to claims for bunker oil pollution damage, obviously if it is in force in the State in which action for bunker oil pollution damage is brought. This is impliedly confirmed by the fact that among the claims excepted from limitation under the LLMC Convention there are not generally claims for oil pollution damage, but specifically claims for oil pollution damage 'within the meaning' of the CLC 1969, and this indicates that the exclusion was due to the need to avoid a conflict between conventions, rather than the intention to exclude a specific category of claims. Even if the fact that certain claims are not expressly excluded does not entail that they are impliedly subject to limitation, since the claims subject to limitation are enumerated in the previous article, in the special case of claims for pollution damage the specific exclusion of certain claims creates a presumption of other claims for pollution damage being instead subject to limitation, even if not specifically mentioned in art. 2. In any event claims for pollution damage are generally covered by art. 2(1) (c) of the LLMC Convention, in which reference is made to claims in respect of (other) loss resulting from the infringement of rights other than contractual rights occurring in direct connection with the operation of the ship.

It appears, therefore, that the LLMC Convention would apply to claims for bunker oil pollution damage and the reference to that Convention in art. 6 of the Bunker Oil Convention indicates that that was also the view of the Conference that adopted this article and approved the resolution previously referred to. Although the formulation of this article is such that the decision whether the benefit of limitation applies or not belongs to the competent court, that court ought to take into consideration the

---

NOTING THAT article 6 of the Convention preserves the right of the shipowner to limit its liability under any applicable national or international regime,

REAFFIRMING that clear rights to limitation of liability are desirable, to enable the shipowner to take out effective insurance cover at reasonable cost,

BELIEVING that limitation amounts must be sufficiently high to permit the payment of full compensation for eligible claims in normal circumstances,

1 URGES all States that have not yet done so, to ratify, or accede to the Protocol of 1996 to amend the Convention on Limitation of Liability for Maritime Claims, 1976;

2 ENCOURAGES States Parties to the Convention on Limitation of Liability for Maritime Claims, 1976 to denounce that Convention with effect from the entry into force of the Protocol of 1996 to amend the Convention on Limitation of Liability for Maritime Claims, 1976 for those States Parties, or after a limited period of time;

3 ALSO ENCOURAGES States Parties to the International Convention for Unification of Certain Rules relating to the Limitation of Liability of Owners of Sea-Going Vessels, 1924 and the International Convention relating to Limitation of Liability of Owners of Sea-Going Ships, 1957 to denounce those Conventions with effect from the entry into force of the Protocol of 1996 to amend the Convention on Limitation of Liability for Maritime Claims, 1976 for those States Parties;

4 RECOMMENDS that States, when implementing the Convention in their national law, make clear which limitation of liability regime is applicable according to article 6 of the Convention.

26 Patrick Griggs, 'International Convention on Civil Liability for Bunker Oil Pollution Damage', *supra*, note 2.

more specific reference to the LLMC Convention in the subsequent art. 7(1), pursuant to which the amount for which insurance or other financial security must be provided by the registered owner must be 'equal to the limits of liability under the applicable national limitation regime, but in all cases, not exceeding an amount calculated in accordance with the Convention on Limitation of Liability for Maritime Claims, 1976 as amended'. The effect of this latter provision appears actually to be that of incorporating into the Bunker Oil Convention the limits of liability of the LLMC Convention as the ceiling of the insurance or other financial security.

6 COMPULSORY INSURANCE OR FINANCIAL SECURITY

Similarly to the provisions on compulsory insurance of the owner under art. 12 of the HNS Convention, the provisions on compulsory insurance in art. 7 of the Bunker Oil Convention mirror those in art. VII of the CLC 1992, but differ from them – and in this case from those in art. 13 of the HNS Convention. This will be discussed in the following analysis, which for convenience will be made as far as possible under the same titles used for the analysis of art. VII of the CLC 1992.

6.1 Who is bound to insure

Art. 7(1) so provides:

The registered owner of a ship having a gross tonnage greater than 1000 registered in a State Party shall be required to maintain insurance or other financial security, such as the guarantee of a bank or similar financial institution, to cover the liability of the registered owner for pollution damage in an amount equal to the limits of liability under the applicable national or international limitation regime, but in all cases, not exceeding an amount calculated in accordance with the Convention on Limitation of Liability for Maritime Claims, 1976, as amended.

The person bound to maintain insurance or other financial security is, as with the CLC 1992 and the HNS Convention, the registered owner of the ship. But while under both of these Conventions the person liable is – except for ships owned by a State and operated by a company which in that State is registered as the operator – the registered owner, under the Bunker Oil Convention the person liable is the 'shipowner'. According to the definition in art. 1(3) this includes, in addition to the registered owner, the bareboat charterer and the operator of the ship. However, the obligation to maintain insurance or other guarantee lies with the registered owner only and the insurance or guarantee covers only his liability and not that of the bareboat charterer, manager or operator.

Similarly to the CLC 1992, the obligation arises above a minimum tonnage, but for bunker oil the minimum tonnage is only 1,000 GT[27] and no reference is made to the quantity of (bunker) oil carried by the ship.[28] Since, however, no provision

---

27 On the insurance threshold see the report submitted to the Conference by Australia (LEG/CONF.12/6 of 18 January 2001).

28 A study on the relationship between the gross tonnage of ships and bunker fuel oil capacity has been made by Lloyd's Register of Shipping in respect of ships with a gross tonnage greater than 500 tons and circulated with a Note of the IMO Secretariat of 5 December 2000 (LEG/CONF.12/4).

INTERNATIONAL MARITIME CONVENTIONS

on limitation of liability exists in the Bunker Oil Convention, reference is made, as in art. 6, to the applicable national or international limitation regime, but if such limit is above that calculated in accordance with the LLMC Convention, the LLMC Convention limit applies.

A facultative additional exclusion is also allowed with reference to the area in which the ships are operating. Art. 7(15) provides:

15 A State may, at the time of ratification, acceptance, approval of, or accession to this Convention, or at any time thereafter, declare that this article does not apply to ships operating exclusively within the area of that State referred to in article 2(a)(i). [29]

The area referred to in art. 2(a)(i) is the territorial sea of the State and, therefore, the exclusion is allowed only if the ships to which it refers operate exclusively within the territorial sea.

6.2 The nature and amount of the security provided

The nature of the coverage is also in this case, as under the CLC and the HNS Convention, an insurance or a guarantee of a bank or of a similar financial institution.[30] The amount of the security must be 'equal to the limits of liability under the applicable national or international limitation regime'. As for the CLC the use of the plural – 'limits of liability', does not appear to be appropriate since there is only one limit. The limit is not indicated in the Bunker Oil Convention, but reference is made primarily to the limits under the applicable national or international limitation regime, the identity of which must be based on the relevant provisions of the law of the State in a court of which the benefit of limitation is invoked. The last part of the article reading 'such as the Convention on Limitation of Liability for Maritime Claims, 1976, as amended' does not entail the application of that Convention: the initial words 'such as' clearly indicate that reference to the LLMC Convention is made as an example of a convention of limitation of liability governing also liability for oil pollution damage,[31] but does not exclude the applicability of other conventions. If therefore the State in a court of which the benefit of limitation is invoked is a party to one of the limitation conventions presently in force, the Limitation Convention of 1957[32] or the LLMC Convention of 1976,[33] the applicable limit of liability will be that in force in the relevant State and, therefore, in view also of the

---

29 A declaration to that effect has been made by the People's Republic of China.
30 *Supra*, Chapter 11, para. 9.2 and *infra*, Chapter 14, para. 8.2.
31 *Supra*, para. 5.
32 The States Parties to that Convention on 31 December 2013 were Belize, Dominican Republic, Fiji, Ghana, Grenada, Iceland, Iran, Israel, Lebanon, Luxembourg, Madagascar, Monaco, Papua New Guinea, Portugal, Seychelles, Solomon Islands, St Vincent and the Grenadines, United Arab Republic and Zaire. See Vol. II, Chapter 10, para. 1.
33 The limits of liability were increased by the Protocol of 1996. See Vol. II, Chapter 11, para. 8.1. The States Parties only to the Convention of 1976 are Algeria, Azerbaijan, Bahamas, Barbados, Benin, China, Congo, Dominica, Egypt, Equatorial Guinea, Georgia, Guyana, Kiribati, Mauritius, Mexico, New Zealand, Nigeria, Singapore, Switzerland, Trinidad and Tobago, United Arab Emirates, Vanuatu, Yemen. The States Parties to the Protocol of 1996 are Albania, Antigua and Barbuda, Australia, Belgium, Bulgaria, Canada, Cook Islands, Congo, Croatia, Cyprus, Denmark, Estonia, Finland, France, Germany, Greece, Hungary, Iceland, India, Ireland, Jamaica, Japan, Latvia, Liberia, Lithuania, Luxembourg, Malaysia, Malta, Marshall Island, Mongolia, Netherlands, New Zealand, Niue, Norway, Palau, Poland,

6.3 Evidence of the insurance or other financial security

Art. 7(2) so provides:

2 A certificate attesting that insurance or other financial security is in force in accordance with the provisions of this Convention shall be issued to each ship after the appropriate authority of a State Party has determined that the requirements of paragraph 1 have been complied with. With respect to a ship registered in a State Party such certificate shall be issued or certified by the appropriate authority of the State of the ship's registry; with respect to a ship not registered in a State Party it may be issued or certified by the appropriate authority of any State Party. This certificate shall be in the form of the model set out in the annex to this Convention and shall contain the following particulars:

(a) name of ship, distinctive number or letters and port of registry;
(b) name and principal place of business of the registered owner;
(c) IMO ship identification number;
(d) type and duration of security;
(e) name and principal place of business of insurer or other person giving security and, where appropriate, place of business where the insurance or security is established;
(f) period of validity of the certificate which shall not be longer than the period of validity of the insurance or other security.

The wording of the opening sentence of this paragraph is identical to that in art. 12(2) of the HNS Convention and therefore reference is made to the comments thereunder.[34] Also the enumeration of the particulars corresponds to that in art. 12(2) of that Convention. In the period of validity of the certificate reference is instead made to the comments under the corresponding provision in art. VII(2) of the CLC Convention.[35]

6.4 Authorities that may issue the certificate and notices required

Art. 7(3)(a) so provides:

3(a) A State Party may authorize either an institution or an organization recognized by it to issue the certificate referred to in paragraph 2. Such institution or organization shall inform that State of the issue of each certificate. In all cases, the State Party shall fully guarantee the completeness and accuracy of the certificate so issued and shall undertake to ensure the necessary arrangements to satisfy this obligation.

This provision differs from the corresponding provisions in art. VII(2) of the CLC and in art. 12(2) of the HNS Convention. While such Conventions merely provide that the certificates must be issued 'or certified' by the appropriate authority of the State of the ship's registry, art. 7(3) of the Bunker Oil Convention is more specific: it indicates the characters of the entities that may issue the certificate in lieu of the

---

Romania, Russian Federation, Samoa, Serbia, Sierra Leone, Spain, St Lucia, Sweden, Syrian Arab Republic, Tonga, Turkey, Tuvalu, United Kingdom. See Vol. II, Chapter 11, para. 8.4.

34 *Infra*, Chapter 14, para. 8.3.
35 *Supra*, Chapter 11, para. 9.4.

State by mentioning that they may either be an institution or an organisation recognised by the State and provides that 'in all cases' the State shall fully guarantee the completeness and accuracy of the certificate and shall undertake 'to ensure the necessary arrangements to satisfy this obligation'. The description of the nature of the entity that may issue the certificate as an 'institution' or an 'organization' is very generic, but the relevant requirement is that it must be recognised by the State. The object of the guarantee of the State is not clear: which is the obligation the State undertakes to satisfy? If it is the guarantee of the accuracy and completeness of the certificate, what else should have been required? What would be the nature of the 'necessary arrangements'?

Art. 3(b), for which there is no corresponding rule in the CLC and the HNS Convention, provides:

(b) A State Party shall notify the Secretary-General of:

    (i)   the specific responsibilities and conditions of the authority delegated to an institution or organization recognised by it;
    (ii) the withdrawal of such authority; and
    (iii) the date from which such authority or withdrawal of such authority takes effect.

An authority delegated shall not take effect prior to three months from the date on which notification to that effect was given to the Secretary-General.

Since pursuant to the last sentence the delegation may only take effect after three months from the date of the notification to the Secretary General, the purpose of the notice seems to be that of enabling IMO to assess the propriety of the delegation.

Finally art. 7(3)(c) provides:

(c)   The institution or organization authorized to issue certificates in accordance with this paragraph shall, as a minimum, be authorized to withdraw these certificates if the conditions under which they have been issued are not maintained. In all cases the institution or organization shall report such withdrawal to the State on whose behalf the certificate was issued.

This provision is difficult to understand. The institution or organisation ought not to be authorised 'as a minimum' to withdraw the certificates, but rather should be required to do that and be held responsible if it fails to take that action.

6.5 Language of the certificate

Art. 7(4) so provides:

4   The certificate shall be in the official language or languages of the issuing State. If the language used is not English, French or Spanish, the text shall include a translation into one of these languages and, where the State so decides, the official language of the State may be omitted.

Spanish has been added to English and French, as in art. 4*bis* of the Athens Convention and in art. 12(4) of the HNS Convention.

6.6 International validity of the certificate

Art. 7 so provides in paragraphs 9, 11 and 12:

9   Certificates issued or certified under the authority of a State Party shall be accepted by other States Parties for the purposes of this Convention and shall be regarded by other States Parties as having the same force as certificates issued or certified by them even if issued or certified in respect of a ship not registered in a State Party. A State Party may at any time request consultation with the issuing or certifying State should it believe that the insurer or guarantor named in the insurance certificate is not financially capable of meeting the obligations imposed by this Convention.
    [. . .]
11 A State Party shall not permit a ship under its flag to which this article applies to operate at any time, unless a certificate has been issued under paragraphs 2 or 14.
12 Subject to the provisions of this article, each State Party shall ensure, under its national law, that insurance or other security, to the extent specified in paragraph 1, is in force in respect of any ship having a gross tonnage greater than 1000, wherever registered, entering or leaving a port in its territory, or arriving at or leaving an offshore facility in its territorial sea.

While the corresponding provisions in the CLC apply to ships carrying more than 2,000 tons of oil in bulk as cargo[36] and those in the HNS Convention apply to ships actually carrying hazardous and noxious substances, irrespective of the quantity and whether in bulk or packaged,[37] the restriction of the scope of application of the provisions on compulsory insurance in the Bunker Oil Convention is based on the gross tonnage of the ships, and apply to all ships having a tonnage greater than 1,000 GT: it would in fact have been impossible to make reference to the quantity of bunker oil actually on board or to the volume of the bunkers, because the control of the existence of the obligation to insure the liability would have been practically impossible. Although the definition of ship is very wide, for the application of the Convention it is necessary that ships require oil for their operation or propulsion. It is however very difficult, if not impossible, that a ship having a gross tonnage greater than 1,000 is not provided with engines, except perhaps nuclear ships; but nuclear propulsion is at present used only for warships, to which the Convention does not apply. As for the CLC and the HNS Convention, although the obligation to maintain insurance binds only the registered owners of ships registered in States Parties, owners of ships not registered in States Parties must also provide their ships with the certificate mentioned in art. 7(2) if they wish to trade with States Parties.

6.7 The obligation for the ships to carry on board the certificate

Art. 7(5) so provides:

5   The certificate shall be carried on board the ship and a copy shall be deposited with the authorities who keep the record of the ship's registry or, if the ship is not registered in a State Party, with the authorities issuing or certifying the certificate.

Although an identical provision may be found in both the CLC and the HNS Convention,[38] in the Bunker Oil Convention the obligation is not absolute. Article 7(13) so in fact provides:

---

36 *Supra*, Chapter 11, para. 9.
37 *Infra*, Chapter 14, para. 8.
38 Article VII(4) of the CLC and art. 12(4) of the HNS Convention.

13 Notwithstanding the provisions of paragraph 5, a State Party may notify the Secretary-General that, for the purposes of paragraph 12, ships are not required to carry on board or to produce the certificate required by paragraph 2, when entering or leaving ports or arriving at or leaving from offshore facilities in its territory, provided that the State Party which issues the certificate required by paragraph 2 has notified the Secretary-General that it maintains records in an electronic format, accessible to all States Parties, attesting the existence of the certificate and enabling States Parties to discharge their obligations under paragraph 12.

Therefore, this provision lays down an exception to the rule of paragraph 5 pursuant to which the certificate must be carried on board; and since paragraph 12 requires each State Party to ensure under its national law that insurance or other security is in force in respect of any ship entering or leaving a port in its territory or arriving at or leaving an offshore facility in its territorial sea, paragraph 13 states that such obligation is met if the State Party which has issued the certificate has notified the Secretary General as required by this paragraph. Although the notice must be given to the Secretary General of IMO, the condition for the exemption from compliance with paragraph 12 is that records in electronic format are maintained by the relevant State attesting the existence of the certificate and such records be accessible to all State Parties. It is assumed that the simplest way for the State Party in a port that the relevant ship enters to become aware of this is for the Master of the ship to inform the Port Authority that the certificate has been uploaded on the site of the State Party in the register of which the ship is registered.

6.8 Direct action against the insurer or guarantor

Art. 7(10) so provides:

10 Any claim for compensation for pollution damage may be brought directly against the insurer or other person providing financial security for the registered owner's liability for pollution damage. In such a case the defendant may invoke the defences (other than bankruptcy or winding up of the shipowner) which the shipowner would have been entitled to invoke, including limitation pursuant to article 6. Furthermore, even if the shipowner is not entitled to limitation of liability according to article 6, the defendant may limit liability to an amount equal to the amount of the insurance or other financial security required to be maintained in accordance with paragraph 1. Moreover, the defendant may invoke the defence that the pollution damage resulted from the wilful misconduct of the shipowner, but the defendant shall not invoke any other defence which the defendant might have been entitled to invoke in proceedings brought by the shipowner against the defendant. The defendant shall in any event have the right to require the shipowner to be joined in the proceedings.

This provision also exists in the CLC and in the HNS Convention, and in both cases the wording is rather unsatisfactory.[39] The failure to draw a distinction between the benefit of limitation granted to the shipowner and the ceiling of the insurance or financial security, reference to which is made in paragraph 1 has been remedied in the provision now under consideration, for reference is made to both. However, the wording in both is inappropriate.

As regards the owner's limitation, it is inappropriate to state that the insurer or

---

39 *Supra*, Chapter 11, para. 9.9 for the CLC and *infra*, Chapter 14, para. 8.7 for the HNS Convention.

provider of financial security may invoke the 'limitation pursuant to article 6', for art. 6 does not grant the benefit of limitation, but merely states that nothing in the Convention shall affect the right of the shipowner and the persons providing insurance or other financial security to limit liability under any applicable national or international regime: therefore this provision does not grant limitation to the shipowner but merely provides that that right, if it existed under the applicable national or international regime, was not affected.

As regards the limitation of liability to an amount equal to the amount of insurance or other financial security, reference to it as a 'limitation' is inappropriate: in fact it is in both cases a contractual ceiling of the insurance cover or of the guarantee.

6.9 Ships owned by a Contracting State

Art. 7(14) so provides:

14 If insurance or other financial security is not maintained in respect of a ship owned by a State Party, the provisions of this article relating thereto shall not be applicable to such ship, but the ship shall carry a certificate issued by the appropriate authority of the State of the ship's registry stating that the ship is owned by that State and that the ship's liability is covered within the limit prescribed in accordance with paragraph 1. Such a certificate shall follow as closely as possible the model prescribed by paragraph 2.

The wording of this provision is the same as that included in art. VII(12) of the CLC and in art. 12(12) of the HNS Convention and therefore reference is made to the comments under the former of such Conventions.[40]

6.10 Facultative exclusion of ships operating exclusively within the area of a State

Art. 7(15) so provides:

15 A State may, at the time of ratification, acceptance, approval of, or accession to this Convention, or at any time thereafter, declare that this article does not apply to ships operating exclusively within the area of that State referred to in article 2(a)(i).[41]

7 TIME FOR SUIT

Art. 8 so provides:

Rights to compensation under this Convention shall be extinguished unless an action is brought thereunder within three years from the date when the damage occurred. However,

---

40 *Supra*, Chapter 11, para. 9.10.
41 Such a declaration has been made by China in the following terms:

Article 7 of the Convention shall not apply to the ships operating exclusively within the inland waterways of the People's Republic of China.

It has also been made by Estonia in the following terms:

Based on the article 7 paragraph 15 of the Convention, article 7 does not apply to ships operating exclusively within the waters of the Republic of Estonia.

INTERNATIONAL MARITIME CONVENTIONS

in no case shall an action be brought more than six years from the date of the incident which caused the damage. Where the incident consists of a series of occurrences, the six years' period shall run from the date of the first such occurrence.

The wording of this provision is exactly the same as that in art. VIII of the CLC 1992 and therefore reference is made to the comments thereunder.[42]

8 JURISDICTION

Art. 9 so provides:

1 Where an incident has caused pollution damage in the territory, including the territorial sea, or in an area referred to in article 2(a)(ii) of one or more States Parties, or preventive measures have been taken to prevent or minimise pollution damage in such territory, including the territorial sea, or in such area, actions for compensation against the shipowner, insurer or other person providing security for the shipowner's liability may be brought only in the courts of any such States Parties.[43]
2 Reasonable notice of any action taken under paragraph 1 shall be given to each defendant.
3 Each State Party shall ensure that its courts have jurisdiction to entertain actions for compensation under this Convention.

The question whether courts in different States may be seised by different claimants when pollution damage has been caused or preventive measures have been taken in different States Parties, to which it has been suggested should be given a negative answer in respect of the CLC after a limitation fund has been constituted,[44] should be similarly be given a negative answer where the shipowner or person or persons providing insurance or other financial security will, on the basis of art. 6 of the Bunker Oil Convention, seek to limit his liability under the applicable national law or international regime.

9 RECOGNITION AND ENFORCEMENT OF JUDGMENTS

Art. 10 so provides:

1 Any judgment given by a Court with jurisdiction in accordance with article 9 which is enforceable in the State of origin where it is no longer subject to ordinary forms of review, shall be recognised in any State Party, except:

---

42 *Supra*, Chapter 11, para. 9.

43 Although within the European Union jurisdiction is a matter exclusively within the competence of the EU, in connection with this Convention the individual ratification of or accession to this Convention has been authorised by a Council Decision, reference to which has been made in the instrument of ratification of Germany. The Member States that have ratified or acceded to this Convention are Belgium, Bulgaria, Cyprus, Denmark, Estonia, Finland, France, Germany, Ireland, Italy, Lithuania, Luxembourg, Malta, Netherlands, Poland, Romania, Slovakia, Spain and Sweden. These States have declared that judgments on matters covered by the Convention shall, when given by a court in another Member State, be recognised and enforced according to the relevant Community rules on the subject. The declarations differ in that some States have generally referred to other Member States of the EU, while other States have identified the relevant States to which the declaration applied.

44 *Supra*, Chapter 11, para. 11.

BUNKER OIL POLLUTION DAMAGE CONVENTION, 2001

(a) where the judgment was obtained by fraud; or
(b) where the defendant was not given reasonable notice and a fair opportunity to present his or her case.
2 A judgment recognised under paragraph 1 shall be enforceable in each State Party as soon as the formalities required in that State have been complied with. The formalities shall not permit the merits of the case to be re-opened.

This is a standard provision, that reproduces word for word that in art. X of the CLC and, therefore, reference is made to the comment made thereunder.[45]

10 SUPERSESSION CLAUSE

Art. 11 so provides:

This Convention shall supersede any Convention in force or open for signature, ratification or accession at the date on which this Convention is opened for signature, but only to the extent that such Convention would be in conflict with it; however nothing in this article shall affect the obligations of States Parties to States not party to this Convention arising under such Convention.

The last sentence of this article is meant to comply with the provisions of art. 30(4) (b) of the Vienna Convention on the Law of Treaties. An identical provision is included in the CLC (art. XII) and in the HNS Convention (art. 42).

---

45 *Supra*, Chapter 11, para. 12.

CHAPTER 14

International Convention on Liability and Compensation for Damage in Connection with the Carriage of Hazardous and Noxious Substances by Sea, 1996

1 THE HISTORY OF THE CONVENTION

These were the fundamental questions that required consideration in order to establish the scope of application of this new convention:

(a) What should be the substances, other than oil within the meaning given to it in the CLC?
(b) What should be the damages to which the future convention should apply?
(c) Who should provide the funds for the settlement of claims arising out of such damages?

In respect of the first issue it was decided that, as it was done with the CLC, the method to be adopted should be that of a definition of such substances: a task much more difficult than that of the definition of 'oil' given the great variety of substances that, in addition to oil, could cause damages. In respect of the second issue, which was linked to the solution adopted for the first, it was decided that the damages should include not only damage to the environment, but also loss of life and personal injuries. In respect of the third issue, the same two-tier solution adopted by the CLC, accompanied by the owner's compulsory insurance and the Fund Convention was chosen; but more difficulties had arisen in respect of whether contributions to the fund should be provided by the shippers or the receivers of the hazardous and noxious substances.

The Convention was adopted on 3 May 1996, but at the end of 2008, over 12 years after its adoption, it had been acceded to by only 14 States, out of which only three[1] had a tonnage in excess of 2 million tons, the required number of States with tonnage in excess of 2 million tons being four, pursuant to art. 46 of the Convention. An enquiry into the underlying reasons that had inhibited the entry into force of the Convention was carried out by the IMO Secretariat. It appeared that these had included the heavy burden on States having to report the vast range of packaged substances received by them pursuant to art. 21(3) of the Convention, the fact that, in the case of LNG cargoes, the title holder, who would be the person responsible for making contributions, may not be subject to the jurisdiction of a State Party and the possible non-submission of contributing cargo reports on ratification of the Convention and annually thereafter.[2]

---

1 Cyprus, Liberia and the Russian Federation.
2 Annex to doc. LEG 98/4/1 of 18 January 2011, para. 4.

With a view to curing those difficulties a Protocol to the Convention was adopted on 30 April 2010 with amendments, *inter alia*, to the definition of hazardous and noxious substances in art. 1(5), including the new definitions of 'Bulk HNS' and 'Packaged HNS' required for the amendment of art. 9 in which distinct limits were adopted for hazardous and noxious substances.

Four Resolutions were also adopted by the Conference:[3] with the first, the Assembly of the IOPC Fund was requested to set up the HNS Fund; with the second, States Parties to the 2010 HNS Protocol, Member States of IMO and other appropriate organisations as well as the maritime industry were requested to provide assistance to those States which required support in the consideration of adoption and implementation of the Protocol; with the third, States were invited to give early and urgent consideration to acceptance of the Protocol, in order to avoid the contemporary existence of two different regimes, that of the HNS 1996 and that created by the Protocol; with the fourth, the Legal Committee of IMO was invited to reconsider its overview of the 1996 HNS Convention in light of the adoption of the Protocol.

The efforts to encourage the adoption of the HNS Convention, as amended by the 2010 Protocol (reference to which was made as the '2010 HNS Convention') continued in the following years.

On 28 January 2011, an Overview of the 2010 HNS Convention was prepared by the IMO Secretariat and submitted to the Legal Committee for its comments and decisions as appropriate.[4] During the HNS Workshop held at IMO Headquarters on 12 and 13 November 2012, Guidelines on reporting of HNS contributing cargo were prepared and endorsed by the IMO Legal Committee at its 100th session on 19 April 2013. At the time of endorsing the Guidelines it was agreed that States should continue to monitor and coordinate ratification and accession timelines and that the IMO and the IOPC Funds should continue their work to promote the entry into force of the HNS Protocol. At a subsequent informal meeting that took place on 24 October 2013, during a subsequent meeting of the IOPC Funds, it was agreed that an Informal Correspondence Group be constituted to continue the dialogue among States aiming at resolving implementation issues. At the 101st session of the Legal Committee, the following Terms of Reference for the Correspondence Group were submitted by Canada, Denmark, France, Germany, the Netherlands and Norway:[5]

1   to provide a forum for an exchange of views concerning HNS implementation issues and to monitor and inform the implementation process in States;
2   to provide, with a view to encouraging early entry into force of the 2010 HNS Convention at a global level, and for the benefit of both potential States Parties and affected industries seeking a coordinated approach to ratification, accession or acceptance, guidance and assistance on issues regarding the implementation and operation of the Convention such as, but not limited, to:
  (a) the collection of information on contributing cargo, the development of appropriate reporting and verification systems, and the contribution system in accordance with the *Guidelines on reporting of HNS contributing cargo*;
  (b) the acceptability of insurance or other financial security for the purpose of article 12 of the 2010 HNS Convention;

---

3 LEG/CONF.17/11 of 4 May 2010.
4 Guidelines on Implementation of the HNS Protocol 2010: LEG 98/4/1.
5 LEG 101/3, 14 March 2014, p. 3.

INTERNATIONAL MARITIME CONVENTIONS

   (c)   assisting the IOPC Fund 1992 with the development of the various documents and decisions required for the first sessions of the HNS Assembly, in accordance with resolution 1 on setting up the HNS Fund agreed to at the international conference which adopted the 2010 HNS Protocol; and

3   to report to the Legal Committee on a regular basis.

However no success has so far been achieved towards the entry into force of the HNS Convention 2010. As at 30 September 2014, no State had deposited an instrument of ratification or accession to the Convention as amended by the Protocol.[6]

2 THE STRUCTURE OF THE CONVENTION

While in respect of oil pollution damage there are, owing to their history, two separate conventions – the CLC Convention which regulates the liability of the owners of ships carrying oil and the Fund Convention which regulates the contribution of the cargo – in respect of damage in connection with the carriage of hazardous and noxious substances both aspects are regulated in the same convention. Its structure is therefore different. The Convention is divided into six chapters: the first containing general provisions applicable to the whole Convention; the second containing rules on the liability of the owner as the CLC does for oil; the third containing rules on the establishment and the administration of the International Fund; the fourth, again of a general nature, containing rules on claims and actions; the fifth on transitional provisions; and the sixth on final clauses. This commentary follows the structure of the Convention.

I – GENERAL PROVISIONS

3 SCOPE OF APPLICATION

The scope of application of the Convention is defined with reference to the nature of the damage, the substances that may cause the damage, and the area in which the damage is caused.

---

6 One of the difficulties with which States are confronted has been indicated as follows in para. 1 of the 'Guidelines on reporting of HNS contributing cargo' previously referred to:

> The HNS Protocol requires, under article 20, paragraph 4, that an expression of consent to be bound by this Protocol must be accompanied by the submission of data on the total quantity of contributing cargo received during the preceding calendar year.
> This poses a challenge, since the procedure for reporting contributing cargo requires a number of decisions from the first HNS Fund Assembly to ensure uniform application. Since the Assembly cannot be convened until the treaty enters into force, there is a need to put reporting regulations in place prior to ratification.

The provision referred to in the above statement has become art. 45 of HNS 2010, paras. 4 and 5 of which are quoted below:

> 4 An expression of consent to be bound by this Protocol shall be accompanied by the submission to the Secretary-General of data on the total quantities of contributing cargo liable for contributions received in that State during the preceding calendar year in respect of the general account and each separate account.
> 5 An expression of consent which is not accompanied by the data referred to in paragraph 4 shall not be accepted by the Secretary-General.

3.1 Nature of the damage

The following definition of damage is given in art. 1(6):

6 'Damage' means:
    (a) loss of life or personal injury on board or outside the ship carrying the hazardous and noxious substances caused by those substances;
    (b) loss of or damage to property outside the ship carrying the hazardous and noxious substances caused by those substances;
    (c) loss or damage by contamination of the environment caused by the hazardous and noxious substances, provided that compensation for impairment of the environment other than loss of profit from such impairment shall be limited to costs of reasonable measures of reinstatement actually undertaken or to be undertaken; and
    (d) the costs of preventive measures and further loss or damage caused by preventive measures.
    Where it is not reasonably possible to separate damage caused by the hazardous and noxious substances from that caused by other factors, all such damage shall be deemed to be caused by the hazardous and noxious substances except if, and to the extent that, the damage caused by other factors is damage of a type referred to in article 4, paragraph 3.
    In this paragraph, 'caused by those substances' means caused by the hazardous or noxious nature of the substances.

This definition, and consequently the scope of application of the Convention, is much wider than that in art. 1(6) of the CLC, since it includes, in addition to loss or damage by contamination of the environment and cost of preventive measures, loss of life or personal injury and loss of or damage to property caused by noxious or hazardous substances.

With respect to loss of life or personal injury the occurrence may be either on board the ship or outside, provided it is caused by the hazardous or noxious substances carried on the ship, and its character and the limits are the same as those of oil pollution damage under the CLC 1992.

With respect to loss of or damage to property, such property must be outside the ship, either at sea or ashore, while the Convention does not apply to claims in respect of loss or damage to property on board the ship caused by the hazardous or noxious substances carried on that ship and the rule on preventive measures mirrors that in art. I(6)(b) of CLC 1992.

With respect to loss or damage by contamination of the environment, the limits in respect of compensation for impairment of the environment other than loss of profit from such impairment are the same as those set out in art. I(6) of the CLC 1992 in respect of pollution damage.

It is on the contrary a new rule that where damage is jointly caused by hazardous and noxious substances and by other factors and it is not reasonably possible to separate damage caused by the hazardous and noxious substances from that caused by other factors, in which event all such damage shall be deemed to be caused by the hazardous and noxious substances. This presumption, however, does not operate where, and to the extent to which, the damage caused by other factors is damage of a type referred to in art. 4(3), wherein reference is made to pollution damage as defined in the CLC 1969 as amended and to damage caused by a radioactive material of class 7 either in the International Maritime Dangerous Goods

Code, as amended, or in the International Maritime Solid Bulk Cargoes Code, as amended.[7]

The reason why the presumption does not operate is that pursuant to art. 4(2) the Convention does not apply to damage caused by such material. However, the question remains on the basis of which criterion the proportion of the damage caused by hazardous and noxious substances may be established, where separation of such damage from that caused by radioactive material is not possible.[8] Perhaps the only reasonable criterion is that causation be apportioned equally: a criterion adopted in art. 4 of the 1910 Collision Convention when it is not possible to establish the degree of fault.[9]

3.2 Substances causing the damage

Art. 4(1) states:

1   This Convention shall apply to claims, other than claims arising out of any contract for the carriage of goods and passengers, for damage arising from the carriage of hazardous and noxious substances by sea.

The substances that may cause the damage, globally referred to as 'hazardous and noxious substances', are so defined in art. 1(5) followed by a comment when necessary:

5   'Hazardous and noxious substances (HNS)' means:
   (a)   any substances, materials and articles carried on board a ship as cargo, referred to in (i) to (vii) below:

Reference to substances carried as cargo indicates clearly that bunker oil is excluded from the scope of application of this Convention.

(i)   oils, carried in bulk, as defined in regulation 1 of Annex I to the International Convention for the Prevention of Pollution from Ships, 1973, as modified by the Protocol of 1978 relating thereto, as amended;

---

7 *Infra*, para. 3.2.

8 The final words of this provision 'except if, and to the extent that . . .' were added following a proposal of the United Kingdom delegation, which explained the reasons of its suggestion as follows (LEG/CONF 10/6(a)/27 of 9 April 1996):

    6 The UK delegation submits that article 4(3) should take precedence over article 1(6). As currently drafted, there would be conflict between the two provisions if an incident caused damage of a type referred to in article 4(3) which it was not reasonably possible to separate from HNS damage. For example, if a tanker laden with persistent oil explodes in port, it may not be reasonably possible to separate the loss of profit due to the physical damage to the port infrastructure from the loss of profit due to measures taken to minimise pollution.

    7 Clarifying that article 4(3) takes precedence over article 1(6) would ensure that the parties who share the costs of compensation under the HNS Convention would not find themselves liable for costs which, in normal circumstances, would have been borne by other parties. Claimants should not suffer. Provided that States Parties to the HNS Convention are also parties to the other international conventions referred to in article 4(3), or have equivalent provisions in national law, claimants would be entitled to compensation both for the HNS damage and the other damage. Even if it were not reasonably possible to separate the damage, the national courts or the appropriate international organisations would be able to reach a pragmatic decision on how the costs of compensation payments should be shared.

9 Volume II, Chapter 1, para. 3.3.

Appendix I to Annex I to MARPOL[10] consists of a 'List of oils' that includes asphalt solutions, oils, distillates, gas oil, gasoline blending stocks, gasoline, jet fuels and naphtha and, therefore, does not include the oils reference to which is made in art. 1(5) of the CLC.

(ii) noxious liquid substances, carried in bulk, as defined in regulation 1.10 of Annex II to the International Convention for the Prevention of Pollution from Ships, 1973, as modified by the Protocol of 1978 relating thereto, as amended, and those substances and mixtures provisionally categorized as falling in pollution category X, Y or Z in accordance with regulation 6.3 of the said Annex II;

Regulation 1.10 of Annex II to MARPOL states:

Noxious liquid substance means any substance indicated in the Pollution Category column of chapter 17 or 18 of the International Bulk Chemical Code or provisionally assessed under the provisions of regulation 6.3 as falling into category X, Y or Z.

Regulation 6.3 of Annex II to MARPOL states:

3 Where it is proposed to carry a liquid substance in bulk which has not been categorized under paragraph 1 of this regulation,[11] the Governments of Parties to this Convention involved in the proposed operation shall establish and agree on a provisional assessment for the proposed operation on the basis of the guidelines referred to in paragraph 2 of this regulation.[12] Until full agreement among the Governments involved has been reached, the substance shall not be carried. As soon as possible, but not later than 30 days after the agreement has been reached, the Government of the producing shipping country, initiating the agreement concerned, shall notify the Organization and provide details of the substance and the provisional assessment for annual circulation to all Parties for their information. The Organization shall maintain a register of all such substances and their provisional assessment until such time as the substances are formally included in the IBC Code.

---

10 On MARPOL see *supra* Chapter 3.
11 Paragraph 1 of reg. 6 states:

For the purpose of the regulations of this Annex, noxious liquid substances shall be divided into four categories as follows:
1 Category X: Noxious Liquid Substances which, if discharged into the sea from tank cleaning or deballasting operations, are deemed to present a major hazard to either marine resources or human health and, therefore, justify the prohibition of the discharge into the marine environment;
2 Category Y: Noxious Liquid Substances which, if discharged into the sea from tank cleaning or deballasting operations, are deemed to present a hazard to either marine resources or human health or cause harm to amenities or other legitimate uses of the sea and therefore justify a limitation on the quality and quantity of the discharge into the marine environment;
3 Category Z: Noxious Liquid Substances which, if discharged into the sea from tank cleaning or deballasting operations, are deemed to present a minor hazard to either marine resources or human health and therefore justify less stringent restrictions on the quality and quantity of the discharge into the marine environment; and
4 Other Substances: Substances indicated as OS (Other Substances) in the pollution category column of chapter 18 of the International Bulk Chemical Code which have been evaluated and found to fall outside Category X, Y or Z as defined in regulation 6.1 of this Annex because they are, at present, considered to present no harm to marine resources, human health, amenities or other legitimate uses of the sea when discharged into the sea from tank cleaning of deballasting operations. The discharge of bilge or ballast water or other residues or mixtures containing only substances referred to as 'Other Substances' shall not be subject to any requirements of the Annex.

12 Paragraph 2 of reg. 6 states:

2 Guidelines for use in the categorization of noxious liquid substances are given in appendix 1 to this Annex. Such appendix is published in the consolidated 2011 edition of MARPOL at p. 185–187.

INTERNATIONAL MARITIME CONVENTIONS

   (iii)   Dangerous liquid substances carried in bulk listed in chapter 17 of the International Code for the Construction and Equipment of Ships Carrying Dangerous Chemicals in Bulk as amended, and the dangerous products for which the preliminary suitable conditions for the carriage have been prescribed by the Administration and port administrations involved in accordance with paragraph 1.1.6 of the Code.

The chapeau of chapter 17 of this Code states:

Mixtures of noxious liquid substances presenting pollution hazards only, and which are assessed or provisionally assessed under regulation 6.3 of MARPOL Annex II, may be carried under the requirements of the Code applicable to the appropriate position of the entry in this chapter or Noxious Liquid Substances, not otherwise specified (n.o.s.).

The substances enumerated in this chapter are published at pages 88–249 of the Code. The initial explanatory note relating to the 'Product name' may be of interest:

The product name shall be used in the shipping document for any cargo offered for bulk shipments. Any additional name may be included in brackets after the product name. In some cases, the product names are not identical with the names given in previous issues of the Code.

   (iv)   dangerous, hazardous and harmful substances, materials and articles in packaged form covered by the International Maritime Dangerous Goods Code, as amended;

Although this provision does not help very much in the identification of the substances, material and articles mentioned in the IMDG Code, it would appear that reference should be made to Chapter 4.1 of the Code on 'Use of packaging, including intermediate bulk containers (IBCs) and large packaging', in which specific packing instructions are provided in respect of specific categories of goods.

   (v)   liquefied gases as listed in chapter 19 of the International Code for the Construction and Equipment of Ships Carrying Liquefied Gases in Bulk, as amended, and the products for which preliminary suitable conditions for the carriage have been prescribed by the Administration and port administrations involved in accordance with paragraph 1.1.6 of the Code.

The IGC Code, adopted by resolution of the Maritime Safety Committee of IMO 5(48) of 17 June 1983, states in paragraph 1 of its Preamble:

The purpose of this Code is to provide an international standard for the safe carriage by sea in bulk of liquefied gases and certain other substances listed in chapter 19 of the Code,[13] by prescribing the design and construction standards of ships involved in such carriage and the equipment they should carry so as to minimize the risk to the ship, to its crew and to the environment, having regard to the nature of the product involved.

   (vi)   liquid substances carried in bulk with a flashpoint not exceeding 60°C (measured by a closed-cup test),

---

   13 The substances listed are the following:

   Acetaldehyde, Ammonia, anhydrous, Butadiene, Butane, Butane-propane mixtures, Butylenes, Chlorine, Diethyl ether,* Dimethylamine, Ethane, Ethyl chloride, Ethylene, Ethylene oxide, Ethylene oxide propylene oxide mixtures with ethylene oxide content of not more than 30% by weight,* Isoprene,* Isopropylamine,* Methane (LNG), Methyl acetylene propadiene mixtures, Methyl bromide, Methyl chloride, Monoethylamine,* Nitrogen, Pentanes (all isomers),* Pentene (all isomers),* Propane, Propylene, Propylene oxide,* Refrigerant gases such as: dichlorodifluoromethane, dichloromonofluoromethane, dichlorotetrafluoroethane, monochlorodifluoromethane, monochlorotetrafluoroethane, monochlorotrifluoromethane; Sulphur dioxide, Vinyl chloride, Vinyl ethyl ether,* Vinylidene chloride.*

   * Also covered by IBC Code.

214

(vii) solid bulk materials possessing chemical hazards covered by the International Maritime Solid Bulk Cargoes Code, as amended, to the extent that these substances are also subject to the provisions of the International Maritime Dangerous Goods Code in effect in 1996, when carried in packaged form.

The solid bulk cargos which may possess a chemical hazard during transport are the object of regulation in Section 9 of the IMSBC Code adopted by Resolution MSC.268(85) of 4 December 2008. They are included in the definition of HNS in art. 1(5)(a) of the HNS Convention and consequently subject to its rules only if they are subject to the provisions of the IMDG Code.

(b) residues from the previous carriage in bulk of substances referred to in (a)(i) to (iii) and (v) to (vii) above.

While in the CLC reference to residues is made in the definition of ship in order to limit the application of the Convention to ships capable of carrying oil and other cargo performing a voyage following that with cargo on board to the existence during such voyage of residues of a prior voyage with cargo on board, in the HNS Convention they are included in the definition of hazardous and noxious substances. The reason for such difference is that while in the CLC the characteristics of the ships are a determinant factor for the application of the Convention, in the HNS Convention they are not as it appears from the following very generic definition of ship in its art. 1(1):

'Ship' means any seagoing vessel and seaborne craft, of any type whatsoever.

3.3 Area in which the damage is caused

Art. 3 states:

This Convention shall apply exclusively:
(a) to any damage caused in the territory, including the territorial sea, of a State Party;
(b) to damage by contamination of the environment caused in the exclusive economic zone of a State Party, established in accordance with international law, or, if a State Party has not established such a zone, in an area beyond and adjacent to the territorial sea of that State determined by that State in accordance with international law and extending not more than 200 nautical miles from the baselines from which the breadth of its territorial sea is measured;
(c) to damage, other than damage by contamination of the environment, caused outside the territory, including the territorial sea, of any State, if this damage has been caused by a substance carried on board a ship registered in a State Party or, in the case of an unregistered ship, on board a ship entitled to fly the flag of a State Party; and
(d) to preventive measures, wherever taken.

The nature of the damage to which the Convention applies varies according to the area in which the damage is caused and the flag of the ship that carries the substance that has caused the damage.

(a) Damage caused in the territory, including the territorial sea, of a State Party: the Convention applies to any damage covered by the definition in art. 1(6), namely loss of life or personal injury, loss of or damage to property, loss or damage by contamination of the environment.

(b) Damage caused in the Exclusive Economic Zone of State Party or area beyond and adjacent to the territorial sea of that State determined by that State: the Convention applies only in respect of damage by contamination of the environment.

(c) Damage caused outside the territory, including the territorial sea, of any State, by a substance carried on board a ship registered in a State Party or, in the case of an unregistered ship, on board a ship entitled to fly the flag of a State Party: the Convention applies only in respect of damage other than by contamination of the environment, such damage being either loss of life or personal injury or loss or damage to property.

3.4 Exclusions from the scope of application

3.4.1 Exclusions related to the basis of the claims

Art. 4(1) states:

1 This Convention shall apply to claims, other than claims arising out of any contract for the carriage of goods and passengers, for damage arising from the carriage of hazardous and noxious substances by sea.

The effect of the exclusion of claims arising out of any contract for the carriage of goods and passengers appears to be that the Convention does not apply to claims for damage to goods owned by a shipper caused by hazardous and noxious substances carried on board the ship.

3.4.2 Exclusions based on the character or the cause of the damage

Art. 4(3) states:

3 This Convention shall not apply:
   (a) to pollution damage as defined in the International Convention on Civil Liability for Oil Pollution Damage, 1969, as amended, whether or not compensation is payable in respect of it under that Convention; and
   (b) to damage caused by a radioactive material of class 7 either in the International Maritime Dangerous Goods Code, as amended, or in appendix B of the Code of Safe Practice for Solid Bulk Cargoes, as amended.

The exclusion under (a) is obvious, since the HNS Convention aims to complement the CLC and the Fund Convention by covering damage caused by substances other than oil as defined in art. 1(5) of the CLC.

The reference in the exclusion under (b) to damage caused by a radioactive material of class 7 either in the International Maritime Dangerous Goods Code, as amended, or in the International Maritime Solid Bulk Cargoes Code, as amended is unclear, for in the Code Class 7 is not a specific class of radioactive materials, but rather is the class relating to radioactive materials: since there is in Chapter 2.7 of the Code entitled 'Class 7 – Radioactive materials' a definition of such materials, it is suggested that the meaning of that provision is 'radioactive materials as defined in Class 7 of the IMDG Code'.

Class 7 of the IMSBC Code,[14] is the class of radioactive materials defined in section 9.2.2.6:

The materials in this class are any materials containing radionuclides where both the activity concentration and the total activity in the consignment exceeds the value specified in 7.7.7.2.1 to 7.7.7.2.6 of the IMDG Code.

3.4.3 Exclusion of warships and ships owned or operated by States

Art. 4 states in paragraphs 4, 5 and 6:

4 Except as provided in paragraph 5, the provisions of this Convention shall not apply to warships, naval auxiliary or other ships owned or operated by a State and used, for the time being, only on Government non-commercial service.
5 A State Party may decide to apply this Convention to its warships or other vessels described in paragraph 4, in which case it shall notify the Secretary-General thereof specifying the terms and conditions of such application.
6 With respect to ships owned by a State Party and used for commercial purposes, each State shall be subject to suit in the jurisdictions set forth in article 38 and shall waive all defences based on its status as a sovereign State.

These provisions reproduce those in art. XI of the CLC, previously considered.[15]

3.4.4 Exclusions allowed to States Parties

Art. 5(1) states:

1 A State may, at the time of ratification, acceptance, approval of, or accession to, this Convention, or any time thereafter, declare that this Convention does not apply to ships:
   (a) which do not exceed 200 gross tonnage; and
   (b) which carry hazardous and noxious substances only in packaged form; and
   (c) while they are engaged on voyages between ports or facilities of that State.

The conjunction 'and' between (a) and (b) and between (b) and (c) indicates that the requirements mentioned under (b) and (c) are cumulative to that under (a). Consequently the liberty granted to States Parties is restricted to ships which do not exceed 200 gross tons only where they carry the substances mentioned in (b) and perform the voyages mentioned in (c).

This is confirmed by the following wording of paragraph 2 that allows two neighbouring States to exclude the application of the Convention when the ships mentioned in paragraph 1 are engaged in voyages between ports and facilities of such States:

2 Where two neighbouring States agree that this Convention does not apply also to ships which are covered by paragraph 1(a) and (b) while engaged on voyages between ports or facilities of those States, the States concerned may declare that the exclusion from the application of this Convention declared under paragraph 1 covers also ships referred to in this paragraph.

---

14 In the original text of this article, reference was made to Appendix B of the Code of Safe Practice for Solid Bulk Cargoes, which has been replaced by the IMSBC Code, adopted by the Maritime Safety Committee of IMO in 2008 and entered into force on 1 January 2011.
15 *Supra*, Chapter 11, para. 2.2.

However, the exclusion of its application is not global as the liability of the HNS Fund does not cease to exist except where the damage is caused in the State or States, reference to which is made in paragraphs 1 and 2. Art. 5(5) states:

5   The HNS Fund is not liable to pay compensation for damage caused by substances carried by a ship to which the Convention does not apply pursuant to a declaration made under paragraph 1 or 2, to the extent that:
(a)   the damage as defined in article 1, paragraph 6(a), (b) or (c) was caused in:
(i)   the territory, including the territorial sea, of the State which has made the declaration, or in the case of neighbouring States which have made a declaration under paragraph 2, of either of them; or
(ii)   the exclusive economic zone, or area mentioned in article 3(b), of the State or States referred to in (i);
(b)   the damage includes measures taken to prevent or minimize such damage.

II – LIABILITY OF THE OWNER

4 THE DEFINITION OF 'OWNER'

The definition of 'owner' in art. 1(3) is the same as that in art. 1(3) of the CLC 1992:[16]

3   'Owner' means the person or persons registered as the owner of the ship or, in the absence of registration, the person or persons owning the ship. However, in the case of a ship owned by a State and operated by a company which in that State is registered as the ship's operator, 'owner' shall mean such company.

Therefore, except in the situation mentioned in the second sentence, which at least at the time when the CLC was adopted was usual in socialist countries, only the registered owner is liable and, where a ship is chartered by demise, the charterer is not liable under the Convention, albeit its liability may exist vis-à-vis the registered owner, if so provided in the charter party.

The opinion that the HNS Convention should be based on a principle of shared responsibility between shipowners and cargo owners and that liability of shipowners should, as in the CLC, be strict had been supported by a large majority, but different views had been put forward in respect of the limits of shipowners' liability.[17]

5 THE BASIS OF LIABILITY AND THE ALLOCATION OF THE BURDEN OF PROOF

Article 7(1) states:

1   Except as provided in paragraphs 2 and 3, the owner at the time of an incident shall be liable for damage caused by any hazardous and noxious substances in connection with their carriage by sea on board the ship, provided that if an incident consists of a series of

---

16 *Supra*, Chapter 11, para. 9.1.

17 *Inter alia*, the suggestion had been made by the Swedish delegation that such limits be fixed at sufficiently high levels in order that the intervention of the HNS Fund be not too frequent (LEG/CONF.10/6(a)/11 of 13 February 1996).

occurrences having the same origin the liability shall attach to the owner at the time of the first of such occurrences.

The claimant, therefore, has the burden of proving the loss or damage and that such loss or damage has been caused by hazardous or noxious substances as defined in art. 1(5) in connection with their carriage on board a ship of which the defendant is the owner. 'In connection with the carriage' does not restrict the liability of the owner to the time when the goods were on board the ship: the loss or damage may have occurred before loading, provided the substances were under the control of the shipowner or after they had left the ship following an event occurred during transportation as well as following their discharge, provided they were still under the control of the shipowner.

The liability of the shipowner, which is exclusively governed by the provisions of the Convention,[18] is strict, but not absolute. Art. 7(2) states:

2 No liability shall attach to the owner if the owner proves that:

(a) the damage resulted from an act of war, hostilities, civil war, insurrection or a natural phenomenon of an exceptional, inevitable and irresistible character; or
(b) the damage was wholly caused by an act or omission done with the intent to cause damage by a third party; or
(c) the damage was wholly caused by the negligence or other wrongful act of any Government or other authority responsible for the maintenance of lights or other navigational aids in the exercise of that function; or
(d) the failure of the shipper or any other person to furnish information concerning the hazardous and noxious nature of the substances shipped either
    (i) has caused the damage, wholly or partly; or
    (ii) has led the owner not to obtain insurance in accordance with article 12;
provided that neither the owner nor its servants or agents knew or ought reasonably to have known of the hazardous and noxious nature of the substances shipped.

The exclusions under (a), (b) and (c) are the same as those in art. III(2) of the CLC and reference is made to their analysis under that article.[19] The exclusion under (d) originates from art. 5(4)(c) of the Convention on Civil Liability for Damage caused during Carriage of Dangerous Goods by Road, Rail and Inland Navigation Vessels of 1989.

Art. 7(3) states:

If the owner proves that the damage resulted wholly or partly either from an act or omission done with intent to cause damage by the person who suffered the damage or from the negligence of that person, the owner may be exonerated wholly or partially from liability to such person.

This exception originates from the CLC and reproduces its art. III(3) verbatim. The first alternative is obvious, but very unlikely to occur. The second – negligence of the person who suffered the damage – may occur, for example, if the package of HNS, although properly made, had been broken by other goods that instead had shifted in the hold owing to their inappropriate packaging or, if following a collision, fire broke out in bulk HNS and extended to the colliding ship, liable for the collision.

---

18 Article 7(4) states:

    4 No claim for compensation for damage shall be made against the owner otherwise than in accordance with this Convention.

19 *Supra*, Chapter 11, para. 5.

INTERNATIONAL MARITIME CONVENTIONS

6 THE RULE ON THE CHANNELLING OF LIABILITY

Art. 7 states in paragraphs 5 and 6:

5 Subject to paragraph 6, no claim for compensation for damage under this Convention or
   otherwise may be made against:
   (a) the servants or agents of the owner or the members of the crew;
   (b) the pilot or any other person who, without being a member of the crew, performs
        services for the ship;
   (c) any charterer (howsoever described, including a bareboat charterer), manager or
        operator of the ship;
   (d) any person performing salvage operations with the consent of the owner or on the
        instructions of a competent public authority;
   (e) any person taking preventive measures; and
   (f) the servants or agents of persons mentioned in (c), (d) and (e);
        unless the damage resulted from their personal act or omission, committed with the
        intent to cause such damage, or recklessly and with knowledge that such damage
        would probably result.
6 Nothing in this Convention shall prejudice any existing right of recourse of the owner
   against any third party, including, but not limited to, the shipper or the receiver of the
   substance causing the damage, or the persons indicated in paragraph 5.

Although the provisions in paragraph 5 existed already, in identical terms, in art.
III(4) of CLC 1992, they originate from a draft of this Convention. Their history, as
well as the analysis of each of its sub-paragraphs, have already been the object of a
commentary in connection with the CLC 1992.[20]

7 THE LIMITATION OF LIABILITY OF THE OWNER

7.1 The limits of liability

In its original text, art. 9(1) stated:

1 The owner of a ship shall be entitled to limit liability under this Convention in respect of
   any one incident to an aggregate amount calculated as follows:

   (a) 10 million units of account for a ship not exceeding 2,000 units of tonnage; and
   (b) for a ship with a tonnage in excess thereof, the following amount in addition to that
        mentioned in (a):
        for each unit of tonnage from 2,001 to 50,000 units of tonnage, 1,500 units of
        account;
        for each unit of tonnage in excess of 50,000 units of tonnage, 360 units of account;
   provided, however, that this aggregate amount shall not in any event exceed 100 million
   units of account.

It was, however, deemed more appropriate to adopt different limits according to
whether the HNS were in bulk or packaged and to increase the limits in respect of
packaged HNS, such increase being of 15 per cent.

Article 9(1) was consequently amended by keeping the original text in force in
respect of bulk HNS and adopting a new paragraph in respect of packaged HNS,

---

20 *Supra*, Chapter 11, para. 3.3.

such new limits applying where the damage is caused both by bulk and packaged HNS where it is impossible to determine whether the damage originates from bulk or packaged HNS. The amended art. 9(1), adopted by the Protocol of 2010, consequently provides as follows:

1 The owner of a ship shall be entitled to limit liability under this Convention in respect of any one incident to an aggregate amount calculated as follows:

(a) Where the damage has been caused by bulk HNS:
   (i) 10 million units of account for a ship not exceeding 2,000 units of tonnage; and
   (ii) for a ship with a tonnage in excess thereof, the following amount in addition to that mentioned in (i):
   for each unit of tonnage from 2,001 to 50,000 units of tonnage, 1,500 units of account;
   for each unit of tonnage in excess of 50,000 units of tonnage, 360 units of account;
   provided, however, that this aggregate amount shall not in any event exceed 100 million units of account.

(b) Where the damage has been caused by packaged HNS, or where the damage has been caused by both bulk HNS and packaged HNS, or where it is not possible to determine whether the damage originating from that ship has been caused by bulk HNS or by packaged HNS:
   (i) 11.5 million units of account for a ship not exceeding 2,000 units of tonnage; and
   (ii) for a ship with a tonnage in excess thereof, the following amount in addition to that mentioned in (i):
   for each unit of tonnage from 2,001 to 50,000 units of tonnage, 1,725 units of account;
   for each unit of tonnage in excess of 50,000 units of tonnage, 414 units of account;
   provided, however, that this aggregate amount shall not in any event exceed 115 million units of account.

A comparison between the limits adopted in the 1992 CLC and the 2010 HNS Convention may be of some interest:

CLC	HNS 1996	HNS 2010	
Ships up to 5,000 GT: 4,510,000	Ships up to 2,000 GT: 10,000,000	*Bulk HNS*	*Packaged HNS*
– for each addi-tional ton: 631	– for each addi-tional ton up to 50,000 GT: 1,500	– ships up to 2,000: 10,000,000	– ships up to 2,000: 11,500,000
– ceiling: 89,770,000 being the limit for a tanker of 140,118 GT	– for each ton in excess: 360	– for each addi-tional ton up to 50,000: 1,500	– for each additional ton up to 50,000: 1,725
	– ceiling: 100,000,000 being the limit for a ship of 100,000 GT	– for each ton above 50,000: 360	– for each ton above 50,000: 414
		– ceiling: 100,000,000 being the limit for a ship of 100,000 GT	– ceiling: 115,000,000 being the limit for a ship of 100,000 GT

* Figures in SDRs.

The ceiling under the CLC is equal to the limit for a tanker of 140.118 GT, whereas the ceiling under the HNS Convention 2010 is equal both for bulk and packaged HNS to the limit for a ship of 100,000 GT.

7.2 The limitation fund

7.2.1 Where the fund may be constituted

Art. 9(3) states:

> 3 The owner shall, for the purpose of benefiting from the limitation provided for in para-graph 1, constitute a fund for the total sum representing the limit of liability established in accordance with paragraph 1 with the court or other competent authority of any one of the States Parties in which action is brought under article 38 or, if no action is brought, with any court or other competent authority in any one of the States Parties in which an action can be brought under article 38. The fund can be constituted either by depositing the sum or by producing a bank guarantee or other guarantee, acceptable under the law of the State Party where the fund is constituted, and considered to be adequate by the court or other competent authority.

Similarly to the CLC, and differently from the LLMC Convention, the constitution of the limitation fund is a condition precedent to the right of the owner to invoke the benefit of limitation.

As regards the jurisdiction in which the fund may be constituted, the scheme of art. 9(3) of the HNS Convention mirrors that of the CLC. As under art. V(3) of the CLC, there are two alternatives. The first is that actions have already been brought and the second that no action has yet been brought. In the first case, the owner has a choice in that he may constitute the fund in any one of the courts in which actions have been brought; this implies that if only one action has been brought he has no choice: he must constitute the fund in the court in which the action has been brought. The second (although it makes reference, as art. V(3) of the CLC, to the provisions on the jurisdiction in respect of actions for compensation) differs because the jurisdictions under art. 38 of the HNS Convention differ from that in the corresponding provision of the CLC: while art. IX(1) of the CLC considers only incidents causing pollution damage in the territory, including the territorial sea or the EEZ or equivalent area of Contracting States, art. 38 of the HNS Convention also considers damage caused outside all such areas.[21]

7.2.2 How the fund may be constituted

The ways in which the fund may be constituted are the same as those indicated in art. V(3) of the CLC: it may be constituted either by depositing the full amount or by producing a bank or 'other' guarantee acceptable under the law of the State Party where the fund is constituted. The requirement of acceptability under the law of the relevant State Party applies both to the bank guarantee and to the 'other' guarantee: it can refer, *inter alia*, to the financial responsibility of the bank or other guarantor,

---

21 *Infra*, para. 9.

to their being authorised to operate in the State in which the fund is constituted and to the conditions under which the guarantee may be enforceable, such as the mere enforceability of the order on the distribution of the fund or its finality.

7.2.3 The distribution of the fund

The basic rule in all limitation conventions is that the fund must be distributed among the claimants in proportion to their established claims.[22] That means 'established' in the limitation proceedings by the court or other competent authority with which the fund has been constituted. This is confirmed by the reference in the French text of all conventions to 'créances admises'. That rule is, however, subject to exceptions, the basic one being that priority is given to claims in respect of loss of life or personal injury. This is the case also for the HNS Convention, art. 9(4) of which makes the general rule of distribution in proportion to the established claims subject to art. 11, which states:

Claims in respect of death or personal injury have priority over other claims save to the extent that the aggregate of such claims exceeds two-thirds of the total amount established in accordance with article 9, paragraph 1.

Although this wording is not very clear, its purpose is the same as that achieved by art. 6 of the LLMC Convention. This provides, in paragraph 1, two separate limits in respect of claims for loss of life and personal injury and in respect of other claims; and then provides in paragraph 2 that where the amount available in respect of claims for loss of life and personal injury is insufficient to pay such claims, the amount calculated for other claims shall be available for settlement of the unpaid balance of claims for loss of life and personal injury, such unpaid balance however ranking rateably with the other claims.

The other exception relates to the possible setting aside of a part of the compensation in order to enable the person liable to exercise in the future a right of subrogation. Art. 9(7) states:

7 Where owners or other persons establish that they may be compelled to pay at a later date in whole or in part any such amount of compensation, with regard to which the right of subrogation would have been enjoyed under paragraphs 5 or 6 had the compensation been paid before the fund was distributed, the court or other competent authority of the State where the fund has been constituted may order that a sufficient sum shall be provisionally set aside to enable such person at such later date to enforce the claim against the fund.

An identical provision may be found in art. V(5) of CLC 1992[23] which, in turn, is based on that in art. 12(4) of the LLMC Convention and originates from art. 3(4) of the Limitation Convention 1957. The reference to 'other persons', which replaces the reference to 'any other person' in both the CLC and the LLMC Convention, cannot include any of the persons against whom, pursuant to art. 7(5), no claim for compensation for damage can be brought under the Convention, and thus, first of all, against the servants or agents of the owners and the members of the crew. It

---

22 LLMC Convention, art. 12(1); CLC, art. V(4); HNS Convention, art. 9(4).
23 *Supra*, Chapter 11, para. 6.3.

does instead include the insurer or other person providing financial security for the owner's liability for damage pursuant to art. 12, against whom direct action by the claimants may be brought pursuant to art. 12(8).

7.3 The loss of the right to limit

Art. 9.2 states:

2   The owner shall not be entitled to limit liability under this Convention if it is proved that the damage resulted from the personal act or omission of the owner, committed with the intent to cause such damage, or recklessly and with knowledge that such damage would probably result.

The provision on the loss of the right to limit adopted in all maritime conventions is the same, except that in some[24] the reference is not qualified, it being made to the intent to cause damage or knowledge that damage would probably occur and in others, including the CLC 1992,[25] the reference is instead qualified, it being made to the intent to cause *such* damage. For the reasons indicated in the comment on the identical provision of the CLC 1992,[26] it is suggested that for the purposes of the HNS Convention what would trigger the loss of the benefit of limitation and should be proved by the claimants is that the owner acted recklessly and with knowledge that his act or omission would have caused damage as defined in art. 1(6)(a) or (b) or (c).

8 THE COMPULSORY INSURANCE OF THE OWNER

Although generally the provisions on compulsory insurance in art. 12 mirror those in art. VII of the CLC 1992, they differ from them in some respects that will be mentioned in the following analysis, that for convenience will be made under the same titles as those used for the analysis of art. VII of the CLC 1992.

8.1 Who is bound to insure

Art. 12(1) states:

1. The owner of a ship registered in a State Party and actually carrying hazardous and noxious substances shall be required to maintain insurance or other financial security, such as the guarantee of a bank or similar financial institution, in the sums fixed by applying the limits of liability prescribed in article 9, paragraph 1, to cover liability for damage under this Convention.

While under the CLC the obligation arises only for owners of ships carrying more than 2,000 tons of oil, under this Convention no minimum quantity of HNS is required. Instead, similarly to the CLC, although the obligation to insure arises only in respect of ships registered in a State Party, nevertheless insurance is a condition

---

24 Warsaw Convention 1929 as amended by the Hague Protocol of 1955, art. 26 and Hague-Visby Rules, art. 4(5)(e), Vol. I, Chapter 4, para. 7.10.
25 *Supra*, Chapter 11, para. 7.
26 *Ibid.*

for any ship, of whatever nationality, being allowed to enter a port in the territory of a State Party. Art. 12(11) states:

11 Subject to the provisions of this article, each State Party shall ensure, under its national law, that insurance or other security in the sums specified in paragraph 1 is in force in respect of any ship, wherever registered, entering or leaving a port in its territory, or arriving at or leaving an offshore facility in its territorial sea.

The obligation arises in respect of ships actually carrying HNS. However, since the compulsory insurance certificate mentioned in art. 12(2) must, pursuant to art. 12(4), be carried on board, it is practically impossible that it be issued after the hazardous or noxious substances have been loaded on the ship. In practice, since any ship, both in the liner and tramp trade,[27] may carry occasionally such substances, all ships ought to be provided with such certificate, and consequently carry insurance in accordance with art. 12.

8.2 The nature and amount of the security required

Art. 12(1) states:

1 The owner of a ship registered in a State Party and actually carrying hazardous and noxious substances shall be required to maintain insurance or other financial security, such as the guarantee of a bank or similar financial institution, in the sums fixed by applying the limits of liability prescribed in article 9, paragraph 1, to cover liability for damage under this Convention.

The alternative natures of the security are the same as that under the CLC and under the Athens Convention, as amended by its Protocol of 2002: either insurance or 'other financial security'. The use of the words 'such as' that, after the reference to insurance or other financial security, precede the reference to the guarantee of a bank or similar financial institution, indicates that the security may also be different, even though it must have the character of a financial security, the essence of which consists of an obligation to provide a sum of money.

As for the CLC, the use of the plural, 'limits of liability', was not appropriate under the HNS Convention 1996, because the limit was one, and consisted of the aggregate amount calculated pursuant to art. 9(1). It is instead more appropriate under the HNS Convention 2010, in which the limits are two, one where the damage has been caused by bulk HNS and one where the damage has been caused by packaged HNS. Probably it would have been more appropriate to use, rather than the words 'sum fixed by applying the limits', wording such as 'sum calculated on the basis of the rules set out in article 9'.

8.3 Evidence of the insurance or other financial security

Art. 12(2) states:

2 A compulsory insurance certificate attesting that insurance or other financial security is in force in accordance with the provisions of this Convention shall be issued to each ship

---

27 Which in the Rotterdam Rules is called 'non-liner transportation': Vol. I, Chapter 3, para. 5.3.

after the appropriate authority of a State Party has determined that the requirements of paragraph 1 have been complied with. With respect to a ship registered in a State Party such compulsory insurance certificate shall be issued or certified by the appropriate authority of the State of the ship's registry; with respect to a ship not registered in a State Party it may be issued or certified by the appropriate authority of any State Party. This compulsory insurance certificate shall be in the form of the model set out in Annex I and shall contain the following particulars:

(a) name of the ship, distinctive number or letters and port of registry;
(b) name and principal place of business of the owner;
(c) IMO ship identification number;
(d) type and duration of security;
(e) name and principal place of business of insurer or other person giving security and, where appropriate, place of business where the insurance or security is established; and
(f) period of validity of certificate, which shall not be longer than the period of validity of the insurance or other security.

8.3.1 The name given to the document

The certificate attesting that insurance or other financial security is in force in accordance with the provisions of the Convention (reference to which is made in the CLC merely as a 'certificate') in the HNS Convention is called a 'compulsory insurance certificate': a name that appears incorrect both because the certificate may attest either that insurance or other financial security is in force and because what is compulsory is, pursuant to art. 11(1), the maintenance by the owner of an insurance and, pursuant to paragraph 4, the carrying on board of such certificate, that must, pursuant to art. 11(2), be in the form of the model set out in Annex I; this must be issued or certified by the appropriate authority of the State of the ship's registry.

The description of the authority that must issue the certificate as 'the appropriate authority of the State of the ship's registry' indicates that the authority which issues the certificate must be an entity of the relevant State to which the power has been granted to issue the certificate. The provision that such authority must, prior to issuing the certificate, determine that the requirements of paragraph 1 have been complied with places on the State of the ship's registry the burden of verifying that the insurance or other financial security is issued for a sum equal to or higher than the limit of liability prescribed in art. 9(1). In consideration of the limit varying according to whether the substances are bulk or packaged HNS, and that, for the reasons previously indicated, it is unlikely that the insurance or other financial security will be issued for an individual shipment, the relevant limit of liability must necessarily always be that based on the carriage of packaged HNS.

8.3.2 The identification of the ship

While in art. VII(2)(a) of the CLC only the indication of the name and port of registry of the ship is required, the HNS Convention also requires the indication of the distinctive number or letters. Such distinctive element differs from the IMO ship identification number, which must be marked on all passenger ships of 100 GT or more and all cargo ships of 300 GT or more,[28] since in the form of the certificate annexed to the Convention there appear, after the box in which the name of the ship must be indicated, two other boxes, in which the distinctive number or letters and the IMO ship identification number must be indicated. The requirement in art. 12(2)(a) that in addition to the name, the distinctive number or letters must be indicated, may not be complied with in respect of ships registered in States in which no such number is given, these ships being identified by their name and port of registry.[29]

8.3.3 The effect of the cessation of validity of the certificate

Art. 12(5) states:

5 An insurance or other financial security shall not satisfy the requirements of this article if it can cease, for reasons other than the expiry of the period of validity of the insurance or security specified in the certificate under paragraph 2, before three months have elapsed from the date on which notice of its termination is given to the authorities referred to in paragraph 4, unless the compulsory insurance certificate has been issued within the said period. The foregoing provisions shall similarly apply to any modification which results in the insurance or security no longer satisfying the requirements of this article.

The fundamental requirement is that the period of validity of the certificate has not expired and this is impliedly stated in paragraph 1, pursuant to which the owner is required 'to maintain insurance or other financial security'. Its date of expiry must be indicated in the certificate. In the model certificate annexed to the Convention, one of the pieces of information that must be provided is the 'duration of security': although 'duration' indicates a period of time (e.g. one year), in this case that would not be satisfactory information for the purposes of the insurance certificate. However in the explanatory notes it is stated under no. 4 that 'the entry "Duration of the Security" must stipulate the date in which such security takes effect' and since the certificate must state the date of its expiry, the two dates would convey the information on the period of validity of the security. The question remains whether this explanatory note is brought to the knowledge of the person to whom the certificate of insurance is produced. As regards the possible causes that can entail the cessation of the insurance or security there are the failure to pay the insurance premium or the commission due on the guarantee, in respect of which, therefore, a three-month advance notice of termination is required. Such notice must be given to the authority that keeps the record of the ship's registry, with whom a copy of the insurance certificate must be deposited pursuant to paragraph 4; obviously that authority ought to take action in order to collect the certificate from the ship.

---

28 The ship identification number was adopted in 1987 by Resolution A.600(15) and became mandatory as of 1 January 1996.

29 This is the case, for example in Italy, where pursuant to art. 140 of the Navigation Code, ships that may sail on the high seas are identified by a name and the port of registry, distinctive numbers being given instead to ships intended only for the coastwise navigation.

8.4 Conditions of issue and validity of the certificate

Art. 12(6) states:

1 For the purpose of fulfilling its function under article 13, paragraph 1(a), the HNS Fund shall pay compensation to any person suffering damage if such person has been unable to obtain full and adequate compensation for the damage under the terms of chapter II:
   (a) because no liability for the damage arises under chapter II;
   (b) because the owner liable for the damage under chapter II is financially incapable of meeting the obligations under this Convention in full and any financial security that may be provided under chapter II does not cover or is insufficient to satisfy the claims for compensation for damage; an owner being treated as financially incapable of meeting these obligations and a financial security being treated as insufficient if the person suffering the damage has been unable to obtain full satisfaction of the amount of compensation due under chapter II after having taken all reasonable steps to pursue the available legal remedies;
   (c) because the damage exceeds the owner's liability under the terms of chapter II.
2 Expenses reasonably incurred or sacrifices reasonably made by the owner voluntarily to prevent or minimize damage shall be treated as damage for the purposes of this article.
   (. . . . .)
6 The State of the ship's registry shall, subject to the provisions of this article, determine the conditions of issue and validity of the compulsory insurance certificate.

There is a significant difference between the conditions of issue and those of validity. While, in fact, third parties do not need to know the conditions of issue of the compulsory insurance certificate, they are instead interested to know if it is available and the conditions of its validity, in order to establish whether or not the document is valid. As observed in connection with the identical provision in art. VII(6) of the CLC,[30] given the international character of the certificates, which become a sort of passport for the entry of ships into ports of States Parties, there ought to be as much uniformity as possible in respect of the conditions of their validity.

8.5 Language of the certificate

Art. 12(4) states:

3 The compulsory insurance certificate shall be in the official language or languages of the issuing State. If the language used is neither English, nor French nor Spanish, the text shall include a translation into one of these languages.

The only difference between this provision and that in art. VII(3) of the CLC is that, under art. 4*bis* of the Athens Convention as amended by the 2002 Protocol, there are now three official languages of the certificates, with Spanish having been added to English and French.

8.6 International validity of the certificate

Art. 12(7) states:

7 Compulsory insurance certificates issued or certified under the authority of a State Party in accordance with paragraph 2 shall be accepted by other States Parties for the purposes

---

30 *Supra*, Chapter 11, para. 7.2.

of this Convention and shall be regarded by other States Parties as having the same force
as compulsory insurance certificates issued or certified by them even if issued or certified
in respect of a ship not registered in a State Party. A State Party may at any time request
consultation with the issuing or certifying State should it believe that the insurer or guarantor named in the compulsory insurance certificate is not financially capable of meeting
the obligations imposed by this Convention.

The 'acceptance' of the certificates by other States Parties is very likely related to
the right and obligation of all States Parties to make entry into their ports of any
ship subject to insurance or other security, as required by paragraph 1, being in force
and to the need for their courts to establish the existence of such insurance or other
security in case any claim for damage caused by HNS is brought against the owners
of the ship by which such substances are carried and of an application to arrest that
ship. It is unlikely that the consultation with the State that has issued or certified
the certificate, where doubts arise in respect of the financial capability of the insurer
or guarantor would take place when a ship requests permission to enter into a port
of the relevant State, as such consultation would very likely require a significant
amount of time. It could only be useful in order to decide whether to allow the entry
of that ship on future occasions.

8.7 Direct action against the insurer or guarantor

Art. 12(8) states:

8 Any claim for compensation for damage may be brought directly against the insurer or
other person providing financial security for the owner's liability for damage. In such
case the defendant may, even if the owner is not entitled to limitation of liability, benefit
from the limit of liability prescribed in accordance with paragraph 1. The defendant may
further invoke the defences (other than the bankruptcy or winding up of the owner) which
the owner would have been entitled to invoke. Furthermore, the defendant may invoke
the defence that the damage resulted from the wilful misconduct of the owner, but the
defendant shall not invoke any other defence which the defendant might have been entitled to invoke in proceedings brought by the owner against the defendant. The defendant
shall in any event have the right to require the owner to be joined in the proceedings.

This provision, as practically all the other provisions in this article, reproduces that
in art. VII(8) of the CLC; therefore reference is made to the comments made thereunder.[31] There are, however, some slight differences that are worthy of consideration. While art. VII(8) of the CLC provides that the insurer or guarantor may, even
if the owner is not entitled to limitation of liability, avail itself of the limits of liability
prescribed in art. V(1), in art. 12(8) of the HNS Convention it is provided that the
insurer or guarantor may 'benefit' from the limit prescribed in accordance with
paragraph 1. Therefore they do not invoke the 'benefit' of limitation granted to the
owner under art. 9(1), but merely invoke the ceiling of the insurance or guarantee
which is equal to the limit prescribed in art. 9. That entails that where they have
insured or guaranteed the owner's liability for an amount in excess of the limit under
art. 9(1) they would not be entitled to invoke that limit, but only the higher limit
of their cover. It appears that the sentence 'may, even if the owner is not entitled to

---

31 *Supra*, Chapter 11, para. 9.8.

limitation of liability, benefit from the limit of liability prescribed in accordance with paragraph 1' is misleading, for the two limits are of an entirely different legal nature: the first is really a 'benefit', as the owner's liability would otherwise be limited to the actual amount of the damage, while the second is the contractual limit of an obligation that arises which is limited in its amount.

8.8 Ships owned by a State Party

Art. 12(12) states:

12   If insurance or other financial security is not maintained in respect of a ship owned by a State Party, the provisions of this article relating thereto shall not be applicable to such ship, but the ship shall carry a compulsory insurance certificate issued by the appropriate authorities of the State of the ship's registry stating that the ship is owned by that State and that the ship's liability is covered within the limit prescribed in accordance with paragraph 1. Such a compulsory insurance certificate shall follow as closely as possible the model prescribed by paragraph 2.

The expression 'compulsory insurance certificate' is misleading, because the State would not issue an insurance certificate, but merely a statement that it warrants payment of claims up to the amount indicated in paragraph 1. The expression 'compulsory insurance certificate' is used in this Convention in respect of the certificate, reference to which is made in paragraph 2, but in respect of a ship owned by a State Party the document issued by the State is not likely to be precisely in the form of Annex I to the Convention. The wording used in art. VII(12) of the CLC appears to be more appropriate.[32]

8.9 When the obligation for ships to carry on board a certificate is compulsory

Art. 12 states in paragraphs 10 and 11:

10   A State Party shall not permit a ship under its flag to which this article applies to trade unless a certificate has been issued under paragraph 2 or 12.
11   Subject to the provisions of this article, each State Party shall ensure, under its national law, that insurance or other security in the sums specified in paragraph 1 is in force in respect of any ship, wherever registered, entering or leaving a port in its territory, or arriving at or leaving an offshore facility in its territorial sea.

The obligation for States Parties not to permit a ship under their flag to trade arises when art. 12 applies and therefore arises in respect of ships actually carrying hazardous and noxious substances. This is also the case for art. 11, which applies generally to all ships, whether flying the flag of a State Party or not, and the different wording used in order to make reference to art. 12 – 'subject to the provisions of this article' instead of 'to which this article applies' – is probably due to the fact that art. 12 does not directly apply to ships flying the flag of non-parties States.

---

32 *Supra*, Chapter 11, para. 9.10.

III – COMPENSATION BY THE INTERNATIONAL HNS FUND

9 ESTABLISHMENT OF THE FUND

Art. 13 states:

1 The International Hazardous and Noxious Substances Fund (HNS Fund) is hereby established with the following aims:
   (a) to provide compensation for damage in connection with the carriage of hazardous and noxious substances by sea, to the extent that the protection afforded by chapter II is inadequate or not available; and
   (b) to give effect to the related tasks set out in article 15.

2 The HNS Fund shall in each State Party be recognized as a legal person capable under the laws of that State of assuming rights and obligations and of being a party in legal proceedings before the courts of that State. Each State Party shall recognize the Director as the legal representative of the HNS Fund.

Paragraph 1 of this article is of great importance because, besides being the basis of the birth of the Fund, sets out its function and the conditions for its availability. Its function is to provide compensation for damage in connection with the carriage by sea of HNS: a purpose wider than that of the Fund for Compensation for Oil Pollution Damage, because of the much wider notion of damage in the HNS Convention as compared with the CLC, incorporated in the Fund Convention 1992, and because the damage is not only that caused outside the ship by escape or discharge (of oil), but more generally the relevant damage occurring 'in connection with' the carriage of HNS by sea. The conditions for its availability are practically the same, even though the terminology used differs: in the Fund Convention reference is made to the protection afforded by the CLC being inadequate, whilst in the HNS Convention, reference is made to the protection afforded in the previous chapter II being 'inadequate or not available'. However, in the Fund Convention the concept of 'inadequacy' includes the absence of liability and the financial incapability of the owner.

10 WHEN COMPENSATION MUST BE PAID BY THE FUND

The rules governing payment by the Fund of compensation to persons suffering damage are set out in art. 14 and are divided in four groups. First there are set out in paragraph 1 the conditions under which the obligation of the Fund may arise, such conditions being that the persons suffering damage have been unable to obtain 'full and adequate compensation' for the damage as defined in art. 1(6) of the Convention for one of the causes indicated in that paragraph. Secondly there are set out in paragraph 3 the situations in which the obligation of the Fund is excluded. Thirdly there are set out in paragraph 4 the situations in which the Fund may be exonerated in whole or in part from its obligation. Fourthly there are set out in paragraphs 5 through to 7 rules on the limit of the obligation of the Fund and on the criteria for the distribution of the global amount available.

10.1 Conditions required for the payment by the Fund

Art. 14 states in paragraphs (1) and (2):

1 For the purpose of fulfilling its function under article 13, paragraph 1(a), the HNS Fund shall pay compensation to any person suffering damage if such person has been unable to obtain full and adequate compensation for the damage under the terms of chapter II:
   (a) because no liability for the damage arises under chapter II;
   (b) because the owner liable for the damage under chapter II is financially incapable of meeting the obligations under this Convention in full and any financial security that may be provided under chapter II does not cover or is insufficient to satisfy the claims for compensation for damage; an owner being treated as financially incapable of meeting these obligations and a financial security being treated as insufficient if the person suffering the damage has been unable to obtain full satisfaction of the amount of compensation due under chapter II after having taken all reasonable steps to pursue the available legal remedies;
   (c) because the damage exceeds the owner's liability under the terms of chapter II.

2 Expenses reasonably incurred or sacrifices reasonably made by the owner voluntarily to prevent or minimize damage shall be treated as damage for the purposes of this article.

The provisions in such paragraphs correspond to those in art. 4(1) of the 1992 Fund Convention and, therefore, reference is made to their analysis.[33]

10.2 When payment of compensation is not due

Art. 14(3) states in paragraphs (3) and (4):

3 The HNS Fund shall incur no obligation under the preceding paragraphs if:
   (a) it proves that the damage resulted from an act of war, hostilities, civil war or insurrection or was caused by hazardous and noxious substances which had escaped or been discharged from a warship or other ship owned or operated by a State and used, at the time of the incident, only on Government non-commercial service; or
   (b) the claimant cannot prove that there is a reasonable probability that the damage resulted from an incident involving one or more ships.
4 If the HNS Fund proves that the damage resulted wholly or partly either from an act or omission done with intent to cause damage by the person who suffered the damage or from the negligence of that person, the HNS Fund may be exonerated wholly or partially from its obligation to pay compensation to such person. The HNS Fund shall in any event be exonerated to the extent that the owner may have been exonerated under article 7, paragraph 3. However, there shall be no such exoneration of the HNS Fund with regard to preventive measures.

Also the provisions in such paragraphs correspond to those in art. 4(2) and (3) of the 1992 Fund Convention and, therefore, reference is made to their analysis.[34]

---

33 *Supra*, Chapter 12, para. 5.2.
34 *Ibid.*

10.3 The amount of compensation payable by the Fund

10.3.1 The general structure of the relevant rules

The general structure of such rules, contained in paragraphs 5, 6 and 7 of art. 14, is based on that contained in paragraphs 4, 5 and 6 of the Fund Convention 1992, reference to which will be made where necessary in the analysis that follows.

10.3.2 The general aggregate amount

Art. 14(5)(a) states:

5(a)   Except as otherwise provided in subparagraph (b), the aggregate amount of compensation payable by the HNS Fund under this article shall in respect of any one incident be limited, so that the total sum of that amount and any amount of compensation actually paid under chapter II for damage within the scope of application of this Convention as defined in article 3 shall not exceed 250 million units of account.

Since the amount payable by the Fund complements the amount payable by the owner, there will follow a review of the entity of such complement in each of the three situations envisaged in art. 14(1).

(a) Where the owner is not liable for the damage
From the comparison between the situations in which the owner is not liable pursuant to art. 7(2) and (3) and those in which the HNS Fund is not liable, it appears that the Fund would be bound to settle the whole aggregate amount of compensation where:

(i)   the damage resulted from a natural phenomenon of an exceptional, inevitable and irresistible character in respect of which the owner is not liable under art. 7(2)(a);
(ii)   the damage was wholly caused by an act or omission done with the intent to cause damage by a third party;
(iii) the damage was wholly caused by the negligence or other wrongful act of any Government or other authority for which the owner is not responsible pursuant to art. 7 (2)(c);
(iv)   the damage was caused by the failure of the shipper or any other person to furnish information concerning the hazardous or noxious nature of the substances shipped, for which the owner is not responsible pursuant to art. 7 (2)(d).

In any one of such circumstances the Fund would be bound to provide compensation within the limit set in art. 14(5)(a).

(b) Where the owner is financially incapable of meeting his obligation, no financial security is available and the person suffering the damage has been unable to obtain satisfaction of the amount of compensation
The Fund would be bound to contribute within the aforesaid limit.

INTERNATIONAL MARITIME CONVENTIONS

(c) Where the damage exceeds the owner's liability

Since the limit of the owner's liability is based on the gross tonnage of the carrying ship and increases with the increase of the tonnage to a maximum of 100 million SDRs where damage is caused by bulk HNS and 115 million where damage is caused by packaged HNS, the contribution of the Fund correspondingly decreases as it appears from the following examples, in which the sums are units of account:

Ship carrying bulk HNS:

     2,000 GT   Owner limit 10,000,000
                       Fund maximum liability: 240,000,000
     50,000 GT   Owner limit 82,000,000
                       Fund maximum liability: 168,000,000
     100,000 GT   Owner limit 100,000,000
                       Fund maximum liability: 150,000,000

Ships carrying packaged HNS:

     2,000 GT   Owner limit 11,500,000
                       Fund maximum liability 238,500,000
     50,000 GT   Owner limit 94,300,000
                       Fund maximum liability: 155,700,000
     100,000 GT   Owner limit 115,000,000 SDRs
                       Fund maximum liability: 135,000,000

The situation where there is no payment by the owner is considered in art. 14(7) which states:

> 7 The Assembly of the HNS Fund may decide that, in exceptional cases, compensation in accordance with this Convention can be paid even if the owner has not constituted a fund in accordance with chapter II. In such cases paragraph 5(d) applies accordingly.[35]

Art. 14(5)(b), reference to which is made in art. 14(5)(a), states:

> (b) The aggregate amount of compensation payable by the HNS Fund under this article for damage resulting from a natural phenomenon of an exceptional, inevitable and irresistible character shall not exceed 250 million units of account.

This provision relates to a situation in which the owner is not liable pursuant to art. 7(2)(a) and, therefore, there would be no contribution by the owner and its insurers or guarantors, but nevertheless the ceiling of the aggregate amount payable remains the same and will be borne exclusively by the Fund. No reference is made to the other causes of damage for which the owner is not liable pursuant to the above provision because also the Fund is not liable pursuant to art. 14(3)(a).

---

35 Paragraph 5(d) states:

(d) The amounts mentioned in this article shall be converted into national currency on the basis of the value of that currency with reference to the Special Drawing Right on the date of the decision of the Assembly of the HNS Fund as to the first date of payment of compensation.

10.3.3 Distribution among the claimants of the amount available

Art. 14(6) states:

6   Where the amount of established claims against the HNS Fund exceeds the aggregate amount of compensation payable under paragraph 5, the amount available shall be distributed in such a manner that the proportion between any established claim and the amount of compensation actually recovered by the claimant under this Convention shall be the same for all claimants. Claims in respect of death or personal injury shall have priority over other claims, however, save to the extent that the aggregate of such claims exceeds two-thirds of the total amount established in accordance with paragraph 5.

The rules on the distribution of the HNS Fund are the same as those applicable to the fund constituted by the owner in arts. 9(4) and 11, except that in this case the special provision on the priority of claims in respect of death and personal injury follows the general provision. Also in the provision now under consideration the criterion to be followed in case the aggregate of the death and personal injury claims exceeds two-thirds of the total amount of the fund is not expressly indicated. It is, however, implied that the criterion is the same as for the LLMC Convention, pursuant to which such claims for the unpaid balance rank rateably with the other claims.

10.4 Related tasks of the HNS Fund

Art. 15 enumerates the tasks of the HNS Fund related to the fulfilling by it of its functions under art. 13, that include the consideration of the claims made against the Fund and the preparation of an estimate in the form of a budget for each calendar year of expenditure and income.

10.5 Contributions

The rules on contributions are set out in details in arts. 16 through 23 and among those deserving special attention are those relating to the accounts in which contributions must be paid.

Art. 16 in the section 'General provisions on contributions', states in its paragraphs, 1, 2, 3 and 4:

1   The HNS Fund shall have a general account, which shall be divided into sectors.
2   The HNS Fund shall, subject to article 19, paragraphs 3 and 4, also have separate accounts in respect of:
(a) oil as defined in article 1, paragraph 5(a)(i) (oil account);
(b) liquefied natural gases of light hydrocarbons with methane as the main constituent (LNG) (LNG account); and
(c) liquefied petroleum gases of light hydrocarbons with propane and butane as the main constituents (LPG) (LPG account).
3   There shall be initial contributions and, as required, annual contributions to the HNS Fund.
4   Contributions to the HNS Fund shall be made into the general account in accordance with article 18, to separate accounts in accordance with article 19 and to either the general account or separate accounts in accordance with article 20 or article 21, paragraph 5.

Subject to article 19, paragraph 6, the general account shall be available to compensate damage caused by hazardous and noxious substances covered by that account, and a separate account shall be available to compensate damage caused by a hazardous and noxious substance covered by that account.

From art. 18 it appears that contribution in respect of all HNS is payable to the general account except the substances mentioned in art. 16(2). However, the operation of the separate accounts, into which contribution of such substances should be paid, has been postponed and until such accounts will become operative such contribution is payable into the general account. Art. 18, in the section 'Annual contribution to the general account', enumerates in paragraph 1 the substances in respect of which contribution must be paid into the general account and then states in paragraph 2:

2 Annual contributions shall also be payable to the general account by persons who would have been liable to pay contributions to a separate account in accordance with article 19, paragraph 1 and paragraph 1*bis*, had its operation not been postponed or suspended in accordance with article 19. Each separate account the operation of which has been postponed or suspended under article 19 shall form a separate sector within the general account.

Art. 19, in the section 'Annual contribution to separate accounts', states in paragraphs 2 and 3:

2 Subject to paragraph 3, the separate accounts referred to in paragraph 1 and paragraph 1*bis* above shall become effective at the same time as the general account.
3 The initial operation of a separate account referred to in article 16, paragraph 2 shall be postponed until such time as the quantities of contributing cargo in respect of that account during the preceding calendar year, or such other year as the Assembly may decide, exceed the following levels:
   (a) 350 million tonnes of contributing cargo in respect of the oil account;
   (b) 20 million tonnes of contributing cargo in respect of the LNG account; and
   (c) 15 million tonnes of contributing cargo in respect of the LPG account.

It appears, therefore, that the operation of the separate accounts cannot coincide with the entry into force of the Convention because, even if prior to such entry into force the quantities of contributing cargo have exceeded the levels specified in art. 19(3), a decision of the Assembly will be required and since an Assembly may only be convened after the entry into force of the Convention, the operation of the separate account(s) may consequently start at the earliest in the year following that during which the Convention has entered into force.

IV – CLAIMS AND ACTIONS

11 LIMITATION OF ACTIONS

In art. 37 there are separate rules in respect of claims against the owner and claims against the Fund, the term used in this provision being, as in the CLC Convention, 'right of compensation'.
Art. 37(1) states in respect of claims against the owner:

1 Rights to compensation under chapter II shall be extinguished unless an action is brought thereunder within three years from the date when the person suffering the damage knew or ought reasonably to have known of the damage and of the identity of the owner.

Whilst in the majority of maritime conventions the lapse of the time limit entails the bar of the right to bring an action against the debtor, in the HNS Convention, as in the CLC, the lapse of the time limit entails the extinction of the substantive right.

The commencement of the three-year period is linked to two distinct events that may have occurred at different dates: (a) the date when the person suffering damage knew or ought reasonably to have known of the damage; and (b) the date when the person suffering damage knew or ought reasonably to have known of the identity of the owner of the ship that carried the hazardous and noxious substances.

The burden of proof of the date when the time has commenced to run rests on the defendant who invokes the extinction of the right, such defendant being either the owner of the ship or his insurer or guarantor. Although it would be difficult for him to prove when the claimant knew of the damage and who was the owner of the ship, in particular when the claim relates to loss of or damage to property (such knowledge would not raise problems when the claim is in respect of loss of life or personal injury on board the ship), this provision allows him alternatively to prove that the claimant should reasonably have known of both the damage and the identity of the person liable. By knowledge of the damage is meant general knowledge of damage within the meaning of art. 1(6)(a), (b) or (c) having been caused, but not specific knowledge of the amount of the damage. Loss of life, in respect of which the event is unique in its character, is an exception to this. For personal injury, the fact that a person has been injured and probably the general character of such injury and for loss of or damage to property, the existence of a loss or damage, and not respectively its precise extent or nature, should suffice in order to allow the time to commence to run. The position in respect of loss or damage by contamination of the environment should be similar to this. If the claimant is a fisherman, the general knowledge that the contamination may cause a loss of future catches, and if the claimant is the owner of a beach resort, the fear that the contamination of the beach would reduce the number of his customers should suffice. The time may commence to run even when the claimant did not actually know which ship had caused the damage and who her owner was, but he should reasonably have known that.

Art. 37(2) states in respect of claims against the Fund:

2 Rights to compensation under chapter III shall be extinguished unless an action is brought thereunder or a notification has been made pursuant to article 39, paragraph 7, within three years from the date when the person suffering the damage knew or ought reasonably to have known of the damage.

The comments made in respect of the rights of compensation against the owner or his insurer or guarantor apply also in respect of the rights of compensation against the Fund except that in this latter case the lapse of the period is prevented also by a notification to the Fund, as provided by art. 39(7).[36] This provision is identical to

---

36 Art. 39(7) states:

7 Without prejudice to the provisions of paragraph 5, where an action under this Convention for compensation for damage has been brought against an owner or the owner's guarantor before a

that in art. 7(6) of the Fund Convention 1992; therefore reference is made to its analysis.[37]

For the same reason for which a longer time limit running from the date of the incident has been provided in respect of actions against the Oil Pollution Fund, a similar longer time limit is provided in art. 37(3) of the HNS Convention; in this case, however, such longer period being ten years.[38]

12 JURISDICTION

As with the case of limitation of actions, the fact that this Convention regulates both the liability of the owner and that of the Fund, which instead had, by necessity rather than choice, been the object of distinct conventions in respect of oil pollution damage, there are two distinct articles on jurisdiction in chapter IV, the first with rules on the jurisdiction in respect of action against the owner and the second with rules on the jurisdiction in respect of actions against the Fund.

12.1 Jurisdiction in respect of actions against the owner

The connecting factors differ according to whether damage has been caused or preventive measures have been taken: (1) in the territory, including the territorial sea or in the exclusive economic zone or area adjacent to the territorial sea mentioned in art. 3(b), or (2) exclusively outside the territory, including the territorial sea. The distinction between these two alternatives is not clear since there appears to be a partial overlap. Paragraphs (1) and (2) of art. 38 in fact identify them:

1 Where an incident has caused damage in the territory, including the territorial sea or in an area referred to in article 3(b), of one or more States Parties, or preventive measures have been taken to prevent or minimize damage in such territory including the territorial sea or in such area . . ., actions for compensation may be brought against the owner or other person providing financial security for the owner's liability only in the courts of any such States Parties.
2 Where an incident has caused damage exclusively outside the territory, including the territorial sea, of any State and either the conditions for application of this Convention set out in article 3(c) have been fulfilled or preventive measures to prevent or minimize such damage have been taken, . . .

---

competent court in a State Party, each party to the proceedings shall be entitled under the national law of that State to notify the HNS Fund of the proceedings. Where such notification has been made in accordance with the formalities required by the law of the court seised and in such time and in such a manner that the HNS Fund has in fact been in a position effectively to intervene as a party to the proceedings, any judgment rendered by the court in such proceedings shall, after it has become final and enforceable in the State where the judgment was given, become binding upon the HNS Fund in the sense that the facts and findings in that judgment may not be disputed by the HNS Fund even if the HNS Fund has not actually intervened in the proceedings.

37 *Supra*, Chapter 12, para. 5.6.
38 Art. 37(3) states:

3 In no case, however, shall an action be brought later than ten years from the date of the incident which caused the damage.

(a) the State Party where the ship is registered or, in the case of an unregistered ship, the State Party whose flag the ship is entitled to fly; or

(b) the State Party where the owner has habitual residence or where the principal place of business of the owner is established; or

(c) the State Party where a fund has been constituted in accordance with article 9, paragraph 3.

The apparent overlapping relates to the area referred to in art. 3(b), being the exclusive economic zone or the area adjacent to the territorial sea mentioned in art. 3(b) that is expressly included in paragraph 1 and impliedly included also in paragraph 2, since no reference to it is made among the areas to which paragraph 2 does not apply. The conclusion appears to be that where damage has been caused exclusively in that area or in that area and on the high seas the claimant has the choice between the jurisdictions indicated in paragraph 2.

When paragraph 1 applies, the courts of competent jurisdiction are those in whose territory, including the territorial sea or EEZ or other area adjacent to the territorial sea mentioned in art. 3(b), the damage has been caused or preventive measures have been taken. When paragraph 2 applies, the courts enumerated therein may have jurisdiction.

12.2 Jurisdiction in respect of actions against the HNS Fund or actions taken by the Fund

Although the caption of this article appears to place actions against and action by the Fund on the same level, the possible actions taken by the Fund, reference to which is made in paragraph 5, relate only to the right to intervene as a party to legal proceedings instituted by the claimants against the owner or his guarantor and, as will be seen, would be a defence, rather than an action.

The basic rule is contained in paragraph (1) which states:

1 Subject to the subsequent provisions of this article, any action against the HNS Fund for compensation under article 14 shall be brought only before a court having jurisdiction under article 38 in respect of actions against the owner who is liable for damage caused by the relevant incident or before a court in a State Party which would have been competent if an owner had been liable.

The courts that have jurisdiction are, therefore, the same as those with jurisdiction in actions against the owner and his guarantor. This provision applies when no action has yet been brought against the owner; otherwise the action against the Fund should be brought in the court in which such action has been brought. Paragraph 4 states:

4 Where an action for compensation for damage has been brought before a court against the owner or the owner's guarantor, such court shall have exclusive jurisdiction over any action against the HNS Fund for compensation under the provisions of article 14 in respect of the same damage.

The purpose of this rule is to ensure that the same court decides on all claims for compensation of damages arising out of the same incident, whether brought against the owner or the Fund. But whilst there is only one Fund, and this is known to all claimants, that may not always be the case for the identity of the ship responsible for the incident. This situation is covered by paragraph 2 as follows:

2 In the event that the ship carrying the hazardous or noxious substances which caused the damage has not been identified, the provisions of article 38, paragraph 1, shall apply *mutatis mutandis* to actions against the HNS Fund.

As jurisdiction, pursuant to paragraph (1), is based on the incident that caused the damage having occurred in the territory, including the territorial sea or in the EEZ or alternatively in the area referred to in art. 3(b), it would not be possible to identify the court having jurisdiction for actions against the Fund on the basis of its provisions. A strict interpretation of the combined provisions of art. 39(1) and (2) would consequently prevent any action against the Fund. It would appear, in fact, that pursuant to art. 3(c), the Convention would not apply since the conditions for its application to damage other than contamination of the environment caused outside the area previously mentioned is that such damage has been caused by a substance carried on board a ship registered in a State Party or flying the flag of a State Party.

12.3 Whether and to what extent a judgment rendered against the owner is binding on the Fund

Art. 39(7) states:

7 Without prejudice to the provisions of paragraph 5, where an action under this Convention for compensation for damage has been brought against an owner or the owner's guarantor before a competent court in a State Party, each party to the proceedings shall be entitled under the national law of that State to notify the HNS Fund of the proceedings. Where such notification has been made in accordance with the formalities required by the law of the court seised and in such time and in such a manner that the HNS Fund has in fact been in a position effectively to intervene as a party to the proceedings, any judgment rendered by the court in such proceedings shall, after it has become final and enforceable in the State where the judgment was given, become binding upon the HNS Fund in the sense that the facts and findings in that judgment may not be disputed by the HNS Fund even if the HNS Fund has not actually intervened in the proceedings.

This provision is identical to that in art. 7(6) of the Fund Convention and reference is therefore made to the comments in respect of that article.[39]

13 RECOGNITION AND ENFORCEMENT OF JUDGMENTS

Distinct rules are set out in art. 40 in respect of recognition and enforcement of judgments against the owner and against the HNS Fund.

---

39 *Supra*, chapter 12, para. 5.7.5.

13.1 Judgements against the owner

Art. 40 states in paragraphs (1) and (2):

1 Any judgement given by a court with jurisdiction in accordance with article 38, which is enforceable in the State of origin where it is no longer subject to ordinary forms of review, shall be recognized in any State Party, except:
 (a) where the judgement was obtained by fraud; or
 (b) where the defendant was not given reasonable notice and a fair opportunity to present the case.
2 A judgement recognized under paragraph 1 shall be enforceable in each State Party as soon as the formalities required in that State have been complied with. The formalities shall not permit the merits of the case to be re-opened.

The wording of the provisions on recognition and enforcement of judgments has become standard in recent maritime conventions and is the same as that in art. X of the CLC. Reference is therefore made to the comments thereunder.[40]

14 JUDGMENTS AGAINST THE HNS FUND

Art. 40(3) states:

3 Subject to any decision concerning the distribution referred to in article 14, paragraph 6, any judgment given against the HNS Fund by a court having jurisdiction in accordance with article 39, paragraphs 1 and 3 shall, when it has become enforceable in the State of origin and is in that State no longer subject to ordinary forms of review, be recognized and enforceable in each State Party.

Judgments given against the Fund in respect of claims for compensation under art. 14 would. of course. be for the full amount recognised to the relevant claimant or claimants. However, the obligation of the Fund is limited to the amount specified in art. 14(5)[41] and pursuant to art. 14(6) where the amount of the established claims exceeds the aggregate amount of compensation payable under paragraph (5), the amount is distributed on a pro rata basis to all the claimants, as is done under the LLMC Convention.

In respect of judgments against the Fund, the conditions laid down in the preceding paragraphs in respect of judgments against the owner are not mentioned, but it appears that they should apply anyhow.

15 SUBROGATION AND RECOURSE

15.1 Subrogation of the Fund in the rights against the owner or guarantor

Art.41(1) states:

1 The HNS Fund shall, in respect of any amount of compensation for damage paid by the HNS Fund in accordance with article 14, paragraph 1, acquire by subrogation

---

40 *Supra*, Chapter 11, para. 12.
41 *Supra*, para. 10.3.1.

the rights that the person so compensated may enjoy against the owner or the owner's guarantor.

Out of the three situations mentioned in art. 14(1) those under (a) and (c), which cover respectively the situations where the owner is not liable and that where the damage exceeds his liability, do not give rise to any possible subrogation because the person suffering damage would have no right against the owner. Therefore, the only one that would give rise to subrogation is that under (b); this, however, would give little hope to the Fund, since it refers to the situation where the owner is insolvent and the financial security is insufficient.

15.2 Right of recourse or subrogation of the Fund against other persons

Art. 41(2) states:

> 2 Nothing in this Convention shall prejudice any rights of recourse or subrogation of the HNS Fund against any person, including persons referred to in article 7, paragraph 2(d), other than those referred to in the previous paragraph, in so far as they can limit their liability. In any event the right of the HNS Fund to subrogation against such persons shall not be less favourable than that of an insurer of the person to whom compensation has been paid.

If the conditions for the application of art. 7(2)(d) materialise, the right (of recourse) against the shipper is more likely to yield a positive result. It would appear that a similar right could be enforced against the third party which has intentionally caused the damage and against a government or other authority in case of damage caused by negligence in the maintenance of lights or other navigational aids reference to which is made in art. 7(2)(b) and (c).

15.3 Right of subrogation or recourse against the Fund

Art. 41(3) states:

> 3 Without prejudice to any other rights of subrogation or recourse against the HNS Fund which may exist, a State Party or agency thereof which has paid compensation for damage in accordance with provisions of national law shall acquire by subrogation the rights which the person so compensated would have enjoyed under this Convention.

The exercise of a right of recourse or subrogation against the Fund is based on the assumption that a State Party has enacted legislation pursuant to which it is bound to pay compensation in lieu of the Fund or prior to payment by the Fund. The most likely situation is that where the payment mechanism that must be observed by the Fund is considered too slow and that the persons damaged are in urgent need of the payment of the compensation that should be payable by the Fund pursuant to art. 14(1) and (6) where applicable. It is obviously within those limits that the exercise of such right (that appears to be qualified as a right of subrogation) is conceivable.

16 SUPERSESSION CLAUSE

Art. 42 states:

This Convention shall supersede any Convention in force or open for signature, ratification or accession at the date on which this Convention is opened for signature, but only to the extent that such convention would be in conflict with it; however nothing in this article shall affect the obligations of States Parties to States not party to this Convention arising under such Convention.

The last sentence of this article is meant to comply with the provisions of art. 30(4)(b) of the Vienna Convention on the Law of Treaties.[42] Since rules on the limitation of liability of the shipowner are contained also in the Convention on Limitation of liability 1957 and in the LLMC Convention 1976–1996, it is necessary to consider which is the effect of the above provision if an action will be brought in a State party to the HNS Convention against the owner of a ship registered in a State party to one of such Conventions. As stated in respect of the CLC,[43] the provisions of the Convention on Limitation of Liability 1957 would prevail if an action were brought in a State party to the HNS Convention against the owner of a ship registered in a State party to the said Limitation Convention that is not a party to the HNS Convention. A conflict with the LLMC Convention would instead be avoided pursuant to its art. 18(1), as amended by art. 7 of the 1996 Protocol, which states:

1 Any State may, at the time of signature, ratification, acceptance, approval or accession, or at any time thereafter, reserve the right:
   (a) to exclude the application of article 2, paragraphs 1(d) and (e);
   (b) to exclude claims for damage within the meaning of the International Convention on Liability and Compensation for damage in Connection with the Carriage of Hazardous and Noxious Substances by Sea, 1996 or of any amendment or protocol thereto.
   No other reservation shall be admissible to the substantive provisions of this Convention.

Of course, the operation of this provision requires an express statement by each individual State and, therefore, the question arises as to whether, in case of such statement being omitted, the provisions of the CLC 1992 on the limits of liability would prevail over those of the HNS Convention.

V – TRANSITIONAL PROVISIONS

Art. 44 provides that the final clauses of the Convention shall be the final clauses of the Protocol of 2010 and, therefore, they replace the Final Clauses of the HNS Convention 1996. Whilst originally they were numbered from 20 to 29, they have been re-renumbered from 45 onwards.

---

42 An identical provision is included in the CLC Convention (art. XII) and in the Bunker Oil Convention (art. 11).

43 *Supra*, Chapter 11, para. 12.

INTERNATIONAL MARITIME CONVENTIONS

VI – FINAL CLAUSES

17 SIGNATURE, RATIFICATION, ACCEPTANCE, APPROVAL AND ACCESSION

17.1 General provisions

Art. 45 states in paragraphs 1–3:

1 This Protocol shall be open for signature at the Headquarters of the Organization from 1 November 2010 to 31 October 2011 and shall thereafter remain open for accession.
2 Subject to the provisions in paragraphs 4 and 5, States may express their consent to be bound by this Protocol by:
 (a) signature without reservation as to ratification, acceptance or approval; or
 (b) signature subject to ratification, acceptance or approval followed by ratification, acceptance or approval; or
 (c) accession.
3 Ratification, acceptance, approval or accession shall be effected by the deposit of an instrument to that effect with the Secretary-General.

Prior to 31 October 2011, the Protocol had been signed, subject to ratification, by Canada, Denmark, France, Germany, Greece, the Netherlands, Norway and Turkey and no State deposited an instrument of ratification or accession subsequently.

17.2 Submission of data on total quantities of contributing cargo

The obligation for States to submit data on the total quantities of contributing cargo that have expressed their consent to be bound by the Convention in one of the manners indicated in art. 45(2) arises before the Convention enters into force. It arises as from the date on which they have expressed their consent and continues on the basis of the provisions of art. 45, until the date when the Convention enters into force. It will thereafter be replaced by the provisions of art. 21. The significant difference between the period preceding and the period following the entry into force of the Convention is that during the former there cannot be an obligation to pay contributions and therefore the term 'contributing cargo' is not appropriate: it is the cargo that would contribute if it is received after the date of entry into force of the Convention. Consequently, the failure to submit data cannot entail the breach of an obligation under arts. 19 or 21. It may only affect the State which has expressed its consent to be bound by the Convention. As will be seen, the consequence of the omission varies if it relates to the year preceding the expression of the consent to be bound or to the subsequent years.

The reason for this requirement is due to the fact that pursuant to art. 46, one of the conditions for the entry into force of the Convention is that the Secretary-General must have received information in accordance with art. 45(4) and (6), that the persons in the States that have expressed consent to be bound have during the preceding calendar year received a total quantity of at least 40 million tonnes of cargo contributing to the general account.

HNS CONVENTION, 1996

17.2.1 Initial submission of data on total quantities of contributing cargo

Art. 45(4) and(5) states:

4 An expression of consent to be bound by this Protocol shall be accompanied by the submission to the Secretary-General of data on the total quantities of contributing cargo liable for contributions received in that State during the preceding calendar year in respect of the general account and each separate account.
5 An expression of consent which is not accompanied by the data referred to in paragraph 4 shall not be accepted by the Secretary-General.

It appears, therefore, that the consent by a State to be bound, if not accompanied by the data on the total quantities of contributing cargo received is ineffective. The consequence would be that it is irrelevant in order to establish the number of States Parties for the purpose of the entry into force of the Convention.

17.2.2 Subsequent submission of data on total quantities of contributing cargo

Art. 45(6) and (7) so instead provide:

6 Each State which has expressed its consent to be bound by this Protocol shall annually thereafter on or before 31 May until this Protocol enters into force for that State, submit to the Secretary-General data on the total quantities of contributing cargo liable for contributions received in that State during the preceding calendar year in respect of the general account and each separate account.
7 A State which has expressed its consent to be bound by this Protocol and which has not submitted the data on contributing cargo required under paragraph 6 for any relevant years shall, before the entry into force of the Protocol for that State, be temporarily suspended from being a Contracting State until it has submitted the required data.

It appears that these rules apply where the relevant State has complied with the rule set out in paragraph 4, because otherwise that State would not have expressed a consent to be bound. The consequence of the subsequent omission to submit data for the subsequent years (on the assumption that the Protocol has not meanwhile entered into force) is merely a temporary suspension of its character of Contracting State. The consequence would be that it would not provisionally be relevant for the application of art. 46 that sets out the conditions for the entry into force of the Protocol.

The difficulties that the requirement to submit data on the total quantities of cargo liable for contribution might give rise to were stressed as follows in the Guidelines on reporting of HNS contributing cargo adopted during the HNS Workshop held at IMO Headquarters on 12 and 13 November 2012 and endorsed by the IMO Legal Committee at its 100th session on 19 April 2013:[44]

The 2010 HNS Protocol requires, under article 20,[45] paragraph 4, that an expression of consent to be bound by this Protocol must be accompanied by the submission of data on the total quantity of contributing cargo received during the preceding calendar year. This poses a challenge, since the procedure for reporting contributing cargo data requires a number of decisions from the first HNS Fund Assembly to ensure uniform application. Since the

---

44 LEG 98/4/1.
45 This has become art. 45.

245

Assembly cannot be convened until the treaty enters into force, there is a need to put reporting regulations in place prior to ratification.

17.3 Withdrawal of the consent to be bound

Art. 45(8) states:

> 8 A State which has expressed its consent to be bound by the International Convention on
> Liability and Compensation for Damage in Connection with the Carriage of Hazardous
> and Noxious Substances by Sea, 1996 shall be deemed to have withdrawn this consent on
> the date on which it has signed this Protocol or deposited an instrument of ratification,
> acceptance, approval or accession in accordance with paragraph 2.

This appears to be a provision peculiar to this Convention. Generally in all conventions there are provisions on the denunciation, available after a convention has
entered into force, but not on the 'withdrawal' of the instrument of ratification,
acceptance, approval or accession during the period preceding the entry into force
of the convention. The reason for this provision appears to be due to another peculiar characteristic of the HNS Convention, namely the action required under the
preceding paragraphs of this article prior to the entry into force of the Convention
of the State that has expressed its consent to be bound. The retrospective effect of
the withdrawal has the purpose of nullifying the submission, if any, to the Secretary-
General of the data on the total quantities of contributing cargo reference to which
is made in paragraphs 4 and 6.

18 ENTRY INTO FORCE OF THE CONVENTION

Initially no express condition was required for the entry into force of the maritime conventions; subsequently the condition required became the ratification or
acceptance of or accession to a given convention by a minimum number of States,
such number varying from a minimum of two to a maximum of 20; more recently
there was added the condition of a minimum global tonnage and then, in the HNS
Convention, the requirement of a minimum quantity of contributing cargo.

The following table provides an overview of the criteria adopted in a number of
maritime conventions:

Convention	No. of States required for entry into force	No. of States with required minimum tonnage	Minimum tonnage of contributing cargo
Collision 1910	–	–	–
Salvage 1910	–	–	–
Arrest 1952	2	–	–
Arrest 1999	10	–	–
Hague-Visby	–	–	–
Hamburg Rules	20	–	–
Rotterdam Rules	20	–	–

Athens Convention	10	–	–
MLM 1926	–	–	–
MLM 1993	10	–	–
Limitation 1957	10	5 with 1 million tons	–
LLMC 1976	12	–	–
CLC 1992	10	4 with 1 million tons	–
Fund 1992	8	–	–
Supplementary Fund	8	–	450 million tons
Bunker Oil	18	5 with 1 million tons	–
HNS	12	4 with 2 million tons	40 million tons

Art. 46(1) states:

1   This Protocol shall enter into force eighteen months after the date on which the following conditions are fulfilled:

(a)   at least twelve States, including four States each with not less than 2 million units of gross tonnage, have expressed their consent to be bound by it; and
(b)   the Secretary-General has received information in accordance with article 45, paragraphs 4 and 6, that those persons in such States who would be liable to contribute pursuant to article 18, paragraphs 1(a) and (c), of the Convention, as amended by this Protocol, have received during the preceding calendar year a total quantity of at least 40 million tonnes of cargo contributing to the general account.

The condition under (a) may at present be considered to be usual. That under (b) may be found in all recent limitation and oil conventions. That under (c) has been added first in the Supplementary Fund Convention and then in the HNS Convention.

A minimum quantity of contributing cargo is required only for the functioning of the Fund, but in view of the strict linkage between the liability of the owner and the compensation by the Fund, it has become a condition for the entry into force of the whole Convention.

For the purposes of the entry into force of the Convention, the relevant account is only the general account, the substances referred to in art. 18(a) and (c) being those in respect of which contributions are payable to such account. It would appear, therefore, that the contributions, if any, payable into the general account because the operation of the separate accounts has been postponed or suspended are not relevant for the purposes of art. 46(1).

19 AMENDMENT OF LIMITS

The provisions in art. 48 on the amendment of the limits, that obviously apply only to the limit of liability of the owner set out in art. 9, are practically identical to those set out in respect of the limits of liability of the owner under the CLC 1992,[46] except that:

---

46 Chapter 11, para. 6.2.

INTERNATIONAL MARITIME CONVENTIONS

(a) The relationship that must be taken into account pursuant to art. 15(5) of the CLC between the limits in art. V(1) of the CLC and art. 4(4) of the Fund Convention 1992 has been replaced by the relationship between the limits in art. 9(1) of the HNS Convention and those in art. 14(5).

(b) The provision in art. 48(7)(a) excluding amendment prior to the lapse of five years from a specified date makes reference to the date when the Convention was opened for signature instead of to the date when the CLC Protocol has entered into force.

20 TERMINATION

Pursuant to art. 51 the Convention ceases to be in force either as a consequence of the reduction of the number of States Parties below six or of the total quantity of contributing cargo below 30 million tons. However, in this latter case, some flexibility is allowed to the Assembly if the contributing cargo, albeit being less than 30 million tons, is more than 25 million. In art. 38 of the Fund Convention the only situation considered is instead that where the number of States Parties falls below three.

APPENDICES: PART I

THE PREVENTIVE CONVENTIONS

APPENDIX 1

International Convention Relating to Intervention on the High Seas in Cases of Oil Pollution Casualties, 1969 and Protocol of 1973

1969 International Convention Relating to Intervention on the High Seas in Cases of Oil Pollution Casualties

THE STATES PARTIES TO THE PRESENT CONVENTION,

CONSCIOUS of the need to protect the interests of their peoples against the grave consequences of a maritime casualty resulting in danger of oil pollution of sea and coastlines,

CONVINCED that under these circumstances measures of an exceptional character to protect such interests might be necessary on the high seas and that these measures do not affect the principle of freedom of the high seas,

HAVE AGREED as follows:

Article I

1. Parties to the present Convention may take such measures on the high seas as may be necessary to prevent, mitigate or eliminate grave and imminent danger to their coastline or related interests from pollution or threat of pollution of the sea by oil, following upon a maritime casualty or acts related to such a casualty, which may reasonably be expected to result in major harmful consequences.

2. However, no measures shall be taken under the present Convention against any warship or other ship owned or operated by a State and used, for the time being, only on government non-commercial service.

Article II

For the purposes of the present Convention:

1. 'maritime casualty' means a collision of ships, stranding or other incident of navigation, or other occurrence on board a ship or external to it resulting in material damage or imminent threat of material damage to a ship or cargo;

2. 'ship' means:
   (a) any sea-going vessel of any type whatsoever, and
   (b) any floating craft, with the exception of an installation or device engaged in the exploration and exploitation of the resources of the sea-bed and the ocean floor and the subsoil thereof;

3. 'oil' means crude oil, fuel oil, diesel oil and lubricating oil;

251

APPENDIX 1

4. 'related interests' means the interests of a coastal State directly affected or threatened by the maritime casualty, such as:

    (a)   maritime coastal, port or estuarine activities, including fisheries activities, constituting an essential means of livelihood of the persons concerned;

    (b)   tourist attractions of the area concerned;

    (c)   the health of the coastal population and the well-being of the area concerned, including conservation of living marine resources and of wildlife;

5. 'Organization' means the Inter-Governmental Maritime Consultative Organization.

Article III

When a coastal State is exercising the right to take measures in accordance with Article I, the following provisions shall apply:

    (a)   before taking any measures, a coastal State shall proceed to consultations with other States affected by the maritime casualty, particularly with the flag State or States;

    (b)   the coastal State shall notify without delay the proposed measures to any persons physical or corporate known to the coastal State, or made known to it during the consultations, to have interests which can reasonably be expected to be affected by those measures. The coastal State shall take into account any views they may submit;

    (c)   before any measure is taken, the coastal State may proceed to a consultation with independent experts, whose names shall be chosen from a list maintained by the Organization;

    (d)   in cases of extreme urgency requiring measures to be taken immediately, the coastal State may take measures rendered necessary by the urgency of the situation, without prior notification or consultation or without continuing consultations already begun;

    (e)   a coastal State shall, before taking such measures and during their course, use its best endeavours to avoid any risk to human life, and to afford persons in distress any assistance of which they may stand in need, and in appropriate cases to facilitate repatriation of ships' crews, and to raise no obstacle thereto;

    (f)   measures which have been taken in application of Article I shall be notified without delay to the States and to the known physical or corporate persons concerned, as well as to the Secretary-General of the Organization.

Article IV

1. Under the supervision of the Organization, there shall be set up and maintained the list of experts contemplated by Article III of the present Convention, and the Organization shall make necessary and appropriate regulations in connection therewith, including the determination of the required qualifications.

2. Nominations to the list may be made by Member States of the Organization and by Parties to this Convention. The experts shall be paid on the basis of services rendered by the States utilizing those services.

Article V

1. Measures taken by the coastal State in accordance with Article I shall be proportionate to the damage actual or threatened to it.

2. Such measures shall not go beyond what is reasonably necessary to achieve the end mentioned in Article I and shall cease as soon as that end has been achieved; they shall not

unnecessarily interfere with the rights and interests of the flag State, third States and of any persons, physical or corporate, concerned.

3. In considering whether the measures are proportionate to the damage, account shall be taken of:

    (a)   the extent and probability of imminent damage if those measures are not taken; and

    (b)   the likelihood of those measures being effective; and

    (c)   the extent of the damage which may be caused by such measures.

Article VI

Any party which has taken measures in contravention of the provisions of the present Convention causing damage to others, shall be obliged to pay compensation to the extent of the damage caused by measures which exceed those reasonably necessary to achieve the end mentioned in Article I.

Article VII

Except as specifically provided, nothing in the present Convention shall prejudice any otherwise applicable right, duty, privilege or immunity or deprive any of the Parties or any interested physical or corporate person of any remedy otherwise applicable.

Article VIII

1. Any controversy between the Parties as to whether measures taken under Article I were in contravention of the provisions of the present Convention, to whether compensation is obliged to be paid under Article VI, and to the amount of such compensation shall, if settlement by negotiation between the Parties involved or between the Party which took the measures and the physical or corporate claimants has not been possible, and if the Parties do not otherwise agree, be submitted upon request of any of the Parties concerned to conciliation or, if conciliation does not succeed, to arbitration, as set out in the Annex to the present Convention.

2. The Party which took the measures shall not be entitled to refuse a request for conciliation or arbitration under provisions of the preceding paragraph solely on the grounds that any remedies under municipal law in its own courts have not been exhausted.

Article IX

1. The present Convention shall remain open for signature until 31 December 1970 and shall thereafter remain open for accession.

2. States Members of the United Nations or any of the Specialized Agencies or of the International Atomic Energy Agency or Parties to the Statute of the International Court of Justice may become Parties to this Convention by:

    (a)   signature without reservation as to ratification, acceptance or approval;

    (b)   signature subject to ratification, acceptance or approval followed by ratification, acceptance or approval; or

    (c)   accession.

Article X

1. Ratification, acceptance, approval or accession shall be effected by the deposit of a formal instrument to that effect with the Secretary-General of the Organization.

APPENDIX 1

2. Any instrument of ratification, acceptance, approval or accession deposited after the entry into force of an amendment to the present Convention with respect to all existing Parties or after the completion of all measures required for the entry into force of the amendment with respect to those Parties shall be deemed to apply to the Convention as modified by the amendment.

Article XI

1. The present Convention shall enter into force on the ninetieth day following the date on which Governments of fifteen States have either signed it without reservation as to ratification, acceptance or approval or have deposited instruments of ratification, acceptance, approval or accession with the Secretary-General of the Organization.

2. For each State which subsequently ratifies, accepts, approves or accedes to it the present Convention shall come into force on the ninetieth day after deposit by such State of the appropriate instrument.

Article XII

1. The present Convention may be denounced by any Party at any time after the date on which the Convention comes into force for that State.

2. Denunciation shall be effected by the deposit of an instrument with the Secretary-General of the Organization.

3. A denunciation shall take effect one year, or such longer period as may be specified in the instrument of denunciation, after its deposit with the Secretary-General of the Organization.

Article XIII

1. The United Nations where it is the administering authority for a territory, or any State Party to the present Convention responsible for the international relations of a territory, shall as soon as possible consult with the appropriate authorities of such territories or take such other measures as may be appropriate, in order to extend the present Convention to that territory and may at any time by notification in writing to the Secretary-General of the Organization declare that the present Convention shall extend to such territory.

2. The present Convention shall, from the date of receipt of the notification or from such other date as may be specified in the notification, extend to the territory named therein.

3. The United Nations, or any Party which has made a declaration under paragraph 1 of this Article may at any time after the date on which the Convention has been so extended to any territory declare by notification in writing to the Secretary-General of the Organization that the present Convention shall cease to extend to any such territory named in the notification.

4. The present Convention shall cease to extend to any territory mentioned in such notification one year, or such longer period as may be specified therein, after the date of receipt of the notification by the Secretary-General of the Organization.

Article XIV

1. A Conference for the purpose of revising or amending the present Convention may be convened by the Organization.

2. The Organization shall convene a Conference of the States Parties to the present Convention for revising or amending the present Convention at the request of not less than one-third of the Parties.

APPENDIX 1

Article XV

1. The present Convention shall be deposited with the Secretary-General of the Organization.

2. The Secretary-General of the Organization shall:
 (a) inform all States which have signed or acceded to the Convention of:
  (i) each new signature or deposit of instrument together with the date thereof;
  (ii) the deposit of any instrument of denunciation of this Convention together with the date of the deposit;
  (iii) the extension of the present convention to any territory under paragraph 1 of Article XIII and of the termination of any such extension under the provisions of paragraph 4 of that Article stating in each case the date on which the present Convention has been or will cease to be so extended;
 (b) transmit certified true copies of the present Convention to all Signatory States and to all States which accede to the present Convention.

Article XVI

As soon as the present Convention comes into force, the text shall be transmitted by the Secretary-General of the Organization to the Secretariat of the United Nations for registration and publication in accordance with Article 102 of the Charter of the United Nations.

Article XVII

The present Convention is established in a single copy in the English and French languages, both texts being equally authentic. Official translations in the Russian and Spanish languages shall be prepared and deposited with the signed original.

IN WITNESS WHEREOF the undersigned being duly authorized by their respective Governments for that purpose have signed the present Convention.

DONE at Brussels this twenty-ninth day of November 1969.

[Signatures not reproduced here.]

★ ★ ★

APPENDIX 1

ANNEX

Chapter I Conciliation

Article 1

Provided the Parties concerned do not decide otherwise, the procedure for conciliation shall be in accordance with the rules set out in this Chapter.

Article 2

1. A Conciliation Commission shall be established upon the request of one Party addressed to another in application of Article VIII of the Convention.
2. The request for conciliation submitted by a Party shall consist of a statement of the case together with any supporting documents.
3. If a procedure has been initiated between two Parties, any other Party the nationals or property of which have been affected by the same measures, or which is a Coastal State having taken similar measures, may join in the conciliation procedure by giving written notice to the Parties which have originally initiated the procedure unless either of the latter Parties object to such joinder.

Article 3

1. The Conciliation Commission shall be composed of three members: one nominated by the coastal State which took the measures, one nominated by the State the nationals or property of which have been affected by those measures and a third, who shall preside over the Commission and shall be nominated by agreement between the two original members.
2. The Conciliators shall be selected from a list previously drawn up in accordance with the procedure set out in Article 4 below.
3. If within a period of 60 days from the date of receipt of the request for conciliation, the Party to which such request is made has not given notice to the other Party to the controversy of the nomination of the Conciliator for whose selection it is responsible, or if, within a period of 30 days from the date of nomination of the second of the members of the Commission to be designated by the Parties, the first two Conciliators have not been able to designate by common agreement the Chairman of the Commission, the Secretary-General of the Organization shall upon request of either Party and within a period of 30 days, proceed to the required nomination. The members of the Commission thus nominated shall be selected from the list prescribed in the preceding paragraph.
4. In no case shall the Chairman of the Commission be or have been a national of one of the original Parties to the procedure, whatever the method of his nomination.

Article 4

1. The list prescribed in Article 3 above shall consist of qualified persons designated by the Parties and shall be kept up to date by the Organization. Each Party may designate for inclusion on the list four persons, who shall not necessarily be its nationals. The nominations shall be for periods of six years each and shall be renewable.
2. In the case of the decease or resignation of a person whose name appears on the list, the Party which nominated such persons shall be permitted to nominate a replacement for the remainder of the term of office.

APPENDIX 1

Article 5

1. Provided the Parties do not agree otherwise, the Conciliation Commission shall establish its own procedures, which shall in all cases permit a fair hearing. As regards examination, the Commission, unless it unanimously decides otherwise, shall conform with the provisions of Chapter III of The Hague Convention for the Peaceful Settlement of International Disputes of 18 October 1907.

2. The Parties shall be represented before the Conciliation Commission by agents whose duty shall be to act as intermediaries between the parties and the Commission. Each of the Parties may seek also the assistance of advisers and experts nominated by it for this purpose and may request the hearing of all persons whose evidence the Party considers useful.

3. The Commission shall have the right to request explanations from agents, advisers and experts of the Parties as well as from any persons whom, with the consent of their Governments, it may deem useful to call.

Article 6

Provided the Parties do not agree otherwise, decisions of the Conciliation Commission shall be taken by a majority vote and the Commission shall not pronounce on the substance of the controversy unless all its members are present.

Article 7

The Parties shall facilitate the work of the Conciliation Commission and in particular, in accordance with their legislation, and using all means at their disposal:
    (a)   provide the Commission with the necessary documents and information;
    (b)   enable the Commission to enter their territory, to hear witnesses or experts, and to visit the scene.

Article 8

The task of the Conciliation Commission will be to clarify the matters under dispute, to assemble for this purpose all relevant information by means of examination or other means, and to endeavour to reconcile the Parties. After examining the case, the Commission shall communicate to the Parties a recommendation which appears to the Commission to be appropriate to the matter and shall fix a period of not more than 90 days within which the Parties are called upon to state whether or not they accept the recommendation.

Article 9

The recommendation shall be accompanied by a statement of reasons. If the recommendation does not represent in whole or in part the unanimous opinion of the Commission, any Conciliator shall be entitled to deliver a separate opinion.

Article 10

A conciliation shall be deemed unsuccessful if, 90 days after the Parties have been notified of the recommendation, either Party shall not have notified the other Party of its acceptance of the recommendation. Conciliation shall likewise be deemed unsuccessful if the Commission shall not have been established within the period prescribed in the third paragraph of Article 3

APPENDIX 1

above, or provided the Parties have not agreed otherwise, if the Commission shall not have issued its recommendation within one year from the date on which the Chairman of the Commission was nominated.

Article 11

1. Each member of the Commission shall receive the remuneration for his work, such remuneration to be fixed by agreement between the Parties which shall each contribute an equal proportion.
2. Contributions for miscellaneous expenditure incurred by the work of the Commission shall be apportioned in the same manner.

Article 12

The parties to the controversy may at any time during the conciliation procedure decide in agreement to have recourse to a different procedure for settlement of disputes.

Chapter II   Arbitration

Article 13

1. Arbitration procedure, unless the Parties decide otherwise, shall be in accordance with the rules set out in this Chapter.
2. Where conciliation is unsuccessful, a request for arbitration may only be made within a period of 180 days following the failure of conciliation.

Article 14

The Arbitration Tribunal shall consist of three members: one Arbitrator nominated by the coastal State which took the measures, one Arbitrator nominated by the State the national or property of which have been affected by those measures, and another Arbitrator who shall be nominated by agreement between the two first-named, and shall act as its Chairman.

Article 15

1. If, at the end of a period of 60 days from the nomination of the second Arbitrator, the Chairman of the Tribunal shall not have been nominated, the Secretary-General of the Organization upon request of either Party shall within a further period of 60 days proceed to such nomination, selecting from a list of qualified persons previously drawn up on accordance with the provisions of Article 4 above. This list shall be separate from the list of experts prescribed in Article IV of the Convention and from the list of Conciliators prescribed in Article 4 of the present Annex; the name of the same person may, however, appear both on the list of Conciliators and on the list of Arbitrators. A person who has acted as Conciliator in a dispute may not, however, be chosen to act as Arbitrator in the same matter.
2. If, within a period of 60 days from the date of the receipt of the request, one of the Parties shall not have nominated the member of the Tribunal for whose designation it is responsible, the other Party may directly inform the Secretary-General of the Organization who shall nominate the Chairman of the Tribunal within a period of 60 days, selecting him from the list prescribed in paragraph 1 of the present Article.
3. The Chairman of the Tribunal shall, upon nomination, request the Party which has not

APPENDIX 1

provided an Arbitrator, to do so in the same manner and under the same conditions. If the Party does not make the required nomination, the Chairman of the Tribunal shall request the Secretary-General of the Organization to make the nomination in the form and conditions prescribed in the preceding paragraph.

4. The Chairman of the Tribunal, if nominated under the provisions of the present Article, shall not be or have been a national of one of the Parties concerned, except with the consent of the other Party or Parties.

5. In the case of the decease or default of an Arbitrator for whose nomination one of the Parties is responsible, the said Party shall nominate a replacement within a period of 60 days from the date of decease or default. Should the said party not make the nomination, the arbitration shall proceed under the remaining Arbitrators. In the case of decease or default of the Chairman of the Tribunal, a replacement shall be nominated in accordance with the provisions of Article 14 above, or in the absence of agreement between the members of the Tribunal within a period of 60 days of the decease or default according to the provisions of the present Article.

Article 16

If a procedure has been initiated between two Parties, any other Party, the nationals or property of which have been affected by the same measures or which is a coastal State having taken similar measures, may join in the arbitration procedure by giving written notice to the Parties which have originally initiated the procedure unless either of the latter Parties object to such joinder.

Article 17

Any Arbitration Tribunal established under the provisions of the present Annex shall decide its own rules of procedure.

Article 18

1. Decisions of the Tribunal both as to its procedure and its place of meeting and as to any controversy laid before it, shall be taken by majority vote of its members; the absence or abstention of one of the members of the Tribunal for whose nomination the Parties were responsible shall not constitute an impediment to the Tribunal reaching a decision. In cases of equal voting, the Chairman shall cast the deciding vote.

2. The Parties shall facilitate the work of the Tribunal and in particular, in accordance with their legislation, and using all means at their disposal:
    (a)   provide the Tribunal with the necessary documents and information;
    (b)   enable the Tribunal to enter their territory, to hear witnesses or experts, and to visit the scene.

3. Absence or default of one Party shall not constitute an impediment to the procedure.

Article 19

1. The award of the Tribunal shall be accompanied by a statement of reasons. It shall be final and without appeal. The Parties shall immediately comply with the award.

2. Any controversy which may arise between the Parties as regards interpretation and execution of the award may be submitted by either Party for judgment to the Tribunal which made the award, or, if it is not available, to another Tribunal constituted for this purpose in the same manner as the original Tribunal.

★ ★ ★

APPENDIX 1

Protocol Relating to Intervention on the High Seas in Cases of Pollution by Substances other than Oil, 1973

THE PARTIES TO THE PRESENT PROTOCOL,

BEING PARTIES to the International Convention relating to Intervention on the High Seas in Cases of Oil Pollution Casualties, done at Brussels on 29 November 1969,
TAKING INTO ACCOUNT the Resolution on International Co-operation concerning Pollutants other than Oil adopted by the International Legal Conference on Marine Pollution Damage, 1969,
FURTHER TAKING INTO ACCOUNT that pursuant to the Resolution, the Inter-Governmental Maritime Consultative Organization has intensified its work, in collaboration with all interested international organizations, on all aspects of pollution by substances other than oil,

HAVE AGREED as follows:

Article I

1. Parties to the present Protocol may take such measures on the high seas as may be necessary to prevent, mitigate or eliminate grave and imminent danger to their coastline or related interests from pollution or threat of pollution by substances other than oil following upon a maritime casualty or acts related to such a casualty, which may reasonably be expected to result in major harmful consequences.
    2. 'Substances other than oil' as referred to in paragraph 1 shall be:
      (a)   those substances enumerated in a list which shall be established by an appropriate body designated by the Organization and which shall be annexed to the present Protocol, and
      (b)   those other substances which are liable to create hazards to human health, to harm living resources and marine life, to damage amenities or to interfere with other legitimate uses of the sea.
    3. Whenever an intervening Party takes action with regard to a substance referred to in paragraph 2(b) above that Party shall have the burden of establishing that the substance, under the circumstances present at the time of the intervention, could reasonably pose a grave and imminent danger analogous to that posed by any of the substances enumerated in the list referred to in paragraph 2(a) above.

Article II

1. The provisions of paragraph 2 of Article I and of Articles II to VIII of the Convention Relating to Intervention on the High Seas in Cases of Oil Pollution Casualties, 1969, and the Annex thereto as they relate to oil, shall be applicable with regard to the substances referred to in Article I of the present Protocol.
    2. For the purpose of the present Protocol the list of experts referred to in Articles III(c) and IV of the Convention shall be extended to include experts qualified to give advice in relation to substances other than oil. Nominations to the list may be made by Member States of the Organization and by Parties to the present Protocol.

APPENDIX 1

Article III

1. The list referred to in paragraph 2(a) of Article I shall be maintained by the appropriate body designated by the Organization.

2. Any amendment to the list proposed by a Party to the present Protocol shall be submitted to the Organization and circulated by it to all Members of the Organization and all Parties to the present Protocol at least three months prior to its consideration by the appropriate body.

3. Parties to the present Protocol whether or not Members of the Organization shall be entitled to participate in the proceedings of the appropriate body.

4. Amendments shall be adopted by a two-thirds majority of only the Parties to the present Protocol present and voting.

5. If adopted in accordance with paragraph 4 above, the amendment shall be communicated by the Organization to all Parties to the present Protocol for acceptance.

6. The amendment shall be deemed to have been accepted at the end of a period of six months after it has been communicated, unless within that period an objection to the amendment has been communicated to the Organization by not less than one-third of the Parties to the present Protocol.

7. An amendment deemed to have been accepted in accordance with paragraph 6 above shall enter into force three months after its acceptance for all Parties to the present Protocol, with the exception of those which before that date have made a declaration of non-acceptance of the said amendment.

Article IV

1. The present Protocol shall be open for signature by the States which have signed the Convention referred to in Article II or acceded thereto, and by any State invited to be represented at the International Conference on Marine Pollution 1973. The Protocol shall remain open for signature from 15 January 1974 until 31 December 1974 at the Headquarters of the Organization.

2. Subject to paragraph 4 of this Article, the present Protocol shall be subject to ratification, acceptance or approval by the States which have signed it.

3. Subject to paragraph 4, this Protocol shall be open for accession by States which did not sign it.

4. The present Protocol may be ratified, accepted, approved or acceded to only by States which have ratified, accepted, approved or acceded to the Convention referred to in Article II.

Article V

1. Ratification, acceptance, approval or accession shall be effected by the deposit of a formal instrument to that effect with the Secretary-General of the Organizations.

2. Any instrument of ratification, acceptance, approval or accession deposited after the entry into force of an amendment to the present Protocol with respect to all existing Parties or after the completion of all measures required for the entry into force of the amendment with respect to all existing Parties shall be deemed to apply to the Protocol as modified by the amendment.

Article VI

1. The present Protocol shall enter into force on the ninetieth day following the date on which fifteen States have deposited instruments of ratification, acceptance, approval or

APPENDIX 1

accession with the Secretary-General of the Organization, provided however that the present Protocol shall not enter into force before the Convention referred to in Article II has entered into force.

2. For each State which subsequently ratifies, accepts, approves or accedes to it, the present Protocol shall enter into force on the ninetieth day after the deposit by such State of the appropriate instrument.

Article VII

1. The present Protocol may be denounced by any Party at any time after the date on which the Protocol enters into force for that Party.

2. Denunciation shall be effected by the deposit of an instrument to that effect with the Secretary-General of the Organization.

3. Denunciation shall take effect one year, or such longer period as may be specified in the instrument of denunciation, after its deposit with the Secretary-General of the Organization.

4. Denunciation of the Convention referred to in Article II by a Party shall be deemed to be a denunciation of the present Protocol by that Party. Such denunciation shall take effect on the same day as the denunciation of the Convention takes effect in accordance with paragraph 3 of Article XII of that Convention.

Article VIII

1. A conference for the purpose of revising or amending the present Protocol may be convened by the Organization.

2. The Organization shall convene a conference of Parties to the present Protocol for the purpose of revising or amending it at the request of not less than one-third of the Parties.

Article IX

1. The present Protocol shall be deposited with the Secretary-General of the Organization.

2. The Secretary-General of the Organization shall:
   (a)   inform all States which have signed the present Protocol or acceded thereto of:
       (i)   each new signature or deposit of an instrument together with the date thereof;
       (ii)   the date of entry into force of the present Protocol;
       (iii)   the deposit of any instrument of denunciation of the present Protocol together with the date on which the denunciation takes effect;
       (iv)   any amendments to the present Protocol or its Annex and any objection or declaration of non-acceptance of the said amendment;
   (b)   transmit certified true copies of the present Protocol to all States which have signed the present Protocol or acceded thereto.

Article X

As soon as the present Protocol enters into force, a certified true copy thereof shall be transmitted by the Secretary-General of the Organization to the Secretariat of the United Nations for registration and publication in accordance with Article 102 of the Charter of the United Nations.

APPENDIX 1

Article XI

The present Protocol is established in a single original in the English, French, Russian and Spanish languages, all four texts being equally authentic.

IN WITNESS WHEREOF the undersigned being duly authorized for that purpose have signed the present Protocol.

DONE AT LONDON this second day of November one thousand nine hundred and seventy-three.

[Signatures not reproduced here.]

★ ★ ★

ANNEX

List of substances established by the Marine Environment Protection Committee of the Organization in accordance with paragraph 2(a) of Article I

(The list of the substances is not reproduced)

APPENDIX 2

International Convention on Oil Pollution Preparedness, Response and Co-Operation, 1990 (OPRC Convention) with its Protocol of 2000 (OPRC-HNS Protocol)

International Convention on Oil Pollution Preparedness, Response and Co-operation, 1990

THE PARTIES TO THE PRESENT CONVENTION,

CONSCIOUS of the need to preserve the human environment in general and the marine environment in particular,

RECOGNIZING the serious threat posed to the marine environment by oil pollution incidents involving ships, offshore units, sea ports and oil handling facilities,

MINDFUL of the importance of precautionary measures and prevention in avoiding oil pollution in the first instance, and the need for strict application of existing international instruments dealing with maritime safety and marine pollution prevention, particularly the International Convention for the Safety of Life at Sea, 1974, as amended, and the International Convention for the Prevention of Pollution from Ships, 1973, as modified by the Protocol of 1978 relating thereto, as amended, and also the speedy development of enhanced standards for the design, operation and maintenance of ships carrying oil, and of offshore units,

MINDFUL ALSO that, in the event of an oil pollution incident, prompt and effective action is essential in order to minimize the damage which may result from such an incident,

EMPHASIZING the importance of effective preparation for combating oil pollution incidents and the important role which the oil and shipping industries have in this regard,

RECOGNIZING FURTHER the importance of mutual assistance and international co-operation relating to matters including the exchange of information respecting the capabilities of States to respond to oil pollution incidents, the preparation of oil pollution contingency plans, the exchange of reports of incidents of significance which may affect the marine environment or the coastline and related interests of States, and research and development respecting means of combating oil pollution in the marine environment,

TAKING ACCOUNT of the 'polluter pays' principle as a general principle of international environmental law,

TAKING ACCOUNT ALSO of the importance of international instruments on liability and compensation for oil pollution damage, including the 1969 International Convention on Civil Liability for Oil Pollution Damage (CLC); and the 1971 International Convention on the Establishment of an International Fund for Compensation for Oil Pollution Damage (FUND); and the compelling need for early entry into force of the 1984 Protocols to the CLC and FUND Conventions,

TAKING ACCOUNT FURTHER of the importance of bilateral and multilateral agreements and arrangements including regional conventions and agreements,

BEARING IN MIND the relevant provisions of the United Nations Convention on the Law of the Sea, in particular of its part XII,

APPENDIX 2

BEING AWARE of the need to promote international co-operation and to enhance existing national, regional and global capabilities concerning oil pollution preparedness and response, taking into account the special needs of the developing countries and particularly small island States,

CONSIDERING that these objectives may best be achieved by the conclusion of an International Convention on Oil Pollution Preparedness, Response and Co-operation,

HAVE AGREED as follows:

Article 1 – General provisions

(1) Parties undertake, individually or jointly, to take all appropriate measures in accordance with the provisions of this Convention and the Annex thereto to prepare for and respond to an oil pollution incident.

(2) The Annex to this Convention shall constitute an integral part of the Convention and a reference to this Convention constitutes at the same time a reference to the Annex.

(3) This Convention shall not apply to any warship, naval auxiliary or other ship owned or operated by a State and used, for the time being, only on government non-commercial service. However, each Party shall ensure by the adoption of appropriate measures not impairing the operations or operational capabilities of such ships owned or operated by it, that such ships act in a manner consistent, so far as is reasonable and practicable, with this Convention.

Article 2 – Definitions

For the purposes of this Convention:

(1) 'Oil' means petroleum in any form including crude oil, fuel oil, sludge, oil refuse and refined products.

(2) 'Oil pollution incident' means an occurrence or series of occurrences having the same origin, which results or may result in a discharge of oil and which poses or may pose a threat to the marine environment, or to the coastline or related interests of one or more States, and which requires emergency action or other immediate response.

(3) 'Ship' means a vessel of any type whatsoever operating in the marine environment and includes hydrofoil boats, air-cushion vehicles, submersibles, and floating craft of any type.

(4) 'Offshore unit' means any fixed or floating offshore installation or structure engaged in gas or oil exploration, exploitation or production activities, or loading or unloading of oil.

(5) 'Sea ports and oil handling facilities' means those facilities which present a risk of an oil pollution incident and includes, inter alia, sea ports, oil terminals, pipelines and other oil handling facilities.

(6) 'Organization' means the International Maritime Organization.

(7) 'Secretary-General' means the Secretary-General of the Organization.

Article 3 – Oil pollution emergency plans

(1)(a) Each Party shall require that ships entitled to fly its flag have on board a shipboard oil pollution emergency plan as required by and in accordance with the provisions adopted by the Organization for this purpose.

(b) A ship required to have on board an oil pollution emergency plan in accordance with subparagraph (a) is subject, while in a port or at an offshore terminal under the jurisdiction of a Party, to inspection by officers duly authorized by that Party, in

265

APPENDIX 2

accordance with the practices provided for in existing international agreements or its national legislation.

(2) Each Party shall require that operators of offshore units under its jurisdiction have oil pollution emergency plans, which are co-ordinated with the national system established in accordance with article 6 and approved in accordance with procedures established by the competent national authority.

(3) Each Party shall require that authorities or operators in charge of such sea ports and oil handling facilities under its jurisdiction as it deems appropriate have oil pollution emergency plans or similar arrangements which are co-ordinated with the national system established in accordance with article 6 and approved in accordance with procedures established by the competent national authority.

Article 4 – Oil pollution reporting procedures

(1) Each Party shall:
  (a) require masters or other persons having charge of ships flying its flag and persons having charge of offshore units under its jurisdiction to report without delay any event on their ship or offshore unit involving a discharge or probable discharge of oil:
      (i) in the case of a ship, to the nearest coastal State;
      (ii) in the case of an offshore unit, to the coastal State to whose jurisdiction the unit is subject;
  (b) require masters or other persons having charge of ships flying its flag and persons having charge of offshore units under its jurisdiction to report without delay any observed event at sea involving a discharge of oil or the presence of oil:
      (i) in the case of a ship, to the nearest coastal State;
      (ii) in the case of an offshore unit, to the coastal State to whose jurisdiction the unit is subject;
  (c) require persons having charge of sea ports and oil handling facilities under its jurisdiction to report without delay any event involving a discharge or probable discharge of oil or the presence of oil to the competent national authority;
  (d) instruct its maritime inspection vessels or aircraft and other appropriate services or officials to report without delay any observed event at sea or at a sea port or oil handling facility involving a discharge of oil or the presence of oil to the competent national authority or, as the case may be, to the nearest coastal State;
  (e) request the pilots of civil aircraft to report without delay any observed event at sea involving a discharge of oil or the presence of oil to the nearest coastal State.

(2) Reports under paragraph (1)(a)(i) shall be made in accordance with the requirements developed by the Organization and based on the guidelines and general principles adopted by the Organization. Reports under paragraph (1)(a)(ii), (b), (c) and (d) shall be made in accordance with the guidelines and general principles adopted by the Organization to the extent applicable.

Article 5 – Action on receiving an oil pollution report

(1) Whenever a Party receives a report referred to in article 4 or pollution information provided by other sources, it shall:
  (a) assess the event to determine whether it is an oil pollution incident;
  (b) assess the nature, extent and possible consequences of the oil pollution incident; and

APPENDIX 2

(c) then, without delay, inform all States whose interests are affected or likely to be affected by such oil pollution incident, together with
  (i) details of its assessments and any action it has taken, or intends to take, to deal with the incident, and
  (ii) further information as appropriate, until the action taken to respond to the incident has been concluded or until joint action has been decided by such States.

(2) When the severity of such oil pollution incident so justifies, the Party should provide the Organization directly or, as appropriate, through the relevant regional organization or arrangements with the information referred to in paragraph (1)(b) and (c).

(3) When the severity of such oil pollution incident so justifies, other States affected by it are urged to inform the Organization directly or, as appropriate, through the relevant regional organizations or arrangements of their assessment of the extent of the threat to their interests and any action taken or intended.

(4) Parties should use, in so far as practicable, the oil pollution reporting system developed by the Organization when exchanging information and communicating with other States and with the Organization.

Article 6 – National and regional systems for preparedness and response

(1) Each Party shall establish a national system for responding promptly and effectively to oil pollution incidents. This system shall include as a minimum:
  (a) the designation of:
    (i) the competent national authority or authorities with responsibility for oil pollution preparedness and response;
    (ii) the national operational contact point or points, which shall be responsible for the receipt and transmission of oil pollution reports as referred to in article 4; and
    (iii) an authority which is entitled to act on behalf of the State to request assistance or to decide to render the assistance requested;
  (b) a national contingency plan for preparedness and response which includes the organizational relationship of the various bodies involved, whether public or private, taking into account guidelines developed by the Organization.

(2) In addition, each Party, within its capabilities either individually or through bilateral or multilateral co-operation and, as appropriate, in co-operation with the oil and shipping industries, port authorities and other relevant entities, shall establish:
  (a) a minimum level of pre-positioned oil spill combating equipment, commensurate with the risk involved, and programmes for its use;
  (b) a programme of exercises for oil pollution response organizations and training of relevant personnel;
  (c) detailed plans and communication capabilities for responding to an oil pollution incident. Such capabilities should be continuously available; and
  (d) a mechanism or arrangement to co-ordinate the response to an oil pollution incident with, if appropriate, the capabilities to mobilize the necessary resources.

(3) Each Party shall ensure that current information is provided to the Organization, directly or through the relevant regional organization or arrangements, concerning:
  (a) the location, telecommunication data and, if applicable, areas of responsibility of authorities and entities referred to in paragraph (1)(a);
  (b) information concerning pollution response equipment and expertise in disciplines

APPENDIX 2

related to oil pollution response and marine salvage which may be made available
to other States, upon request; and

(c)   its national contingency plan.

Article 7 – International co-operation in pollution response

(1) Parties agree that, subject to their capabilities and the availability of relevant resources, they will co-operate and provide advisory services, technical support and equipment for the purpose of responding to an oil pollution incident, when the severity of such incident so justi-fies, upon the request of any Party affected or likely to be affected. The financing of the costs for such assistance shall be based on the provisions set out in the Annex to this Convention.

(2) A Party which has requested assistance may ask the Organization to assist in identify-ing sources of provisional financing of the costs referred to in paragraph (1).

(3) In accordance with applicable international agreements, each Party shall take neces-sary legal or administrative measures to facilitate:

(a)   the arrival and utilization in and departure from its territory of ships, aircraft and other modes of transport engaged in responding to an oil pollution incident or transporting personnel, cargoes, materials and equipment required to deal with such an incident; and

(b)   the expeditious movement into, through, and out of its territory of personnel, cargoes, materials and equipment referred to in subparagraph (a).

Article 8 – Research and development

(1) Parties agree to co-operate directly or, as appropriate, through the Organization or relevant regional organizations or arrangements in the promotion and exchange of results of research and development programmes relating to the enhancement of the state-of-the-art of oil pollution preparedness and response, including technologies and techniques for surveil-lance, containment, recovery, dispersion, clean-up and otherwise minimizing or mitigating the effects of oil pollution, and for restoration.

(2) To this end, Parties undertake to establish directly or, as appropriate, through the Organization or relevant regional organizations or arrangements, the necessary links between Parties' research institutions.

(3) Parties agree to co-operate directly or through the Organization or relevant regional organizations or arrangements to promote, as appropriate, the holding on a regular basis of international symposia on relevant subjects, including technological advances in oil pollution combating techniques and equipment.

(4) Parties agree to encourage, through the Organization or other competent international organizations, the development of standards for compatible oil pollution combating tech-niques and equipment.

Article 9 – Technical co-operation

(1) Parties undertake directly or through the Organization and other international bodies, as appropriate, in respect of oil pollution preparedness and response, to provide support for those Parties which request technical assistance:

(a)   to train personnel;

(b)   to ensure the availability of relevant technology, equipment and facilities;

(c)   to facilitate other measures and arrangements to prepare for and respond to oil pollution incidents; and

APPENDIX 2

(d)   to initiate joint research and development programmes.

(2) Parties undertake to co-operate actively, subject to their national laws, regulations and policies, in the transfer of technology in respect of oil pollution preparedness and response.

Article 10 – Promotion of bilateral and multilateral co-operation in preparedness and response

Parties shall endeavour to conclude bilateral or multilateral agreements for oil pollution preparedness and response. Copies of such agreements shall be communicated to the Organization which should make them available on request to Parties.

Article 11 – Relation to other conventions and international agreements

Nothing in this Convention shall be construed as altering the rights or obligations of any Party under any other convention or international agreement.

Article 12 – Institutional arrangements

(1) Parties designate the Organization, subject to its agreement and the availability of adequate resources to sustain the activity, to perform the following functions and activities:
(a)   information services:
    (i)   to receive, collate and disseminate on request the information provided by Parties (see, for example, articles 5(2) and (3), 6(3) and 10) and relevant information provided by other sources; and
    (ii)   to provide assistance in identifying sources of provisional financing of costs (see, for example, article 7(2));
(b)   education and training:
    (i)   to promote training in the field of oil pollution preparedness and response (see, for example, article 9); and
    (ii)   to promote the holding of international symposia (see, for example, article 8(3));
(c)   technical services:
    (i)   to facilitate co-operation in research and development (see, for example, articles 8(1), (2) and (4) and 9(1)(d));
    (ii)   to provide advice to States establishing national or regional response capabilities; and
    (iii) to analyse the information provided by Parties (see, for example, articles 5(2) and (3), 6(3) and 8(1)) and relevant information provided by other sources and provide advice or information to States;
(d)   technical assistance:
    (i)   to facilitate the provision of technical assistance to States establishing national or regional response capabilities; and
    (ii)   to facilitate the provision of technical assistance and advice, upon the request of States faced with major oil pollution incidents.

(2) In carrying out the activities specified in this article, the Organization shall endeavour to strengthen the ability of States individually or through regional arrangements to prepare for and combat oil pollution incidents, drawing upon the experience of States, regional agreements and industry arrangements and paying particular attention to the needs of developing countries.

(3) The provisions of this article shall be implemented in accordance with a programme developed and kept under review by the Organization.

269

APPENDIX 2

Article 13 – Evaluation of the Convention

Parties shall evaluate within the Organization the effectiveness of the Convention in the light of its objectives, particularly with respect to the principles underlying co-operation and assistance.

Article 14 – Amendments

(1) This Convention may be amended by one of the procedures specified in the following paragraphs.

(2) Amendment after consideration by the Organization:

    (a) Any amendment proposed by a Party to the Convention shall be submitted to the Organization and circulated by the Secretary-General to all Members of the Organization and all Parties at least six months prior to its consideration.

    (b) Any amendment proposed and circulated as above shall be submitted to the Marine Environment Protection Committee of the Organization for consideration.

    (c) Parties to the Convention, whether or not Members of the Organization, shall be entitled to participate in the proceedings of the Marine Environment Protection Committee.

    (d) Amendments shall be adopted by a two-thirds majority of only the Parties to the Convention present and voting.

    (e) If adopted in accordance with subparagraph (d), amendments shall be communicated by the Secretary-General to all Parties to the Convention for acceptance.

    (f) (i) An amendment to an article or the Annex of the Convention shall be deemed to have been accepted on the date on which it is accepted by two thirds of the Parties.

       (ii) An amendment to an appendix shall be deemed to have been accepted at the end of a period to be determined by the Marine Environment Protection Committee at the time of its adoption, which period shall not be less than ten months, unless within that period an objection is communicated to the Secretary-General by not less than one third of the Parties.

    (g) (i) An amendment to an article or the Annex of the Convention accepted in conformity with subparagraph (f)(i) shall enter into force six months after the date on which it is deemed to have been accepted with respect to the Parties which have notified the Secretary-General that they have accepted it.

       (ii) An amendment to an appendix accepted in conformity with subparagraph (f)(ii) shall enter into force six months after the date on which it is deemed to have been accepted with respect to all Parties with the exception of those which, before that date, have objected to it. A Party may at any time withdraw a previously communicated objection by submitting a notification to that effect to the Secretary-General.

(3) Amendment by a Conference:

    (a) Upon the request of a Party, concurred with by at least one third of the Parties, the Secretary-General shall convene a Conference of Parties to the Convention to consider amendments to the Convention.

    (b) An amendment adopted by such a Conference by a two-thirds majority of those Parties present and voting shall be communicated by the Secretary-General to all Parties for their acceptance.

    (c) Unless the Conference decides otherwise, the amendment shall be deemed to have

APPENDIX 2

been accepted and shall enter into force in accordance with the procedures specified in paragraph (2)(f) and (g).

(4) The adoption and entry into force of an amendment constituting an addition of an Annex or an appendix shall be subject to the procedure applicable to an amendment to the Annex.

(5) Any Party which has not accepted an amendment to an article or the Annex under paragraph (2)(f)(i) or an amendment constituting an addition of an Annex or an appendix under paragraph (4) or has communicated an objection to an amendment to an appendix under paragraph (2)(f)(ii) shall be treated as a non-Party only for the purpose of the application of such amendment. Such treatment shall terminate upon the submission of a notification of acceptance under paragraph (2)(f)(i) or withdrawal of the objection under paragraph (2)(g)(ii).

(6) The Secretary-General shall inform all Parties of any amendment which enters into force under this article, together with the date on which the amendment enters into force.

(7) Any notification of acceptance of, objection to, or withdrawal of objection to, an amendment under this article shall be communicated in writing to the Secretary-General who shall inform Parties of such notification and the date of its receipt.

(8) An appendix to the Convention shall contain only provisions of a technical nature.

Article 15 – Signature, ratification, acceptance, approval and accession

(1) This Convention shall remain open for signature at the Headquarters of the Organization from 30 November 1990 until 29 November 1991 and shall thereafter remain open for accession. Any State may become Party to this Convention by:
   (a)   signature without reservation as to ratification, acceptance or approval; or
   (b)   signature subject to ratification, acceptance or approval, followed by ratification, acceptance or approval; or
   (c)   accession.

(2) Ratification, acceptance, approval or accession shall be effected by the deposit of an instrument to that effect with the Secretary-General.

Article 16 – Entry into force

(1) This Convention shall enter into force twelve months after the date on which not less than fifteen States have either signed it without reservation as to ratification, acceptance or approval or have deposited the requisite instruments of ratification, acceptance, approval or accession in accordance with article 15.

(2) For States which have deposited an instrument of ratification, acceptance, approval or accession in respect of this Convention after the requirements for entry into force thereof have been met but prior to the date of entry into force, the ratification, acceptance, approval or accession shall take effect on the date of entry into force of this Convention or three months after the date of deposit of the instrument, whichever is the later date.

(3) For States which have deposited an instrument of ratification, acceptance, approval or accession after the date on which this Convention entered into force, this Convention shall become effective three months after the date of deposit of the instrument.

(4) After the date on which an amendment to this Convention is deemed to have been accepted under article 14, any instrument of ratification, acceptance, approval or accession deposited shall apply to this Convention as amended.

Article 17 – Denunciation

APPENDIX 2

(1) This Convention may be denounced by any Party at any time after the expiry of five years from the date on which this Convention enters into force for that Party.

(2) Denunciation shall be effected by notification in writing to the Secretary-General.

(3) A denunciation shall take effect twelve months after receipt of the notification of denunciation by the Secretary-General or after the expiry of any longer period which may be indicated in the notification.

Article 18 – Depositary

(1) This Convention shall be deposited with the Secretary-General.

(2) The Secretary-General shall:
   (a) inform all States which have signed this Convention or acceded thereto of:
      (i)   each new signature or deposit of an instrument of ratification, acceptance, approval or accession, together with the date thereof;
      (ii) the date of entry into force of this Convention; and
      (iii) the deposit of any instrument of denunciation of this Convention together with the date on which it was received and the date on which the denunciation takes effect;
   (b) transmit certified true copies of this Convention to the Governments of all States which have signed this Convention or acceded thereto.

(3) As soon as this Convention enters into force, a certified true copy thereof shall be transmitted by the depositary to the Secretary-General of the United Nations for registration and publication in accordance with Article 102 of the Charter of the United Nations.

Article 19 – Languages

This Convention is established in a single original in the Arabic, Chinese, English, French, Russian and Spanish languages, each text being equally authentic.

IN WITNESS WHEREOF the undersigned, being duly authorized by their respective Governments for that purpose, have signed this Convention

DONE AT London this thirtieth day of November one thousand nine hundred and ninety.

★ ★ ★

APPENDIX 2

ANNEX

Reimbursement of costs of assistance

(1)(a)   Unless an agreement concerning the financial arrangements governing actions of Parties to deal with oil pollution incidents has been concluded on a bilateral or multilateral basis prior to the oil pollution incident, Parties shall bear the costs of their respective actions in dealing with pollution in accordance with subparagraph (i) or subparagraph (ii).

    (i)   If the action was taken by one Party at the express request of another Party, the requesting Party shall reimburse to the assisting Party the cost of its action. The requesting Party may cancel its request at any time, but in that case it shall bear the costs already incurred or committed by the assisting Party.

    (ii)   If the action was taken by a Party on its own initiative, this Party shall bear the costs of its action.

  (b)   The principles laid down in subparagraph (a) shall apply unless the Parties concerned otherwise agree in any individual case.

(2)   Unless otherwise agreed, the costs of action taken by a Party at the request of another Party shall be fairly calculated according to the law and current practice of the assisting Party concerning the reimbursement of such costs.

(3)   The Party requesting assistance and the assisting Party shall, where appropriate, co-operate in concluding any action in response to a compensation claim. To that end, they shall give due consideration to existing legal regimes. Where the action thus concluded does not permit full compensation for expenses incurred in the assistance operation, the Party requesting assistance may ask the assisting Party to waive reimbursement of the expenses exceeding the sums compensated or to reduce the costs which have been calculated in accordance with paragraph (2).

It may also request a postponement of the reimbursement of such costs. In considering such a request, assisting Parties shall give due consideration to the needs of the developing countries.

(4)   The provisions of this Convention shall not be interpreted as in any way prejudicing the rights of Parties to recover from third parties the costs of actions to deal with pollution or the threat of pollution under other applicable provisions and rules of national and international law.

Special attention shall be paid to the 1969 International Convention on Civil Liability for Oil Pollution Damage and the 1971 International Convention on the Establishment of an International Fund for Compensation for Oil Pollution Damage or any subsequent amendment to those Conventions.

★ ★ ★

APPENDIX 2

Protocol on Preparedness, Response and Co-Operation to Pollution Incidents by Hazardous and Noxious Substances, 2000

THE PARTIES TO THE PRESENT PROTOCOL,

BEING PARTIES to the International Convention on Oil Pollution Preparedness, Response and Co-operation, done at London on 30 November 1990,
TAKING INTO ACCOUNT Resolution 10, on the expansion of the scope of the International Convention on Oil Pollution Preparedness, Response and Co-operation 1990, to include hazardous and noxious substances, adopted by the Conference on International Co-operation on Oil Pollution Preparedness and Response 1990,
FURTHER TAKING INTO ACCOUNT that pursuant to Resolution 10 of the Conference on International Co-operation on Oil Pollution Preparedness and Response 1990, the International Maritime Organization has intensified its work, in collaboration with all interested international organizations, on all aspects of preparedness, response and co-operation to pollution incidents by hazardous and noxious substances,
TAKING ACCOUNT of the 'polluter pays' principle as a general principle of international environmental law,
BEING MINDFUL of the development of a strategy for incorporating the precautionary approach in the policies of the International Maritime Organization,
MINDFUL ALSO that, in the event of a pollution incident by hazardous and noxious substances, prompt and effective action is essential in order to minimize the damage which may result from such an incident,

HAVE AGREED as follows:

Article 1 – General provisions

(1) Parties undertake, individually or jointly, to take all appropriate measures in accordance with the provisions of this Protocol and the Annex thereto to prepare for and respond to a pollution incident by hazardous and noxious substances.

(2) The Annex to this Protocol shall constitute an integral part of this Protocol and a reference to this Protocol constitutes at the same time a reference to the Annex.

(3) This Protocol shall not apply to any warship, naval auxiliary or other ship owned or operated by a State and used, for the time being, only on government non-commercial service. However, each Party shall ensure by the adoption of appropriate measures not impairing the operations or operational capabilities of such ships owned or operated by it, that such ships act in a manner consistent, so far as is reasonable and practicable, with this Protocol.

Article 2 – Definitions

For the purposes of this Protocol:

(1) *Pollution incident by hazardous and noxious substances* (hereinafter referred to as 'pollution incident') means any occurrence or series of occurrences having the same origin, including fire or explosion, which results or may result in a discharge, release or emission of hazardous and noxious substances and which poses or may pose a threat to the marine environment, or to the coastline or related interests of one or more States, and which requires emergency action or immediate response.

(2) *Hazardous and noxious substances* means any substance other than oil which, if introduced into the marine environment is likely to create hazards to human health, to harm living

274

APPENDIX 2

resources and marine life, to damage amenities or to interfere with other legitimate uses of the sea.

(3) *Sea ports and hazardous and noxious substances handling facilities* means those ports or facilities where such substances are loaded into or unloaded from ships.

(4) *Organization* means the International Maritime Organization.

(5) *Secretary-General* means the Secretary-General of the Organization.

(6) *OPRC Convention* means the International Convention on Oil Pollution Preparedness, Response and Co-operation, 1990.

Article 3 – Emergency plans and reporting

(1) Each Party shall require that ships entitled to fly its flag have on-board a pollution incident emergency plan and shall require masters or other persons having charge of such ships to follow reporting procedures to the extent required. Both planning requirements and reporting procedures shall be in accordance with applicable provisions of the conventions developed within the Organization which have entered into force for that Party. On-board pollution incident emergency plans for offshore units, including Floating Production, Storage and Offloading Facilities and Floating Storage Units, should be dealt with under national provisions and/or company environmental management systems, and are excluded from the application of this article.

(2) Each Party shall require that authorities or operators in charge of sea ports and hazardous and noxious substances handling facilities under its jurisdiction as it deems appropriate have pollution incident emergency plans or similar arrangements for hazardous and noxious substances that it deems appropriate which are co-ordinated with the national system established in accordance with article 4 and approved in accordance with procedures established by the competent national authority.

(3) When the appropriate authorities of a Party learn of a pollution incident, they shall notify other States whose interests are likely to be affected by such incident.

Article 4 – National and regional systems for preparedness and response

(1) Each Party shall establish a national system for responding promptly and effectively to pollution incidents. This system shall include as a minimum:
- (a) the designation of:
  - (i) the competent national authority or authorities with responsibility for preparedness for and response to pollution incidents;
  - (ii) the national operational contact point or points; and
  - (iii) an authority which is entitled to act on behalf of the State to request assistance or to decide to render the assistance requested;
- (b) a national contingency plan for preparedness and response which includes the organizational relationship of the various bodies involved, whether public or private, taking into account guidelines developed by the Organization.

(2) In addition, each Party within its capabilities either individually or through bilateral or multilateral co-operation and, as appropriate, in co-operation with the shipping industries and industries dealing with hazardous and noxious substances, port authorities and other relevant entities, shall establish:
- (a) a minimum level of pre-positioned equipment for responding to pollution incidents commensurate with the risk involved, and programmes for its use;
- (b) a programme of exercises for pollution incident response organizations and training of relevant personnel;

APPENDIX 2

    (c) detailed plans and communication capabilities for responding to a pollution inci-
dent. Such capabilities should be continuously available; and

    (d) a mechanism or arrangement to co-ordinate the response to a pollution incident
with, if appropriate, the capabilities to mobilize the necessary resources.

(3) Each Party shall ensure that current information is provided to the Organization,
directly or through the relevant regional organization or arrangements, concerning:

    (a) the location, telecommunication data and, if applicable, areas of responsibility of
authorities and entities referred to in paragraph (1)(a);

    (b) information on pollution response equipment and expertise in disciplines related
to pollution incident response and marine salvage which may be made available to
other States, upon request; and

    (c) its national contingency plan.

Article 5 – International co-operation in pollution response

(1) Parties agree that, subject to their capabilities and the availability of relevant
resources, they will co-operate and provide advisory services, technical support and equipment for the purpose of responding to a pollution incident, when the severity of the incident so justifies, upon the request of any Party affected or likely to be affected. The
financing of the costs for such assistance shall be based on the provisions set out in the
Annex to this Protocol.

(2) A Party which has requested assistance may ask the Organization to assist in identifying sources of provisional financing of the costs referred to in paragraph (1).

(3) In accordance with applicable international agreements, each Party shall take necessary legal or administrative measures to facilitate:

    (a) the arrival and utilization in and departure from its territory of ships,
aircraft and other modes of transport engaged in responding to a pollution incident or transporting personnel, cargoes, materials and equipment
required to deal with such an incident; and

    (b) the expeditious movement into, through, and out of its territory of person-
nel, cargoes, materials and equipment referred to in subparagraph (a).

Article 6 – Research and development

(1) Parties agree to co-operate directly or, as appropriate, through the Organization or
relevant regional organizations or arrangements in the promotion and exchange of results of
research and development programmes relating to the enhancement of the state-of-the-art of
preparedness for and response to pollution incidents, including technologies and techniques
for surveillance, containment, recovery, dispersion, clean-up and otherwise minimizing or
mitigating the effects of pollution incidents, and for restoration.

(2) To this end, Parties undertake to establish directly or, as appropriate, through the
Organization or relevant regional organizations or arrangements, the necessary links between
Parties' research institutions.

(3) Parties agree to co-operate directly or through the Organization or relevant regional
organizations or arrangements to promote, as appropriate, the holding on a regular basis of
international symposia on relevant subjects, including technological advances in techniques
and equipment for responding to pollution incidents.

(4) Parties agree to encourage, through the Organization or other competent international
organizations, the development of standards for compatible hazardous and noxious substances pollution combating techniques and equipment.

APPENDIX 2

Article 7 – Technical co-operation

(1) Parties undertake directly or through the Organization and other international bodies, as appropriate, in respect of preparedness for and response to pollution incidents, to provide support for those Parties which request technical assistance:
  (a) to train personnel;
  (b) to ensure the availability of relevant technology, equipment and facilities;
  (c) to facilitate other measures and arrangements to prepare for and respond to pollution incidents; and
  (d) to initiate joint research and development programmes.

(2) Parties undertake to co-operate actively, subject to their national laws, regulations and policies, in the transfer of technology in respect of preparedness for and response to pollution incidents.

Article 8 – Promotion of bilateral and multilateral co-operation in preparedness and response

Parties shall endeavour to conclude bilateral or multilateral agreements for preparedness for and response to pollution incidents. Copies of such agreements shall be communicated to the Organization which should make them available on request to the Parties.

Article 9 – Relation to other conventions and other agreements

Nothing in this Protocol shall be construed as altering the rights or obligations of any Party under any other convention or international agreement.

Article 10 – Institutional arrangements

(1) Parties designate the Organization, subject to its agreement and the availability of adequate resources to sustain the activity, to perform the following functions and activities:
  (a) information services:
      (i)   to receive, collate and disseminate on request the information provided by Parties and relevant information provided by other sources; and
      (ii) to provide assistance in identifying sources of provisional financing of costs;
  (b) education and training:
      (i)   to promote training in the field of preparedness for and response to pollution incidents; and
      (ii) to promote the holding of international symposia;
  (c) technical services:
      (i)   to facilitate co-operation in research and development;
      (ii) to provide advice to States establishing national or regional response capabilities; and
      (iii) to analyse the information provided by Parties and relevant information provided by other sources and provide advice or information to States;
  (d) technical assistance:
      (i)   to facilitate the provision of technical assistance to States establishing national or regional response capabilities; and
      (ii) to facilitate the provision of technical assistance and advice, upon the request of States faced with major pollution incidents.

(2) In carrying out the activities specified in this article, the Organization shall endeavour to strengthen the ability of States individually or through regional arrangements to prepare

APPENDIX 2

for and combat pollution incidents, drawing upon the experience of States, regional agreements and industry arrangements and paying particular attention to the needs of developing countries.

(3) The provisions of this article shall be implemented in accordance with a programme developed and kept under review by the Organization.

Article 11 – Evaluation of the Protocol

Parties shall evaluate within the Organization the effectiveness of the Protocol in the light of its objectives, particularly with respect to the principles underlying co-operation and assistance.

Article 12 – Amendments

(1) this Protocol may be amended by one of the procedures specified in the following paragraphs.

(2) Amendment after consideration by the Organization:
   (a) Any amendment proposed by a Party to the Protocol shall be submitted to the Organization and circulated by the Secretary-General to all Members of the Organization and all Parties at least six months prior to its consideration.
   (b) Any amendment proposed and circulated as above shall be submitted to the Marine Environment Protection Committee of the Organization for consideration.
   (c) Parties to the Protocol, whether or not Members of the Organization, shall be entitled to participate in the proceedings of the Marine Environment Protection Committee.
   (d) Amendments shall be adopted by a two thirds majority of only the Parties to the Protocol present and voting.
   (e) If adopted in accordance with subparagraph (d), amendments shall be communicated by the Secretary-General to all Parties to the Protocol for acceptance.
   (f) (i) An amendment to an article or the Annex of the Protocol shall be deemed to have been accepted on the date on which two thirds of the Parties have notified the Secretary-General that they have accepted it.
       (ii) An amendment to an appendix shall be deemed to have been accepted at the end of a period to be determined by the Marine Environment Protection Committee at the time of its adoption, in accordance with subparagraph (d), which period shall not be less than ten months, unless within that period an objection is communicated to the Secretary-General by not less than one third of the Parties.
   (g) (i) An amendment to an article or the Annex of the Protocol accepted in conformity with subparagraph (f)(i) shall enter into force six months after the date on which it is deemed to have been accepted with respect to the Parties which have notified the Secretary-General that they have accepted it.
       (ii) An amendment to an appendix accepted in conformity with subparagraph (f)(ii) shall enter into force six months after the date on which it is deemed to have been accepted with respect to all Parties with the exception of those which, before that date, have objected to it. A Party may at any time withdraw a previously communicated objection by submitting a notification to that effect to the Secretary-General.

(3) Amendment by a Conference:
   (a) Upon the request of a Party, concurred with by at least one third of the Parties,

APPENDIX 2

the Secretary-General shall convene a Conference of Parties to the Protocol to consider amendments to the Protocol.

(b) An amendment adopted by such a Conference by a two thirds majority of those Parties present and voting shall be communicated by the Secretary-General to all Parties for their acceptance.

(c) Unless the Conference decides otherwise, the amendment shall be deemed to have been accepted and shall enter into force in accordance with the procedures specified in paragraph (2)(f) and (g).

(4) The adoption and entry into force of an amendment constituting an addition of an Annex or an appendix shall be subject to the procedure applicable to an amendment to the Annex.

(5) Any Party which:

(a) has not accepted an amendment to an article or the Annex under paragraph (2)(f)(i); or

(b) has not accepted an amendment constituting an addition of an Annex or an appendix under paragraph (4); or

(c) has communicated an objection to an amendment to an appendix under paragraph (2)(f)(ii)

shall be treated as a non-Party only for the purpose of the application of such amendment. Such treatment shall terminate upon the submission of a notification of acceptance under paragraph (2)(f)(i) or withdrawal of the objection under paragraph (2)(g)(ii).

(6) The Secretary-General shall inform all Parties of any amendment which enters into force under this article, together with the date on which the amendment enters into force.

(7) Any notification of acceptance of, objection to, or withdrawal of objection to, an amendment under this article shall be communicated in writing to the Secretary-General who shall inform Parties of such notification and the date of its receipt.

(8) An appendix to the Protocol shall contain only provisions of a technical nature.

Article 13 – Signature, ratification, acceptance, approval and accession

(1) This Protocol shall remain open for signature at the Headquarters of the Organization from 15 March 2000 until 14 March 2001 and shall thereafter remain open for accession. Any State party to the OPRC Convention may become Party to this Protocol by:

(a) signature without reservation as to ratification, acceptance or approval; or

(b) signature subject to ratification, acceptance or approval, followed by ratification, acceptance or approval; or

(c) accession.

(2) Ratification, acceptance, approval or accession shall be effected by the deposit of an instrument to that effect with the Secretary-General.

Article 14 – States with more than one system of law

(1) If a State party to the OPRC Convention comprises two or more territorial units in which different systems of law are applicable in relation to matters dealt with in this Protocol, it may at the time of signature, ratification, acceptance, approval or accession declare that this Protocol shall extend to all its territorial units or only to one or more of them to which the application of the OPRC Convention has been extended, and may modify this declaration by submitting another declaration at any time.

(2) Any such declarations shall be notified to the depositary in writing and shall state expressly the territorial unit or units to which the Protocol applies. In the case of

APPENDIX 2

modification the declaration shall state expressly the territorial unit or units to which the application of the Protocol shall be further extended and the date on which such extension takes effect.

Article 15 – Entry into force

(1) This Protocol shall enter into force twelve months after the date on which not less than fifteen States have either signed it without reservation as to ratification, acceptance or approval or have deposited the requisite instruments of ratification, acceptance, approval or accession in accordance with article 13.

(2) For States which have deposited an instrument of ratification, acceptance, approval or accession in respect of this Protocol after the requirements for entry into force thereof have been met but prior to the date of entry into force, the ratification, acceptance, approval or accession shall take effect on the date of entry into force of this Protocol or three months after the date of deposit of the instrument, whichever is the later date.

(3) For States which have deposited an instrument of ratification, acceptance, approval or accession after the date on which this Protocol entered into force, this Protocol shall become effective three months after the date of deposit of the instrument.

(4) After the date on which an amendment to this Protocol is deemed to have been accepted under article 12, any instrument of ratification, acceptance, approval or accession deposited shall apply to this Protocol as amended.

Article 16 – Denunciation

(1) This Protocol may be denounced by any Party at any time after the expiry of five years from the date on which this Protocol enters into force for that Party.

(2) Denunciation shall be effected by notification in writing to the Secretary-General.

(3) A denunciation shall take effect twelve months after receipt of the notification of denunciation by the Secretary-General or after the expiry of any longer period which may be indicated in the notification.

(4) A Party denouncing the OPRC Convention also automatically denounces the Protocol.

Article 17 – Depositary

(1) This Protocol shall be deposited with the Secretary-General.

(2) The Secretary-General shall:
   (a)   inform all States which have signed this Protocol or acceded thereto of:
      (i)   each new signature or deposit of an instrument of ratification, acceptance, approval or accession, together with the date thereof;
      (ii)   any declaration made under article 14;
      (iii)   the date of entry into force of this Protocol; and
      (iv)   the deposit of any instrument of denunciation of this Protocol together with the date on which it was received and the date on which the denunciation takes effect;
   (b)   transmit certified true copies of this Protocol to the Governments of all States which have signed this Protocol or acceded thereto.

(3) As soon as this Protocol enters into force, a certified true copy thereof shall be transmitted by the depositary to the Secretary-General of the United Nations for registration and publication in accordance with Article 102 of the Charter of the United Nations.

APPENDIX 2

Article 18 – Languages

This Protocol is established in a single original in the Arabic, Chinese, English, French, Russian and Spanish languages, each text being equally authentic.

IN WITNESS WHEREOF the undersigned, being duly authorized by their respective Governments for that purpose, have signed this Protocol.

DONE AT London this fifteenth day of March two thousand.

APPENDIX 3

International Convention for the Prevention of Pollution from Ships (MARPOL), 1973 and Protocol of 1978

International Convention for the Prevention of Pollution from Ships (MARPOL), 1973

THE PARTIES TO THE CONVENTION,

BEING CONSCIOUS of the need to preserve the human environment in general and the marine environment in particular,

RECOGNIZING that deliberate, negligent or accidental release of oil and other harmful substances from ships constitutes a serious source of pollution,

RECOGNIZING ALSO the importance of the International Convention for the Prevention of Pollution of the Sea by Oil, 1954, as being the first multilateral instrument to be concluded with the prime objective of protecting the environment, and appreciating the significant contribution which that Convention has made in preserving the seas and coastal environment from pollution,

DESIRING to achieve the complete elimination of intentional pollution of the marine environment by oil and other harmful substances and the minimization of accidental discharge of such substances,

CONSIDERING that this object may best be achieved by establishing rules not limited to oil pollution having a universal purport,

HAVE AGREED as follows:

Article 1 – General obligations under the Convention

(1) The Parties to the Convention undertake to give effect to the provisions of the present Convention and those Annexes thereto by which they are bound, in order to prevent the pollution of the marine environment by the discharge of harmful substances or effluents containing such substances in contravention of the Convention.

(2) Unless expressly provided otherwise, a reference to the present Convention constitutes at the same time a reference to its Protocols and to the Annexes.

Article 2 – Definitions

For the purposes of the present Convention, unless expressly provided otherwise:

(1) Regulation means the regulations contained in the Annexes to the present Convention.

(2) Harmful substance means any substance which, if introduced into the sea, is liable to create hazards to human health, to harm living resources and marine life, to damage amenities or to interfere with other legitimate uses of the sea, and includes any substance subject to control by the present Convention.

APPENDIX 3

(3) (a) Discharge, in relation to harmful substances or effluents containing such substances, means any release howsoever caused from a ship and includes any escape, disposal, spilling, leaking, pumping, emitting or emptying;

(b) Discharge does not include:

(i) dumping within the meaning of the Convention on the Prevention of Marine Pollution by Dumping of Wastes and Other Matter, done at London on 13 November 1972; or

(ii) release of harmful substances directly arising from the exploration, exploitation and associated offshore processing of sea-bed mineral resources; or

(iii) release of harmful substances for purposes of legitimate scientific research into pollution abatement or control.

(4) Ship means a vessel of any type whatsoever operating in the marine environment and includes hydrofoil boats, air-cushion vehicles, submersibles, floating craft and fixed or floating platforms.

(5) Administration means the Government of the State under whose authority the ship is operating. With respect to a ship entitled to fly a flag of any State, the Administration is the Government of that State. With respect to fixed or floating platforms engaged in exploration and exploitation of the sea-bed and subsoil thereof adjacent to the coast over which the coastal State exercises sovereign rights for the purposes of exploration and exploitation of their natural resources, the Administration is the Government of the coastal State concerned.

(6) Incident means an event involving the actual or probable discharge into the sea of a harmful substance, or effluents containing such a substance.

(7) Organization means the Inter-Governmental Maritime Consultative Organization.*

Article 3 – Application

(1) The present Convention shall apply to:

(a) ships entitled to fly the flag of a Party to the Convention; and

(b) ships not entitled to fly the flag of a Party but which operate under the authority of a Party.

(2) Nothing in the present article shall be construed as derogating from or extending the sovereign rights of the Parties under international law over the sea-bed and subsoil thereof adjacent to their coasts for the purposes of exploration and exploitation of their natural resources.

(3) The present Convention shall not apply to any warship, naval auxiliary or other ship owned or operated by a State and used, for the time being, only on government non-commercial service. However, each Party shall ensure by the adoption of appropriate measures not impairing the operations or operational capabilities of such ships owned or operated by it, that such ships act in a manner consistent, so far as is reasonable and practicable, with the present Convention.

Article 4 – Violation

(1) Any violation of the requirements of the present Convention shall be prohibited and sanctions shall be established therefor under the law of the Administration of the ship concerned wherever the violation occurs. If the Administration is informed of such a violation

---

* The name of the Organization was changed to 'International Maritime Organization' by virtue of amendments to the Organization's Convention which entered into force on 22 May 1982.

APPENDIX 3

and is satisfied that sufficient evidence is available to enable proceedings to be brought in respect of the alleged violation, it shall cause such proceedings to be taken as soon as possible, in accordance with its law.

(2) Any violation of the requirements of the present Convention within the jurisdiction of any Party to the Convention shall be prohibited and sanctions shall be established therefor under the law of that Party. Whenever such a violation occurs, that Party shall either:

(a) cause proceedings to be taken in accordance with its law; or
(b) furnish to the Administration of the ship such information and evidence as may be in its possession that a violation has occurred.

(3) Where information or evidence with respect to any violation of the present Convention by a ship is furnished to the Administration of that ship, the Administration shall promptly inform the Party which has furnished the information or evidence, and the Organization, of the action taken.

(4) The penalties specified under the law of a Party pursuant to the present article shall be adequate in severity to discourage violations of the present Convention and shall be equally severe irrespective of where the violations occur.

Article 5 – Certificates and special rules on inspection of ships

(1) Subject to the provisions of paragraph (2) of the present article a certificate issued under the authority of a Party to the Convention in accordance with the provisions of the regulations shall be accepted by the other Parties and regarded for all purposes covered by the present Convention as having the same validity as a certificate issued by them.

(2) A ship required to hold a certificate in accordance with the provisions of the regulations is subject, while in the ports or offshore terminals under the jurisdiction of a Party, to inspection by officers duly authorized by that Party. Any such inspection shall be limited to verifying that there is on board a valid certificate, unless there are clear grounds for believing that the condition of the ship or its equipment does not correspond substantially with the particulars of that certificate. In that case, or if the ship does not carry a valid certificate, the Party carrying out the inspection shall take such steps as will ensure that the ship shall not sail until it can proceed to sea without presenting an unreasonable threat of harm to the marine environment. That Party may, however, grant such a ship permission to leave the port or offshore terminal for the purpose of proceeding to the nearest appropriate repair yard available.

(3) If a Party denies a foreign ship entry to the ports or offshore terminals under its jurisdiction or takes any action against such a ship for the reason that the ship does not comply with the provisions of the present Convention, the Party shall immediately inform the consul or diplomatic representative of the Party whose flag the ship is entitled to fly, or if this is not possible, the Administration of the ship concerned. Before denying entry or taking such action the Party may request consultation with the Administration of the ship concerned. Information shall also be given to the Administration when a ship does not carry a valid certificate in accordance with the provisions of the regulations.

(4) With respect to the ship of non-Parties to the Convention, Parties shall apply the requirements of the present Convention as may be necessary to ensure that no more favourable treatment is given to such ships.

Article 6 – Detection of violations and enforcement of the Convention

(1) Parties to the Convention shall co-operate in the detection of violations and the enforcement of the provisions of the present Convention, using all appropriate and practica-

APPENDIX 3

ble measures of detection and environmental monitoring, adequate procedures for reporting and accumulation of evidence.

(2) A ship to which the present Convention applies may, in any port or offshore terminal of a Party, be subject to inspection by officers appointed or authorized by that Party for the purpose of verifying whether the ship has discharged any harmful substances in violation of the provisions of the regulations. If an inspection indicates a violation of the Convention, a report shall be forwarded to the Administration for any appropriate action.

(3) Any Party shall furnish to the Administration evidence, if any, that the ship has discharged harmful substances or effluents containing such substances in violation of the provisions of the regulations. If it is practicable to do so, the competent authority of the former Party shall notify the master of the ship of the alleged violation.

(4) Upon receiving such evidence, the Administration so informed shall investigate the matter, and may request the other Party to furnish further or better evidence of the alleged contravention. If the Administration is satisfied that sufficient evidence is available to enable proceedings to be brought in respect of the alleged violation, it shall cause such proceedings to be taken in accordance with its law as soon as possible. The Administration shall promptly inform the Party which has reported the alleged violation, as well as the Organization, of the action taken.

(5) A Party may also inspect a ship to which the present Convention applies when it enters the ports or offshore terminals under its jurisdiction, if a request for an investigation is received from any Party together with sufficient evidence that the ship has discharged harmful substances or effluents containing such substances in any place. The report of such investigation shall be sent to the Party requesting it and to the Administration so that the appropriate action may be taken under the present Convention.

Article 7 – Undue delay to ships

(1) All possible efforts shall be made to avoid a ship being unduly detained or delayed under articles 4, 5 or 6 of the present Convention.

(2) When a ship is unduly detained or delayed under articles 4, 5 or 6 of the present Convention, it shall be entitled to compensation for any loss or damage suffered.

Article 8 – Reports on incidents involving harmful substances

(1) A report of an incident shall be made without delay to the fullest extent possible in accordance with the provisions of Protocol I to the present Convention.

(2) Each Party to the Convention shall:
    (a)   make all arrangements necessary for an appropriate officer or agency to receive and process all reports on incidents; and
    (b)   notify the Organization with complete details of such arrangements for circulation to other Parties and Member States of the Organization.

(3) Whenever a Party receives a report under the provisions of the present article, that Party shall relay the report without delay to:
    (a)   the Administration of the ship involved; and
    (b)   any other State which may be affected.

(4) Each Party to the Convention undertakes to issue instructions to its maritime inspection vessels and aircraft and to other appropriate services, to report to its authorities any incident referred to in Protocol I to the present Convention. That Party shall, if it considers it appropriate, report accordingly to the Organization and to any other Party concerned.

APPENDIX 3

Article 9 – Other treaties and interpretation

(1) Upon its entry into force, the present Convention supersedes the International Convention for the Prevention of Pollution of the Sea by Oil, 1954, as amended, as between Parties to that Convention.

(2) Nothing in the present Convention shall prejudice the codification and development of the law of the sea by the United Nations Conference on the Law of the Sea convened pursuant to resolution 2750 C(XXV) of the General Assembly of the United Nations nor the present or future claims and legal views of any State concerning the law of the sea and the nature and extent of coastal and flag State jurisdiction.

(3) The term 'jurisdiction' in the present Convention shall be construed in the light of international law in force at the time of application or interpretation of the present Convention.

Article 10 – Settlement of disputes

Any dispute between two or more Parties to the Convention concerning the interpretation or application of the present Convention shall, if settlement by negotiation between the Parties involved has not been possible, and if these Parties do not otherwise agree, be submitted upon request of any of them to arbitration as set out in Protocol II to the present Convention.

Article 11 – Communication of information

(1) The Parties to the Convention undertake to communicate to the Organization:
  (a) the text of laws, orders, decrees and regulations and other instruments which have been promulgated on the various matters within the scope of the present Convention;
  (b) a list of non-governmental agencies which are authorized to act on their behalf in matters relating to the design, construction and equipment of ships carrying harmful substances in accordance with the provisions of the regulations:*
  (c) a sufficient number of specimens of their certificates issued under the provisions of the regulations;
  (d) a list of reception facilities including their location, capacity and available facilities and other characteristics;
  (e) official reports or summaries of official reports in so far as they show the results of the application of the present Convention; and
  (f) an annual statistical report, in a form standardized by the Organization, of penalties actually imposed for infringement of the present Convention.

(2) The Organization shall notify Parties of the receipt of any communications under the present article and circulate to all Parties any information communicated to it under subparagraphs (1)(b) to (f) of the present article.

Article 12 – Casualties to ships

(1) Each Administration undertakes to conduct an investigation of any casualty occurring to any of its ships subject to the provisions of the regulations if such casualty has produced a major deleterious effect upon the marine environment.

(2) Each Party to the Convention undertakes to supply the Organization with information

---

* The text of this subparagraph is replaced by that contained in article III of the 1978 Protocol.

APPENDIX 3

concerning the findings of such investigation, when it judges that such information may assist in determining what changes in the present Convention might be desirable.

Article 13 – Signature, ratification, acceptance, approval and accession

(1) The present Convention shall remain open for signature at the Headquarters of the Organization from 15 January 1974 until 31 December 1974 and shall thereafter remain open for accession. States may become Parties to the present Convention by:
- (a) signature without reservation as to ratification, acceptance or approval; or
- (b) signature subject to ratification, acceptance or approval, followed by ratification, acceptance or approval; or
- (c) accession.

(2) Ratification, acceptance, approval or accession shall be effected by the deposit of an instrument to that effect with the Secretary-General of the Organization.

(3) The Secretary-General of the Organization shall inform all States which have signed the present Convention or acceded to it of any signature or of the deposit of any new instrument of ratification, acceptance, approval or accession and the date of its deposit.

Article 14 – Optional annexes

(1) A State may at the time of signing, ratifying, accepting, approving or acceding to the present Convention declare that it does not accept any one or all of Annexes III, IV and V (hereinafter referred to as 'Optional Annexes') of the present Convention. Subject to the above, Parties to the Convention shall be bound by any Annex in its entirety.

(2) A State which has declared that it is not bound by an Optional Annex may at any time accept such Annex by depositing with the Organization an instrument of the kind referred to in article 13(2).

(3) A State which makes a declaration under paragraph (1) of the present article in respect of an Optional Annex and which has not subsequently accepted that Annex in accordance with paragraph (2) of the present article shall not be under any obligation nor entitled to claim any privileges under the present Convention in respect of matters related to such Annex and all references to Parties in the present Convention shall not include that State in so far as matters related to such Annex are concerned.

(4) The Organization shall inform the States which have signed or acceded to the present Convention of any declaration under the present article as well as the receipt of any instrument deposited in accordance with the provisions of paragraph (2) of the present article.

Article 15 – Entry in force

(1) The present Convention shall enter into force 12 months after the date on which not less than 15 States, the combined merchant fleets of which constitute not less than 50 per cent of the gross tonnage of the world's merchant shipping, have become parties to it in accordance with article 13.

(2) An Optional Annex shall enter into force 12 months after the date on which the conditions stipulated in paragraph (1) of the present article have been satisfied in relation to that Annex.

(3) The Organization shall inform the States which have signed the present Convention or acceded to it of the date on which it enters into force and of the date on which an Optional Annex enters into force in accordance with paragraph (2) of the present article.

(4) For States which have deposited an instrument of ratification, acceptance, approval

APPENDIX 3

or accession in respect of the present Convention or any Optional Annex after the requirements for entry into force thereof have been met but prior to the date of entry into force, the
ratification, acceptance, approval or accession shall take effect on the date of entry into force
of the Convention or such Annex or three months after the date of deposit of the instrument
whichever is the later date.

(5) For States which have deposited an instrument of ratification, acceptance, approval or
accession after the date on which the Convention or an Optional Annex entered into force,
the Convention or the Optional Annex shall become effective three months after the date of
deposit of the instrument.

(6) After the date on which all the conditions required under article 16 to bring an
amendment to the present Convention or an Optional Annex into force have been fulfilled,
any instrument of ratification, acceptance, approval or accession deposited shall apply to the
Convention or Annex as amended.

Article 16 – Amendments

(1) The present Convention may be amended by any of the procedures specified in the
following paragraphs.

(2) Amendments after consideration by the Organization:

    (a)   any amendment proposed by a Party to the Convention shall be submitted to
          the Organization and circulated by its Secretary-General to all Members of the
          Organization and all Parties at least six months prior to its consideration;

    (b)   any amendment proposed and circulated as above shall be submitted to an appro-
          priate body by the Organization for consideration;

    (c)   Parties to the Convention, whether or not Members of the Organization, shall be
          entitled to participate in the proceedings of the appropriate body;

    (d)   amendments shall be adopted by a two-thirds majority of only the Parties to the
          Convention present and voting;

    (e)   if adopted in accordance with subparagraph (d) above, amendments shall be com-
          municated by the Secretary-General of the Organization to all the Parties to the
          Convention for acceptance;

    (f)   an amendment shall be deemed to have been accepted in the following circumstances:

        (i)   an amendment to an article of the Convention shall be deemed to have
              been accepted on the date on which it is accepted by two thirds of the
              Parties, the combined merchant fleets of which constitute not less than
              50 per cent of the gross tonnage of the world's merchant fleet;

        (ii)   an amendment to an Annex to the Convention shall be deemed to have
              been accepted in accordance with the procedure specified in subparagraph
              (f)(iii) unless the appropriate body, at the time of its adoption, determines
              that the amendment shall be deemed to have been accepted on the date on
              which it is accepted by two thirds of the Parties, the combined merchant
              fleets of which constitute not less than 50 per cent of the gross tonnage of
              the world's merchant fleet. Nevertheless, at any time before the entry into
              force of an amendment to an Annex to the Convention, a Party may notify
              the Secretary-General of the Organization that its express approval will be
              necessary before the amendment enters into force for it. The latter shall
              bring such notification and the date of its receipt to the notice of Parties;

       (iii)   an amendment to an appendix to an Annex to the Convention shall be
              deemed to have been accepted at the end of a period to be determined by the
              appropriate body at the time of its adoption, which period shall be not less

APPENDIX 3

than ten months, unless within that period an objection is communicated to the Organization by not less than one third of the Parties or by the Parties the combined merchant fleets of which constitute not less than 50 per cent of the gross tonnage of the world's merchant fleet whichever condition is fulfilled;

    (iv) an amendment to Protocol I to the Convention shall be subject to the same procedures as for the amendments to the Annexes to the Convention, as provided for in subparagraphs (f)(ii) or (f)(iii) above;

    (v) an amendment to Protocol II to the Convention shall be subject to the same procedures as for the amendments to an article of the Convention, as provided for in subparagraph (f)(i) above;

  (g) the amendment shall enter into force under the following conditions:

    (i) in the case of an amendment to an article of the Convention, to Protocol II, or to Protocol I or to an Annex to the Convention not under the procedure specified in subparagraph (f)(iii), the amendment accepted in conformity with the foregoing provisions shall enter into force six months after the date of its acceptance with respect to the Parties which have declared that they have accepted it;

    (ii) in the case of an amendment to Protocol I, to an appendix to an Annex or to an Annex to the Convention under the procedure specified in subparagraph (f)(iii), the amendment deemed to have been accepted in accordance with the foregoing conditions shall enter into force six months after its acceptance for all the Parties with the exception of those which, before that date, have made a declaration that they do not accept it or a declaration under subparagraph (f)(ii), that their express approval is necessary.

(3) Amendment by a Conference:

  (a) Upon the request of a Party, concurred in by at least one third of the Parties, the Organization shall convene a Conference of Parties to the Convention to consider amendments to the present Convention.

  (b) Every amendment adopted by such a Conference by a two thirds majority of those present and voting of the Parties shall be communicated by the Secretary-General of the Organization to all Contracting Parties for their acceptance.

  (c) Unless the Conference decides otherwise, the amendment shall be deemed to have been accepted and to have entered into force in accordance with the procedures specified for that purpose in paragraph (2)(f) and (g) above.

(4) (a) In the case of an amendment to an Optional Annex, a reference in the present article to a 'Party to the Convention' shall be deemed to mean a reference to a Party bound by that Annex.

  (b) Any Party which has declined to accept an amendment to an Annex shall be treated as a non-Party only for the purpose of application of that amendment.

(5) The adoption and entry into force of a new annex shall be subject to the same procedures as for the adoption and entry into force of an amendment to an article of the Convention.

(6) Unless expressly provided otherwise, any amendment to the present Convention made under this article, which relates to the structure of a ship, shall apply only to ships for which the building contract is placed, or in the absence of a building contract, the keel of which is laid, on or after the date on which the amendment comes into force.

(7) Any amendment to a Protocol or to an Annex shall relate to the substance of that Protocol or Annex and shall be consistent with the articles of the present Convention.

(8) The Secretary-General of the Organization shall inform all Parties of any amendments which enter into force under the present article, together with the date on which each such amendment enters into force.

APPENDIX 3

(9) Any declaration of acceptance or of objection to an amendment under the present article shall be notified in writing to the Secretary-General of the Organization. The latter shall bring such notification and the date of its receipt to the notice of the Parties to the Convention.

Article 17 – Promotion of technical co-operation

The Parties to the Convention shall promote, in consultation with the Organization and other international bodies, with assistance and coordination by the Executive Director of the United Nations Environment Programme, support for those Parties which request technical assistance for:

   (a)   the training of scientific and technical personnel;
   (b)   the supply of necessary equipment and facilities for reception and monitoring;
   (c)   the facilitation of other measures and arrangements to prevent or mitigate pollution of the marine environment by ships; and
   (d)   the encouragement of research;
       preferably within the countries concerned, so furthering the aims and purposes of the present Convention.

Article 18 – Denunciation

(1) The present Convention or any Optional Annex may be denounced by any Parties to the Convention at any time after the expiry of five years from the date on which the Convention or such Annex enters into force for that Party.

(2) Denunciation shall be effected by notification in writing to the Secretary-General of the Organization who shall inform all the other Parties of any such notification received and of the date of its receipt as well as the date on which such denunciation takes effect.

(3) A denunciation shall take effect 12 months after receipt of the notification of denunciation by the Secretary-General of the Organization or after the expiry of any other longer period which may be indicated in the notification.

Article 19 – Deposit and registration

(1) The present Convention shall be deposited with the Secretary-General of the Organization who shall transmit certified true copies thereof to all States which have signed the present Convention or acceded to it.

(2) As soon as the present Convention enters into force, the text shall be transmitted by the Secretary-General of the Organization to the Secretary-General of the United Nations for registration and publication, in accordance with Article 102 of the Charter of the United Nations.

Article 20 – Languages

The present Convention is established in a single copy in the English, French, Russian and Spanish languages, each text being equally authentic. Official translations in the Arabic, German, Italian and Japanese languages shall be prepared and deposited with the signed original.

IN WITNESS WHEREOF the undersigned being duly authorized by their respective Governments for that purpose have signed the present Convention.

DONE AT LONDON this second day of November, one thousand nine hundred and seventy-three.

★ ★ ★

290

APPENDIX 3

Protocol of 1978 relating to the International Convention for the Prevention of Pollution from Ships, 1973

THE PARTIES TO THE PRESENT PROTOCOL,

RECOGNIZING the significant contribution which can be made by the International Convention for the Prevention of Pollution from Ships, 1973, to the protection of the marine environment from pollution from ships,

RECOGNIZING ALSO the need to improve further the prevention and control of marine pollution from ships, particularly oil tankers,

RECOGNIZING FURTHER the need for implementing the Regulations for the Prevention of Pollution by Oil contained in Annex I of that Convention as early and as widely as possible,

ACKNOWLEDGING HOWEVER the need to defer the application of Annex II of that Convention until certain technical problems have been satisfactorily resolved,

CONSIDERING that these objectives may best be achieved by the conclusion of a Protocol relating to the International Convention for the Prevention of Pollution from Ships, 1973,

HAVE AGREED as follows:

Article I – General obligations

1. The Parties to the present Protocol undertake to give effect to the provisions of:
   (a) the present Protocol and the Annex hereto which shall constitute an integral part of the present Protocol; and
   (b) the International Convention for the Prevention of Pollution from Ships, 1973 (hereinafter referred to as 'the Convention'), subject to the modifications and additions set out in the present Protocol.

2. The provisions of the Convention and the present Protocol shall be read and interpreted together as one single instrument.

3. Every reference to the present Protocol constitutes at the same time a reference to the Annex hereto.

Article II – Implementation of Annex II of the Convention

1. Notwithstanding the provisions of article 14(1) of the Convention, the Parties to the present Protocol agree that they shall not be bound by the provisions of Annex II of the Convention for a period of three years from the date of entry into force of the present Protocol or for such longer period as may be decided by a two-thirds majority of the Parties to the present Protocol in the Marine Environment Protection Committee (hereinafter referred to as 'the Committee') of the Inter-Governmental Maritime Consultative Organization (hereinafter referred to as 'the Organization').

2. During the period specified in paragraph 1 of this article, the Parties to the present Protocol shall not be under any obligations nor entitled to claim any privileges under the Convention in respect of matters relating to Annex II of the Convention and all reference to Parties in the Convention shall not include the Parties to the present Protocol in so far as matters relating to that Annex are concerned.

APPENDIX 3

Article III – Communication of information

The text of article 11(1)(b) of the Convention is replaced by the following:

'a list of nominated surveyors or recognized organizations which are authorized to act on their behalf in the administration of matters relating to the design, construction, equipment and operation of ships carrying harmful substances in accordance with the provisions of the regulations for circulation to the Parties for information of their officers. The Administration shall therefore notify the Organization of the specific responsibilities and conditions of the authority delegated to nominated surveyors or recognized organizations.'

Article IV – Signature, ratification, acceptance, approval and accession

1. The present Protocol shall be open for signature at the Headquarters of the Organization from 1 June 1978 to 31 May 1979 and shall thereafter remain open for accession. States may become Parties to the present Protocol by:
    (a)   signature without reservation as to ratification, acceptance or approval; or
    (b)   signature, subject to ratification, acceptance or approval, followed by ratification, acceptance or approval; or
    (c)   accession.

2. Ratification, acceptance, approval or accession shall be effected by the deposit of an instrument to that effect with the Secretary-General of the Organization.

Article V – Entry into force

1. The present Protocol shall enter into force 12 months after the date on which not less than 15 States, the combined merchant fleets of which constitute not less than 50 per cent of the gross tonnage of the world's merchant shipping, have become Parties to it in accordance with article IV of the present Protocol.

2. Any instrument of ratification, acceptance, approval or accession deposited after the date on which the present Protocol enters into force shall take effect three months after the date of deposit.

3. After the date on which an amendment to the present Protocol is deemed to have been accepted in accordance with article 16 of the Convention, any instrument of ratification, acceptance, approval or accession deposited shall apply to the present Protocol as amended.

Article VI – Amendments

The procedures set out in article 16 of the Convention in respect of amendments to the articles, an Annex and an appendix to an Annex of the Convention shall apply respectively to amendments to the articles, the Annex and an appendix to the Annex of the present Protocol.

Article VII – Denunciation

1. The present Protocol may be denounced by any Party to the present Protocol at any time after the expiry of five years from the date on which the Protocol enters into force for that Party.

2. Denunciation shall be effected by the deposit of an instrument of denunciation with the Secretary-General of the Organization.

3. A denunciation shall take effect 12 months after receipt of the notification by the

APPENDIX 3

Secretary-General of the Organization or after the expiry of any other longer period which may be indicated in the notification.

Article VIII – Depositary

1. The present Protocol shall be deposited with the Secretary-General of the Organization (hereinafter referred to as 'the Depositary').

2. The Depositary shall:
  (a) inform all States which have signed the present Protocol or acceded thereto of:
      (i) each new signature or deposit of an instrument of ratification, acceptance, approval or accession, together with the date thereof;
      (ii) the date of entry into force of the present Protocol;
      (iii) the deposit of any instrument of denunciation of the present Protocol together with the date on which it was received and the date on which the denunciation takes effect;
      (iv) any decision made in accordance with article II(1) of the present Protocol;
  (b) transmit certified true copies of the present Protocol to all States which have signed the present Protocol or acceded thereto.

3. As soon as the present Protocol enters into force, a certified true copy thereof shall be transmitted by the Depositary to the Secretariat of the United Nations for registration and publication in accordance with Article 102 of the Charter of the United Nations.

Article IX – Languages

The present Protocol is established in a single original in the English, French, Russian and Spanish languages, each text being equally authentic.

Official translations in the Arabic, German, Italian and Japanese languages shall be prepared and deposited with the signed original.

IN WITNESS WHEREOF the undersigned being duly authorized by their respective Governments for that purpose have signed the present Protocol.

DONE AT LONDON this seventeenth day of February one thousand nine hundred and seventy-eight.

APPENDIX 4

International Convention for the Safety of Life at Sea, 1974 and Protocol of 1988 (SOLAS)

International Convention for the Safety of Life at Sea, 1974

The Contracting Governments:

BEING DESIROUS of promoting safety of life at sea by establishing in a common agreement uniform principles and rules directed thereto,
CONSIDERING that this end may best be achieved by the conclusion of a Convention to replace the International Convention for the Safety of Life at Sea, 1960, taking account of developments since that Convention was concluded,

HAVE AGREED as follows:

Article I – General obligations under the Convention

(a) The Contracting Governments undertake to give effect to the provisions of the present Convention and the annex thereto, which shall constitute an integral part of the present Convention. Every reference to the present Convention constitutes at the same time a reference to the annex.

(b) The Contracting Governments undertake to promulgate all laws, decrees, orders and regulations and to take all other steps which may be necessary to give the present Convention full and complete effect, so as to ensure that, from the point of view of safety of life, a ship is fit for the service for which it is intended.

Article II – Application

The present Convention shall apply to ships entitled to fly the flag of States the Governments of which are Contracting Governments.

Article III – Laws, regulations

The Contracting Governments undertake to communicate to and deposit with the Secretary-General of the Inter-Governmental Maritime Consultative Organization (hereinafter referred to as 'the Organization'):

(a) a list of non-governmental agencies which are authorized to act in their behalf in the administration of measures for safety of life at sea for circulation to the Contracting Governments for the information of their officers;

(b) the text of laws, decrees, orders and regulations which shall have been promulgated on the various matters within the scope of the present Convention;

APPENDIX 4

(c) a sufficient number of specimens of their certificates issued under the provisions of the present Convention for circulation to the Contracting Governments for the information of their officers.

Article IV – Cases of force majeure

(a) A ship, which is not subject to the provisions of the present Convention at the time of its departure on any voyage, shall not become subject to the provisions of the present Convention on account of any deviation from its intended voyage due to stress of weather or any other case of force majeure.

(b) Persons who are on board a ship by reason of force majeure or in consequence of the obligation laid upon the master to carry shipwrecked or other persons shall not be taken into account for the purpose of ascertaining the application to a ship of any provisions of the present Convention.

Article V – Carriage of persons in emergency

(a) For the purpose of evacuating persons in order to avoid a threat to the security of their lives a Contracting Government may permit the carriage of a larger number of persons in its ships than is otherwise permissible under the present Convention.

(b) Such permission shall not deprive other Contracting Governments of any right of control under the present Convention over such ships which come within their ports.

(c) Notice of any such permission, together with a statement of the circumstances, shall be sent to the Secretary-General of the Organization by the Contracting Government granting such permission.

Article VI – Prior treaties and conventions

(a) As between the Contracting Governments, the present Convention replaces and abrogates the International Convention for the Safety of Life at Sea which was signed in London on 17 June 1960.

(b) All other treaties, conventions and arrangements relating to safety of life at sea, or matters appertaining thereto, at present in force between Governments parties to the present Convention shall continue to have full and complete effect during the terms thereof as regards:
  (i) ships to which the present Convention does not apply;
  (ii) ships to which the present Convention applies, in respect of matters for which it has not expressly provided.

(c) To the extent, however, that such treaties, conventions or arrangements conflict with the provisions of the present Convention, the provisions of the present Convention shall prevail.

(d) All matters which are not expressly provided for in the present Convention remain subject to the legislation of the Contracting Governments.

Article VII – Special rules drawn up by agreement

When in accordance with the present Convention special rules are drawn up by agreement between all or some of the Contracting Governments, such rules shall be communicated to the Secretary-General of the Organization for circulation to all Contracting Governments.

APPENDIX 4

Article VIII – Amendments

(a) The present Convention may be amended by either of the procedures specified in the following paragraphs.

(b) Amendments after consideration within the Organization:

  (i) Any amendment proposed by a Contracting Government shall be submitted to the Secretary-General of the Organization, who shall then circulate it to all Members of the Organization and all Contracting Governments at least six months prior to its consideration.

  (ii) Any amendment proposed and circulated as above shall be referred to the Maritime Safety Committee of the Organization for consideration.

  (iii) Contracting Governments of States, whether or not Members of the Organization, shall be entitled to participate in the proceedings of the Maritime Safety Committee for the consideration and adoption of amendments.

  (iv) Amendments shall be adopted by a two-thirds majority of the Contracting Governments present and voting in the Maritime Safety Committee expanded as provided for in subparagraph (iii) of this paragraph (hereinafter referred to as 'the expanded Maritime Safety Committee') on condition that at least one third of the Contracting Governments shall be present at the time of voting.

  (v) Amendments adopted in accordance with subparagraph (iv) of this paragraph shall be communicated by the Secretary-General of the Organization to all Contracting Governments for acceptance.

  (vi) (1) An amendment to an article of the Convention or to chapter I of the annex shall be deemed to have been accepted on the date on which it is accepted by two thirds of the Contracting Governments.

(2) An amendment to the annex other than chapter I shall be deemed to have been accepted:

  (aa) at the end of two years from the date on which it is communicated to Contracting Governments for acceptance; or

  (bb) at the end of a different period, which shall not be less than one year, if so determined at the time of its adoption by a two-thirds majority of the Contracting Governments present and voting in the expanded Maritime Safety Committee.

However, if within the specified period either more than one third of Contracting Governments, or Contracting Governments the combined merchant fleets of which constitute not less than fifty per cent of the gross tonnage of the world's merchant fleet, notify the Secretary-General of the Organization that they object to the amendment, it shall be deemed not to have been accepted.

  (vii) (1) An amendment to an article of the Convention or to chapter I of the annex shall enter into force with respect to those Contracting Governments which have accepted it, six months after the date on which it is deemed to have been accepted, and with respect to each Contracting Government which accepts it after that date, six months after the date of that Contracting Government's acceptance.

  (2) An amendment to the annex other than chapter I shall enter into force with respect to all Contracting Governments, except those which have objected to the amendment under subparagraph (vi)(2) of this paragraph and which have not withdrawn such objections, six months after the date on which it is deemed to have been accepted. However, before the date set for entry into force, any Contracting Government may give notice to the Secretary-General

296

APPENDIX 4

of the Organization that it exempts itself from giving effect to that amendment for a period not longer than one year from the date of its entry into force, or for such longer period as may be determined by a two-thirds majority of the Contracting Governments present and voting in the expanded Maritime Safety Committee at the time of the adoption of the amendment.

(c) Amendment by a Conference:

    (i) Upon the request of a Contracting Government concurred in by at least one third of the Contracting Governments, the Organization shall convene a Conference of Contracting Governments to consider amendments to the present Convention.

    (ii) Every amendment adopted by such a Conference by a two-thirds majority of the Contracting Governments present and voting shall be communicated by the Secretary-General of the Organization to all Contracting Governments for acceptance.

    (iii) Unless the Conference decides otherwise, the amendment shall be deemed to have been accepted and shall enter into force in accordance with the procedures specified in subparagraphs (b)(vi) and (b)(vii) respectively of this article, provided that references in these paragraphs to the expanded Maritime Safety Committee shall be taken to mean references to the Conference.

(d)   (i) A Contracting Government which has accepted an amendment to the annex which has entered into force shall not be obliged to extend the benefit of the present Convention in respect of the certificates issued to a ship entitled to fly the flag of a State the Government of which, pursuant to the provisions of subparagraph (b)(vi)(2) of this article, has objected to the amendment and has not withdrawn such an objection, but only to the extent that such certificates relate to matters covered by the amendment in question.

    (ii) A Contracting Government which has accepted an amendment to the annex which has entered into force shall extend the benefit of the present Convention in respect of the certificates issued to a ship entitled to fly the flag of a State the Government of which, pursuant to the provisions of subparagraph (b)(vii)(2) of this article, has notified the Secretary-General of the Organization that it exempts itself from giving effect to the amendment.

(e) Unless expressly provided otherwise, any amendment to the present Convention made under this article, which relates to the structure of a ship, shall apply only to ships the keels of which are laid or which are at a similar stage of construction, on or after the date on which the amendment enters into force.

(f) Any declaration of acceptance of, or objection to, an amendment or any notice given under subparagraph (b)(vii)(2) of this article shall be submitted in writing to the Secretary-General of the Organization, who shall inform all Contracting Governments of any such submission and the date of its receipt.

(g) The Secretary-General of the Organization shall inform all Contracting Governments of any amendments which enter into force under this article, together with the date on which each such amendment enters into force.

Article IX – Signature, ratification, acceptance, approval and accession

(a) The present Convention shall remain open for signature at the Headquarters of the Organization from 1 November 1974 until 1 July 1975 and shall thereafter remain open for accession. States may become parties to the present Convention by:

    (i) signature without reservation as to ratification, acceptance or approval; or

APPENDIX 4

    (ii)   signature subject to ratification, acceptance or approval, followed by ratification, acceptance or approval; or

    (iii) accession.

(b) Ratification, acceptance, approval or accession shall be effected by the deposit of an instrument to that effect with the Secretary-General of the Organization.

(c) The Secretary-General of the Organization shall inform the Governments of all States which have signed the present Convention or acceded to it of any signature or of the deposit of any instrument of ratification, acceptance, approval or accession and the date of its deposit.

Article X – Entry into force

(a) The present Convention shall enter into force twelve months after the date on which not less than twenty-five States, the combined merchant fleets of which constitute not less than fifty per cent of the gross tonnage of the world's merchant shipping, have become parties to it in accordance with article IX.

(b) Any instrument of ratification, acceptance, approval or accession deposited after the date on which the present Convention enters into force shall take effect three months after the date of deposit.

(c) After the date on which an amendment to the present Convention is deemed to have been accepted under article VIII, any instrument of ratification, acceptance, approval or accession deposited shall apply to the Convention as amended.

Article XI – Denunciation

(a) The present Convention may be denounced by any Contracting Government at any time after the expiry of five years from the date on which the Convention enters into force for that Government.

(b) Denunciation shall be effected by the deposit of an instrument of denunciation with the Secretary-General of the Organization who shall notify all the other Contracting Governments of any instrument of denunciation received and of the date of its receipt as well as the date on which such denunciation takes effect.

(c) A denunciation shall take effect one year, or such longer period as may be specified in the instrument of denunciation, after its receipt by the Secretary-General of the Organization.

Article XII – Deposit and registration

(a) The present Convention shall be deposited with the Secretary-General of the Organization who shall transmit certified true copies thereof to the Governments of all States which have signed the present Convention or acceded to it.

(b) As soon as the present Convention enters into force, the text shall be transmitted by the Secretary-General of the Organization to the Secretary-General of the United Nations for registration and publication, in accordance with Article 102 of the Charter of the United Nations.

Article XIII – Languages

The present Convention is established in a single copy in the Chinese, English, French, Russian and Spanish languages, each text being equally authentic. Official translations in

APPENDIX 4

the Arabic, German and Italian languages shall be prepared and deposited with the signed original.

IN WITNESS WHEREOF the undersigned, being duly authorized by their respective Governments for that purpose, have signed the present Convention.

DONE AT LONDON this first day of November one thousand nine hundred and seventy four.

* * *

APPENDIX 4

Protocol of 1988 Relating to the International Convention for the Safety of Life at Sea, 1974

THE PARTIES TO THE PRESENT PROTOCOL,

BEING PARTIES to the International Convention for the Safety of Life at Sea, done at London on 1 November 1974,

RECOGNIZING the need for the introduction into the above-mentioned Convention of provisions for survey and certification harmonized with corresponding provisions in other international instruments,

CONSIDERING that this need may best be met by the conclusion of a Protocol relating to the International Convention for the Safety of Life at Sea, 1974,

HAVE AGREED as follows:

Article I – General obligations

1. The Parties to the present Protocol undertake to give effect to the provisions of the present Protocol and the annex hereto, which shall constitute an integral part of the present Protocol. Every reference to the present Protocol constitutes at the same time a reference to the annex hereto.

2. As between the Parties to the present Protocol, the provisions of the International Convention for the Safety of Life at Sea, 1974, as amended (hereinafter referred to as 'the Convention') shall apply subject to the modifications and additions set out in the present Protocol.

3. With respect to ships entitled to fly the flag of a State which is not a Party to the Convention and the present Protocol, the Parties to the present Protocol shall apply the requirements of the Convention and the present Protocol as may be necessary to ensure that no more favourable treatment is given to such ships.

Article II – Prior treaties

1. As between the Parties to the present Protocol, the present Protocol replaces and abrogates the Protocol of 1978 relating to the Convention.

2. Notwithstanding any other provisions of the present Protocol, any certificate issued under, and in accordance with, the provisions of the Convention and any supplement to such certificate issued under, and in accordance with, the provisions of the Protocol of 1978 relating to the Convention which is current when the present Protocol enters into force in respect of the Party by which the certificate or supplement was issued, shall remain valid until it expires under the terms of the Convention or the Protocol of 1978 relating to the Convention, as the case may be.

3. A Party to the present Protocol shall not issue certificates under, and in accordance with, the provisions of the International Convention for the Safety of Life at Sea, 1974, as adopted on 1 November 1974.

Article III – Communication of information

The Parties to the present Protocol undertake to communicate to, and deposit with, the Secretary-General of the International Maritime Organization (hereinafter referred to as 'the Organization'):

    (a)   the text of laws, decrees, orders and regulations and other instruments which

APPENDIX 4

have been promulgated on the various matters within the scope of the present Protocol;

(b) a list of nominated surveyors or recognized organizations which are authorized to act on their behalf in the administration of measures for safety of life at sea for circulation to the Parties for information of their officers, and a notification of the specific responsibilities and conditions of the authority delegated to those nominated surveyors or recognized organizations; and

(c) a sufficient number of specimens of their certificates issued under the provision of the present Protocol.

Article IV – Signature, ratification, acceptance, approval and accession

1. The present Protocol shall be open for signature at the Headquarters of the Organization from 1 March 1989 to 28 February 1990 and shall thereafter remain open for accession. Subject to the provisions of paragraph 3, States may express their consent to be bound by the present Protocol by:

(a) signature without reservation as to ratification, acceptance or approval; or

(b) signature subject to ratification, acceptance or approval, followed by ratification, acceptance or approval; or

(c) accession.

2. Ratification, acceptance, approval or accession shall be effected by the deposit of an instrument to that effect with the Secretary-General of the Organization.

3. The present Protocol may be signed without reservation, ratified, accepted, approved or acceded to only by States which have signed without reservation, ratified, accepted, approved or acceded to the Convention.

Article V – Entry into force

1. The present Protocol shall enter into force twelve months after the date on which both the following conditions have been met:

(a) not less than fifteen States, the combined merchant fleets of which constitute not less than fifty per cent of the gross tonnage of the world's merchant shipping, have expressed their consent to be bound by it in accordance with article IV, and

(b) the conditions for the entry into force of the Protocol of 1988 relating to the International Convention on Load Lines, 1966, have been met, provided that the present Protocol shall not enter into force before 1 February 1992.

2. For States which have deposited an instrument of ratification, acceptance, approval or accession in respect of the present Protocol after the conditions for entry into force thereof have been met but prior to the date of entry into force, the ratification, acceptance, approval or accession shall take effect on the date of entry into force of the present Protocol or three months after the date of deposit of the instrument, whichever is the later date.

3. Any instrument of ratification, acceptance, approval or accession deposited after the date on which the present Protocol enters into force shall take effect three months after the date of deposit.

4. After the date on which an amendment to the present Protocol is deemed to have been accepted under article VI, any instrument of ratification, acceptance, approval or accession deposited shall apply to the present Protocol as amended.

301

APPENDIX 4

Article VI – Amendments

The procedures set out in article VIII of the Convention shall apply to amendments to the present Protocol, provided that:
- (a) references in that article to the Convention and to Contracting Governments shall be taken to mean references to the present Protocol and to the Parties to the present Protocol respectively;
- (b) amendments to the articles of the present Protocol and to the Annex thereto shall be adopted and brought into force in accordance with the procedure applicable to amendments to the articles of the Convention or to chapter I of the annex thereto; and
- (c) amendments to the appendix to the annex to the present Protocol may be adopted and brought into force in accordance with the procedure applicable to amendments to the annex to the Convention other than chapter I.

Article VII – Denunciation

1. The present Protocol may be denounced by any Party at any time after the expiry of five years from the date on which the present Protocol enters into force for that Party.

2. Denunciation shall be effected by the deposit of an instrument of denunciation with the Secretary-General of the Organization.

3. A denunciation shall take effect one year, or such longer period as may be specified in the instrument of denunciation, after its receipt by the Secretary-General of the Organization.

4. A denunciation of the Convention by a Party shall be deemed to be a denunciation of the present Protocol by that Party. Such denunciation shall take effect on the same date as denunciation of the Convention takes effect according to paragraph (c) of article XI of the Convention.

Article VIII – Depositary

1. The present Protocol shall be deposited with the Secretary-General of the Organization (hereinafter referred to as 'the depositary').

2. The depositary shall:
- (a) inform the Governments of all States which have signed the present Protocol or acceded thereto of:
  - (i) each new signature or deposit of an instrument of ratification, acceptance, approval or accession, together with the date thereof;
  - (ii) the date of entry into force of the present Protocol;
  - (iii) the deposit of any instrument of denunciation of the present Protocol together with the date on which it was received and the date on which the denunciation takes effect;
- (b) transmit certified true copies of the present Protocol to the Governments of all States which have signed the present Protocol or acceded thereto.

3. As soon as the present Protocol enters into force, a certified true copy thereof shall be transmitted by the depositary to the Secretariat of the United Nations for registration and publication in accordance with Article 102 of the Charter of the United Nations.

APPENDIX 4

Article IX – Languages

The present Protocol is established in a single original in the Arabic, Chinese, English, French, Russian and Spanish languages, each text being equally authentic. An official translation into the Italian language shall be prepared and deposited with the signed original.

DONE AT LONDON this eleventh day of November one thousand nine hundred and eighty-eight.

IN WITNESS WHEREOF the undersigned, being duly authorized by their respective Governments for that purpose, have signed the present Protocol.

APPENDIX 5

Convention on the Prevention of Marine Pollution by Dumping of Wastes and Other Matter, 1972 and Protocol of 1996

Convention on the Prevention of Marine Pollution by Dumping of Wastes and Other Matter, 1972

THE CONTRACTING PARTIES TO THIS CONVENTION,

RECOGNIZING that the marine environment and the living organisms which it supports are of vital importance to humanity, and all people have an interest in assuring that it is so managed that its quality and resources are not impaired;

RECOGNIZING that the capacity of the sea to assimilate wastes and render them harmless, and its ability to regenerate natural resources, is not unlimited;

RECOGNIZING that States have, in accordance with the Charter of the United Nations and the principles of international law, the sovereign right to exploit their own resources pursuant to their own environmental policies, and the responsibility to ensure that activities within their jurisdiction or control do not cause damage to the environment of other States or of areas beyond the limits of national jurisdiction;

RECALLING resolution 2749(XXV) of the General Assembly of the United Nations on the principles governing the sea-bed and the ocean floor and the subsoil thereof, beyond the limits of national jurisdiction;

NOTING that marine pollution originates in many sources, such as dumping and discharges through the atmosphere, rivers, estuaries, outfalls and pipelines, and that it is important that States use the best practicable means to prevent such pollution and develop products and processes which will reduce the amount of harmful wastes to be disposed of;

BEING CONVINCED that international action to control the pollution of the sea by dumping can and must be taken without delay but that this action should not preclude discussion of measures to control other sources of marine pollution as soon as possible; and

WISHING to improve protection of the marine environment by encouraging States with a common interest in particular geographical areas to enter into appropriate agreements supplementary to this Convention;

HAVE AGREED as follows:

Article I

Contracting Parties shall individually and collectively promote the effective control of all sources of pollution of the marine environment, and pledge themselves especially to take all practicable steps to prevent the pollution of the sea by the dumping of waste and other matter that is liable to create hazards to human health, to harm living resources and marine life, to damage amenities or to interfere with other legitimate uses of the sea.

APPENDIX 5

Article II

Contracting Parties shall, as provided for in the following articles, take effective measures individually, according to their scientific, technical and economic capabilities, and collectively, to prevent marine pollution caused by dumping and shall harmonize their policies in this regard.

Article III

For the purposes of this Convention:
1 (a) 'Dumping' means:
     (i)   any deliberate disposal at sea of wastes or other matter from vessels, aircraft, platforms or other man-made structures at sea;
     (ii) any deliberate disposal at sea of vessels, aircraft, platforms or other man-made structures at sea.
  (b) 'Dumping' does not include:
     (i)   the disposal at sea of wastes or other matter incidental to, or derived from the normal operations of vessels, aircraft, platforms or other man-made structures at sea and their equipment, other than wastes or other matter transported by or to vessels, aircraft, platforms or other man-made structures at sea, operating for the purpose of disposal of such matter or derived from the treatment of such wastes or other matter on such vessels, aircraft, platforms or structures;
     (ii) placement of matter for a purpose other than the mere disposal thereof, provided that such placement is not contrary to the aims of this Convention.
  (c) The disposal of wastes or other matter directly arising from, or related to the exploration, exploitation and associated off-shore processing of sea-bed mineral resources will not be covered by the provisions of this Convention.

2. 'Vessels and aircraft' means waterborne or airborne craft of any type whatsoever. This expression includes air cushioned craft and floating craft, whether self-propelled or not.

3. 'Sea' means all marine waters other than the internal waters of States.

4. 'Wastes or other matter' means material and substance of any kind, form or description.

5. 'Special permit' means permission granted specifically on application in advance and in accordance with Annex II and Annex III.

6. 'General permit' means permission granted in advance and in accordance with Annex III.

7. 'The Organization' means the Organization designated by the Contracting Parties in accordance with article XIV(2).

Article IV

1. In accordance with the provisions of this Convention Contracting Parties shall prohibit the dumping of any wastes or other matter in whatever form or condition except as otherwise specified below:
  (a) the dumping of wastes or other matter listed in Annex I is prohibited;
  (b) the dumping of wastes or other matter listed in Annex II requires a prior special permit;
  (c) the dumping of all other wastes or matter requires a prior general permit.

2. Any permit shall be issued only after careful consideration of all the factors set forth in Annex III, including prior studies of the characteristics of the dumping site, as set forth in sections B and C of that Annex.

APPENDIX 5

3.   No provision of this Convention is to be interpreted as preventing a Contracting Party from prohibiting, insofar as that Party is concerned, the dumping of wastes or other matter not mentioned in Annex I. That Party shall notify such measures to the Organization.

Article V

1. The provisions of article IV shall not apply when it is necessary to secure the safety of human life or of vessels, aircraft, platforms or other man-made structures at sea in cases of *force majeure* caused by stress of weather, or in any case which constitutes a danger to human life or a real threat to vessels, aircraft, platforms or other man-made structures at sea, if dumping appears to be the only way of averting the threat and if there is every probability that the damage consequent upon such dumping will be less than would otherwise occur. Such dumping shall be so conducted as to minimize the likelihood of damage to human or marine life and shall be reported forthwith to the Organization.

2. A Contracting Party may issue a special permit as an exception to article IV(1)(a), in emergencies, posing unacceptable risk relating to human health and admitting no other feasible solution. Before doing so the Party shall consult any other country or countries that are likely to be affected and the Organization which, after consulting other Parties, and international organizations as appropriate, shall, in accordance with article XIV promptly recommend to the Party the most appropriate procedures to adopt. The Party shall follow these recommendations to the maximum extent feasible consistent with the time within which action must be taken and with the general obligation to avoid damage to the marine environment and shall inform the Organization of the action it takes. The Parties pledge themselves to assist one another in such situations.

3. Any Contracting Party may waive its rights under paragraph (2) at the time of, or subsequent to ratification of, or accession to this Convention.

Article VI

1. Each Contracting Party shall designate an appropriate authority or authorities to:
   (a)   issue special permits which shall be required prior to, and for, the dumping of matter listed in Annex II and in the circumstances provided for in article V(2);
   (b)   issue general permits which shall be required prior to, and for, the dumping of all other matter;
   (c)   keep records of the nature and quantities of all matter permitted to be dumped and the location, time and method of dumping;
   (d)   monitor individually, or in collaboration with other Parties and competent international organizations, the condition of the seas for the purposes of this Convention.

2. The appropriate authority or authorities of a contracting Party shall issue prior special or general permits in accordance with paragraph (1) in respect of matter intended for dumping:
   (a)   loaded in its territory;
   (b)   loaded by a vessel or aircraft registered in its territory or flying its flag, when the loading occurs in the territory of a State not party to this Convention.

3. In issuing permits under sub-paragraphs (1)(a) and (b) above, the appropriate authority or authorities shall comply with Annex III, together with such additional criteria, measures and requirements as they may consider relevant.

4. Each Contracting Party, directly or through a Secretariat established under a regional agreement, shall report to the Organization, and where appropriate to other Parties, the information specified in sub-paragraphs(c) and (d) of paragraph (1) above, and the criteria, measures and requirements it adopts in accordance with paragraph (3) above. The

306

APPENDIX 5

procedure to be followed and the nature of such reports shall be agreed by the Parties in consultation.

Article VII

1. Each Contracting Party shall apply the measures required to implement the present Convention to all:
   (a) vessels and aircraft registered in its territory or flying its flag;
   (b) vessels and aircraft loading in its territory or territorial seas matter which is to be dumped;
   (c) vessels and aircraft and fixed or floating platforms under its jurisdiction believed to be engaged in dumping.

2. Each Party shall take in its territory appropriate measures to prevent and punish conduct in contravention of the provisions of this Convention.

3. The Parties agree to co-operate in the development of procedures for the effective application of this Convention particularly on the high seas, including procedures for the reporting of vessels and aircraft observed dumping in contravention of the Convention.

4. This Convention shall not apply to those vessels and aircraft entitled to sovereign immunity under international law. However, each Party shall ensure by the adoption of appropriate measures that such vessels and aircraft owned or operated by it act in a manner consistent with the object and purpose of this Convention, and shall inform the Organization accordingly.

5. Nothing in this Convention shall affect the right of each Party to adopt other measures, in accordance with the principles of international law, to prevent dumping at sea.

Article VIII

In order to further the objectives of this Convention, the Contracting Parties with common interests to protect the marine environment in a given geographical area shall endeavour, taking into account characteristic regional features, to enter into regional agreements consistent with this Convention for the prevention of pollution, especially by dumping. The Contracting Parties to the present Convention shall endeavour to act consistently with the objectives and provisions of such regional agreements, which shall be notified to them by the Organization. Contracting Parties shall seek to co-operate with the Parties to regional agreements in order to develop harmonized procedures to be followed by Contracting Parties to the different conventions concerned. Special attention shall be given to co-operation in the field of monitoring and scientific research.

Article IX

The Contracting Parties shall promote, through collaboration within the Organization and other international bodies, support for those Parties which request it for:
   (a) the training of scientific and technical personnel;
   (b) the supply of necessary equipment and facilities for research and monitoring;
   (c) the disposal and treatment of waste and other measures to prevent or mitigate pollution caused by dumping;
preferably within the countries concerned, so furthering the aims and purposes of this Convention.

APPENDIX 5

Article X

In accordance with the principles of international law regarding State responsibility for damage to the environment of other States or to any other area of the environment, caused by dumping of wastes and other matter of all kinds, the Contracting Parties undertake to develop procedures for the assessment of liability and the settlement of disputes regarding dumping.

Article XI

The Contracting Parties shall at their first consultative meeting consider procedures for the settlement of disputes concerning the interpretation and application of this Convention.

Article XII

The Contracting Parties pledge themselves to promote, within the competent specialized agencies and other international bodies, measures to protect the marine environment against pollution caused by:

(a) hydrocarbons, including oil and their wastes;
(b) other noxious or hazardous matter transported by vessels for purposes other than dumping;
(c) wastes generated in the course of operation of vessels, aircraft, platforms and other man-made structures at sea;
(d) radio-active pollutants from all sources, including vessels;
(e) agents of chemical and biological warfare;
(f) wastes or other matter directly arising from, or related to the exploration, exploitation and associated off-shore processing of sea-bed mineral resources.

The Parties will also promote, within the appropriate international organization, the codification of signals to be used by vessels engaged in dumping.

Article XIII

Nothing in this Convention shall prejudice the codification and development of the law of the sea by the United Nations Conference on the Law of the Sea convened pursuant to resolution 2750 C(XXV) of the General Assembly of the United Nations nor the present or future claims and legal views of any State concerning the law of the sea and the nature and extent of coastal and flag State jurisdiction. The Contracting Parties agree to consult at a meeting to be convened by the Organization after the Law of the Sea Conference, and in any case not later than 1976, with a view to defining the nature and extent of the right and the responsibility of a coastal State to apply the Convention in a zone adjacent to its coast.

Article XIV

1. The Government of the United Kingdom of Great Britain and Northern Ireland as a depositary shall call a meeting of the Contracting Parties not later than three months after the entry into force of this Convention to decide on organizational matters.

2. The Contracting Parties shall designate a competent Organization existing at the time of that meeting to be responsible for secretariat duties in relation to this Convention. Any Party to this Convention not being a member of this Organization shall make an appropriate contribution to the expenses incurred by the Organization in performing these duties.

3. The Secretariat duties of the Organization shall include:

APPENDIX 5

(a) the convening of consultative meetings of the Contracting Parties not less frequently than once every two years and of special meetings of the Parties at any time
on the request of two thirds of the Parties;

(b) preparing and assisting, in consultation with the Contracting Parties and appropriate International Organizations, in the development and implementation of procedures referred to in sub-paragraph (4)(e) of this article;

(c) considering enquiries by, and information from the Contracting Parties, consulting
with them and with the appropriate International Organizations, and providing recommendations to the Parties on questions related to, but not specifically covered by
the Convention;

(d) conveying to the Parties concerned all notifications received by the Organization in
accordance with articles IV(3), V(1) and (2), VI(4), XV, XX and XXI.

Prior to the designation of the Organization these functions shall, as necessary, be performed by the depositary, who for this purpose shall be the Government of the United
Kingdom of Great Britain and Northern Ireland.

4. Consultative or special meetings of the Contracting Parties shall keep under continuing
review the implementation of this Convention and may, *inter alia*:

(a) review and adopt amendments to this Convention and its Annexes in accordance
with article XV;

(b) invite the appropriate scientific body or bodies to collaborate with and to advise
the Parties or the Organization on any scientific or technical aspect relevant to this
Convention, including particularly the content of the Annexes;

(c) receive and consider reports made pursuant to article VI(4);

(d) promote co-operation with and between regional organizations concerned with the
prevention of marine pollution;

(e) develop or adopt, in consultation with appropriate International Organizations,
procedures referred to in article V(2), including basic criteria for determining
exceptional and emergency situations, and procedures for consultative advice and
the safe disposal of matter in such circumstances, including the designation of
appropriate dumping areas, and recommend accordingly;

(f) consider any additional action that may be required.

5. The Contracting Parties at their first consultative meeting shall establish rules of
procedure as necessary.

Article XV

1.(a) At meetings of the Contracting Parties called in accordance with article XIV amendments to this Convention may be adopted by a two-thirds majority of those present. An
amendment shall enter into force for the Parties which have accepted it on the sixtieth day
after two thirds of the Parties shall have deposited an instrument of acceptance of the amendment with the Organization. Thereafter the amendment shall enter into force for any other
Party 30 days after that Party deposits its instrument of acceptance of the amendment.

(b) The Organization shall inform all Contracting Parties of any request made for a special
meeting under article XIV and of any amendments adopted at meetings of the Parties and of
the date on which each such amendment enters into force for each Party.

2. Amendments to the Annexes will be based on scientific or technical considerations.
Amendments to the annexes approved by a two-thirds majority of those present at a meeting
called in accordance with article XIV shall enter into force for each Contracting Party immediately on notification of its acceptance to the Organization and 100 days after approval by
the meeting for all other Parties except for those which before the end of the 100 days make

309

APPENDIX 5

a declaration that they are not able to accept the amendment at that time. Parties should endeavour to signify their acceptance of an amendment to the Organization as soon as possible after approval at a meeting. A Party may at any time substitute an acceptance for a previous declaration of objection and the amendment previously objected to shall thereupon enter into force for that Party.

3. An acceptance or declaration of objection under this article shall be made by the deposit of an instrument with the Organization. The Organization shall notify all Contracting Parties of the receipt of such instruments.

4. Prior to the designation of the Organization, the Secretarial functions herein attributed to it shall be performed temporarily by the Government of the United Kingdom of Great Britain and Northern Ireland, as one of the depositaries of this Convention.

Article XVI

This Convention shall be open for signature by any State at London, Mexico City, Moscow and Washington from 29 December 1972 until 31 December 1973.

Article XVII

This Convention shall be subject to ratification. The instruments of ratification shall be deposited with the Governments of Mexico, the Union of Soviet Socialist Republics, the United Kingdom of Great Britain and Northern Ireland, and the United States of America.

Article XVIII

After 31 December 1973, this Convention shall be open for accession by any State. The instruments of accession shall be deposited with the Governments of Mexico, the Union of Soviet Socialist Republics, the United Kingdom of Great Britain and Northern Ireland, and the United States of America.

Article XIX

1. This Convention shall enter into force on the thirtieth day following the date of deposit of the fifteenth instrument of ratification or accession.

2. For each Contracting Party ratifying or acceding to the Convention after the deposit of the fifteenth instrument of ratification or accession, the Convention shall enter into force on the thirtieth day after deposit by such Party of its instrument of ratification or accession.

Article XX

The depositaries shall inform Contracting Parties:
- (a) of signatures to this Convention and of the deposit of instruments of ratification, accession or withdrawal, in accordance with articles XVI, XVII, XVIII and XXI, and
- (b) of the date on which this Convention will enter into force, in accordance with article XIX.

Article XXI

Any Contracting Party may withdraw from this Convention by giving six months' notice in writing to a depositary, which shall promptly inform all Parties of such notice.

APPENDIX 5

Article XXII

The original of this Convention of which the English, French, Russian and Spanish texts are equally authentic, shall be deposited with the Governments of Mexico, the Union of Soviet Socialist Republics, the United Kingdom of Great Britain and Northern Ireland and the United States of America who shall send certified copies thereof to all States.

IN WITNESS WHEREOF the undersigned Plenipotentiaries, being duly authorized thereto by their respective Governments, have signed the present Convention.

DONE in quadruplicate at London, Mexico City, Moscow and Washington, this twenty-ninth day of December, 1972.

★ ★ ★

APPENDIX 5

1996 Protocol to the Convention on the Prevention of Marine Pollution by Dumping of Wastes and Other Matter, 1972

(as amended in 2006)

THE CONTRACTING PARTIES TO THIS PROTOCOL,

STRESSING the need to protect the marine environment and to promote the sustainable use and conservation of marine resources,

NOTING in this regard the achievements within the framework of the Convention on the Prevention of Marine Pollution by Dumping of Wastes and Other Matter, 1972 and especially the evolution towards approaches based on precaution and prevention,

NOTING FURTHER the contribution in this regard by complementary regional and national instruments which aim to protect the marine environment and which take account of specific circumstances and needs of those regions and States,

REAFFIRMING the value of a global approach to these matters and in particular the importance of continuing co-operation and collaboration between Contracting Parties in implementing the Convention and the Protocol,

RECOGNIZING that it may be desirable to adopt, on a national or regional level, more stringent measures with respect to prevention and elimination of pollution of the marine environment from dumping at sea than are provided for in international conventions or other types of agreements with a global scope,

TAKING INTO ACCOUNT relevant international agreements and actions, especially the United Nations Convention on the Law of the Sea, 1982, the Rio Declaration on Environment and Development and Agenda 21,

RECOGNIZING ALSO the interests and capacities of developing States and in particular small island developing States,

BEING CONVINCED that further international action to prevent, reduce and where practicable eliminate pollution of the sea caused by dumping can and must be taken without delay to protect and preserve the marine environment and to manage human activities in such a manner that the marine ecosystem will continue to sustain the legitimate uses of the sea and will continue to meet the needs of present and future generations,

HAVE AGREED as follows:

Article 1 – Definitions

For the purposes of this Protocol:

1. 'Convention' means the Convention on the Prevention of Marine Pollution by Dumping of Wastes and Other Matter, 1972, as amended.

2. 'Organization' means the International Maritime Organization.

3. 'Secretary-General' means the Secretary-General of the Organization.

4.   .1   'Dumping' means:

        .1   any deliberate disposal into the sea of wastes or other matter from vessels, aircraft, platforms or other man-made structures at sea;

        .2   any deliberate disposal into the sea of vessels, aircraft, platforms or other man-made structures at sea;

        .3   any storage of wastes or other matter in the seabed and the subsoil thereof from vessels, aircraft, platforms or other man-made structures at sea; and

APPENDIX 5

     .4 any abandonment or toppling at site of platforms or other man-made structures at sea, for the sole purpose of deliberate disposal.

  .2 'Dumping' does not include:

     .1 the disposal into the sea of wastes or other matter incidental to, or derived from the normal operations of vessels, aircraft, platforms or other man-made structures at sea and their equipment, other than wastes or other matter transported by or to vessels, aircraft, platforms or other man-made structures at sea, operating for the purpose of disposal of such matter or derived from the treatment of such wastes or other matter on such vessels, aircraft, platforms or other man-made structures;

     .2 placement of matter for a purpose other than the mere disposal thereof, provided that such placement is not contrary to the aims of this Protocol; and

     .3 notwithstanding paragraph 4.1.4, abandonment in the sea of matter (e.g., cables, pipelines and marine research devices) placed for a purpose other than the mere disposal thereof.

  .3 The disposal or storage of wastes or other matter directly arising from, or related to the exploration, exploitation and associated off-shore processing of seabed mineral resources is not covered by the provisions of this Protocol.

5.   .1 'Incineration at sea' means the combustion on board a vessel, platform or other man-made structure at sea of wastes or other matter for the purpose of their deliberate disposal by thermal destruction.

     .2 'Incineration at sea' does not include the incineration of wastes or other matter on board a vessel, platform, or other man-made structure at sea if such wastes or other matter were generated during the normal operation of that vessel, platform or other man-made structure at sea.

6. 'Vessels and aircraft' means waterborne or airborne craft of any type whatsoever. This expression includes air-cushioned craft and floating craft, whether self-propelled or not.

7. 'Sea' means all marine waters other than the internal waters of States, as well as the seabed and the subsoil thereof; it does not include sub-seabed repositories accessed only from land.

8. 'Wastes or other matter' means material and substance of any kind, form or description.

9. 'Permit' means permission granted in advance and in accordance with relevant measures adopted pursuant to article 4.1.2 or 8.2.

10. 'Pollution' means the introduction, directly or indirectly, by human activity, of wastes or other matter into the sea which results or is likely to result in such deleterious effects as harm to living resources and marine ecosystems, hazards to human health, hindrance to marine activities, including fishing and other legitimate uses of the sea, impairment of quality for use of sea water and reduction of amenities.

Article 2 – Objectives

Contracting Parties shall individually and collectively protect and preserve the marine environment from all sources of pollution and take effective measures, according to their scientific, technical and economic capabilities, to prevent, reduce and where practicable eliminate pollution caused by dumping or incineration at sea of wastes or other matter. Where appropriate, they shall harmonize their policies in this regard.

Article 3 – General Obligations

1. In implementing this Protocol, Contracting Parties shall apply a precautionary approach to environmental protection from dumping of wastes or other matter whereby appropriate

APPENDIX 5

preventative measures are taken when there is reason to believe that wastes or other matter introduced into the marine environment are likely to cause harm even when there is no conclusive evidence to prove a causal relation between inputs and their effects.

2. Taking into account the approach that the polluter should, in principle, bear the cost of pollution, each Contracting Party shall endeavour to promote practices whereby those it has authorized to engage in dumping or incineration at sea bear the cost of meeting the pollution prevention and control requirements for the authorized activities, having due regard to the public interest.

3. In implementing the provisions of this Protocol, Contracting Parties shall act so as not to transfer, directly or indirectly, damage or likelihood of damage from one part of the environment to another or transform one type of pollution into another.

4. No provision of this Protocol shall be interpreted as preventing Contracting Parties from taking, individually or jointly, more stringent measures in accordance with international law with respect to the prevention, reduction and where practicable elimination of pollution.

Article 4 – Dumping of wastes or other matter

1. .1 Contracting Parties shall prohibit the dumping of any wastes or other matter with the exception of those listed in Annex 1.
   .2 The dumping of wastes or other matter listed in Annex 1 shall require a permit. Contracting Parties shall adopt administrative or legislative measures to ensure that issuance of permits and permit conditions comply with provisions of Annex 2. Particular attention shall be paid to opportunities to avoid dumping in favour of environmentally preferable alternatives.

2. No provision of this Protocol shall be interpreted as preventing a Contracting Party from prohibiting, insofar as that Contracting Party is concerned, the dumping of wastes or other matter mentioned in Annex 1. That Contracting Party shall notify the Organization of such measures.

Article 5 – Incineration at sea

Contracting Parties shall prohibit incineration at sea of wastes or other matter.

Article 6 – Export of wastes or other matter

Contracting Parties shall not allow the export of wastes or other matter to other countries for dumping or incineration at sea.

Article 7 – Internal Waters

1. Notwithstanding any other provision of this Protocol, this Protocol shall relate to internal waters only to the extent provided for in paragraphs 2 and 3.

2. Each Contracting Party shall at its discretion either apply the provisions of this Protocol or adopt other effective permitting and regulatory measures to control the deliberate disposal of wastes or other matter in marine internal waters where such disposal would be 'dumping' or 'incineration at sea' within the meaning of article 1, if conducted at sea.

3. Each Contracting Party should provide the Organization with information on legislation and institutional mechanisms regarding implementation, compliance and enforcement in marine internal waters. Contracting Parties should also use their best efforts to provide on a

314

APPENDIX 5

voluntary basis summary reports on the type and nature of the materials dumped in marine internal waters.

Article 8 – Exceptions

1. The provisions of articles 4.1 and 5 shall not apply when it is necessary to secure the safety of human life or of vessels, aircraft, platforms or other man-made structures at sea in cases of force majeure caused by stress of weather, or in any case which constitutes a danger to human life or a real threat to vessels, aircraft, platforms or other man-made structures at sea, if dumping or incineration at sea appears to be the only way of averting the threat and if there is every probability that the damage consequent upon such dumping or incineration at sea will be less than would otherwise occur. Such dumping or incineration at sea shall be conducted so as to minimize the likelihood of damage to human or marine life and shall be reported forthwith to the Organization.

2. A Contracting Party may issue a permit as an exception to articles 4.1 and 5, in emergencies posing an unacceptable threat to human health, safety, or the marine environment and admitting of no other feasible solution. Before doing so the Contracting Party shall consult any other country or countries that are likely to be affected and the Organization which, after consulting other Contracting Parties, and competent international organizations as appropriate, shall, in accordance with article 18.1.6 promptly recommend to the Contracting Party the most appropriate procedures to adopt. The Contracting Party shall follow these recommendations to the maximum extent feasible consistent with the time within which action must be taken and with the general obligation to avoid damage to the marine environment and shall inform the Organization of the action it takes. The Contracting Parties pledge themselves to assist one another in such situations.

3. Any Contracting Party may waive its rights under paragraph 2 at the time of, or subsequent to ratification of, or accession to this Protocol.

Article 9 – Issuance of permits and reporting

1. Each Contracting Party shall designate an appropriate authority or authorities to:
  .1 issue permits in accordance with this Protocol;
  .2 keep records of the nature and quantities of all wastes or other matter for which dumping permits have been issued and where practicable the quantities actually dumped and the location, time and method of dumping; and
  .3 monitor individually, or in collaboration with other Contracting Parties and competent international organizations, the condition of the sea for the purposes of this Protocol.

2. The appropriate authority or authorities of a Contracting Party shall issue permits in accordance with this Protocol in respect of wastes or other matter intended for dumping or, as provided for in article 8.2, incineration at sea:
  .1 loaded in its territory; and
  .2 loaded onto a vessel or aircraft registered in its territory or flying its flag, when the loading occurs in the territory of a State not a Contracting Party to this Protocol.

3. In issuing permits, the appropriate authority or authorities shall comply with the requirements of article 4, together with such additional criteria, measures and requirements as they may consider relevant.

4. Each Contracting Party, directly or through a secretariat established under a regional agreement, shall report to the Organization and where appropriate to other Contracting Parties:

315

APPENDIX 5

  .1 the information specified in paragraphs 1.2 and 1.3;

  .2 the administrative and legislative measures taken to implement the provisions of this Protocol, including a summary of enforcement measures; and

  .3 the effectiveness of the measures referred to in paragraph 4.2 and any problems encountered in their application.

The information referred to in paragraphs 1.2 and 1.3 shall be submitted on an annual basis. The information referred to in paragraphs 4.2 and 4.3 shall be submitted on a regular basis.

5. Reports submitted under paragraphs 4.2 and 4.3 shall be evaluated by an appropriate subsidiary body as determined by the Meeting of Contracting Parties. This body will report its conclusions to an appropriate Meeting or Special Meeting of Contracting Parties.

Article 10 – Application and enforcement

1. Each Contracting Party shall apply the measures required to implement this Protocol to all:

  .1 vessels and aircraft registered in its territory or flying its flag;

  .2 vessels and aircraft loading in its territory the wastes or other matter which are to be dumped or incinerated at sea; and

  .3 vessels, aircraft and platforms or other man-made structures believed to be engaged in dumping or incineration at sea in areas within which it is entitled to exercise jurisdiction in accordance with international law.

2. Each Contracting Party shall take appropriate measures in accordance with international law to prevent and if necessary punish acts contrary to the provisions of this Protocol.

3. Contracting Parties agree to co-operate in the development of procedures for the effective application of this Protocol in areas beyond the jurisdiction of any State, including procedures for the reporting of vessels and aircraft observed dumping or incinerating at sea in contravention of this Protocol.

4. This Protocol shall not apply to those vessels and aircraft entitled to sovereign immunity under international law. However, each Contracting Party shall ensure by the adoption of appropriate measures that such vessels and aircraft owned or operated by it act in a manner consistent with the object and purpose of this Protocol and shall inform the Organization accordingly.

5. A State may, at the time it expresses its consent to be bound by this Protocol, or at any time thereafter, declare that it shall apply the provisions of this Protocol to its vessels and aircraft referred to in paragraph 4, recognising that only that State may enforce those provisions against such vessels and aircraft.

Article 11 – Compliance Procedures

1. No later than two years after the entry into force of this Protocol, the Meeting of Contracting Parties shall establish those procedures and mechanisms necessary to assess and promote compliance with this Protocol. Such procedures and mechanisms shall be developed with a view to allowing for the full and open exchange of information, in a constructive manner.

2. After full consideration of any information submitted pursuant to this Protocol and any recommendations made through procedures or mechanisms established under paragraph 1, the Meeting of Contracting Parties may offer advice, assistance or co-operation to Contracting Parties and non-Contracting Parties.

APPENDIX 5

Article 12 – Regional co-operation

In order to further the objectives of this Protocol, Contracting Parties with common interests to protect the marine environment in a given geographical area shall endeavour, taking into account characteristic regional features, to enhance regional co-operation including the conclusion of regional agreements consistent with this Protocol for the prevention, reduction and where practicable elimination of pollution caused by dumping or incineration at sea of wastes or other matter. Contracting Parties shall seek to co-operate with the parties to regional agreements in order to develop harmonized procedures to be followed by Contracting Parties to the different conventions concerned.

Article 13 – Technical co-operation and assistance

1. Contracting Parties shall, through collaboration within the Organization and in coordination with other competent international organizations, promote bilateral and multilateral support for the prevention, reduction and where practicable elimination of pollution caused by dumping as provided for in this Protocol to those Contracting Parties that request it for:
   .1 training of scientific and technical personnel for research, monitoring and enforcement, including as appropriate the supply of necessary equipment and facilities, with a view to strengthening national capabilities;
   .2 advice on implementation of this Protocol;
   .3 information and technical co-operation relating to waste minimization and clean production processes;
   .4 information and technical co-operation relating to the disposal and treatment of waste and other measures to prevent, reduce and where practicable eliminate pollution caused by dumping; and
   .5 access to and transfer of environmentally sound technologies and corresponding know-how, in particular to developing countries and countries in transition to market economies, on favourable terms, including on concessional and preferential terms, as mutually agreed, taking into account the need to protect intellectual property rights as well as the special needs of developing countries and countries in transition to market economies.
2. The Organization shall perform the following functions:
   .1 forward requests from Contracting Parties for technical co-operation to other Contracting Parties, taking into account such factors as technical capabilities;
   .2 co-ordinate requests for assistance with other competent international organizations, as appropriate; and
   .3 subject to the availability of adequate resources, assist developing countries and those in transition to market economies, which have declared their intention to become Contracting Parties to this Protocol, to examine the means necessary to achieve full implementation.

Article 14 – Scientific and technical research

1. Contracting Parties shall take appropriate measures to promote and facilitate scientific and technical research on the prevention, reduction and where practicable elimination of pollution by dumping and other sources of marine pollution relevant to this Protocol. In particular, such research should include observation, measurement, evaluation and analysis of pollution by scientific methods.

APPENDIX 5

2. Contracting Parties shall, to achieve the objectives of this Protocol, promote the availability of relevant information to other Contracting Parties who request it on:

.1 scientific and technical activities and measures undertaken in accordance with this Protocol;

.2 marine scientific and technological programmes and their objectives; and

.3 the impacts observed from the monitoring and assessment conducted pursuant to article 9.1.3.

Article 15 – Responsibility and liability

In accordance with the principles of international law regarding State responsibility for damage to the environment of other States or to any other area of the environment, the Contracting Parties undertake to develop procedures regarding liability arising from the dumping or incineration at sea of wastes or other matter.

Article 16 – Settlement of disputes

1. Any disputes regarding the interpretation or application of this Protocol shall be resolved in the first instance through negotiation, mediation or conciliation, or other peaceful means chosen by parties to the dispute.

2. If no resolution is possible within twelve months after one Contracting Party has notified another that a dispute exists between them, the dispute shall be settled, at the request of a party to the dispute, by means of the Arbitral Procedure set forth in Annex 3, unless the parties to the dispute agree to use one of the procedures listed in paragraph 1 of Article 287 of the 1982 United Nations Convention on the Law of the Sea. The parties to the dispute may so agree, whether or not they are also States Parties to the 1982 United Nations Convention on the Law of the Sea.

3. In the event an agreement to use one of the procedures listed in paragraph 1 of Article 287 of the 1982 United Nations Convention on the Law of the Sea is reached, the provisions set forth in Part XV of that Convention that are related to the chosen procedure would also apply, *mutatis mutandis.*

4. The twelve month period referred to in paragraph 2 may be extended for another twelve months by mutual consent of the parties concerned.

5. Notwithstanding paragraph 2, any State may, at the time it expresses its consent to be bound by this Protocol, notify the Secretary-General that, when it is a party to a dispute about the interpretation or application of article 3.1 or 3.2, its consent will be required before the dispute may be settled by means of the Arbitral Procedure set forth in Annex 3.

Article 17 – International co-operation

Contracting Parties shall promote the objectives of this Protocol within the competent international organizations.

Article 18 – Meetings of contracting parties

1. Meetings of Contracting Parties or Special Meetings of Contracting Parties shall keep under continuing review the implementation of this Protocol and evaluate its effectiveness with a view to identifying means of strengthening action, where necessary, to prevent, reduce and where practicable eliminate pollution caused by dumping and incineration at sea of

APPENDIX 5

wastes or other matter. To these ends, Meetings of Contracting Parties or Special Meetings of Contracting Parties may:

.1 review and adopt amendments to this Protocol in accordance with articles 21 and 22;

.2 establish subsidiary bodies, as required, to consider any matter with a view to facilitating the effective implementation of this Protocol;

.3 invite appropriate expert bodies to advise the Contracting Parties or the Organization on matters relevant to this Protocol;

.4 promote co-operation with competent international organizations concerned with the prevention and control of pollution;

.5 consider the information made available pursuant to article 9.4;

.6 develop or adopt, in consultation with competent international organizations, procedures referred to in article 8.2, including basic criteria for determining exceptional and emergency situations, and procedures for consultative advice and the safe disposal of matter at sea in such circumstances;

.7 consider and adopt resolutions; and

.8 consider any additional action that may be required.

2. The Contracting Parties at their first Meeting shall establish rules of procedure as necessary.

Article 19 – Duties of the organization

1. The Organization shall be responsible for Secretariat duties in relation to this Protocol. Any Contracting Party to this Protocol not being a member of this Organization shall make an appropriate contribution to the expenses incurred by the Organization in performing these duties.

2. Secretariat duties necessary for the administration of this Protocol include:

.1 convening Meetings of Contracting Parties once per year, unless otherwise decided by Contracting Parties, and Special Meetings of Contracting Parties at any time on the request of two-thirds of the Contracting Parties;

.2 providing advice on request on the implementation of this Protocol and on guidance and procedures developed thereunder;

.3 considering enquiries by, and information from Contracting Parties, consulting with them and with the competent international organizations, and providing recommendations to Contracting Parties on questions related to, but not specifically covered by, this Protocol;

.4 preparing and assisting, in consultation with Contracting Parties and the competent international organizations, in the development and implementation of procedures referred to in article 18.1.6;

.5 conveying to the Contracting Parties concerned all notifications received by the Organization in accordance with this Protocol; and

.6 preparing, every two years, a budget and a financial account for the administration of this Protocol which shall be distributed to all Contracting Parties.

3. The Organization shall, subject to the availability of adequate resources, in addition to the requirements set out in article 13.2.3.

.1 collaborate in assessments of the state of the marine environment; and

.2 co-operate with competent international organizations concerned with the prevention and control of pollution.

APPENDIX 5

Article 20 – Annexes

Annexes to this Protocol form an integral part of this Protocol.

Article 21 – Amendment of the Protocol

1. Any Contracting Party may propose amendments to the articles of this Protocol. The text of a proposed amendment shall be communicated to Contracting Parties by the Organization at least six months prior to its consideration at a Meeting of Contracting Parties or a Special Meeting of Contracting Parties.

2. Amendments to the articles of this Protocol shall be adopted by a two-thirds majority vote of the Contracting Parties which are present and voting at the Meeting of Contracting Parties or Special Meeting of Contracting Parties designated for this purpose.

3. An amendment shall enter into force for the Contracting Parties which have accepted it on the sixtieth day after two-thirds of the Contracting Parties shall have deposited an instrument of acceptance of the amendment with the Organization. Thereafter the amendment shall enter into force for any other Contracting Party on the sixtieth day after the date on which that Contracting Party has deposited its instrument of acceptance of the amendment.

4. The Secretary-General shall inform Contracting Parties of any amendments adopted at Meetings of Contracting Parties and of the date on which such amendments enter into force generally and for each Contracting Party.

5. After entry into force of an amendment to this Protocol, any State that becomes a Contracting Party to this Protocol shall become a Contracting Party to this Protocol as amended, unless two-thirds of the Contracting Parties present and voting at the Meeting or Special Meeting of Contracting Parties adopting the amendment agree otherwise.

Article 22 – Amendment of the annexes

1. Any Contracting Party may propose amendments to the Annexes to this Protocol. The text of a proposed amendment shall be communicated to Contracting Parties by the Organization at least six months prior to its consideration by a Meeting of Contracting Parties or Special Meeting of Contracting Parties.

2. Amendments to the Annexes other than Annex 3 will be based on scientific or technical considerations and may take into account legal, social and economic factors as appropriate. Such amendments shall be adopted by a two-thirds majority vote of the Contracting Parties present and voting at a Meeting of Contracting Parties or Special Meeting of Contracting Parties designated for this purpose.

3. The Organization shall without delay communicate to Contracting Parties amendments to the Annexes that have been adopted at a Meeting of Contracting Parties or Special Meeting of Contracting Parties.

4. Except as provided in paragraph 7, amendments to the Annexes shall enter into force for each Contracting Party immediately on notification of its acceptance to the Organization or 100 days after the date of their adoption at a Meeting of Contracting Parties, if that is later, except for those Contracting Parties which before the end of the 100 days make a declaration that they are not able to accept the amendment at that time. A Contracting Party may at any time substitute an acceptance for a previous declaration of objection and the amendment previously objected to shall thereupon enter into force for that Contracting Party.

APPENDIX 5

5. The Secretary-General shall without delay notify Contracting Parties of instruments of acceptance or objection deposited with the Organization.

6. A new Annex or an amendment to an Annex which is related to an amendment to the articles of this Protocol shall not enter into force until such time as the amendment to the articles of this Protocol enters into force.

7. With regard to amendments to Annex 3 concerning the Arbitral Procedure and with regard to the adoption and entry into force of new Annexes the procedures on amendments to the articles of this Protocol shall apply.

Article 23 – Relationship between the Protocol and the Convention

This Protocol will supersede the Convention as between Contracting Parties to this Protocol which are also Parties to the Convention.

Article 24 – Signature, ratification, acceptance, approval and accession

1. This Protocol shall be open for signature by any State at the Headquarters of the Organization from 1 April 1997 to 31 March 1998 and shall thereafter remain open for accession by any State.

2. States may become Contracting Parties to this Protocol by:
   .1 signature not subject to ratification, acceptance or approval; or
   .2 signature subject to ratification, acceptance or approval, followed by ratification, acceptance or approval; or
   .3 accession.

3. Ratification, acceptance, approval or accession shall be effected by the deposit of an instrument to that effect with the Secretary-General.

Article 25 – Entry into force

1. This Protocol shall enter into force on the thirtieth day following the date on which:
   .1 at least 26 States have expressed their consent to be bound by this Protocol in accordance with article 24; and
   .2 at least 15 Contracting Parties to the Convention are included in the number of States referred to in paragraph 1.1.

2. For each State that has expressed its consent to be bound by this Protocol in accordance with article 24 following the date referred to in paragraph 1, this Protocol shall enter into force on the thirtieth day after the date on which such State expressed its consent.

Article 26 – Transitional period

1. Any State that was not a Contracting Party to the Convention before 31 December 1996 and that expresses its consent to be bound by this Protocol prior to its entry into force or within five years after its entry into force may, at the time it expresses its consent, notify the Secretary-General that, for reasons described in the notification, it will not be able to comply with specific provisions of this Protocol other than those provided in paragraph 2, for a transitional period that shall not exceed that described in paragraph 4.

2. No notification made under paragraph 1 shall affect the obligations of a Contracting Party to this Protocol with respect to incineration at sea or the dumping of radioactive wastes or other radioactive matter.

APPENDIX 5

3. Any Contracting Party to this Protocol that has notified the Secretary-General under paragraph 1 that, for the specified transitional period, it will not be able to comply, in part or in whole, with article 4.1 or article 9 shall nonetheless during that period prohibit the dumping of wastes or other matter for which it has not issued a permit, use its best efforts to adopt administrative or legislative measures to ensure that issuance of permits and permit conditions comply with the provisions of Annex 2, and notify the Secretary-General of any permits issued.

4. Any transitional period specified in a notification made under paragraph 1 shall not extend beyond five years after such notification is submitted.

5. Contracting Parties that have made a notification under paragraph 1 shall submit to the first Meeting of Contracting Parties occurring after deposit of their instrument of ratification, acceptance, approval or accession a programme and timetable to achieve full compliance with this Protocol, together with any requests for relevant technical co-operation and assistance in accordance with article 13 of this Protocol.

6. Contracting Parties that have made a notification under paragraph 1 shall establish procedures and mechanisms for the transitional period to implement and monitor submitted programmes designed to achieve full compliance with this Protocol. A report on progress toward compliance shall be submitted by such Contracting Parties to each Meeting of Contracting Parties held during their transitional period for appropriate action.

Article 27 – Withdrawal

1. Any Contracting Party may withdraw from this Protocol at any time after the expiry of two years from the date on which this Protocol enters into force for that Contracting Party.

2. Withdrawal shall be effected by the deposit of an instrument of withdrawal with the Secretary-General.

3. A withdrawal shall take effect one year after receipt by the Secretary-General of the instrument of withdrawal or such longer period as may be specified in that instrument.

Article 28 – Depositary

1. This Protocol shall be deposited with the Secretary-General.

2. In addition to the functions specified in articles 10.5, 16.5, 21.4, 22.5 and 26.5, the Secretary-General shall:

  .1 inform all States which have signed this Protocol or acceded thereto of:

      .1 each new signature or deposit of an instrument of ratification, acceptance, approval or accession, together with the date thereof;

      .2 the date of entry into force of this Protocol; and

      .3 the deposit of any instrument of withdrawal from this Protocol together with the date on which it was received and the date on which the withdrawal takes effect.

  .2 transmit certified copies of this Protocol to all States which have signed this Protocol or acceded thereto.

3. As soon as this Protocol enters into force, a certified true copy thereof shall be transmitted by the Secretary-General to the Secretariat of the United Nations for registration and publication in accordance with Article 102 of the Charter of the United Nations.

APPENDIX 5

Article 29 – Authentic texts

This Protocol is established in a single original in the Arabic, Chinese, English, French, Russian and Spanish languages, each text being equally authentic.

IN WITNESS WHEREOF the undersigned being duly authorized by their respective Governments for that purpose have signed this Protocol

DONE AT LONDON, this seventh day of November, one thousand nine hundred and ninety-six.

★ ★ ★

APPENDIX 5

ANNEX 1

Wastes or other matter that may be considered for dumping

1 The following wastes or other matter are those that may be considered for dumping being mindful of the Objectives and General Obligations of this Protocol set out in articles 2 and 3:

.1 dredged material;

.2 sewage sludge;

.3 fish waste, or material resulting from industrial fish processing operations;

.4 vessels and platforms or other man-made structures at sea;

.5 inert, inorganic geological material;

.6 organic material of natural origin;

.7 bulky items primarily comprising iron, steel, concrete and similarly unharmful materials for which the concern is physical impact, and limited to those circumstances where such wastes are generated at locations, such as small islands with isolated communities, having no practicable access to disposal options other than dumping; and

.8 Carbon dioxide streams from carbon dioxide capture processes for sequestration.

2. The wastes or other matter listed in paragraphs 1.4 and 1.7 may be considered for dumping, provided that material capable of creating floating debris or otherwise contributing to pollution of the marine environment has been removed to the maximum extent and provided that the material dumped poses no serious obstacle to fishing or navigation.

3. Notwithstanding the above, materials listed in paragraphs 1.1 to 1.8 containing levels of radioactivity greater than *de minimis* (exempt) concentrations as defined by the IAEA and adopted by Contracting Parties, shall not be considered eligible for dumping; provided further that within 25 years of 20 February 1994, and at each 25 year interval thereafter, Contracting Parties shall complete a scientific study relating to all radioactive wastes and other radioactive matter other than high level wastes or matter, taking into account such other factors as Contracting Parties consider appropriate and shall review the prohibition on dumping of such substances in accordance with the procedures set forth in article 22.

4. Carbon dioxide streams referred to in paragraph 1.8 may only be considered for dumping, if:

.1 disposal is into a sub-seabed geological formation; and

.2 they consist overwhelmingly of carbon dioxide. They may contain incidental associated substances derived from the source material and the capture and sequestration processes used; and

.3 no wastes or other matter are added for the purpose of disposing of those wastes or other matter.

★ ★ ★

APPENDIX 5

ANNEX 2

Assessment of wastes or other matter that may be considered for dumping

GENERAL

1. The acceptance of dumping under certain circumstances shall not remove the obligations under this Annex to make further attempts to reduce the necessity for dumping.

WASTE PREVENTION AUDIT

2. The initial stages in assessing alternatives to dumping should, as appropriate, include an evaluation of:

    .1   types, amounts and relative hazard of wastes generated;

    .2   details of the production process and the sources of wastes within that process; and

    .3   feasibility of the following waste reduction/prevention techniques:

        .1   product reformulation;

        .2   clean production technologies;

        .3   process modification;

        .4   input substitution; and

        .5   on-site, closed-loop recycling.

3. In general terms, if the required audit reveals that opportunities exist for waste prevention at source, an applicant is expected to formulate and implement a waste prevention strategy, in collaboration with relevant local and national agencies, which includes specific waste reduction targets and provision for further waste prevention audits to ensure that these targets are being met. Permit issuance or renewal decisions shall assure compliance with any resulting waste reduction and prevention requirements.

4. For dredged material and sewage sludge, the goal of waste management should be to identify and control the sources of contamination. This should be achieved through implementation of waste prevention strategies and requires collaboration between the relevant local and national agencies involved with the control of point and non-point sources of pollution. Until this objective is met, the problems of contaminated dredged material may be addressed by using disposal management techniques at sea or on land.

Consideration of waste management options

5. Applications to dump wastes or other matter shall demonstrate that appropriate consideration has been given to the following hierarchy of waste management options, which implies an order of increasing environmental impact:

    .1   re-use;

    .2   off-site recycling;

    .3   destruction of hazardous constituents;

    .4   treatment to reduce or remove the hazardous constituents; and

    .5   disposal on land, into air and in water.

6. A permit to dump wastes or other matter shall be refused if the permitting authority determines that appropriate opportunities exist to re-use, recycle or treat the waste without undue risks to human health or the environment or disproportionate costs. The practical availability of other means of disposal should be considered in the light of a comparative risk assessment involving both dumping and the alternatives.

Chemical, physical and biological properties

7. A detailed description and characterization of the waste is an essential precondition for the consideration of alternatives and the basis for a decision as to whether a waste may be

APPENDIX 5

dumped. If a waste is so poorly characterized that proper assessment cannot be made of its potential impacts on human health and the environment, that waste shall not be dumped.

8. Characterization of the wastes and their constituents shall take into account:

.1 origin, total amount, form and average composition;
.2 properties: physical, chemical, biochemical and biological;
.3 toxicity;
.4 persistence: physical, chemical and biological; and
.5 accumulation and biotransformation in biological materials or sediments.

Action List

9. Each Contracting Party shall develop a national Action List to provide a mechanism for screening candidate wastes and their constituents on the basis of their potential effects on human health and the marine environment. In selecting substances for consideration in an Action List, priority shall be given to toxic, persistent and bioaccumulative substances from anthropogenic sources (e.g., cadmium, mercury, organohalogens, petroleum hydrocarbons, and, whenever relevant, arsenic, lead, copper, zinc, beryllium, chromium, nickel and vanadium, organosilicon compounds, cyanides, fluorides and pesticides or their by-products other than organohalogens). An Action List can also be used as a trigger mechanism for further waste prevention considerations.

10. An Action List shall specify an upper level and may also specify a lower level. The upper level should be set so as to avoid acute or chronic effects on human health or on sensitive marine organisms representative of the marine ecosystem. Application of an Action List will result in three possible categories of waste:

.1 wastes which contain specified substances, or which cause biological responses, exceeding the relevant upper level shall not be dumped, unless made acceptable for dumping through the use of management techniques or processes;
.2 wastes which contain specified substances, or which cause biological responses, below the relevant lower levels should be considered to be of little environmental concern in relation to dumping; and
.3 wastes which contain specified substances, or which cause biological responses, below the upper level but above the lower level require more detailed assessment before their suitability for dumping can be determined.

Dump-site selection

11. Information required to select a dump-site shall include:

.1 physical, chemical and biological characteristics of the water-column and the seabed;
.2 location of amenities, values and other uses of the sea in the area under consideration;
.3 assessment of the constituent fluxes associated with dumping in relation to existing fluxes of substances in the marine environment; and
.4 economic and operational feasibility.

Assessment of potential effects

12. Assessment of potential effects should lead to a concise statement of the expected consequences of the sea or land disposal options, i.e., the 'Impact Hypothesis'. It provides a basis for deciding whether to approve or reject the proposed disposal option and for defining environmental monitoring requirements.

APPENDIX 5

13. The assessment for dumping should integrate information on waste characteristics, conditions at the proposed dump-site(s), fluxes, and proposed disposal techniques and specify the potential effects on human health, living resources, amenities and other legitimate uses of the sea. It should define the nature, temporal and spatial scales and duration of expected impacts based on reasonably conservative assumptions.

14. An analysis of each disposal option should be considered in the light of a comparative assessment of the following concerns: human health risks, environmental costs, hazards, (including accidents), economics and exclusion of future uses. If this assessment reveals that adequate information is not available to determine the likely effects of the proposed disposal option then this option should not be considered further. In addition, if the interpretation of the comparative assessment shows the dumping option to be less preferable, a permit for dumping should not be given.

15. Each assessment should conclude with a statement supporting a decision to issue or refuse a permit for dumping.

Monitoring

16. Monitoring is used to verify that permit conditions are met – compliance monitoring – and that the assumptions made during the permit review and site selection process were correct and sufficient to protect the environment and human health-field monitoring. It is essential that such monitoring programmes have clearly defined objectives.

Permit and permit conditions

17. A decision to issue a permit should only be made if all impact evaluations are completed and the monitoring requirements are determined. The provisions of the permit shall ensure, as far as practicable, that environmental disturbance and detriment are minimized and the benefits maximized. Any permit issued shall contain data and information specifying:

  .1 the types and sources of materials to be dumped;
  .2 the location of the dump-site(s);
  .3 the method of dumping; and
  .4 monitoring and reporting requirements.

18. Permits should be reviewed at regular intervals, taking into account the results of monitoring and the objectives of monitoring programmes. Review of monitoring results will indicate whether field programmes need to be continued, revised or terminated and will contribute to informed decisions regarding the continuance, modification or revocation of permits. This provides an important feedback mechanism for the protection of human health and the marine environment.

***

327

APPENDIX 5

ANNEX 3

Arbitral procedure

Article 1

1. An Arbitral Tribunal (hereinafter referred to as the 'Tribunal') shall be established upon the request of a Contracting Party addressed to another Contracting Party in application of article 16 of this Protocol. The request for arbitration shall consist of a statement of the case together with any supporting documents.
2. The requesting Contracting Party shall inform the Secretary-General of:
    .1   its request for arbitration; and
    .2   the provisions of this Protocol the interpretation or application of which is, in its opinion, the subject of disagreement.
3. The Secretary-General shall transmit this information to all Contracting States.

Article 2

1. The Tribunal shall consist of a single arbitrator if so agreed between the parties to the dispute within 30 days from the date of receipt of the request for arbitration.
2. In the case of the death, disability or default of the arbitrator, the parties to a dispute may agree upon a replacement within 30 days of such death, disability or default.

Article 3

1. Where the parties to a dispute do not agree upon a Tribunal in accordance with article 2 of this Annex, the Tribunal shall consist of three members:
    .1   one arbitrator nominated by each party to the dispute; and
    .2   a third arbitrator who shall be nominated by agreement between the two first named and who shall act as its Chairman.
2. If the Chairman of a Tribunal is not nominated within 30 days of nomination of the second arbitrator, the parties to a dispute shall, upon the request of one party, submit to the Secretary-General within a further period of 30 days an agreed list of qualified persons. The Secretary-General shall select the Chairman from such list as soon as possible. He shall not select a Chairman who is or has been a national of one party to the dispute except with the consent of the other party to the dispute.
3. If one party to a dispute fails to nominate an arbitrator as provided in paragraph 1.1 within 60 days from the date of receipt of the request for arbitration, the other party may request the submission to the Secretary-General within a period of 30 days of an agreed list of qualified persons. The Secretary-General shall select the Chairman of the Tribunal from such list as soon as possible. The Chairman shall then request the party which has not nominated an arbitrator to do so. If this party does not nominate an arbitrator within 15 days of such request, the Secretary-General shall, upon request of the Chairman, nominate the arbitrator from the agreed list of qualified persons.
4. In the case of the death, disability or default of an arbitrator, the party to the dispute who nominated him shall nominate a replacement within 30 days of such death, disability or default. If the party does not nominate a replacement, the arbitration shall proceed with the remaining arbitrators. In the case of the death, disability or default of the Chairman, a replacement shall be nominated in accordance with the provision of paragraphs 1.2 and 2 within 90 days of such death, disability or default.
5. A list of arbitrators shall be maintained by the Secretary-General and composed of

328

APPENDIX 5

qualified persons nominated by the Contracting Parties. Each Contracting Party may designate for inclusion in the list four persons who shall not necessarily be its nationals. If the parties to the dispute have failed within the specified time limits to submit to the Secretary-General an agreed list of qualified persons as provided for in paragraphs 2, 3 and 4, the Secretary-General shall select from the list maintained by him the arbitrator or arbitrators not yet nominated.

Article 4

The Tribunal may hear and determine counter-claims arising directly out of the subject matter of the dispute.

Article 5

Each party to the dispute shall be responsible for the costs entailed by the preparation of its own case. The remuneration of the members of the Tribunal and of all general expenses incurred by the arbitration shall be borne equally by the parties to the dispute. The Tribunal shall keep a record of all its expenses and shall furnish a final statement thereof to the parties.

Article 6

Any Contracting Party which has an interest of a legal nature which may be affected by the decision in the case may, after giving written notice to the parties to the dispute which have originally initiated the procedure, intervene in the arbitration procedure with the consent of the Tribunal and at its own expense. Any such intervenor shall have the right to present evidence, briefs and oral argument on the matters giving rise to its intervention, in accordance with procedures established pursuant to article 7 of this Annex, but shall have no rights with respect to the composition of the Tribunal.

Article 7

A Tribunal established under the provisions of this Annex shall decide its own rules of procedure.

Article 8

1. Unless a Tribunal consists of a single arbitrator, decisions of the Tribunal as to its procedure, its place of meeting, and any question related to the dispute laid before it, shall be taken by majority vote of its members. However, the absence or abstention of any member of the Tribunal who was nominated by a party to the dispute shall not constitute an impediment to the Tribunal reaching a decision. In case of equal voting, the vote of the Chairman shall be decisive.

2. The parties to the dispute shall facilitate the work of the Tribunal and in particular shall, in accordance with their legislation and using all means at their disposal:
   .1 provide the Tribunal with all necessary documents and information; and
   .2 enable the Tribunal to enter their territory, to hear witnesses or experts, and to visit the scene.

3. The failure of a party to the dispute to comply with the provisions of paragraph 2 shall not preclude the Tribunal from reaching a decision and rendering an award.

APPENDIX 5

Article 9

The Tribunal shall render its award within five months from the time it is established unless it finds it necessary to extend that time limit for a period not to exceed five months. The award of the Tribunal shall be accompanied by a statement of reasons for the decision. It shall be final and without appeal and shall be communicated to the Secretary-General who shall inform the Contracting Parties. The parties to the dispute shall immediately comply with the award.

APPENDIX 6

International Convention for the Control and Management of Ships' Ballast Water and Sediments, 2004

THE PARTIES TO THIS CONVENTION,

RECALLING Article 196(1) of the 1982 United Nations Convention on the Law of the Sea (UNCLOS), which provides that 'States shall take all measures necessary to prevent, reduce and control pollution of the marine environment resulting from the use of technologies under their jurisdiction or control, or the intentional or accidental introduction of species, alien or new, to a particular part of the marine environment, which may cause significant and harmful changes thereto,'

NOTING the objectives of the 1992 Convention on Biological Diversity (CBD) and that the transfer and introduction of Harmful Aquatic Organisms and Pathogens via ships' ballast water threatens the conservation and sustainable use of biological diversity as well as decision IV/5 of the 1998 Conference of the Parties (COP 4) to the CBD concerning the conservation and sustainable use of marine and coastal ecosystems, as well as decision VI/23 of the 2002 Conference of the Parties (COP 6) to the CBD on alien species that threaten ecosystems, habitats or species, including guiding principles on invasive species,

NOTING FURTHER that the 1992 United Nations Conference on Environment and Development (UNCED) requested the International Maritime Organization (the Organization) to consider the adoption of appropriate rules on ballast water discharge,

MINDFUL of the precautionary approach set out in Principle 15 of the Rio Declaration on Environment and Development and referred to in resolution MEPC.67(37), adopted by the Organization's Marine Environment Protection Committee on 15 September 1995,

ALSO MINDFUL that the 2002 World Summit on Sustainable Development, in paragraph 34(b) of its Plan of Implementation, calls for action at all levels to accelerate the development of measures to address invasive alien species in ballast water,

CONSCIOUS that the uncontrolled discharge of Ballast Water and Sediments from ships has led to the transfer of Harmful Aquatic Organisms and Pathogens, causing injury or damage to the environment, human health, property and resources,

RECOGNIZING the importance placed on this issue by the Organization through Assembly resolutions A.774(18) in 1993 and A.868(20) in 1997, adopted for the purpose of addressing the transfer of Harmful Aquatic Organisms and Pathogens,

RECOGNIZING FURTHER that several States have taken individual action with a view to prevent, minimize and ultimately eliminate the risks of introduction of Harmful Aquatic Organisms and Pathogens through ships entering their ports, and also that this issue, being of worldwide concern, demands action based on globally applicable regulations together with guidelines for their effective implementation and uniform interpretation,

DESIRING to continue the development of safer and more effective Ballast Water Management options that will result in continued prevention, minimization and ultimate elimination of the transfer of Harmful Aquatic Organisms and Pathogens,

APPENDIX 6

RESOLVED to prevent, minimize and ultimately eliminate the risks to the environment, human health, property and resources arising from the transfer of Harmful Aquatic Organisms and Pathogens through the control and management of ships' Ballast Water and Sediments, as well as to avoid unwanted side-effects from that control and to encourage developments in related knowledge and technology,

CONSIDERING that these objectives may best be achieved by the conclusion of an International Convention for the Control and Management of Ships' Ballast Water and Sediments,

HAVE AGREED as follows:

Article 1 – Definitions

For the purpose of this Convention, unless expressly provided otherwise:

1 'Administration' means the Government of the State under whose authority the ship is operating. With respect to a ship entitled to fly a flag of any State, the Administration is the Government of that State. With respect to floating platforms engaged in exploration and exploitation of the sea-bed and subsoil thereof adjacent to the coast over which the coastal State exercises sovereign rights for the purposes of exploration and exploitation of its natural resources, including Floating Storage Units (FSUs) and Floating Production Storage and Offloading Units (FPSOs), the Administration is the Government of the coastal State concerned.

2. 'Ballast Water' means water with its suspended matter taken on board a ship to control trim, list, draught, stability or stresses of the ship.

3. 'Ballast Water Management' means mechanical, physical, chemical, and biological processes, either singularly or in combination, to remove, render harmless, or avoid the uptake or discharge of Harmful Aquatic Organisms and Pathogens within Ballast Water and Sediments.

4. 'Certificate' means the International Ballast Water Management Certificate.

5. 'Committee' means the Marine Environment Protection Committee of the Organization.

6. 'Convention' means the International Convention for the Control and Management of Ships' Ballast Water and Sediments.

7. 'Gross tonnage' means the gross tonnage calculated in accordance with the tonnage measurement regulations contained in Annex I to the International Convention on Tonnage Measurement of Ships, 1969 or any successor Convention.

8. 'Harmful Aquatic Organisms and Pathogens' means aquatic organisms or pathogens which, if introduced into the sea including estuaries, or into fresh water courses, may create hazards to the environment, human health, property or resources, impair biological diversity or interfere with other legitimate uses of such areas.

9. 'Organization' means the International Maritime Organization.

10. 'Secretary-General' means the Secretary-General of the Organization.

11. 'Sediments' means matter settled out of Ballast Water within a ship.

12. 'Ship' means a vessel of any type whatsoever operating in the aquatic environment and includes submersibles, floating craft, floating platforms, FSUs and FPSOs.

Article 2 – General Obligations

1. Parties undertake to give full and complete effect to the provisions of this Convention and the Annex thereto in order to prevent, minimize and ultimately eliminate the transfer of Harmful Aquatic Organisms and Pathogens through the control and management of ships' Ballast Water and Sediments.

APPENDIX 6

2. The Annex forms an integral part of this Convention. Unless expressly provided otherwise, a reference to this Convention constitutes at the same time a reference to the Annex.

3. Nothing in this Convention shall be interpreted as preventing a Party from taking, individually or jointly with other Parties, more stringent measures with respect to the prevention, reduction or elimination of the transfer of Harmful Aquatic Organisms and Pathogens through the control and management of ships' Ballast Water and Sediments, consistent with international law.

4. Parties shall endeavour to co-operate for the purpose of effective implementation, compliance and enforcement of this Convention.

5. Parties undertake to encourage the continued development of Ballast Water Management and standards to prevent, minimize and ultimately eliminate the transfer of Harmful Aquatic Organisms and Pathogens through the control and management of ships' Ballast Water and Sediments.

6. Parties taking action pursuant to this Convention shall endeavour not to impair or damage their environment, human health, property or resources, or those of other States.

7. Parties should ensure that Ballast Water Management practices used to comply with this Convention do not cause greater harm than they prevent to their environment, human health, property or resources, or those of other States.

8. Parties shall encourage ships entitled to fly their flag, and to which this Convention applies, to avoid, as far as practicable, the uptake of Ballast Water with potentially Harmful Aquatic Organisms and Pathogens, as well as Sediments that may contain such organisms, including promoting the adequate implementation of recommendations developed by the Organization.

9. Parties shall endeavour to co-operate under the auspices of the Organization to address threats and risks to sensitive, vulnerable or threatened marine ecosystems and biodiversity in areas beyond the limits of national jurisdiction in relation to Ballast Water Management.

Article 3 – Application

1. Except as expressly provided otherwise in this Convention, this Convention shall apply to:
    (a)   ships entitled to fly the flag of a Party; and
    (b)   ships not entitled to fly the flag of a Party but which operate under the authority of a Party.
2. This Convention shall not apply to:
    (a)   ships not designed or constructed to carry Ballast Water;
    (b)   ships of a Party which only operate in waters under the jurisdiction of that Party, unless the Party determines that the discharge of Ballast Water from such ships would impair or damage their environment, human health, property or resources, or those of adjacent or other States;
    (c)   ships of a Party which only operate in waters under the jurisdiction of another Party, subject to the authorization of the latter Party for such exclusion. No Party shall grant such authorization if doing so would impair or damage their environment, human health, property or resources, or those of adjacent or other States. Any Party not granting such authorization shall notify the Administration of the ship concerned that this Convention applies to such ship;
    (d)   ships which only operate in waters under the jurisdiction of one Party and on the high seas, except for ships not granted an authorization pursuant to sub-paragraph (c), unless such Party determines that the discharge of Ballast Water from such ships would impair or damage their environment, human health, property or resources, or those of adjacent of other States;

APPENDIX 6

(e) any warship, naval auxiliary or other ship owned or operated by a State and used, for the time being, only on government non-commercial service. However, each Party shall ensure, by the adoption of appropriate measures not impairing operations or operational capabilities of such ships owned or operated by it, that such ships act in a manner consistent, so far as is reasonable and practicable, with this Convention; and

(f) permanent Ballast Water in sealed tanks on ships, that is not subject to discharge.

3. With respect to ships of non-Parties to this Convention, Parties shall apply the requirements of this Convention as may be necessary to ensure that no more favourable treatment is given to such ships.

Article 4 – Control of the Transfer of Harmful Aquatic Organisms and Pathogens Through Ships' Ballast Water and Sediments

1. Each Party shall require that ships to which this Convention applies and which are entitled to fly its flag or operating under its authority comply with the requirements set forth in this Convention, including the applicable standards and requirements in the Annex, and shall take effective measures to ensure that those ships comply with those requirements.

2. Each Party shall, with due regard to its particular conditions and capabilities, develop national policies, strategies or programmes for Ballast Water Management in its ports and waters under its jurisdiction that accord with, and promote the attainment of the objectives of this Convention.

Article 5 – Sediment Reception Facilities

1. Each Party undertakes to ensure that, in ports and terminals designated by that Party where cleaning or repair of ballast tanks occurs, adequate facilities are provided for the reception of Sediments, taking into account the Guidelines developed by the Organization. Such reception facilities shall operate without causing undue delay to ships and shall provide for the safe disposal of such Sediments that does not impair or damage their environment, human health, property or resources or those of other States.

2. Each Party shall notify the Organization for transmission to the other Parties concerned of all cases where the facilities provided under paragraph 1 are alleged to be inadequate.

Article 6 – Scientific and Technical Research and Monitoring

1. Parties shall endeavour, individually or jointly, to:

(a) promote and facilitate scientific and technical research on Ballast Water Management; and

(b) monitor the effects of Ballast Water Management in waters under their jurisdiction.

Such research and monitoring should include observation, measurement, sampling, evaluation and analysis of the effectiveness and adverse impacts of any technology or methodology as well as any adverse impacts caused by such organisms and pathogens that have been identified to have been transferred through ships' Ballast Water.

2. Each Party shall, to further the objectives of this Convention, promote the availability of relevant information to other Parties who request it on:

(a) scientific and technology programmes and technical measures undertaken with respect to Ballast Water Management; and

(b) the effectiveness of Ballast Water Management deduced from any monitoring and assessment programmes.

334

APPENDIX 6

Article 7 – Survey and certification

1. Each Party shall ensure that ships flying its flag or operating under its authority and subject to survey and certification are so surveyed and certified in accordance with the regulations in the Annex.

2. A Party implementing measures pursuant to Article 2.3 and Section C of the Annex shall not require additional survey and certification of a ship of another Party, nor shall the Administration of the ship be obligated to survey and certify additional measures imposed by another Party. Verification of such additional measures shall be the responsibility of the Party implementing such measures and shall not cause undue delay to the ship.

Article 8 – Violations

1. Any violation of the requirements of this Convention shall be prohibited and sanctions shall be established under the law of the Administration of the ship concerned, wherever the violation occurs. If the Administration is informed of such a violation, it shall investigate the matter and may request the reporting Party to furnish additional evidence of the alleged violation. If the Administration is satisfied that sufficient evidence is available to enable proceedings to be brought in respect of the alleged violation, it shall cause such proceedings to be taken as soon as possible, in accordance with its law. The Administration shall promptly inform the Party that reported the alleged violation, as well as the Organization, of any action taken. If the Administration has not taken any action within 1 year after receiving the information, it shall so inform the Party which reported the alleged violation.

2. Any violation of the requirements of this Convention within the jurisdiction of any Party shall be prohibited and sanctions shall be established under the law of that Party. Whenever such a violation occurs, that Party shall either:
   (a) cause proceedings to be taken in accordance with its law; or
   (b) furnish to the Administration of the ship such information and evidence as may be in its possession that a violation has occurred.

3. The sanctions provided for by the laws of a Party pursuant to this Article shall be adequate in severity to discourage violations of this Convention wherever they occur.

Article 9 – Inspection of Ships

1. A ship to which this Convention applies may, in any port or offshore terminal of another Party, be subject to inspection by officers duly authorized by that Party for the purpose of determining whether the ship is in compliance with this Convention. Except as provided in paragraph 2 of this Article, any such inspection is limited to:
   (a) verifying that there is onboard a valid Certificate, which, if valid shall be accepted; and
   (b) inspection of the Ballast Water record book, and/or
   (c) a sampling of the ship's Ballast Water, carried out in accordance with the guidelines to be developed by the Organization. However, the time required to analyse the samples shall not be used as a basis for unduly delaying the operation, movement or departure of the ship.

2. Where a ship does not carry a valid Certificate or there are clear grounds for believing that:
   (a) the condition of the ship or its equipment does not correspond substantially with the particulars of the Certificate; or
   (b) the master or the crew are not familiar with essential shipboard procedures relating to Ballast Water Management, or have not implemented such procedures; a detailed inspection may be carried out.

335

APPENDIX 6

3. In the circumstances given in paragraph 2 of this Article, the Party carrying out the inspection shall take such steps as will ensure that the ship shall not discharge Ballast Water until it can do so without presenting a threat of harm to the environment, human health, property or resources.

Article 10 – Detection of Violations and Control of Ships

1. Parties shall co-operate in the detection of violations and the enforcement of the provisions of this Convention.

2. If a ship is detected to have violated this Convention, the Party whose flag the ship is entitled to fly, and/or the Party in whose port or offshore terminal the ship is operating, may, in addition to any sanctions described in Article 8 or any action described in Article 9, take steps to warn, detain, or exclude the ship. The Party in whose port or offshore terminal the ship is operating, however, may grant such a ship permission to leave the port or offshore terminal for the purpose of discharging Ballast Water or proceeding to the nearest appropriate repair yard or reception facility available, provided doing so does not present a threat of harm to the environment, human health, property or resources.

3. If the sampling described in Article 9.1(c) leads to a result, or supports information received from another port or offshore terminal, indicating that the ship poses a threat to the environment, human health, property or resources, the Party in whose waters the ship is operating shall prohibit such ship from discharging Ballast Water until the threat is removed.

4. A Party may also inspect a ship when it enters the ports or offshore terminals under its jurisdiction, if a request for an investigation is received from any Party, together with sufficient evidence that a ship is operating or has operated in violation of a provision in this Convention. The report of such investigation shall be sent to the Party requesting it and to the competent authority of the Administration of the ship concerned so that appropriate action may be taken.

Article 11 – Notification of Control Actions

1. If an inspection conducted pursuant to Article 9 or 10 indicates a violation of this Convention, the ship shall be notified. A report shall be forwarded to the Administration, including any evidence of the violation.

2. In the event that any action is taken pursuant to Article 9.3, 10.2 or 10.3, the officer carrying out such action shall forthwith inform, in writing, the Administration of the ship concerned, or if this is not possible, the consul or diplomatic representative of the ship concerned, of all the circumstances in which the action was deemed necessary. In addition, the recognized organization responsible for the issue of certificates shall be notified.

3. The port State authority concerned shall, in addition to parties mentioned in paragraph 2, notify the next port of call of all relevant information about the violation, if it is unable to take action as specified in Article 9.3, 10.2 or 10.3 or if the ship has been allowed to proceed to the next port of call.

Article 12 – Undue Delay to Ships

1. All possible efforts shall be made to avoid a ship being unduly detained or delayed under Article 7.2, 8, 9 or 10.

2. When a ship is unduly detained or delayed under Article 7.2, 8, 9 or 10, it shall be entitled to compensation for any loss or damage suffered.

APPENDIX 6

Article 13 – Technical Assistance, Co-operation and Regional Co-operation

1. Parties undertake, directly or through the Organization and other international bodies, as appropriate, in respect of the control and management of ships' Ballast Water and Sediments, to provide support for those Parties which request technical assistance:
    (a)   to train personnel;
    (b)   to ensure the availability of relevant technology, equipment and facilities;
    (c)   to initiate joint research and development programmes; and
    (d)   to undertake other action aimed at the effective implementation of this Convention and of guidance developed by the Organization related thereto.

2. Parties undertake to co-operate actively, subject to their national laws, regulations and policies, in the transfer of technology in respect of the control and management of ships' Ballast Water and Sediments.

3. In order to further the objectives of this Convention, Parties with common interests to protect the environment, human health, property and resources in a given geographical area, in particular, those Parties bordering enclosed and semi-enclosed seas, shall endeavour, taking into account characteristic regional features, to enhance regional co-operation, including through the conclusion of regional agreements consistent with this Convention. Parties shall seek to co-operate with the Parties to regional agreements to develop harmonized procedures.

Article 14 – Communication of information

1. Each Party shall report to the Organization and, where appropriate, make available to other Parties the following information:
    (a)   any requirements and procedures relating to Ballast Water Management, including its laws, regulations, and guidelines for implementation of this Convention;
    (b)   the availability and location of any reception facilities for the environmentally safe disposal of Ballast Water and Sediments; and
    (c)   any requirements for information from a ship which is unable to comply with the provisions of this Convention for reasons specified in regulations A-3 and B-4 of the Annex.

2. The Organization shall notify Parties of the receipt of any communications under the present Article and circulate to all Parties any information communicated to it under sub-paragraphs 1(b) and (c) of this Article.

Article 15 – Dispute Settlement

Parties shall settle any dispute between them concerning the interpretation or application of this Convention by negotiation, enquiry, mediation, conciliation, arbitration, judicial settlement, resort to regional agencies or arrangements or other peaceful means of their own choice.

Article 16 – Relationship to International Law and Other Agreements

Nothing in this Convention shall prejudice the rights and obligations of any State under customary international law as reflected in the United Nations Convention on the Law of the Sea.

APPENDIX 6

Article 17 – Signature, Ratification, Acceptance, Approval and Accession

1. This Convention shall be open for signature by any State at the Headquarters of the Organization from 1 June 2004 to 31 May 2005 and shall thereafter remain open for accession by any State.

2. States may become Parties to the Convention by:
   (a) signature not subject to ratification, acceptance, or approval; or
   (b) signature subject to ratification, acceptance, or approval, followed by ratification, acceptance or approval; or
   (c) accession.

3. Ratification, acceptance, approval or accession shall be effected by the deposit of an instrument to that effect with the Secretary-General.

4. If a State comprises two or more territorial units in which different systems of law are applicable in relation to matters dealt with in this Convention, it may at the time of signature, ratification, acceptance, approval, or accession declare that this Convention shall extend to all its territorial units or only to one or more of them and may modify this declaration by submitting another declaration at any time.

5. Any such declaration shall be notified to the Depositary in writing and shall state expressly the territorial unit or units to which this Convention applies.

Article 18 – Entry into Force

1. This Convention shall enter into force twelve months after the date on which not less than thirty States, the combined merchant fleets of which constitute not less than thirty-five percent of the gross tonnage of the world's merchant shipping, have either signed it without reservation as to ratification, acceptance or approval, or have deposited the requisite instrument of ratification, acceptance, approval or accession in accordance with Article 17.

2. For States which have deposited an instrument of ratification, acceptance, approval or accession in respect of this Convention after the requirements for entry into force thereof have been met, but prior to the date of entry in force, the ratification, acceptance, approval or accession shall take effect on the date of entry into force of this Convention or three months after the date of deposit of instrument, whichever is the later date.

3. Any instrument of ratification, acceptance, approval or accession deposited after the date on which this Convention enters into force shall take effect three months after the date of deposit.

4. After the date on which an amendment to this Convention is deemed to have been accepted under Article 19, any instrument of ratification, acceptance, approval or accession deposited shall apply to this Convention as amended.

Article 19 – Amendments

1. This Convention may be amended by either of the procedures specified in the following paragraphs.

2. Amendments after consideration within the Organization:
   (a) Any Party may propose an amendment to this Convention. A proposed amendment shall be submitted to the Secretary-General, who shall then circulate it to the Parties and Members of the Organization at least six months prior to its consideration.
   (b) An amendment proposed and circulated as above shall be referred to the Committee for consideration. Parties, whether or not Members of the Organization, shall be

APPENDIX 6

entitled to participate in the proceedings of the Committee for consideration and adoption of the amendment.

(c) Amendments shall be adopted by a two-thirds majority of the Parties present and voting in the Committee, on condition that at least one-third of the Parties shall be present at the time of voting.

(d) Amendments adopted in accordance with subparagraph (c) shall be communicated by the Secretary-General to the Parties for acceptance.

(e) An amendment shall be deemed to have been accepted in the following circumstances:

    (i) An amendment to an article of this Convention shall be deemed to have been accepted on the date on which two-thirds of the Parties have notified the Secretary-General of their acceptance of it.

    (ii) An amendment to the Annex shall be deemed to have been accepted at the end of twelve months after the date of adoption or such other date as determined by the Committee. However, if by that date more than one-third of the Parties notify the Secretary-General that they object to the amendment, it shall be deemed not to have been accepted.

(f) An amendment shall enter into force under the following conditions:

    (i) An amendment to an article of this Convention shall enter into force for those Parties that have declared that they have accepted it six months after the date on which it is deemed to have been accepted in accordance with subparagraph (e)(i).

    (ii) An amendment to the Annex shall enter into force with respect to all Parties six months after the date on which it is deemed to have been accepted, except for any Party that has:

        (1) notified its objection to the amendment in accordance with subparagraph (e)(ii) and that has not withdrawn such objection; or

        (2) notified the Secretary-General, prior to the entry into force of such amendment, that the amendment shall enter into force for it only after a subsequent notification of its acceptance.

(g) (i) A Party that has notified an objection under subparagraph (f)(ii)(1) may subsequently notify the Secretary-General that it accepts the amendment. Such amendment shall enter into force for such Party six months after the date of its notification of acceptance, or the date on which the amendment enters into force, whichever is the later date.

    (ii) If a Party that has made a notification referred to in subparagraph (f)(ii)(2) notifies the Secretary-General of its acceptance with respect to an amendment, such amendment shall enter into force for such Party six months after the date of its notification of acceptance, or the date on which the amendment enters into force, whichever is the later date.

3. Amendment by a Conference:

(a) Upon the request of a Party concurred in by at least one-third of the Parties, the Organization shall convene a Conference of Parties to consider amendments to this Convention.

(b) An amendment adopted by such a Conference by a two-thirds majority of the Parties present and voting shall be communicated by the Secretary-General to all Parties for acceptance.

(c) Unless the Conference decides otherwise, the amendment shall be deemed to have been accepted and shall enter into force in accordance with the procedures specified in paragraphs 2(e) and (f) respectively.

APPENDIX 6

4. Any Party that has declined to accept an amendment to the Annex shall be treated as a non-Party only for the purpose of application of that amendment.

5. Any notification under this Article shall be made in writing to the Secretary-General.

6. The Secretary-General shall inform the Parties and Members of the Organization of:

(a) any amendment that enters into force and the date of its entry into force generally and for each Party; and

(b) any notification made under this Article.

Article 20 – Denunciation

1. This Convention may be denounced by any Party at any time after the expiry of two years from the date on which this Convention enters into force for that Party.

2. Denunciation shall be effected by written notification to the Depositary, to take effect one year after receipt or such longer period as may be specified in that notification.

Article 21 – Depositary

1. This Convention shall be deposited with the Secretary-General, who shall transmit certified copies of this Convention to all States which have signed this Convention or acceded thereto.

2. In addition to the functions specified elsewhere in this Convention, the Secretary-General shall:

(a) inform all States that have signed this Convention, or acceded thereto, of:

(i) each new signature or deposit of an instrument of ratification, acceptance, approval or accession, together with the date thereof;

(ii) the date of entry into force of this Convention; and

(iii) the deposit of any instrument of denunciation from the Convention, together with the date on which it was received and the date on which the denunciation takes effect; and

(b) as soon as this Convention enters into force, transmit the text thereof to the Secretariat of the United Nations for registration and publication in accordance with Article 102 of the Charter of the United Nations.

Article 22 – Languages

This Convention is established in a single original in the Arabic, Chinese, English, French, Russian and Spanish languages, each text being equally authentic.

DONE AT LONDON this thirteenth day of February, two thousand and four.

IN WITNESS WHEREOF the undersigned, being duly authorised by their respective Governments for that purpose, have signed this Convention.

★ ★ ★

APPENDIX 6

ANNEX

Regulations for the control and

management of ships' ballast water and sediments

Section A – General provisions[3]

Regulation A-1 – Definitions

For the purposes of this Annex:

1 'Anniversary date' means the day and the month of each year corresponding to the date of expiry of the Certificate.

2 'Ballast Water Capacity' means the total volumetric capacity of any tanks, spaces or compartments on a ship used for carrying, loading or discharging Ballast Water, including any multi-use tank, space or compartment designed to allow carriage of Ballast Water.

3 'Company' means the owner of the ship or any other organization or person such as the manager, or the bareboat charterer, who has assumed the responsibility for operation of the ship from the owner of the ship and who on assuming such responsibility has agreed to take over all the duties and responsibilities imposed by the International Safety Management Code[1].

4 'Constructed' in respect of a ship means a stage of construction where:

   .1   the keel is laid; or

   .2   construction identifiable with the specific ship begins;

   .3   assembly of the ship has commenced comprising at least 50 tonnes or 1 percent of the estimated mass of all structural material, whichever is less; or

   .4   the ship undergoes a major conversion.

5 'Major conversion' means a conversion of a ship:

   .1   which changes its ballast water carrying capacity by 15 percent or greater, or

   .2   which changes the ship type, or

   .3   which, in the opinion of the Administration, is projected to prolong its life by ten years or more, or

   .4   which results in modifications to its ballast water system other than component replacement-in-kind. Conversion of a ship to meet the provisions of regulation D-1 shall not be deemed to constitute a major conversion for the purpose of this Annex.

6 'From the nearest land' means from the baseline from which the territorial sea of the territory in question is established in accordance with international law except that, for the purposes of the Convention, 'from the nearest land' off the north-eastern coast of Australia shall mean from a line drawn from a point on the coast of Australia in

latitude 11°00′ S, longitude 142°08′ E

to a point in latitude 10°35′ S, longitude 141°55′ E

thence to a point latitude 10°00′ S, longitude 142°00′ E

thence to a point latitude 9°10′ S, longitude 143°52′ E

thence to a point latitude 9°00′ S, longitude 144°30′ E

thence to a point latitude 10°41′ S, longitude 145°00′ E

thence to a point latitude 13°00′ S, longitude 145°00′ E

thence to a point latitude 15°00′ S, longitude 146°00′ E

thence to a point latitude 17°30′ S, longitude 147°00′ E

thence to a point latitude 21°00′ S, longitude 152°55′ E

thence to a point latitude 24°30′ S, longitude 154°00′ E

thence to a point on the coast of Australia in latitude 24°42′ S, longitude 153°15′ E.

---

1 Refer to the ISM Code adopted by the Organization by resolution A.741 (18), as amended.

APPENDIX 6

7 'Active Substance' means a substance or organism, including a virus or a fungus, that has a general or specific action on or against Harmful Aquatic Organisms and Pathogens.

Regulation A-2 – General Applicability

Except where expressly provided otherwise, the discharge of Ballast Water shall only be conducted through Ballast Water Management in accordance with the provisions of this Annex.

Regulation A-3 – Exceptions

The requirements of regulation B-3, or any measures adopted by a Party pursuant to Article 2.3 and Section C, shall not apply to:

1 the uptake or discharge of Ballast Water and Sediments necessary for the purpose of ensuring the safety of a ship in emergency situations or saving life at sea; or

2 the accidental discharge or ingress of Ballast Water and Sediments resulting from damage to a ship or its equipment:

    .1   provided that all reasonable precautions have been taken before and after the occurrence of the damage or discovery of the damage or discharge for the purpose of preventing or minimizing the discharge; and

    .2   unless the owner, Company or officer in charge wilfully or recklessly caused damage; or

3 the uptake and discharge of Ballast Water and Sediments when being used for the purpose of avoiding or minimizing pollution incidents from the ship; or

4 the uptake and subsequent discharge on the high seas of the same Ballast Water and Sediments; or

5 the discharge of Ballast Water and Sediments from a ship at the same location where the whole of that Ballast Water and those Sediments originated and provided that no mixing with unmanaged Ballast Water and Sediments from other areas has occurred. If mixing has occurred, the Ballast Water taken from other areas is subject to Ballast Water Management in accordance with this Annex.

Regulation A-4 – Exemptions

1 A Party or Parties, in waters under their jurisdiction, may grant exemptions to any requirements to apply regulations B-3 or C-1, in addition to those exemptions contained elsewhere in this Convention, but only when they are:

    .1   granted to a ship or ships on a voyage or voyages between specified ports or locations; or to a ship which operates exclusively between specified ports or locations;

    .2   effective for a period of no more than five years subject to intermediate review;

    .3   granted to ships that do not mix Ballast Water or Sediments other than between the ports or locations specified in paragraph 1.1; and

    .4   granted based on the Guidelines on risk assessment developed by the Organization.

2 Exemptions granted pursuant to paragraph 1 shall not be effective until after communication to the Organization and circulation of relevant information to the Parties.

3 Any exemptions granted under this regulation shall not impair or damage the environment, human health, property or resources of adjacent or other States. Any State that the Party determines may be adversely affected shall be consulted, with a view to resolving any identified concerns.

4 Any exemptions granted under this regulation shall be recorded in the Ballast Water record book.

APPENDIX 6

Regulation A-5 – Equivalent compliance

Equivalent compliance with this Annex for pleasure craft used solely for recreation or competition or craft used primarily for search and rescue, less than 50 metres in length overall, and with a maximum Ballast Water capacity of 8 cubic metres, shall be determined by the Administration taking into account Guidelines developed by the Organization.

Section B – Management and control requirements for ships

Regulation B-1 – Ballast water management plan

Each ship shall have on board and implement a Ballast Water Management plan. Such a plan shall be approved by the Administration taking into account Guidelines developed by the Organization. The Ballast Water Management plan shall be specific to each ship and shall at least:

1 detail safety procedures for the ship and the crew associated with Ballast Water Management as required by this Convention;

2 provide a detailed description of the actions to be taken to implement the Ballast Water Management requirements and supplemental Ballast Water Management practices as set forth in this Convention;

3 detail the procedures for the disposal of Sediments:

.1 at sea; and

.2 to shore;

4 include the procedures for coordinating shipboard Ballast Water Management that involves discharge to the sea with the authorities of the State into whose waters such discharge will take place;

5 designate the officer on board in charge of ensuring that the plan is properly implemented;

6 contain the reporting requirements for ships provided for under this Convention; and

7 be written in the working language of the ship. If the language used is not English, French or Spanish, a translation into one of these languages shall be included.

Regulation B-2 – Ballast water record book

1 Each ship shall have on board a Ballast Water record book that may be an electronic record system, or that may be integrated into another record book or system and, which shall at least contain the information specified in Appendix II.

2 Ballast Water record book entries shall be maintained on board the ship for a minimum period of two years after the last entry has been made and thereafter in the Company's control for a minimum period of three years.

3 In the event of the discharge of Ballast Water pursuant to regulations A-3, A-4 or B-3.6 or in the event of other accidental or exceptional discharge of Ballast Water not otherwise exempted by this Convention, an entry shall be made in the Ballast Water record book describing the circumstances of, and the reason for, the discharge.

4 The Ballast Water record book shall be kept readily available for inspection at all reasonable times and, in the case of an unmanned ship under tow, may be kept on the towing ship.

5 Each operation concerning Ballast Water shall be fully recorded without delay in the Ballast Water record book. Each entry shall be signed by the officer in charge of the operation concerned and each completed page shall be signed by the master. The entries in the Ballast Water record book shall be in a working language of the ship. If that language is not English, French or Spanish the entries shall contain a translation into one of those languages. When

343

APPENDIX 6

entries in an official national language of the State whose flag the ship is entitled to fly are also used, these shall prevail in case of a dispute or discrepancy.

6 Officers duly authorized by a Party may inspect the Ballast Water record book on board any ship to which this regulation applies while the ship is in its port or offshore terminal, and may make a copy of any entry, and require the master to certify that the copy is a true copy. Any copy so certified shall be admissible in any judicial proceeding as evidence of the facts stated in the entry. The inspection of a Ballast Water record book and the taking of a certified copy shall be performed as expeditiously as possible without causing the ship to be unduly delayed.

Regulation B-3 – Ballast water management for ships

1 A ship constructed before 2009:
- .1 with a Ballast Water Capacity of between 1,500 and 5,000 cubic metres, inclusive, shall conduct Ballast Water Management that at least meets the standard described in regulation D-1 or regulation D-2 until 2014, after which time it shall at least meet the standard described in regulation D-2;
- .2 with a Ballast Water Capacity of less than 1,500 or greater than 5,000 cubic metres shall conduct Ballast Water Management that at least meets the standard described in regulation D-1 or regulation D-2 until 2016, after which time it shall at least meet the standard described in regulation D-2.

2 A ship to which paragraph 1 applies shall comply with paragraph 1 not later than the first intermediate or renewal survey, whichever occurs first, after the anniversary date of delivery of the ship in the year of compliance with the standard applicable to the ship.

3 A ship constructed in or after 2009 with a Ballast Water Capacity of less than 5,000 cubic metres shall conduct Ballast Water Management that at least meets the standard described in regulation D-2.

4 A ship constructed in or after 2009, but before 2012, with a Ballast Water Capacity of 5,000 cubic metres or more shall conduct Ballast Water Management in accordance with paragraph 1.2.

5 A ship constructed in or after 2012 with a Ballast Water Capacity of 5000 cubic metres or more shall conduct Ballast Water Management that at least meets the standard described in regulation D-2.

6 The requirements of this regulation do not apply to ships that discharge Ballast Water to a reception facility designed taking into account the Guidelines developed by the Organization for such facilities.

7 Other methods of Ballast Water Management may also be accepted as alternatives to the requirements described in paragraphs 1 to 5, provided that such methods ensure at least the same level of protection to the environment, human health, property or resources, and are approved in principle by the Committee.

Regulation B-4 – Ballast water exchange

1 A ship conducting Ballast Water exchange to meet the standard in regulation D-1 shall:
- .1 whenever possible, conduct such Ballast Water exchange at least 200 nautical miles from the nearest land and in water at least 200 metres in depth, taking into account the Guidelines developed by the Organization;
- .2 in cases where the ship is unable to conduct Ballast Water exchange in accordance with paragraph 1.1, such Ballast Water exchange shall be conducted taking into account the Guidelines described in paragraph 1.1 and as far from the nearest land

APPENDIX 6

as possible, and in all cases at least 50 nautical miles from the nearest land and in water at least 200 metres in depth.

2 In sea areas where the distance from the nearest land or the depth does not meet the parameters described in paragraph 1.1 or 1.2, the port State may designate areas, in consultation with adjacent or other States, as appropriate, where a ship may conduct Ballast Water exchange, taking into account the Guidelines described in paragraph 1.1.

3 A ship shall not be required to deviate from its intended voyage, or delay the voyage, in order to comply with any particular requirement of paragraph 1.

4 A ship conducting Ballast Water exchange shall not be required to comply with paragraphs 1 or 2, as appropriate, if the master reasonably decides that such exchange would threaten the safety or stability of the ship, its crew, or its passengers because of adverse weather, ship design or stress, equipment failure, or any other extraordinary condition.

5 When a ship is required to conduct Ballast Water exchange and does not do so in accordance with this regulation, the reasons shall be entered in the Ballast Water record book.

Regulation B-5 – Sediment management for ships

1 All ships shall remove and dispose of Sediments from spaces designated to carry Ballast Water in accordance with the provisions of the ship's Ballast Water Management plan.

2 Ships described in regulation B-3.3 to B-3.5 should, without compromising safety or operational efficiency, be designed and constructed with a view to minimize the uptake and undesirable entrapment of Sediments, facilitate removal of Sediments, and provide safe access to allow for Sediment removal and sampling, taking into account guidelines developed by the Organization. Ships described in regulation B-3.1 should, to the extent practicable, comply with this paragraph.

Regulation B-6 – Duties of officers and crew

Officers and crew shall be familiar with their duties in the implementation of Ballast Water Management particular to the ship on which they serve and shall, appropriate to their duties, be familiar with the ship's Ballast Water Management plan.

Section C – Special requirements in certain areas

Regulation C-1 – Additional measures

1 If a Party, individually or jointly with other Parties, determines that measures in addition to those in Section B are necessary to prevent, reduce, or eliminate the transfer of Harmful Aquatic Organisms and Pathogens through ships' Ballast Water and Sediments, such Party or Parties may, consistent with international law, require ships to meet a specified standard or requirement.

2 Prior to establishing standards or requirements under paragraph 1, a Party or Parties should consult with adjacent or other States that may be affected by such standards or requirements.

3 A Party or Parties intending to introduce additional measures in accordance with paragraph 1 shall:

    .1   take into account the Guidelines developed by the Organization.

    .2   communicate their intention to establish additional measure(s) to the Organization at least 6 months, except in emergency or epidemic situations, prior to the projected date of implementation of the measure(s). Such communication shall include:

APPENDIX 6

   .1   the precise co-ordinates where additional measure(s) is/are applicable;

   .2   the need and reasoning for the application of the additional measure(s), including, whenever possible, benefits;

   .3   a description of the additional measure(s); and

   .4   any arrangements that may be provided to facilitate ships' compliance with the additional measure(s).

  .3 To the extent required by customary international law as reflected in the United Nations Convention on the Law of the Sea, as appropriate, obtain the approval of the Organization.

4 A Party or Parties, in introducing such additional measures, shall endeavour to make available all appropriate services, which may include but are not limited to notification to mariners of areas, available and alternative routes or ports, as far as practicable, in order to ease the burden on the ship.

5 Any additional measures adopted by a Party or Parties shall not compromise the safety and security of the ship and in any circumstances not conflict with any other convention with which the ship must comply.

6 A Party or Parties introducing additional measures may waive these measures for a period of time or in specific circumstances as they deem fit.

Regulation C-2 – Warnings concerning ballast water

Uptake in certain areas and related flag state measures

1 A Party shall endeavour to notify mariners of areas under their jurisdiction where ships should not uptake Ballast Water due to known conditions. The Party shall include in such notices the precise coordinates of the area or areas, and, where possible, the location of any alternative area or areas for the uptake of Ballast Water. Warnings may be issued for areas:

   .1   known to contain outbreaks, infestations, or populations of Harmful Aquatic Organisms and Pathogens (e.g., toxic algal blooms) which are likely to be of relevance to Ballast Water uptake or discharge;

   .2   near sewage outfalls; or

   .3   where tidal flushing is poor or times during which a tidal stream is known to be more turbid.

2 In addition to notifying mariners of areas in accordance with the provisions of paragraph 1, a Party shall notify the Organization and any potentially affected coastal States of any areas identified in paragraph 1 and the time period such warning is likely to be in effect. The notice to the Organization and any potentially affected coastal States shall include the precise coordinates of the area or areas, and, where possible, the location of any alternative area or areas for the uptake of Ballast Water. The notice shall include advice to ships needing to uptake Ballast Water in the area, describing arrangements made for alternative supplies. The Party shall also notify mariners, the Organization, and any potentially affected coastal States when a given warning is no longer applicable.

Regulation C-3 – Communication of Information

The Organization shall make available, through any appropriate means, information communicated to it under regulations C-1 and C-2.

APPENDIX 6

Section D – Standards for ballast water management

Regulation D-1 – Ballast water exchange standard

1 Ships performing Ballast Water exchange in accordance with this regulation shall do so with an efficiency of at least 95 percent volumetric exchange of Ballast Water.

2 For ships exchanging Ballast Water by the pumping-through method, pumping through three times the volume of each Ballast Water tank shall be considered to meet the standard described in paragraph 1. Pumping through less than three times the volume may be accepted provided the ship can demonstrate that at least 95 percent volumetric exchange is met.

Regulation D-2 – Ballast water performance standard

1 Ships conducting Ballast Water Management in accordance with this regulation shall discharge less than 10 viable organisms per cubic metre greater than or equal to 50 micrometres in minimum dimension and less than 10 viable organisms per millilitre less than 50 micrometres in minimum dimension and greater than or equal to 10 micrometres in minimum dimension; and discharge of the indicator microbes shall not exceed the specified concentrations described in paragraph 2.

2 Indicator microbes, as a human health standard, shall include:

.1 Toxicogenic Vibrio cholerae (O1 and O139) with less than 1 colony forming unit (cfu) per 100 millilitres or less than 1 cfu per 1 gram (wet weight) zooplankton samples;

.2 Escherichia coli less than 250 cfu per 100 millilitres;

.3 Intestinal Enterococci less than 100 cfu per 100 milliliters.

Regulation D-3 – Approval requirements for ballast water management systems

1 Except as specified in paragraph 2, Ballast Water Management systems used to comply with this Convention must be approved by the Administration taking into account Guidelines developed by the Organization.

2 Ballast Water Management systems which make use of Active Substances or preparations containing one or more Active Substances to comply with this Convention shall be approved by the Organization, based on a procedure developed by the Organization. This procedure shall describe the approval and withdrawal of approval of Active Substances and their proposed manner of application. At withdrawal of approval, the use of the relevant Active Substance or Substances shall be prohibited within 1 year after the date of such withdrawal.

3 Ballast Water Management systems used to comply with this Convention must be safe in terms of the ship, its equipment and the crew.

Regulation D-4 – Prototype ballast water treatment technologies

1 For any ship that, prior to the date that the standard in regulation D-2 would otherwise become effective for it, participates in a programme approved by the Administration to test and evaluate promising Ballast Water treatment technologies, the standard in regulation D-2 shall not apply to that ship until five years from the date on which the ship would otherwise be required to comply with such standard.

2 For any ship that, after the date on which the standard in regulation D-2 has become effective for it, participates in a programme approved by the Administration, taking into account Guidelines developed by the Organization, to test and evaluate promising Ballast

347

APPENDIX 6

Water technologies with the potential to result in treatment technologies achieving a standard higher than that in regulation D-2, the standard in regulation D-2 shall cease to apply to that ship for five years from the date of installation of such technology.

3 In establishing and carrying out any programme to test and evaluate promising Ballast Water technologies, Parties shall:

.1 take into account Guidelines developed by the Organization, and

.2 allow participation only by the minimum number of ships necessary to effectively test such technologies.

4 Throughout the test and evaluation period, the treatment system must be operated consistently and as designed.

Regulation D-5 Review of standards by the organization

1 At a meeting of the Committee held no later than three years before the earliest effective date of the standard set forth in regulation D-2, the Committee shall undertake a review which includes a determination of whether appropriate technologies are available to achieve the standard, an assessment of the criteria in paragraph 2, and an assessment of the socio-economic effect(s) specifically in relation to the developmental needs of developing countries, particularly small island developing States. The Committee shall also undertake periodic reviews, as appropriate, to examine the applicable requirements for ships described in regulation B-3.1 as well as any other aspect of Ballast Water Management addressed in this Annex, including any Guidelines developed by the Organization.

2 Such reviews of appropriate technologies shall also take into account:

.1 safety considerations relating to the ship and the crew;

.2 environmental acceptability, i.e., not causing more or greater environmental impacts than they solve;

.3 practicability, i.e., compatibility with ship design and operations;

.4 cost effectiveness, i.e., economics; and

.5 biological effectiveness in terms of removing, or otherwise rendering not viable, Harmful Aquatic Organisms and Pathogens in Ballast Water.

3 The Committee may form a group or groups to conduct the review(s) described in paragraph 1. The Committee shall determine the composition, terms of reference and specific issues to be addressed by any such group formed. Such groups may develop and recommend proposals for amendment of this Annex for consideration by the Parties. Only Parties may participate in the formulation of recommendations and amendment decisions taken by the Committee.

4 If, based on the reviews described in this regulation, the Parties decide to adopt amendments to this Annex, such amendments shall be adopted and enter into force in accordance with the procedures contained in Article 19 of this Convention.

Section E – Survey and certification requirements for ballast water management

Regulation E-1 – Surveys

1 Ships of 400 gross tonnage and above to which this Convention applies, excluding floating platforms, FSUs and FPSOs, shall be subject to surveys specified below:

.1 An initial survey before the ship is put in service or before the Certificate required under regulation E-2 or E-3 is issued for the first time. This survey shall verify that the Ballast Water Management plan required by regulation B-1 and any associated

348

APPENDIX 6

structure, equipment, systems, fitting, arrangements and material or processes comply fully with the requirements of this Convention.

.2 A renewal survey at intervals specified by the Administration, but not exceeding five years, except where regulation E-5.2, E-5.5, E-5.6, or E-5.7 is applicable. This survey shall verify that the Ballast Water Management plan required by regulation B-1 and any associated structure, equipment, systems, fitting, arrangements and material or processes comply fully with the applicable requirements of this Convention.

.3 An intermediate survey within three months before or after the second Anniversary date or within three months before or after the third Anniversary date of the Certificate, which shall take the place of one of the annual surveys specified in paragraph 1.4. The intermediate surveys shall ensure that the equipment, associated systems and processes for Ballast Water Management fully comply with the applicable requirements of this Annex and are in good working order. Such intermediate surveys shall be endorsed on the Certificate issued under regulation E-2 or E-3.

.4 An annual survey within three months before or after each Anniversary date, including a general inspection of the structure, any equipment, systems, fittings, arrangements and material or processes associated with the Ballast Water Management plan required by regulation B-1 to ensure that they have been maintained in accordance with paragraph 9 and remain satisfactory for the service for which the ship is intended. Such annual surveys shall be endorsed on the Certificate issued under regulation E-2 or E-3.

.5 An additional survey either general or partial, according to the circumstances, shall be made after a change, replacement, or significant repair of the structure, equipment, systems, fittings, arrangements and material necessary to achieve full compliance with this Convention. The survey shall be such as to ensure that any such change, replacement, or significant repair has been effectively made, so that the ship complies with the requirements of this Convention. Such surveys shall be endorsed on the Certificate issued under regulation E-2 or E-3.

2 The Administration shall establish appropriate measures for ships that are not subject to the provisions of paragraph 1 in order to ensure that the applicable provisions of this Convention are complied with.

3 Surveys of ships for the purpose of enforcement of the provisions of this Convention shall be carried out by officers of the Administration. The Administration may, however, entrust the surveys either to surveyors nominated for the purpose or to organizations recognized by it.

4. An Administration nominating surveyors or recognizing organizations to conduct surveys, as described in paragraph 3 shall, as a minimum, empower such nominated surveyors or recognized organizations to:

.1 require a ship that they survey to comply with the provisions of this Convention; and

.2 carry out surveys and inspections if requested by the appropriate authorities of a port State that is a Party.

5 The Administration shall notify the Organization of the specific responsibilities and conditions of the authority delegated to the nominated surveyors or recognized organizations, for circulation to Parties for the information of their officers.

6 When the Administration, a nominated surveyor, or a recognized organization determines that the ship's Ballast Water Management does not conform to the particulars of the Certificate required under regulation E-2 or E-3 or is such that the ship is not fit to proceed to sea without presenting a threat of harm to the environment, human health, property or

APPENDIX 6

resources such surveyor or organization shall immediately ensure that corrective action is taken to bring the ship into compliance. A surveyor or organization shall be notified immediately, and it shall ensure that the Certificate is not issued or is withdrawn as appropriate. If the ship is in the port of another Party, the appropriate authorities of the port State shall be notified immediately. When an officer of the Administration, a nominated surveyor, or a recognized organization has notified the appropriate authorities of the port State, the Government of the port State concerned shall give such officer, surveyor or organization any necessary assistance to carry out their obligations under this regulation, including any action described in Article 9.

7 Whenever an accident occurs to a ship or a defect is discovered which substantially affects the ability of the ship to conduct Ballast Water Management in accordance with this Convention, the owner, operator or other person in charge of the ship shall report at the earliest opportunity to the Administration, the recognized organization or the nominated surveyor responsible for issuing the relevant Certificate, who shall cause investigations to be initiated to determine whether a survey as required by paragraph 1 is necessary. If the ship is in a port of another Party, the owner, operator or other person in charge shall also report immediately to the appropriate authorities of the port State and the nominated surveyor or recognized organization shall ascertain that such report has been made.

8 In every case, the Administration concerned shall fully guarantee the completeness and efficiency of the survey and shall undertake to ensure the necessary arrangements to satisfy this obligation.

9 The condition of the ship and its equipment, systems and processes shall be maintained to conform with the provisions of this Convention to ensure that the ship in all respects will remain fit to proceed to sea without presenting a threat of harm to the environment, human health, property or resources.

10 After any survey of the ship under paragraph 1 has been completed, no change shall be made in the structure, any equipment, fittings, arrangements or material associated with the Ballast Water Management plan required by regulation B-1 and covered by the survey without the sanction of the Administration, except the direct replacement of such equipment or fittings.

Regulation E-2 – Issuance or endorsement of a certificate

1 The Administration shall ensure that a ship to which regulation E-1 applies is issued a Certificate after successful completion of a survey conducted in accordance with regulation E-1. A Certificate issued under the authority of a Party shall be accepted by the other Parties and regarded for all purposes covered by this Convention as having the same validity as a Certificate issued by them.

2 Certificates shall be issued or endorsed either by the Administration or by any person or organization duly authorized by it. In every case, the Administration assumes full responsibility for the Certificate.

Regulation E-3 – Issuance or endorsement of a certificate by another party

1 At the request of the Administration, another Party may cause a ship to be surveyed and, if satisfied that the provisions of this Convention are complied with, shall issue or authorize the issuance of a Certificate to the ship, and where appropriate, endorse or authorize the endorsement of that Certificate on the ship, in accordance with this Annex.

2 A copy of the Certificate and a copy of the survey report shall be transmitted as soon as possible to the requesting Administration.

3 A Certificate so issued shall contain a statement to the effect that it has been issued at the

350

APPENDIX 6

request of the Administration and it shall have the same force and receive the same recognition as a Certificate issued by the Administration.

4 No Certificate shall be issued to a ship entitled to fly the flag of a State which is not a Party.

Regulation E-4 – Form of the certificate

The Certificate shall be drawn up in the official language of the issuing Party, in the form set forth in Appendix I. If the language used is neither English, French nor Spanish, the text shall include a translation into one of these languages.

Regulation E-5 – Duration and validity of the certificate

1 A Certificate shall be issued for a period specified by the Administration that shall not exceed five years.

2 For renewal surveys:

.1 Notwithstanding the requirements of paragraph 1, when the renewal survey is completed within three months before the expiry date of the existing Certificate, the new Certificate shall be valid from the date of completion of the renewal survey to a date not exceeding five years from the date of expiry of the existing Certificate.

.2 When the renewal survey is completed after the expiry date of the existing Certificate, the new Certificate shall be valid from the date of completion of the renewal survey to a date not exceeding five years from the date of expiry of the existing Certificate.

.3 When the renewal survey is completed more than three months before the expiry date of the existing Certificate, the new Certificate shall be valid from the date of completion of the renewal survey to a date not exceeding five years from the date of completion of the renewal survey.

3 If a Certificate is issued for a period of less than five years, the Administration may extend the validity of the Certificate beyond the expiry date to the maximum period specified in paragraph 1, provided that the surveys referred to in regulation E-1.1.3 applicable when a Certificate is issued for a period of five years are carried out as appropriate.

4 If a renewal survey has been completed and a new Certificate cannot be issued or placed on board the ship before the expiry date of the existing Certificate, the person or organization authorized by the Administration may endorse the existing Certificate and such a Certificate shall be accepted as valid for a further period which shall not exceed five months from the expiry date.

5 If a ship at the time when the Certificate expires is not in a port in which it is to be surveyed, the Administration may extend the period of validity of the Certificate but this extension shall be granted only for the purpose of allowing the ship to complete its voyage to the port in which it is to be surveyed, and then only in cases where it appears proper and reasonable to do so. No Certificate shall be extended for a period longer than three months, and a ship to which such extension is granted shall not, on its arrival in the port in which it is to be surveyed, be entitled by virtue of such extension to leave that port without having a new Certificate. When the renewal survey is completed, the new Certificate shall be valid to a date not exceeding five years from the date of expiry of the existing Certificate before the extension was granted.

6 A Certificate issued to a ship engaged on short voyages which has not been extended under the foregoing provisions of this regulation may be extended by the Administration for a period of grace of up to one month from the date of expiry stated on it. When the renewal

351

APPENDIX 6

survey is completed, the new Certificate shall be valid to a date not exceeding five years from the date of expiry of the existing Certificate before the extension was granted.

7 In special circumstances, as determined by the Administration, a new Certificate need not be dated from the date of expiry of the existing Certificate as required by paragraph 2.2, 5 or 6 of this regulation. In these special circumstances, the new Certificate shall be valid to a date not exceeding five years from the date of completion of the renewal survey.

8 If an annual survey is completed before the period specified in regulation E-1, then:

   .1   the Anniversary date shown on the Certificate shall be amended by endorsement to a date which shall not be more than three months later than the date on which the survey was completed;

   .2   the subsequent annual or intermediate survey required by regulation E-1 shall be completed at the intervals prescribed by that regulation using the new Anniversary date;

   .3   the expiry date may remain unchanged provided one or more annual surveys, as appropriate, are carried out so that the maximum intervals between the surveys prescribed by regulation E-1 are not exceeded.

9 A Certificate issued under regulation E-2 or E-3 shall cease to be valid in any of the following cases:

   .1   if the structure, equipment, systems, fittings, arrangements and material necessary to comply fully with this Convention is changed, replaced or significantly repaired and the Certificate is not endorsed in accordance with this Annex;

   .2   upon transfer of the ship to the flag of another State. A new Certificate shall only be issued when the Party issuing the new Certificate is fully satisfied that the ship is in compliance with the requirements of regulation E-1. In the case of a transfer between Parties, if requested within three months after the transfer has taken place, the Party whose flag the ship was formerly entitled to fly shall, as soon as possible, transmit to the Administration copies of the Certificates carried by the ship before the transfer and, if available, copies of the relevant survey reports;

   .3   if the relevant surveys are not completed within the periods specified under regulation E-1.1; or

   .4   if the Certificate is not endorsed in accordance with regulation E-1.1.

APPENDIX 7

International Convention on Standards of Training, Certification and Watchkeeping for Seafarers, 1978*

THE PARTIES TO THIS CONVENTION,

DESIRING to promote safety of life and property at sea and the protection of the marine environment by establishing in common agreement international standards of training, certification and watchkeeping for seafarers,

CONSIDERING that this end may best be achieved by the conclusion of an International Convention on Standards of Training, Certification and Watchkeeping for Seafarers,

HAVE AGREED as follows:

Article I – General obligations under the Convention

(1) The Parties undertake to give effect to the provisions of the Convention and the Annex thereto, which shall constitute an integral part of the Convention. Every reference to the Convention constitutes at the same time a reference to the Annex.

(2) The Parties undertake to promulgate all laws, decrees, orders and regulations and to take all other steps which may be necessary to give the Convention full and complete effect, so as to ensure that, from the point of view of safety of life and property at sea and the protection of the marine environment, seafarers on board ships are qualified and fit for their duties.

Article II – Definitions

For the purpose of the Convention, unless expressly provided otherwise:
- (a) 'Party' means a State for which the Convention has entered into force;
- (b) 'Administration' means the Government of the Party whose flag the ship is entitled to fly;
- (c) 'Certificate' means a valid document, by whatever name it may be known, issued by or under the authority of the Administration or recognized by the Administration authorizing the holder to serve as stated in this document or as authorized by national regulations;
- (d) 'Certificated' means properly holding a certificate;
- (e) 'Organization' means the Inter-Governmental Maritime Consultative Organization (IMCO);
- (f) 'Secretary-General' means the Secretary-General of the Organization;
- (g) 'Sea-going ship' means a ship other than those which navigate exclusively in inland

---

* Without the Annex, amended by the Conference of 1995.

APPENDIX 7

waters or in waters within, or closely adjacent to, sheltered waters or areas where port regulations apply;

(h) 'Fishing vessel' means a vessel used for catching fish, whales, seals, walrus or other living resources of the sea;

(i) 'Radio Regulations' means the Radio Regulations annexed to, or regarded as being annexed to, the most recent International Telecommunication Convention which may be in force at any time.

Article III – Application

The Convention shall apply to seafarers serving on board sea-going ships entitled to fly the flag of a Party except to those serving on board:

(a) warships, naval auxiliaries or other ships owned or operated by a State and engaged only on governmental non-commercial service; however, each Party shall ensure by the adoption of appropriate measures not impairing the operations or operational capabilities of such ships owned or operated by it, that the persons serving on board such ships meet the requirements of the Convention so far as is reasonable and practicable;

(b) fishing vessels;

(c) pleasure yachts not engaged in trade; or

(d) wooden ships of primitive build.

Article IV – Communication of information

(1) The Parties shall communicate as soon as practicable to the Secretary-General:

(a) the text of laws, decrees, orders, regulations and instruments promulgated on the various matters within the scope of the Convention;

(b) full details, where appropriate, of contents and duration of study courses, together with their national examination and other requirements for each certificate issued in compliance with the Convention;

(c) a sufficient number of specimen certificates issued in compliance with the Convention.

(2) The Secretary-General shall notify all Parties of the receipt of any communication under paragraph (1)(a) and, *inter alia*, for the purposes of Articles IX and X, shall, on request, provide them with any information communicated to him under paragraphs (1)(b) and (c).

Article V – Other treaties and interpretation

(1) All prior treaties, conventions and arrangements relating to standards of training, certification and watchkeeping for seafarers in force between the Parties, shall continue to have full and complete effect during the terms thereof as regards:

(a) seafarers to whom this Convention does not apply;

(b) seafarers to whom this Convention applies, in respect of matters for which it has not expressly provided.

(2) To the extent, however, that such treaties, conventions or arrangements conflict with the provisions of the Convention, the Parties shall review their commitments under such treaties, conventions and arrangements with a view to ensuring that there is no conflict between these commitments and their obligations under the Convention.

(3) All matters which are not expressly provided for in the Convention remain subject to the legislation of Parties.

APPENDIX 7

(4) Nothing in the Convention shall prejudice the codification and development of the law of the sea by the United Nations Conference on the Law of the Sea convened pursuant to resolution 2750C(XXV) of the General Assembly of the United Nations, nor the present or future claims and legal views of any State concerning the law of the sea and the nature and extent of coastal and flag State jurisdiction.

Article VI – Certificates

(1) Certificates for masters, officers or ratings shall be issued to those candidates who, to the satisfaction of the Administration, meet the requirements for service, age, medical fitness, training, qualification and examinations in accordance with the appropriate provisions of the Annex to the Convention.

(2) Certificates for masters and officers, issued in compliance with this Article, shall be endorsed by the issuing Administration in the form as prescribed in Regulation I/2 of the Annex. If the language used is not English, the endorsement shall include a translation into that language.

Article VII – Transitional provisions

(1) A certificate of competency or of service in a capacity for which the Convention requires a certificate and which before entry into force of the Convention for a Party is issued in accordance with the laws of that Party or the Radio Regulations, shall be recognized as valid for service after entry into force of the Convention for that Party.

(2) After the entry into force of the Convention for a Party, its Administration may continue to issue certificates of competency in accordance with its previous practices for a period not exceeding five years. Such certificates shall be recognized as valid for the purpose of the Convention. During this transitional period such certificates shall be issued only to seafarers who had commenced their sea service before entry into force of the Convention for that Party within the specific ship department to which those certificates relate. The Administration shall ensure that all other candidates for certification shall be examined and certificated in accordance with the Convention.

(3) A Party may, within two years after entry into force of the Convention for that Party, issue a certificate of service to seafarers who hold neither an appropriate certificate under the Convention nor a certificate of competency issued under its laws before entry into force of the Convention for that Party but who have:

(a) served in the capacity for which they seek a certificate of service for not less than three years at sea within the last seven years preceding entry into force of the Convention for that Party;

(b) produced evidence that they have performed that service satisfactorily;

(c) satisfied the Administration as to medical fitness, including eyesight and hearing, taking into account their age at the time of application.

For the purpose of the Convention, a certificate of service issued under this paragraph shall be regarded as the equivalent of a certificate issued under the Convention.

Article VIII – Dispensation

(1) In circumstances of exceptional necessity, Administrations, if in their opinion this does not cause danger to persons, property or the environment, may issue a dispensation permitting a specified seafarer to serve in a specified ship for a specified period not exceeding six months in a capacity, other than that of the radio officer or radiotelephone operator, except

APPENDIX 7

as provided by the relevant Radio Regulations, for which he does not hold the appropriate certificate, provided that the person to whom the dispensation is issued shall be adequately qualified to fill the vacant post in a safe manner, to the satisfaction of the Administration. However, dispensations shall not be granted to a master or chief engineer officer, except in circumstances of *force majeure* and then only for the shortest possible period.

(2) Any dispensation granted for a post shall be granted only to a person properly certificated to fill the post immediately below. Where certification of the post below is not required by the Convention, a dispensation may be issued to a person whose qualification and experience are, in the opinion of the Administration, of a clear equivalence to the requirements for the post to be filled, provided that, if such a person holds no appropriate certificate, he shall be required to pass a test accepted by the Administration as demonstrating that such a dispensation may safely be issued. In addition, Administrations shall ensure that the post in question is filled by the holder of an appropriate certificate as soon as possible.

(3) Parties shall, as soon as possible after 1 January of each year, send a report to the Secretary-General giving information of the total number of dispensations in respect of each capacity for which a certificate is required that have been issued during the year to sea-going ships, together with information as to the numbers of those ships above and below 1,600 gross register tons respectively.

Article IX – Equivalents

(1) The Convention shall not prevent an Administration from retaining or adopting other educational and training arrangements, including those involving sea-going service and shipboard organization especially adapted to technical developments and to special types of ships and trades, provided that the level of sea-going service, knowledge and efficiency as regards navigational and technical handling of ship and cargo ensures a degree of safety at sea and has a preventive effect as regards pollution at least equivalent to the requirements of the Convention.

(2) Details of such arrangements shall be reported as early as practicable to the Secretary-General who shall circulate such particulars to all Parties.

Article X – Control

(1) Ships, except those excluded by Article III, are subject, while in the ports of a Party, to control by officers duly authorized by that Party to verify that all seafarers serving on board who are required to be certificated by the Convention are so certificated or hold an appropriate dispensation. Such certificates shall be accepted unless there are clear grounds for believing that a certificate has been fraudulently obtained or that the holder of a certificate is not the person to whom that certificate was originally issued.

(2) In the event that any deficiencies are found under paragraph (1) or under the procedures specified in Regulation I/4 – 'Control Procedures', the officer carrying out the control shall forthwith inform, in writing, the master of the ship and the Consul or, in his absence, the nearest diplomatic representative or the maritime authority of the State whose flag the ship is entitled to fly, so that appropriate action may be taken. Such notification shall specify the details of the deficiencies found and the grounds on which the Party determines that these deficiencies pose a danger to persons, property or the environment.

(3) In exercising the control under paragraph (1) if, taking into account the size and type of the ship and the length and nature of the voyage, the deficiencies referred to in paragraph (3) of Regulation I/4 are not corrected and it is determined that this fact poses a danger to persons, property or the environment, the Party carrying out the control shall take steps to

356

APPENDIX 7

ensure that the ship will not sail unless and until these requirements are met to the extent that the danger has been removed. The facts concerning the action taken shall be reported promptly to the Secretary-General.

(4) When exercising control under this Article, all possible efforts shall be made to avoid a ship being unduly detained or delayed. If a ship is so detained or delayed it shall be entitled to compensation for any loss or damage resulting therefrom.

(5) This Article shall be applied as may be necessary to ensure that no more favourable treatment is given to ships entitled to fly the flag of a non-Party than is given to ships entitled to fly the flag of a Party.

Article XI – Promotion of technical co-operation

(1) Parties to the Convention shall promote, in consultation with, and with the assistance of, the Organization, support for those Parties which request technical assistance for:
  (a) training of administrative and technical personnel;
  (b) establishment of institutions for the training of seafarers;
  (c) supply of equipment and facilities for training institutions;
  (d) development of adequate training programmes, including practical training on sea-going ships; and
  (e) facilitation of other measures and arrangements to enhance the qualifications of seafarers;
preferably on a national, sub-regional or regional basis, to further the aims and purposes of the Convention, taking into account the special needs of developing countries in this regard.

(2) On its part, the Organization shall pursue the aforesaid efforts, as appropriate, in consultation or association with other international organizations, particularly the International Labour Organisation.

Article XII – Amendments

(1) The Convention may be amended by either of the following procedures:
  (a) amendments after consideration within the Organization:
      (i)   any amendment proposed by a Party shall be submitted to the Secretary-General, who shall then circulate it to all Members of the Organization, all Parties and the Director-General of the International Labour Office at least six months prior to its consideration;
      (ii)   any amendment so proposed and circulated shall be referred to the Maritime Safety Committee of the Organization for consideration;
      (iii) Parties, whether or not Members of the Organization, shall be entitled to participate in the proceedings of the Maritime Safety Committee for consideration and adoption of amendments;
      (iv)   amendments shall be adopted by a two-thirds majority of the Parties present and voting in the Maritime Safety Committee expanded as provided for in sub-paragraph (a)(iii) (hereinafter referred to as the 'expanded Maritime Safety Committee') on condition that at least one third of the Parties shall be present at the time of voting;
      (v)   amendments so adopted shall be communicated by the Secretary-General to all Parties for acceptance;
      (vi)   an amendment to an Article shall be deemed to have been accepted on the date on which it is accepted by two thirds of the Parties;

APPENDIX 7

    (vii)   an amendment to the Annex shall be deemed to have been accepted:

        1. at the end of two years from the date on which it is communicated to Parties for acceptance; or

        2. at the end of a different period, which shall not be less than one year, if so determined at the time of its adoption by a two-thirds majority of the Parties present and voting in the expanded Maritime Safety Committee;

    however, the amendments shall be deemed not to have been accepted if within the specified period either more than one third of Parties, or Parties the combined merchant fleets of which constitute not less than fifty per cent of the gross tonnage of the world's merchant shipping of ships of 100 gross register tons or more, notify the Secretary-General that they object to the amendment;

    (viii) an amendment to an Article shall enter into force with respect to those Parties which have accepted it, six months after the date on which it is deemed to have been accepted, and with respect to each Party which accepts it after that date, six months after the date of that Party's acceptance;

    (ix) an amendment to the Annex shall enter into force with respect to all Parties, except those which have objected to the amendment under sub-paragraph (a)(vii) and which have not withdrawn such objections, six months after the date on which it is deemed to have been accepted. Before the date determined for entry into force, any Party may give notice to the Secretary-General that it exempts itself from giving effect to that amendment for a period not longer than one year from the date of its entry into force, or for such longer period as may be determined by a two-thirds majority of the Parties present and voting in the expanded Maritime Safety Committee at the time of the adoption of the amendment; or

  (b)   amendment by a conference:

    (i) upon the request of a Party concurred in by at least one third of the Parties, the Organization shall convene, in association or consultation with the Director-General of the International Labour Office, a conference of Parties to consider amendments to the Convention;

    (ii) every amendment adopted by such a conference by a two-thirds majority of the Parties present and voting shall be communicated by the Secretary-General to all Parties for acceptance;

    (iii) unless the conference decides otherwise, the amendment shall be deemed to have been accepted and shall enter into force in accordance with the procedures specified in sub-paragraph (a)(vi) and (a)(viii) or sub-paragraphs (a)(vii) and (a)(ix) respectively, provided that references in these sub-paragraphs to the expanded Maritime Safety Committee shall be taken to mean references to the conference.

(2) Any declaration of acceptance of, or objection to, an amendment or any notice given under paragraph (1)(a)(ix) shall be submitted in writing to the Secretary-General, who shall inform all Parties of any such submission and the date of its receipt.

(3) The Secretary-General shall inform all Parties of any amendments which enter into force, together with the date on which each such amendment enters into force.

APPENDIX 7

Article XIII – Signature, ratification, acceptance, approval and accession

(1) The Convention shall remain open for signature at the Headquarters of the Organization from 1 December 1978 until 30 November 1979 and shall thereafter remain open for accession. Any State may become a Party by:
    (a)   signature without reservation as to ratification, acceptance or approval; or
    (b)   signature subject to ratification, acceptance or approval, followed by ratification, acceptance or approval; or
    (c)   accession.

(2) Ratification, acceptance, approval or accession shall be effected by the deposit of an instrument to that effect with the Secretary-General.

(3) The Secretary-General shall inform all States that have signed the Convention or acceded to it and the Director-General of the International Labour Office of any signature or of the deposit of any instrument of ratification, acceptance, approval or accession and the date of its deposit.

Article XIV – Entry into force

(1) The Convention shall enter into force twelve months after the date on which not less than twenty-five States, the combined merchant fleets of which constitute not less than fifty per cent of the gross tonnage of the world's merchant shipping of ships of 100 gross register tons or more, have either signed it without reservation as to ratification, acceptance or approval or deposited the requisite instruments of ratification, acceptance, approval or accession in accordance with Article XIII.

(2) The Secretary-General shall inform all States that have signed the Convention or acceded to it of the date on which it enters into force.

(3) Any instrument of ratification, acceptance, approval or accession deposited during the twelve months referred to in paragraph (1) shall take effect on the coming into force of the Convention or three months after the deposit of such instrument, whichever is the later date.

(4) Any instrument of ratification, acceptance, approval or accession deposited after the date on which the Convention enters into force shall take effect three months after the date of deposit.

(5) After the date on which an amendment is deemed to have been accepted under Article XII, any instrument of ratification, acceptance, approval or accession deposited shall apply to the Convention as amended.

Article XV – Denunciation

(1) The Convention may be denounced by any Party at any time after five years from the date on which the Convention entered into force for that Party.

(2) Denunciation shall be effected by notification in writing to the Secretary-General who shall inform all other Parties and the Director-General of the International Labour Office of any such notification received and of the date of its receipt as well as the date on which such denunciation takes effect.

(3) A denunciation shall take effect twelve months after receipt of the notification of denunciation by the Secretary-General or after any longer period which may be indicated in the notification.

APPENDIX 7

Article XVI – Deposit and registration

(1) The Convention shall be deposited with the Secretary-General who shall transmit certified true copies thereof to all States that have signed the Convention or acceded to it.

(2) As soon as the Convention enters into force, the Secretary-General shall transmit the text to the Secretary-General of the United Nations for registration and publication, in accordance with Article 102 of the Charter of the United Nations.

Article XVII – Languages

The Convention is established in a single copy in the Chinese, English, French, Russian and Spanish languages, each text being equally authentic. Official translations in the Arabic and German languages shall be prepared and deposited with the signed original.

IN WITNESS WHEREOF the undersigned, being duly authorized by their respective Governments for that purpose, have signed the Convention.

DONE AT LONDON this seventh day of July, one thousand nine hundred and seventy-eight.

(Annex omitted)

APPENDIX 8

Nairobi International Convention on the Removal of Wrecks, 2007

Preamble

THE STATES PARTIES TO THE PRESENT CONVENTION,

CONSCIOUS of the fact that wrecks, if not removed, may pose a hazard to navigation or the marine environment,

CONVINCED of the need to adopt uniform international rules and procedures to ensure the prompt and effective removal of wrecks and payment of compensation for the costs therein involved,

NOTING that many wrecks may be located in States' territory, including the territorial sea,

RECOGNIZING the benefits to be gained through uniformity in legal regimes governing responsibility and liability for removal of hazardous wrecks,

BEARING IN MIND the importance of the United Nations Convention on the Law of the Sea, done at Montego Bay on 10 December 1982, and of the customary international law of the sea, and the consequent need to implement the present Convention in accordance with such provisions,

HAVE AGREED as follows:

Article 1 – Definitions

For the purposes of this Convention:

1. 'Convention area' means the exclusive economic zone of a State Party, established in accordance with international law or, if a State Party has not established such a zone, an area beyond and adjacent to the territorial sea of that State determined by that State in accordance with international law and extending not more than 200 nautical miles from the baselines from which the breadth of its territorial sea is measured.

2. 'Ship' means a seagoing vessel of any type whatsoever and includes hydrofoil boats, air-cushion vehicles, submersibles, floating craft and floating platforms, except when such platforms are on location engaged in the exploration, exploitation or production of sea-bed mineral resources.

3. 'Maritime casualty' means a collision of ships, stranding or other incident of navigation, or other occurrence on board a ship or external to it resulting in material damage or imminent threat of material damage to a ship or its cargo.

4. 'Wreck', following upon a maritime casualty, means:
   (a) a sunken or stranded ship; or
   (b) any part of a sunken or stranded ship, including any object that is or has been on board such a ship; or
   (c) any object that is lost at sea from a ship and that is stranded, sunken or adrift at sea; or

361

APPENDIX 8

(d) a ship that is about, or may reasonably be expected, to sink or to strand, where effective measures to assist the ship or any property in danger are not already being taken.

5. 'Hazard' means any condition or threat that:

(a) poses a danger or impediment to navigation; or

(b) may reasonably be expected to result in major harmful consequences to the marine environment, or damage to the coastline or related interests of one or more States.

6. 'Related interests' means the interests of a coastal State directly affected or threatened by a wreck, such as:

(a) maritime coastal, port and estuarine activities, including fisheries activities, constituting an essential means of livelihood of the persons concerned;

(b) tourist attractions and other economic interests of the area concerned;

(c) the health of the coastal population and the well-being of the area concerned, including conservation of marine living resources and of wildlife; and

(d) offshore and underwater infrastructure.

7. 'Removal' means any form of prevention, mitigation or elimination of the hazard created by a wreck. 'Remove', 'removed' and 'removing' shall be construed accordingly.

8. 'Registered owner' means the person or persons registered as the owner of the ship or, in the absence of registration, the person or persons owning the ship at the time of the maritime casualty. However, in the case of a ship owned by a State and operated by a company which in that State is registered as the operator of the ship, 'registered owner' shall mean such company.

9. 'Operator of the ship' means the owner of the ship or any other organization or person such as the manager, or the bareboat charterer, who has assumed the responsibility for operation of the ship from the owner of the ship and who, on assuming such responsibility, has agreed to take over all duties and responsibilities established under the International Safety Management Code, as amended.

10. 'Affected State' means the State in whose Convention area the wreck is located.

11. 'State of the ship's registry' means, in relation to a registered ship, the State of registration of the ship and, in relation to an unregistered ship, the State whose flag the ship is entitled to fly.

12. 'Organization' means the International Maritime Organization.

13. 'Secretary-General' means the Secretary-General of the Organization.

Article 2 – Objectives and general principles

1. A State Party may take measures in accordance with this Convention in relation to the removal of a wreck which poses a hazard in the Convention area.

2. Measures taken by the Affected State in accordance with paragraph 1 shall be proportionate to the hazard.

3. Such measures shall not go beyond what is reasonably necessary to remove a wreck which poses a hazard and shall cease as soon as the wreck has been removed; they shall not unnecessarily interfere with the rights and interests of other States including the State of the ship's registry, and of any person, physical or corporate, concerned.

4. The application of this Convention within the Convention area shall not entitle a State Party to claim or exercise sovereignty or sovereign rights over any part of the high seas.

5. States Parties shall endeavour to co-operate when the effects of a maritime casualty resulting in a wreck involve a State other than the Affected State.

APPENDIX 8

Article 3 – Scope of application

1. Except as otherwise provided in this Convention, this Convention shall apply to wrecks in the Convention area.

2. A State Party may extend the application of this Convention to wrecks located within its territory, including the territorial sea, subject to article 4, paragraph 4. In that case, it shall notify the Secretary-General accordingly, at the time of expressing its consent to be bound by this Convention or at any time thereafter. When a State Party has made a notification to apply this Convention to wrecks located within its territory, including the territorial sea, this is without prejudice to the rights and obligations of that State to take measures in relation to wrecks located in its territory, including the territorial sea, other than locating, marking and removing in accordance with this Convention. The provisions of articles 10, 11 and 12 of this Convention shall not apply to any measures so taken other than those referred to in articles 7, 8 and 9 of this Convention.

3. When a State Party has made a notification under paragraph 2, the 'Convention area' of the Affected State shall include the territory, including the territorial sea, of that State Party.

4. A notification made under paragraph 2 above shall take effect for that State Party, if made before entry into force of this Convention for that State Party, upon entry into force. If notification is made after entry into force of this Convention for that State Party, it shall take effect six months after its receipt by the Secretary-General.

5. A State Party that has made a notification under paragraph 2 may withdraw it at any time by means of a notification of withdrawal to the Secretary-General. Such notification of withdrawal shall take effect six months after its receipt by the Secretary-General, unless the notification specifies a later date.

Article 4 – Exclusions

1. This Convention shall not apply to measures taken under the International Convention relating to Intervention on the High Seas in Cases of Oil Pollution Casualties, 1969, as amended, or the Protocol relating to Intervention on the High Seas in Cases of Pollution by Substances other than Oil, 1973, as amended.

2. This Convention shall not apply to any warship or other ship owned or operated by a State and used, for the time being, only on Government non-commercial service, unless that State decides otherwise.

3. Where a State Party decides to apply this Convention to its warships or other ships as described in paragraph 2, it shall notify the Secretary-General thereof, specifying the terms and conditions of such application.

4. (a) When a State Party has made a notification under article 3, paragraph 2, the following provisions of this Convention shall not apply in its territory, including the territorial sea:

      (i)   Article 2, paragraph 4

      (ii) Article 9, paragraphs 1, 5, 7, 8, 9 and 10

      (iii) Article 15

  (b) Article 9, paragraph 4, insofar as it applies to the territory, including the territorial sea of a State Party, shall read:

'Subject to the national law of the Affected State, the registered owner may contract with any salvor or other person to remove the wreck determined to constitute a hazard on behalf of the owner. Before such removal commences, the Affected State may lay down conditions for such removal only to the extent necessary to ensure that the removal proceeds in a manner that is consistent with considerations of safety and protection of the marine environment.'

APPENDIX 8

Article 5 – Reporting wrecks

1. A State Party shall require the master and the operator of a ship flying its flag to report to the Affected State without delay when that ship has been involved in a maritime casualty resulting in a wreck. To the extent that the reporting obligation under this article has been fulfilled either by the master or the operator of the ship, the other shall not be obliged to report.

2. Such reports shall provide the name and the principal place of business of the registered owner and all the relevant information necessary for the Affected State to determine whether the wreck poses a hazard in accordance with article 6, including:

    (a)   the precise location of the wreck;

    (b)   the type, size and construction of the wreck;

    (c)   the nature of the damage to, and the condition of, the wreck;

    (d)   the nature and quantity of the cargo, in particular any hazardous and noxious substances; and

    (e)   the amount and types of oil, including bunker oil and lubricating oil, on board.

Article 6 – Determination of hazard

When determining whether a wreck poses a hazard, the following criteria should be taken into account by the Affected State:

    (a)   the type, size and construction of the wreck;

    (b)   depth of the water in the area;

    (c)   tidal range and currents in the area;

    (d)   particularly sensitive sea areas identified and, as appropriate, designated in accordance with guidelines adopted by the Organization, or a clearly defined area of the exclusive economic zone where special mandatory measures have been adopted pursuant to article 211, paragraph 6, of the United Nations Convention on the Law of the Sea, 1982;

    (e)   proximity of shipping routes or established traffic lanes;

    (f)   traffic density and frequency;

    (g)   type of traffic;

    (h)   nature and quantity of the wreck's cargo, the amount and types of oil (such as bunker oil and lubricating oil) on board the wreck and, in particular, the damage likely to result should the cargo or oil be released into the marine environment;

    (i)   vulnerability of port facilities;

    (j)   prevailing meteorological and hydrographical conditions;

    (k)   submarine topography of the area;

    (l)   height of the wreck above or below the surface of the water at lowest astronomical tide;

    (m)   acoustic and magnetic profiles of the wreck;

    (n)   proximity of offshore installations, pipelines, telecommunications cables and similar structures; and

    (o)   any other circumstances that might necessitate the removal of the wreck.

Article 7 – Locating wrecks

1. Upon becoming aware of a wreck, the Affected State shall use all practicable means, including the good offices of States and organizations, to warn mariners and the States concerned of the nature and location of the wreck as a matter of urgency.

2. If the Affected State has reason to believe that a wreck poses a hazard, it shall ensure that all practicable steps are taken to establish the precise location of the wreck.

APPENDIX 8

Article 8 – Marking of wrecks

1. If the Affected State determines that a wreck constitutes a hazard, that State shall ensure that all reasonable steps are taken to mark the wreck.

2. In marking the wreck, all practicable steps shall be taken to ensure that the markings conform to the internationally accepted system of buoyage in use in the area where the wreck is located.

3. The Affected State shall promulgate the particulars of the marking of the wreck by use of all appropriate means, including the appropriate nautical publications.

Article 9 – Measures to facilitate the removal of wrecks

1. If the Affected State determines that a wreck constitutes a hazard, that State shall immediately:
   (a) inform the State of the ship's registry and the registered owner; and
   (b) proceed to consult the State of the ship's registry and other States affected by the wreck regarding measures to be taken in relation to the wreck.

2. The registered owner shall remove a wreck determined to constitute a hazard.

3. When a wreck has been determined to constitute a hazard, the registered owner, or other interested party, shall provide the competent authority of the Affected State with evidence of insurance or other financial security as required by article 12.

4. The registered owner may contract with any salvor or other person to remove the wreck determined to constitute a hazard on behalf of the owner. Before such removal commences, the Affected State may lay down conditions for such removal only to the extent necessary to ensure that the removal proceeds in a manner that is consistent with considerations of safety and protection of the marine environment.

5. When the removal referred to in paragraphs 2 and 4 has commenced, the Affected State may intervene in the removal only to the extent necessary to ensure that the removal proceeds effectively in a manner that is consistent with considerations of safety and protection of the marine environment.

6. The Affected State shall:
   (a) set a reasonable deadline within which the registered owner must remove the wreck taking into account the nature of the hazard determined in accordance with article 6;
   (b) inform the registered owner in writing of the deadline it has set and specify that, if the registered owner does not remove the wreck within that deadline, it may remove the wreck at the registered owner's expense; and
   (c) inform the registered owner in writing that it intends to intervene immediately in circumstances where the hazard becomes particularly severe.

7. If the registered owner does not remove the wreck within the deadline set in accordance with paragraph 6(a), or the registered owner cannot be contacted, the Affected State may remove the wreck by the most practical and expeditious means available, consistent with considerations of safety and protection of the marine environment.

8. In circumstances where immediate action is required and the Affected State has informed the State of the ship's registry and the registered owner accordingly, it may remove the wreck by the most practical and expeditious means available, consistent with considerations of safety and protection of the marine environment.

9. States Parties shall take appropriate measures under their national law to ensure that their registered owners comply with paragraphs 2 and 3.

10. States Parties give their consent to the Affected State to act under paragraphs 4 to 8, where required.

365

APPENDIX 8

11. The information referred to in this article shall be provided by the Affected State to the registered owner identified in the reports referred to in article 5, paragraph 2.

Article 10 – Liability of the owner

1. Subject to article 11, the registered owner shall be liable for the costs of locating, marking and removing the wreck under articles 7, 8 and 9, respectively, unless the registered owner proves that the maritime casualty that caused the wreck:

    (a)   resulted from an act of war, hostilities, civil war, insurrection, or a natural phenomenon of an exceptional, inevitable and irresistible character;

    (b)   was wholly caused by an act or omission done with intent to cause damage by a third party; or

    (c)   was wholly caused by the negligence or other wrongful act of any Government or other authority responsible for the maintenance of lights or other navigational aids in the exercise of that function.

2. Nothing in this Convention shall affect the right of the registered owner to limit liability under any applicable national or international regime, such as the Convention on Limitation of Liability for Maritime Claims, 1976, as amended.

3. No claim for the costs referred to in paragraph 1 may be made against the registered owner otherwise than in accordance with the provisions of this Convention. This is without prejudice to the rights and obligations of a State Party that has made a notification under article 3, paragraph 2, in relation to wrecks located in its territory, including the territorial sea, other than locating, marking and removing in accordance with this Convention.

4. Nothing in this article shall prejudice any right of recourse against third parties.

Article 11 – Exceptions to liability

1. The registered owner shall not be liable under this Convention for the costs mentioned in article 10, paragraph 1 if, and to the extent that, liability for such costs would be in conflict with:

    (a)   the International Convention on Civil Liability for Oil Pollution Damage, 1969, as amended;

    (b)   the International Convention on Liability and Compensation for Damage in Connection with the Carriage of Hazardous and Noxious Substances by Sea, 1996, as amended;

    (c)   the Convention on Third Party Liability in the Field of Nuclear Energy, 1960, as amended, or the Vienna Convention on Civil Liability for Nuclear Damage, 1963, as amended; or national law governing or prohibiting limitation of liability for nuclear damage; or

    (d)   the International Convention on Civil Liability for Bunker Oil Pollution Damage, 2001, as amended;

provided that the relevant convention is applicable and in force.

2. To the extent that measures under this Convention are considered to be salvage under applicable national law or an international convention, such law or convention shall apply to questions of the remuneration or compensation payable to salvors to the exclusion of the rules of this Convention.

Article 12 – Compulsory insurance or other financial security

1. The registered owner of a ship of 300 gross tonnage and above and flying the flag of a State Party shall be required to maintain insurance or other financial security, such as

APPENDIX 8

a guarantee of a bank or similar institution, to cover liability under this Convention in an amount equal to the limits of liability under the applicable national or international limitation regime, but in all cases not exceeding an amount calculated in accordance with article 6(1)(b) of the Convention on Limitation of Liability for Maritime Claims, 1976, as amended.

2. A certificate attesting that insurance or other financial security is in force in accordance with the provisions of this Convention shall be issued to each ship of 300 gross tonnage and above by the appropriate authority of the State of the ship's registry after determining that the requirements of paragraph 1 have been complied with. With respect to a ship registered in a State Party such certificate shall be issued or certified by the appropriate authority of the State of the ship's registry; with respect to a ship not registered in a State Party it may be issued or certified by the appropriate authority of any State Party. This compulsory insurance certificate shall be in the form of the model set out in the annex to this Convention, and shall contain the following particulars:

(a)   name of the ship, distinctive number or letters and port of registry;
(b)   gross tonnage of the ship;
(c)   name and principal place of business of the registered owner;
(d)   IMO ship identification number;
(e)   type and duration of security;
(f)   name and principal place of business of insurer or other person giving security and, where appropriate, place of business where the insurance or security is established;
(g)   period of validity of the certificate, which shall not be longer than the period of validity of the insurance or other security.

3. (a)   A State Party may authorize either an institution or an organization recognized by it to issue the certificate referred to in paragraph 2. Such institution or organization shall inform that State of the issue of each certificate. In all cases, the State Party shall fully guarantee the completeness and accuracy of the certificate so issued and shall undertake to ensure the necessary arrangements to satisfy this obligation.

(b)   A State Party shall notify the Secretary-General of:
(i)   the specific responsibilities and conditions of the authority delegated to an institution or organization recognized by it;
(ii)   the withdrawal of such authority; and
(iii)   the date from which such authority or withdrawal of such authority takes effect.

An authority delegated shall not take effect prior to three months from the date on which notification to that effect was given to the Secretary-General.

(c)   The institution or organization authorized to issue certificates in accordance with this paragraph shall, as a minimum, be authorized to withdraw these certificates if the conditions under which they have been issued are not maintained. In all cases the institution or organization shall report such withdrawal to the State on whose behalf the certificate was issued.

4. The certificate shall be in the official language or languages of the issuing State. If the language used is not English, French or Spanish, the text shall include a translation into one of these languages and, where the State so decides, the official language(s) of the State may be omitted.

5. The certificate shall be carried on board the ship and a copy shall be deposited with the authorities who keep the record of the ship's registry or, if the ship is not registered in a State Party, with the authorities issuing or certifying the certificate.

6. An insurance or other financial security shall not satisfy the requirements of this article if it can cease for reasons other than the expiry of the period of validity of the insurance or security specified in the certificate under paragraph 2 before three months have elapsed from

APPENDIX 8

the date on which notice of its termination is given to the authorities referred to in paragraph 5 unless the certificate has been surrendered to these authorities or a new certificate has been issued within the said period. The foregoing provisions shall similarly apply to any modification, which results in the insurance or security no longer satisfying the requirements of this article.

7. The State of the ship's registry shall, subject to the provisions of this article and having regard to any guidelines adopted by the Organization on the financial responsibility of the registered owners, determine the conditions of issue and validity of the certificate.

8. Nothing in this Convention shall be construed as preventing a State Party from relying on information obtained from other States or the Organization or other international organizations relating to the financial standing of providers of insurance or financial security for the purposes of this Convention. In such cases, the State Party relying on such information is not relieved of its responsibility as a State issuing the certificate required by paragraph 2.

9. Certificates issued and certified under the authority of a State Party shall be accepted by other States Parties for the purposes of this Convention and shall be regarded by other States Parties as having the same force as certificates issued or certified by them, even if issued or certified in respect of a ship not registered in a State Party. A State Party may at any time request consultation with the issuing or certifying State should it believe that the insurer or guarantor named in the certificate is not financially capable of meeting the obligations imposed by this Convention.

10. Any claim for costs arising under this Convention may be brought directly against the insurer or other person providing financial security for the registered owner's liability. In such a case the defendant may invoke the defences (other than the bankruptcy or winding up of the registered owner) that the registered owner would have been entitled to invoke, including limitation of liability under any applicable national or international regime. Furthermore, even if the registered owner is not entitled to limit liability, the defendant may limit liability to an amount equal to the amount of the insurance or other financial security required to be maintained in accordance with paragraph 1. Moreover, the defendant may invoke the defence that the maritime casualty was caused by the wilful misconduct of the registered owner, but the defendant shall not invoke any other defence which the defendant might have been entitled to invoke in proceedings brought by the registered owner against the defendant. The defendant shall in any event have the right to require the registered owner to be joined in the proceedings.

11. A State Party shall not permit any ship entitled to fly its flag to which this article applies to operate at any time unless a certificate has been issued under paragraphs 2 or 14.

12. Subject to the provisions of this article, each State Party shall ensure, under its national law, that insurance or other security to the extent required by paragraph 1 is in force in respect of any ship of 300 gross tonnage and above, wherever registered, entering or leaving a port in its territory, or arriving at or leaving an offshore facility in its territorial sea.

13. Notwithstanding the provisions of paragraph 5, a State Party may notify the Secretary-General that, for the purposes of paragraph 12, ships are not required to carry on board or to produce the certificate required by paragraph 2, when entering or leaving a port in its territory or arriving at or leaving from an offshore facility in its territorial sea, provided that the State Party which issues the certificate required by paragraph 2 has notified the Secretary-General that it maintains records in an electronic format, accessible to all States Parties, attesting the existence of the certificate and enabling States Parties to discharge their obligations under paragraph 12.

14. If insurance or other financial security is not maintained in respect of a ship owned by a State Party, the provisions of this article relating thereto shall not be applicable to such ship, but the ship shall carry a certificate issued by the appropriate authority of the State of

APPENDIX 8

registry stating that it is owned by that State and that the ship's liability is covered within the limits prescribed in paragraph 1. Such a certificate shall follow as closely as possible the model prescribed by paragraph 2.

Article 13 – Time limits

Rights to recover costs under this Convention shall be extinguished unless an action is brought hereunder within three years from the date when the hazard has been determined in accordance with this Convention. However, in no case shall an action be brought after six years from the date of the maritime casualty that resulted in the wreck. Where the maritime casualty consists of a series of occurrences, the six-year period shall run from the date of the first occurrence.

Article 14 – Amendment provisions

1. At the request of not less than one third of States Parties, a conference shall be convened by the Organization for the purpose of revising or amending this Convention.

2. Any consent to be bound by this Convention expressed after the date of entry into force of an amendment to this Convention shall be deemed to apply to this Convention, as amended.

Article 15 – Settlement of disputes

1. Where a dispute arises between two or more States Parties regarding the interpretation or application of this Convention, they shall seek to resolve their dispute, in the first instance, through negotiation, enquiry, mediation, conciliation, arbitration, judicial settlement, resort to regional agencies or arrangements or other peaceful means of their choice.

2. If no settlement is possible within a reasonable period of time not exceeding twelve months after one State Party has notified another that a dispute exists between them, the provisions relating to the settlement of disputes set out in Part XV of the United Nations Convention on the Law of the Sea, 1982, shall apply *mutatis mutandis*, whether or not the States party to the dispute are also States Parties to the United Nations Convention on the Law of the Sea, 1982.

3. Any procedure chosen by a State Party to this Convention and to the United Nations Convention on the Law of the Sea, 1982, pursuant to Article 287 of the latter shall apply to the settlement of disputes under this Article, unless that State Party, when ratifying, accepting, approving or acceding to this Convention, or at any time thereafter, chooses another procedure pursuant to Article 287 for the purpose of the settlement of disputes arising out of this Convention.

4. A State Party to this Convention which is not a Party to the United Nations Convention on the Law of the Sea, 1982, when ratifying, accepting, approving or acceding to this Convention or at any time thereafter shall be free to choose, by means of a written declaration, one or more of the means set out in Article 287, paragraph 1, of the United Nations Convention on the Law of the Sea, 1982, for the purpose of settlement of disputes under this Article. Article 287 shall apply to such a declaration, as well as to any dispute to which such State is party, which is not covered by a declaration in force. For the purpose of conciliation and arbitration, in accordance with Annexes V and VII of the United Nations Convention on the Law of the Sea, 1982, such State shall be entitled to nominate conciliators and arbitrators to be included in the lists referred to in Annex V, Article 2, and Annex VII, Article 2, for the settlement of disputes arising out of this Convention.

APPENDIX 8

5. A declaration made under paragraphs 3 and 4 shall be deposited with the Secretary-General who shall transmit copies thereof to the States Parties.

Article 16 – Relationship to other conventions and international agreements

Nothing in this Convention shall prejudice the rights and obligations of any State under the United Nations Convention on the Law of the Sea, 1982, and under the customary international law of the sea.

Article 17 – Signature, ratification, acceptance, approval and accession

1. This Convention shall be open for signature at the Headquarters of the Organization from 19 November 2007 until 18 November 2008 and shall thereafter remain open for accession.
    (a)   States may express their consent to be bound by this Convention by:
          (i)   signature without reservation as to ratification, acceptance or approval; or
          (ii)   signature subject to ratification, acceptance or approval, followed by ratification, acceptance or approval; or
         (iii)   accession.
    (b)   Ratification, acceptance, approval or accession shall be effected by the deposit of an instrument to that effect with the Secretary-General.

Article 18 – Entry into force

1. This Convention shall enter into force twelve months following the date on which ten States have either signed it without reservation as to ratification, acceptance or approval or have deposited instruments of ratification, acceptance, approval or accession with the Secretary-General.
2. For any State which ratifies, accepts, approves or accedes to this Convention after the conditions in paragraph 1 for entry into force have been met, this Convention shall enter into force three months following the date of deposit by such State of the appropriate instrument, but not before this Convention has entered into force in accordance with paragraph 1.

Article 19 – Denunciation

1. This Convention may be denounced by a State Party at any time after the expiry of one year following the date on which this Convention comes into force for that State.
2. Denunciation shall be effected by the deposit of an instrument to that effect with the Secretary-General.
3. A denunciation shall take effect one year, or such longer period as may be specified in the instrument of denunciation, following its receipt by the Secretary-General.

Article 20 – Depositary

1. This Convention shall be deposited with the Secretary General.
2. The Secretary-General shall:
    (a)   inform all States which have signed or acceded to this Convention of:
          (i)   each new signature or deposit of an instrument of ratification, acceptance, approval or accession, together with the date thereof;
         (ii)   the date of entry into force of this Convention;

APPENDIX 8

(iii) the deposit of any instrument of denunciation of this Convention together with the date of the deposit and the date on which the denunciation takes effect; and

(iv) other declarations and notifications received pursuant to this Convention; and

(b) transmit certified true copies of this Convention to all States that have signed or acceded to this Convention.

3. As soon as this Convention enters into force, a certified true copy of the text shall be transmitted by the Secretary-General to the Secretary-General of the United Nations for registration and publication in accordance with Article 102 of the Charter of the United Nations.

Article 21 – Languages

This Convention is established in a single original in the Arabic, Chinese, English, French, Russian and Spanish languages, each text being equally authentic.

Done at NAIROBI this eighteenth day of May two thousand and seven.

IN WITNESS WHEREOF the undersigned, being duly authorized by their respective Governments for that purpose, have signed this Convention.

APPENDICES: PART II

THE LIABILITY CONVENTIONS

APPENDIX 9

International Convention on Civil Liability for Oil Pollution Damage, 1992 (CLC 1992)

THE STATES PARTIES TO THE PRESENT CONVENTION,

CONSCIOUS of the dangers of pollution posed by the worldwide maritime carriage of oil in bulk, CONVINCED of the need to ensure that adequate compensation is available to persons who suffer damage caused by pollution resulting from the escape or discharge of oil from ships, DESIRING to adopt uniform international rules and procedures for determining questions of liability and providing adequate compensation in such cases,

HAVE AGREED as follows:

Article I

For the purposes of this Convention:

1. 'Ship' means any sea-going vessel and seaborne craft of any type whatsoever constructed or adapted for the carriage of oil in bulk as cargo, provided that a ship capable of carrying oil and other cargoes shall be regarded as a ship only when it is actually carrying oil in bulk as cargo and during any voyage following such carriage unless it is proved that it has no residues of such carriage of oil in bulk aboard.

2. 'Person' means any individual or partnership or any public or private body, whether corporate or not, including a State or any of its constituent subdivisions.

3. 'Owner' means the person or persons registered as the owner of the ship or, in the absence of registration, the person or persons owning the ship. However in the case of a ship owned by a State and operated by a company which in that State is registered as the ship's operator, 'owner' shall mean such company.

4. 'State of the ship's registry' means in relation to registered ships the State of registration of the ship, and in relation to unregistered ships the State whose flag the ship is flying.

5. 'Oil' means any persistent hydrocarbon mineral oil such as crude oil, fuel oil, heavy diesel oil and lubricating oil, whether carried on board a ship as cargo or in the bunkers of such a ship.

6. 'Pollution damage' means:
   - (a) loss or damage caused outside the ship by contamination resulting from the escape or discharge of oil from the ship, wherever such escape or discharge may occur, provided that compensation for impairment of the environment other than loss of profit from such impairment shall be limited to costs of reasonable measures of reinstatement actually undertaken or to be undertaken;
   - (b) the costs of preventive measures and further loss or damage caused by preventive measures.

7. 'Preventive measures' means any reasonable measures taken by any person after an incident has occurred to prevent or minimize pollution damage.

APPENDIX 9

8. 'Incident' means any occurrence, or series of occurrences having the same origin, which causes pollution damage or creates a grave and imminent threat of causing such damage.

9. 'Organization' means the International Maritime Organization.

10. '1969 Liability Convention' means the International Convention on Civil Liability for Oil Pollution Damage, 1969. For States Parties to the Protocol of 1976 to that Convention, the term shall be deemed to include the 1969 Liability Convention as amended by that Protocol.

Article II

This Convention shall apply exclusively:

    (a)   to pollution damage caused:

        (i)   in the territory, including the territorial sea, of a Contracting State, and

        (ii)   in the exclusive economic zone of a Contracting State, established in accordance with international law, or, if a Contracting State has not established such a zone, in an area beyond and adjacent to the territorial sea of that State determined by that State in accordance with international law and extending not more than 200 nautical miles from the baselines from which the breadth of its territorial sea is measured;

    (b)   to preventive measures, wherever taken, to prevent or minimize such damage.

Article III

1. Except as provided in paragraphs 2 and 3 of this Article, the owner of a ship at the time of an incident, or, where the incident consists of a series of occurrences, at the time of the first such occurrence, shall be liable for any pollution damage caused by the ship as a result of the incident.

2. No liability for pollution damage shall attach to the owner if he proves that the damage:

    (a)   resulted from an act of war, hostilities, civil war, insurrection or a natural phenomenon of an exceptional, inevitable and irresistible character, or

    (b)   was wholly caused by an act or omission done with intent to cause damage by a third party, or

    (c)   was wholly caused by the negligence or other wrongful act of any Government or other authority responsible for the maintenance of lights or other navigational aids in the exercise of that function.

3. If the owner proves that the pollution damage resulted wholly or partially either from an act or omission done with intent to cause damage by the person who suffered the damage or from the negligence of that person, the owner may be exonerated wholly or partially from his liability to such person.

4. No claim for compensation for pollution damage may be made against the owner otherwise than in accordance with this Convention. Subject to paragraph 5 of this Article, no claim for compensation for pollution damage under this Convention or otherwise may be made against:

    (a)   the servants or agents of the owner or the members of the crew;

    (b)   the pilot or any other person who, without being a member of the crew, performs services for the ship;

    (c)   any charterer (howsoever described, including a bareboat charterer), manager or operator of the ship;

    (d)   any person performing salvage operations with the consent of the owner or on the instructions of a competent public authority;

APPENDIX 9

(e)   any person taking preventive measures;

(f)   all servants or agents of persons mentioned in subparagraphs (c), (d) and (e);
unless the damage resulted from their personal act or omission, committed with the intent to cause such damage, or recklessly and with knowledge that such damage would probably result.

5. Nothing in this Convention shall prejudice any right of recourse of the owner against third parties.

Article IV

When an incident involving two or more ships occurs and pollution damage results therefrom, the owners of all the ships concerned, unless exonerated under Article III, shall be jointly and severally liable for all such damage which is not reasonably separable.

Article V

1. The owner of a ship shall be entitled to limit his liability under this Convention in respect of any one incident to an aggregate amount calculated as follows:

(a)   4,510,000 units of account[1] for a ship not exceeding 5,000 units of tonnage;

(b)   for a ship with a tonnage in excess thereof, for each additional unit of tonnage, 631 units of account[1] in addition to the amount mentioned in sub-paragraph (a);
provided, however, that this aggregate amount shall not in any event exceed 89,770,000 units of account[1].

2. The owner shall not be entitled to limit his liability under this Convention if it is proved that the pollution damage resulted from his personal act or omission, committed with the intent to cause such damage, or recklessly and with knowledge that such damage would probably result.

3. For the purpose of availing himself of the benefit of limitation provided for in paragraph 1 of this Article the owner shall constitute a fund for the total sum representing the limit of his liability with the Court or other competent authority of any one of the Contracting States in which action is brought under Article IX or, if no action is brought, with any Court or other competent authority in any one of the Contracting States in which an action can be brought under Article IX. The fund can be constituted either by depositing the sum or by producing a bank guarantee or other guarantee, acceptable under the legislation of the Contracting State where the fund is constituted, and considered to be adequate by the Court or other competent authority.

4. The fund shall be distributed among the claimants in proportion to the amounts of their established claims.

5. If before the fund is distributed the owner or any of his servants or agents or any person providing him insurance or other financial security has as a result of the incident in question, paid compensation for pollution damage, such person shall, up to the amount he has paid, acquire by subrogation the rights which the person so compensated would have enjoyed under this Convention.

6. The right of subrogation provided for in paragraph 5 of this Article may also be exercised by a person other than those mentioned therein in respect of any amount of compensation for pollution damage which he may have paid but only to the extent that such subrogation is permitted under the applicable national law.

7. Where the owner or any other person establishes that he may be compelled to pay at a later

---

1 Lower amounts applied to incidents occurring before 1 November 2003.

APPENDIX 9

date in whole or in part any such amount of compensation, with regard to which such person would have enjoyed a right of subrogation under paragraphs 5 or 6 of this Article, had the compensation been paid before the fund was distributed, the Court or other competent authority of the State where the fund has been constituted may order that a sufficient sum shall be provisionally set aside to enable such person at such later date to enforce his claim against the fund.

8. Claims in respect of expenses reasonably incurred or sacrifices reasonably made by the owner voluntarily to prevent or minimize pollution damage shall rank equally with other claims against the fund.

9. (a) The 'unit of account' referred to in paragraph 1 of this Article is the Special Drawing Right as defined by the International Monetary Fund. The amounts mentioned in paragraph 1 shall be converted into national currency on the basis of the value of that currency by reference to the Special Drawing Right on the date of the constitution of the fund referred to in paragraph 3. The value of the national currency, in terms of the Special Drawing Right, of a Contracting State which is a member of the International Monetary Fund shall be calculated in accordance with the method of valuation applied by the International Monetary Fund in effect on the date in question for its operations and transactions. The value of the national currency, in terms of the Special Drawing Right, of a Contracting State which is not a member of the International Monetary Fund shall be calculated in a manner determined by that State.

(b) Nevertheless, a Contracting State which is not a member of the International Monetary Fund and whose law does not permit the application of the provisions of paragraph 9(a) may, at the time of ratification, acceptance, approval of or accession to this Convention or at any time thereafter, declare that the unit of account referred to in paragraph 9(a) shall be equal to 15 gold francs. The gold franc referred to in this paragraph corresponds to sixty-five and a half milligrammes of gold of millesimal fineness nine hundred. The conversion of the gold franc into the national currency shall be made according to the law of the State concerned.

(c) The calculation mentioned in the last sentence of paragraph 9(a) and the conversion mentioned in paragraph 9(b) shall be made in such manner as to express in the national currency of the Contracting State as far as possible the same real value for the amounts in paragraph 1 as would result from the application of the first three sentences of paragraph 9(a). Contracting States shall communicate to the depositary the manner of calculation pursuant to paragraph 9(a), or the result of the conversion in paragraph 9(b) as the case may be, when depositing an instrument of ratification, acceptance, approval of or accession to this Convention and whenever there is a change in either.

10. For the purpose of this Article the ship's tonnage shall be the gross tonnage calculated in accordance with the tonnage measurement regulations contained in Annex I of the International Convention on Tonnage Measurement of Ships, 1969.

11. The insurer or other person providing financial security shall be entitled to constitute a fund in accordance with this Article on the same conditions and having the same effect as if it were constituted by the owner. Such a fund may be constituted even if, under the provisions of paragraph 2, the owner is not entitled to limit his liability, but its constitution shall in that case not prejudice the rights of any claimant against the owner.

Article VI

1. Where the owner, after an incident, has constituted a fund in accordance with Article V, and is entitled to limit his liability,

APPENDIX 9

(a) no person having a claim for pollution damage arising out of that incident shall be entitled to exercise any right against any other assets of the owner in respect of such claim;

(b) the Court or other competent authority of any Contracting State shall order the release of any ship or other property belonging to the owner which has been arrested in respect of a claim for pollution damage arising out of that incident, and shall similarly release any bail or other security furnished to avoid such arrest.

2. The foregoing shall, however, only apply if the claimant has access to the Court administering the fund and the fund is actually available in respect of his claim.

Article VII

1. The owner of a ship registered in a Contracting State and carrying more than 2,000 tons of oil in bulk as cargo shall be required to maintain insurance or other financial security, such as the guarantee of a bank or a certificate delivered by an international compensation fund, in the sums fixed by applying the limits of liability prescribed in Article V, paragraph 1 to cover his liability for pollution damage under this Convention.

2. A certificate attesting that insurance or other financial security is in force in accordance with the provisions of this Convention shall be issued to each ship after the appropriate authority of a Contracting State has determined that the requirements of paragraph 1 have been complied with. With respect to a ship registered in a Contracting State such certificate shall be issued or certified by the appropriate authority of the State of the ship's registry; with respect to a ship not registered in a Contracting State it may be issued or certified by the appropriate authority of any Contracting State. This certificate shall be in the form of the annexed model and shall contain the following particulars:

(a) name of ship and port of registration;

(b) name and principal place of business of owner;

(c) type of security;

(d) name and principal place of business of insurer or other person giving security and, where appropriate, place of business where the insurance or security is established;

(e) period of validity of certificate which shall not be longer than the period of validity of the insurance or other security.

3. The certificate shall be in the official language or languages of the issuing State. If the language used is neither English nor French, the text shall include a translation into one of these languages.

4. The certificate shall be carried on board the ship and a copy shall be deposited with the authorities who keep the record of the ship's registry or, if the ship is not registered in a Contracting State, with the authorities of the State issuing or certifying the certificate.

5. An insurance or other financial security shall not satisfy the requirements of this Article if it can cease, for reasons other than the expiry of the period of validity of the insurance or security specified in the certificate under paragraph 2 of this Article, before three months have elapsed from the date on which notice of its termination is given to the authorities referred to in paragraph 4 of this Article, unless the certificate has been surrendered to these authorities or a new certificate has been issued within the said period. The foregoing provisions shall similarly apply to any modification which results in the insurance or security no longer satisfying the requirements of this Article.

6. The State of registry shall, subject to the provisions of this Article, determine the conditions of issue and validity of the certificate.

7. Certificates issued or certified under the authority of a Contracting State in accordance with paragraph 2 shall be accepted by other Contracting States for the purposes of this

Convention and shall be regarded by other Contracting States as having the same force as certificates issued by them even if issued or certified in respect of a ship not registered in a Contracting State. A Contracting State may at any time request consultation with the issuing or certifying State should it believe that the insurer or guarantor named in the certificate is not financially capable of meeting the obligations imposed by this Convention.

8. Any claim for compensation for pollution damage may be brought directly against the insurer or other person providing financial security for the owner's liability for pollution damage. In such case the defendant may, even if the owner is not entitled to limit his liability according to Article V, paragraph 2, avail himself of the limits of liability prescribed in Article V, paragraph 1. He may further avail himself of the defences (other than the bankruptcy or winding up of the owner) which the owner himself would have been entitled to invoke. Furthermore, the defendant may avail himself of the defence that the pollution damage resulted from the wilful misconduct of the owner himself, but the defendant shall not avail himself of any other defence which he might have been entitled to invoke in proceedings brought by the owner against him. The defendant shall in any event have the right to require the owner to be joined in the proceedings.

9. Any sums provided by insurance or by other financial security maintained in accordance with paragraph 1 of this Article shall be available exclusively for the satisfaction of claims under this Convention.

10. A Contracting State shall not permit a ship under its flag to which this Article applies to trade unless a certificate has been issued under paragraph 2 or 12 of this Article.

11. Subject to the provisions of this Article, each Contracting State shall ensure, under its national legislation, that insurance or other security to the extent specified in paragraph 1 of this Article is in force in respect of any ship, wherever registered, entering or leaving a port in its territory, or arriving at or leaving an off-shore terminal in its territorial sea, if the ship actually carries more than 2,000 tons of oil in bulk as cargo.

12. If insurance or other financial security is not maintained in respect of a ship owned by a Contracting State, the provisions of this Article relating thereto shall not be applicable to such ship, but the ship shall carry a certificate issued by the appropriate authorities of the State of the ship's registry stating that the ship is owned by that State and that the ship's liability is covered within the limits prescribed by Article V, paragraph 1. Such a certificate shall follow as closely as practicable the model prescribed by paragraph 2 of this Article.

Article VIII

Rights of compensation under this Convention shall be extinguished unless an action is brought thereunder within three years from the date when the damage occurred. However, in no case shall an action be brought after six years from the date of the incident which caused the damage. Where this incident consists of a series of occurrences, the six years' period shall run from the date of the first such occurrence.

Article IX

1. Where an incident has caused pollution damage in the territory, including the territorial sea or an area referred to in Article II, of one or more Contracting States or preventive measures have been taken to prevent or minimize pollution damage in such territory including the territorial sea or area, actions for compensation may only be brought in the Courts of any such Contracting State or States. Reasonable notice of any such action shall be given to the defendant.

2. Each Contracting State shall ensure that its Courts possess the necessary jurisdiction to entertain such actions for compensation.

APPENDIX 9

3. After the fund has been constituted in accordance with Article V the Courts of the State in which the fund is constituted shall be exclusively competent to determine all matters relating to the apportionment and distribution of the fund.

Article X

1. Any judgment given by a Court with jurisdiction in accordance with Article IX which is enforceable in the State of origin where it is no longer subject to ordinary forms of review, shall be recognized in any Contracting State, except:
   (a) where the judgment was obtained by fraud; or
   (b) where the defendant was not given reasonable notice and a fair opportunity to present his case.

2. A judgment recognized under paragraph 1 of this Article shall be enforceable in each Contracting State as soon as the formalities required in that State have been complied with. The formalities shall not permit the merits of the case to be re-opened.

Article XI

1. The provisions of this Convention shall not apply to warships or other ships owned or operated by a State and used, for the time being, only on government non-commercial service.

2. With respect to ships owned by a Contracting State and used for commercial purposes, each State shall be subject to suit in the jurisdictions set forth in Article IX and shall waive all defences based on its status as a sovereign State.

Article XII

This Convention shall supersede any International Conventions in force or open for signature, ratification or accession at the date on which the Convention is opened for signature, but only to the extent that such Conventions would be in conflict with it; however, nothing in this Article shall affect the obligations of Contracting States to non-Contracting States arising under such International Conventions.

Article XII bis – Transitional provisions

The following transitional provisions shall apply in the case of a State which at the time of an incident is a Party both to this Convention and to the 1969 Liability Convention:
   (a) where an incident has caused pollution damage within the scope of this Convention, liability under this Convention shall be deemed to be discharged if, and to the extent that, it also arises under the 1969 Liability Convention;
   (b) where an incident has caused pollution damage within the scope of this Convention, and the State is a Party both to this Convention and to the International Convention on the Establishment of an International Fund for Compensation for Oil Pollution Damage, 1971, liability remaining to be discharged after the application of sub-paragraph (a) of this Article shall arise under this Convention only to the extent that pollution damage remains uncompensated after application of the said 1971 Convention;
   (c) in the application of Article III, paragraph 4, of this Convention the expression 'this Convention' shall be interpreted as referring to this Convention or the 1969 Liability Convention, as appropriate;

APPENDIX 9

(d) in the application of Article V, paragraph 3, of this Convention the total sum of the fund to be constituted shall be reduced by the amount by which liability has been deemed to be discharged in accordance with sub-paragraph (a) of this Article.

Article XII ter – Final clauses

The final clauses of this Convention shall be Articles 12 to 18 of the Protocol of 1992 to amend the 1969 Liability Convention. References in this Convention to Contracting States shall be taken to mean references to the Contracting States of that Protocol.

Final Clauses of the Protocol of 1992 to amend the 1969 Civil Liability Convention

Article 12 – Signature, ratification, acceptance, approval and accession

1. This Protocol shall be open for signature at London from 15 January 1993 to 14 January 1994 by all States.

2. Subject to paragraph 4, any State may become a Party to this Protocol by:
   (a) signature subject to ratification, acceptance or approval followed by ratification, acceptance or approval; or
   (b) accession.

3. Ratification, acceptance, approval or accession shall be effected by the deposit of a formal instrument to that effect with the Secretary-General of the Organization.

4. Any Contracting State to the International Convention on the Establishment of an International Fund for Compensation for Oil Pollution Damage, 1971, hereinafter referred to as the 1971 Fund Convention, may ratify, accept, approve or accede to this Protocol only if it ratifies, accepts, approves or accedes to the Protocol of 1992 to amend that Convention at the same time, unless it denounces the 1971 Fund Convention to take effect on the date when this Protocol enters into force for that State.

5. A State which is a Party to this Protocol but not a Party to the 1969 Liability Convention shall be bound by the provisions of the 1969 Liability Convention as amended by this Protocol in relation to other States Parties hereto, but shall not be bound by the provisions of the 1969 Liability Convention in relation to States Parties thereto.

6. Any instrument of ratification, acceptance, approval or accession deposited after the entry into force of an amendment to the 1969 Liability Convention as amended by this Protocol shall be deemed to apply to the Convention so amended, as modified by such amendment.

Article 13 – Entry into force

1. This Protocol shall enter into force twelve months following the date on which ten States including four States each with not less than one million units of gross tanker tonnage have deposited instruments of ratification, acceptance, approval or accession with the Secretary-General of the Organization.

2. However, any Contracting State to the 1971 Fund Convention may, at the time of the deposit of its instrument of ratification, acceptance, approval or accession in respect of this Protocol, declare that such instrument shall be deemed not to be effective for the purposes of this Article until the end of the six-month period in Article 31 of the Protocol of 1992 to amend the 1971 Fund Convention. A State which is not a Contracting State to the 1971 Fund Convention but which deposits an instrument of ratification, acceptance, approval or

APPENDIX 9

accession in respect of the Protocol of 1992 to amend the 1971 Fund Convention may also make a declaration in accordance with this paragraph at the same time.

3. Any State which has made a declaration in accordance with the preceding paragraph may withdraw it at any time by means of a notification addressed to the Secretary-General of the Organization. Any such withdrawal shall take effect on the date the notification is received, provided that such State shall be deemed to have deposited its instrument of ratification, acceptance, approval or accession in respect of this Protocol on that date.

4. For any State which ratifies, accepts, approves or accedes to it after the conditions in paragraph 1 for entry into force have been met, this Protocol shall enter into force twelve months following the date of deposit by such State of the appropriate instrument.

Article 14 – Revision and amendment

1. A Conference for the purpose of revising or amending the 1992 Liability Convention may be convened by the Organization.

2. The Organization shall convene a Conference of Contracting States for the purpose of revising or amending the 1992 Liability Convention at the request of not less than one third of the Contracting States.

Article 15 – Amendments of limitation amounts

1. Upon the request of at least one quarter of the Contracting States any proposal to amend the limits of liability laid down in Article V, paragraph 1, of the 1969 Liability Convention as amended by this Protocol shall be circulated by the Secretary-General to all Members of the Organization and to all Contracting States.

2. Any amendment proposed and circulated as above shall be submitted to the Legal Committee of the Organization for consideration at a date at least six months after the date of its circulation.

3. All Contracting States to the 1969 Liability Convention as amended by this Protocol, whether or not Members of the Organization, shall be entitled to participate in the proceedings of the Legal Committee for the consideration and adoption of amendments.

4. Amendments shall be adopted by a two-thirds majority of the Contracting States present and voting in the Legal Committee, expanded as provided for in paragraph 3, on condition that at least one half of the Contracting States shall be present at the time of voting.

5. When acting on a proposal to amend the limits, the Legal Committee shall take into account the experience of incidents and in particular the amount of damage resulting therefrom, changes in the monetary values and the effect of the proposed amendment on the cost of insurance. It shall also take into account the relationship between the limits in Article V, paragraph 1, of the 1969 Liability Convention as amended by this Protocol and those in Article 4, paragraph 4, of the International Convention on the Establishment of an International Fund for Compensation for Oil Pollution Damage, 1992.

6. (a) No amendment of the limits of liability under this Article may be considered before 15 January 1998 nor less than five years from the date of entry into force of a previous amendment under this Article. No amendment under this Article shall be considered before this Protocol has entered into force.

   (b) No limit may be increased so as to exceed an amount which corresponds to the limit laid down in the 1969 Liability Convention as amended by this Protocol increased by 6 per cent per year calculated on a compound basis from 15 January 1993.

   (c) No limit may be increased so as to exceed an amount which corresponds to the

383

APPENDIX 9

limit laid down in the 1969 Liability Convention as amended by this Protocol multiplied by 3.

7. Any amendment adopted in accordance with paragraph 4 shall be notified by the Organization to all Contracting States. The amendment shall be deemed to have been accepted at the end of a period of eighteen months after the date of notification, unless within that period not less than one quarter of the States that were Contracting States at the time of the adoption of the amendment by the Legal Committee have communicated to the Organization that they do not accept the amendment in which case the amendment is rejected and shall have no effect.

8. An amendment deemed to have been accepted in accordance with paragraph 7 shall enter into force eighteen months after its acceptance.

9. All Contracting States shall be bound by the amendment, unless they denounce this Protocol in accordance with Article 16, paragraphs 1 and 2, at least six months before the amendment enters into force. Such denunciation shall take effect when the amendment enters into force.

10. When an amendment has been adopted by the Legal Committee but the eighteen-month period for its acceptance has not yet expired, a State which becomes a Contracting State during that period shall be bound by the amendment if it enters into force. A State which becomes a Contracting State after that period shall be bound by an amendment which has been accepted in accordance with paragraph 7. In the cases referred to in this paragraph, a State becomes bound by an amendment when that amendment enters into force, or when this Protocol enters into force for that State, if later.

Article 16 – Denunciation

1. This Protocol may be denounced by any Party at any time after the date on which it enters into force for that Party.

2. Denunciation shall be effected by the deposit of an instrument with the Secretary-General of the Organization.

3. A denunciation shall take effect twelve months, or such longer period as may be specified in the instrument of denunciation, after its deposit with the Secretary-General of the Organization.

4. As between the Parties to this Protocol, denunciation by any of them of the 1969 Liability Convention in accordance with Article XVI thereof shall not be construed in any way as a denunciation of the 1969 Liability Convention as amended by this Protocol.

5. Denunciation of the Protocol of 1992 to amend the 1971 Fund Convention by a State which remains a Party to the 1971 Fund Convention shall be deemed to be a denunciation of this Protocol. Such denunciation shall take effect on the date on which denunciation of the Protocol of 1992 to amend the 1971 Fund Convention takes effect according to Article 34 of that Protocol.

Article 17 – Depositary

1. This Protocol and any amendments accepted under Article 15 shall be deposited with the Secretary-General of the Organization.

2. The Secretary-General of the Organization shall:
  (a) inform all States which have signed or acceded to this Protocol of:
      (i) each new signature or deposit of an instrument together with the date thereof;
      (ii) each declaration and notification under Article 13 and each declaration

APPENDIX 9

and communication under Article V, paragraph 9, of the 1992 Liability Convention;

(iii)   the date of entry into force of this Protocol;

(iv)   any proposal to amend limits of liability which has been made in accordance with Article 15, paragraph 1;

(v)   any amendment which has been adopted in accordance with Article 15, paragraph 4;

(vi)   any amendment deemed to have been accepted under Article 15, paragraph 7, together with the date on which that amendment shall enter into force in accordance with paragraphs 8 and 9 of that Article;

(vii)   the deposit of any instrument of denunciation of this Protocol together with the date of the deposit and the date on which it takes effect;

(viii)   any denunciation deemed to have been made under Article 16, paragraph 5;

(ix)   any communication called for by any Article of this Protocol;

(b)   transmit certified true copies of this Protocol to all Signatory States and to all States which accede to this Protocol.

3. As soon as this Protocol enters into force, the text shall be transmitted by the Secretary-General of the Organization to the Secretariat of the United Nations for registration and publication in accordance with Article 102 of the Charter of the United Nations.

Article 18 – Languages

This Protocol is established in a single original in the Arabic, Chinese, English, French, Russian and Spanish languages, each text being equally authentic.

DONE AT LONDON this twenty-seventh day of November one thousand nine hundred and ninety-two.

IN WITNESS WHEREOF the undersigned, being duly authorized by their respective Governments for that purpose, have signed this Protocol.

APPENDIX 10

Consolidated text of the International Convention on the Establishment of an International Fund for Compensation for Oil Pollution Damage, 1992, as amended by its Protocol of 2000 and its Supplementary Protocol of 2003 (The Fund Convention)

Consolidated text of the International Convention on the Establishment of an International Fund for Compensation for Oil Pollution Damage, 1992, as amended by its Protocol of 2000

The States Parties to the present Convention,

BEING PARTIES to the International Convention on Civil Liability for Oil Pollution Damage, adopted at Brussels on 29 November 1969,

CONSCIOUS of the dangers of pollution posed by the world-wide maritime carriage of oil in bulk,

CONVINCED of the need to ensure that adequate compensation is available to persons who suffer damage caused by pollution resulting from the escape or discharge of oil from ships,

CONSIDERING that the International Convention of 29 November 1969, on Civil Liability for Oil Pollution Damage, by providing a regime for compensation for pollution damage in Contracting States and for the costs of measures, wherever taken, to prevent or minimize such damage, represents a considerable progress towards the achievement of this aim,

CONSIDERING HOWEVER that this regime does not afford full compensation for victims of oil pollution damage in all cases while it imposes an additional financial burden on shipowners,

CONSIDERING FURTHER that the economic consequences of oil pollution damage resulting from the escape or discharge of oil carried in bulk at sea by ships should not exclusively be borne by the shipping industry but should in part be borne by the oil cargo interests,

CONVINCED of the need to elaborate a compensation and indemnification system supplementary to the International Convention on Civil Liability for Oil Pollution Damage with a view to ensuring that full compensation will be available to victims of oil pollution incidents and that the shipowners are at the same time given relief in respect of the additional financial burdens imposed on them by the said Convention,

TAKING NOTE of the Resolution on the Establishment of an International Compensation Fund for Oil Pollution Damage which was adopted on 29 November 1969 by the International Legal Conference on Marine Pollution Damage,

APPENDIX 10

HAVE AGREED as follows:

Article 1

For the purposes of this Convention:

1. '1992 Liability Convention' means the International Convention on Civil Liability for Oil Pollution Damage, 1992.

1bis. '1971 Fund Convention' means the International Convention on the Establishment of an International Fund for Compensation for Oil Pollution Damage, 1971. For States Parties to the Protocol of 1976 to that Convention, the term shall be deemed to include the 1971 Fund Convention as amended by that Protocol.

2. 'Ship', 'Person', 'Owner', 'Oil', 'Pollution Damage', 'Preventive Measures', 'Incident', and 'Organization' have the same meaning as in Article I of the 1992 Liability Convention.

3. 'Contributing Oil' means crude oil and fuel oil as defined in sub-paragraphs (a) and (b) below:

   (a) 'Crude Oil' means any liquid hydrocarbon mixture occurring naturally in the earth whether or not treated to render it suitable for transportation. It also includes crude oils from which certain distillate fractions have been removed (sometimes referred to as 'topped crudes') or to which certain distillate fractions have been added (sometimes referred to as 'spiked' or 'reconstituted' crudes).

   (b) 'Fuel Oil' means heavy distillates or residues from crude oil or blends of such materials intended for use as a fuel for the production of heat or power of a quality equivalent to the 'American Society for Testing and Materials' Specification for Number Four Fuel Oil (Designation D 396–69)', or heavier.

4. 'Unit of account' has the same meaning as in Article V, paragraph 9, of the 1992 Liability Convention.

5. 'Ship's tonnage' has the same meaning as in Article V, paragraph 10, of the 1992 Liability Convention.

6. 'Ton', in relation to oil, means a metric ton.

7. 'Guarantor' means any person providing insurance or other financial security to cover an owner's liability in pursuance of Article VII, paragraph 1, of the 1992 Liability Convention.

8. 'Terminal installation' means any site for the storage of oil in bulk which is capable of receiving oil from waterborne transportation, including any facility situated off-shore and linked to such site.

9. Where an incident consists of a series of occurrences, it shall be treated as having occurred on the date of the first such occurrence.

Article 2

1. An International Fund for compensation for pollution damage, to be named 'The International Oil Pollution Compensation Fund 1992' and hereinafter referred to as 'the Fund', is hereby established with the following aims:

   (a) to provide compensation for pollution damage to the extent that the protection afforded by the 1992 Liability Convention is inadequate;

   (b) to give effect to the related purposes set out in this Convention.

2. The Fund shall in each Contracting State be recognized as a legal person capable under the laws of that State of assuming rights and obligations and of being a party in legal proceedings before the courts of that State. Each Contracting State shall recognize the Director of the Fund (hereinafter referred to as 'The Director') as the legal representative of the Fund.

387

APPENDIX 10

Article 3

This Convention shall apply exclusively:
- (a)   to pollution damage caused:
    - (i)   in the territory, including the territorial sea, of a Contracting State, and
    - (ii)   in the exclusive economic zone of a Contracting State, established in accordance with international law, or, if a Contracting State has not established such a zone, in an area beyond and adjacent to the territorial sea of that State determined by that State in accordance with international law and extending not more than 200 nautical miles from the baselines from which the breadth of its territorial sea is measured;
- (b)   to preventive measures, wherever taken, to prevent or minimize such damage.

Compensation

Article 4

1 For the purpose of fulfilling its function under Article 2, paragraph 1(a), the Fund shall pay compensation to any person suffering pollution damage if such person has been unable to obtain full and adequate compensation for the damage under the terms of the 1992 Liability Convention,
- (a)   because no liability for the damage arises under the 1992 Liability Convention;
- (b)   because the owner liable for the damage under the 1992 Liability Convention is financially incapable of meeting his obligations in full and any financial security that may be provided under Article VII of that Convention does not cover or is insufficient to satisfy the claims for compensation for the damage; an owner being treated as financially incapable of meeting his obligations and a financial security being treated as insufficient if the person suffering the damage has been unable to obtain full satisfaction of the amount of compensation due under the 1992 Liability Convention after having taken all reasonable steps to pursue the legal remedies available to him;
- (c)   because the damage exceeds the owner's liability under the 1992 Liability Convention as limited pursuant to Article V, paragraph 1, of that Convention or under the terms of any other international Convention in force or open for signature, ratification or accession at the date of this Convention.

Expenses reasonably incurred or sacrifices reasonably made by the owner voluntarily to prevent or minimize pollution damage shall be treated as pollution damage for the purposes of this Article.

2. The Fund shall incur no obligation under the preceding paragraph if:
- (a)   it proves that the pollution damage resulted from an act of war, hostilities, civil war or insurrection or was caused by oil which has escaped or been discharged from a warship or other ship owned or operated by a State and used, at the time of the incident, only on Government non-commercial service; or
- (b)   the claimant cannot prove that the damage resulted from an incident involving one or more ships.

3. If the Fund proves that the pollution damage resulted wholly or partially either from an act or omission done with the intent to cause damage by the person who suffered the damage or from the negligence of that person, the Fund may be exonerated wholly or partially from its obligation to pay compensation to such person. The Fund shall in any event be exonerated to the extent that the shipowner may have been exonerated under Article III, paragraph 3, of

APPENDIX 10

the 1992 Liability Convention. However, there shall be no such exoneration of the Fund with regard to preventive measures.

4. (a) Except as otherwise provided in sub-paragraphs (b) and (c) of this paragraph, the aggregate amount of compensation payable by the Fund under this Article shall in respect of any one incident be limited, so that the total sum of that amount and the amount of compensation actually paid under the 1992 Liability Convention for pollution damage within the scope of application of this Convention as defined in Article 3 shall not exceed 203,000,000 units of account.

(b) Except as otherwise provided in sub-paragraph (c), the aggregate amount of compensation payable by the Fund under this Article for pollution damage resulting from a natural phenomenon of an exceptional, inevitable and irresistible character shall not exceed 203,000,000 units of account.

(c) The maximum amount of compensation referred to in sub-paragraphs (a) and (b) shall be 300,740,000 units of account with respect to any incident occurring during any period when there are three Parties to this Convention in respect of which the combined relevant quantity of contributing oil received by persons in the territories of such Parties, during the preceding calendar year, equalled or exceeded 600 million tons.

(d) Interest accrued on a fund constituted in accordance with Article V, paragraph 3, of the 1992 Liability Convention, if any, shall not be taken into account for the computation of the maximum compensation payable by the Fund under this Article.

(e) The amounts mentioned in this Article shall be converted into national currency on the basis of the value of that currency by reference to the Special Drawing Right on the date of the decision of the Assembly of the Fund as to the first date of payment of compensation.

5. Where the amount of established claims against the Fund exceeds the aggregate amount of compensation payable under paragraph 4, the amount available shall be distributed in such a manner that the proportion between any established claim and the amount of compensation actually recovered by the claimant under this Convention shall be the same for all claimants.

6. The Assembly of the Fund may decide that, in exceptional cases, compensation in accordance with this Convention can be paid even if the owner of the ship has not constituted a fund in accordance with Article V, paragraph 3, of the 1992 Liability Convention. In such case paragraph 4(e) of this Article applies accordingly.

7. The Fund shall, at the request of a Contracting State, use its good offices as necessary to assist that State to secure promptly such personnel, material and services as are necessary to enable the State to take measures to prevent or mitigate pollution damage arising from an incident in respect of which the Fund may be called upon to pay compensation under this Convention.

8. The Fund may on conditions to be laid down in the Internal Regulations provide credit facilities with a view to the taking of preventive measures against pollution damage arising from a particular incident in respect of which the Fund may be called upon to pay compensation under this Convention.

Article 5

(1971 Article 5 deleted)

Article 6

Rights to compensation under Article 4 shall be extinguished unless an action is brought thereunder or a notification has been made pursuant to Article 7, paragraph 6, within three

APPENDIX 10

years from the date when the damage occurred. However, in no case shall an action be brought after six years from the date of the incident which caused the damage.

Article 7

1. Subject to the subsequent provisions of this Article, any action against the Fund for compensation under Article 4 of this Convention shall be brought only before a court competent under Article IX of the 1992 Liability Convention in respect of actions against the owner who is or who would, but for the provisions of Article III, paragraph 2, of that Convention, have been liable for pollution damage caused by the relevant incident.

2. Each Contracting State shall ensure that its courts possess the necessary jurisdiction to entertain such actions against the Fund as are referred to in paragraph 1.

3. Where an action for compensation for pollution damage has been brought before a court competent under Article IX of the 1992 Liability Convention against the owner of a ship or his guarantor, such court shall have exclusive jurisdictional competence over any action against the Fund for compensation under the provisions of Article 4 of this Convention in respect of the same damage. However, where an action for compensation for pollution damage under the 1992 Liability Convention has been brought before a court in a State Party to the 1992 Liability Convention but not to this Convention, any action against the Fund under Article 4 of this Convention shall at the option of the claimant be brought either before a court of the State where the Fund has its headquarters or before any court of a State Party to this Convention competent under Article IX of the 1992 Liability Convention.

4. Each Contracting State shall ensure that the Fund shall have the right to intervene as a party to any legal proceedings instituted in accordance with Article IX of the 1992 Liability Convention before a competent court of that State against the owner of a ship or his guarantor.

5. Except as otherwise provided in paragraph 6, the Fund shall not be bound by any judgment or decision in proceedings to which it has not been a party or by any settlement to which it is not a party.

6. Without prejudice to the provisions of paragraph 4, where an action under the 1992 Liability Convention for compensation for pollution damage has been brought against an owner or his guarantor before a competent court in a Contracting State, each party to the proceedings shall be entitled under the national law of that State to notify the Fund of the proceedings. Where such notification has been made in accordance with the formalities required by the law of the court seized and in such time and in such a manner that the Fund has in fact been in a position effectively to intervene as a party to the proceedings, any judgment rendered by the court in such proceedings shall, after it has become final and enforceable in the State where the judgment was given, become binding upon the Fund in the sense that the facts and findings in that judgment may not be disputed by the Fund even if the Fund has not actually intervened in the proceedings.

Article 8

Subject to any decision concerning the distribution referred to in Article 4, paragraph 5, any judgment given against the Fund by a court having jurisdiction in accordance with Article 7, paragraphs 1 and 3, shall, when it has become enforceable in the State of origin and is in that State no longer subject to ordinary forms of review, be recognized and enforceable in each Contracting State on the same conditions as are prescribed in Article X of the 1992 Liability Convention.

390

APPENDIX 10

Article 9

1. The Fund shall, in respect of any amount of compensation for pollution damage paid by the Fund in accordance with Article 4, paragraph 1, of this Convention, acquire by subrogation the rights that the person so compensated may enjoy under the 1992 Liability Convention against the owner or his guarantor.

2. Nothing in this Convention shall prejudice any right of recourse or subrogation of the Fund against persons other than those referred to in the preceding paragraph. In any event the right of the Fund to subrogation against such person shall not be less favourable than that of an insurer of the person to whom compensation has been paid.

3. Without prejudice to any other rights of subrogation or recourse against the Fund which may exist, a Contracting State or agency thereof which has paid compensation for pollution damage in accordance with provisions of national law shall acquire by subrogation the rights which the person so compensated would have enjoyed under this Convention.

Contributions

Article 10

1. Annual contributions to the Fund shall be made in respect of each Contracting State by any person who, in the calendar year referred to in Article 12, paragraph 2(a) or (b), has received in total quantities exceeding 150,000 tons:
  (a) in the ports or terminal installations in the territory of that State contributing oil carried by sea to such ports or terminal installations; and
  (b) in any installations situated in the territory of that Contracting State contributing oil which has been carried by sea and discharged in a port or terminal installation of a non-Contracting State, provided that contributing oil shall only be taken into account by virtue of this sub-paragraph on first receipt in a Contracting State after its discharge in that non-Contracting State.
2. (a) For the purposes of paragraph 1, where the quantity of contributing oil received in the territory of a Contracting State by any person in a calendar year when aggregated with the quantity of contributing oil received in the same Contracting State in that year by any associated person or persons exceeds 150,000 tons, such person shall pay contributions in respect of the actual quantity received by him notwithstanding that that quantity did not exceed 150,000 tons.
  (b) 'Associated person' means any subsidiary or commonly controlled entity. The question whether a person comes within this definition shall be determined by the national law of the State concerned.

Article 11

(1971 Article 11 deleted)

Article 12

1. With a view to assessing the amount of annual contributions due, if any, and taking account of the necessity to maintain sufficient liquid funds, the Assembly shall for each calendar year make an estimate in the form of a budget of:
  (i) *Expenditure*

APPENDIX 10

(a) costs and expenses of the administration of the Fund in the relevant year and any deficit from operations in preceding years;

(b) payments to be made by the Fund in the relevant year for the satisfaction of claims against the Fund due under Article 4, including repayment on loans previously taken by the Fund for the satisfaction of such claims, to the extent that the aggregate amount of such claims in respect of any one incident does not exceed four million units of account;

(c) payments to be made by the Fund in the relevant year for the satisfaction of claims against the Fund due under Article 4, including repayments on loans previously taken by the Fund for the satisfaction of such claims, to the extent that the aggregate amount of such claims in respect of any one incident is in excess of four million units of account;

(ii) *Income*

(a) surplus funds from operations in preceding years, including any interest;

(b) annual contributions, if required to balance the budget;

(c) any other income.

2. The Assembly shall decide the total amount of contributions to be levied. On the basis of that decision, the Director shall, in respect of each Contracting State, calculate for each person referred to in Article 10 the amount of his annual contribution:

(a) in so far as the contribution is for the satisfaction of payments referred to in paragraph 1(i)(a) and (b) on the basis of a fixed sum for each ton of contributing oil received in the relevant State by such persons during the preceding calendar year; and

(b) in so far as the contribution is for the satisfaction of payments referred to in paragraph 1(i)(c) of this Article on the basis of a fixed sum for each ton of contributing oil received by such person during the calendar year preceding that in which the incident in question occurred, provided that State was a Party to this Convention at the date of the incident.

3. The sums referred to in paragraph 2 above shall be arrived at by dividing the relevant total amount of contributions required by the total amount of contributing oil received in all Contracting States in the relevant year.

4. The annual contribution shall be due on the date to be laid down in the Internal Regulations of the Fund. The Assembly may decide on a different date of payment.

5. The Assembly may decide, under conditions to be laid down in the Financial Regulations of the Fund, to make transfers between funds received in accordance with Article 12.2(a) and funds received in accordance with Article 12.2(b).

Article 13

1. The amount of any contribution due under Article 12 and which is in arrears shall bear interest at a rate which shall be determined in accordance with the Internal Regulations of the Fund, provided that different rates may be fixed for different circumstances.

2. Each Contracting State shall ensure that any obligation to contribute to the Fund arising under this Convention in respect of oil received within the territory of that State is fulfilled and shall take any appropriate measures under its law, including the imposing of such sanctions as it may deem necessary, with a view to the effective execution of any such obligation; provided, however, that such measures shall only be directed against those persons who are under an obligation to contribute to the Fund.

3. Where a person who is liable in accordance with the provisions of Articles 10 and 12 to make contributions to the Fund does not fulfil his obligations in respect of any such contribution or any part thereof and is in arrears, the Director shall take all appropriate action against such person on behalf of the Fund with a view to the recovery of the amount due. However,

APPENDIX 10

where the defaulting contributor is manifestly insolvent or the circumstances otherwise so warrant, the Assembly may, upon recommendation of the Director, decide that no action shall be taken or continued against the contributor.

Article 14

1. Each Contracting State may at the time when it deposits its instrument of ratification or accession or at any time thereafter declare that it assumes itself obligations that are incumbent under this Convention on any person who is liable to contribute to the Fund in accordance with Article 10, paragraph 1, in respect of oil received within the territory of that State. Such declaration shall be made in writing and shall specify which obligations are assumed.

2. Where a declaration under paragraph 1 is made prior to the entry into force of this Convention in accordance with Article 40, it shall be deposited with the Secretary-General of the Organization who shall after the entry into force of the Convention communicate the declaration to the Director.

3. A declaration under paragraph 1 which is made after the entry into force of this Convention shall be deposited with the Director.

4. A declaration made in accordance with this Article may be withdrawn by the relevant State giving notice thereof in writing to the Director. Such notification shall take effect three months after the Director's receipt thereof.

5. Any State which is bound by a declaration made under this Article shall, in any proceedings brought against it before a competent court in respect of any obligation specified in the declaration, waive any immunity that it would otherwise be entitled to invoke.

Article 15

1. Each Contracting State shall ensure that any person who receives contributing oil within its territory in such quantities that he is liable to contribute to the Fund appears on a list to be established and kept up to date by the Director in accordance with the subsequent provisions of this Article.

2. For the purposes set out in paragraph 1, each Contracting State shall communicate, at a time and in the manner to be prescribed in the Internal Regulations, to the Director the name and address of any person who in respect of that State is liable to contribute to the Fund pursuant to Article 10, as well as data on the relevant quantities of contributing oil received by any such person during the preceding calendar year.

3. For the purposes of ascertaining who are, at any given time, the persons liable to contribute to the Fund in accordance with Article 10, paragraph 1, and of establishing, where applicable, the quantities of oil to be taken into account for any such person when determining the amount of his contribution, the list shall be prima facie evidence of the facts stated therein.

4. Where a Contracting State does not fulfil its obligations to submit to the Director the communication referred to in paragraph 2 and this results in a financial loss for the Fund, that Contracting State shall be liable to compensate the Fund for such loss. The Assembly shall, on the recommendation of the Director, decide whether such compensation shall be payable by that Contracting State.

Organization and administration

Article 16

The Fund shall have an Assembly and a Secretariat headed by a Director.

APPENDIX 10

Assembly

Article 17

The Assembly shall consist of all Contracting States to this Convention.

Article 18

The functions of the Assembly shall be:
1. to elect at each regular session its Chairman and two Vice-Chairmen who shall hold office until the next regular session;
2. to determine its own rules of procedure, subject to the provisions of this Convention;
3. to adopt Internal Regulations necessary for the proper functioning of the Fund;
4. to appoint the Director and make provisions for the appointment of such other personnel as may be necessary and determine the terms and conditions of service of the Director and other personnel;
5. to adopt the annual budget and fix the annual contributions;
6. to appoint auditors and approve the accounts of the Fund;
7. to approve settlements of claims against the Fund, to take decisions in respect of the distribution among claimants of the available amount of compensation in accordance with Article 4, paragraph 5, and to determine the terms and conditions according to which provisional payments in respect of claims shall be made with a view to ensuring that victims of pollution damage are compensated as promptly as possible;
8. (deleted).
9. to establish any temporary or permanent subsidiary body it may consider to be necessary, to define its terms of reference and to give it the authority needed to perform the functions entrusted to it; when appointing the members of such body, the Assembly shall endeavour to secure an equitable geographical distribution of members and to ensure that the Contracting States, in respect of which the largest quantities of contributing oil are being received, are appropriately represented; the Rules of Procedure of the Assembly may be applied, mutatis mutandis, for the work of such subsidiary body;
10. to determine which non-Contracting States and which inter-governmental and international non-governmental organizations shall be admitted to take part, without voting rights, in meetings of the Assembly and subsidiary bodies;
11. to give instructions concerning the administration of the Fund to the Director and subsidiary bodies;
12. (deleted);
13. to supervise the proper execution of the Convention and of its own decisions;
14. to perform such other functions as are allocated to it under the Convention or are otherwise necessary for the proper operation of the Fund.

Article 19

1. Regular sessions of the Assembly shall take place once every calendar year upon convocation by the Director.

2. Extraordinary sessions of the Assembly shall be convened by the Director at the request of at least one third of the members of the Assembly and may be convened on the Director's own initiative after consultation with the Chairman of the Assembly. The Director shall give members at least thirty days' notice of such sessions.

APPENDIX 10

Article 20

A majority of the members of the Assembly shall constitute a quorum for its meetings.

Articles 21–27

(1971 Articles 21–27 deleted)

Secretariat

Article 28

1. The Secretariat shall comprise the Director and such staff as the administration of the Fund may require.
2. The Director shall be the legal representative of the Fund.

Article 29

1. The Director shall be the chief administrative officer of the Fund. Subject to the instructions given to him by the Assembly, he shall perform those functions which are assigned to him by this Convention, the Internal Regulations of the Fund and the Assembly.
2. The Director shall in particular:
   (a) appoint the personnel required for the administration of the Fund;
   (b) take all appropriate measures with a view to the proper administration of the Fund's assets;
   (c) collect the contributions due under this Convention while observing in particular the provisions of Article 13, paragraph 3;
   (d) to the extent necessary to deal with claims against the Fund and carry out the other functions of the Fund, employ the services of legal, financial and other experts;
   (e) take all appropriate measures for dealing with claims against the Fund within the limits and on conditions to be laid down in the Internal Regulations, including the final settlement of claims without the prior approval of the Assembly where these Regulations so provide;
   (f) prepare and submit to the Assembly the financial statements and budget estimates for each calendar year;
   (g) prepare, in consultation with the Chairman of the Assembly, and publish a report of the activities of the Fund during the previous calendar year;
   (h) prepare, collect and circulate the papers, documents, agenda, minutes and information that may be required for the work of the Assembly and subsidiary bodies.

Article 30

In the performance of their duties the Director and the staff and experts appointed by him shall not seek or receive instructions from any Government or from any authority external to the Fund. They shall refrain from any action which might reflect on their position as international officials. Each Contracting State on its part undertakes to respect the exclusively international character of the responsibilities of the Director and the staff and experts appointed by him, and not to seek to influence them in the discharge of their duties.

APPENDIX 10

Finances

Article 31

1. Each Contracting State shall bear the salary, travel and other expenses of its own delegation to the Assembly and of its representatives on subsidiary bodies.
2. Any other expenses incurred in the operation of the Fund shall be borne by the Fund.

Voting

Article 32

The following provisions shall apply to voting in the Assembly:
    (a)   each member shall have one vote;
    (b)   except as otherwise provided in Article 33, decisions of the Assembly shall be by a majority vote of the members present and voting;
    (c)   decisions where a three-fourths or a two-thirds majority is required shall be by a three-fourths or two-thirds majority vote, as the case may be, of those present;
    (d)   for the purpose of this Article the phrase 'members present' means 'members present at the meeting at the time of the vote', and the phrase 'members present and voting' means 'members present and casting an affirmative or negative vote'.
Members who abstain from voting shall be considered as not voting.

Article 33

The following decisions of the Assembly shall require a two-thirds majority:
    (a)   a decision under Article 13, paragraph 3, not to take or continue action against a contributor;
    (b)   the appointment of the Director under Article 18, paragraph 4;
    (c)   the establishment of subsidiary bodies, under Article 18, paragraph 9, and matters relating to such establishment.

Article 34

1. The Fund, its assets, income, including contributions, and other property shall enjoy in all Contracting States exemption from all direct taxation.
2. When the Fund makes substantial purchases of movable or immovable property, or has important work carried out which is necessary for the exercise of its official activities and the cost of which includes indirect taxes or sales taxes, the Governments of Member States shall take, whenever possible, appropriate measures for the remission or refund of the amount of such duties and taxes.
3. No exemption shall be accorded in the case of duties, taxes or dues which merely constitute payment for public utility services.
4. The Fund shall enjoy exemption from all customs duties, taxes and other related taxes on articles imported or exported by it or on its behalf for its official use. Articles thus imported shall not be transferred either for consideration or gratis on the territory of the country into which they have been imported except on conditions agreed by the Government of that country.
5. Persons contributing to the Fund and victims and owners of ships receiving compensation from the Fund shall be subject to the fiscal legislation of the State where they are taxable, no special exemption or other benefit being conferred on them in this respect.

APPENDIX 10

6. Information relating to individual contributors supplied for the purpose of this Convention shall not be divulged outside the Fund except in so far as it may be strictly necessary to enable the Fund to carry out its functions including the bringing and defending of legal proceedings.

7. Independently of existing or future regulations concerning currency or transfers, Contracting States shall authorize the transfer and payment of any contribution to the Fund and of any compensation paid by the Fund without any restriction.

Transitional Provisions

Article 35

Claims for compensation under Article 4 arising from incidents occurring after the date of entry into force of this Convention may not be brought against the Fund earlier than the one hundred and twentieth day after that date.

Article 36

The Secretary-General of the Organization shall convene the first session of the Assembly. This session shall take place as soon as possible after entry into force of this Convention and, in any case, not more than thirty days after such entry into force.

Article 36 bis

The following transitional provisions shall apply in the period, hereinafter referred to as the transitional period, commencing with the date of entry into force of this Convention and ending with the date on which the denunciations provided for in Article 31 of the 1992 Protocol to amend the 1971 Fund Convention take effect:

(a) In the application of paragraph 1(a) of Article 2 of this Convention, the reference to the 1992 Liability Convention shall include reference to the International Convention on Civil Liability for Oil Pollution Damage, 1969, either in its original version or as amended by the Protocol thereto of 1976 (referred to in this Article as 'the 1969 Liability Convention'), and also the 1971 Fund Convention.

(b) Where an incident has caused pollution damage within the scope of this Convention, the Fund shall pay compensation to any person suffering pollution damage only if, and to the extent that, such person has been unable to obtain full and adequate compensation for the damage under the terms of the 1969 Liability Convention, the 1971 Fund Convention and the 1992 Liability Convention, provided that, in respect of pollution damage within the scope of this Convention in respect of a Party to this Convention but not a Party to the 1971 Fund Convention, the Fund shall pay compensation to any person suffering pollution damage only if, and to the extent that, such person would have been unable to obtain full and adequate compensation had that State been party to each of the above-mentioned Conventions.

(c) In the application of Article 4 of this Convention, the amount to be taken into account in determining the aggregate amount of compensation payable by the Fund shall also include the amount of compensation actually paid under the 1969 Liability Convention, if any, and the amount of compensation actually paid or deemed to have been paid under the 1971 Fund Convention.

(d) Paragraph 1 of Article 9 of this Convention shall also apply to the rights enjoyed under the 1969 Liability Convention.

APPENDIX 10

Article 36 ter

1. Subject to paragraph 4 of this Article, the aggregate amount of the annual contributions payable in respect of contributing oil received in a single Contracting State during a calendar year shall not exceed 27.5% of the total amount of annual contributions pursuant to the 1992 Protocol to amend the 1971 Fund Convention, in respect of that calendar year.

2. If the application of the provisions in paragraphs 2 and 3 of Article 12 would result in the aggregate amount of the contributions payable by contributors in a single Contracting State in respect of a given calendar year exceeding 27.5% of the total annual contributions, the contributions payable by all contributors in that State shall be reduced pro rata so that their aggregate contributions equal 27.5% of the total annual contributions to the Fund in respect of that year.

3. If the contributions payable by persons in a given Contracting State shall be reduced pursuant to paragraph 2 of this Article, the contributions payable by persons in all other Contracting States shall be increased pro rata so as to ensure that the total amount of contributions payable by all persons liable to contribute to the Fund in respect of the calendar year in question will reach the total amount of contributions decided by the Assembly.

4. The provisions in paragraphs 1 to 3 of this Article shall operate until the total quantity of contributing oil received in all Contracting States in a calendar year has reached 750 million tons or until a period of 5 years after the date of entry into force of the said 1992 Protocol has elapsed, whichever occurs earlier.

Article 36 quater

Notwithstanding the provisions of this Convention, the following provisions shall apply to the administration of the Fund during the period in which both the 1971 Fund Convention and this Convention are in force:

(a)   The Secretariat of the Fund, established by the 1971 Fund Convention (hereinafter referred to as 'the 1971 Fund'), headed by the Director, may also function as the Secretariat and the Director of the Fund.

(b)   If, in accordance with sub-paragraph (a), the Secretariat and the Director of the 1971 Fund also perform the function of Secretariat and Director of the Fund, the Fund shall be represented, in cases of conflict of interests between the 1971 Fund and the Fund, by the Chairman of the Assembly of the Fund.

(c)   The Director and the staff and experts appointed by him, performing their duties under this Convention and the 1971 Fund Convention, shall not be regarded as contravening the provisions of Article 30 of this Convention in so far as they discharge their duties in accordance with this Article.

(d)   The Assembly of the Fund shall endeavour not to take decisions which are incompatible with decisions taken by the Assembly of the 1971 Fund. If differences of opinion with respect to common administrative issues arise, the Assembly of the Fund shall try to reach a consensus with the Assembly of the 1971 Fund, in a spirit of mutual co-operation and with the common aims of both organizations in mind.

(e)   The Fund may succeed to the rights, obligations and assets of the 1971 Fund if the Assembly of the 1971 Fund so decides, in accordance with Article 44, paragraph 2, of the 1971 Fund Convention.

(f)   The Fund shall reimburse to the 1971 Fund all costs and expenses arising from administrative services performed by the 1971 Fund on behalf of the Fund.

APPENDIX 10

Article 36 quinquies

Final clauses

The final clauses of this Convention shall be Articles 28 to 39 of the Protocol of 1992 to amend the 1971 Fund Convention. References in this Convention to Contracting States shall be taken to mean references to the Contracting States of that Protocol.

Final Clauses of the Protocol of 1992 to amend the 1971 Fund Convention

Article 28 – Signature, ratification, acceptance, approval and accession

1. This Protocol shall be open for signature at London from 15 January 1993 to 14 January 1994 by any State which has signed the 1992 Liability Convention.

2. Subject to paragraph 4, this Protocol shall be ratified, accepted or approved by States which have signed it.

3. Subject to paragraph 4, this Protocol is open for accession by States which did not sign it.

4. This Protocol may be ratified, accepted, approved or acceded to only by States which have ratified, accepted, approved or acceded to the 1992 Liability Convention.

5. Ratification, acceptance, approval or accession shall be effected by the deposit of a formal instrument to that effect with the Secretary-General of the Organization.

6. A State which is a Party to this Protocol but is not a Party to the 1971 Fund Convention shall be bound by the provisions of the 1971 Fund Convention as amended by this Protocol in relation to other Parties hereto, but shall not be bound by the provisions of the 1971 Fund Convention in relation to Parties thereto.

7. Any instrument of ratification, acceptance, approval or accession deposited after the entry into force of an amendment to the 1971 Fund Convention as amended by this Protocol shall be deemed to apply to the Convention so amended, as modified by such amendment.

Article 29 – Information on contributing oil

1. Before this Protocol comes into force for a State, that State shall, when depositing an instrument referred to in Article 28, paragraph 5, and annually thereafter at a date to be determined by the Secretary-General of the Organization, communicate to him the name and address of any person who in respect of that State would be liable to contribute to the Fund pursuant to Article 10 of the 1971 Fund Convention as amended by this Protocol as well as data on the relevant quantities of contributing oil received by any such person in the territory of that State during the preceding calendar year.

2. During the transitional period, the Director shall, for Parties, communicate annually to the Secretary-General of the Organization data on quantities of contributing oil received by persons liable to contribute to the Fund pursuant to Article 10 of the 1971 Fund Convention as amended by this Protocol.

Article 30 – Entry into force

1. This Protocol shall enter into force twelve months following the date on which the following requirements are fulfilled:
   (a) at least eight States have deposited instruments of ratification, acceptance, approval or accession with the Secretary-General of the Organization; and
   (b) the Secretary-General of the Organization has received information in accordance

APPENDIX 10

with Article 29 that those persons who would be liable to contribute pursuant to Article 10 of the 1971 Fund Convention as amended by this Protocol have received during the preceding calendar year a total quantity of at least 450 million tons of contributing oil.

2. However, this Protocol shall not enter into force before the 1992 Liability Convention has entered into force.

3. For each State which ratifies, accepts, approves or accedes to this Protocol after the conditions in paragraph 1 for entry into force have been met, the Protocol shall enter into force twelve months following the date of the deposit by such State of the appropriate instrument.

4. Any State may, at the time of the deposit of its instrument of ratification, acceptance, approval or accession in respect of this Protocol declare that such instrument shall not take effect for the purpose of this Article until the end of the six-month period Article 31.

5. Any State which has made a declaration in accordance with the preceding paragraph may withdraw it at any time by means of a notification addressed to the Secretary-General of the Organization. Any such withdrawal shall take effect on the date the notification is received, and any State making such a withdrawal shall be deemed to have deposited its instrument of ratification, acceptance, approval or accession in respect of this Protocol on that date.

6. Any State which has made a declaration under Article 13, paragraph 2, of the Protocol of 1992 to amend the 1969 Liability Convention shall be deemed to have also made a declaration under paragraph 4 of this Article. Withdrawal of a declaration under the said Article 13, paragraph 2, shall be deemed to constitute withdrawal also under paragraph 5 of this Article.

Article 31 – Denunciation of the 1969 and 1971 Conventions

Subject to Article 30, within six months following the date on which the following requirements are fulfilled:

    (a)   at least eight States have become Parties to this Protocol or have deposited instruments of ratification, acceptance, approval or accession with the Secretary-General of the Organization, whether or not subject to Article 30, paragraph 4, and

    (b)   the Secretary-General of the Organization has received information in accordance with Article 29 that those persons who are or would be liable to contribute pursuant to Article 10 of the 1971 Fund Convention as amended by this Protocol have received during the preceding calendar year a total quantity of at least 750 million tons of contributing oil;

each Party to this Protocol and each State which has deposited an instrument of ratification, acceptance, approval or accession, whether or not subject to Article 30, paragraph 4, shall, if Party thereto, denounce the 1971 Fund Convention and the 1969 Liability Convention with effect twelve months after the expiry of the above-mentioned six-month period.

Article 32 – Revision and amendment

1. A conference for the purpose of revising or amending the 1992 Fund Convention may be convened by the Organization.

2. The Organization shall convene a Conference of Contracting States for the purpose of revising or amending the 1992 Fund Convention at the request of not less than one third of all Contracting States.

APPENDIX 10

Article 33 – Amendment of compensation limits

1. Upon the request of at least one quarter of the Contracting States, any proposal to amend the limits of amounts of compensation laid down in Article 4, paragraph 4, of the 1971 Fund Convention as amended by this Protocol shall be circulated by the Secretary-General to all Members of the Organization and to all Contracting States.

2. Any amendment proposed and circulated as above shall be submitted to the Legal Committee of the Organization for consideration at a date at least six months after the date of its circulation.

3. All Contracting States to the 1971 Fund Convention as amended by this Protocol, whether or not Members of the Organization, shall be entitled to participate in the proceedings of the Legal Committee for the consideration and adoption of amendments.

4. Amendments shall be adopted by a two-thirds majority of the Contracting States present and voting in the Legal Committee, expanded as provided for in paragraph 3, on condition that at least one half of the Contracting States shall be present at the time of voting.

5. When acting on a proposal to amend the limits, the Legal Committee shall take into account the experience of incidents and in particular the amount of damage resulting therefrom and changes in the monetary values. It shall also take into account the relationship between the limits in Article 4, paragraph 4, of the 1971 Fund Convention as amended by this Protocol and those in Article V, paragraph 1, of the International Convention on Civil Liability for Oil Pollution Damage, 1992.

6. (a) No amendment of the limits under this Article may be considered before 15 January 1998 nor less than five years from the date of entry into force of a previous amendment under this Article. No amendment under this Article shall be considered before this Protocol has entered into force.

(b) No limit may be increased so as to exceed an amount which corresponds to the limit laid down in the 1971 Fund Convention as amended by this Protocol increased by six per cent per year calculated on a compound basis from 15 January 1993.

(c) No limit may be increased so as to exceed an amount which corresponds to the limit laid down in the 1971 Fund Convention as amended by this Protocol multiplied by three.

7. Any amendment adopted in accordance with paragraph 4 shall be notified by the Organization to all Contracting States. The amendment shall be deemed to have been accepted at the end of a period of eighteen months after the date of notification unless within that period not less than one quarter of the States that were Contracting States at the time of the adoption of the amendment by the Legal Committee have communicated to the Organization that they do not accept the amendment in which case the amendment is rejected and shall have no effect.

8. An amendment deemed to have been accepted in accordance with paragraph 7 shall enter into force eighteen months after its acceptance.

9. All Contracting States shall be bound by the amendment, unless they denounce this Protocol in accordance with Article 34, paragraphs 1 and 2, at least six months before the amendment enters into force. Such denunciation shall take effect when the amendment enters into force.

10. When an amendment has been adopted by the Legal Committee but the eighteen-month period for its acceptance has not yet expired, a State which becomes a Contracting State during that period shall be bound by the amendment if it enters into force. A State which becomes a Contracting State after that period shall be bound by an amendment which has been accepted in accordance with paragraph 7. In the cases referred to in this paragraph,

APPENDIX 10

a State becomes bound by an amendment when that amendment enters into force, or when this Protocol enters into force for that State, if later.

Article 34 – Denunciation

1. This Protocol may be denounced by any Party at any time after the date on which it enters into force for that Party.

2. Denunciation shall be effected by the deposit of an instrument with the Secretary-General of the Organization.

3. A denunciation shall take effect twelve months, or such longer period as may be specified in the instrument of denunciation, after its deposit with the Secretary-General of the Organization.

4. Denunciation of the 1992 Liability Convention shall be deemed to be a denunciation of this Protocol. Such denunciation shall take effect on the date on which denunciation of the Protocol of 1992 to amend the 1969 Liability Convention takes effect according to Article 16 of that Protocol.

5. Any Contracting State to this Protocol which has not denounced the 1971 Fund Convention and the 1969 Liability Convention as required by Article 31 shall be deemed to have denounced this Protocol with effect twelve months after the expiry of the six-month period mentioned in that Article. As from the date on which the denunciations provided for in Article 31 take effect, any Party to this Protocol which deposits an instrument of ratification, acceptance, approval or accession to the 1969 Liability Convention shall be deemed to have denounced this Protocol with effect from the date on which such instrument takes effect.

6. As between the Parties to this Protocol, denunciation by any of them of the 1971 Fund Convention in accordance with Article 41 thereof shall not be construed in any way as a denunciation of the 1971 Fund Convention as amended by this Protocol.

7. Notwithstanding a denunciation of this Protocol by a Party pursuant to this Article, any provisions of this Protocol relating to the obligations to make contributions under Article 10 of the 1971 Fund Convention as amended by this Protocol with respect to an incident referred to in Article 12, paragraph 2(b), of that amended Convention and occurring before the denunciation takes effect shall continue to apply.

Article 35 – Extraordinary sessions of the Assembly

1. Any Contracting State may, within ninety days after the deposit of an instrument of denunciation the result of which it considers will significantly increase the level of contributions for the remaining Contracting States, request the Director to convene an extraordinary session of the Assembly. The Director shall convene the Assembly to meet not later than sixty days after receipt of the request.

2. The Director may convene, on his own initiative, an extraordinary session of the Assembly to meet within sixty days after the deposit of any instrument of denunciation, if he considers that such denunciation will result in a significant increase in the level of contributions of the remaining Contracting States.

3. If the Assembly at an extraordinary session convened in accordance with paragraph 1 or 2 decides that the denunciation will result in a significant increase in the level of contributions for the remaining Contracting States, any such State may, not later than one hundred and twenty days before the date on which the denunciation takes effect, denounce this Protocol with effect from the same date.

APPENDIX 10

Article 36 – Termination

1. This Protocol shall cease to be in force on the date when the number of Contracting States falls below three.

2. States which are bound by this Protocol on the day before the date it ceases to be in force shall enable the Fund to exercise its functions as described under Article 37 of this Protocol and shall, for that purpose only, remain bound by this Protocol.

Article 37 – Winding up of the Fund

1. If this Protocol ceases to be in force, the Fund shall nevertheless:
   (a) meet its obligations in respect of any incident occurring before the Protocol ceased to be in force;
   (b) be entitled to exercise its rights to contributions to the extent that these contributions are necessary to meet the obligations under subparagraph (a), including expenses for the administration of the Fund necessary for this purpose.

2. The Assembly shall take all appropriate measures to complete the winding up of the Fund including the distribution in an equitable manner of any remaining assets among those persons who have contributed to the Fund.

3. For the purposes of this Article the Fund shall remain a legal person.

Article 38 – Depositary

1. This Protocol and any amendments accepted under Article 33 shall be deposited with the Secretary-General of the Organization.

2. The Secretary-General of the Organization shall:
   (a) inform all States which have signed or acceded to this Protocol of:
      (i) each new signature or deposit of an instrument together with the date thereof;
      (ii) each declaration and notification under Article 30 including declarations and withdrawals deemed to have been made in accordance with that Article;
      (iii) the date of entry its force of this Protocol;
      (iv) the date by which denunciations provided for in Article 31 are required to be made;
      (v) any proposal to amend limits of amounts of compensation which has been made in accordance with Article 33, paragraph 1;
      (vi) any amendment which has been adopted in accordance with Article 33, paragraph 4;
      (vii) any amendment deemed to have been accepted under Article 33, paragraph 7, together with the date on which that amendment shall enter into force in accordance with paragraphs 8 and 9 of that Article;
      (viii) the deposit of an instrument of denunciation of this Protocol together with the date of the deposit and the date on which it takes effect;
      (ix) any denunciation deemed to have been made under Article 34, paragraph 5;
      (x) any communication called for by any Article in this Protocol;
   (b) transmit certified true copies of this Protocol to all Signatory States and to all States which accede to the Protocol.

3. As soon as this Protocol enters into force, the text shall be transmitted by the Secretary-General of the Organization to the Secretariat of the United Nations for registration and publication in accordance with Article 102 of the Charter of the United Nations.

APPENDIX 10

Article 39 – Languages

This Protocol is established in a single original in the Arabic, Chinese, English, French, Russian and Spanish languages, each text being equally authentic.

DONE AT LONDON this twenty-seventh day of November one thousand nine hundred and ninety-two.

IN WITNESS WHEREOF the undersigned being duly authorized for that purpose have signed this Protocol.

★ ★ ★

APPENDIX 10

Protocol of 2003 to the International Convention on the Establishment of an International Fund for Compensation for Oil Pollution Damage, 1992

THE CONTRACTING STATES TO THE PRESENT PROTOCOL,

BEARING IN MIND the International Convention on Civil Liability for Oil Pollution Damage, 1992 (hereinafter the 1992 Liability Convention),

HAVING CONSIDERED the International Convention on the Establishment of an International Fund for Compensation for Oil Pollution Damage, 1992 (hereinafter the 1992 Fund Convention),

AFFIRMING the importance of maintaining the viability of the international oil pollution liability and compensation system,

NOTING that the maximum compensation afforded by the 1992 Fund Convention might be insufficient to meet compensation needs in certain circumstances in some Contracting States to that Convention,

RECOGNIZING that a number of Contracting States to the 1992 Liability and 1992 Fund Conventions consider it necessary as a matter of urgency to make available additional funds for compensation through the creation of a supplementary scheme to which States may accede if they so wish,

BELIEVING that the supplementary scheme should seek to ensure that victims of oil pollution damage are compensated in full for their loss or damage and should also alleviate the difficulties faced by victims in cases where there is a risk that the amount of compensation available under the 1992 Liability and 1992 Fund Conventions will be insufficient to pay established claims in full and that as a consequence the International Oil Pollution Compensation Fund, 1992, has decided provisionally that it will pay only a proportion of any established claim,

CONSIDERING that accession to the supplementary scheme will be open only to Contracting States to the 1992 Fund Convention,

HAVE AGREED as follows:

General provisions

Article 1

For the purposes of this Protocol:

1. '1992 Liability Convention' means the International Convention on Civil Liability for Oil Pollution Damage, 1992;

2. '1992 Fund Convention' means the International Convention on the Establishment of an International Fund for Compensation for Oil Pollution Damage, 1992;

3. '1992 Fund' means the International Oil Pollution Compensation Fund, 1992, established under the 1992 Fund Convention;

4. 'Contracting State' means a Contracting State to this Protocol, unless stated otherwise;

5. When provisions of the 1992 Fund Convention are incorporated by reference into this Protocol, 'Fund' in that Convention means 'Supplementary Fund', unless stated otherwise;

6. 'Ship', 'Person', 'Owner', 'Oil', 'Pollution Damage', 'Preventive Measures' and 'Incident' have the same meaning as in article I of the 1992 Liability Convention;

7. 'Contributing Oil', 'Unit of Account', 'Ton', 'Guarantor' and 'Terminal installation' have the same meaning as in article 1 of the 1992 Fund Convention, unless stated otherwise;

8. 'Established claim' means a claim which has been recognised by the 1992 Fund or been accepted as admissible by decision of a competent court binding upon the 1992 Fund

405

APPENDIX 10

not subject to ordinary forms of review and which would have been fully compensated if the limit set out in article 4, paragraph 4, of the 1992 Fund Convention had not been applied to that incident;

9. 'Assembly' means the Assembly of the International Oil Pollution Compensation Supplementary Fund, 2003, unless otherwise indicated;

10. 'Organization' means the International Maritime Organization;

11. 'Secretary-General' means the Secretary-General of the Organization.

Article 2

1. An International Supplementary Fund for compensation for pollution damage, to be named 'The International Oil Pollution Compensation Supplementary Fund, 2003' (hereinafter the Supplementary Fund), is hereby established.

2. The Supplementary Fund shall in each Contracting State be recognized as a legal person capable under the laws of that State of assuming rights and obligations and of being a party in legal proceedings before the courts of that State. Each Contracting State shall recognize the Director of the Supplementary Fund as the legal representative of the Supplementary Fund.

Article 3

This Protocol shall apply exclusively:
    (a)   to pollution damage caused:
        (i)   in the territory, including the territorial sea, of a Contracting State, and
        (ii)   in the exclusive economic zone of a Contracting State, established in accordance with international law, or, if a Contracting State has not established such a zone, in an area beyond and adjacent to the territorial sea of that State determined by that State in accordance with international law and extending not more than 200 nautical miles from the baselines from which the breadth of its territorial sea is measured;
    (b)   to preventive measures, wherever taken, to prevent or minimize such damage.

Supplementary Compensation

Article 4

1. The Supplementary Fund shall pay compensation to any person suffering pollution damage if such person has been unable to obtain full and adequate compensation for an established claim for such damage under the terms of the 1992 Fund Convention, because the total damage exceeds, or there is a risk that it will exceed, the applicable limit of compensation laid down in article 4, paragraph 4, of the 1992 Fund Convention in respect of any one incident.

2. (a)   The aggregate amount of compensation payable by the Supplementary Fund under this article shall in respect of any one incident be limited, so that the total sum of that amount together with the amount of compensation actually paid under the 1992 Liability Convention and the 1992 Fund Convention within the scope of application of this Protocol shall not exceed 750 million units of account.

    (b)   The amount of 750 million units of account mentioned in paragraph 2(a) shall be converted into national currency on the basis of the value of that currency by reference to the Special Drawing Right on the date determined by the Assembly

APPENDIX 10

of the 1992 Fund for conversion of the maximum amount payable under the 1992 Liability and 1992 Fund Conventions.

3. Where the amount of established claims against the Supplementary Fund exceeds the aggregate amount of compensation payable under paragraph 2, the amount available shall be distributed in such a manner that the proportion between any established claim and the amount of compensation actually recovered by the claimant under this Protocol shall be the same for all claimants.

4. The Supplementary Fund shall pay compensation in respect of established claims as defined in article 1, paragraph 8, and only in respect of such claims.

Article 5

The Supplementary Fund shall pay compensation when the Assembly of the 1992 Fund has considered that the total amount of the established claims exceeds, or there is a risk that the total amount of established claims will exceed the aggregate amount of compensation available under article 4, paragraph 4, of the 1992 Fund Convention and that as a consequence the Assembly of the 1992 Fund has decided provisionally or finally that payments will only be made for a proportion of any established claim. The Assembly of the Supplementary Fund shall then decide whether and to what extent the Supplementary Fund shall pay the proportion of any established claim not paid under the 1992 Liability Convention and the 1992 Fund Convention.

Article 6

1. Subject to article 15, paragraphs 2 and 3, rights to compensation against the Supplementary Fund shall be extinguished only if they are extinguished against the 1992 Fund under article 6 of the 1992 Fund Convention.

2. A claim made against the 1992 Fund shall be regarded as a claim made by the same claimant against the Supplementary Fund.

Article 7

1. The provisions of article 7, paragraphs 1, 2, 4, 5 and 6, of the 1992 Fund Convention shall apply to actions for compensation brought against the Supplementary Fund in accordance with article 4, paragraph 1, of this Protocol.

2. Where an action for compensation for pollution damage has been brought before a court competent under article IX of the 1992 Liability Convention against the owner of a ship or his guarantor, such court shall have exclusive jurisdictional competence over any action against the Supplementary Fund for compensation under the provisions of article 4 of this Protocol in respect of the same damage.

However, where an action for compensation for pollution damage under the 1992 Liability Convention has been brought before a court in a Contracting State to the 1992 Liability Convention but not to this Protocol, any action against the Supplementary Fund under article 4 of this Protocol shall at the option of the claimant be brought either before a court of the State where the Supplementary Fund has its headquarters or before any court of a Contracting State to this Protocol competent under article IX of the 1992 Liability Convention.

3. Notwithstanding paragraph 1, where an action for compensation for pollution damage against the 1992 Fund has been brought before a court in a Contracting State to the 1992 Fund Convention but not to this Protocol, any related action against the Supplementary

APPENDIX 10

Fund shall, at the option of the claimant, be brought either before a court of the State where the Supplementary Fund has its headquarters or before any court of a Contracting State competent under paragraph 1.

Article 8

1. Subject to any decision concerning the distribution referred to in article 4, paragraph 3 of this Protocol, any judgment given against the Supplementary Fund by a court having jurisdiction in accordance with article 7 of this Protocol, shall, when it has become enforceable in the State of origin and is in that State no longer subject to ordinary forms of review, be recognized and enforceable in each Contracting State on the same conditions as are prescribed in article X of the 1992 Liability Convention.

2. A Contracting State may apply other rules for the recognition and enforcement of judgments, provided that their effect is to ensure that judgments are recognised and enforced at least to the same extent as under paragraph 1.

Article 9

1. The Supplementary Fund shall, in respect of any amount of compensation for pollution damage paid by the Supplementary Fund in accordance with article 4, paragraph 1, of this Protocol, acquire by subrogation the rights that the person so compensated may enjoy under the 1992 Liability Convention against the owner or his guarantor.

2. The Supplementary Fund shall acquire by subrogation the rights that the person compensated by it may enjoy under the 1992 Fund Convention against the 1992 Fund.

3. Nothing in this Protocol shall prejudice any right of recourse or subrogation of the Supplementary Fund against persons other than those referred to in the preceding paragraphs. In any event the right of the Supplementary Fund to subrogation against such person shall not be less favourable than that of an insurer of the person to whom compensation has been paid.

4. Without prejudice to any other rights of subrogation or recourse against the Supplementary Fund which may exist, a Contracting State or agency thereof which has paid compensation for pollution damage in accordance with provisions of national law shall acquire by subrogation the rights which the person so compensated would have enjoyed under this Protocol.

Contributions

Article 10

1. Annual contributions to the Supplementary Fund shall be made in respect of each Contracting State by any person who, in the calendar year referred to in article 11, paragraph 2(a) or (b), has received in total quantities exceeding 150,000 tons:
    (a) in the ports or terminal installations in the territory of that State contributing oil carried by sea to such ports or terminal installations; and
    (b) in any installations situated in the territory of that Contracting State contributing oil which has been carried by sea and discharged in a port or terminal installation of a non-Contracting State, provided that contributing oil shall only be taken into account by virtue of this sub-paragraph on first receipt in a Contracting State after its discharge in that non-Contracting State.

2. The provisions of article 10, paragraph 2, of the 1992 Fund Convention shall apply in respect of the obligation to pay contributions to the Supplementary Fund.

APPENDIX 10

Article 11

1. With a view to assessing the amount of annual contributions due, if any, and taking account of the necessity to maintain sufficient liquid funds, the Assembly shall for each calendar year make an estimate in the form of a budget of:

(i) *Expenditure*

(a) costs and expenses of the administration of the Supplementary Fund in the relevant year and any deficit from operations in preceding years;

(b) payments to be made by the Supplementary Fund in the relevant year for the satisfaction of claims against the Supplementary Fund due under article 4, including repayments on loans previously taken by the Supplementary Fund for the satisfaction of such claims;

(ii) *Income*

(a) surplus funds from operations in preceding years, including any interest;

(b) annual contributions, if required to balance the budget;

(c) any other income.

2. The Assembly shall decide the total amount of contributions to be levied. On the basis of that decision, the Director of the Supplementary Fund shall, in respect of each Contracting State, calculate for each person referred to in article 10, the amount of that person's annual contribution:

(a) in so far as the contribution is for the satisfaction of payments referred to in paragraph 1(i)(a) on the basis of a fixed sum for each ton of contributing oil received in the relevant State by such person during the preceding calendar year; and

(b) in so far as the contribution is for the satisfaction of payments referred to in paragraph 1(i)(b) on the basis of a fixed sum for each ton of contributing oil received by such person during the calendar year preceding that in which the incident in question occurred, provided that State was a Contracting State to this Protocol at the date of the incident.

3. The sums referred to in paragraph 2 shall be arrived at by dividing the relevant total amount of contributions required by the total amount of contributing oil received in all Contracting States in the relevant year.

4. The annual contribution shall be due on the date to be laid down in the Internal Regulations of the Supplementary Fund. The Assembly may decide on a different date of payment.

5. The Assembly may decide, under conditions to be laid down in the Financial Regulations of the Supplementary Fund, to make transfers between funds received in accordance with paragraph 2(a) and funds received in accordance with paragraph 2(b).

Article 12

1. The provisions of article 13 of the 1992 Fund Convention shall apply to contributions to the Supplementary Fund.

2. A Contracting State itself may assume the obligation to pay contributions to the Supplementary Fund in accordance with the procedure set out in article 14 of the 1992 Fund Convention.

Article 13

1. Contracting States shall communicate to the Director of the Supplementary Fund information on oil receipts in accordance with article 15 of the 1992 Fund Convention

APPENDIX 10

provided, however, that communications made to the Director of the 1992 Fund under article 15, paragraph 2, of the 1992 Fund Convention shall be deemed to have been made also under this Protocol.

2. Where a Contracting State does not fulfil its obligations to submit the communication referred to in paragraph 1 and this results in a financial loss for the Supplementary Fund, that Contracting State shall be liable to compensate the Supplementary Fund for such loss. The Assembly shall, on the recommendation of the Director of the Supplementary Fund, decide whether such compensation shall be payable by that Contracting State.

Article 14

1. Notwithstanding article 10, for the purposes of this Protocol there shall be deemed to be a minimum receipt of 1 million tons of contributing oil in each Contracting State.

2. When the aggregate quantity of contributing oil received in a Contracting State is less than 1 million tons, the Contracting State shall assume the obligations that would be incumbent under this Protocol on any person who would be liable to contribute to the Supplementary Fund in respect of oil received within the territory of that State in so far as no liable person exists for the aggregated quantity of oil received.

Article 15

1. If in a Contracting State there is no person meeting the conditions of article 10, that Contracting State shall for the purposes of this Protocol inform the Director of the Supplementary Fund thereof.

2. No compensation shall be paid by the Supplementary Fund for pollution damage in the territory, territorial sea or exclusive economic zone or area determined in accordance with article 3(a)(ii), of this Protocol, of a Contracting State in respect of a given incident or for preventive measures, wherever taken, to prevent or minimize such damage, until the obligations to communicate to the Director of the Supplementary Fund according to article 13, paragraph 1 and paragraph 1 of this article have been complied with in respect of that Contracting State for all years prior to the occurrence of that incident. The Assembly shall determine in the Internal Regulations the circumstances under which a Contracting State shall be considered as having failed to comply with its obligations.

3. Where compensation has been denied temporarily in accordance with paragraph 2, compensation shall be denied permanently in respect of that incident if the obligations to communicate to the Director of the Supplementary Fund under article 13, paragraph 1 and paragraph 1 of this article, have not been complied with within one year after the Director of the Supplementary Fund has notified the Contracting State of its failure to report.

4. Any payments of contributions due to the Supplementary Fund shall be set off against compensation due to the debtor, or the debtor's agents.

Organization and administration

Article 16

1. The Supplementary Fund shall have an Assembly and a Secretariat headed by a Director.

2. Articles 17 to 20 and 28 to 33 of the 1992 Fund Convention shall apply to the Assembly, Secretariat and Director of the Supplementary Fund.

3. Article 34 of the 1992 Fund Convention shall apply to the Supplementary Fund.

APPENDIX 10

Article 17

1. The Secretariat of the 1992 Fund, headed by the Director of the 1992 Fund, may also function as the Secretariat and the Director of the Supplementary Fund.

2. If, in accordance with paragraph 1, the Secretariat and the Director of the 1992 Fund also perform the function of Secretariat and Director of the Supplementary Fund, the Supplementary Fund shall be represented in cases of conflict of interests between the 1992 Fund and the Supplementary Fund, by the Chairman of the Assembly.

3. The Director of the Supplementary Fund, and the staff and experts appointed by the Director of the Supplementary Fund, performing their duties under this Protocol and the 1992 Fund Convention, shall not be regarded as contravening the provisions of article 30 of the 1992 Fund Convention as applied by article 16, paragraph 2, of this Protocol in so far as they discharge their duties in accordance with this article.

4. The Assembly shall endeavour not to take decisions which are incompatible with decisions taken by the Assembly of the 1992 Fund. If differences of opinion with respect to common administrative issues arise, the Assembly shall try to reach a consensus with the Assembly of the 1992 Fund, in a spirit of mutual co-operation and with the common aims of both organizations in mind.

5. The Supplementary Fund shall reimburse the 1992 Fund all costs and expenses arising from administrative services performed by the 1992 Fund on behalf of the Supplementary Fund.

Article 18

Transitional provisions

1. Subject to paragraph 4, the aggregate amount of the annual contributions payable in respect of contributing oil received in a single Contracting State during a calendar year shall not exceed 20% of the total amount of annual contributions pursuant to this Protocol in respect of that calendar year.

2. If the application of the provisions in article 11, paragraphs 2 and 3, would result in the aggregate amount of the contributions payable by contributors in a single Contracting State in respect of a given calendar year exceeding 20% of the total annual contributions, the contributions payable by all contributors in that State shall be reduced pro rata so that their aggregate contributions equal 20% of the total annual contributions to the Supplementary Fund in respect of that year.

3. If the contributions payable by persons in a given Contracting State shall be reduced pursuant to paragraph 2, the contributions payable by persons in all other Contracting States shall be increased pro rata so as to ensure that the total amount of contributions payable by all persons liable to contribute to the Supplementary Fund in respect of the calendar year in question will reach the total amount of contributions decided by the Assembly.

4. The provisions in paragraphs 1 to 3 shall operate until the total quantity of contributing oil received in all Contracting States in a calendar year, including the quantities referred to in article 14, paragraph 1, has reached 1,000 million tons or until a period of 10 years after the date of entry into force of this Protocol has elapsed, whichever occurs earlier.

APPENDIX 10

Final clauses

Article 19 – Signature, ratification, acceptance, approval and accession

  1. This Protocol shall be open for signature at London from 31 July 2003 to 30 July 2004.
  2. States may express their consent to be bound by this Protocol by:
    (a) signature without reservation as to ratification, acceptance or approval; or
    (b) signature subject to ratification, acceptance or approval followed by ratification, acceptance or approval; or
    (c) accession.
  3. Only Contracting States to the 1992 Fund Convention may become Contracting States to this Protocol.
  4. Ratification, acceptance, approval or accession shall be effected by the deposit of a formal instrument to that effect with the Secretary-General.

Article 20 – Information on contributing oil

Before this Protocol comes into force for a State, that State shall, when signing this Protocol in accordance with article 19, paragraph 2(a), or when depositing an instrument referred to in article 19, paragraph 4 of this Protocol, and annually thereafter at a date to be determined by the Secretary-General, communicate to the Secretary-General the name and address of any person who in respect of that State would be liable to contribute to the Supplementary Fund pursuant to article 10 as well as data on the relevant quantities of contributing oil received by any such person in the territory of that State during the preceding calendar year.

Article 21 – Entry into force

  1. This Protocol shall enter into force three months following the date on which the following requirements are fulfilled:
    (a) at least eight States have signed the Protocol without reservation as to ratification, acceptance or approval, or have deposited instruments of ratification, acceptance, approval or accession with the Secretary-General; and
    (b) the Secretary-General has received information from the Director of the 1992 Fund that those persons who would be liable to contribute pursuant to article 10 have received during the preceding calendar year a total quantity of at least 450 million tons of contributing oil, including the quantities referred to in article 14, paragraph 1.
  2. For each State which signs this Protocol without reservation as to ratification, acceptance or approval, or which ratifies, accepts, approves or accedes to this Protocol, after the conditions in paragraph 1 for entry into force have been met, the Protocol shall enter into force three months following the date of the deposit by such State of the appropriate instrument.
  3. Notwithstanding paragraphs 1 and 2, this Protocol shall not enter into force in respect of any State until the 1992 Fund Convention enters into force for that State.

Article 22 – First session of the Assembly

The Secretary-General shall convene the first session of the Assembly. This session shall take place as soon as possible after the entry into force of this Protocol and, in any case, not more than thirty days after such entry into force.

412

APPENDIX 10

Article 23 – Revision and amendment

1. A conference for the purpose of revising or amending this Protocol may be convened by the Organization.

2. The Organization shall convene a Conference of Contracting States for the purpose of revising or amending this Protocol at the request of not less than one third of all Contracting States.

Article 24 – Amendment of compensation limit

1. Upon the request of at least one quarter of the Contracting States, any proposal to amend the limit of the amount of compensation laid down in article 4, paragraph 2 (a), shall be circulated by the Secretary-General to all Members of the Organization and to all Contracting States.

2. Any amendment proposed and circulated as above shall be submitted to the Legal Committee of the Organization for consideration at a date at least six months after the date of its circulation.

3. All Contracting States to this Protocol, whether or not Members of the Organization, shall be entitled to participate in the proceedings of the Legal Committee for the consideration and adoption of amendments.

4. Amendments shall be adopted by a two-thirds majority of the Contracting States present and voting in the Legal Committee, expanded as provided for in paragraph 3, on condition that at least one half of the Contracting States shall be present at the time of voting.

5. When acting on a proposal to amend the limit, the Legal Committee shall take into account the experience of incidents and in particular the amount of damage resulting changes in the monetary values.

6. (a) No amendments of the limit under this article may be considered before the date of entry into force of this Protocol nor less than three years from the date of entry into force of a previous amendment under this article.

   (b) The limit may not be increased so as to exceed an amount which corresponds to the limit laid down in this Protocol increased by six per cent per year calculated on a compound basis from the date when this Protocol is opened for signature to the date on which the Legal Committee's decision comes into force.

   (c) The limit may not be increased so as to exceed an amount which corresponds to the limit laid down in this Protocol multiplied by three.

7. Any amendment adopted in accordance with paragraph 4 shall be notified by the Organization to all Contracting States. The amendment shall be deemed to have been accepted at the end of a period of twelve months after the date of notification, unless within that period not less than one quarter of the States that were Contracting States at the time of the adoption of the amendment by the Legal Committee have communicated to the Organization that they do not accept the amendment, in which case the amendment is rejected and shall have no effect.

8. An amendment deemed to have been accepted in accordance with paragraph 7 shall enter into force twelve months after its acceptance.

9. All Contracting States shall be bound by the amendment, unless they denounce this Protocol in accordance with article 26, paragraphs 1 and 2, at least six months before the amendment enters into force. Such denunciation shall take effect when the amendment enters into force.

10 When an amendment has been adopted by the Legal Committee but the twelve-month period for its acceptance has not yet expired, a State which becomes a Contracting State

APPENDIX 10

during that period shall be bound by the amendment if it enters into force. A State which becomes a Contracting State after that period shall be bound by an amendment which has been accepted in accordance with paragraph 7.

In the cases referred to in this paragraph, a State becomes bound by an amendment when that amendment enters into force, or when this Protocol enters into force for that State, if later.

Article 25 – Protocols to the 1992 Fund Convention

1. If the limits laid down in the 1992 Fund Convention have been increased by a Protocol thereto, the limit laid down in article 4, paragraph 2(a), may be increased by the same amount by means of the procedure set out in article 24. The provisions of article 24, paragraph 6, shall not apply in such cases.

2. If the procedure referred to in paragraph 1 has been applied, any subsequent amendment of the limit laid down in article 4, paragraph 2, by application of the procedure in article 24 shall, for the purpose of article 24, paragraphs 6(b) and (c), be calculated on the basis of the new limit as increased in accordance with paragraph 1.

Article 26 – Denunciation

1. This Protocol may be denounced by any Contracting State at any time after the date on which it enters into force for that Contracting State.

2. Denunciation shall be effected by the deposit of an instrument with the Secretary-General.

3. A denunciation shall take effect twelve months, or such longer period as may be specified in the instrument of denunciation, after its deposit with the Secretary-General.

4. Denunciation of the 1992 Fund Convention shall be deemed to be a denunciation of this Protocol. Such denunciation shall take effect on the date on which denunciation of the Protocol of 1992 to amend the 1971 Fund Convention takes effect according to article 34 of that Protocol.

5. Notwithstanding a denunciation of the present Protocol by a Contracting State pursuant to this article, any provisions of this Protocol relating to the obligations to make contributions to the Supplementary Fund with respect to an incident referred to in article 11, paragraph 2(b), and occurring before the denunciation takes effect, shall continue to apply.

Article 27 – Extraordinary sessions of the Assembly

1. Any Contracting State may, within ninety days after the deposit of an instrument of denunciation the result of which it considers will significantly increase the level of contributions for the remaining Contracting States, request the Director of the Supplementary Fund to convene an extraordinary session of the Assembly. The Director of the Supplementary Fund shall convene the Assembly to meet not later than sixty days after receipt of the request.

2. The Director of the Supplementary Fund may take the initiative to convene an extraordinary session of the Assembly to meet within sixty days after the deposit of any instrument of denunciation, if the Director of the Supplementary Fund considers that such denunciation will result in a significant increase in the level of contributions of the remaining Contracting States.

3. If the Assembly at an extraordinary session convened in accordance with paragraph 1 or 2 decides that the denunciation will result in a significant increase in the level of contributions for the remaining Contracting States, any such State may, not later than one hundred and twenty days before the date on which the denunciation takes effect, denounce this Protocol with effect from the same date.

APPENDIX 10

Article 28 – Termination

1. This Protocol shall cease to be in force on the date when the number of Contracting States falls below seven or the total quantity of contributing oil received in the remaining Contracting States, including the quantities referred to in article 14, paragraph 1, falls below 350 million tons, whichever occurs earlier.

2. States which are bound by this Protocol on the day before the date it ceases to be in force shall enable the Supplementary Fund to exercise its functions as described in article 29 and shall, for that purpose only, remain bound by this Protocol.

Article 29 – Winding up of the Supplementary Fund

1. If this Protocol ceases to be in force, the Supplementary Fund shall nevertheless:

(a) meet its obligations in respect of any incident occurring before the Protocol ceased to be in force;

(b) be entitled to exercise its rights to contributions to the extent that these contributions are necessary to meet the obligations under paragraph 1(a), including expenses for the administration of the Supplementary Fund necessary for this purpose.

2. The Assembly shall take all appropriate measures to complete the winding up of the Supplementary Fund, including the distribution in an equitable manner of any remaining assets among those persons who have contributed to the Supplementary Fund.

3. For the purposes of this article the Supplementary Fund shall remain a legal person.

Article 30 – Depositary

1. This Protocol and any amendments accepted under article 24 shall be deposited with the Secretary-General.

2. The Secretary-General shall:

(a) inform all States which have signed or acceded to this Protocol of:

(i) each new signature or deposit of an instrument together with the date thereof;

(ii) the date of entry into force of this Protocol;

(iii) any proposal to amend the limit of the amount of compensation which has been made in accordance with article 24, paragraph 1;

(iv) any amendment which has been adopted in accordance with article 24, paragraph 4;

(v) any amendment deemed to have been accepted under article 24, paragraph 7, together with the date on which that amendment shall enter into force in accordance with paragraphs 8 and 9 of that article;

(vi) the deposit of an instrument of denunciation of this Protocol together with the date of the deposit and the date on which it takes effect;

(vii) any communication called for by any article in this Protocol;

(b) transmit certified true copies of this Protocol to all Signatory States and to all States which accede to the Protocol.

3. As soon as this Protocol enters into force, the text shall be transmitted by the Secretary-General to the Secretariat of the United Nations for registration and publication in accordance with Article 102 of the Charter of the United Nations.

APPENDIX 10

Article 31 – Languages

This Protocol is established in a single original in the Arabic, Chinese, English, French, Russian and Spanish languages, each text being equally authentic.

DONE AT LONDON this sixteenth day of May, two thousand and three.

IN WITNESS WHEREOF the undersigned, being duly authorised by their respective Governments for that purpose, have signed this Protocol.

APPENDIX 11

International Convention on Civil Liability for Bunker Oil Pollution Damage, 2001

Article 1 (Definitions)

For the purposes of this Convention:

1. 'Ship' means any seagoing vessel and seaborne craft, of any type whatsoever.

2. 'Person' means any individual or partnership or any public or private body, whether corporate or not, including a State or any of its constituent subdivisions.

3. 'Shipowner' means the owner, including the registered owner, bareboat charterer, manager and operator of the ship.

4. 'Registered owner' means the person or persons registered as the owner of the ship or, in the absence of registration, the person or persons owning the ship. However, in the case of a ship owned by a State and operated by a company which in that State is registered as the ship's operator, 'registered owner' shall mean such company.

5. 'Bunker oil' means any hydrocarbon mineral oil, including lubricating oil, used or intended to be used for the operation or propulsion of the ship, and any residues of such oil.

6. 'Civil Liability Convention' means the International Convention on Civil Liability for Oil Pollution Damage, 1992, as amended.

7. 'Preventive measures' means any reasonable measures taken by any person after an incident has occurred to prevent or minimize pollution damage.

8. 'Incident' means any occurrence or series of occurrences having the same origin, which causes pollution damage or creates a grave and imminent threat of causing such damage.

9. 'Pollution damage' means:
   (a) loss or damage caused outside the ship by contamination resulting from the escape or discharge of bunker oil from the ship, wherever such escape or discharge may occur, provided that compensation for impairment of the environment other than loss of profit from such impairment shall be limited to costs of reasonable measures of reinstatement actually undertaken or to be undertaken; and
   (b) the costs of preventive measures and further loss or damage caused by preventive measures.

10. 'State of the ship's registry' means, in relation to a registered ship, the State of registration of the ship and, in relation to an unregistered ship, the State whose flag the ship is entitled to fly.

11. 'Gross tonnage' means gross tonnage calculated in accordance with the tonnage measurement regulations contained in Annex 1 of the International Convention on Tonnage Measurement of Ships, 1969.

12. 'Organization' means the International Maritime Organization.

13. 'Secretary-General' means the Secretary-General of the Organization.

APPENDIX 11

Article 2 (Scope of application)

This Convention shall apply exclusively:
  (a) to pollution damage caused:
      (i) in the territory, including the territorial sea, of a State Party, and
      (ii) in the exclusive economic zone of a State Party, established in accordance with international law, or, if a State Party has not established such a zone, in an area beyond and adjacent to the territorial sea of that State determined by that State in accordance with international law and extending not more than 200 nautical miles from the baselines from which the breadth of its territorial sea is measured;
  (b) to preventive measures, wherever taken, to prevent or minimize such damage.

Article 3 (Liability of the shipowner)

1. Except as provided in paragraphs 3 and 4, the shipowner at the time of an incident shall be liable for pollution damage caused by any bunker oil on board or originating from the ship, provided that, if an incident consists of a series of occurrences having the same origin, the liability shall attach to the shipowner at the time of the first of such occurrences.

2. Where more than one person is liable in accordance with paragraph 1, their liability shall be joint and several.

3. No liability for pollution damage shall attach to the shipowner if the shipowner proves that:
  (a) the damage resulted from an act of war, hostilities, civil war, insurrection or a natural phenomenon of an exceptional, inevitable and irresistible character; or
  (b) the damage was wholly caused by an act or omission done with the intent to cause damage by a third party; or
  (c) the damage was wholly caused by the negligence or other wrongful act of any Government or other authority responsible for the maintenance of lights or other navigational aids in the exercise of that function.

4. If the shipowner proves that the pollution damage resulted wholly or partially either from an act or omission done with intent to cause damage by the person who suffered the damage or from the negligence of that person, the shipowner may be exonerated wholly or partially from liability to such person.

5. No claim for compensation for pollution damage shall be made against the shipowner otherwise than in accordance with this Convention.

6. Nothing in this Convention shall prejudice any right of recourse of the shipowner which exists independently of this Convention.

Article 4 (Exclusions)

1. This Convention shall not apply to pollution damage as defined in the Civil Liability Convention, whether or not compensation is payable in respect of it under that Convention.

2. Except as provided in paragraph 3, the provisions of this Convention shall not apply to warships, naval auxiliary or other ships owned or operated by a State and used, for the time being, only on Government non-commercial service.

3. A State Party may decide to apply this Convention to its warships or other ships described in paragraph 2, in which case it shall notify the Secretary-General thereof specifying the terms and conditions of such application.

4. With respect to ships owned by a State Party and used for commercial purposes, each

418

APPENDIX 11

State shall be subject to suit in the jurisdictions set forth in article 9 and shall waive all defences based on its status as a sovereign State.

Article 5 (Incidents involving two or more ships)

When an incident involving two or more ships occurs and pollution damage results therefrom, the shipowners of all the ships concerned, unless exonerated under article 3, shall be jointly and severally liable for all such damage which is not reasonably separable.

Article 6 (Limitation of liability)

Nothing in this Convention shall affect the right of the shipowner and the person or persons providing insurance or other financial security to limit liability under any applicable national or international regime, such as the Convention on Limitation of Liability for Maritime Claims, 1976, as amended.

Article 7 (Compulsory insurance or financial security)

1. The registered owner of a ship having a gross tonnage greater than 1000 registered in a State Party shall be required to maintain insurance or other financial security, such as the guarantee of a bank or similar financial institution, to cover the liability of the registered owner for pollution damage in an amount equal to the limits of liability under the applicable national or international limitation regime, but in all cases, not exceeding an amount calculated in accordance with the Convention on Limitation of Liability for Maritime Claims, 1976, as amended.

2. A certificate attesting that insurance or other financial security is in force in accordance with the provisions of this Convention shall be issued to each ship after the appropriate authority of a State Party has determined that the requirements of paragraph 1 have been complied with. With respect to a ship registered in a State Party such certificate shall be issued or certified by the appropriate authority of the State of the ship's registry; with respect to a ship not registered in a State Party it may be issued or certified by the appropriate authority of any State Party. This certificate shall be in the form of the model set out in the annex to this Convention and shall contain the following particulars:

   (a) name of ship, distinctive number or letters and port of registry;
   (b) name and principal place of business of the registered owner;
   (c) IMO ship identification number;
   (d) type and duration of security;
   (e) name and principal place of business of insurer or other person giving security and, where appropriate, place of business where the insurance or security is established;
   (f) period of validity of the certificate which shall not be longer than the period of validity of the insurance or other security.

3. (a) A State Party may authorize either an institution or an organization recognized by it to issue the certificate referred to in paragraph 2. Such institution or organization shall inform that State of the issue of each certificate. In all cases, the State Party shall fully guarantee the completeness and accuracy of the certificate so issued and shall undertake to ensure the necessary arrangements to satisfy this obligation.

   (b) A State Party shall notify the Secretary-General of:
       (i) the specific responsibilities and conditions of the authority delegated to an institution or organization recognised by it;
       (ii) the withdrawal of such authority; and

419

APPENDIX 11

(iii) the date from which such authority or withdrawal of such authority takes effect.

An authority delegated shall not take effect prior to three months from the date on which notification to that effect was given to the Secretary-General.

(c) The institution or organization authorized to issue certificates in accordance with this paragraph shall, as a minimum, be authorized to withdraw these certificates if the conditions under which they have been issued are not maintained. In all cases the institution or organization shall report such withdrawal to the State on whose behalf the certificate was issued.

4. The certificate shall be in the official language or languages of the issuing State. If the language used is not English, French or Spanish, the text shall include a translation into one of these languages and, where the State so decides, the official language of the State may be omitted.

5. The certificate shall be carried on board the ship and a copy shall be deposited with the authorities who keep the record of the ship's registry or, if the ship is not registered in a State Party, with the authorities issuing or certifying the certificate.

6. An insurance or other financial security shall not satisfy the requirements of this article if it can cease, for reasons other than the expiry of the period of validity of the insurance or security specified in the certificate under paragraph 2 of this article, before three months have elapsed from the date on which notice of its termination is given to the authorities referred to in paragraph 5 of this article, unless the certificate has been surrendered to these authorities or a new certificate has been issued within the said period. The foregoing provisions shall similarly apply to any modification which results in the insurance or security no longer satisfying the requirements of this article.

7. The State of the ship's registry shall, subject to the provisions of this article, determine the conditions of issue and validity of the certificate.

8. Nothing in this Convention shall be construed as preventing a State Party from relying on information obtained from other States or the Organization or other international organisations relating to the financial standing of providers of insurance or financial security for the purposes of this Convention. In such cases, the State Party relying on such information is not relieved of its responsibility as a State issuing the certificate required by paragraph 2.

9. Certificates issued or certified under the authority of a State Party shall be accepted by other States Parties for the purposes of this Convention and shall be regarded by other States Parties as having the same force as certificates issued or certified by them even if issued or certified in respect of a ship not registered in a State Party. A State Party may at any time request consultation with the issuing or certifying State should it believe that the insurer or guarantor named in the insurance certificate is not financially capable of meeting the obligations imposed by this Convention.

10. Any claim for compensation for pollution damage may be brought directly against the insurer or other person providing financial security for the registered owner's liability for pollution damage. In such a case the defendant may invoke the defences (other than bankruptcy or winding up of the shipowner) which the shipowner would have been entitled to invoke, including limitation pursuant to article 6. Furthermore, even if the shipowner is not entitled to limitation of liability according to article 6, the defendant may limit liability to an amount equal to the amount of the insurance or other financial security required to be maintained in accordance with paragraph 1. Moreover, the defendant may invoke the defence that the pollution damage resulted from the wilful misconduct of the shipowner, but the defendant shall not invoke any other defence which the defendant might have been entitled to invoke in proceedings brought by the shipowner against the defendant. The defendant shall in any event have the right to require the shipowner to be joined in the proceedings.

APPENDIX 11

11. A State Party shall not permit a ship under its flag to which this article applies to operate at any time, unless a certificate has been issued under paragraphs 2 or 14.

12. Subject to the provisions of this article, each State Party shall ensure, under its national law, that insurance or other security, to the extent specified in paragraph 1, is in force in respect of any ship having a gross tonnage greater than 1000, wherever registered, entering or leaving a port in its territory, or arriving at or leaving an offshore facility in its territorial sea.

13. Notwithstanding the provisions of paragraph 5, a State Party may notify the Secretary-General that, for the purposes of paragraph 12, ships are not required to carry on board or to produce the certificate required by paragraph 2, when entering or leaving ports or arriving at or leaving from offshore facilities in its territory, provided that the State Party which issues the certificate required by paragraph 2 has notified the Secretary-General that it maintains records in an electronic format, accessible to all States Parties, attesting the existence of the certificate and enabling States Parties to discharge their obligations under paragraph 12.

14. If insurance or other financial security is not maintained in respect of a ship owned by a State Party, the provisions of this article relating thereto shall not be applicable to such ship, but the ship shall carry a certificate issued by the appropriate authority of the State of the ship's registry stating that the ship is owned by that State and that the ship's liability is covered within the limit prescribed in accordance with paragraph 1. Such a certificate shall follow as closely as possible the model prescribed by paragraph 2.

15. A State may, at the time of ratification, acceptance, approval of, or accession to this Convention, or at any time thereafter, declare that this article does not apply to ships operating exclusively within the area of that State referred to in article 2(a)(i).

Article 8 (Time limits)

Rights to compensation under this Convention shall be extinguished unless an action is brought thereunder within three years from the date when the damage occurred. However, in no case shall an action be brought more than six years from the date of the incident which caused the damage. Where the incident consists of a series of occurrences, the six years' period shall run from the date of the first such occurrence.

Article 9 (Jurisdiction)

1. Where an incident has caused pollution damage in the territory, including the territorial sea, or in an area referred to in article 2(a)(ii) of one or more States Parties, or preventive measures have been taken to prevent or minimise pollution damage in such territory, including the territorial sea, or in such area, actions for compensation against the shipowner, insurer or other person providing security for the shipowner's liability may be brought only in the courts of any such States Parties.

2. Reasonable notice of any action taken under paragraph 1 shall be given to each defendant.

3. Each State Party shall ensure that its courts have jurisdiction to entertain actions for compensation under this Convention.

Article 10 (Recognition and enforcement)

1. Any judgement given by a Court with jurisdiction in accordance with article 9 which is enforceable in the State of origin where it is no longer subject to ordinary forms of review, shall be recognised in any State Party, except:

APPENDIX 11

    (a)   where the judgement was obtained by fraud; or

    (b)   where the defendant was not given reasonable notice and a fair opportunity to present his or her case.

2. A judgement recognised under paragraph 1 shall be enforceable in each State Party as soon as the formalities required in that State have been complied with. The formalities shall not permit the merits of the case to be re-opened.

Article 11 (Supersession clause)

This Convention shall supersede any Convention in force or open for signature, ratification or accession at the date on which this Convention is opened for signature, but only to the extent that such Convention would be in conflict with it; however, nothing in this article shall affect the obligations of States Parties to States not party to this Convention arising under such Convention.

Article 12 (Signature, ratification, acceptance, approval and accession)

1. This Convention shall be open for signature at the Headquarters of the Organization from 1 October 2001 until 30 September 2002 and shall thereafter remain open for accession.

2. States may express their consent to be bound by this Convention by:

    (a)   signature without reservation as to ratification, acceptance or approval;

    (b)   signature subject to ratification, acceptance or approval followed by ratification, acceptance or approval; or

    (c)   accession.

3. Ratification, acceptance, approval or accession shall be effected by the deposit of an instrument to that effect with the Secretary-General.

4. Any instrument of ratification, acceptance, approval or accession deposited after the entry into force of an amendment to this Convention with respect to all existing State Parties, or after the completion of all measures required for the entry into force of the amendment with respect to those State Parties shall be deemed to apply to this Convention as modified by the amendment.

Article 13 (States with more than one system of law)

1. If a State has two or more territorial units in which different systems of law are applicable in relation to matters dealt with in this Convention, it may at the time of signature, ratification, acceptance, approval or accession declare that this Convention shall extend to all its territorial units or only to one or more of them and may modify this declaration by submitting another declaration at any time.

2. Any such declaration shall be notified to the Secretary-General and shall state expressly the territorial units to which this Convention applies.

3. In relation to a State Party which has made such a declaration:

    (a)   in the definition of 'registered owner' in article 1(4), references to a State shall be construed as references to such a territorial unit;

    (b)   references to the State of a ship's registry and, in relation to a compulsory insurance certificate, to the issuing or certifying State, shall be construed as referring to the territorial unit respectively in which the ship is registered and which issues or certifies the certificate;

    (c)   references in this Convention to the requirements of national law shall be

APPENDIX 11

construed as references to the requirements of the law of the relevant territorial unit; and

(d) references in articles 9 and 10 to courts, and to judgements which must be recognized in States Parties, shall be construed as references respectively to courts of, and to judgements which must be recognized in, the relevant territorial unit.

Article 14 (Entry into force)

1. This Convention shall enter into force one year following the date on which eighteen States, including five States each with ships whose combined gross tonnage is not less than 1 million, have either signed it without reservation as to ratification, acceptance or approval or have deposited instruments of ratification, acceptance, approval or accession with the Secretary General.

2. For any State which ratifies, accepts, approves or accedes to it after the conditions in paragraph 1 for entry into force have been met, this Convention shall enter into force three months after the date of deposit by such State of the appropriate instrument.

Article 15 (Denunciation)

1. This Convention may be denounced by any State Party at any time after the date on which this Convention comes into force for that State.

2. Denunciation shall be effected by the deposit of an instrument with the Secretary-General.

3. A denunciation shall take effect one year, or such longer period as may be specified in the instrument of denunciation, after its deposit with the Secretary-General.

Article 16 (Revision or amendment)

1. A conference for the purpose of revising or amending this Convention may be convened by the Organization.

2. The Organization shall convene a conference of the States Parties for revising or amending this Convention at the request of not less than one-third of the States Parties.

Article 17 (Depositary)

1. This Convention shall be deposited with the Secretary-General.

2. The Secretary-General shall:

(a) inform all States which have signed or acceded to this Convention of:
   (i) each new signature or deposit of instrument together with the date thereof;
   (ii) the date of entry into force of this Convention;
   (iii) the deposit of any instrument of denunciation of this Convention together with the date of the deposit and the date on which the denunciation takes effect; and
   (iv) other declarations and notifications made under this Convention.

(b) transmit certified true copies of this Convention to all Signatory States and to all States which accede to this Convention.

APPENDIX 11

Article 18 (Transmission to United Nations)

As soon as this Convention comes into force, the text shall be transmitted by the Secretary-General to the Secretariat of the United Nations for registration and publication in accordance with Article 102 of the Charter of the United Nations.

Article 19 (Languages)

This Convention is established in a single original in the Arabic, Chinese, English, French, Russian and Spanish languages, each text being equally authentic.

Done at London this twenty-third day of March, two thousand and one.

APPENDIX 12

International Convention on Liability and Compensation for Damage in Connection with the Carriage of Hazardous and Noxious Substances by Sea, 1996

(London, 3 May 1996)

THE STATES PARTIES TO THE PRESENT CONVENTION,

CONSCIOUS of the dangers posed by the world-wide carriage by sea of hazardous and noxious substances,

CONVINCED of the need to ensure that adequate, prompt and effective compensation is available to persons who suffer damage caused by incidents in connection with the carriage by sea of such substances,

DESIRING to adopt uniform international rules and procedures for determining questions of liability and compensation in respect of such damage,

CONSIDERING that the economic consequences of damage caused by the carriage by sea of hazardous and noxious substances should be shared by the shipping industry and the cargo interests involved,

HAVE AGREED as follows:

Chapter I

General Provisions

Definitions

Article 1

For the purposes of this Convention:

1. 'Ship' means any seagoing vessel and seaborne craft, of any type whatsoever.

2. 'Person' means any individual or partnership or any public or private body, whether corporate or not, including a State or any of its constituent subdivisions.

3. 'Owner' means the person or persons registered as the owner of the ship or, in the absence of registration, the person or persons owning the ship. However, in the case of a ship owned by a State and operated by a company which in that State is registered as the ship's operator, 'owner' shall mean such company.

4. 'Receiver' means either:
   (a) the person who physically receives contributing cargo discharged in the ports and terminals of a State Party; provided that if at the time of receipt the person who physically receives the cargo acts as an agent for another who is subject to the jurisdiction of any State Party, then the principal shall be deemed to be the receiver, if the agent discloses the principal to the HNS Fund; or

425

APPENDIX 12

(b) the person in the State Party who in accordance with the national law of that State Party is deemed to be the receiver of contributing cargo discharged in the ports and terminals of a State Party, provided that the total contributing cargo received according to such national law is substantially the same as that which would have been received under (a).

5. 'Hazardous and noxious substances' (HNS) means:

(a) any substances, materials and articles carried on board a ship as cargo, referred to in (i) to (vii) below:

(i) oils carried in bulk listed in appendix I of Annex I to the International Convention for the Prevention of Pollution from Ships, 1973, as modified by the Protocol of 1978 relating thereto, as amended;

(ii) noxious liquid substances carried in bulk referred to in appendix II of Annex II to the International Convention for the Prevention of Pollution from Ships, 1973, as modified by the Protocol of 1978 relating thereto, as amended, and those substances and mixtures provisionally categorized as falling in pollution category A, B, C or D in accordance with regulation 3(4) of the said Annex II;

(iii) dangerous liquid substances carried in bulk listed in Chapter 17 of the International Code for the Construction and Equipment of Ships Carrying Dangerous Chemicals in Bulk, 1983, as amended, and the dangerous products for which the preliminary suitable conditions for the carriage have been prescribed by the Administration and port administrations involved in accordance with paragraph 1.1.3 of the Code;

(iv) dangerous, hazardous and harmful substances, materials and articles in packaged form covered by the International Maritime Dangerous Goods Code, as amended;

(v) liquefied gases as listed in Chapter 19 of the International Code for the Construction and Equipment of Ships carrying Liquefied Gases in Bulk, 1983, as amended, and the products for which preliminary suitable conditions for the carriage have been prescribed by the Administration and port administrations involved in accordance with paragraph 1.1.6 of the Code;

(vi) liquid substances carried in bulk with a flashpoint not exceeding 60deg.C (measured by a closed cup test);

(vii) solid bulk materials possessing chemical hazards covered by appendix B of the Code of Safe Practice for Solid Bulk Cargoes, as amended, to the extent that these substances are also subject to the provisions of the International Maritime Dangerous Goods Code when carried in packaged form; and

(b) residues from the previous carriage in bulk of substances referred to in (a)(i) to (iii) and (v) to (vii) above.

6. 'Damage' means:

(a) loss of life or personal injury on board or outside the ship carrying the hazardous and noxious substances caused by those substances;

(b) loss of or damage to property outside the ship carrying the hazardous and noxious substances caused by those substances;

(c) loss or damage by contamination of the environment caused by the hazardous and noxious substances, provided that compensation for impairment of the environment other than loss of profit from such impairment shall be limited to costs of reasonable measures of reinstatement actually undertaken or to be undertaken; and

(d) the costs of preventive measures and further loss or damage caused by preventive measures.

APPENDIX 12

Where it is not reasonably possible to separate damage caused by the hazardous and noxious substances from that caused by other factors, all such damage shall be deemed to be caused by the hazardous and noxious substances except if, and to the extent that, the damage caused by other factors is damage of a type referred to in Article 4, paragraph 3.

In this paragraph, 'caused by those substances' means caused by the hazardous or noxious nature of the substances.

7. 'Preventive measures' means any reasonable measures taken by any person after an incident has occurred to prevent or minimize damage.

8. 'Incident' means any occurrence or series of occurrences having the same origin, which causes damage or creates a grave and imminent threat of causing damage.

9. 'Carriage by sea' means the period from the time when the hazardous and noxious substances enter any part of the ship's equipment, on loading, to the time they cease to be present in any part of the ship's equipment, on discharge. If no ship's equipment is used, the period begins and ends respectively when the hazardous and noxious substances cross the ship's rail.

10. 'Contributing cargo' means any hazardous and noxious substances which are carried by sea as cargo to a port or terminal in the territory of a State Party and discharged in that State. Cargo in transit which is transferred directly, or through a port or terminal, from one ship to another, either wholly or in part, in the course of carriage from the port or terminal of original loading to the port or terminal of final destination shall be considered as contributing cargo only in respect of receipt at the final destination.

11. The 'HNS Fund' means the International Hazardous and Noxious Substances Fund established under Article 13.

12. 'Unit of account' means the Special Drawing Right as defined by the International Monetary Fund.

13. 'State of the ship's registry' means in relation to a registered ship the State of registration of the ship, and in relation to an unregistered ship the State whose flag the ship is entitled to fly.

14. 'Terminal' means any site for the storage of hazardous and noxious substances received from waterborne transportation, including any facility situated off-shore and linked by pipeline or otherwise to such site.

15. 'Director' means the Director of the HNS Fund.

16. 'Organization' means the International Maritime Organization.

17. 'Secretary-General' means the Secretary-General of the Organization.

Annexes

Article 2

The Annexes to this Convention shall constitute an integral part of this Convention.

Scope of application

Article 3

This Convention shall apply exclusively:
> (a) to any damage caused in the territory, including the territorial sea, of a State Party;
> (b) to damage by contamination of the environment caused in the exclusive economic zone of a State Party, established in accordance with international law, or, if a State Party has not established such a zone, in an area beyond and adjacent to the territorial sea of that State determined by that State in accordance with international

APPENDIX 12

law and extending not more than 200 nautical miles from the baselines from which the breadth of its territorial sea is measured;

(c) to damage, other than damage by contamination of the environment, caused outside the territory, including the territorial sea, of any State, if this damage has been caused by a substance carried on board a ship registered in a State Party or, in the case of an unregistered ship, on board a ship entitled to fly the flag of a State Party; and

(d) to preventive measures, wherever taken.

Article 4

1. This Convention shall apply to claims, other than claims arising out of any contract for the carriage of goods and passengers, for damage arising from the carriage of hazardous and noxious substances by sea.

2. This Convention shall not apply to the extent that its provisions are incompatible with those of the applicable law relating to workers' compensation or social security schemes.

3. This Convention shall not apply:

(a) to pollution damage as defined in the International Convention on Civil Liability for Oil Pollution Damage, 1969, as amended, whether or not compensation is payable in respect of it under that Convention; and

(b) to damage caused by a radioactive material of class 7 either in the International Maritime Dangerous Goods Code, as amended, or in appendix B of the Code of Safe Practice for Solid Bulk Cargoes, as amended.

4. Except as provided in paragraph 5, the provisions of this Convention shall not apply to warships, naval auxiliary or other ships owned or operated by a State and used, for the time being, only on Government non-commercial service.

5. A State Party may decide to apply this Convention to its warships or other vessels described in paragraph 4, in which case it shall notify the Secretary-General thereof specifying the terms and conditions of such application.

6. With respect to ships owned by a State Party and used for commercial purposes, each State shall be subject to suit in the jurisdictions set forth in Article 38 and shall waive all defences based on its status as a sovereign State.

Article 5

1. A State may, at the time of ratification, acceptance, approval of, or accession to, this Convention, or any time thereafter, declare that this Convention does not apply to ships:

(a) which do not exceed 200 gross tonnage; and

(b) which carry hazardous and noxious substances only in packaged form; and

(c) while they are engaged on voyages between ports or facilities of that State.

2. Where two neighbouring States agree that this Convention does not apply also to ships which are covered by paragraph 1(a) and (b) while engaged on voyages between ports or facilities of those States, the States concerned may declare that the exclusion from the application of this Convention declared under paragraph 1 covers also ships referred to in this paragraph.

3. Any State which has made the declaration under paragraph 1 or 2 may withdraw such declaration at any time.

4. A declaration made under paragraph 1 or 2, and the withdrawal of the declaration made under paragraph 3, shall be deposited with the Secretary-General who shall, after the entry into force of this Convention, communicate it to the Director.

5. Where a State has made a declaration under paragraph 1 or 2 and has not withdrawn

APPENDIX 12

it, hazardous and noxious substances carried on board ships covered by that paragraph shall not be considered to be contributing cargo for the purpose of application of Articles 18, 20, Article 21, paragraph 5 and Article 43.

6. The HNS Fund is not liable to pay compensation for damage caused by substances carried by a ship to which the Convention does not apply pursuant to a declaration made under paragraph 1 or 2, to the extent that:

(a)   the damage as defined in Article 1, paragraph 6(a), (b) or (c) was caused in:

    (i)   the territory, including the territorial sea, of the State which has made the declaration, or in the case of neighbouring States which have made a declaration under paragraph 2, of either of them; or

    (ii)   the exclusive economic zone, or area mentioned in Article 3(b), of the State or States referred to in (i);

(b)   the damage includes measures taken to prevent or minimize such damage.

Duties of state parties

Article 6

Each State Party shall ensure that any obligation arising under this Convention is fulfilled and shall take appropriate measures under its law including the imposing of sanctions as it may deem necessary, with a view to the effective execution of any such obligation.

Chapter II

Liability

Liability of the owner

Article 7

1. Except as provided in paragraphs 2 and 3, the owner at the time of an incident shall be liable for damage caused by any hazardous and noxious substances in connection with their carriage by sea on board the ship, provided that if an incident consists of a series of occurrences having the same origin the liability shall attach to the owner at the time of the first of such occurrences.

2. No liability shall attach to the owner if the owner proves that:

(a)   the damage resulted from an act of war, hostilities, civil war, insurrection or a natural phenomenon of an exceptional, inevitable and irresistible character; or

(b)   the damage was wholly caused by an act or omission done with the intent to cause damage by a third party; or

(c)   the damage was wholly caused by the negligence or other wrongful act of any Government or other authority responsible for the maintenance of lights or other navigational aids in the exercise of that function; or

(d)   the failure of the shipper or any other person to furnish information concerning the hazardous and noxious nature of the substances shipped either

    (i)   has caused the damage, wholly or partly; or

    (ii)   has led the owner not to obtain insurance in accordance with Article 12;

provided that neither the owner nor its servants or agents knew or ought reasonably to have known of the hazardous and noxious nature of the substances shipped.

3. If the owner proves that the damage resulted wholly or partly either from an act or

APPENDIX 12

omission done with intent to cause damage by the person who suffered the damage or from the negligence of that person, the owner may be exonerated wholly or partially from liability to such person.

4. No claim for compensation for damage shall be made against the owner otherwise than in accordance with this Convention.

5. Subject to paragraph 6, no claim for compensation for damage under this Convention or otherwise may be made against:

    (a)   the servants or agents of the owner or the members of the crew;

    (b)   the pilot or any other person who, without being a member of the crew, performs services for the ship;

    (c)   any charterer (howsoever described, including a bareboat charterer), manager or operator of the ship;

    (d)   any person performing salvage operations with the consent of the owner or on the instructions of a competent public authority;

    (e)   any person taking preventive measures; and

    (f)   the servants or agents of persons mentioned in (c), (d) and (e);

unless the damage resulted from their personal act or omission, committed with the intent to cause such damage, or recklessly and with knowledge that such damage would probably result.

6. Nothing in this Convention shall prejudice any existing right of recourse of the owner against any third party, including, but not limited to, the shipper or the receiver of the substance causing the damage, or the persons indicated in paragraph 5.

Incidents involving two or more ships

Article 8

1. Whenever damage has resulted from an incident involving two or more ships each of which is carrying hazardous and noxious substances, each owner, unless exonerated under Article 7, shall be liable for the damage. The owners shall be jointly and severally liable for all such damage which is not reasonably separable.

2. However, owners shall be entitled to the limits of liability applicable to each of them under Article 9.

3. Nothing in this Article shall prejudice any right of recourse of an owner against any other owner.

Limitation of liability

Article 9

1. The owner of a ship shall be entitled to limit liability under this Convention in respect of any one incident to an aggregate amount calculated as follows:

    (a)   10 million units of account for a ship not exceeding 2,000 units of tonnage; and

    (b)   for a ship with a tonnage in excess thereof, the following amount in addition to that mentioned in (a):

        for each unit of tonnage from 2,001 to 50,000 units of tonnage, 1,500 units of account;

        for each unit of tonnage in excess of 50,000 units of tonnage, 360 units of account;

   provided, however, that this aggregate amount shall not in any event exceed 100 million units of account.

APPENDIX 12

2. The owner shall not be entitled to limit liability under this Convention if it is proved that the damage resulted from the personal act or omission of the owner, committed with the intent to cause such damage, or recklessly and with knowledge that such damage would probably result.

3. The owner shall, for the purpose of benefitting from the limitation provided for in paragraph 1, constitute a fund for the total sum representing the limit of liability established in accordance with paragraph 1 with the court or other competent authority of any one of the States Parties in which action is brought under Article 38 or, if no action is brought, with any court or other competent authority in any one of the States Parties in which an action can be brought under Article 38. The fund can be constituted either by depositing the sum or by producing a bank guarantee or other guarantee, acceptable under the law of the State Party where the fund is constituted, and considered to be adequate by the court or other competent authority.

4. Subject to the provisions of Article 11, the fund shall be distributed among the claimants in proportion to the amounts of their established claims.

5. If before the fund is distributed the owner or any of the servants or agents of the owner or any person providing to the owner insurance or other financial security has as a result of the incident in question, paid compensation for damage, such person shall, up to the amount that person has paid, acquire by subrogation the rights which the person so compensated would have enjoyed under this Convention.

6. The right of subrogation provided for in paragraph 5 may also be exercised by a person other than those mentioned therein in respect of any amount of compensation for damage which such person may have paid but only to the extent that such subrogation is permitted under the applicable national law.

7. Where owners or other persons establish that they may be compelled to pay at a later date in whole or in part any such amount of compensation, with regard to which the right of subrogation would have been enjoyed under paragraphs 5 or 6 had the compensation been paid before the fund was distributed, the court or other competent authority of the State where the fund has been constituted may order that a sufficient sum shall be provisionally set aside to enable such person at such later date to enforce the claim against the fund.

8. Claims in respect of expenses reasonably incurred or sacrifices reasonably made by the owner voluntarily to prevent or minimize damage shall rank equally with other claims against the fund.

9. (a) The amounts mentioned in paragraph 1 shall be converted into national currency on the basis of the value of that currency by reference to the Special Drawing Right on the date of the constitution of the fund referred to in paragraph 3. The value of the national currency, in terms of the Special Drawing Right, of a State Party which is a member of the International Monetary Fund, shall be calculated in accordance with the method of valuation applied by the International Monetary Fund in effect on the date in question for its operations and transactions. The value of the national currency, in terms of the Special Drawing Right, of a State Party which is not a member of the International Monetary Fund, shall be calculated in a manner determined by that State.

   (b) Nevertheless, a State Party which is not a member of the International Monetary Fund and whose law does not permit the application of the provisions of paragraph 9(a) may, at the time of ratification, acceptance, approval of or accession to this Convention or at any time thereafter, declare that the unit of account referred to in paragraph 9(a) shall be equal to 15 gold francs. The gold franc referred to in this paragraph corresponds to sixty-five-and-a-half milligrammes of gold of millesimal

APPENDIX 12

fineness nine hundred. The conversion of the gold franc into the national currency shall be made according to the law of the State concerned.

(c) The calculation mentioned in the last sentence of paragraph 9(a) and the conversion mentioned in paragraph 9(b) shall be made in such manner as to express in the national currency of the State Party as far as possible the same real value for the amounts in paragraph 1 as would result from the application of the first two sentences of paragraph 9(a). States Parties shall communicate to the Secretary-General the manner of calculation pursuant to paragraph 9(a), or the result of the conversion in paragraph 9(b) as the case may be, when depositing an instrument of ratification, acceptance, approval of or accession to this Convention and whenever there is a change in either.

10. For the purpose of this Article the ship's tonnage shall be the gross tonnage calculated in accordance with the tonnage measurement regulations contained in Annex I of the International Convention on Tonnage Measurement of Ships, 1969.

11. The insurer or other person providing financial security shall be entitled to constitute a fund in accordance with this Article on the same conditions and having the same effect as if it were constituted by the owner. Such a fund may be constituted even if, under the provisions of paragraph 2, the owner is not entitled to limitation of liability, but its constitution shall in that case not prejudice the rights of any claimant against the owner.

Article 10

1. Where the owner, after an incident, has constituted a fund in accordance with Article 9 and is entitled to limit liability:

(a) no person having a claim for damage arising out of that incident shall be entitled to exercise any right against any other assets of the owner in respect of such claim; and

(b) the court or other competent authority of any State Party shall order the release of any ship or other property belonging to the owner which has been arrested in respect of a claim for damage arising out of that incident, and shall similarly release any bail or other security furnished to avoid such arrest.

2. The foregoing shall, however, only apply if the claimant has access to the court administering the fund and the fund is actually available in respect of the claim.

Death and injury

Article 11

Claims in respect of death or personal injury have priority over other claims save to the extent that the aggregate of such claims exceeds two-thirds of the total amount established in accordance with Article 9, paragraph 1.

Compulsory insurance of the owner

Article 12

1. The owner of a ship registered in a State Party and actually carrying hazardous and noxious substances shall be required to maintain insurance or other financial security, such as the guarantee of a bank or similar financial institution, in the sums fixed by applying the limits of liability prescribed in Article 9, paragraph 1, to cover liability for damage under this Convention.

432

APPENDIX 12

2. A compulsory insurance certificate attesting that insurance or other financial security is in force in accordance with the provisions of this Convention shall be issued to each ship after the appropriate authority of a State Party has determined that the requirements of paragraph 1 have been complied with. With respect to a ship registered in a State Party such compulsory insurance certificate shall be issued or certified by the appropriate authority of the State of the ship's registry; with respect to a ship not registered in a State Party it may be issued or certified by the appropriate authority of any State Party. This compulsory insurance certificate shall be in the form of the model set out in Annex I and shall contain the following particulars:

   (a) name of the ship, distinctive number or letters and port of registry;

   (b) name and principal place of business of the owner;

   (c) IMO ship identification number;

   (d) type and duration of security;

   (e) name and principal place of business of insurer or other person giving security and, where appropriate, place of business where the insurance or security is established; and

   (f) period of validity of certificate, which shall not be longer than the period of validity of the insurance or other security.

3. The compulsory insurance certificate shall be in the official language or languages of the issuing State. If the language used is neither English, nor French nor Spanish, the text shall include a translation into one of these languages.

4. The compulsory insurance certificate shall be carried on board the ship and a copy shall be deposited with the authorities who keep the record of the ship's registry or, if the ship is not registered in a State Party, with the authority of the State issuing or certifying the certificate.

5. An insurance or other financial security shall not satisfy the requirements of this Article if it can cease, for reasons other than the expiry of the period of validity of the insurance or security specified in the certificate under paragraph 2, before three months have elapsed from the date on which notice of its termination is given to the authorities referred to in paragraph 4, unless the compulsory insurance certificate has been issued within the said period. The foregoing provisions shall similarly apply to any modification which results in the insurance or security no longer satisfying the requirements of this Article.

6. The State of the ship's registry shall, subject to the provisions of this Article, determine the conditions of issue and validity of the compulsory insurance certificate.

7. Compulsory insurance certificates issued or certified under the authority of a State Party in accordance with paragraph 2 shall be accepted by other States Parties for the purposes of this Convention and shall be regarded by other States Parties as having the same force as compulsory insurance certificates issued or certified by them even if issued or certified in respect of a ship not registered in a State Party. A State Party may at any time request consultation with the issuing or certifying State should it believe that the insurer or guarantor named in the compulsory insurance certificate is not financially capable of meeting the obligations imposed by this Convention.

8. Any claim for compensation for damage may be brought directly against the insurer or other person providing financial security for the owner's liability for damage. In such case the defendant may, even if the owner is not entitled to limitation of liability, benefit from the limit of liability prescribed in accordance with paragraph 1. The defendant may further invoke the defences (other than the bankruptcy or winding up of the owner) which the owner would have been entitled to invoke. Furthermore, the defendant may invoke the defence that the damage resulted from the wilful misconduct of the owner, but the defendant shall not invoke any other defence which the defendant might have been entitled to invoke in proceedings

APPENDIX 12

brought by the owner against the defendant. The defendant shall in any event have the right to require the owner to be joined in the proceedings.

9. Any sums provided by insurance or by other financial security maintained in accordance with paragraph 1 shall be available exclusively for the satisfaction of claims under this Convention.

10. A State Party shall not permit a ship under its flag to which this Article applies to trade unless a certificate has been issued under paragraph 2 or 12.

11. Subject to the provisions of this Article, each State Party shall ensure, under its national law, that insurance or other security in the sums specified in paragraph 1 is in force in respect of any ship, wherever registered, entering or leaving a port in its territory, or arriving at or leaving an offshore facility in its territorial sea.

12. If insurance or other financial security is not maintained in respect of a ship owned by a State Party, the provisions of this Article relating thereto shall not be applicable to such ship, but the ship shall carry a compulsory insurance certificate issued by the appropriate authorities of the State of the ship's registry stating that the ship is owned by that State and that the ship's liability is covered within the limit prescribed in accordance with paragraph 1. Such a compulsory insurance certificate shall follow as closely as possible the model prescribed by paragraph 2.

Chapter III

Compensation by the international hazardous and noxious substances fund (HNS Fund)

Establishment of the HNS Fund

Article 13

1. The International Hazardous and Noxious Substances Fund (HNS Fund) is hereby established with the following aims:
   (a) to provide compensation for damage in connection with the carriage of hazardous and noxious substances by sea, to the extent that the protection afforded by Chapter II is inadequate or not available; and
   (b) to give effect to the related tasks set out in Article 15.

2. The HNS Fund shall in each State Party be recognized as a legal person capable under the laws of that State of assuming rights and obligations and of being a party in legal proceedings before the courts of that State. Each State Party shall recognize the Director as the legal representative of the HNS Fund.

Compensation

Article 14

1. For the purpose of fulfilling its function under Article 13, paragraph 1(a), the HNS Fund shall pay compensation to any person suffering damage if such person has been unable to obtain full and adequate compensation for the damage under the terms of Chapter II:
   (a) because no liability for the damage arises under Chapter II;
   (b) because the owner liable for the damage under Chapter II is financially incapable of meeting the obligations under this Convention in full and any financial security that may be provided under Chapter II does not cover or is insufficient to satisfy the

434

APPENDIX 12

claims for compensation for damage; an owner being treated as financially incapable of meeting these obligations and a financial security being treated as insufficient if the person suffering the damage has been unable to obtain full satisfaction of the amount of compensation due under Chapter II after having taken all reasonable steps to pursue the available legal remedies;

(c) because the damage exceeds the owner's liability under the terms of Chapter II.

2. Expenses reasonably incurred or sacrifices reasonably made by the owner voluntarily to prevent or minimize damage shall be treated as damage for the purposes of this Article.

3. The HNS Fund shall incur no obligation under the preceding paragraphs if:

(a) it proves that the damage resulted from an act of war, hostilities, civil war or insurrection or was caused by hazardous and noxious substances which had escaped or been discharged from a warship or other ship owned or operated by a State and used, at the time of the incident, only on Government non-commercial service; or

(b) the claimant cannot prove that there is a reasonable probability that the damage resulted from an incident involving one or more ships.

4. If the HNS Fund proves that the damage resulted wholly or partly either from an act or omission done with intent to cause damage by the person who suffered the damage or from the negligence of that person, the HNS Fund may be exonerated wholly or partially from its obligation to pay compensation to such person. The HNS Fund shall in any event be exonerated to the extent that the owner may have been exonerated under Article 7, paragraph 3. However, there shall be no such exoneration of the HNS Fund with regard to preventive measures.

5. (a) Except as otherwise provided in subparagraph (b), the aggregate amount of compensation payable by the HNS Fund under this Article shall in respect of any one incident be limited, so that the total sum of that amount and any amount of compensation actually paid under Chapter II for damage within the scope of application of this Convention as defined in Article 3 shall not exceed 250 million units of account.

(b) The aggregate amount of compensation payable by the HNS Fund under this Article for damage resulting from a natural phenomenon of an exceptional, inevitable and irresistible character shall not exceed 250 million units of account.

(c) Interest accrued on a fund constituted in accordance with Article 9, paragraph 3, if any, shall not be taken into account for the computation of the maximum compensation payable by the HNS Fund under this Article.

(d) The amounts mentioned in this Article shall be converted into national currency on the basis of the value of that currency with reference to the Special Drawing Right on the date of the decision of the Assembly of the HNS Fund as to the first date of payment of compensation.

6. Where the amount of established claims against the HNS Fund exceeds the aggregate amount of compensation payable under paragraph 5, the amount available shall be distributed in such a manner that the proportion between any established claim and the amount of compensation actually recovered by the claimant under this Convention shall be the same for all claimants. Claims in respect of death or personal injury shall have priority over other claims, however, save to the extent that the aggregate of such claims exceeds two-thirds of the total amount established in accordance with paragraph 5.

7. The Assembly of the HNS Fund may decide that, in exceptional cases, compensation in accordance with this Convention can be paid even if the owner has not constituted a fund in accordance with Chapter II. In such cases paragraph 5(d) applies accordingly.

435

APPENDIX 12

Related tasks of the HNS Fund

Article 15

For the purpose of fulfilling its function under Article 13, paragraph 1(a), the HNS Fund shall have the following tasks:
  (a) to consider claims made against the HNS Fund;
  (b) to prepare an estimate in the form of a budget for each calendar year of:
      Expenditure:
          (i)   costs and expenses of the administration of the HNS Fund in the relevant year and any deficit from operations in the preceding years; and
          (ii) payments to be made by the HNS Fund in the relevant year;
      Income:
          (iii) surplus funds from operations in preceding years, including any interest;
          (iv) initial contributions to be paid in the course of the year;
          (v)   annual contributions if required to balance the budget; and
          (vi) any other income;
  (c) to use at the request of a State Party its good offices as necessary to assist that State to secure promptly such personnel, material and services as are necessary to enable the State to take measures to prevent or mitigate damage arising from an incident in respect of which the HNS Fund may be called upon to pay compensation under this Convention; and
  (d) to provide, on conditions laid down in the internal regulations, credit facilities with a view to the taking of preventive measures against damage arising from a particular incident in respect of which the HNS Fund may be called upon to pay compensation under this Convention.

General provisions on contributions

Article 16

  1. The HNS Fund shall have a general account, which shall be divided into sectors.
  2. The HNS Fund shall, subject to Article 19, paragraphs 3 and 4, also have separate accounts in respect of:
      (a) oil as defined in Article 1, paragraph 5(a)(i) (oil account);
      (b) liquefied natural gases of light hydrocarbons with methane as the main constituent (LNG) (LNG account); and
      (c) liquefied petroleum gases of light hydrocarbons with propane and butane as the main constituents (LPG) (LPG account).
  3. There shall be initial contributions and, as required, annual contributions to the HNS Fund.
  4. Contributions to the HNS Fund shall be made into the general account in accordance with Article 18, to separate accounts in accordance with Article 19 and to either the general account or separate accounts in accordance with Article 20 or Article 21, paragraph 5. Subject to Article 19, paragraph 6, the general account shall be available to compensate damage caused by hazardous and noxious substances covered by that account, and a separate account shall be available to compensate damage caused by a hazardous and noxious substance covered by that account.
  5. For the purposes of Article 18, Article 19, paragraph 1(a)(i), paragraph 1(a)(ii) and paragraph 1(c), Article 20 and Article 21, paragraph 5, where the quantity of a given type of contributing cargo received in the territory of a State Party by any person in a calendar

APPENDIX 12

year when aggregated with the quantities of the same type of cargo received in the same State Party in that year by any associated person or persons exceeds the limit specified in the respective subparagraphs, such a person shall pay contributions in respect of the actual quantity received by that person notwithstanding that that quantity did not exceed the respective limit.

6. 'Associated person' means any subsidiary or commonly controlled entity. The question whether a person comes within this definition shall be determined by the national law of the State concerned.

General provisions on annual contributions

Article 17

1. Annual contributions to the general account and to each separate account shall be levied only as required to make payments by the account in question.

2. Annual contributions payable pursuant to Articles 18, 19 and Article 21, paragraph 5 shall be determined by the Assembly and shall be calculated in accordance with those Articles on the basis of the units of contributing cargo received or, in respect of cargoes referred to in Article 19, paragraph 1(b), discharged during the preceding calendar year or such other year as the Assembly may decide.

3. The Assembly shall decide the total amount of annual contributions to be levied to the general account and to each separate account. Following that decision the Director shall, in respect of each State Party, calculate for each person liable to pay contributions in accordance with Article 18, Article 19, paragraph 1 and Article 21, paragraph 5, the amount of that person's annual contribution to each account, on the basis of a fixed sum for each unit of contributing cargo reported in respect of the person during the preceding calendar year or such other year as the Assembly may decide. For the general account, the abovementioned fixed sum per unit of contributing cargo for each sector shall be calculated pursuant to the regulations contained in Annex II to this Convention. For each separate account, the fixed sum per unit of contributing cargo referred to above shall be calculated by dividing the total annual contribution to be levied to that account by the total quantity of cargo contributing to that account.

4. The Assembly may also levy annual contributions for administrative costs and decide on the distribution of such costs between the sectors of the general account and the separate accounts.

5. The Assembly shall also decide on the distribution between the relevant accounts and sectors of amounts paid in compensation for damage caused by two or more substances which fall within different accounts or sectors, on the basis of an estimate of the extent to which each of the substances involved contributed to the damage.

Annual contributions to the general account

Article 18

1. Subject to Article 16, paragraph 5, annual contributions to the general account shall be made in respect of each State Party by any person who was the receiver in that State in the preceding calendar year, or such other year as the Assembly may decide, of aggregate quantities exceeding 20,000 tonnes of contributing cargo, other than substances referred to in Article 19, paragraph 1, which fall within the following sectors:
(a)   solid bulk materials referred to in Article 1, paragraph 5(a)(vii);

437

APPENDIX 12

(b) substances referred to in paragraph 2; and
(c) other substances.

2. Annual contributions shall also be payable to the general account by persons who would have been liable to pay contributions to a separate account in accordance with Article 19, paragraph 1 had its operation not been postponed or suspended in accordance with Article 19. Each separate account the operation of which has been postponed or suspended under Article 19 shall form a separate sector within the general account.

Annual contributions to separate accounts

Article 19

1. Subject to Article 16, paragraph 5, annual contributions to separate accounts shall be made in respect of each State Party:
  (a) in the case of the oil account,
    (i) by any person who has received in that State in the preceding calendar year, or such other year as the Assembly may decide, total quantities exceeding 150,000 tonnes of contributing oil as defined in Article 1, paragraph 3 of the International Convention on the Establishment of an International Fund for Compensation for Oil Pollution Damage, 1971, as amended, and who is or would be liable to pay contributions to the International Oil Pollution Compensation Fund in accordance with Article 10 of that Convention; and
    (ii) by any person who was the receiver in that State in the preceding calendar year, or such other year as the Assembly may decide, of total quantities exceeding 20,000 tonnes of other oils carried in bulk listed in appendix I of Annex I to the International Convention for the Prevention of Pollution from Ships, 1973, as modified by the Protocol of 1978 relating thereto, as amended;
  (b) in the case of the LNG account, by any person who in the preceding calendar year, or such other year as the Assembly may decide, immediately prior to its discharge, held title to an LNG cargo discharged in a port or terminal of that State;
  (c) in the case of the LPG account, by any person who in the preceding calendar year, or such other year as the Assembly may decide, was the receiver in that State of total quantities exceeding 20,000 tonnes of LPG.

2. Subject to paragraph 3, the separate accounts referred to in paragraph 1 above shall become effective at the same time as the general account.

3. The initial operation of a separate account referred to in Article 16, paragraph 2 shall be postponed until such time as the quantities of contributing cargo in respect of that account during the preceding calendar year, or such other year as the Assembly may decide, exceed the following levels:
  (a) 350 million tonnes of contributing cargo in respect of the oil account;
  (b) 20 million tonnes of contributing cargo in respect of the LNG account; and
  (c) 15 million tonnes of contributing cargo in respect of the LPG account.

4. The Assembly may suspend the operation of a separate account if:
  (a) the quantities of contributing cargo in respect of that account during the preceding calendar year fall below the respective level specified in paragraph 3; or
  (b) when six months have elapsed from the date when the contributions were due, the total unpaid contributions to that account exceed ten per cent of the most recent levy to that account in accordance with paragraph 1.

APPENDIX 12

5. The Assembly may reinstate the operation of a separate account which has been suspended in accordance with paragraph 4.

6. Any person who would be liable to pay contributions to a separate account the operation of which has been postponed in accordance with paragraph 3 or suspended in accordance with paragraph 4, shall pay into the general account the contributions due by that person in respect of that separate account. For the purpose of calculating future contributions, the postponed or suspended separate account shall form a new sector in the general account and shall be subject to the HNS points system defined in Annex II.

Initial contributions

Article 20

1. In respect of each State Party, initial contributions shall be made of an amount which shall for each person liable to pay contributions in accordance with Article 16, paragraph 5, Articles 18, 19 and Article 21, paragraph 5 be calculated on the basis of a fixed sum, equal for the general account and each separate account, for each unit of contributing cargo received or, in the case of LNG, discharged in that State, during the calendar year preceding that in which this Convention enters into force for that State.

2. The fixed sum and the units for the different sectors within the general account as well as for each separate account referred to in paragraph 1 shall be determined by the Assembly.

3. Initial contributions shall be paid within three months following the date on which the HNS Fund issues invoices in respect of each State Party to persons liable to pay contributions in accordance with paragraph 1.

Reports

Article 21

1. Each State Party shall ensure that any person liable to pay contributions in accordance with Articles 18, 19 or paragraph 5 of this Article appears on a list to be established and kept up to date by the Director in accordance with the provisions of this Article.

2. For the purposes set out in paragraph 1, each State Party shall communicate to the Director, at a time and in the manner to be prescribed in the internal regulations of the HNS Fund, the name and address of any person who in respect of the State is liable to pay contributions in accordance with Articles 18, 19 or paragraph 5 of this Article, as well as data on the relevant quantities of contributing cargo for which such a person is liable to contribute in respect of the preceding calendar year.

3. For the purposes of ascertaining who are, at any given time, the persons liable to pay contributions in accordance with Articles 18, 19 or paragraph 5 of this Article and of establishing, where applicable, the quantities of cargo to be taken into account for any such person when determining the amount of the contribution, the list shall be *prima facie* evidence of the facts stated therein.

4. Where a State Party does not fulfil its obligations to communicate to the Director the information referred to in paragraph 2 and this results in a financial loss for the HNS Fund, that State Party shall be liable to compensate the HNS Fund for such loss. The Assembly shall, on the recommendation of the Director, decide whether such compensation shall be payable by a State Party.

5. In respect of contributing cargo carried from one port or terminal of a State Party to another port or terminal located in the same State and discharged there, States Parties shall

439

APPENDIX 12

have the option of submitting to the HNS Fund a report with an annual aggregate quantity for each account covering all receipts of contributing cargo, including any quantities in respect of which contributions are payable pursuant to Article 16, paragraph 5. The State Party shall, at the time of reporting, either:

(a) notify the HNS Fund that that State will pay the aggregate amount for each account in respect of the relevant year in one lump sum to the HNS Fund; or

(b) instruct the HNS Fund to levy the aggregate amount for each account by invoicing individual receivers or, in the case of LNG, the title holder who discharges within the jurisdiction of that State Party, for the amount payable by each of them. These persons shall be identified in accordance with the national law of the State concerned.

Non-payment of contributions

Article 22

1. The amount of any contribution due under Articles 18, 19, 20 or Article 21, paragraph 5 and which is in arrears shall bear interest at a rate which shall be determined in accordance with the internal regulations of the HNS Fund, provided that different rates may be fixed for different circumstances.

2. Where a person who is liable to pay contributions in accordance with Articles 18, 19, 20 or Article 21, paragraph 5 does not fulfil the obligations in respect of any such contribution or any part thereof and is in arrears, the Director shall take all appropriate action, including court action, against such a person on behalf of the HNS Fund with a view to the recovery of the amount due. However, where the defaulting contributor is manifestly insolvent or the circumstances otherwise so warrant, the Assembly may, upon recommendation of the Director, decide that no action shall be taken or continued against the contributor.

Optional liability of states parties for the payment of contributions

Article 23

1. Without prejudice to Article 21, paragraph 5, a State Party may at the time when it deposits its instrument of ratification, acceptance, approval or accession or at any time thereafter declare that it assumes responsibility for obligations imposed by this Convention on any person liable to pay contributions in accordance with Articles 18, 19, 20 or Article 21, paragraph 5 in respect of hazardous and noxious substances received or discharged in the territory of that State. Such a declaration shall be made in writing and shall specify which obligations are assumed.

2. Where a declaration under paragraph 1 is made prior to the entry into force of this Convention in accordance with Article 46, it shall be deposited with the Secretary-General who shall after the entry into force of this Convention communicate the declaration to the Director.

3. A declaration under paragraph 1 which is made after the entry into force of this Convention shall be deposited with the Director.

4. A declaration made in accordance with this Article may be withdrawn by the relevant State giving notice thereof in writing to the Director. Such a notification shall take effect three months after the Director's receipt thereof.

5. Any State which is bound by a declaration made under this Article shall, in any proceedings brought against it before a competent court in respect of any obligation specified in the declaration, waive any immunity that it would otherwise be entitled to invoke.

APPENDIX 12

Organization and administration

Article 24

The HNS Fund shall have an Assembly and a Secretariat headed by the Director.

Assembly

Article 25

The Assembly shall consist of all States Parties to this Convention.

Article 26

The functions of the Assembly shall be:
- (a) to elect at each regular session its President and two Vice-Presidents who shall hold office until the next regular session;
- (b) to determine its own rules of procedure, subject to the provisions of this Convention;
- (c) to develop, apply and keep under review internal and financial regulations relating to the aim of the HNS Fund as described in Article 13, paragraph 1(a), and the related tasks of the HNS Fund listed in Article 15;
- (d) to appoint the Director and make provisions for the appointment of such other personnel as may be necessary and determine the terms and conditions of service of the Director and other personnel;
- (e) to adopt the annual budget prepared in accordance with Article 15(b);
- (f) to consider and approve as necessary any recommendation of the Director regarding the scope of definition of contributing cargo;
- (g) to appoint auditors and approve the accounts of the HNS Fund;
- (h) to approve settlements of claims against the HNS Fund, to take decisions in respect of the distribution among claimants of the available amount of compensation in accordance with Article 14 and to determine the terms and conditions according to which provisional payments in respect of claims shall be made with a view to ensuring that victims of damage are compensated as promptly as possible;
- (i) to establish a Committee on Claims for Compensation with at least 7 and not more than 15 members and any temporary or permanent subsidiary body it may consider to be necessary, to define its terms of reference and to give it the authority needed to perform the functions entrusted to it; when appointing the members of such body, the Assembly shall endeavour to secure an equitable geographical distribution of members and to ensure that the States Parties are appropriately represented; the Rules of Procedure of the Assembly may be applied, *mutatis mutandis*, for the work of such subsidiary body;
- (j) to determine which States not party to this Convention, which Associate Members of the Organization and which intergovernmental and international non-governmental organizations shall be admitted to take part, without voting rights, in meetings of the Assembly and subsidiary bodies;
- (k) to give instructions concerning the administration of the HNS Fund to the Director and subsidiary bodies;
- (l) to supervise the proper execution of this Convention and of its own decisions;
- (m) to review every five years the implementation of this Convention with particular

441

APPENDIX 12

reference to the performance of the system for the calculation of levies and the contribution mechanism for domestic trade; and

(n) to perform such other functions as are allocated to it under this Convention or are otherwise necessary for the proper operation of the HNS Fund.

Article 27

1. Regular sessions of the Assembly shall take place once every calendar year upon convocation by the Director.

2. Extraordinary sessions of the Assembly shall be convened by the Director at the request of at least one-third of the members of the Assembly and may be convened on the Director's own initiative after consultation with the President of the Assembly. The Director shall give members at least thirty days' notice of such sessions.

Article 28

A majority of the members of the Assembly shall constitute a quorum for its meetings.

Secretariat

Article 29

1. The Secretariat shall comprise the Director and such staff as the administration of the HNS Fund may require.

2. The Director shall be the legal representative of the HNS Fund.

Article 30

1. The Director shall be the chief administrative officer of the HNS Fund. Subject to the instructions given by the Assembly, the Director shall perform those functions which are assigned to the Director by this Convention, the internal regulations of the HNS Fund and the Assembly.

2. The Director shall in particular:

(a) appoint the personnel required for the administration of the HNS Fund;

(b) take all appropriate measures with a view to the proper administration of the assets of the HNS Fund;

(c) collect the contributions due under this Convention while observing in particular the provisions of Article 22, paragraph 2;

(d) to the extent necessary to deal with claims against the HNS Fund and to carry out the other functions of the HNS Fund, employ the services of legal, financial and other experts;

(e) take all appropriate measures for dealing with claims against the HNS Fund, within the limits and on conditions to be laid down in the internal regulations of the HNS Fund, including the final settlement of claims without the prior approval of the Assembly where these regulations so provide;

(f) prepare and submit to the Assembly the financial statements and budget estimates for each calendar year;

(g) prepare, in consultation with the President of the Assembly, and publish a report on the activities of the HNS Fund during the previous calendar year; and

APPENDIX 12

(h) prepare, collect and circulate the documents and information which may be required for the work of the Assembly and subsidiary bodies.

Article 31

In the performance of their duties the Director and the staff and experts appointed by the Director shall not seek or receive instructions from any Government or from any authority external to the HNS Fund. They shall refrain from any action which might adversely reflect on their position as international officials. Each State Party on its part undertakes to respect the exclusively international character of the responsibilities of the Director and the staff and experts appointed by the Director, and not to seek to influence them in the discharge of their duties.

Finances

Article 32

1. Each State Party shall bear the salary, travel and other expenses of its own delegation to the Assembly and of its representatives on subsidiary bodies.

2. Any other expenses incurred in the operation of the HNS Fund shall be borne by the HNS Fund.

Voting

Article 33

The following provisions shall apply to voting in the Assembly:
(a) each member shall have one vote;
(b) except as otherwise provided in Article 34, decisions of the Assembly shall be made by a majority vote of the members present and voting;
(c) decisions where a two-thirds majority is required shall be a two-thirds majority vote of members present; and
(d) for the purpose of this Article the phrase 'members present' means 'members present at the meeting at the time of the vote', and the phrase 'members present and voting' means 'members present and casting an affirmative or negative vote'. Members who abstain from voting shall be considered as not voting.

Article 34

The following decisions of the Assembly shall require a two-thirds majority:
(a) a decision under Article 19, paragraphs 4 or 5 to suspend or reinstate the operation of a separate account;
(b) a decision under Article 22, paragraph 2, not to take or continue action against a contributor;
(c) the appointment of the Director under Article 26(d);
(d) the establishment of subsidiary bodies, under Article 26(i), and matters relating to such establishment; and
(e) a decision under Article 51, paragraph 1, that this Convention shall continue to be in force.

APPENDIX 12

Tax exemptions and currency regulations

Article 35

1. The HNS Fund, its assets, income, including contributions, and other property necessary for the exercise of its functions as described in Article 13, paragraph 1, shall enjoy in all States Parties exemption from all direct taxation.

2. When the HNS Fund makes substantial purchases of movable or immovable property, or of services which are necessary for the exercise of its official activities in order to achieve its aims as set out in Article 13, paragraph 1, the cost of which include indirect taxes or sales taxes, the Governments of the States Parties shall take, whenever possible, appropriate measures for the remission or refund of the amount of such duties and taxes. Goods thus acquired shall not be sold against payment or given away free of charge unless it is done according to conditions approved by the Government of the State having granted or supported the remission or refund.

3. No exemption shall be accorded in the case of duties, taxes or dues which merely constitute payment for public utility services.

4. The HNS Fund shall enjoy exemption from all customs duties, taxes and other related taxes on articles imported or exported by it or on its behalf for its official use. Articles thus imported shall not be transferred either for consideration or gratis on the territory of the country into which they have been imported except on conditions agreed by the Government of that country.

5. Persons contributing to the HNS Fund as well as victims and owners receiving compensation from the HNS Fund shall be subject to the fiscal legislation of the State where they are taxable, no special exemption or other benefit being conferred on them in this respect.

6. Notwithstanding existing or future regulations concerning currency or transfers, States Parties shall authorize the transfer and payment of any contribution to the HNS Fund and of any compensation paid by HNS Fund without any restriction.

Confidentiality of information

Article 36

Information relating to individual contributors supplied for the purpose of this Convention shall not be divulged outside the HNS Fund except in so far as it may be strictly necessary to enable the HNS Fund to carry out its functions including the bringing and defending of legal proceedings.

Chapter IV

Claims and actions

Limitation of actions

Article 37

1. Rights to compensation under Chapter II shall be extinguished unless an action is brought thereunder within three years from the date when the person suffering the damage knew or ought reasonably to have known of the damage and of the identity of the owner.

2. Rights to compensation under Chapter III shall be extinguished unless an action is

APPENDIX 12

brought thereunder or a notification has been made pursuant to Article 39, paragraph 7, within three years from the date when the person suffering the damage knew or ought reasonably to have known of the damage.

3. In no case, however, shall an action be brought later than ten years from the date of the incident which caused the damage.

4. Where the incident consists of a series of occurrences, the ten-year period mentioned in paragraph 3 shall run from the date of the last of such occurrences.

Jurisdiction in respect of action against the owner

Article 38

1. Where an incident has caused damage in the territory, including the territorial sea or in an area referred to in Article 3(b), of one or more States Parties, or preventive measures have been taken to prevent or minimize damage in such territory including the territorial sea or in such area, actions for compensation may be brought against the owner or other person providing financial security for the owner's liability only in the courts of any such States Parties.

2. Where an incident has caused damage exclusively outside the territory, including the territorial sea, of any State and either the conditions for application of this Convention set out in Article 3(c) have been fulfilled or preventive measures to prevent or minimize such damage have been taken, actions for compensation may be brought against the owner or other person providing financial security for the owner's liability only in the courts of:

(a)   the State Party where the ship is registered or, in the case of an unregistered ship, the State Party whose flag the ship is entitled to fly; or

(b)   the State Party where the owner has habitual residence or where the principal place of business of the owner is established; or

(c)   the State Party where a fund has been constituted in accordance with Article 9, paragraph 3.

3. Reasonable notice of any action taken under paragraph 1 or 2 shall be given to the defendant.

4. Each State Party shall ensure that its courts have jurisdiction to entertain actions for compensation under this Convention.

5. After a fund under Article 9 has been constituted by the owner or by the insurer or other person providing financial security in accordance with Article 12, the courts of the State in which such fund is constituted shall have exclusive jurisdiction to determine all matters relating to the apportionment and distribution of the fund.

Jurisdiction in respect of action against the HNS Fund or taken by the HNS Fund

Article 39

1. Subject to the subsequent provisions of this Article, any action against the HNS Fund for compensation under Article 14 shall be brought only before a court having jurisdiction under Article 38 in respect of actions against the owner who is liable for damage caused by the relevant incident or before a court in a State Party which would have been competent if an owner had been liable.

2. In the event that the ship carrying the hazardous or noxious substances which caused the damage has not been identified, the provisions of Article 38, paragraph 1, shall apply *mutatis mutandis* to actions against the HNS Fund.

445

APPENDIX 12

3. Each State Party shall ensure that its courts have jurisdiction to entertain such actions against the HNS Fund as are referred to in paragraph 1.

4. Where an action for compensation for damage has been brought before a court against the owner or the owner's guarantor, such court shall have exclusive jurisdiction over any action against the HNS Fund for compensation under the provisions of Article 14 in respect of the same damage.

5. Each State Party shall ensure that the HNS Fund shall have the right to intervene as a party to any legal proceedings instituted in accordance with this Convention before a competent court of that State against the owner or the owner's guarantor.

6. Except as otherwise provided in paragraph 7, the HNS Fund shall not be bound by any judgement or decision in proceedings to which it has not been a party or by any settlement to which it is not a party.

7. Without prejudice to the provisions of paragraph 5, where an action under this Convention for compensation for damage has been brought against an owner or the owner's guarantor before a competent court in a State Party, each party to the proceedings shall be entitled under the national law of that State to notify the HNS Fund of the proceedings. Where such notification has been made in accordance with the formalities required by the law of the court seized and in such time and in such a manner that the HNS Fund has in fact been in a position effectively to intervene as a party to the proceedings, any judgement rendered by the court in such proceedings shall, after it has become final and enforceable in the State where the judgement was given, become binding upon the HNS Fund in the sense that the facts and findings in that judgement may not be disputed by the HNS Fund even if the HNS Fund has not actually intervened in the proceedings.

Recognition and enforcement

Article 40

1. Any judgement given by a court with jurisdiction in accordance with Article 38, which is enforceable in the State of origin where it is no longer subject to ordinary forms of review, shall be recognized in any State Party, except:
   (a)   where the judgement was obtained by fraud; or
   (b)   where the defendant was not given reasonable notice and a fair opportunity to present the case.

2. A judgement recognized under paragraph 1 shall be enforceable in each State Party as soon as the formalities required in that State have been complied with. The formalities shall not permit the merits of the case to be re-opened.

3. Subject to any decision concerning the distribution referred to in Article 14, paragraph 6, any judgement given against the HNS Fund by a court having jurisdiction in accordance with Article 39, paragraphs 1 and 3 shall, when it has become enforceable in the State of origin and is in that State no longer subject to ordinary forms of review, be recognized and enforceable in each State Party.

APPENDIX 12

Subrogation and recourse

Article 41

1. The HNS Fund shall, in respect of any amount of compensation for damage paid by the HNS Fund in accordance with Article 14, paragraph 1, acquire by subrogation the rights that the person so compensated may enjoy against the owner or the owner's guarantor.

2. Nothing in this Convention shall prejudice any rights of recourse or subrogation of the HNS Fund against any person, including persons referred to in Article 7, paragraph 2(d), other than those referred to in the previous paragraph, in so far as they can limit their liability. In any event the right of the HNS Fund to subrogation against such persons shall not be less favourable than that of an insurer of the person to whom compensation has been paid.

3. Without prejudice to any other rights of subrogation or recourse against the HNS Fund which may exist, a State Party or agency thereof which has paid compensation for damage in accordance with provisions of national law shall acquire by subrogation the rights which the person so compensated would have enjoyed under this Convention.

Supersession clause

Article 42

This Convention shall supersede any convention in force or open for signature, ratification or accession at the date on which this Convention is opened for signature, but only to the extent that such convention would be in conflict with it; however, nothing in this Article shall affect the obligations of States Parties to States not party to this Convention arising under such convention.

Chapter V

Transitional provisions

Information on contributing cargo

Article 43

When depositing an instrument referred to in Article 45, paragraph 3, and annually thereafter until this Convention enters into force for a State, that State shall submit to the Secretary-General data on the relevant quantities of contributing cargo received or, in the case of LNG, discharged in that State during the preceding calendar year in respect of the general account and each separate account.

First session of the Assembly

Article 44

The Secretary-General shall convene the first session of the Assembly. This session shall take place as soon as possible after the entry into force of this Convention and, in any case, not more than thirty days after such entry into force.

447

APPENDIX 12

Chapter VI

Final clauses

Signature, ratification, acceptance, approval and accession

Article 45

1. This Convention shall be open for signature at the Headquarters of the Organization from 1 October 1996 to 30 September 1997 and shall thereafter remain open for accession.
2. States may express their consent to be bound by this Convention by:
   (a) signature without reservation as to ratification, acceptance or approval; or
   (b) signature subject to ratification, acceptance or approval, followed by ratification, acceptance or approval; or
   (c) accession.
3. Ratification, acceptance, approval or accession shall be effected by the deposit of an instrument to that effect with the Secretary-General.

Entry into force

Article 46

1. This Convention shall enter into force eighteen months after the date on which the following conditions are fulfilled:
   (a) at least twelve States, including four States each with not less than 2 million units of gross tonnage, have expressed their consent to be bound by it, and
   (b) the Secretary-General has received information in accordance with Article 43 that those persons in such States who would be liable to contribute pursuant to Article 18, paragraphs 1(a) and (c) have received during the preceding calendar year a total quantity of at least 40 million tonnes of cargo contributing to the general account.
2. For a State which expresses its consent to be bound by this Convention after the conditions for entry into force have been met, such consent shall take effect three months after the date of expression of such consent, or on the date on which this Convention enters into force in accordance with paragraph 1, whichever is the later.

Revision and amendment

Article 47

1. A conference for the purpose of revising or amending this Convention may be convened by the Organization.
2. The Secretary-General shall convene a conference of the States Parties to this Convention for revising or amending the Convention, at the request of six States Parties or one-third of the States Parties whichever is the higher figure.
3. Any consent to be bound by this Convention expressed after the date of entry into force of an amendment to this Convention shall be deemed to apply to the Convention as amended.

APPENDIX 12

Amendment of limits

Article 48

1. Without prejudice to the provisions of Article 47, the special procedure in this Article shall apply solely for the purposes of amending the limits set out in Article 9, paragraph 1 and Article 14, paragraph 5.

2. Upon the request of at least one half, but in no case less than six, of the States Parties, any proposal to amend the limits specified in Article 9, paragraph 1, and Article 14, paragraph 5, shall be circulated by the Secretary-General to all Members of the Organization and to all Contracting States.

3. Any amendment proposed and circulated as above shall be submitted to the Legal Committee of the Organization (the Legal Committee) for consideration at a date at least six months after the date of its circulation.

4. All Contracting States, whether or not Members of the Organization, shall be entitled to participate in the proceedings of the Legal Committee for the consideration and adoption of amendments.

5. Amendments shall be adopted by a two-thirds majority of the Contracting States present and voting in the Legal Committee, expanded as provided in paragraph 4, on condition that at least one half of the Contracting States shall be present at the time of voting.

6. When acting on a proposal to amend the limits, the Legal Committee shall take into account the experience of incidents and, in particular, the amount of damage resulting therefrom, changes in the monetary values and the effect of the proposed amendment on the cost of insurance. It shall also take into account the relationship between the limits established in Article 9, paragraph 1, and those in Article 14, paragraph 5.

7. (a) No amendment of the limits under this Article may be considered less than five years from the date this Convention was opened for signature nor less than five years from the date of entry into force of a previous amendment under this Article.

   (b) No limit may be increased so as to exceed an amount which corresponds to a limit laid down in this Convention increased by six per cent per year calculated on a compound basis from the date on which this Convention was opened for signature.

   (c) No limit may be increased so as to exceed an amount which corresponds to a limit laid down in this Convention multiplied by three.

8. Any amendment adopted in accordance with paragraph 5 shall be notified by the Organization to all Contracting States. The amendment shall be deemed to have been accepted at the end of a period of eighteen months after the date of notification, unless within that period no less than one-fourth of the States which were Contracting States at the time of the adoption of the amendment have communicated to the Secretary-General that they do not accept the amendment, in which case the amendment is rejected and shall have no effect.

9. An amendment deemed to have been accepted in accordance with paragraph 8 shall enter into force eighteen months after its acceptance.

10. All Contracting States shall be bound by the amendment, unless they denounce this Convention in accordance with Article 49, paragraphs 1 and 2, at least six months before the amendment enters into force. Such denunciation shall take effect when the amendment enters into force.

11. When an amendment has been adopted but the eighteen month period for its acceptance has not yet expired, a State which becomes a Contracting State during that period shall be bound by the amendment if it enters into force. A State which becomes a Contracting State after that period shall be bound by an amendment which has been accepted in accordance with paragraph 8. In the cases referred to in this paragraph, a State becomes bound by

APPENDIX 12

an amendment when that amendment enters into force, or when this Convention enters into force for that State, if later.

Denunciation

Article 49

1. This Convention may be denounced by any State Party at any time after the date on which it enters into force for that State Party.

2. Denunciation shall be effected by the deposit of an instrument of denunciation with the Secretary-General.

3. Denunciation shall take effect twelve months, or such longer period as may be specified in the instrument of denunciation, after its deposit with the Secretary-General.

4. Notwithstanding a denunciation by a State Party pursuant to this Article, any provisions of this Convention relating to obligations to make contributions under Articles 18, 19 or Article 21, paragraph 5 in respect of such payments of compensation as the Assembly may decide relating to an incident which occurs before the denunciation takes effect shall continue to apply.

Extraordinary sessions of the Assembly

Article 50

1. Any State Party may, within ninety days after the deposit of an instrument of denunciation the result of which it considers will significantly increase the level of contributions from the remaining States Parties, request the Director to convene an extraordinary session of the Assembly. The Director shall convene the Assembly to meet not less than sixty days after receipt of the request.

2. The Director may take the initiative to convene an extraordinary session of the Assembly to meet within sixty days after the deposit of any instrument of denunciation, if the Director considers that such denunciation will result in a significant increase in the level of contributions from the remaining States Parties.

3. If the Assembly, at an extraordinary session, convened in accordance with paragraph 1 or 2 decides that the denunciation will result in a significant increase in the level of contributions from the remaining States Parties, any such State may, not later than one hundred and twenty days before the date on which the denunciation takes effect, denounce this Convention with effect from the same date.

Cessation

Article 51

1. This Convention shall cease to be in force:
    (a) on the date when the number of States Parties falls below 6; or
    (b) twelve months after the date on which data concerning a previous calendar year were to be communicated to the Director in accordance with Article 21, if the data shows that the total quantity of contributing cargo to the general account in accordance with Article 18, paragraphs 1(a) and (c) received in the States Parties in that preceding calendar year was less than 30 million tonnes.

Notwithstanding (b), if the total quantity of contributing cargo to the general account in accordance with Article 18, paragraphs 1(a) and (c) received in the States Parties in the

APPENDIX 12

preceding calendar year was less than 30 million tonnes but more than 25 million tonnes, the Assembly may, if it considers that this was due to exceptional circumstances and is not likely to be repeated, decide before the expiry of the abovementioned twelve month period that the Convention shall continue to be in force. The Assembly may not, however, take such a decision in more than two subsequent years.

2. States which are bound by this Convention on the day before the date it ceases to be in force shall enable the HNS Fund to exercise its functions as described under Article 52 and shall, for that purpose only, remain bound by this Convention.

Winding up of the HNS Fund

Article 52

1. If this Convention ceases to be in force, the HNS Fund shall nevertheless:
    (a) meet its obligations in respect of any incident occurring before this Convention ceased to be in force; and
    (b) be entitled to exercise its rights to contributions to the extent that these contributions are necessary to meet the obligations under (a), including expenses for the administration of the HNS Fund necessary for this purpose.
2. The Assembly shall take all appropriate measures to complete the winding up of the HNS Fund including the distribution in an equitable manner of any remaining assets among those persons who have contributed to the HNS Fund.
3. For the purposes of this Article the HNS Fund shall remain a legal person.

Depositary

Article 53

1. This Convention and any amendment adopted under Article 48 shall be deposited with the Secretary-General.
2. The Secretary-General shall:
    (a) inform all States which have signed this Convention or acceded thereto, and all Members of the Organization, of:
        (i)   each new signature or deposit of an instrument of ratification, acceptance, approval or accession together with the date thereof;
        (ii)   the date of entry into force of this Convention;
        (iii) any proposal to amend the limits on the amounts of compensation which has been made in accordance with Article 48, paragraph 2;
        (iv) any amendment which has been adopted in accordance with Article 48, paragraph 5;
        (v)   any amendment deemed to have been accepted under Article 48, paragraph 8, together with the date on which that amendment shall enter into force in accordance with paragraphs 9 and 10 of that Article;
        (vi) the deposit of any instrument of denunciation of this Convention together with the date on which it is received and the date on which the denunciation takes effect; and
        (vii) any communication called for by any Article in this Convention; and
    (b) transmit certified true copies of this Convention to all States which have signed this Convention or acceded thereto.
3. As soon as this Convention enters into force, a certified true copy thereof shall be

451

APPENDIX 12

transmitted by the depositary to the Secretary-General of the United Nations for registration and publication in accordance with Article 102 of the Charter of the United Nations.

Languages

Article 54

This Convention is established in a single original in the Arabic, Chinese, English, French, Russian and Spanish languages, each text being equally authentic.

DONE at London this third day of May one thousand nine hundred and ninety-six.

IN WITNESS WHEREOF the undersigned, being duly authorized by their respective Governments for that purpose, have signed this Convention.

★ ★ ★

APPENDIX 12

Protocol of 2010 to the International Convention on Liability and Compensation for Damage in Connection with the Carriage of Hazardous and Noxious Substances by Sea, 1996

THE STATES PARTIES TO THIS PROTOCOL,

RECOGNIZING the significant contribution that can be made by the International Convention on Liability and Compensation for Damage in Connection with the Carriage of Hazardous and Noxious Substances by Sea, 1996 (the Convention), to the prompt, adequate and effective compensation of persons who suffer damage caused by incidents in connection with the carriage of hazardous and noxious substances by sea, as well as to the preservation of the marine environment,

RECOGNIZING ALSO that, over many years, a large number of States have consistently expressed their determination to establish a robust and effective compensation regime for the maritime carriage of hazardous and noxious substances based on a system of shared liability and have worked towards a uniform implementation of the Convention,

ACKNOWLEDGING, HOWEVER, that certain issues have been identified as inhibiting the entry into force of the Convention and, consequently, the implementation of the international regime contained therein,

DETERMINED to resolve these issues without embarking on a comprehensive revision of the Convention,

AWARE OF the need to take into account the possible impact on developing countries, as well as the interests of those States which have already ratified the Convention or have almost completed the ratification process,

RECALLING the principles enshrined in IMO resolution A.998(25) 'Need for capacity-building for the development and implementation of new, and amendments to existing, instruments', adopted on 29 November 2007,

CONSIDERING that these objectives may best be achieved by the conclusion of a Protocol to the Convention,

HAVE AGREED as follows:

Article 1 – Definitions

For the purposes of this Protocol:

1 'Convention' means the International Convention on Liability and Compensation for Damage in Connection with the Carriage of Hazardous and Noxious Substances by Sea, 1996.

2 'Organization' means the International Maritime Organization.

3 'Secretary-General' means the Secretary-General of the Organization.

Article 2 – General obligations

The Parties to this Protocol shall give effect to the provisions of this Protocol and the provisions of the Convention, as amended by this Protocol.

Article 3

1 Article 1, paragraph 5 of the Convention is replaced by the following text:

5 'Hazardous and noxious substances (HNS)' means:

453

APPENDIX 12

(a) any substances, materials and articles carried on board a ship as cargo, referred to in (i) to (vii) below:

    (i) oils, carried in bulk, as defined in regulation 1 of Annex I to the International Convention for the Prevention of Pollution from Ships, 1973, as modified by the Protocol of 1978 relating thereto, as amended;

    (ii) noxious liquid substances, carried in bulk, as defined in regulation 1.10 of Annex II to the International Convention for the Prevention of Pollution from Ships, 1973, as modified by the Protocol of 1978 relating thereto, as amended, and those substances and mixtures provisionally categorized as falling in pollution category X, Y or Z in accordance with regulation 6.3 of the said Annex II;

    (iii) dangerous liquid substances carried in bulk listed in chapter 17 of the International Code for the Construction and Equipment of Ships Carrying Dangerous Chemicals in Bulk, as amended, and the dangerous products for which the preliminary suitable conditions for the carriage have been prescribed by the Administration and port administrations involved in accordance with paragraph 1.1.6 of the Code;

    (iv) dangerous, hazardous and harmful substances, materials and articles in packaged form covered by the International Maritime Dangerous Goods Code, as amended;

    (v) liquefied gases as listed in chapter 19 of the International Code for the Construction and Equipment of Ships Carrying Liquefied Gases in Bulk, as amended, and the products for which preliminary suitable conditions for the carriage have been prescribed by the Administration and port administrations involved in accordance with paragraph 1.1.6 of the Code;

    (vi) liquid substances carried in bulk with a flashpoint not exceeding 60°C (measured by a closed-cup test);

    (vii) solid bulk materials possessing chemical hazards covered by the International Maritime Solid Bulk Cargoes Code, as amended, to the extent that these substances are also subject to the provisions of the International Maritime Dangerous Goods Code in effect in 1996, when carried in packaged form; and

(b) residues from the previous carriage in bulk of substances referred to in (a)(i) to (iii) and (v) to (vii) above.

2 The following text is added as article 1, paragraphs 5*bis* and 5*ter* of the Convention:

5*bis* 'Bulk HNS' means any hazardous and noxious substances referred to in article 1, paragraph 5(a)(i) to (iii) and (v) to (vii) and paragraph 5(b).

5*ter* 'Packaged HNS' means any hazardous and noxious substances referred to in article 1, paragraph 5(a)(iv).

3 Article 1, paragraph 10 of the Convention is replaced by the following text:

10 'Contributing cargo' means any bulk HNS which is carried by sea as cargo to a port or terminal in the territory of a State Party and discharged in that State. Cargo in transit which is transferred directly, or through a port or terminal, from one ship to another, either wholly or in part, in the course of carriage from the port or terminal of original loading to the port or terminal of final destination shall be considered as contributing cargo only in respect of receipt at the final destination.

Article 4

Article 3(d) of the convention is replaced by the following text:

(d) to preventive measures, wherever taken, to prevent or minimize such damage as referred to in (a), (b) and (c) above.

454

APPENDIX 12

Article 5

Article 4, paragraph 3(b) of the Convention is replaced by the following text:

3(b) to damage caused by a radioactive material of class 7 either in the International Maritime Dangerous Goods Code, as amended, or in the International Maritime Solid Bulk Cargoes Code, as amended.

Article 6

Article 5, paragraph 5 of the Convention is deleted, and paragraph 6 becomes paragraph 5.

Article 7

Article 9, paragraph 1 of the Convention is replaced by the following text:

1 The owner of a ship shall be entitled to limit liability under this Convention in respect of any one incident to an aggregate amount calculated as follows:

(a) Where the damage has been caused by bulk HNS:

(i) 10 million units of account for a ship not exceeding 2,000 units of tonnage; and

(ii) for a ship with a tonnage in excess thereof, the following amount in addition to that mentioned in (i):

for each unit of tonnage from 2,001 to 50,000 units of tonnage, 1,500 units of account;

for each unit of tonnage in excess of 50,000 units of tonnage, 360 units of account;

provided, however, that this aggregate amount shall not in any event exceed 100 million units of account.

(b) Where the damage has been caused by packaged HNS, or where the damage has been caused by both bulk HNS and packaged HNS, or where it is not possible to determine whether the damage originating from that ship has been caused by bulk HNS or by packaged HNS:

(i) 11.5 million units of account for a ship not exceeding 2,000 units of tonnage; and

(ii) for a ship with a tonnage in excess thereof, the following amount in addition to that mentioned in (i):

for each unit of tonnage from 2,001 to 50,000 units of tonnage, 1,725 units of account;

for each unit of tonnage in excess of 50,000 units of tonnage, 414 units of account;

provided, however, that this aggregate amount shall not in any event exceed 115 million units of account.

Article 8

In article 16, paragraph 5 of the Convention, the reference to 'paragraph 1(c)' is replaced by a reference to 'paragraph 1(b)'.

Article 9

1 Article 17, paragraph 2 of the Convention is replaced by the following text:

2 Annual contributions payable pursuant to articles 18, 19 and article 21, paragraph

APPENDIX 12

5 shall be determined by the Assembly and shall be calculated in accordance with those articles on the basis of the units of contributing cargo received during the preceding calendar year or such other year as the Assembly may decide.

2 In article 17, paragraph 3 of the Convention, a reference to 'and paragraph 1*bis*,' is inserted immediately after the words 'article 19, paragraph 1'.

Article 10

In article 18, paragraphs 1 and 2 of the Convention, a reference to 'and paragraph 1*bis*,' is inserted immediately after the words 'article 19, paragraph 1' in both paragraphs.

Article 11

1 In article 19, paragraph 1(b) of the Convention is deleted and paragraph 1(c) becomes paragraph 1(b).

2 In article 19 of the Convention, after paragraph 1, a new paragraph is inserted as follows:

1*bis* (a)   In the case of the LNG account, subject to article 16, paragraph 5, annual contributions to the LNG account shall be made in respect of each State Party by any person who in the preceding calendar year, or such other year as the Assembly may decide, was the receiver in that State of any quantity of LNG.

(b)   However, any contributions shall be made by the person who, immediately prior to its discharge, held title to an LNG cargo discharged in a port or terminal of that State (the titleholder) where:

(i)   the titleholder has entered into an agreement with the receiver that the titleholder shall make such contributions; and

(ii)   the receiver has informed the State Party that such an agreement exists.

(c)   If the titleholder referred to in subparagraph (b) above does not make the contributions or any part thereof, the receiver shall make the remaining contributions. The Assembly shall determine in the internal regulations the circumstances under which the titleholder shall be considered as not having made the contributions and the arrangements in accordance with which the receiver shall make any remaining contributions.

(d)   Nothing in this paragraph shall prejudice any rights of recourse or reimbursement of the receiver that may arise between the receiver and the titleholder under the applicable law.

3 In article 19, paragraph 2 of the Convention, a reference to 'and paragraph 1*bis*' is inserted immediately after the words 'paragraph 1'.

Article 12

Article 20, paragraph 1 of the Convention is replaced by the following text:

1 In respect of each State Party, initial contributions shall be made of an amount which shall, for each person liable to pay contributions in accordance with article 16, paragraph 5, articles 18, 19 and article 21, paragraph 5, be calculated on the basis of a fixed sum, equal for the general account and each separate account, for each unit of contributing cargo received in that State during the calendar year preceding that in which this Convention enters into force for that State.

APPENDIX 12

Article 13

1 Article 21, paragraph 4 of the Convention is replaced by the following text:
4 If in a State Party there is no person liable to pay contributions in accordance with articles 18, 19 or paragraph 5 of this article, that State Party shall, for the purposes of this Convention, inform the Director of the HNS Fund thereof.
2 Article 21, paragraph 5(b) of the Convention is replaced by the following text:

5(b)   instruct the HNS Fund to levy the aggregate amount for each account by invoicing individual receivers or, in the case of LNG, the titleholder if article 19, paragraph 1*bis*(b) is applicable, for the amount payable by each of them. If the titleholder does not make the contributions or any part thereof, the HNS Fund shall levy the remaining contributions by invoicing the receiver of the LNG cargo. These persons shall be identified in accordance with the national law of the State concerned.

Article 14

The following text is added as article 21*bis* of the Convention:

Article 21bis – Non-reporting

1 Where a State Party does not fulfil its obligations under article 21, paragraph 2, and this results in a financial loss for the HNS Fund, that State Party shall be liable to compensate the HNS Fund for such loss. The Assembly shall, upon recommendation of the Director, decide whether such compensation shall be payable by a State.
2 No compensation for any incident shall be paid by the HNS Fund for damage in the territory, including the territorial sea, of a State Party in accordance with article 3(a), the exclusive economic zone or other area of a State Party in accordance with article 3(b), or damage in accordance with article 3(c) in respect of a given incident or for preventive measures, wherever taken, in accordance with article 3(d), until the obligations under article 21, paragraphs 2 and 4 have been complied with in respect of that State Party for all years prior to the occurrence of an incident for which compensation is sought. The Assembly shall determine in the internal regulations of the HNS Fund the circumstances under which a State Party shall be considered as not having fulfilled these obligations.
3 Where compensation has been denied temporarily in accordance with paragraph 2, compensation shall be denied permanently if the obligations under article 21, paragraphs 2 and 4 have not been fulfilled within one year after the Director has notified the State Party of its failure to fulfil these obligations.
4 Any payments of contributions due to the HNS Fund shall be set off against compensation due to the debtor or the debtor's agents.
5 Paragraphs 2 to 4 shall not apply to claims in respect of death or personal injury.

Article 15

Article 23, paragraph 1 of the Convention is replaced by the following text:
1 Without prejudice to article 21, paragraph 5 a State Party may, at the time when it signs without reservation as to ratification, acceptance or approval, or deposits its instrument of ratification, acceptance, approval or accession or at any time thereafter, declare that it assumes responsibility for obligations imposed by this Convention on any person liable to pay contributions in accordance with articles 18, 19, 20 or article 21, paragraph 5, in respect of

APPENDIX 12

hazardous and noxious substances received in the territory of that State. Such a declaration shall be made in writing and shall specify which obligations are assumed.

Article 16

Article 43 of the Convention is deleted, and article 44 is renumbered as article 43.

Article 17

The model certificate set out in Annex I of the Convention is replaced by the model annexed to this Protocol.

Article 18 – Interpretation and application

1 The Convention and this Protocol shall, as between the Parties to this Protocol, be read and interpreted together as one single instrument.

2 Articles 1 to 44 and Annexes I and II of the Convention, as amended by this Protocol and the annex thereto, together with articles 20 to 29 of this Protocol (the final clauses), shall *mutatis mutandis* constitute and be called the International Convention on Liability and Compensation for Damage in Connection with the Carriage of Hazardous and Noxious Substances by Sea, 2010 (2010 HNS Convention). Articles 20 to 29 of this Protocol shall be renumbered sequentially with the preceding articles of the Convention. References within the final clauses to other articles of the final clauses shall be renumbered accordingly.

Article 19

In chapter VI, the following text is inserted as article 44*bis* of the Convention:

Final clauses of the International Convention on Liability and Compensation for Damage in Connection with the Carriage of Hazardous and Noxious Substances by Sea, 2010

The final clauses of the International Convention on Liability and Compensation for Damage in Connection with the Carriage of Hazardous and Noxious Substances by Sea, 2010 shall be the final clauses of the Protocol of 2010 to the International Convention on Liability and Compensation for Damage in Connection with the Carriage of Hazardous and Noxious Substances by Sea, 1996.

Final clauses

Article 20 – Signature, ratification, acceptance, approval and accession

1 This Protocol shall be open for signature at the Headquarters of the Organization from 1 November 2010 to 31 October 2011 and shall thereafter remain open for accession.

2 Subject to the provisions in paragraphs 4 and 5, States may express their consent to be bound by this Protocol by:

(a) signature without reservation as to ratification, acceptance or approval; or
(b) signature subject to ratification, acceptance or approval, followed by ratification, acceptance or approval; or
(c) accession.

APPENDIX 12

3 Ratification, acceptance, approval or accession shall be effected by the deposit of an instrument to that effect with the Secretary-General.

4 An expression of consent to be bound by this Protocol shall be accompanied by the submission to the Secretary-General of data on the total quantities of contributing cargo liable for contributions received in that State during the preceding calendar year in respect of the general account and each separate account.

5 An expression of consent which is not accompanied by the data referred to in paragraph 4 shall not be accepted by the Secretary-General.

6 Each State which has expressed its consent to be bound by this Protocol shall annually thereafter on or before 31 May until this Protocol enters into force for that State, submit to the Secretary-General data on the total quantities of contributing cargo liable for contributions received in that State during the preceding calendar year in respect of the general account and each separate account.

7 A State which has expressed its consent to be bound by this Protocol and which has not submitted the data on contributing cargo required under paragraph 6 for any relevant years shall, before the entry into force of the Protocol for that State, be temporarily suspended from being a Contracting State until it has submitted the required data.

8 A State which has expressed its consent to be bound by the International Convention on Liability and Compensation for Damage in Connection with the Carriage of Hazardous and Noxious Substances by Sea, 1996 shall be deemed to have withdrawn this consent on the date on which it has signed this Protocol or deposited an instrument of ratification, acceptance, approval or accession in accordance with paragraph 2.

Article 21 – Entry into force

1 This Protocol shall enter into force eighteen months after the date on which the following conditions are fulfilled:
- (a)   at least twelve States, including four States each with not less than 2 million units of gross tonnage, have expressed their consent to be bound by it; and
- (b)   the Secretary-General has received information in accordance with article 20, paragraphs 4 and 6 that those persons in such States who would be liable to contribute pursuant to article 18, paragraphs 1(a) and (c) of the Convention, as amended by this Protocol, have received during the preceding calendar year a total quantity of at least 40 million tonnes of cargo contributing to the general account.

2 For a State which expresses its consent to be bound by this Protocol after the conditions for entry into force have been met, such consent shall take effect three months after the date of expression of such consent, or on the date on which this Protocol enters into force in accordance with paragraph 1, whichever is the later.

Article 22 – Revision and amendment

1 A conference for the purpose of revising or amending the Convention, as amended by this Protocol, may be convened by the Organization.

2 The Secretary-General shall convene a conference of the States Parties to this Protocol, for revising or amending the Convention, as amended by this Protocol, at the request of six States Parties or one-third of the States Parties, whichever is the higher figure.

3 Any instrument of ratification, acceptance, approval or accession deposited after the date of entry into force of an amendment to the Convention, as amended by this Protocol, shall be deemed to apply to the Convention as amended.

APPENDIX 12

Article 23 – Amendment of limits

1 Without prejudice to the provisions of article 22, the special procedure in this article shall apply solely for the purposes of amending the limits set out in article 9, paragraph 1 and article 14, paragraph 5 of the Convention, as amended by this Protocol.

2 Upon the request of at least one half, but in no case less than six, of the States Parties, any proposal to amend the limits specified in article 9, paragraph 1 and article 14, paragraph 5 of the Convention, as amended by this Protocol, shall be circulated by the Secretary-General to all Members of the Organization and to all Contracting States.

3 Any amendment proposed and circulated in accordance with paragraph 2 shall be submitted to the Legal Committee of the Organization (the Legal Committee) for consideration at a date at least six months after the date of its circulation.

4 All Contracting States, whether or not Members of the Organization, shall be entitled to participate in the proceedings of the Legal Committee for the consideration and adoption of amendments.

5 Amendments shall be adopted by a two-thirds majority of the Contracting States present and voting in the Legal Committee, expanded as provided in paragraph 4, on condition that at least one half of the Contracting States shall be present at the time of voting.

6 When acting on a proposal to amend the limits, the Legal Committee shall take into account the experience of incidents, in particular the amount of damage resulting therefrom, changes in the monetary values, and the effect of the proposed amendment on the cost of insurance. It shall also take into account the relationship between the limits established in article 9, paragraph 1 and those in article 14, paragraph 5 of the Convention, as amended by this Protocol.

7 (a) No amendment of the limits under this article may be considered less than five years from the date this Protocol was opened for signature nor less than five years from the date of entry into force of a previous amendment under this article.

   (b) No limit may be increased so as to exceed an amount which corresponds to a limit laid down in this Protocol increased by six per cent per year calculated on a compound basis from the date on which this Protocol was opened for signature.

   (c) No limit may be increased so as to exceed an amount which corresponds to a limit laid down in this Protocol multiplied by three.

8 Any amendment adopted in accordance with paragraph 5 shall be notified by the Organization to all Contracting States. The amendment shall be deemed to have been accepted at the end of a period of eighteen months after the date of notification, unless within that period no less than one-fourth of the States which were Contracting States at the time of the adoption of the amendment have communicated to the Secretary-General that they do not accept the amendment, in which case the amendment is rejected and shall have no effect.

9 An amendment deemed to have been accepted in accordance with paragraph 8 shall enter into force eighteen months after its acceptance.

10 All Contracting States shall be bound by the amendment, unless they denounce this Protocol in accordance with article 24, paragraphs 1 and 2, at least six months before the amendment enters into force. Such denunciation shall take effect when the amendment enters into force.

11 When an amendment has been adopted but the eighteen-month period for its acceptance has not yet expired, a State which becomes a Contracting State during that period shall be bound by the amendment if it enters into force. A State which becomes a Contracting State after that period shall be bound by an amendment which has been accepted in accordance with paragraph 8. In the cases referred to in this paragraph, a State becomes bound by an amendment when that amendment enters into force, or when this Protocol enters into force for that State, if later.

APPENDIX 12

Article 24 – Denunciation

1 This Protocol may be denounced by any State Party at any time after the expiry of one year following the date on which this Protocol enters into force for that State.

2 Denunciation shall be effected by the deposit of an instrument to that effect with the Secretary-General.

3 A denunciation shall take effect twelve months, or such longer period as may be specified in the instrument of denunciation, following its receipt by the Secretary-General.

4 Notwithstanding a denunciation by a State Party pursuant to this article, any provisions of this Protocol relating to obligations to make contributions under articles 18, 19 or article 21, paragraph 5 of the Convention, as amended by this Protocol, in respect of such payments of compensation as the Assembly may decide relating to an incident which occurs before the denunciation takes effect shall continue to apply.

Article 25 – Extraordinary sessions of the Assembly

1 Any State Party may, within ninety days after the deposit of an instrument of denunciation the result of which it considers will significantly increase the level of contributions from the remaining States Parties, request the Director to convene an extraordinary session of the Assembly. The Director shall convene the Assembly to meet not less than sixty days after receipt of the request.

2 The Director may take the initiative to convene an extraordinary session of the Assembly to meet within sixty days after the deposit of any instrument of denunciation, if the Director considers that such denunciation will result in a significant increase in the level of contributions from the remaining States Parties.

3 If the Assembly, at an extraordinary session convened in accordance with paragraph 1 or 2, decides that the denunciation will result in a significant increase in the level of contributions from the remaining States Parties, any such State may, not later than one hundred and twenty days before the date on which the denunciation takes effect, denounce this Protocol with effect from the same date.

Article 26 – Cessation

1 This Protocol shall cease to be in force:
   (a)   on the date when the number of States Parties falls below six; or
   (b)   twelve months after the date on which data concerning a previous calendar year
         were to be communicated to the Director in accordance with article 21 of the
         Convention, as amended by this Protocol, if the data show that the total quantity
         of contributing cargo to the general account in accordance with article 18,
         paragraphs 1(a) and (c) of the Convention, as amended by this Protocol, received
         in the States Parties in that preceding calendar year was less than 30 million tonnes.
Notwithstanding subparagraph (b), if the total quantity of contributing cargo to the general account in accordance with article 18, paragraphs 1(a) and (c) of the Convention, as amended by this Protocol, received in the States Parties in the preceding calendar year was less than 30 million tonnes but more than 25 million tonnes, the Assembly may, if it considers that this was due to exceptional circumstances and is not likely to be repeated, decide before the expiry of the above-mentioned twelve-month period that the Protocol shall continue to be in force. The Assembly may not, however, take such a decision in more than two subsequent years.

2 States which are bound by this Protocol on the day before the date it ceases to be in force

461

APPENDIX 12

shall enable the HNS Fund to exercise its functions as described under article 27 and shall, for that purpose only, remain bound by this Protocol.

Article 27 – Winding up of the HNS Fund

1 If this Protocol ceases to be in force, the HNS Fund shall nevertheless:
    (a)   meet its obligations in respect of any incident occurring before this Protocol ceased to be in force; and
    (b)   be entitled to exercise its rights to contributions to the extent that these contributions are necessary to meet the obligations under (a), including expenses for the administration of the HNS Fund necessary for this purpose.

2 The Assembly shall take all appropriate measures to complete the winding up of the HNS Fund including the distribution in an equitable manner of any remaining assets among those persons who have contributed to the HNS Fund.

3 For the purposes of this article the HNS Fund shall remain a legal person.

Article 28 – Depositary

1 This Protocol and any amendment adopted under article 23 shall be deposited with the Secretary-General.

2 The Secretary-General shall:
    (a)   inform all States which have signed this Protocol or acceded thereto, and all Members of the Organization, of:
        (i)   each new signature or deposit of an instrument of ratification, acceptance, approval or accession, together with the date thereof and the data on contributing cargo submitted in accordance with article 20, paragraph 4;
        (ii)   the data on contributing cargo submitted annually thereafter, in accordance with article 20, paragraph 6, until the date of entry into force of this Protocol;
        (iii)   the date of entry into force of this Protocol;
        (iv)   any proposal to amend the limits on the amounts of compensation which has been made in accordance with article 23, paragraph 2;
        (v)   any amendment which has been adopted in accordance with article 23, paragraph 5;
        (vi)   any amendment deemed to have been accepted under article 23, paragraph 8, together with the date on which that amendment shall enter into force in accordance with article 23, paragraph 9;
        (vii)   the deposit of any instrument of denunciation of this Protocol together with the date on which it is received and the date on which the denunciation takes effect;
        (viii)   any communication called for by any article in this Protocol; and
    (b)   transmit certified true copies of this Protocol to all States that have signed or acceded to it.

3 As soon as this Protocol enters into force, a certified true copy of the text shall be transmitted by the Secretary-General to the Secretary-General of the United Nations for registration and publication in accordance with Article 102 of the Charter of the United Nations.

APPENDIX 12

Article 29 – Languages

This Protocol is established in a single original in the Arabic, Chinese, English, French, Russian and Spanish languages, each text being equally authentic.

DONE AT London this thirtieth day of April two thousand and ten.

IN WITNESS WHEREOF the undersigned, being duly authorized by their respective Governments for that purpose, have signed this Protocol.

INDEX

Africa, West and Central 99–100
agents: hazardous and noxious substances: liability and compensation (1996 Convention) 220, 223; oil pollution damage, civil liability for (CLC 1992) 131, 133, 141, 142
air pollution from ships: MARPOL 73/78 30, 37
air-cushion vehicles 24, 31
air-cushioned craft 43
arbitration: intervention on high seas (1969 Convention and 1973 Protocol) 16–17; wrecks, removal of (2007 Convention) 97, 98
Asia/Pacific Region 99
audit, waste prevention 48
Australia 9, 193, 194, 196–7

ballast tank, corrosion prevention of seawater 39
ballast water and sediments (2004 Convention) 55, 101; achieving purpose, manner of 58–9; burden of proof 58; 'harmful aquatic organisms and pathogens' 58; implementation 59–61; inspection 59; MARPOL 73/78 and 32; recourse, right of 195; scope of application 55–8; 'sediments' 32, 58
Baltic Sea area 35
bank guarantee 88, 139, 146, 222–3, 225
bareboat charter registration 56
bareboat charterer: civil liability for bunker oil pollution damage (2001 Convention) 193, 194–5, 199; civil liability for oil pollution damage (CLC 1992) 130, 133; hazardous and noxious substances: liability and compensation (1996 Convention) 220
Belgium 5–6, 127
black, grey and white list 105
Black Sea area 35, 100
bulk carriers 39
bunker oil and HNS Convention 1996 212
bunker oil pollution damage, civil liability for (2001 Convention) 101, 189; basis of liability 196; burden of proof 195; enforcement of judgments 206–7; exclusions from liability 196; geographical scope 190; insurance or

other financial security 93, 195, 199–205; international validity of certificate 203; jurisdiction 206; language of certificate 202; limitation of liability 93, 196–9; 'oil' 190–1; parties to 189; person(s) liable 192–5; recognition of judgments 206–7; scope of application 190–2; 'ship' 190, 191, 203; 'shipowner' 193–4; supersession clause 207; time limits 202, 205–6; time for suit 205–6; wrecks, removal of (2007 Convention) 93, 94, 95
bunker oil pollution damage and CLC 1992 121
burden of proof: ballast water and sediments (2004 Convention) 58; bunker oil pollution damage, civil liability for (2001 Convention) 195; dumping of wastes (1972 Convention as amended by 1996 Protocol) 46; Fund Convention 1992 163, 166–7, 179; HNS Convention 1996 218–19, 237; intervention on high seas 11, 20; MARPOL 73/78 31; oil pollution damage, civil liability for (CLC 1992) 121, 135, 138, 139–40, 142, 143, 166; wrecks, removal of (2007 Convention) 93

Cameroon 11
Canada 209–10, 244; civil liability for oil pollution 131, 193, 194, 196–7; intervention on high seas 4–5, 9, 10, 12, 13, 14, 15–16
Caribbean 99
certificates: insurance or other financial security: Bunker Oil Convention 2001 201–4; insurance or other financial security: CLC 1992 144–50, 151–2; insurance or other financial security: HNS Convention 1996 225–9, 230; insurance or other financial security: wrecks (2007 Convention) 95, 96; MARPOL 73/78 30, 33–4, 36, 37; SOLAS Convention 1974 39
charts, nautical 135
chemical tankers 72, 74–5
civil law countries 131, 153, 170
classification societies 132
Coastguard vessels 44
common law countries 153, 170

INDEX

compensation: bunker oil pollution damage, civil liability for (2001 Convention) *see separate entry*; hazardous and noxious substances: liability and compensation (1996 Convention) *see separate entry*; intervention on high seas (1969 Convention and 1973 Protocol): for damage caused by measures taken 15–16; oil pollution damage, civil liability for (CLC 1992) *see separate entry*; oil pollution damage and Fund Convention *see separate entry*; port state control: European Directive 2009/16/EC 109

conciliation: intervention on high seas (1969 Convention and 1973 Protocol) 16–17; wrecks, removal of (2007 Convention) 97

construction and equipment of ships: SOLAS Convention 1974 – dangerous goods 40

consultation: dumping of wastes (1972 Convention as amended by 1996 Protocol) 49; intervention on high seas (1969 Convention and 1973 Protocol) 10–13, 25, 26, 49; removal of wrecks (2007 Convention) 83, 87, 90, 91

Cook Islands 137

crew: HNS Convention 1996 220, 223; intervention on high seas (1969 Convention and 1973 Protocol) 13; oil pollution damage, civil liability for (CLC 1992) 131–2, 141; standards of training, certification and watchkeeping for seafarers (1978 Convention) *see separate entry*

criminal law: MARPOL 73/78 33

Cyprus 208

dangerous goods: European Traffic Monitoring and Information System Directive 111–12; SOLAS Convention 1974 40

dangerous or polluting goods: traffic monitoring and information system (Directive 2002/59/EC) 111–14; *see also* hazardous and noxious substances

data recorder system 104, 109

Denmark 209–10, 244

deregistration 81

detention of ships: MARPOL 73/78 34, 103; port state control: European Directive 2009/16/EC 109; port state control: Paris MoU 104

dispute settlement: intervention on high seas (1969 Convention and 1973 Protocol) 16–17; removal of wrecks (2007 Convention) 87, 97–8

dumping of wastes (1972 Convention as amended by 1996 Protocol) 41–2; activities regulated 44–5, 80; annual reports 51, 53–4; ashore, disposal from 45; 'dumping' 43, 45; human health 49; human life, safety of 48, 49; implementation 50–1; incineration 44, 45; MARPOL 73/78 and 32, 37; monitor condition of seas 50, 52; obligations of contracting parties 46–9; parties to 41; permits 47–8, 49, 50–3; polluter bears cost 46, 47; precautionary approach 46, 48; purpose 41–2; records 50, 52;

reports to IMO 51, 53–4; scope of application 43–4, 56; sovereign immunity 44; 'vessels and aircraft' 43–4; 'wastes or other matters' 37, 45

ejusdem generis rule 132, 146

employees: hazardous and noxious substances: liability and compensation (1996 Convention) 220, 223; oil pollution damage, civil liability for (CLC 1992) 131, 141, 142

enforcement of judgments: Bunker Oil Convention 2001 206–7; CLC 1992 154; HNS Convention 1996 240–1

estuaries 9, 58, 82

European Union: port state control 100, 106–10; salvage 113–14; traffic monitoring and information system 111–14

exclusive economic zone 83, 113, 123, 125–6, 138, 161, 190, 215, 216, 222, 238–9, 240

experts: intervention on high seas and optional advice 12

Finland 193, 194

fire: SOLAS Convention 1974 39

fisheries 9, 82

fishing vessels 107, 111

fleet/naval auxiliaries 31, 44, 57, 107, 111, 191, 192, 217

floating craft 6, 7, 31, 43

France 81, 83, 117, 146, 209–10, 244

garbage from ships: MARPOL 73/78 30, 37

Germany 15, 209–10, 244

government owned or operated ships used for non-commercial purposes 31, 44, 57–8, 107, 111, 121, 166, 191–2, 217

Greece 244

grey, black and white list 105

guarantee, bank 88, 139, 146, 222–3, 225

Guatemala 11

Gulf Region 100

harmful aquatic organisms and pathogens 58

hazard to navigation: removal of wrecks (2007 Convention) 79, 81–3

hazardous and non-hazardous deficiencies: port state control 103–4, 109

hazardous and noxious substances: 1996 Convention *see* hazardous and noxious substances: liability and compensation; intervention on high seas: other substances (1973 Protocol) 17–22; MARPOL 73/78 29, 36; Protocol of 2000 to 1990 OPRC Convention 26–8; SOLAS Convention 1974 40; *see also* dangerous or polluting goods

hazardous and noxious substances: liability and compensation (1996 Convention) 27, 125–6; amendment of limits 247–8; area in which the damage caused 215–16; basis of liability 218–19; burden of proof 218–19, 237; channelling of liability 220; 'damage' 211; enforcement of judgments 240–1; entry into force 246–7;

466

INDEX

exclusions from scope of application 216–18; final clauses 244–8; history 208–10; insurance of owner 149, 224–30; International HNS Fund 231–6, 239–40; international validity of certificate 228–9; jurisdiction 238–40; language of certificate 228; liability of owner 218–30; limit, loss of right to 224; limitation of actions 236–8; limitation fund 222–4; limitation of liability of owner 220–4, 247–8; nature of the damage 211–12; 'owner' 218; recognition of judgments 240–1; scope of application 210–18; 'ship' 215; signatures 244; structure of 210; submission of data on total quantities of contributing cargo 244–6; subrogation, right of 223, 241–2; substances causing the damage 212–15; supersession clause 207, 243; termination 248; time limits 227, 236–8, 247, 248; transitional provisions 243; withdrawal of the consent to be bound 246; wrecks, removal of (2007 Convention) 94

hazardous ships, monitoring of (Directive 2002/59/EC) 112–13

high seas: hazardous and noxious substances: liability and compensation (1996 Convention) 239; jurisdiction (1958 Convention) 4, 6; oil pollution casualties: intervention on high seas (1969 Convention) *see separate entry*; other substances: intervention on (1973 Protocol) 17–22

history: civil liability for oil pollution damage (CLC 1992) 117–19; Fund Convention 156–60; HNS Convention 1996 208–10; oil pollution casualties: intervention on high seas (1969 Convention) 3–4; other substances: intervention on high seas (1973 Protocol) 17–19

hospital ships 44

hydrofoil boats 24, 31

immunity, sovereign 44, 57, 121, 192

incineration *see* dumping of wastes (1972 Convention as amended by 1996 Protocol)

Indonesia 11

information: dangerous goods, transport of (Directive 2002/59/EC) 112; port state control: information system on inspections (Paris MoU) 105–6; to coastal states on hazardous ships (Directive 2002/59/EC) 112–13

inspection of ships: ballast water and sediments (2004 Convention) 59; MARPOL 73/78 33–4, 35; port state control: European Directive 2009/16/EC 107–9; port state control: Paris MoU 99, 102–6

insurance or other financial security 145; bunker oil pollution damage, civil liability for (2001 Convention) 93, 195, 199–205; hazardous and noxious substances: liability and compensation (1996 Convention) 149, 224–30; oil pollution damage, civil liability for (CLC 1992) 95, 122, 141, 143–52; wrecks, removal of (2007 Convention) 88, 91, 92, 93, 95–6, 145

insurance or other financial security (CLC 1992) 95, 141, 143–52; conditions of issue and validity of certificate 150; direct action against insurer or guarantor 150–1; evidence 146–8; international validity of certificate 150; language of certificate 149; nature and amount of security required 146; oil, definition of 122; party who is bound to insure 145–6; period of validity of certificate 149–50; ships owned by contracting State 151–2; sum insured or secured 146

interest 139, 168, 169, 178

International Chamber of Shipping 194

International Fund 156–60; administration of 180–2; amount of compensation available 167–70; burden of proof 163, 166–7, 179; contributions to 174–80; cooperation of contracting States 179; currency in which contributions must be paid 176; distribution where claims in excess of compensation payable 170; due date for contributions 179; establishment of 161; extinction of right to compensation 170–1; intervene in proceedings, right to 173–4; invoices 179; jurisdiction 171–4; organisation of 180–2; owner has not constituted a fund and payment from 170; rules on payment of compensation 162–74; scope of application 161; time limits 170–1, 179, 180; when compensation not due from 165–7; when judgment or settlement not binding on 173

International Group of P&I Clubs 139, 194

International HNS Fund 231–6; amount of compensation payable by 233–5; budget 235; conditions required for the payment by 232; contributions 235–6; establishment 231; judgments against 241; jurisdiction 239–40; when payment of compensation is not due 232

International Labour Organization (ILO) 106

International Monetary Fund (IMF) 135, 136–7

intervention on high seas: oil pollution casualties: intervention on high seas (1969 Convention) *see separate entry*; other substances (1973 Protocol) 17–22

Ireland 5, 193, 194

Italy 81, 134

Japan 9, 129

joint and several liability 130, 194–5

jurisdiction: bunker oil pollution damage, civil liability for (2001 Convention) 206; Fund Convention 1992 171–4; high seas, vessels sailing on 4, 6; HNS Convention 1996 238–40; oil pollution damage, civil liability for (CLC 1992) 138, 140, 153–4

Latin America Region 99

Liberia 208

liquefied gas tankers 40, 76–7

467

INDEX

Malta 193, 194

MARPOL 73/78: prevention of pollution from ships 29–30, 101, 106, 111; detention of ships 34, 103; 'discharge' 32; general obligations of State parties 32–3; general scope of application 30–1, 56; 'harmful substance' 32; inspection of ships 33–4, 35; main purpose 31–2; national law 33; 'ship' 31; summary of annexes 35–7

mediation: removal of wrecks (2007 Convention) 97

Mediterranean Sea area 35, 100

Monaco 137

monitoring: condition of seas: dumping of wastes (1972 Convention as amended by 1996 Protocol) 50, 52; hazardous goods (Directive 2002/59/EC) 112–13

national law: ballast water and sediments (2004 Convention) 60; dumping of wastes (1972 Convention as amended by 1996 Protocol) 42, 43; Fund Convention 1992 171, 173, 179; hazardous and noxious substances: liability and compensation (1996 Convention) 225; MARPOL 73/78 33; oil pollution damage, civil liability for (CLC 1992) 141, 144, 153; wrecks, removal of (2007 Convention) 87, 88, 95

nautical charts 135

naval/fleet auxiliaries 31, 44, 57, 107, 111, 191, 192, 217

Netherlands 16, 165, 209–10, 244; civil liability for oil pollution 128–9, 193, 194, 196

New Zealand 16

non-persistent oil 8, 122

Norway 152, 165, 193, 194, 196–7, 209–10, 244

notification: Bunker Oil Convention 2001 202; dangerous polluting goods carried on board (Directive 2002/59/EC) 112; Fund Convention 1992 171, 173; hazardous and noxious substances: liability and compensation (1996 Convention) 217; intervention on high seas (1969 Convention and 1973 Protocol) 10–11, 12–13, 26; port state control: Paris MoU 99, 105; wrecks, removal of (2007 Convention) 83, 86, 91, 92

nuclear damage 94; see also radioactive material

offshore units 24, 28

oil pollution and MARPOL 73/78 29, 30, 35–6

oil pollution casualties: intervention on high seas (1969 Convention) 111; arbitration 16–17; 'coastline' 8–9; compensation for damage caused by measures taken 15–16; conciliation 16–17; conditions 7–10, 82; crew 13; geographic scope 6; guidelines for selection of measures 13–15; history 3–4; human life, avoid risk to 13; 'maritime casualty' 4–6; obligations of State that takes measures 10–15, 25–6, 49; 'oil' 8; OPRC Convention 1990: possible conflict with 23, 24–6; other substances (1973 Protocol) 17–22, 27; parties to 19; relationship between Protocol and Convention 20–1; scope of application 4–7, 20; 'ship' 6–7; time limits

17, 22; updating list of other substances 21–2; voluntary discharge of oil 5

oil pollution damage, civil liability for (CLC 1992) 46, 117–19, 216; 'agent' 131; amendment of the limits 137–8; basis of liability 133–5; bunker oil of dry cargo ships 189; burden of proof 121, 135, 138, 139–40, 142, 143, 166; channelling of liability 128–33, 141, 142, 195; 'charterer' 130, 133; conflict with other conventions 155; 'crew' 131–2; enforcement of judgments 154; geographical scope 125–6; intervention on high seas (1969 Convention) 15–16; jurisdiction 138, 140, 153–4; liability insurance 95, 122, 141, 143–52; limit, loss of right to 142–3; limitation fund 138–40, 154; (distribution of) 140–2, 154; limitation of liability of owner 135–40, 142–3, 221–2; 'manager' 133; 'oil' 8, 121, 122; 'operator' 133; 'owner' 127–8; person liable 127–33; 'pollution damage' 122–5; reasonability concept 124; recognition of judgments 154; scope of application 119–26; 'servant' 131; 'ship' 119–21; strict but not absolute liability 134; subrogation rights 141; supersession clause 207; time limits 137, 152–3; wrecks, removal of (2007 Convention) 93, 94

oil pollution damage and Fund Convention 140, 142, 156–60, 216; bunker oil of dry cargo ships 189; International Fund see separate entry; Supplementary Fund 160, 182–8

oil pollution preparedness, response and cooperation (1990 OPRC Convention) 23, 82; comparison of 2000 Protocol with 27–8; geographic scope 24; hazardous and noxious substances: 2000 Protocol 26–8; parties to 23, 27; possible conflict between Intervention Convention and 23, 24–6; scope of application 23–4, 123; 'ship' 24

oil tankers 39, 72, 73–4, 103

P&I Clubs 139, 194

passenger ships 189, 226–7

permits: dumping of wastes (1972 Convention as amended by 1996 Protocol) 47–8, 49, 50–3

Poland 163

polluter bears cost 46, 47

port state control: European Directive 2009/16/EC; classification of ships 108; compensation 109; detention of ships 109; inspections 107–9; origin and purpose 106–7; refusal of access 109–10; 'ship' 107; ships to which it applies 107; time limits 108

port state control: Paris MoU 99–100, 108, 109; black, grey and white list 105; classification of ships 103; criteria for adherence to 100–1; detention of ships 104; duties and powers of port authorities 103–5; information system 105–6; inspections 99, 102–6; organisational structure 101; refusal of access 105, 110; ships to which it applies 102; signatories of 99; time limits 103, 104, 105

468

INDEX

port state control agreements 99–100; port state control: European Directive 2009/16/EC *see separate entry*; port state control: Paris MoU *see separate entry*

precautionary approach: dumping of wastes (1972 Convention as amended by 1996 Protocol) 46, 48

proportionality: intervention on high seas (1969 Convention and 1973 Protocol) 13, 14–15; removal of wrecks (2007 Convention) 81

radioactive material 211–12, 216–17

records: ballast water and sediments (2004 Convention) 59; dumping of wastes (1972 Convention as amended by 1996 Protocol) 50, 52

registration of ships 56, 81, 99; bareboat charter registration 56; Flag and State of 43

reporting: dumping of wastes (1972 Convention as amended by 1996 Protocol) 51, 53–4; Fund Convention 1992: contributions 174–5; incidents and accidents at sea (Directive 2002/59/EC) 113; removal of wrecks (2007 Convention) 89

Romania 16

Russian Federation 208; *see also* Soviet Union

safety of life at sea (1974 SOLAS Convention) 38–40, 100, 106, 111

salvage 44; EU: ships in need of assistance 113–14; hazardous and noxious substances: liability and compensation (1996 Convention) 220; oil pollution, civil liability for (CLC 1992) 133; oil, voluntary discharge of 5; 'vessel' 119–20; wrecks, removal of (2007 Convention) 81, 82, 87, 92–3

Scandinavian delegations 127, 163; *see also* Denmark; Finland; Norway; Sweden

Scotland 164

sewage from ships: MARPOL 73/78 30, 37

ship, meaning of: bunker oil pollution damage, civil liability for (2001 Convention) 190, 191, 203; HNS Convention 1996 215; intervention on high seas (1969 Convention and 1973 Protocol) 6–7; MARPOL 73/78 31; oil pollution damage, civil liability for (CLC 1992) 119–21; oil pollution preparedness, response and cooperation (1990 OPRC Convention) 24; port state control: European Directive 2009/16/EC 107

ships, prevention of pollution from (MARPOL 73/78) 29–30, 101, 106, 111; detention of ships 34, 103; 'discharge' 32; general obligations of State parties 32–3; general scope of application 30–1, 56; 'harmful substance' 32; inspection of ships 33–4, 35; main purpose 31–2; national law 33; 'ship' 31; summary of annexes 35–7

slot charterer 133

South Africa 193, 194, 196–7

sovereign immunity 44, 57, 121, 192

sovereignty, State 16

Soviet Union: civil liability for oil pollution 128, 134, 135; intervention on high seas 13, 16; *see also* Russian Federation

Spain 6

Special Drawing Rights (SDRs) 135–7, 157

standards of training, certification and watchkeeping for seafarers (1978 Convention) 101; chemical tankers 72, 74–5; emergency, occupational safety, security, medical care and survival functions 77–8; engine department 67–72; liquefied gas tankers 76–7; master and deck department 63–6; oil tankers 72, 73–4; ports of State party 62; special requirements 72–7; watchkeeping 78

State owned or operated ships used for non-commercial purposes 31, 44, 57–8, 107, 111, 121, 166, 191–2, 217

structure of ships: SOLAS Convention 1974 39, 40

submersibles 24, 31

subrogation rights 141–2, 223, 241–2

supersession clause 207, 243

Supplementary Fund 160; contributions to 187–8; entry into force and claims in respect of which available 183–4; establishment of 182–3; extinction of right to compensation 186; rules governing payment by 184–6

surveys: SOLAS Convention 1974 39

Sweden 8, 135, 192, 193, 194, 196

Syria 5

tanker, definition of 39

territorial waters 4, 6; bunker oil pollution damage, civil liability for (2001 Convention) 190, 200; Fund Convention 161; hazardous and noxious substances: liability and compensation (1996 Convention) 215, 216, 238–9, 240; oil pollution damage, civil liability for 125–6, 138, 222; oil pollution preparedness, response and cooperation (1990 OPRC Convention) 24; wrecks 79, 83, 86–7, 93–4

time charterer 133

time limits: Bunker Oil Convention 2001 202, 205–6; Fund Convention 1992 170–1, 179, 180; hazardous and noxious substances: liability and compensation (1996 Convention) 227, 236–8, 247, 248; intervention on high seas (1969 Convention and 1973 Protocol) 17, 22; oil pollution damage, civil liability for (CLC 1992) 137, 152–3; port state control: European Directive 2009/16/EC 108; port state control: Paris MoU 103, 104, 105; wrecks, removal of (2007 Convention) 96–7

Torrey Canyon 3, 14, 117

tourism 9, 83

traffic monitoring and information system: European Directive 2002/59/EC 111–14; 'dangerous goods' 111–12

469

INDEX

training, certification and watchkeeping for seafarers, standards of (1978 Convention) 101; chemical tankers 72, 74–5; emergency, occupational safety, security, medical care and survival functions 77–8; engine department 67–72; liquefied gas tankers 76–7; master and deck department 63–6; oil tankers 72, 73–4; ports of State party 62; special requirements 72–7; watchkeeping 78

Turkey 244

United Kingdom 117, 118; civil liability for oil pollution 124, 131, 135, 193, 194, 196–7; deregistration 81; Headquarters of Fund 1992 172, 176; intervention on high seas 3, 7, 11, 14

United States: civil liability for oil pollution 121, 126, 129, 131, 134; intervention on high seas 3, 12, 16

USSR: civil liability for oil pollution 128, 134, 135; intervention on high seas 13, 16; *see also* Russian federation

voyage charterer 133
voyage data recorder system 104, 109

warships 31, 44, 57–8, 107, 111, 121, 166, 191, 192, 203, 217
wastes, dumping of (1972 Convention as amended by 1996 Protocol) 41–2; activities regulated 44–5, 80; annual reports 51, 53–4; ashore, disposal from 45; 'dumping' 43, 45; human health 49; human life, safety of 48,

49; implementation 50–1; incineration 44, 45; MARPOL 73/78 and 32, 37; monitor condition of seas 50, 52; obligations of contracting parties 46–9; parties to 41; permits 47–8, 49, 50–3; polluter bears cost 46, 47; precautionary approach 46, 48; purpose 41–2; records 50, 52; reports to IMO 51, 53–4; scope of application 43–4, 56; sovereign immunity 44; 'vessels and aircraft' 43–4; 'wastes or other matters' 37, 45

watchkeeping 78
West and Central Africa 99–100
whale oil 122
white, grey and black list 105
wrecks, removal of (2007 Convention) 79; coastline or related interests 82–3; consultation 83, 87, 90, 91; Convention area 83; costs 88, 90, 93–5; criteria for determining whether hazard 84–6; dispute settlement 87, 97–8; exceptions to liabilities: owner 93, 94–5; general obligations of State to be complied with when becomes party to 88; geographical scope 83, 86–7; 'hazard' 81–3; insurance or other financial security 88, 91, 92, 93, 95–6, 145; location 90; marking 90–1; MARPOL 73/78 and 32; obligations and liabilities of owner 92–5; obligations of State in whose Convention Area wreck located 90–2; party who may determine whether wreck poses hazard 83; reporting obligation 89, 91; scope of application 79–87; territorial sea 79, 83, 86–7, 93–4; time limits 96–7; 'wreck' 80–1